Communications in Computer and Information Science 1744

More information about this series at https://link.springer.com/bookseries/7899

Ying Tan · Yuhui Shi (Eds.)

Data Mining and Big Data

7th International Conference, DMBD 2022
Beijing, China, November 21–24, 2022
Proceedings, Part I

Editors
Ying Tan
Peking University
Beijing, China

Yuhui Shi
Southern University of Science and Technology
Shenzhen, China

ISSN 1865-0929 ISSN 1865-0937 (electronic)
Communications in Computer and Information Science
ISBN 978-981-19-9296-4 ISBN 978-981-19-9297-1 (eBook)
https://doi.org/10.1007/978-981-19-9297-1

This Springer imprint is published by the registered company Springer Nature Singapore Pte Ltd.
The registered company address is: 152 Beach Road, #21-01/04 Gateway East, Singapore 189721, Singapore

Preface

The Seventh International Conference on Data Mining and Big Data (DMBD 2022) was held in Beijing, China, during November 21–24, 2022. DMBD serves as an international forum for researchers to exchange latest advantages in theories, models, and applications of data mining and big data as well as artificial intelligence techniques. DMBD 2022 was the seventh event after the successful first event (DMBD 2016) on Bali Island, Indonesia, the second event (DMBD 2017) in Fukuoka, Japan, the third event (DMBD 2018) in Shanghai, China, the fourth event (DMBD 2019) in Chiang Mai, Thailand, the fifth event (DMBD 2020) in Belgrade, Serbia, and the sixth event (DMBD 2021) in Guangzhou, China.

These two volumes (CCIS vol. 1744 and CCIS vol. 1745) contain the papers presented at DMBD 2022 covering some major topics of data mining and big data. The conference received 135 submissions. The Program Committee accepted 62 regular papers to be included in the conference program with an acceptance rate of 45.92%. Each submission received at least 3 reviews in an double-blind process. The proceedings contain revised versions of the accepted papers. While revisions are expected to take the referees comments into account, this was not enforced and the authors bear full responsibility for the content of their papers.

DMBD 2022 was organized by the International Association of Swarm and Evolutionary Intelligence (IASEI). It was co-organized by the Computational Intelligence Laboratory at Peking University, the Advanced Institute of Big Data, Beijing, the Key Laboratory of Information System Requirement, the Science and Technology on Information Systems Engineering Laboratory, and the Southern University of Science and Technology and technically co-sponsored by Research Reports on Computer Science (RRCS), the City Brain Technical Committee of the Chinese Institute of Command and Control (CICC), the International Neural Network Society, the Nanjing Kangbo Intelligent Health Academy, Springer, Entropy, MDPI Electronics, and the Beijing Xinghui High-Tech Co. The conference would not have been such a success without the support of these organizations, and we sincerely thank them for their continued assistance and sponsorship.

We would also like to thank the authors who submitted their papers to DMBD 2022, and the conference attendees for their interest and support. We thank the Organizing Committee for their time and effort dedicated to arranging the conference. This allowed us to focus on the paper selection and deal with the scientific program. We thank the Program Committee members and the external reviewers for their hard work in reviewing the submissions; the conference would not have been possible without their expert reviews. Furthermore, this work is partially supported by the National Natural Science Foundation of China (Grant No. 62076010 and 62276008), and also partially supported by the Science and Technology Innovation 2030 - New Generation Artificial Intelligence Major Project (Grant Nos.: 2018AAA0102301 and 2018AAA0100302).

Finally, we thank the EasyChair system and its operators, for making the entire process of managing the conference convenient.

November 2022

Ying Tan
Yuhui Shi

Organization

General Chair

Ying Tan	Peking University, China

Program Committee Chair

Yuhui Shi	Southern University of Science and Technology, China

Advisory Committee Chairs

Xingui He	Peking University, China
Gary G. Yen	Oklahoma State University, USA

Technical Committee Co-chairs

Benjamin W. Wah	The Chinese University of Hong Kong, Hong Kong, China
Guoying Wang	Chongqing University of Posts and Telecommunications, China
Enhong Chen	University of Science and Technology of China, China
Fernando Buarque	University of Pernambuco, Brazil
Haibo He	University of Rhode Island, USA
Jihong Zhu	Tsinghua University, China
Jin Li	Guangzhou University, China
Kay Chen Tan	The Hong Kong Polytechnic University, Hong Kong, China
Nikola Kasabov	Auckland University of Technology, New Zealand
Qirong Tang	Tongji University, China
Yew-Soon Ong	Nanyang Technological University, Singapore
Yi Zhang	Sichuan University, China

Invited Speakers Session Co-chairs

Andres Iglesias	University of Cantabria and Santander, Spain
Shaoqiu Zheng	The 28th Research Institute of China Electronics Technology Group Corporation, Nanjing, China

Special Session Co-chairs

Ben Niu	Shenzhen University, Shenzhen, China
Kun Liu	Advanced Institute of Big Data, China

Publications Co-chairs

Radu-Emil Precup	Politehnica University of Timisoara, Romania
Weiwei Hu	Tencent Corporation, China

Publicity Co-chairs

Eugene Semenkin	Siberian Aerospace University, Russia
Junqi Zhang	Tongji University, China

Finance and Registration Chairs

Andreas Janecek	University of Vienna, Austria
Suicheng Gu	Google Corporation, USA

Conference Secretariat

Maiyue Chen	Peking University, Beijing, China

Program Committee

Muhammad Abulaish	South Asian University, India
Abdelmalek Amine	Tahar Moulay University of Saida, Algeria
Sabri Arik	Istanbul University, Turkey
Nebojsa Bacanin	Singidunum University, Serbia
Carmelo J. A. Bastos Filho	University of Pernambuco, Brazil
Mohamed Ben Aouicha	University of Sfax, Tunisia
Chenyang Bu	Hefei University of Technology, China
Walter Chen	National Taipei University of Technology, Taiwan
Shi Cheng	Shannxi Normal University, China
Zelei Cheng	Purdue University, USA
Khaldoon Dhou	Texas A&M University–Central Texas, USA
Yuxin Ding	Harbin Institute of Technology, Shenzhen, China
Philippe Fournier-Viger	Shenzhen University, China
Hongyuan Gao	Harbin Engineering University, China
Shangce Gao	University of Toyama, Japan
Weifeng Gao	Xidian University, China
Xizhan Gao	University of Jinan, China

Ke Gu	Changsha University of Science and Technology, China
Salekul Islam	United International University, Bangladesh
Roshni Iyer	University of California, Los Angeles, USA
Ziyu Jia	Beijing Jiaotong University, China
Mingyan Jiang	Shandong University, China
Lov Kumar	BITS Pilani, India
Vivek Kumar	Università degli Studi di Cagliari, Italy
Germano Lambert-Torres	PS Solutions, USA
Bin Li	University of Science and Technology of China, China
Xianghong Lin	Northwest Normal University, China
Jian-Wei Liu	China University of Petroleum, Beijing, China
Ju Liu	Shandong University, China
Kun Liu	Advanced Institute of Big Data, China
Qunfeng Liu	Dongguan University of Technology, China
Yi Liu	PLA University of Science and Technology, China
Wenjian Luo	Harbin Institute of Technology, Shenzhen, China
Haoyang Ma	National University of Defense Technology, China
Lianbo Ma	Northeast University, China
Chengying Mao	Jiangxi University of Finance and Economics, China
Seyedfakhredin Musavishavazi	University of Applied Sciences Mittweida, Germany
Sreeja N. K.	PSG College of Technology, India
Qingjian Ni	Southeast University, China
Neelamadhab Padhy	GIET University, India
Mario Pavone	University of Catania, Spain
Yan Pei	University of Aizu, Japan
Xin Peng	Hainan University, China
Mukesh Prasad	University of Technology Sydney, Australia
Radu-Emil Precup	Politehnica University of Timisoara, Romania
Fezan Rasool	LUMS, Pakistan
Jiten Sidhpura	Sardar Patel Institute of Technology, India
Vrijendra Singh	Indian Institute of Information Technology, India
Ying Tan	Peking University, China
Daniel Tang	Institute of Computing Technology, CAS, China
Eva Tuba	University of Belgrade, Serbia
Dujuan Wang	Sichuan University, China
Guoyin Wang	Chongqing University of Posts and Telecommunications, China

Additional Reviewers

Chafekar, Talha
Chen, Changchuan
Deng, Yang
Elbakri, Idris
Han, Yanyang
Huang, Ziheng
Li, Linguo
Li, Zeyu
Liang, Mengnan
Liu, Li
Shengyao, Sun
Wang, Chunyang
Wang, Ruobin
Wang, Wenjun
Wang, Zichong
Xing, Tongtong
Xue, Yu
Yang, Zheng
Zhang, Shiyan
Zhang, Shuai
Zhu, Haifeng

Contents – Part I

Deep Neural Networks

Clustering Methods

Prediction Methods

Classification Methods

Contents – Part II

Identification and Recognition Methods

Optimization Methods

Big Data Analysis

Big-Model Methods

Generating Adversarial Examples and Other Applications

Deep Reinforcement Learning Approach

Heterogeneous Multi-unit Control with Curriculum Learning for Multi-agent Reinforcement Learning

Jiali Chen[1], Kai Jiang[2], Rupeng Liang[2], Jing Wang[2], Shaoqiu Zheng[2(✉)], and Ying Tan[1,3,4,5(✉)]

[1] School of Intelligence Science and Technology, Peking University, Beijing 100871, China
ytan@pku.edu.cn

[2] Nanjing Research Institute of Electronic Engineering, Nanjing 210007, China
zhengshaoqiu1214@foxmail.com

[3] Key Laboratory of Machine Perception (MOE), Peking University, Beijing 100871, China

[4] Institute for Artificial Intelligence, Peking University, Beijing 100871, China

[5] Nanjing Kangbo Intelligent Health Academy, Nanjing 211100, China

Abstract. Heterogeneous Multi-unit control is one of the most concerned topic in multi-agent system, which focuses on controlling agents of different type of functions. Methods that utilize parameter or replay-buffer sharing are able to address the problem of combinatorial explosion under isomorphism assumption, but may lead to divergence under heterogeneous setting. This work use curriculum learning to bypass the barrier of a needle in a haystack that is faced by either joint-action learner or independent learner. According to the experiment on heterogeneous force combat engagements, the independent learner outperforms the baseline learner by 10% of evaluation metrics with curriculum learning, which empirically shows that curriculum learning is able to discover a novel learning trajectory that is not followed by conventional multi-agent learners.

Keywords: Heterogeneous control · Curriculum learning · Multi-agent system

1 Introduction

A series of benchmark has been proposed for determining the performance of multi-agent reinforcement learning, with more agents, more complex agent architecture and sparser rewards indicating better algorithm needed to solve the problem. The StarCraft Multi-Agent Challenge (SMAC [33]) based on the StarCraft

This work is supported by the National Natural Science Foundation of China (Grant No. 62250037, 62276008 and 62076010), and partially supported by Science and Technology Innovation 2030 - 'New Generation Artificial IntelligenceMajor Project (Grant Nos.: 2018AAA0102301 and 2018AAA0100302).

Y. Tan and Y. Shi (Eds.): DMBD 2022, CCIS 1744, pp. 3–16, 2022.
https://doi.org/10.1007/978-981-19-9297-1_1

II Learning Environment (SC2LE [45]) is currently one of the most wildly used benchmark for multi-agent reinforcement learning algorithms, as shown in Fig. 1 However, the performance on SMAC is mostly determined by micromanagement of every single agent rather than collaborative joint actions. Moreover, the agents are with similar action spaces, move and attack, with difference only in attacking range and defense. Yet such setting is still too weak for realistic applications because isomorphism is often violated and requires collaborative joint actions of heterogeneous agents. Besides, tasks are multi-stage and multi-target rather than simply defeating the opponent by elimination.

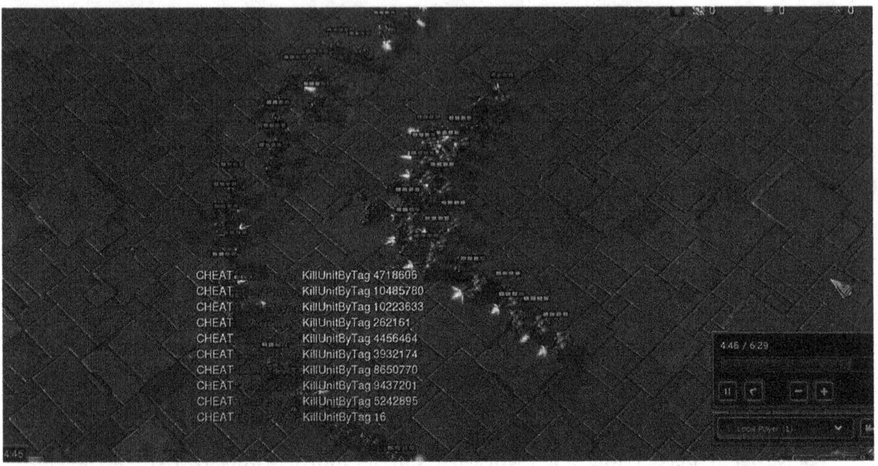

Fig. 1. A snapshot of 27 m vs. 30 m challenge in SMAC

Recently more complex and realistic environments that focuses on heterogeneous agents are being aggressively explored to develop algorithms for policies that are more robust to the dynamics of environment. Different from environments with isomorphism agents, heterogeneity indicates decision structures with little similarity among agents. Agents have different observation spaces and action spaces, thus, neural networks with fixed sizes of input and output can not be directly applied. Furthermore, the optimal parameters and network structures are unique for every agent, which means that a normal technique that tries to reduce the computational cost by sharing information among agents may fail. For example, as shown in Fig. 2, in a heterogeneous force combat engagement task, the view of a tank may be blocked by a nearby forest, and it is only able to move along the facing direction or turn. However, a helicopter is with higher motility and different action space, a control structure different from that of a tank is needed.

Conventional methods like parameter sharing are reconsidered [41–43] since the assumption of similar decision structures is violated under heterogeneous settings. With carefully redesign of the observation spaces, action spaces and

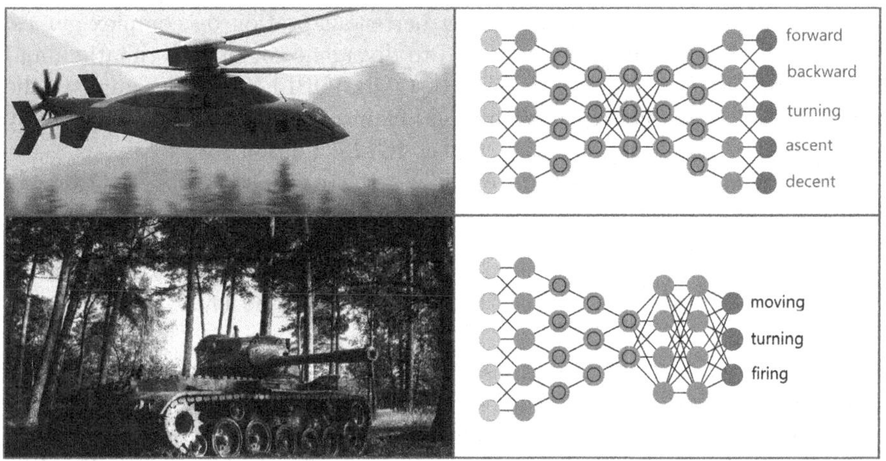

Fig. 2. A tank and a helicopter are heterogeneous agents

neural network structures among all agents, the technique of parameter sharing is able to applied under heterogeneous setting. Meanwhile, this reveals the fact most techniques that developed under the assumption of isomorphism agents failed to directly generalize to heterogeneous setting. As a consequence, methods that fit those benchmarks well are needed to reconsidered if it is over-fitted to isomorphism agents.

2 Related Works

A series of methods is developed under the widely used framework of centralized training and decentralized execution (CTDE [27]). These methods are classified in mainly two classes based on their optimization method, value decomposition or policy gradient.

Value based methods try to fit a value function $Q(s, \boldsymbol{a})$ that is able to evaluate the accumulative rewards of an immediate joint action $\boldsymbol{a}$, by iterating the bellman equation, that is

$$Q(s, \boldsymbol{a}) \leftarrow r + \gamma \max_{\boldsymbol{a}'} Q(s', \boldsymbol{a}') \tag{1}$$

which is a direct utilization of value iteration in single agent reinforcement learning. However, Q function suffers from the curses of dimensions with the increase of the number of agents. To address this problem, alternatives of decomposing the centralized value function are aggressively explored. Linear decomposition [38] assumes that the centralized value function is equal to a linear summation of functions on all agents. QMix [32] consider the monotonic aggregation based on the Individual-Global-Max (IGM) condition. QTRAN [36] claims that monotonic aggregation is not necessary condition for IGM and proposed a method based on affine transformation, showing better adaptation on complex games. WQMix [31] claims that QMix may lead to divergence or underestimation, and therefore proposed a weighted version of QMix. QPLEX [46] decomposes the value function with dueling structure, and claims that it is able to learn every decomposable value function satisfying the IGM condition.

While policy gradient method optimizes the parameters directly from an estimation of accumulative rewards. To formalize, the gradient of neural network weights

$$\nabla J(\theta) = R(\tau)\nabla P(\tau|\theta) \approx \frac{1}{N}\sum_{n=1}^{N} R(\tau_n)\nabla \ln P(\tau_n|\theta) \tag{2}$$

yet it is also necessary to decompose the gradients onto every agent, which is also known as a credit assignment problem [25]. MADDPG [22] uses a centralized critic network to distribute gradients among training agents. COMA [7] introduces counterfactual baseline to reduce the variance of gradients. MAPPO [51] generalizes proximal policy optimization (PPO [35]) to multi-agent environments with 5 proposed techniques. MATRPO [19] generalizes trust region policy optimization (TRPO [34]) to multi-agent environments to acquire a better theoretical guarantee multi-agent reinforcement learning algorithm.

However, methods based on CTDE framework is often assumed that the agents are isomorphism. Although in benchmarks like SMAC there are multiple races or units in an environment, the goals of the challenges and the decision structures of agents are of little difference. Thus algorithms with significant empirical results on these benchmarks may fail under heterogeneous settings. Thus alternatives focus on avoiding the assumption of isomorphism are widely explored.

Some consider independent training of every agent so that heterogeneous agents don't interfere each other. IQL [39] is proposed to learn individual Q function directly from iterating bellman equation independently on every single agent. IPPO [49] applies PPO algorithm directly to multi-agent environments and shows better empirical results than QMix and IQL on several challenges in SMAC. MA2QL [37] applies a minimal modification on IQL to acquire the theoretical guarantee on converging to a Nash Equilibrium [26]. MABCQ [14] exploits value deviation and transition normalization to modify the transition probability to derive an offline decentralized multi-agent algorithm. Yet the assumption of independence may lead to divergence or rather low sample complexity [22], thus these algorithm may lose scalability to the number of agents.

Some applies modern techniques in reinforcement learning or deep learning to address the problem of heterogeneous agents. Graph neural networks [9,50,53] are introduced to describe the relationships between heterogeneous agents, and HMAGQ-Net [23] proposed a graphical description of multi-agent system. Communication [2,20,24] is introduced to stabilize the training of independent learners, which builds channels between agents to achieve better collaboration. DDDQN [5] introduces 3 techniques in reinforcement learning to solve a heterogeneous traffic light control problem. These methods bypass the problem of heterogeneous agents by more expressive neural structures or training methods, but may introduce more computational cost or training difficulty that requires carefully fine tuning.

Some methods are inspired by population based training [6,10,16,21,40,52, 54]. League training [44] is introduced to find weakness of policies. IQ-algorithm [29] introduces an imitation learner to solve a heterogeneous multi-agent problem. Role based learning [47,48] introduces roles to break isomorphism. These methods address directly to the problem of heterogeneous agents, but may requires prior knowledge of the environment. Others focuses on quantifying heterogeneity. Model-free conventions [17] are considered in heterogeneous settings to encourage exploration. FMQ [15] algorithm is proposed to learn to coordinate heterogeneous agents. And communication heterogeneity [3] is considered to provide an analysis tool to describe and quantify heterogeneity during communication.

3 Method

Here we describe an alternative to address the problem of heterogeneous agents by curriculum learning.

3.1 Preliminaries

Consider how a human student learn skills from class. She starts with learning basic concepts and practicing by solving simple problem. As she gets familiar to the newly learnt knowledge, she turns to practice with more difficult problems to become an expert. This is how Curriculum Learning [1] works. To formalize, the preferred curriculum learning is to search for a task selection function [28] $D : H \to T$ where H contains information about past interactions and T is the target task, the objective

$$Obj : \max_{D} \int_{T \sim T_{target}} P_T^N dT \tag{3}$$

indicates the outcome of curriculum learning, where T_{target} denotes the distribution of target tasks, N denotes the number of training steps and P_T^N denotes the fitness on task T after training N steps.

The way to choose a task selection function is one of the most central problem of curriculum learning. The task selection function can be viewed as a control of training trajectory, as shown in Fig. 3, on the skill potential landscape the two training trajectories A and B are of the same starting and target points. However, trajectory A tries to climb through the cliff, which means a rapid increase on training task. This will result in the agent is not prepared to solve the upcoming problem thus getting stuck at the valley. While trajectory B looks for a tortuous path but with slowly ascending difficulty. Therefore although trajectory B is geometrically longer than trajectory A, it is more training friendly. In particular, when the agent is trained directly from the target task, it means to jump vertically from the starting point to the target and is usually the most

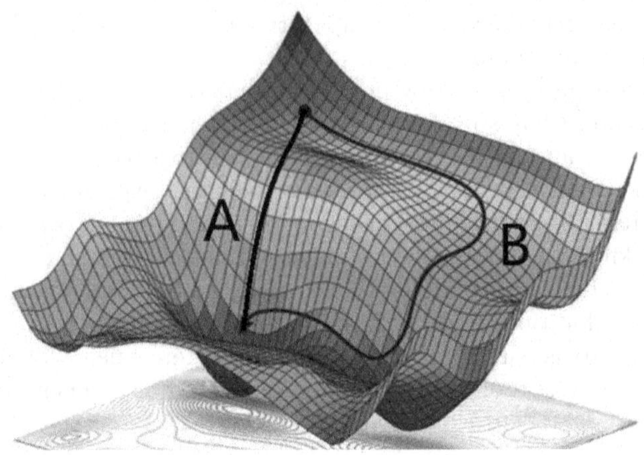

Fig. 3. Different training trajectory means different learning difficulty [13]

difficult trajectory. Therefore, there are tasks that are nearly impossible to learn even with long training time, but can be solved by curriculum learning.

Alternatives to select tasks along training process are broadly explored [28]. BARC [11] determines the initial states to control the difficulties. The reward function is also considered for exploration [4], guidance [8] or intrinsic goals [12]. Others may also consider changing the goal [18,30] during training, which is also known as multi-goal learning.

3.2 Curriculum Learning by Adjusting Opponents

In this work, a curriculum learning task selection by modifying the behaviour of opponents is used, since in heterogeneous force combat engagement problem there are naturally two competitive teams. The difficulty of the task of defeating the opponent can be slowly shifted by interfering the behaviour. Intuitively, consider a talented coach trying to train a teammate by sparring, the coach can conceal his skill in early days and make it all-out when the teammate is trained. Here we proposed two methods that can control the strength of the opponent.

The first method is to blur the observation of the opponent by a vanishing noise, as shown in Fig. 4. To be specific, let the observation of the opponent to be o and now is the j-th round of training, we feed observation

$$o' = o + \frac{N(0, \sigma)}{j} \tag{4}$$

as the input of the opponent. As the decision of the opponent is misled by the noise, it will no longer be a fatal threat that prevents the learner to learn even the basic rules of the game.

Theorem 1. *For a task with continuous action spaces, consider a perfectly trained linear controller G. Under the blurred observation, the distance between*

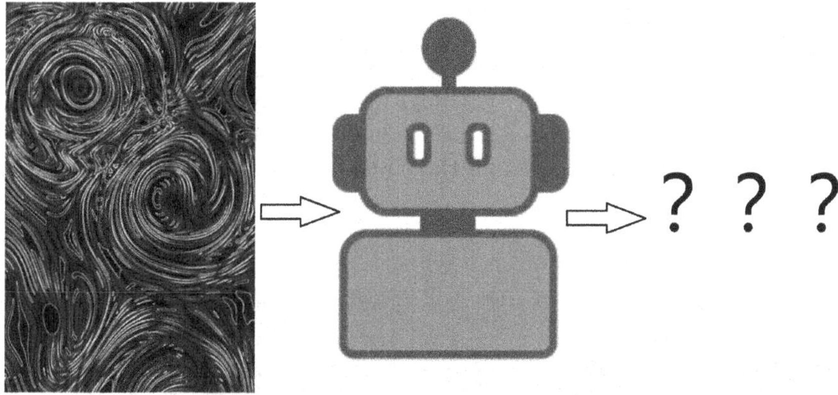

Fig. 4. Control opponent action by blurring observation

the actual behaviour and the best reaction is proportion to a Gaussian with mean 0 *and variance* $\frac{\sigma}{j^2}$.

Proof.

$$||G(o) - G(o')||_1 = ||G(o - o')||_1 \sim ||o - o'|| \sim N(0, \frac{\sigma}{j^2})$$

which indicates that we are able to control an opponent with ascending strength.

The second method is to randomly interfere the action commands of the opponent, which prevent the opponent from acting correctly. For a task with continuous action spaces, the output action a is added by a vanishing Gaussian noise, that is

$$a' = a + \frac{N(0, \sigma)}{j} \tag{5}$$

For a task with discrete action spaces, the action commands are randomly drop with refer to a probability inversely proportion to the number of rounds trained, that is

$$drop(a) = \frac{1}{j} \tag{6}$$

so we derives a method of interfering the behaviour of the opponent, with descending noise away from the best reaction.

4 Experiments

To evaluate the effectiveness of curriculum learning, we adopt the heterogeneous force combat engagements environment.

4.1 Environment and Settings

The task of heterogeneous force combat engagements is to defeat the opponent by destroying the command post. There are multiple agent types including radar, GBAD, destroyer, fighter plane, jammer, bomber and scout. As shown in Fig. 5, agents are highly heterogeneous and the observation is complex.

Fig. 5. A snapshot of the environment

Due to limited speed of the simulator, we utilize distributed training with a cluster of 8 GPUs, with each GPU we collect data from 8 parallel environments. And we compare the performance between the backbone multi-agent reinforcement learning algorithm with or without curriculum learning.

To examine the effectiveness of the two proposed methods of curriculum learning, two sets of contrast experiments are carried out. A hierarchical decision framework with high level instructions from the neural network controller and low level execution by a rule based controller is used. Two sets of rules of the executor are used respectively in two experiments to dispel the effects of rule-based controllers.

4.2 Evaluation

To evaluate the performance of the proposed methods, four metrics summarized from the training process are used.

- asymptotic expected rewards $V_{\pi^*}(S_0)$
- maximum expected rewards $\max_t V_{\pi_t}(s_0)$
- time to converge t_*
- time to reach a threshold of rewards λ, t_λ

concepts of the four metrics are visualized in Fig. 6.

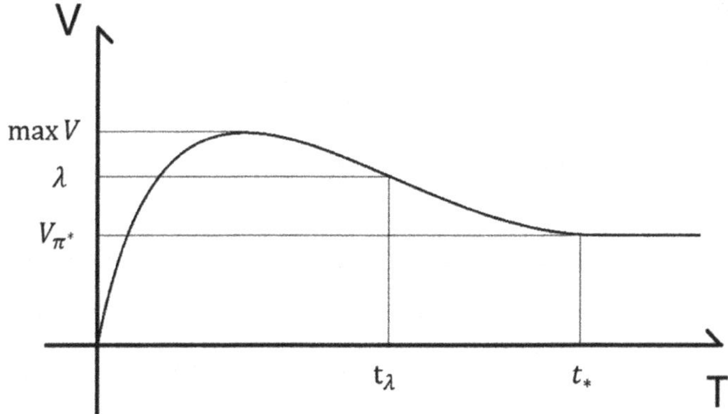

Fig. 6. The metrics used to evaluate an algorithm

4.3 Results

This work first did an experiment on blurring the observation of the opponent. Figure 7 shows the training curves of the baseline algorithm based on rule set A, where 7(a) shows the loss function of PPO and 7(b) shows the expected accumulative rewards.

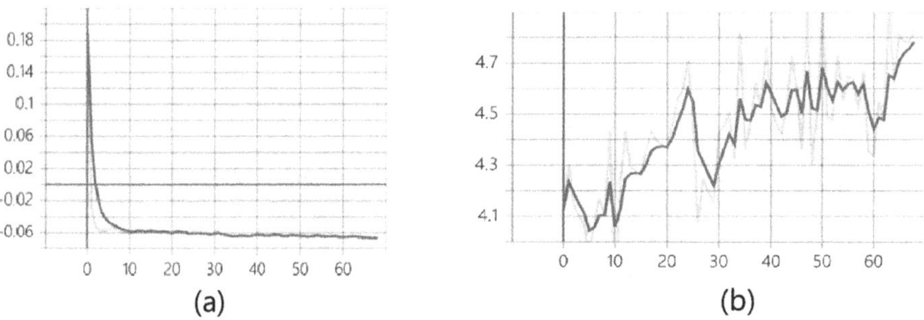

Fig. 7. The loss curve (a) and accumulative rewards (b) of baseline algorithm

As a contrast, Fig. 8 shows the training curves of the curriculum learning based on observation blurring, which also uses the rule set A for its low-level controller. According to the accumulative rewards, the four metrics are summarized in Table 1, where the threshold $\lambda = 4.7$.

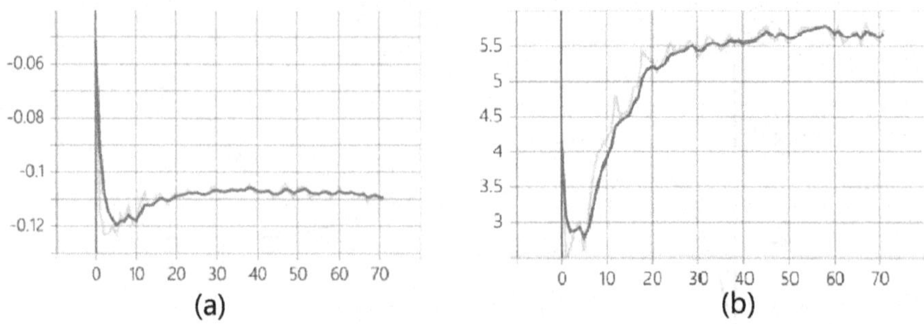

Fig. 8. The loss curve (a) and accumulative rewards (b) of observation blurring

Table 1. Comparison of baseline and observation blurring

Metrics	V_{π^*}	$\max V_{\pi_t}$	t_*	t_λ
Baseline	4.8	4.9	68	62
OB	5.6	5.75	45	18

The second part of the experiment consists of evaluating curriculum learning based on action interference. Figure 9 shows the training curves of the baseline algorithm based on rule set B.

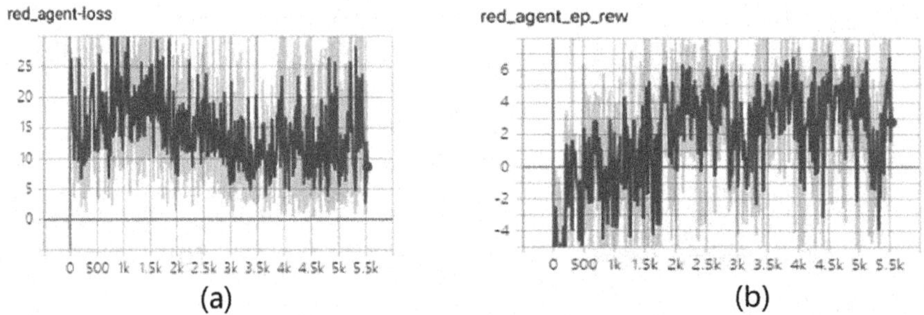

Fig. 9. The loss curve (a) and accumulative rewards (b) of baseline algorithm

While Fig. 10 shows the training curves of curriculum learning based on action interference, which also uses rule set B for low-level control. Table 2 summarizes the metrics of both training process, where $\lambda = 5$.

4.4 Discussion

The experiments reveal that both implementations of curriculum learning, observation blurring and action interference, outperforms the baseline algorithm in

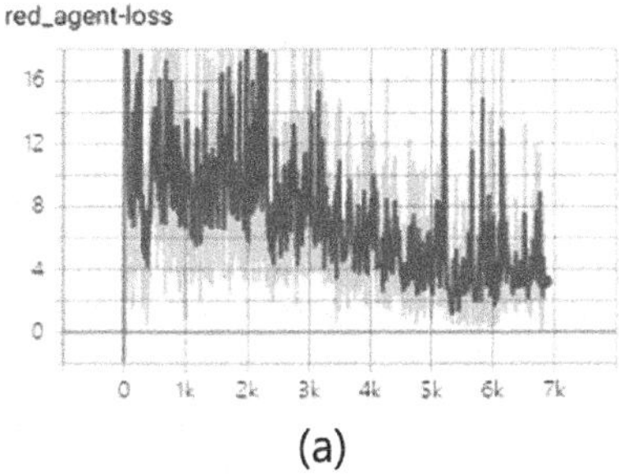

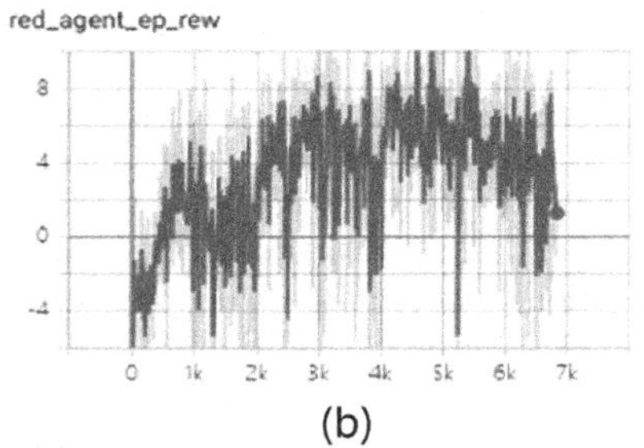

Fig. 10. The loss curve (a) and accumulative rewards (b) of action interference

Table 2. Comparison of baseline and action interference

Metrics	V_{π^*}	$\max V_{\pi_t}$	t_*	t_λ
Baseline	4	7	2000	2000
AI	5	10	2000	1000

policy performance, convergence and sample efficiency. Firstly, as shown in the comparison of $\max V_{\pi_t}$, curriculum learning found policies that gains rewards 10% more than the baseline algorithm. This shows that curriculum learning is able to find better policy, as we are trying to exploit reinforcement learning to find an optimal controller for the problem. Secondly, the comparison of V_{π^*} and t_* also reveals that curriculum learning outperforms the baseline algorithm in asymptotic performance, no matter in convergent point or time to converge. Thirdly, the comparison of t_λ reveals that curriculum learning boosts the sample efficiency for at least 10%. This also in line with expectation, since curriculum learning leverage the training trajectory that is more suitable all along the training process. To sum up, the experiments show a 10% boosting on performance and in turn support the claims this work mentioned above.

5 Conclusion

In this work we proposed an curriculum learning method based on interfering the opponent to solve an heterogeneous force combat. According to the empirical results, the two proposed interfering alternative, observation blurring and action dropping, are both able to achieve a 10% boosting on evaluation metrics.

Although the empirical results show the effectiveness of this method, the theoretically understanding of applying curriculum learning to heterogeneous multi-agent learning problem is still unclear, which we will leave as a future work.

References

1. Bengio, Y., Louradour, J., Collobert, R., Weston, J.: Curriculum learning. In: Proceedings of the 26th Annual International Conference On Machine Learning, pp. 41–48 (2009)
2. Bravo, M., Alvarado, M.: On the pragmatic similarity between agent communication protocols: modeling and measuring. In: On the Move to Meaningful Internet Systems: OTM, pp. 128–137 (2008)
3. Bravo, M., Reyes-Ortiz, J.A., Rodríguez, J., Silva-López, B.: Multi-agent communication heterogeneity. In: 2015 International Conference on Computational Science and Computational Intelligence (CSCI), pp. 583–588. IEEE (2015)
4. Burda, Y., Edwards, H., Storkey, A., Klimov, O.: Exploration by random network distillation. arXiv preprint arXiv:1810.12894 (2018)
5. Calvo, J.A., Dusparic, I.: Heterogeneous multi-agent deep reinforcement learning for traffic lights control. In: AICS, pp. 2–13 (2018)
6. Dorigo, M., Birattari, M., Stutzle, T.: Ant colony optimization. IEEE Comput. Intell. Mag. **1**(4), 28–39 (2006)
7. Foerster, J., Farquhar, G., Afouras, T., Nardelli, N., Whiteson, S.: Counterfactual multi-agent policy gradients. In: Proceedings of the AAAI Conference on Artificial Intelligence, vol. 32 (2018)
8. Fournier, P., Sigaud, O., Chetouani, M., Oudeyer, P.Y.: Accuracy-based curriculum learning in deep reinforcement learning. arXiv preprint arXiv:1806.09614 (2018)
9. Henaff, M., Bruna, J., LeCun, Y.: Deep convolutional networks on graph-structured data. arXiv preprint arXiv:1506.05163 (2015)
10. Hu, W., Tan, Y.: Prototype generation using multiobjective particle swarm optimization for nearest neighbor classification. IEEE Trans. Cybern. **46**(12), 2719–2731 (2015)
11. Ivanovic, B., Harrison, J., Sharma, A., Chen, M., Pavone, M.: BARC: backward reachability curriculum for robotic reinforcement learning. In: 2019 International Conference on Robotics and Automation (ICRA), pp. 15–21. IEEE (2019)
12. Jabri, A., Hsu, K., Gupta, A., Eysenbach, B., Levine, S., Finn, C.: Unsupervised curricula for visual meta-reinforcement learning. In: Advances in Neural Information Processing Systems, vol. 32 (2019)
13. Jain, P., Kar, P., et al.: Non-convex optimization for machine learning. Found. Trends Mach. Learn. **10**(3–4), 142–363 (2017)
14. Jiang, J., Lu, Z.: Offline decentralized multi-agent reinforcement learning. arXiv preprint arXiv:2108.01832 (2021)
15. Kapetanakis, S., Kudenko, D.: Reinforcement learning of coordination in heterogeneous cooperative multi-agent systems. In: Kudenko, D., Kazakov, D., Alonso, E. (eds.) AAMAS 2003-2004. LNCS (LNAI), vol. 3394, pp. 119–131. Springer, Heidelberg (2005). https://doi.org/10.1007/978-3-540-32274-0_8
16. Kennedy, J., Eberhart, R.: Particle swarm optimization. In: Proceedings of ICNN 1995-International Conference on Neural Networks, vol. 4, pp. 1942–1948. IEEE (1995)
17. Köster, R.: Model-free conventions in multi-agent reinforcement learning with heterogeneous preferences. arXiv preprint arXiv:2010.09054 (2020)
18. Lair, N., Colas, C., Portelas, R., Dussoux, J.M., Dominey, P.F., Oudeyer, P.Y.: Language grounding through social interactions and curiosity-driven multi-goal learning. arXiv preprint arXiv:1911.03219 (2019)

19. Li, H., He, H.: Multi-agent trust region policy optimization. arXiv preprint arXiv:2010.07916 (2020)
20. Liu, C.L., Tian, Y.P.: Formation control of multi-agent systems with heterogeneous communication delays. Int. J. Syst. Sci. **40**(6), 627–636 (2009)
21. Liu, L., Zheng, S., Tan, Y.: S-metric based multi-objective fireworks algorithm. In: 2015 IEEE Congress on Evolutionary Computation (CEC), pp. 1257–1264. IEEE (2015)
22. Lowe, R., Wu, Y.I., Tamar, A., Harb, J., Pieter Abbeel, O., Mordatch, I.: Multi-agent actor-critic for mixed cooperative-competitive environments. In: Advances in Neural Information Processing Systems, vol. 30 (2017)
23. Meneghetti, D.D.R., Bianchi, R.A.C.: Towards heterogeneous multi-agent reinforcement learning with graph neural networks. arXiv preprint arXiv:2009.13161 (2020)
24. Meneghetti, D.D.R., da Costa Bianchi, R.A.: Specializing inter-agent communication in heterogeneous multi-agent reinforcement learning using agent class information. arXiv:abs/2012.07617 (2020)
25. Minsky, M.: Steps toward artificial intelligence. Proc. IRE **49**(1), 8–30 (1961)
26. Nash, J.F., Jr.: Equilibrium points in n-person games. Proc. Natl. Acad. Sci. **36**(1), 48–49 (1950)
27. Oliehoek, F.A., Spaan, M.T., Vlassis, N.: Optimal and approximate q-value functions for decentralized Pomdps. J. Artif. Intell. Res. **32**, 289–353 (2008)
28. Portelas, R., Colas, C., Weng, L., Hofmann, K., Oudeyer, P.Y.: Automatic curriculum learning for deep RL: a short survey. arXiv preprint arXiv:2003.04664 (2020)
29. Price, B., Boutilier, C.: Reinforcement learning with imitation in heterogeneous multi-agent systems
30. Racaniere, S., Lampinen, A.K., Santoro, A., Reichert, D.P., Firoiu, V., Lillicrap, T.P.: Automated curricula through setter-solver interactions. arXiv preprint arXiv:1909.12892 (2019)
31. Rashid, T., Farquhar, G., Peng, B., Whiteson, S.: Weighted QMIX: expanding monotonic value function factorisation for deep multi-agent reinforcement learning. Adv. Neural. Inf. Process. Syst. **33**, 10199–10210 (2020)
32. Rashid, T., Samvelyan, M., Schroeder, C., Farquhar, G., Foerster, J., Whiteson, S.: QMIX: monotonic value function factorisation for deep multi-agent reinforcement learning. In: International Conference On Machine Learning, pp. 4295–4304. PMLR (2018)
33. Samvelyan, M., et al.: The StarCraft Multi-Agent Challenge. CoRR abs/1902.04043 (2019)
34. Schulman, J., Levine, S., Abbeel, P., Jordan, M., Moritz, P.: Trust region policy optimization. In: International Conference on Machine Learning, pp. 1889–1897. PMLR (2015)
35. Schulman, J., Wolski, F., Dhariwal, P., Radford, A., Klimov, O.: Proximal policy optimization algorithms. arXiv preprint arXiv:1707.06347 (2017)
36. Son, K., Kim, D., Kang, W.J., Hostallero, D.E., Yi, Y.: QTRAN: learning to factorize with transformation for cooperative multi-agent reinforcement learning. In: International Conference on Machine Learning, pp. 5887–5896. PMLR (2019)
37. Su, K., Zhou, S., Gan, C., Wang, X., Lu, Z.: Ma2QL: a minimalist approach to fully decentralized multi-agent reinforcement learning. arXiv preprint arXiv:2209.08244 (2022)
38. Sunehag, P., et al.: Value-decomposition networks for cooperative multi-agent learning. arXiv preprint arXiv:1706.05296 (2017)

39. Tan, M.: Multi-agent reinforcement learning: independent vs. cooperative agents. In: Proceedings of the Tenth International Conference on Machine Learning, pp. 330–337 (1993)
40. Tan, Y., Zhu, Y.: Fireworks algorithm for optimization. In: Tan, Y., Shi, Y., Tan, K.C. (eds.) ICSI 2010. LNCS, vol. 6145, pp. 355–364. Springer, Heidelberg (2010). https://doi.org/10.1007/978-3-642-13495-1_44
41. Terry, J.K., Grammel, N., Hari, A., Santos, L.: Parameter sharing is surprisingly useful for multi-agent deep reinforcement learning (2020)
42. Terry, J.K., Grammel, N., Hari, A., Santos, L., Black, B.: Revisiting parameter sharing in multi-agent deep reinforcement learning. arXiv preprint arXiv:2005.13625 (2020)
43. Terry, J.K., Grammel, N., Son, S., Black, B.: Parameter sharing for heterogeneous agents in multi-agent reinforcement learning. arXiv:abs/2005.13625 (2020)
44. Vinyals, O., et al.: Grandmaster level in StarCraft ii using multi-agent reinforcement learning. Nature **575**(7782), 350–354 (2019)
45. Vinyals, O., et al.: StarCraft ii: A new challenge for reinforcement learning. arXiv preprint arXiv:1708.04782 (2017)
46. Wang, J., Ren, Z., Liu, T., Yu, Y., Zhang, C.: Qplex: duplex dueling multi-agent q-learning. arXiv preprint arXiv:2008.01062 (2020)
47. Wang, T., Dong, H., Lesser, V., Zhang, C.: Roma: Multi-agent reinforcement learning with emergent roles. arXiv preprint arXiv:2003.08039 (2020)
48. Wang, T., Gupta, T., Mahajan, A., Peng, B., Whiteson, S., Zhang, C.: Rode: learning roles to decompose multi-agent tasks. arXiv preprint arXiv:2010.01523 (2020)
49. de Witt, C.S., et al.: Is independent learning all you need in the StarCraft multi-agent challenge? arXiv preprint arXiv:2011.09533 (2020)
50. Yang, S., Yang, B., Kang, Z., Deng, L.: IHG-MA: Inductive heterogeneous graph multi-agent reinforcement learning for multi-intersection traffic signal control. Neural Netw. **139**, 265–277 (2021). https://doi.org/10.1016/j.neunet.2021.03.015
51. Yu, C., Velu, A., Vinitsky, E., Wang, Y., Bayen, A., Wu, Y.: The surprising effectiveness of ppo in cooperative, multi-agent games. arXiv preprint arXiv:2103.01955 (2021)
52. Zheng, Z., Tan, Y.: Group explosion strategy for searching multiple targets using swarm robotic. In: 2013 IEEE Congress on Evolutionary Computation, pp. 821–828. IEEE (2013)
53. Zhou, J., Cui, G., Zhang, Z., Yang, C., Liu, Z., Sun, M.: Graph neural networks: a review of methods and applications. arXiv:abs/1812.08434 (2020)
54. Zhou, Y., Tan, Y.: GPU-based parallel multi-objective particle swarm optimization. Int. J. Artif. Intell. **7**(A11), 125–141 (2011)

A Deep Reinforcement Learning Approach for Cooperative Target Defense

Yanxue Xiong[1], Zhigang Wang[2], and Liangjun Ke[1](✉)

[1] State Key Laboratory for Manufacturing Systems Engineering, School of Automation Science and Engineering, Xi'an Jiaotong University, Xi'an, China
keljxjtu@xjtu.edu.cn

[2] CETC Key Laboratory of Data Link Technology Xi'an, Xi'an, China

Abstract. This paper considers a new variant of the pursuit-evasion problem, called the cooperative target defense problem with three agents (attacker, targeter, and defender) in a 3D space. The targeter tries to fly as quickly as possible from a starting point to the terminal, while the defender seeks to protect it from the attacker. The problem is difficult to solve under traditional game theory methods, while deep reinforcement learning (DRL) has shown strong adaptability in these complex and higher-dimensional tasks. Inspired by the successful applications of Proximal Policy Optimization (PPO), this paper proposes a PPO-based algorithm for the problem, intending to derive the optimal behavioral policies for both sides. We design the corresponding state space, action space, and rewards of the agents. Three kinds of reward functions are proposed for the attacker and compared by experimental results. Our study provides a good foundation for the cooperative target defense problem.

Keywords: Pursuit-evasion game · Differential game · Deep reinforcement learning · Cooperative target defense

1 Introduction

The pursuit-evasion problem is an important problem in the fields of game theory and artificial intelligence, widely used in aerospace technology, robotics, police security, cyber security, and other fields [6,10]. It has many variants, one of them is Targeter-Attacker-Defender Game (TAD Game) [9]. In this game, there are three agents including an attacker, a targeter, and a defender. The attacker aims to pursue the targeter protected by a defender, while the targeter tries to move from a starting point to a terminal point as soon as possible.

For this game, Von Moll [17], Liang [8,9], and Zhou [19] have solved it based on differential game theory. And later, Fu et al. [3], and Lin et al. have gone further with other methods [10]. But in more complex situations, it becomes difficult or even unworkable for these conventional methods to solve the problem [13,15].

Y. Tan and Y. Shi (Eds.): DMBD 2022, CCIS 1744, pp. 17–26, 2022.
https://doi.org/10.1007/978-981-19-9297-1_2

Reinforcement learning is one of the main paradigms of machine learning, which uses rewards to guide the learning process [14]. As an important tool for multistage decisions, it has been used for the pursuit-evasion problem and its variants [4]. Motivated by the prominent representation ability of deep learning [7], deep reinforcement learning (DRL), a unified framework of reinforcement learning and deep learning, has been widely studied since 2015 [11]. In recent years, deep reinforcement learning has been successfully applied in video games [16], robots [1], and other various fields [2]. Since deep Q-learning was proposed [11], many popular deep reinforcement learning algorithms have been proposed. Among them, the Proximal Policy Optimization (PPO) algorithm [12] is very promising.

In this paper, we consider a special Targeter-Attacker-Defender Game (TAD Game) in which all agents stay in a three-dimensional environment, which is studied for the first time. There are still bottlenecks in the exploration of strategies and the chain reaction caused by the rising dimensionality. To deal with such a complex problem, we design a PPO-based algorithm by taking into account the fundamental characteristics of the agents. Particularly, we propose three ways of reward setting for the attacker. The effectiveness of reward settings and the algorithm is studied according to experimental results.

The remaining of this paper is structured as follows. In Sect. 2, we present the basic process of PPO and MAPPO [18] which is an effective multi-agent version of PPO. In Sect. 3, the formal description of the 3D TAD problem is presented. In Sect. 4, we present the detail of our algorithm. In Sect. 5, the experimental study is presented. The main results are summarized in Sect. 6.

2 Background

The basic process of our algorithm is based on PPO. As reinforcement learning is usually described by a Markov decision process, an agent selects an action a_t in its policy π to interact with the environment under the state s_t. Then it gets a feedback reward r_t and steps into the next state. π is assigned a parameter θ. The training purpose is achieved by using a policy $\pi_{\theta'}$, which has a small difference from π_θ, to collect data as a demonstration to update θ.

The concept of deep learning was introduced in 2006 by G.E. Hinton et al. [5]. It is suggested that Deep Neural Networks (DNN) structure can be used in training sample data, which makes it easier to realize our learning tasks. The classical Actor-Critic network is adopted, in which the actor network outputs actions according to the state; the critic network outputs the value, which is used to evaluate the actions outputted by the actor network.

Thus, for a trajectory $\tau = \{s_1, a_1, s_2, a_2, \ldots, s_t, a_t\}$, the probability of its occurrence is described as $p_\theta(\tau)$. The return can be calculated by Eq. 1 where γ is the discount factor:

$$R(\tau) = \sum_{t=t_0}^{T} \gamma^{t-t_0} r_t. \tag{1}$$

The advantage function is described as

$$A^{\theta}\left(s_t, a_t\right)=\sum_{t=t_0}^{T_n}\left(R\left(\tau^n\right)-b\right)=\sum_{t=t_0}^{T} \gamma^{t-t_0} r_t-b, \tag{2}$$

where the baseline b is usually regarded as the value function.

$$\begin{aligned} & J_{PPO}^{\theta^k}(\theta) \\ & \approx \min \left(\frac{p_\theta\left(a_t \mid s_t\right)}{p_{\theta^k}\left(a_t \mid s_t\right)} A^{\theta^k}\left(s_t, a_t\right), clip\left(\frac{p_\theta\left(a_t \mid s_t\right)}{p_{\theta^k}\left(a_t \mid s_t\right)}, 1-\varepsilon, 1+\varepsilon\right) A^{\theta^k}\left(s_t, a_t\right)\right) .\end{aligned} \tag{3}$$

In order to optimize the objective function of the PPO-clip in Eq. 3, the next step is to update the AC network by backward the loss functions which are

$$\begin{aligned} & loss_{Actor}=-min(\frac{p_\theta\left(a_t \mid s_t\right)}{p_{\theta^k}\left(a_t \mid s_t\right)} A^{\theta^k}\left(s_t, a_t\right), clip(\frac{p_\theta\left(a_t \mid s_t\right)}{p_{\theta^k}\left(a_t \mid s_t\right)}, 1-\varepsilon, 1+\varepsilon) A^{\theta^k}\left(s_t, a_t\right)), \\ & loss_{Critic}=\left(G_t-Value\right)^2, \end{aligned} \tag{4}$$

where G_t is the actual discounted return.

Similar to the PPO algorithm, a centralized value function network is designed in the MAPPO algorithm. With centralized training and decentralized execution, agents are able to interact with each other through a global value function. And some additional techniques are used to improve the efficiency of the algorithm [18].

3 The Problem Description

In this section, we formally describe the cooperative target defense problem. In a three-dimensional environment, there are three agents, namely Attacker(**A**), Targeter(**T**), and Defender(**D**). The task of **A** is to attack **T** which attempts to reach a terminal point safely under the protection of **D**. A demo scenario is shown in Fig. 1.

In this game, these agents play under the following rules:

- **A, T, D** move with constant velocity magnitudes v_A, v_T, v_D $(v_A=v_D>v_T)$ respectively. But each agent can control its yaw and pitch angle to change the moving direction. The change of the yaw and pitch angle must be less than $\pi/2$ and $\pi/4$. The turning radius is determined by its axis length and angle change.
- **T**'s initial position is $T_0\left(x_{T_0}, y_{T_0}, z_{T_0}\right)$, while $ter(\ x_{ter},\ y_{ter},\ z_{ter})$ is its terminal point. The distance between them is denoted as $|T_0-ter|$, and the gaming time is limited within $\Gamma=\frac{|T_0-ter|}{V_T}\times 2$.

Fig. 1. Schematic diagram of the three dimensional Targeter-Attacker-Defender problem

- **A** can capture **T** within the distance of $|V_A|$ around it. T will be captured if the current $A_t\,(x_{A_t}, y_{A_t}, z_{A_t})$ and $T_t\,(x_{T_t}, y_{T_t}, z_{T_t})$ satisfies $|A_t - T_t| \leq V_A$. Similarly, **D**'s capture range and terminal spherical are defined.
- If **A** captures **T** or dispels **T** away from the terminal within the time limit of the game, the game ends and **A** wins; if **T** enters the terminal in time or **D** captures **A** before **T** is captured, the game ends and the TD team wins.

At time t, let $d_{AT}(t)$, $d_{DA}(t)$, and $d_{Tter}(t)$ denote the distance between **A** and **T**, the distance between **D** and **A**, the distance between **T** and terminal respectively. In order to win the game, **A** tries to minimize J_A which is defined as follows:

$$J_A = w_{\mathrm{A}_1} d_{AT}(t) - w_{\mathrm{A}_2} d_{DA}(t), \tag{5}$$

where w_{A_1} and w_{A_2} are two positive weights.

In order to win the game, the TD team tries to minimize J_T and J_D which are defined as follows:

$$\begin{aligned} J_T &= w_{\mathrm{T}_1} d_{Tter}(t) - w_{\mathrm{T}_2} d_{AT}(t), \\ J_D &= d_{DA}(t), \end{aligned} \tag{6}$$

where w_{T_1} and w_{T_2} are two positive weights.

4 The Proposed Algorithm

For the attacker, a PPO algorithm is proposed for policy optimization. Since the targeter and defender are cooperative, a multi-agent PPO [12] is proposed for policy optimization.

4.1 State and Action Space

In the coordinate system $o - xyz$, the motion of each agent can be decomposed into the xoy and yoz planes (see a demo of T in Fig. 2). Then the action space (φ_i, θ_i) is defined by $(\varphi_i \in [0, 2\pi), \theta_i \in [-\pi/2, \pi/2])$ where $i \in \{\mathbf{T,A,D}\}$. φ, θ are the yaw and pitch angle respectively. The state of each agent is $(A_t, D_t, T_t, \varphi_{At}, \theta_{At}, \varphi_{Dt}, \theta_{Dt}, \varphi_{Tt}, \theta_{Tt})$.

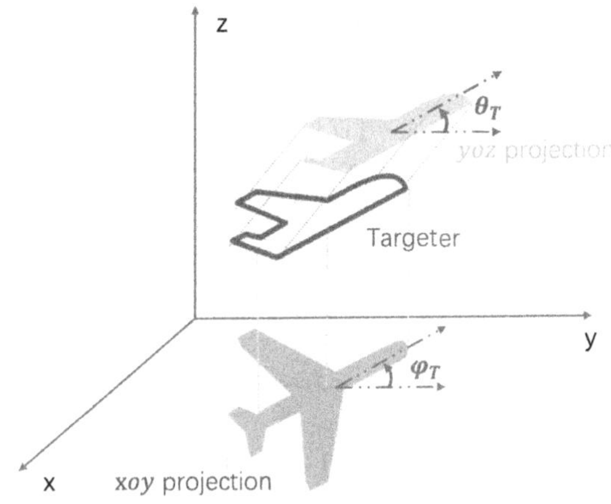

Fig. 2. Illustration of Targeter's action space.

4.2 Reward Functions

For the attacker, the basic idea to define the reward is to encourage it to stay away from the defender and get close to the targeter. Three methods are suggested to define the reward for the attacker according to different considerations.

1) method 1: the reward is defined according to whether **A**'s behavior is favorable for capturing **T** and avoiding **D**. Define $\Delta AT = |A_{t-1} - T_{t-1}| - |A_t - T_t|$, $\Delta AD = |A_{t-1} - D_{t-1}| - |A_t - D_t|$.

$$r_A = \begin{cases} 45/\Gamma & \text{if} \quad \Delta AT > 0.1 \wedge \Delta AD \leq 0.1 \\ 30/\Gamma & \text{if} \quad \Delta AT > 0.1 \wedge \Delta AD > 0.1 \\ 3/\Gamma & \text{if} \quad \Delta AT \leq 0.1 \wedge \Delta AD \leq 0.1 \\ 0 & \text{if} \quad \Delta AT \leq 0.1 \wedge \Delta AD > 0.1 \end{cases}. \tag{7}$$

2) method 2: At the current time, let $\overrightarrow{\sigma_A}$ and $\overrightarrow{\sigma_A}^*$ be **A**'s actual and reference direction respectively where the reference direction is calculated by the velocity of targeter at the last timestep. The angle between them is written as $\Delta\sigma_A$. σ_a stands for the acceptable angular offset. The reward is defined according to the magnitude of $\Delta\sigma_A$.

$$r_A = \begin{cases} max(2 - \Delta\sigma_A/\sigma_a, 1)/\Gamma \times 30 & \text{if} \quad \Delta\sigma_A \leq \sigma_a \\ max(2 - \Delta\sigma_A/\sigma_a, 0)/\Gamma \times 30 & \text{if} \quad \sigma_a < \Delta\sigma_A \leq 2\sigma_a \\ max(1 - \Delta\sigma_A/\sigma_a, -2)/\Gamma \times 30 & \text{if} \quad \Delta\sigma_A > 2\sigma_a \end{cases}. \tag{8}$$

3) method 3: Define λ_t as the distance between A_t and the predicted collision of **A** and **T** at time t. To penalize the occurrence of over-chasing, set a counter C to record the times of the situation. The reward is defined according to

whether λ_t becomes smaller in contrast to λ_{t-1}.

$$r_A = \begin{cases} min(2|\lambda_t - \lambda_{t-1}| + 1, 2)/\Gamma \times 10 & \text{if } \lambda_{t-1} - \lambda_t \geq 0.05 \\ -max(-2|\lambda_t - \lambda_{t-1}|, -1)/\Gamma \times 10 - \gamma^C & \text{if } \lambda_{t-1} - \lambda_t < 0.05 \end{cases}. \tag{9}$$

For the targeter, the reward is given as follows:

$$r_T = w_{\mathrm{T}_1} d_{Tter}(t) - w_{\mathrm{T}_2} d_{AT}(t). \tag{10}$$

For the defender, the reward r_D is given as follows:

$$r_D = d_{DA}(t). \tag{11}$$

5 Experimental Results and Analysis

Experiments are conducted in a simulation environment based on Python version 3.7. The initial angles are $\varphi_i = \theta_i = 0 (i \in \{\mathbf{T,A,D}\})$, speeds are $|V_A| = |V_D| = 0.18, |V_T| = 0.13$, axis lengths are $L = 0.1$ and terminal point is $(0, 0, 0)$. The training process is stopped when the maximum number of episodes reaches 10,000. Take w_{T_1} to be 0.6, w_{T_2} to be 0.4, and γ to be 1.08. When training the attacker, the defender moves towards the attacker and the targeter moves close to the terminal while avoiding the attacker. After that, the TD team is trained.

5.1 The Experimental Study on the Reward Methods for the Attacker

At first, we compare the three methods of defining reward for the attacker. Each model (i.e., each method) is tested for 100 rounds. The winning percentages are shown in Table 1. As seen from Table 1, the attacker trained by method 2 can complete the task the best, while the agent trained by method 1 performs the poorest.

Some policies that attacker had taken are given in Fig. 3. As seen from Fig. 3(a), Fig. 3(b), and Fig. 3(c), once in a safe area, a smart **A** would purely pursue **T** (i.e., without considering **D**). Especially, due to the condition of $|v_A > v_T|$ and the limit in turning angle, as shown in Fig. 3(a) and Fig. 3(b), **A** cannot capture **T** directly through the shortest distance, instead it outflanks **T**. Also, a smart **A** can try its best to pursue **T**, avoiding flying near **D** when there is a threat from **D**, like the policies shown in Fig. 3(d), Fig. 3(e), and Fig. 3(f).

Table 1. **A**'s winning percentage obtained by the three reward methods.

	Method 1	Method 2	Method 3
Winning percentage	0.4800	**0.6253**	0.5763

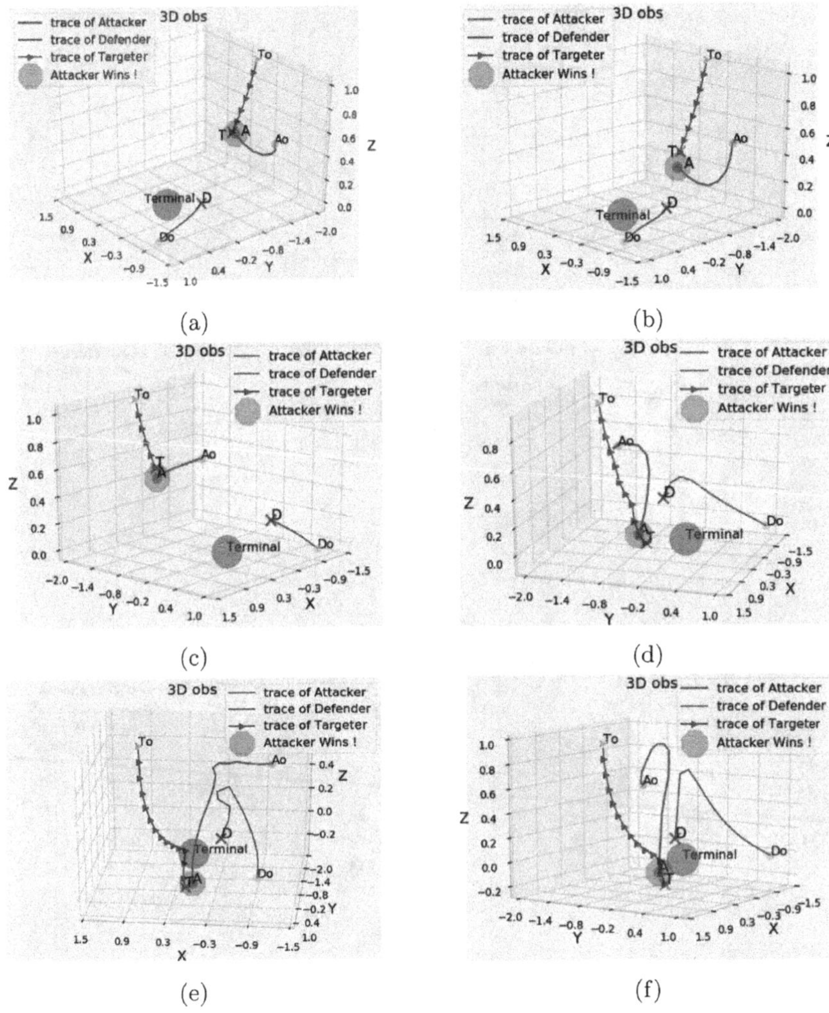

Fig. 3. Several snapshots where attacker successfully completes the task

5.2 The Experimental Study on the Behavior of Defender and Targeter

Figure 4 shows some of the policies the TD team had adopted. According to Fig. 4, when **T** moves straight toward the terminal (see Fig. 4(a) and Fig. 4(b)) or **D** intercepts **A** (see Fig. 4(c)), the whole team can win the game. It is obvious that the agents learn the trick that if both of them try their best to complete their own tasks, the chances of winning can be improved. So they also perform as shown in Fig. 4(d), Fig. 4(e), and Fig. 4(f). Moreover, in Fig. 4(c), the TD team is smart enough to cooperatively win the game. In detail, **T** lures **A** to fall into **D**'s capture region.

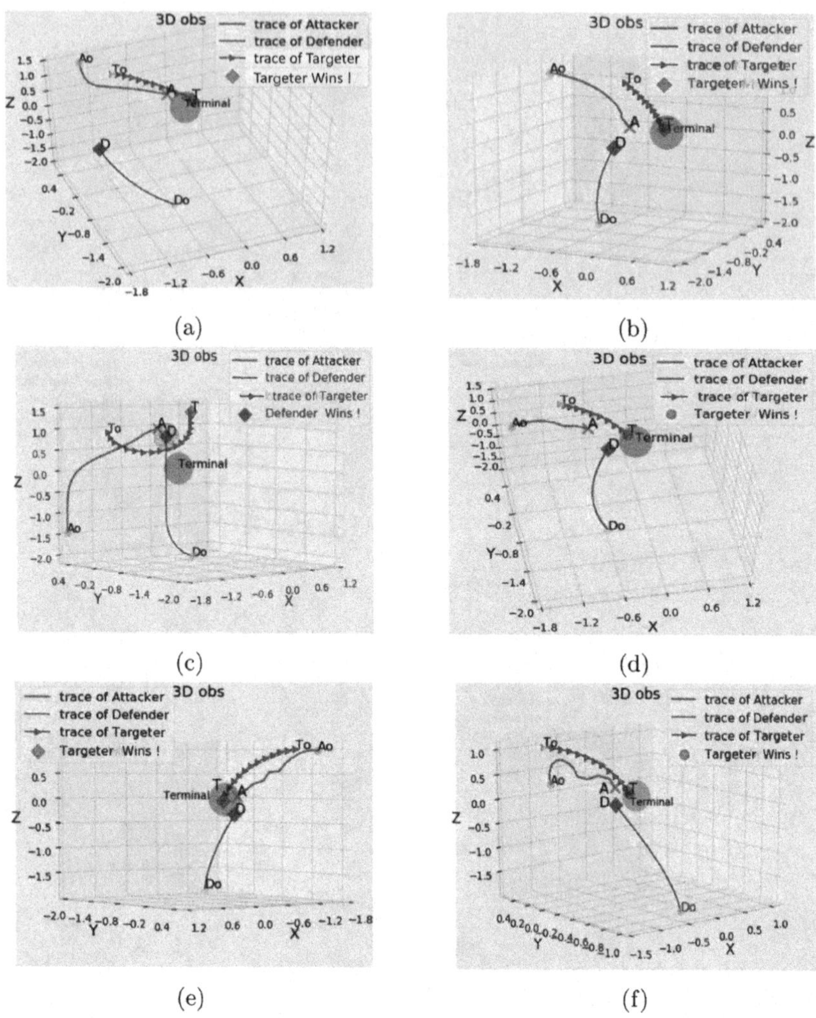

Fig. 4. Several snapshots where the TD team successfully completes the task

6 Conclusion

This paper studies the cooperative target defense problem for the first time. Since this problem is very difficult, we design a Proximal Policy Optimization based algorithm with the aim of obtaining the optimal behavioral policies. For every agent in the game, we design their corresponding state space, action space, and rewards. Moreover, for the attacker, we propose three kinds of reward functions. The experimental results show that method 2 is the best. Moreover, the effectiveness of the proposed algorithm is analyzed.

In the future, it may be interesting to use various reinforcement learning algorithms to deal with the cooperative target defense problem. In addition, it may be better to use the self-play technique to improve the behaviors of these agents.

Acknowledgment. This work was supported by the National Natural Science Foundation of China under Grant 61973244 and Grant 61573277. It is also supported by the open fund of CETC Key Laboratory of Data Link Technology (CLDL-20202101-1).

References

1. Andrychowicz, O.M., et al.: Learning dexterous in-hand manipulation. Int. J. Robot. Res. **39**(1), 3–20 (2020)
2. Degrave, J., et al.: Magnetic control of tokamak plasmas through deep reinforcement learning. Nature **602**(7897), 414–419 (2022)
3. Fu, H., Liu, H.H.T.: Optimal solution of a target defense game with two defenders and a faster intrude. Unmanned Syst. **9**(03), 247–262 (2021)
4. Givigi, S.N., Schwartz, H.M., Lu, X.: A reinforcement learning adaptive fuzzy controller for differential games. J. Intell. Rob. Syst. **59**(1), 3–30 (2010)
5. Hinton, G.E., Osindero, S., Teh, Y.W.: A fast learning algorithm for deep belief nets. Neural Comput. **18**(7), 1527–1554 (2006)
6. Kong, W., Zhou, D., Yang, Z., Zhao, Y., Zhang, K.: UAV autonomous aerial combat maneuver strategy generation with observation error based on state-adversarial deep deterministic policy gradient and inverse reinforcement learning. Electronics **9**(7), 1121 (2020)
7. LeCun, Y., Bengio, Y., Hinton, G.: Deep learning. Nature **521**(7553), 436–444 (2015)
8. Liang, L., Deng, F., Lu, M., Chen, J.: Analysis of role switch for cooperative target defense differential game. IEEE Trans. Autom. Control **66**(2), 902–909 (2020)
9. Liang, L., Deng, F., Peng, Z., Li, X., Zha, W.: A differential game for cooperative target defense. Automatica **102**, 58–71 (2019)
10. Lin, B., Qiao, L., Jia, Z., Sun, Z., Sun, M., Zhang, W.: Control strategies for target-attacker-defender games of USVs. In: 2021 6th International Conference on Automation, Control and Robotics Engineering (CACRE), pp. 191–198 (2021). https://doi.org/10.1109/CACRE52464.2021.9501329
11. Mnih, V., et al.: Human-level control through deep reinforcement learning. Nature **518**(7540), 529–533 (2015)
12. Schulman, J., Wolski, F., Dhariwal, P., Radford, A., Klimov, O.: Proximal policy optimization algorithms. arXiv preprint arXiv:1707.06347 (2017)
13. Sun, W., Tsiotras, P., Lolla, T., Subramani, D.N., Lermusiaux, P.F.: Multiple-pursuer/one-evader pursuit-evasion game in dynamic flowfields. J. Guid. Control. Dyn. **40**(7), 1627–1637 (2017)
14. Sutton, R.S., Barto, A.G.: Reinforcement Learning: An Introduction. MIT Press, Cambridge (2018)
15. Tang, X., Ye, D., Huang, L., Sun, Z., Sun, J.: Pursuit-evasion game switching strategies for spacecraft with incomplete-information. Aerosp. Sci. Technol. **119**, 107112 (2021)
16. Vinyals, O., et al.: Grandmaster level in StarCraft II using multi-agent reinforcement learning. Nature **575**(7782), 350–354 (2019)

17. Von Moll, A., Casbeer, D.W., Garcia, E., Milutinović, D.: Pursuit-evasion of an evader by multiple pursuers. In: 2018 International Conference on Unmanned Aircraft Systems (ICUAS), pp. 133–142. IEEE (2018)
18. Yu, C., Velu, A., Vinitsky, E., Wang, Y., Bayen, A., Wu, Y.: The surprising effectiveness of PPO in cooperative, multi-agent games. arXiv preprint arXiv:2103.01955 (2021)
19. Zhou, Z., Zhang, W., Ding, J., Huang, H., Stipanović, D.M., Tomlin, C.J.: Cooperative pursuit with voronoi partitions. Automatica **72**, 64–72 (2016)

Particle Swarm Based Reinforcement Learning

Jianyu Duan[1], Yanxiao Guo[1], Zhigang Wang[2], and Liangjun Ke[1(✉)]

[1] State Key Laboratory for Manufacturing Systems Engineering, School of Automation Science and Engineering, Xi'an Jiaotong University, Xi'an, China
keljxjtu@xjtu.edu.cn

[2] CETC Key Laboratory of Data Link Technology Xi'an, Xi'an, China

Abstract. With the vigorous development of computer-related technology, the "perception + decision" paradigm of the combination of deep learning and reinforcement learning has become a research hotspot. Nowadays, deep reinforcement learning algorithms have been successfully applied to the fields of games, industry and commerce. However, deep reinforcement learning algorithms often fall into the dilemma of "exploration" and "exploitation", and the effect of these algorithms is easily affected by the quality of hyperparameters. In order to make up for the defects mentioned above, this paper introduces the particle swarm based reinforcement learning framework (PRL). Compared with the standard reinforcement learning algorithms, this framework greatly improves the exploration ability and obtains better scores in a series of gym experimental tests.

Keywords: Reinforcement learning · Particle swarm optimization · Twin delayed deep deterministic policy gradients

1 Introduction

Reinforcement learning (RL) is about an agent interacting with the environment to learn optimal policies through trial and error. It has been widely used to solve a great variety of sequential decision-making problems [16]. Currently, the rise of deep learning has accelerated progress in reinforcement learning, and enabled reinforcement learning to scale to problems that were previously intractable. The research work combining deep learning and reinforcement learning has led to the emergence of various powerful deep reinforcement learning systems, algorithms and agents, which has made remarkable achievements. Such systems not only surpass the capabilities of most classical and non-DL-based reinforcement learning agents, but also excel at tasks that are considered to require extreme human intelligence, creativity, and planning skills [2].

In the field of DRL [6], there are two outstanding classic success stories. The first was the beginning of the DRL revolution, which could learn to play a series of Atari 2600 video games at superhuman levels directly from image pixels [12]. The second prominent success was the development of the hybrid DRL system

Y. Tan and Y. Shi (Eds.): DMBD 2022, CCIS 1744, pp. 27–36, 2022.
https://doi.org/10.1007/978-981-19-9297-1_3

AlphaGo, which defeated the human Go world champion in March 2016 [15]. Unlike the handcrafted rules that dominate chess systems, AlphaGo contains neural networks trained by supervised learning and reinforcement learning, combined with traditional heuristic search algorithms. DRL's end-to-end "perception + decision" system paradigm is very close to the human learning method, has strong universality and gives the intelligent machines strong adaptability. Based on the above unique advantages, deep reinforcement learning technology has been quickly applied to the fields of automatic driving [11], robot control tasks [7], industrial resource scheduling [17] and multi-agent cooperation [13]. However, there are still two major defects in the practical application of deep reinforcement learning: the dilemma of "exploration and exploitation" and fragile convergence properties

A very suitable method to solve these two defects in theory is to integrate RL with heuristic algorithms such as evolutionary algorithm. Shauharda Khadka [9] introduced a scalable framework named Evolutionary Reinforcement Learning which combined RL with neuroevolution and outperforms standard RL algorithms in a range of continuous control benchmark experiments. Besides, evolutionary reinforcement learning [10] and CEM-RL [14] have also been proposed to improve the performance of reinforcement learning algorithms. Cheng [1] used a heuristic algorithm to enrich the experience buffer to accelerate the convergence speed of reinforcement learning algorithms.

Compared with other heuristic algorithms, particle swarm optimization spends less computing resources, and the concept of global optimal solution can just be used as the final network of the whole framework, which is very consistent with the idea of population-based in this paper. So this paper introduces a Particle Swarm Based Reinforcement Learning framework (PRL) (see Fig. 1). Particle swarm optimization [8] is popular swarm intelligence. [18] Inspired by Khadka's work [9], this framework uses a group of reinforcement learning learners with different temporal horizons to explore the solution space. Then, the sampling frequency of each learner will be dynamically allocated by a task manager to improve the exploitation efficiency of solution space. All experiences gained from the interaction between each learner and population are saved in the collective experience replay buffer for all learners to use together. At the same time, the design of particle swarm optimization does not need to add specific hyperparameters that change with the environment, which makes the PRL framework have good universality and stability, and makes up for the defects of reinforcement learning algorithm to a great extent.

2 Background

2.1 Reinforcement Learning Overview

Reinforcement learning is a machine learning method for understanding and automatic processing of goal-oriented decision-making problems [4]. Figure 2 describes the basic process of the interaction between agents and environments:

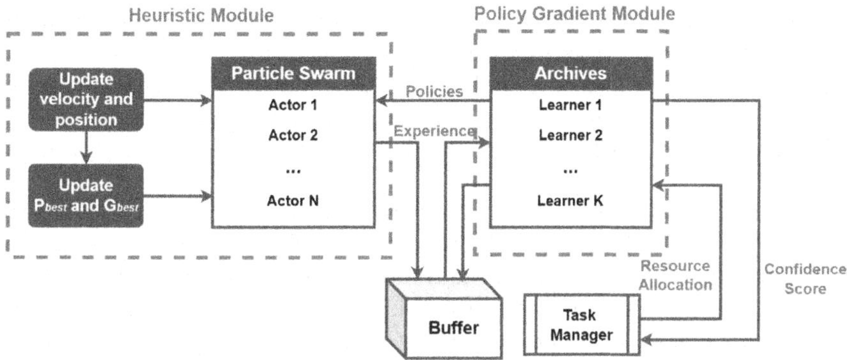

Fig. 1. The overall structure of PRL.

at a certain time t, the agent observes the current state s_t and selects an action a_t according to the strategy π. The environment updates the new state s_{t+1} according to the action a_t of the agent and gives reward feedback r. The agent modifies its action selection strategy π according to the reward feedback and selects a new action at the next time. As a popular reinforcement learning, Twin Delayed Deep Deterministic Policy Gradients (TD3) [19] is chosen as a representation of reinforcement learning in this paper.

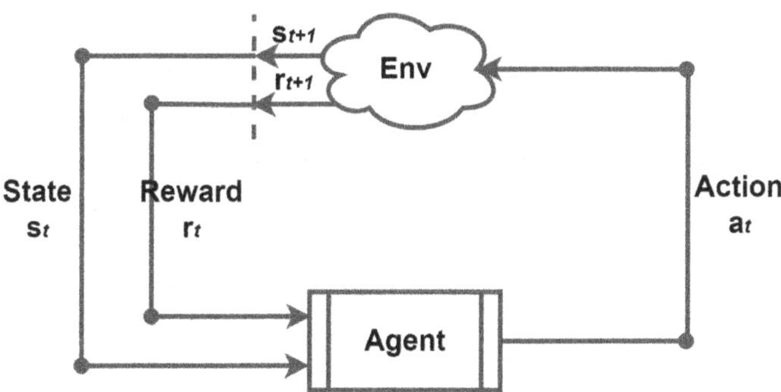

Fig. 2. Interaction process between agent and environment.

2.2 Twin Delayed Deep Deterministic Policy Gradients

TD3 has the following three core points [20]:

- TD3 learns two Q functions at the same time by minimizing the mean square deviation. The two value functions use one Q-target function, and the smaller value given in the two Q functions is used to update the Q-target, which effectively suppresses the overestimation of DDPG.

- TD3 introduces the idea of smoothing and adds Gaussian noise when selecting the action. By estimating the value from similar states and actions, the change of Q function along actions is smoothed, which helps to make the strategy go smoothly.
- TD3 adopts a delayed strategy to update parameters. The research of Fujimoto et al. [5] shows that synchronous training action network and evaluation network will lead to a very unstable training process. However, with the fixed action network, the evaluation network can often converge to the correct results. Therefore, TD3 updates the action network with a lower frequency, which helps to solve the over fitting problem of deterministic policies.

2.3 Particle Swarm Optimization

Particle swarm optimization (PSO) is a simple algorithm for solving optimization problems inspired by the cooperative predation behavior of birds. Each particle has three attributes: position x_i, velocity v_i and fitness value. The particle swarm optimization [3] encodes a set of solutions through the positions of N particles in the search space, and updates the solutions (see Eq. 1 and Eq. 2) by tracking the individual optimal solution P_i and the group optimal solution P_g through the incomplete random search of the calculation method described as follows.

$$v_{id}^{k+1} = wv_{id}^{k} + c_1 r_1 (p_{id}^{k} - p_{id}^{k}) + c_2 r_2 (p_{gd}^{k} - p_{gd}^{k}). \tag{1}$$

$$x_{id}^{k+1} = x_{id}^{k} + v_{id}^{k+1}. \tag{2}$$

The learning factors c_1 and c_2 are updated by the method shown in Eq. 3. In the iterative process, c_1 decreases and c_2 increases. Its goal is to strengthen the global search ability of particles in the early stage and promote particle convergence in the later stage.

$$c_i = (c_{ie} - c_{is})\frac{CurIter}{MaxIter} + c_{is}, i = 1, 2. \tag{3}$$

Due to the advantages of simple implementation, high precision and fast convergence speed, PSO has demonstrated its superiority in solving many practical problems [18].

3 The Proposed Algorithm

3.1 Overall Framework

In this paper, we choose PSO and TD3 to demonstrate how to implement PRL. Algorithm 1 shows the overall pseudo code of the PRL framework.

```
Algorithm 1: PRL
Initialize Archives AR with q learners and allocation A uniformly;
Initialize particle swarm of k actors swarm π; Initialize an empty collective
experience replay buffer;
Initialize collective experience replay buffer R and set A = [ ];
Initialize transfer period o ;
for generation = 1 to ∞ do
    Perform PSO according to Algorithm 4 ;
    Rank the particles based on fitness scores;
    for learner L ∈ AR do
        score, R = Evaluate(L_π, R);
        v'_i = α · score + (1 − α) · v_i;
    end
    T = environment steps taken this generation;
    for t = 1 to T do
        for learner L ∈ AR do
            Perform TD3 learner according to Algorithm 3;
        end
    end
    Compute the UCB scores U and update v according to Eq. 5 and Eq. 4;
    Normalize U to be within [0, 1) and fill up A based on U;
    if generation mod o = 0 then
        Copy the weakest RL actor into particles;
    end
end
```

```
Algorithm 2: Function Evaluate
fitness = 0;
Reset environment and get initial state s_0 ;
Initialize an empty collective experience replay buffer R;
while environment is not done do
    Select action with Gaussian noise;
    Execute action a_t and observe new state s_{t+1}and reward r_t ;
    Append transition (s_t, a_t, r_t, s_{t+1}) to R;
    fitness = fitness + r_t;
    s = s_{t+1};
end
return fitness, R
```

PRL integrates multiple learners' learning results, and all learners are optimized independently in different discounts of Markov processes. The experiences explored by each learner will be regularly stored in the collective experience replay buffer and reused by all learners, which ensures that each learner can collect not only the samples collected by itself, but also the samples collected by other learners or particles, so as to improve the sampling efficiency and exploration ability. The task manager monitors this process by dynamically reallocating computing resources, which is conducive to better learners.

3.2 Module Details

Collective Experience Replay Buffer: As shown in Fig. 3, The collective experience replay buffer will collect transitions from any learner or particle. When the collective experience buffer is full, it will throw away the old experiences to save the new experiences. During iterations, learners will sample experiences in batches from the collective experience replay buffer, repeatedly train the model and update parameters according to these experiences.

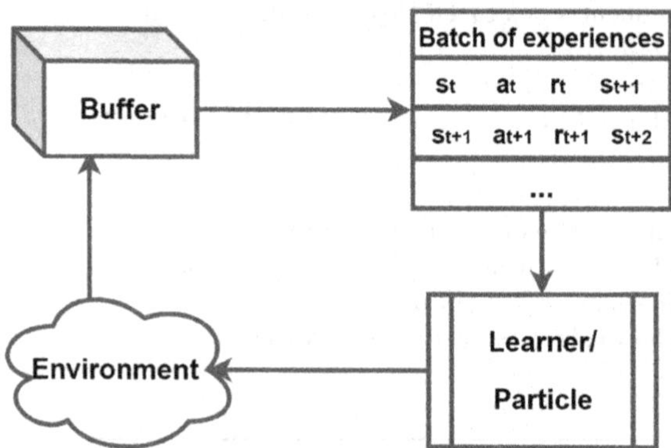

Fig. 3. Working process of collective experience replay buffer.

Learner: Each learner is a standard TD3 algorithm (see Algorithm 3) but discount γ is different, that is, there are differences in the evaluation criteria of each learner. All learners saved in Archives AR build and use the collective experience replay buffer together. In addition, the sampling and updating of each learner are completely independent.

PSO: In the PRL framework, each particle represents an actor network, and all parameters of the actor network are sequentially packaged into a high-dimensional vector as the position information of each particle. The process of updating the position of particles is the parameter updating process of neural networks. The overall pseudo code of particle swarm optimization is shown in Algorithm 4. Particle swarm optimization only updates the neural network through the four fundamental operations of arithmetic, so as to avoid redundant calculation.

Algorithm 3: TD3 Learner

```
Set discount rate = γ, count = 0 and valuev = 0;
Initialize critic network Q_θ1, Q_θ2 and actor network C_Φ with random
parameters θ1,θ2 and Φ;
Initialize target networks θ1' ← θ1, θ2' ← θ2, Φ' ← Φ;
Initialize collective experience replay buffer R;
T = environment steps taken this generation;
for t = 1 to T do
    Sample a random minibatch of T transitions (s_t, a_t, r_t, s_{t+1}) from R;
    Update the critic network Q_θ1, Q_θ2 by the Bellman update;
    if t mod d then
        Update the actor network C_Φ by the deterministic policy gradient;
        Soft update target networks:
        θi' ← τ · θi + (1 − τ) · θi';
        Φ' ← τ · Φ + (1 − τ) · Φ';
    end
end
```

Algorithm 4: PSO

```
Initialize the number of particles n, inertia factor w and learning factors
c_1s, c_1e, c_2s and c_2e;
Initialize the position x_i and velocity v_i of every particle;
Initialize the best personal position p_i and the best personal fitness f_ibest of
each particle;
Initialize the best group position p_g and the best group fitness f_g ;
Initialize maximum number of iterations T_max;
for t = 1 to T_max do
    for i = 1 to n do
        f_i, R = Evaluate(π, R, noise=None);
        if f_i is bigger than f_ibest then
            Update f_ibest, p_i;
            Update p_g and f_g (if f_i is bigger than f_g);
        end
        Update v_i according to Eq. 1 and x_i according to Eq. 2
    end
    Update c_1 and c_2 according to Eq. 3
end
```

Task Manager: The PRL framework sets up multiple learners, and the task manager will dynamically allocate the sampling frequency for the model. In the initial state, the number of initial sampling rounds A_i of each learner is the same. Each learner will store its cumulative number y_i of sampling rounds from the past to the present and a sampling revenue v_i the sampling revenue is obtained by calculating the weighted sum of cumulative returns obtained from interaction with the environment and updated according to Eq. 4:

$$v_i^{'} = \alpha \cdot fitness + (1 - \alpha) \cdot v_i. \tag{4}$$

After the update of each generation, task manager will calculate the confidence score U according to the cumulative number of sampling rounds y_i and sampling income v_i (see Eq. 5)

$$U_i = v_i^n + c \cdot \sqrt{\frac{log(\sum y_i)}{y_i}}. \tag{5}$$

Then normalize U to obtain a probability distribution function, and obtain sampling allocation table A according to this probability distribution. The value in allocation table A is the number of sampling rounds of each learner in the next round. Obviously, the higher the confidence score of a learner, the greater the probability of sampling. The existence of task manager improves the exploration and development efficiency of the whole system.

4 Results

4.1 Domain and Metric

This paper selects the standard experiments on the OpenAI gym platform to test the performance of the PRL framework and compares the performance of the PRL framework with a standard TD3 algorithm. Each algorithm is tested three times regularly in the training process, and the average value is calculated as the algorithm performance result. Figure 4 shows the scores of the PRL framework and standard TD3 in four experimental environments: “Cartpole-v1”, “lunarlander-v2”, “Humanoid-v2” and “Pong-v1”.

4.2 Discussion

The results in Fig. 4 show that the performance of PRL exceeds a single TD3 algorithm in four experiments. The advantages of PRL are very obvious in continuous environments and sparse reward environments. While PRL does not change any hyperparameters in the tests, it has obtained very good results in multiple environments, which undoubtedly helps to improve the universality of reinforcement learning. In addition, it is obvious that particle population gives PRL stronger exploration ability in the environment of sparse reward, so it can get better benefit value in iterations; Secondly, the combination with particle swarm optimization also helps PRL to enhance its development ability at the end of iterations, so that PRL can get a convergent solution in most cases. However, PRL introduces more neural networks, which leads to the operation of PRL algorithm, which needs more computing resources than standard reinforcement learning algorithms. But the cost is acceptable with improved performance.

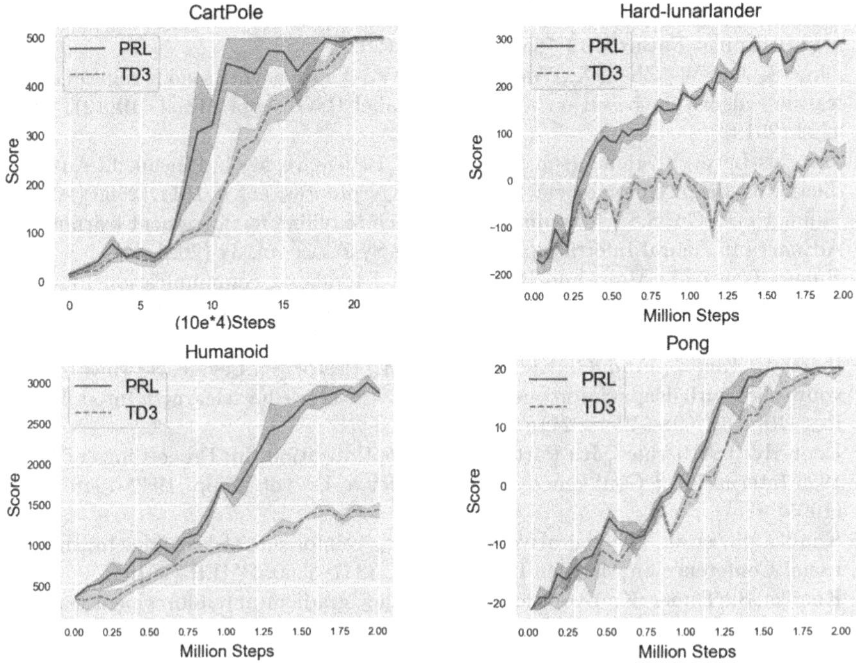

Fig. 4. Comparison results of PRL and TD3.

5 Summary and Future Work

In this paper, particle swarm optimization and TD3 algorithm are used to build the PRL framework. On the one hand, PRL can achieve excellent results in Gym tests without needing the carefully adjustments of hyperparameters, and improve the convergence vulnerability of reinforcement learning. On the other hand, PRL also obviously increases the exploration and exploitation ability of reinforcement learning, and urges agents to find better strategies with good stability. In the future, we will extend PRL to other heuristic algorithms and reinforcement learning algorithms to explore the optimal combination of heuristic algorithms and reinforcement learning algorithms, and apply PRL to more complex environments to test its performance.

Acknowledgement. This work was supported by the National Natural Science Foundation of China under Grant 61973244 and Grant 61573277. It is also supported by the open fund of CETC Key Laboratory of Data Link Technology (CLDL-20202101-1).

References

1. Cheng, C.A., Kolobov, A., Swaminathan, A.: Heuristic-guided reinforcement learning. Adv. Neural. Inf. Process. Syst. **34**, 13550–13563 (2021)

2. Degrave, J., et al.: Magnetic control of tokamak plasmas through deep reinforcement learning. Nature **602**(7897), 414–419 (2022)
3. Ding, S., Du, W., Zhao, X., Wang, L., Jia, W.: A new asynchronous reinforcement learning algorithm based on improved parallel PSO. Appl. Intell. **49**(12), 4211–4222 (2019)
4. François-Lavet, V., Henderson, P., Islam, R., Bellemare, M.G., Pineau, J.: An introduction to deep reinforcement learning. arXiv preprint arXiv:1811.12560 (2018)
5. Fujimoto, S., Gu, S.S.: A minimalist approach to offline reinforcement learning. In: Advances in Neural Information Processing Systems, vol. 34 (2021)
6. Huang, C., et al.: Multi-hop RIS-empowered terahertz communications: a DRL-based hybrid beamforming design. IEEE J. Sel. Areas Commun. **39**(6), 1663–1677 (2021)
7. Ibarz, J., Tan, J., Finn, C., Kalakrishnan, M., Pastor, P., Levine, S.: How to train your robot with deep reinforcement learning: lessons we have learned. Int. J. Robot. Res. **40**(4–5), 698–721 (2021)
8. Kennedy, J., Eberhart, R.: Particle swarm optimization. In: Proceedings of ICNN 1995-International Conference on Neural Networks, vol. 4, pp. 1942–1948. IEEE (1995)
9. Khadka, S., et al.: Collaborative evolutionary reinforcement learning. In: International Conference on Machine Learning, pp. 3341–3350. PMLR (2019)
10. Khadka, S., Tumer, K.: Evolution-guided policy gradient in reinforcement learning. In: Advances in Neural Information Processing Systems, vol. 31 (2018)
11. Kiran, B.R., et al.: Deep reinforcement learning for autonomous driving: a survey. IEEE Trans. Intell. Transp. Syst. (2021)
12. Mnih, V., et al.: Human-level control through deep reinforcement learning. Nature **518**(7540), 529–533 (2015)
13. Movahedi, Z., Bastanfard, A.: Toward competitive multi-agents in polo game based on reinforcement learning. Multimedia Tools Appl. **80**(17), 26773–26793 (2021)
14. Pourchot, A., Sigaud, O.: CEM-RL: combining evolutionary and gradient-based methods for policy search. arXiv preprint arXiv:1810.01222 (2018)
15. Silver, D., et al.: Mastering the game of go with deep neural networks and tree search. Nature **529**(7587), 484–489 (2016)
16. Sutton, R.S., Barto, A.G.: Reinforcement Learning: An Introduction. MIT Press, Cambridge (2018)
17. Wang, B., Liu, F., Lin, W.: Energy-efficient VM scheduling based on deep reinforcement learning. Futur. Gener. Comput. Syst. **125**, 616–628 (2021)
18. Zhan, Z.H., et al.: Matrix-based evolutionary computation. IEEE Trans. Emerg. Top. Comput. Intell. **6**(2), 315–328 (2021)
19. Zhang, F., Li, J., Li, Z.: A TD3-based multi-agent deep reinforcement learning method in mixed cooperation-competition environment. Neurocomputing **411**, 206–215 (2020)
20. Zhou, J., Xue, S., Xue, Y., Liao, Y., Liu, J., Zhao, W.: A novel energy management strategy of hybrid electric vehicle via an improved TD3 deep reinforcement learning. Energy **224**, 120118 (2021)

User's Permission Reasoning Method Based on Knowledge Graph Reward Guidance Reinforcement Learning in Data Center

Yu Pan[1,2], Hongmei Li[3], Wei Li[2], Yi Liu[3], Xiang Li[3], Qibin Zheng[3], and Wei Qin[3](✉)

[1] National University of Defense Technology, Changsha 410073, China
[2] Command and Control Engineering College, Army Engineering University of PLA, Nanjing 210007, China
[3] Academy of Military Science, Beijing 100091, China
xdqinwei@126.com

Abstract. In general, multiple domain cyberspace security assessments are very important for data center security and can be implemented by reasoning user's permissions. However, while existing methods include some information from the physical and social domains, they do not provide a comprehensive representation of cyberspace. Existing reasoning methods are also based on expert given rules, resulting in inefficiency and a low degree of intelligence. To address this challenge, we create a Knowledge Graph (KG) of multiple domain cyberspace in order to provide a standard semantic description of the multiple domain cyberspace. Following that, we proposed a user's permissions reasoning method based on reinforcement learning. All permissions in cyberspace are represented as nodes, and an agent is trained to find all permissions that user can have according to user's initial permissions and cyberspace KG. We set 10 reward setting rules based on the features of cyberspace KG in the reinforcement learning of reward information setting, so that the agent can better locate user's all permissions and avoid blindly finding user's permissions. The results of the experiments showed that the proposed method can successfully reason about user's permissions and increase the intelligence level of the user's permissions reasoning method. At the same time, the F1 value of the proposed method is 6% greater than that of the Translating Embedding (TransE) method.

Keywords: Knowledge graph · Multiple domain cyberspace · Reinforcement learning · Data center · Big data

1 Introduction

Data center security has always been a key issue for cloud services in the era of big data. Artificial intelligence has long been a hot topic for identifying and mitigating cyberspace attacks in data center. Because of the complexity and variety of cyberspace threats, collaborative modeling based on domain expertise has become the standard way to identify them. However, while the component provides physical and social domain

Y. Tan and Y. Shi (Eds.): DMBD 2022, CCIS 1744, pp. 37–49, 2022.
https://doi.org/10.1007/978-981-19-9297-1_4

knowledge, the present approach lacks cyberspace to complete modeling, making it difficult to correctly infer the user's intent.

At this time, the physical domain, information domain, network domain and social domain in cyberspace are mostly described 1. The physical domain is used to represent spatial information such as cities, regions, buildings, rooms, and so on. The typical information of cyberspace is the network domain. The social domain in cyberspace mostly refers to interpersonal relationships. For example, if an attacker and a company's cyberspace administrator were once classmates, the attacker will have an easier time obtaining cyberspace permissions than other attackers. The information domain, which primarily represents digital information such as a user name, password, information.

The main goal of the Knowledge Graph (KG) based description of multiple domain cyberspace is to extract semantic information from the design and configuration of multiple domain cyberspace and to determine the negative effects of event and configuration changes on the security state of cyberspace. The event described in cyberspace to the real quantity and entity relationship and the influence of the properties, as well as the change of entity and entity relationship's influence on the relationship between user permissions, can be defined as firstorder logic corresponding reasoning rules, the event described in cyberspace to the real quantity and entity relationship and the influence of the features, and the change of entity and entity relationship's influence on the relationship between user's permissions, can all be defined as firstorder logic corresponding reasoning rules. Therefore a formal description of the impact of cyberspace security events can be created. The primary goal of this method is to understand how different multiple domain cyberspace attacks interact. Existing reasoning methods, on the other hand, are founded on rules. Firstorder logic defines rules, and the corresponding reasoning rules must be given by experts. However, it has some limitations, such as a low level of intelligent. As a result, determining how to automatically extract user's final permissions from the KG of multiple domains in order to achieve intelligent reasoning of user's final permissions is an issue that merits more investigation.

This process can be divided into three steps: firstly, through theoretical analysis, hierarchical entity features are constructed according to top-down and bottom-up methods, mainly covering various entities in physical domain, information domain, network domain and social domain; Secondly, after determining various entities, it is necessary to sort out the relationships between entities, which are mainly divided into inclusion relationship, dependence relationship, dominance relationship, trust relationship and other types. Finally, after the entities and their relationships are determined, the multiple domain cyberspace KG is constructed to achieve a unified semantic description of multiple domain cyberspace.

By establishing good multiple domain cyberspace semantic information, can be defined first-order logic corresponding reasoning rules, the event described in cyberspace to the real quantity and entity relationship and the influence of the properties, as well as the change of entity and entity relationship's influence on the relationship between user permissions, found that the user is obtained than they should have permissions. So as to achieve the formal description of the impact of network security events. The fundamental purpose of this method is to grasp the interrelation between multiple domain cyberspace attacks. However, the existing reasoning methods are rule based reasoning.

Rules are defined by first-order logic, and the corresponding reasoning rules need to be specified by experts. Therefore, it has certain limitations, that is the level of intelligence is low. Therefore, how to automatically reason user's final permissions from the multiple domain cyberspace KG, so as to realize intelligent reason of user's final permissions is a challenge.

To address this challenge, this paper uses the extraction of multiple domain cyberspace entities and relationship information for the construction of a multiple domain cyberspace KG, the KG to uniformly describe the multiple domain cyberspace. Based on multiple domain cyberspace KG, we proposed a user's permissions reasoning meth-od based on reinforcement learning to realize the user's final permissions, learn how multiple domain cyberspace configuration and cyberspace entity relationships affect the final permissions obtained by users, as well as intelligent reasoning to determine whether the user deserves the permissions. If user's final permissions are more than initial permissions. This indicates that cyberspace configuration has vulnerabilities, and the goal of the proposed method is to increase cyberspace security by further optimizing cyberspace setup.

2 Related Works

KG is essentially a knowledge representation and a semantic network that reveals the relationships between entities [2]. It belongs to the semantic network category and contains real world entities, relationships and events. KG is a knowledge representation, a semantic network that displays relationships between entities, it falls under the semantic network category, which comprises entities, relationships, and events in the actual world.

External objective facts are referred to as information, while external objective rules are inferred and summarized as knowledge. Knowledge is the ability to make connections between entities based on data. To put it another way, objects are made up of information that is represented as a subject predicate object. The KG operates in this way. Previously, the most common method for creating KG was to work from the top down, establishing the KG ontologies and data schema before adding things to the knowledge base. However, as a fundamental knowledge base, this creation approach must use an already organized knowledge base [3].

2.1 Construction Cyberspace KG

In general, the construction of knowledge atlas in cyberspace mainly includes ontology construction, information extraction [4] and knowledge storage [5]. In reference [6], an ontology is developed to model attacks and related entities, and the proposed ontology is only for attacks. In order to represent the concepts and entities related to the field of cyberspace security, reference [7] proposed a cyberspace security ontology based on the ontology of reference [6]. They extend the ontology to provide model relationships that capture the schema structure and security utilization concepts of the U.S. National Vulnerability Database. The ontology includes 11 entity types such as vulnerability, product, means and consequence. Reference [8] extends the ontology proposed in reference [6] and adds rules into the reasoning logic. Their ontology consists of three basic categories: methods, results, and goals.

Information extraction is mainly oriented to open data and can extract usable knowledge units through automation technology. Knowledge unit mainly includes three knowledge elements, entity, relation and feature, and forms a series of high quality fact expression on this basis, which lays a foundation for the construction of the upper pattern layer.

There are two main approaches to information extraction: one is a knowledge-based engineering approach, which relies heavily on extraction rules but allows the system to deal with domain-specific information extraction problems. Most of the early information extraction systems are based on extraction rules. However, the main disadvantage is that it requires the participation of experts. Therefore, the accuracy of extraction system is high. At present, many information extraction systems are based on knowledge engineering [9].

The second main method is based on machine learning [10]. With the rise of artificial intelligence and machine learning, this method has become the mainstream method. The basic steps involve training an information extraction model with a large amount of training data, and then using the information extraction model to extract relevant information. The advantage of this method is that there is no need for experts to define rules in advance and the intelligence level is improved, but a large amount of training data is needed to achieve better experimental results. Reference [11] proposes a system that can identify relevant entities from unstructured text, which mainly solves the problems of network attacks and software vulnerabilities. Reference [12] developed a framework for detecting and extracting vulnerability and attack information from network texts, and then trained a support vector machine to identify potential vulnerabilities. The classifier uses a standard one-word packet vector model. Once potential vulnerability descriptions are identified, the framework uses standard named entity recognition tools to extract security-related entities and concepts. The above methods all describe machine learning methods for automatically extracting relevant information from unstructured text. However, the method cannot accurately identify relevant entities until sufficient training data are obtained.

At the same time, the relationship between information units after information extraction is flat, lacking hierarchy and logic, and there are a lot of redundant or even wrong information fragments. Knowledge storage is the process of integrating knowledge from multiple knowledge bases to form a knowledge base. In this process, the main technologies include reference resolution, entity disambiguation and entity linking. Different knowledge base collects different key knowledge for the same entity, some knowledge base may focus on the description of its own some respects, some knowledge base may focus on the description of the entity and other entities, the relationship between the different knowledge base of knowledge storage of the real purpose is to describe the integration, in order to gain the complete entity description.

2.2 Reasoning Method Based on Knowledge

The practice of reasoning about unknown information based on current knowledge is known as knowledge reasoning. From individual to generic, by starting with known information and extracting new facts from it, or by drawing inferences from a big body of current knowledge. Symbol-based reasoning and statistics-based reasoning are two types of knowledge-based reasoning 13. Symbol-based reasoning is generally based on classical logic (first-order predicate logic or propositional logic) or versions of classical logic in artificial intelligence, such as default logic. Symbolic reasoning can discover logical conflicts between items as well as derive relationships between new entities from existing ones utilizing rules. Machine learning methods are commonly used in statistics-based reasoning approaches to discover new entity associations from KG.

The goal of knowledge reasoning is to figure out how instances and connections in KG are connected. To forecast the type of instances, reference [14] provides an SDType approach that leverages a statistical distribution of characteristics connected by triples or predicates. The approach can be used to create a knowledge graph from a single data source, but it can't be used to reason knowledge across several data sets. Researcher approach has been presented as a tool for automatically inserting entities in the reference [15], whereas linked related datasets [16] employ unique abstract data to extract instance types using specified schema. However, because this method relies on structured text data, it cannot be applied to other databases.

Information refers to external objective facts, and knowledge is the induction and summary of external objective laws. Building connections between entities based on information can be called "knowledge". In other words, objects are made up of knowledge, each of which is represented as a Subject Predicate Object (SPO). This is how the knowledge graph works. Previously, the popular approach to building knowledge graphs was a top-down approach, defining ontologies and data schemas for the knowledge graph before adding entities to the knowledge base. However, this construction method needs to utilize some existing structured knowledge base as its basic knowledge base.

3 Methods

3.1 Unified Description of Multiple Domain Cyberspace Semantic Information Based on KG

In the construction of traditional knowledge atlas of cyberspace, most studies focus on network domain and information domain, which refers to network equipment and processing of network data traffic, and rarely involve physical domain, social domain and other fields. However, with the deepening of the research on cyberspace, academia and the industry have realized that cyberspace not only exists in the domain of cyberspace and digital domain, but also is affected by multiple domain behavior. To address this challenge, we propose a unified semantic information description method based on KG in multiple domain cyberspace. In reference [1], cyberspace should be integrated into physical domain, information domain, network domain, social domain and other domains, so it can be seen that cyberspace has the characteristics of multiple regions.

Firstly, the domain and scope of cyberspace entities are determined, and the relevant data of multi-domain cyberspace are integrated and standardized, providing a top-level model for constructing multiple domain cyberspace knowledge atlas. Second, after determining the scope of related entities, reuse of existing related entities is beneficial to improve construction efficiency.

(1) Entity information extraction

In this paper, we propose that there are 7 types of entity information to be collected, namely: space entity, device entity, port entity, service entity, file entity, information entity and personnel entity.

Space entity belong to physical domains and are used to represent spatial information such as cities, campuses, buildings and rooms. At the same time, the physical domain also has device entities, namely physical entities. Device entity include not only network terminals, such as switches, routers, servers, and user terminals, but also related physical entities, such as keys and access cards. A port entity is located in a network domain and represents the physical ports of various network devices. It also contains not only physical ports but also virtual network ports. The service entity is also located in the network domain and represents the open services on the device, such as HTTP, FTP, and email services. File entity are located in the information domain and represent information entities and digital files, etc. Digital files can also represent digital files stored on terminals or servers. Information entity are located in information domains and are used to represent various types of information, such as user names, passwords, keys, and messages. Personnel entity represent the information of people involved in the network, including attackers, common users and administrators in the social domain.

(2) Semantic information extraction and construction

The KG pulls semantic information from multiple domain cyberspace configuration information to provide a unified semantic description of multiple domain cyberspace. This research focuses on the semantic information while extracting the semantic information of cyberspace setup. The lower level semantic information facilitates the straightforward description of the semantic information of cyberspace configuration, although the model is huge and complex. The extracted fundamental semantic information in the unified description of multiple domain cyberspace based on KG mostly contains entity and relation. The following principles are used to generate the KG from the retrieved data:

Rule A: Group entities into a domain, and then group entities into the appropriate entity type;
Rule B: Extract relationships from cyberspace;
Rule C: Connect related entities with wires and represent their relationships.

3.2 User's Permissions Reasoning Method Based on Reinforcement Learning

We first introduce the basic elements of the RL framework in KG reasoning, including environment, state, action, and reward. As shown in Fig. 1, the input of the agent is a state composed of head and tail entities. The output is the next relationship predicted by the agent.

First, we should collect the following user permissions, including space access permission, device use permission, device control permission, port use permission, port

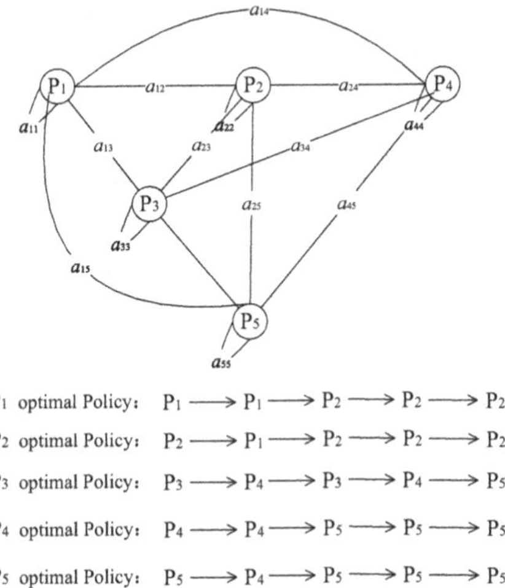

Fig. 1. The reasoning method

control permission, service access permission, service control permission, file control permission, and information known permission.

Space access permission, device use permission, and device control permission belong to the user's permissions 'of the physical domain. Space access permission means that the user can enter the physical space, device use permission means that the user has the device use permission, and device control permission means that the user can control the device. The difference between device use permission and device control permission is that the former means that users can only use the device based on the configured status and cannot modify the configuration parameters of the device, while the latter means that users can modify the configuration parameters of the device, such as the firewall configuration and access control rights. Port access permission, port control permission, and service access permission. Service control permission refers to the network domain permission. Port control permission means that users can use the port to access the service, and port control permission means that users can change the port status or configuration. Service access means that the service request traffic will access the service, but it does not mean that the service can be used normally. The service control permission means that the user can pass the security authentication of the service and use the service normally. For example, the user can use the email service after being authenticated by the email server. File control permission and information known permission refer to information domain permissions. File control permission means that users can read, delete, and modify configuration files. Information known permission means that users know internal secret digital information such as pass-words and keys.

Agent's search for permissions reasoning path is a process of trial and error. The application of reinforcement learning in KG reasoning is based on the assumption that as long as the agent can reach the tail entity Pt from the head entity P1 within a certain number of steps, we can regard this path as a potential reasoning path. DeepPath [17] first introduced reinforcement learning into KG reasoning. The main task is to find the path from head to tail entity in the KG. In this method, the KG is sampled, the policy network is trained, and then the policy network is trained by the artificially designed reward function. We perform reasoning tasks through the agent, and every time the agent takes an action, a state transition will occur and a corresponding reward will be given to it. Our proposed method is consistent with the situational concept in DeepPath. But our method has different with DeepPath in the following details:

(1) In DeepPath, the states are the entities and relations in a KG are naturally discrete atomic symbols. But in our proposed method, the states are the permissions that agent has. In Fig. 1, if agent has P1 permission, the state is agent located in P1; If agent takes action a1 to has permission P2, the state is agent located in P2. (2) In DeepPath, the main task is to find the path from head to tail entity in the KG. In our proposed method, we limit the length of the path to n. In general, if agent has permission Pt, the permissions it's most likely to obtain are the permissions agent closest to finding. For example, in Fig. 1, if user only have permission P1, we use reinforcement learning to find P1's optimal policy (optimal path), and we set n = 5, so we can reason if user has permission P1, he will have permission P2.
(2) In DeepPath, the main task is to find the path from head to tail entity in the KG. In our proposed method, we limit the length of the path to n. In general, if agent has permission Pt, the permissions it's most likely to obtain are the permissions agent closest to finding. For example, in Fig. 1, if user only have permission P1, we use reinforcement learning to find P1's optimal policy (optimal path), and we set n = 5, so we can reason if user has permission P1, he will have permission P2.
(3) In DeepPath, the reward will be given by specialist's experiences. In general, reward has a bigger contribute to the quality of the paths found by the agent. To encourage the agent to find optimal paths, we set the reward based on cyberspace KG, not by specialist's experiences. It is described in detail in the following. And this is our proposed method major innovation.

Next, we will cover each part of reinforcement learning in detail.

Environment: The entire user's permissions is considered to be an environment. This environment will remain unchanged throughout agent training. The environment also defines the interaction between agent and environment. That is, agent will change to a new state by interacting with the environment.

State: State encodes the position of agent in the environment with a vector of fixed length, that is, the position information of agent in the permissions graph.

Action: Our model treats each relationship type as an action. In permissions graph, permissions in graph are discrete atomic symbols. Due to the existing actual permissions, we simulate the symbolic atoms in all states. In our method, each state is the agent‘s position in the KG. The agent will then move from one entity to another when the operation is performed. The two are linked by action only taken by the agent.

We define the action space, where indicates whether the action i is taken, 1 indicates that the action is taken, and 0 indicates no. The agent starts with the head entity, uses the policy network to take the most likely action in the current state, and further searches the path until it reaches the tail entity. The policy function maps the state vector to the probability distribution of all possible actions of A, namely:

where, θ is calculated by the neural network and represents the parameters of the model.

Rewards: Rewards have always been the hardest part of reinforcement learning to set up. Most previous studies have assumed that the model only gets the final reward when it completes the relevant round, and that there is no single step reward. In this method, in addition to the final reward, we also set up different rewards for actions taken at different locations. We call this a KG reward guidance. In general, the reward is related to the length and distance of the path to the head entity. If the weight of path-1 is generally higher than that of path-2. Although both approaches work, the model focuses more on learning from approach 1. Actions taken in close proximity to the target entity have greater impact than actions taken previously. The agent reward set-tings are as follows:

The detail setting is following:

(1) If a user can enter one space and not be prevented by the security rules of that space and another space permission, he can have entered another space permissions. Therefore, the reward between the two permissions is setting r = 1;
(2) If a user has access to a space permission, it has device use permission to all devices in that space. Therefore, the reward between the two permissions is setting r = 1;
(3) If a user has the permission to use a device, it can have the permission to use all ports on the device. Therefore, the reward between the two permissions is setting r = 1;
(4) If a user has the permission to use a port, he can have the permission using the port to access services accessible to the port. Therefore, the reward between the two permissions is setting r = 1;
(5) If a user has the service reachability of a service permission, and he has the password for the service or the service does not have the password, he can obtain the permission control of the service. Therefore, the reward between the two permissions is setting r = 2;
(6) If a user has control a service permission, he can have control the files from that service permission. Therefore, the reward between the two permissions is setting r = 3;
(7) If a user has controlled a service permission, he can have the permission which controlling the information he gets from that service. Therefore, the reward between the two permissions is setting r = 5;
(8) If a user has controlled a file permission, he can have control the information permission in that file. Therefore, the reward between the two permissions is setting r = 10;
(9) If a user has access to a file permission and has the decryption key or the file is not encrypted, he can have the decrypted file permission. Therefore, the reward between the two permissions is setting r = 10;
(10) If a user has controlled a service permission, he can control devices managed by that service. The device can be used and all ports on the device can be controlled. Therefore, the reward between permissions is setting r = 10.

We set the reward information according to the above rules, and at the same time agent takes other actions, we set agent's reward r = 0.

Policy network: We use a fully connected neural network to parameterize the policy function to map the state vector to the probability distribution of all possible actions. The neural network consists of two hidden layers, and the activation function uses ReLU function. The output layer uses SoftMax for normalization functions.

4 Experiments

4.1 Data Sets

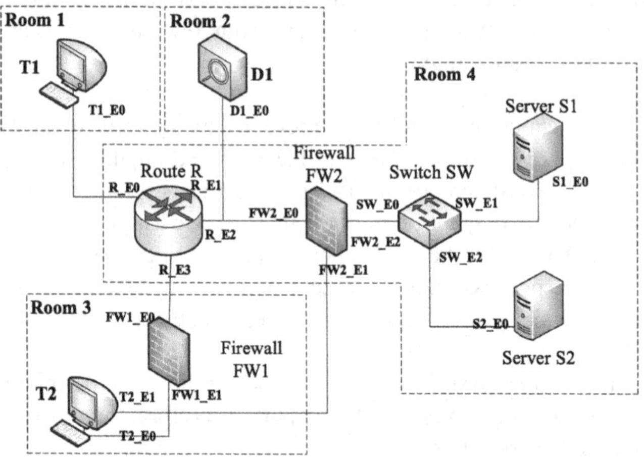

Fig. 2. Experiment environment

The experimental data comes from the real environment of an enterprise network. In this environment, the outermost space is the entire external environment, representing a region, which can refer to campus, company, building, building, etc. Terminal T1 is in room 1, terminal T2 is in room 3, room 2 is in room D1, and room 4 is in room server. Two firewalls, FW1 in room 1, FW2 in room 4, router in room 4, switch in room 4, and two servers, S1 and S2 respectively, are located in room 4. Figure 2 shows the connections between devices.

Method A: Path Ranking Algorithm (PRA) [18]. This method makes use of the characteristics of graph structure, and makes use of the path relationship between entities to perform inference calculation, so as to directly estimate the relationship between two entity nodes. This method basically starts with a single entity node, where you are faced with two choices: either move to a randomly selected node or return to the starting node. The algorithm has only one parameter: restart probability R. Stability is achieved after iteration through countless random walks. The stabilized probability vector contains the score of all nodes in the network to the initial node, that is, the closeness between entity nodes. The node with the highest score is the entity node that can be reasoning.

Method B: Reasoning method Based on Rules (BOR) [1]. Since there are no public permissions reasoning data sets in the previous research, we adopt the rule-based reasoning method based on BOR to conduct user permissions reasoning for the training data sets, and obtain the user's finally permissions. Although reasoning method based on rules has its limitations, but the accuracy rate and recall rate of expert rule making are both 100%, as described in BOR.

Method C: TransE algorithm, whose core idea is to find a mapping function to transform each node in the graph into a low-dimensional dense embedded representation, requiring similar nodes in the graph to have the same distance in the low-dimensional space. The obtained representation vector can be used for downstream tasks, such as node classification, link prediction, visualization, etc. It is also essentially a knowledge-based approach.

Method D: User permissions reasoning based on KG reward guidance reinforcement learning (KGRGRL), which is proposed in this paper.

BOR is a rule-based reasoning method, in which experts specify rules, so its accuracy rate and recall rate are 100%. The main advantage of our proposed method lies in its intelligence and refinement, and there is no public data for user's permissions reasoning. Therefore, the user's permissions reasoning of BOR method is used as training data of other methods to compare its effect.

4.2 Evaluation Criteria

Our judgment criteria for judging the correctness of reasoning are generally divided into two kinds: accuracy rate and recall rate. The definition formula is as follows:

$$\begin{aligned} P &= \frac{TP}{TP + FP} \\ R &= \frac{TP}{TP + FN} \end{aligned} \tag{1}$$

TP is the number of positive samples predicted as positive ones, FP is the number of samples predicted as positive ones, and FN is the number of samples predicted as negative ones.

4.3 Results

The device of our experiment is Intel X Power CPU, 64 GB memory, 2 pieces of Nvidia 2080 Ti GPU, and the operating system is Ubuntu 18.04. The experimental data sets are written by Python 3.6. We set up 5000 users, give them different initial permissions, and then get the corresponding end user permissions through BOR method (Table 1).

From the experimental results, the proposed method of accuracy and recall rate is not equal to zero, shows the proposed method can reason out the user's permissions, and permission to automated reasoning, and not rely on experts given rules, so our proposed method compared with BOR higher intelligent level, has a wider applicability. It can abandon the method of formulate reasoning rules by experts, and let the machine learn rules and features by machine learning, so as to achieve the purpose of user's permissions reasoning.

At the same time, compared with PRA method, the recall rate of the proposed method is greater than that PRA method, and the accuracy and recall rate of the proposed method

Table 1. Experiment results

Method	P	R	$F1$
PRA	30.57%	47.63%	37.24%
TransE	44.56%	56.89%	49.97%
KGRGRL	**50.85%**	**62.08%**	**55.9%**
BOR	100%	100%	100%

are better than PRA method in the data set, indicating that the proposed method has a good effect and can improve the accuracy of existing reasoning methods.

Through the analysis of the experiment results, it was discovered that the user's permissions reasoning based on KG to reason out the user in all possible permissions ability under the current cyberspace configuration, can be based on existing knowledge, reasoning the user's final permissions, abandon the traditional set of reasoning rules through the expert mode, solve the problem of its limited scope of application, and greatly improve the efficiency of reasoning.

5 Conclusion

This paper proposes a unified representation method and a user's permissions reasoning method based on reinforcement learning in multiple domain cyberspace based on KG. Through KG, entities and entity relations in multiple domain cyberspace can be described, so that entities in different domains of cyberspace can be described and expressed uniformly. Through to unify the existing multiple domain cyberspace semantic information description, thus effectively grasp the connection between the multiple domain cyberspace, based on this, reasoning the user's permissions. The reasoning method is to abandon the traditional expert formula mode of reasoning rules in advance, can let the machine learn automatic reasoning rules, reasoning the intelligence of the user's permissions. It has wider applicability and maneuverability and provides a new idea for intelligent reasoning of user's permissions reasoning. Through the experiment of simulation cyberspace environment, it is proved that this method can effectively deduce the user's final permissions under the current cyberspace configuration, and realize the intelligent reasoning of user's permissions. Therefore, the method proposed in this paper is feasible and effective.

This paper proposes a unified semantic description and reasoning method for multiple domain cyberspace based on KG, which can describe the information of different domains in cyberspace, so as to effectively describe and express the whole situation of cyberspace. But at the same time, our experiments are based on small-scale simulation cyberspace environment, and have not been effectively verified in large-scale real cyberspace environment. Next, we hope to be able to verify the correctness and validity of our proposed method in a large real cyberspace.

Acknowledgements. This work was supported by the National Science Foundation for Young Scientists of China (No. 62106281).

References

1. Bai, W., Pan, Z., Guo, S., Chen, Z., Xia, S.: MDC-checker: A novel network risk assessment framework for multiple domain conjurations. Comput. Secur. **86**(Sep.), 388–401 (2019)
2. Eder, J.S.: Knowledge graph based search system. US (2012)
3. Guo, L., Wen, S., Wang, D., Wang, S., Wang, Q., Liu, H.: Overview of cyber threat intelligence description. In: International Conference on Applications and Techniques in Cyber Security and Intelligence, pp. 343–350. Springer, Cham (2021). https://doi.org/10.1007/978-3-030-79197-1
4. Zhao, H.: Knowledge graph oriented information extraction. Hans J. Data Mining **10**(4), 282–302 (2020)
5. Wang, X., Zou, L., Wang, C., Peng, P., Feng, Z.: Research on knowledge graph data management: a survey. J. Softw. **30**(7), 2140 (2019)
6. Undercoffer, J., Joshi, A., Pinkston, J.: Modeling computer attacks: an ontology for intrusion detection. In: Vigna, G., Kruegel, C., Jonsson, E. (eds.) RAID 2003. LNCS, vol. 2820, pp. 113–135. Springer, Heidelberg (2003). https://doi.org/10.1007/978-3-540-45248-5_7
7. Joshi, A., Lal, R., Finin, T., Joshi, A.: Extracting cybersecurity related linked data from text. In: 2013 IEEE Seventh International Conference on Semantic Computing, pp. 252–259. IEEE (2013)
8. More, S., Matthews, M., Joshi, A., Finin, T.: A knowledge-based approach to intrusion detection modeling. In: 2012 IEEE Symposium on Security and Privacy Workshops (2012)
9. Yang, Y., Xu, B., Hu, J., Tong, M., Zhang, P., Zheng, L.: Accurate and ancient method for constructing domain knowledge graph. J. Softw. **29**(10), 2931–2947 (2018)
10. He, Z.H.: Research on knowledge extraction method for Chinese knowledge graph construction, Doctoral thesis. National University of Defense Technology (2017)
11. Lal, R.: Information extraction of cyber security related terms and concepts from unstructured text. Ph.D. thesis, University of Maryland, Baltimore County (2013)
12. Mulwad, V., Li, W., Joshi, A., Finin, T., Viswanathan, K.: Extracting information about security vulnerabilities from web text. In: 2011EEE/WIC/ACM International Conferences on Web Intelligence and Intelligent Agent Technology, vol. 3, pp. 257–260. IEEE (2011)
13. Hui-Xiang, G.U., Yong, Y.U.: Domain ontology and knowledge inference based semantic web application. J. Shanghai Jiaotong Univ. (Chin. Ed.) **38**(4), 583–585 (2004)
14. Paulheim, H., Bizer, C.: Type inference on noisy RDF data. In: Alani, H., et al. (eds.) ISWC 2013. LNCS, vol. 8218, pp. 510–525. Springer, Heidelberg (2013). https://doi.org/10.1007/978-3-642-41335-3_32
15. Gangemi, A., Nuzzolese, A.G., Presutti, V., Draicchio, F., Musetti, A., Ciancarini, P.: Automatic typing of dbpedia entities. In: Cudré-Mauroux, P., et al. (eds.) ISWC 2012. LNCS, vol. 7649, pp. 65–81. Springer, Heidelberg (2012). https://doi.org/10.1007/978-3-642-35176-1_5
16. Kliegr, T.: Linked hypernyms: enriching dbpedia with targeted hypernym discovery. J. Web Semant. **31**, 59–69 (2015)
17. Xiong, W., Hoang, T.-L.-G., Wang, W.Y.: Deeppath: a reinforcement learning method for knowledge graph reasoning. In: EMNLP (2017)
18. Quan, W., Jing, L., Luo, Y., Wang, B., Lin, C.Y.: Knowledge base completion via coupled path ranking. In: Meeting of the Association for Computational Linguistics (2016)

SMPG: Adaptive Soft Update for Masked MADDPG

Yu Zhang[1], Shijia Zhou[3], Ning Guo[1], Tengfei Li[4], Xuechao Zou[1], and Pin Tao[1,2](✉)

[1] Qinghai University, Xining, China
tinkzy@163.com
[2] Tsinghua University, Beijing, China
[3] Jilin Jianzhu University, Changchun, China
[4] University of Chinese Academy of Sciences, Beijing, China

Abstract. In multi-agent systems, deep reinforcement learning policy gradient algorithms can converge excessively slowly or even fail to converge if the agent size as well as the state information quickly grows. We consequently present a policy gradient algorithm for generalised centralised training and decentralised execution (CTDE) based on the principle of masking. We transform the global state information of the critic network in the original (MADDPG) algorithm to the state information of local random agents as the input of the critic network. In addition, we have changed the way Polyak updates the target network so that it can dynamically and adaptively update the target network. Under the new framework, our approach considerably decreases the training strain on the critic network while taking into consideration the efficiency of agent sample learning and speeding up the multi-agent discovery of superior strategies. Combining these two improvements, our suggested approaches can be extended to any other CTDE-based multi-agent deep reinforcement learning algorithms, rather than being limited to the MADDPG conventional multi-agent reinforcement learning algorithm. We made the code publicly available at https://github.com/ZVEzhangyu/SMPG-master.

Keywords: Multi-agent · Reinforcement learning · Masked MADDPG

1 Introduction

With the ongoing inventive development of deep reinforcement learning [12] (RL), strong multi-agent systems have been successfully constructed in many tough fields and attained to beyond human level: AlphaStar [17] attained the level of beating human professional players in StarCraft 2, while AlphaZero [14] achieved the spectacular feat of beating top human players in other chess games after breaking through the Go domain.

These world-beating accomplishments are attributable to the success of distributed training methodologies for RL algorithms such as IMPALA [2] and self-play [14]. The biggest barrier in the application of MARL algorithms to

Y. Tan and Y. Shi (Eds.): DMBD 2022, CCIS 1744, pp. 50–61, 2022.
https://doi.org/10.1007/978-981-19-9297-1_5

real-life production is that the multi-agent systems used in real-world problems need to have fast training speed, stable training process, autonomous learning, and generalization capabilities, which are part of the problem that can be perfectly solved when the number of multi-agent systems is small. Since the number of multi-agent systems in real-world problems is massive, existing policy RL algorithms face difficulties in sampling and poor sample learning utilisation, so off-policy-based reinforcement learning frameworks have been used in recent MARL literature to address these problems, such as MADDPG [6], COMA [3], MAA2C [1], and others. Variants of each distinctive and enhanced method have been presented within this framework, delivering advanced outcomes in a wide range of multi-agent benchmarking scenarios.

In this paper, we revisit the generality of these algorithms on multi-agent policy gradients by investigating the performance of the classical CTDE's off-policy RL algorithm MADDPG in several well-known MARL benchmark environment experimental settings within the multi-agent particle-world environment (MPE) [6]. To compare our experimental results with benchmark MADDPG performance, we experimentally focus on totally cooperative as well as cooperative-competitive mixed super-multi-agent tasks.

Our proposed method achieves the benchmark performance of the original MADDPG paper in all test scenarios, including simple-spread, simple tag, and basic MARL relation case scenarios. Holding all parameters constant, we conducted ablation experiments, and the resultant return convergence curves were all greater than those of the benchmark MADDPG algorithm, and gave practical ideas and improvements for research on CTDE-based policy gradient algorithms. We refer to the modified MADDPG as the Soft-Masked Policy Gradient (SMPG).

Our contributions are summarized as follows:

1. We show that SMPG has minimum parameter and network framework modifications, no domain-specific algorithmic framework as well as hyper-parameter changes. It achieves performance beyond the benchmark MADDPG in all three of the overwhelming number of multi-agent benchmark scenarios.
2. We analyze and obtain the sources of high bias in the value function of MADDPG in a super-multi-agent scenario and the reasons for the lag of soft-polyak in the late stages of multi-agent training. Better performance in policy exploration can be achieved by adaptively updating the target network through masking.
3. We show the influence of each enhancement on the multi-agent strategy under the SMPG ablation experiment. The ablation experiments show that both of our proposed changes have a considerable increase in the capabilities of the multi-agent learning strategy and are more effective when used in combination.

2 Related Work

MARL algorithms typically lie between two frameworks: centralised and decentralised learning. Centralised learning extends to the combined actions of numerous agents by learning a common strategy; decentralised learning focuses on optimising each agent separately, treating the other agents as part of the environment. These approaches have good performance in general game problems. However, in some special game problems, even with low problem complexity, both of the above approaches can introduce instability into multi-agent systems. Recent work has been divided into two main lines to remedy the respective shortcomings of the two frameworks: centralised training decentralised execution (CTDE) and value-based decomposition (VD). The CTDE-based approaches such as MADDPG [6], COMA [3] and MAA2C [1] combine the advantages of centralised and decentralised RL through the actor and critic (AC) framework, which greatly improves the joint strategy of multi-agents in free-model environments VD usually uses Q-functions as the core of the framework of the algorithm to propose a solution to the credit allocation problem among multiple agents, and has since spawned many excellent value function decomposition algorithms: VDN [16] for linear summation of local Q-functions to global Q-functions, QMIX [10] for fitting global Q-functions to supernetworks, QTRAN [15] for decomposing Q-functions on a larger scale based on Value functions while satisfying the IGM (Individual-Global-Max) condition, and QPD [18] based on Q-value path decomposition, etc.

Although many of the single-agent policy gradient algorithms already exist (e.g. PPO [5,13]) have long achieved a level of performance beyond that of humans in continuous tasks. However, the biggest problem to be solved in migrating them to a multi-agent RL framework is the communication exchange between multiple agents and the assignment of credit. MAVEN [7] exploits the mutual information between potential variables of hierarchical control to maximise the learning of a range of different policy behaviours; IPPO [19] & MAPPO [19] have achieved better results in SMAC [11] using decentralised training of independent PPO; FACMAC [9] introduces the idea of value decomposition without monotonic constraints from QMIX to MADDPG. The idea of value decomposition without monotonic constraints in QMIX is introduced into the critic network of MADDPG to avoid the dimensional explosion problem and thus better solve non-monotonic tasks; The communication-based MAIC [20] model improves the efficiency of communication transfer between multiple agents by learning to predict the action choices of teammates and adding regular terms to constrain information transfer.

It is not difficult to see that many existing works have investigated the details of the implementation of PG algorithms for multi-agent in the field of continuous control. After examining the above literature, we find that much of it largely ignores the problem of high variance accumulation due to excessive information input during multi-agent training, which allows multi-agent learning to fall into poorer local optimum solutions, and this is one of the main reasons for including it in our experiments in this paper.

3 Algorithm

3.1 Masked Multi-agent Actor Critic

The Masked Autoencoder (MAE) [4] is He's proposed architecture for a self-supervised learning-based image generation algorithm that, as a denoising autoencoder, corrupts the input signal and learns to reconstruct the original, uncorrupted signal in the process of reducing redundant image block information, as illustrated in Fig. 1(a).

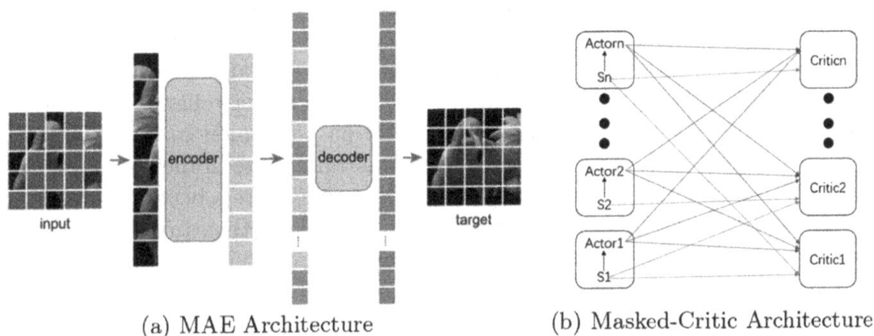

(a) MAE Architecture (b) Masked-Critic Architecture

Fig. 1. In (a), it describes the overall network architecture of the MAE. In (b), the critical input retains the state of the agent corresponding to its own actor network and all agent action information, while the state information of other agents will be randomly masked.

The algorithm of MAE can be described as follows: the main operation of mask is to chunk the input image, mask out some of it at random, and stitch the remaining blocks into the encoder in order. The encoder and decoder sections use an asymmetric encoder-decoder architecture, with the encoder encoding only the unmasked blocks and the decoder encoding the masked blocks as input, resulting in an image the size of the original image. This makes the decoder architecture very lightweight and allows researchers to efficiently train large models as masking out a large proportion of the image blocks (e.g. 75%) results in significant and meaningful self-supervised tasks, with experimental results showing a 3x or more speedup in training large model generation tasks and The accuracy on the self-supervised generation task outperformed that of all Vision Transformers (ViT) variants.

This paper combines the main ideas of MAE to propose a multi-agent deep reinforcement learning algorithm for MADDPG based on information masking. To address the problems that exist in the process of multi-agent collaboration: 1) low learning efficiency 2) a tendency for the training performance of the algorithm to decline significantly as the number of agents increases. Our improvement starts with the design of the collaboration model architecture, which is implemented as follows: First, some of the agent state information is masked randomly according to the masking rate; secondly, the action information of all agents is not masked, mainly because the action information is visible to all agents, and the state information is private information of the agents, so the state information is masked as in Fig. 1(b); the input critic The state information of the critic network is kept in its original order, and the actor network and critic network are updated in the same way as the benchmark MADDPG.

It can be seen that the critic network input to the original MADDPG algorithm is a special case of the SMPG masking rate of 0 in this paper. However, a masking rate of 0 means that the critic network will input private state information of all agents, which is unimaginable in a realistic problem of communication channel consumption between a large number of intelligences, which is one of the problems that MADDPG suffers from. Secondly, although all sampled state information is the true unbiased estimate, MADDPG's over-reliance on all state information leads to a high variance accumulation phenomenon, which in turn makes it exponentially less likely that the agents will update in the correct gradient direction, making it difficult for the algorithm to explore a better strategy. In contrast, SMPG can reduce the variance accumulation of the samples, although it requires sacrificing some of the agents' state information visibility as a cost, i.e. increasing the sampling bias, but as the number of agent iterations increases, the data bias generated in the random masking process will eventually cancel each other out, so it does not affect the convergence of the algorithm. Third, the role played by the random masking approach of SMPG proposed in this paper is similar to that of experience pool replay, i.e., it breaks the problems of data correlation and static distribution between each agent, making the agent model more stable and increasing the spatial dimension of agent exploration, and reducing the phenomenon of agent overfitting.

3.2 Adaptive Polyak Update

Polyak Average Target Update. The Polyak Average Parameter Update was first applied in the Proritized DQN [12] article, which dates back to 2015. For DQN [8], the loss function of its network is through Q-Learning: From the loss function

$$E_{\pi_\omega}\left[r+\gamma \max_{a'} Q\left(s', a', \omega\right)-Q(s, a, \omega)\right]. \tag{1}$$

the predicted Q-value $Q(s,a,\omega)$ and the target Q-value $Q\left(s',a',\omega\right)$of the DQN use the same network parameters ω and model, which results in an overestimation of the target Q when the predicted Q occurs. Due to the instability of the sample data collected by the agent, it is bound to cause fluctuations in the agent learning process, which to a certain extent increases the chance of oscillation and divergence in the agent strategy model. To solve the overestimation problem, Prioritized DQN proposed an update method for Polyak average soft update target network. Specifically, the weights of the target value network ω' are updated by slowly tracking the weights of the current value network ω:

$$\omega' = \tau\omega + (1-\tau)\omega'. \tag{2}$$

where $0 \leq \tau \leq 1$. The Polyak average update method can effectively control the magnitude of each target Q value update and improve the stability of the agent in learning the optimal policy.

Polyak average updates are not only used in the DQN classical framework, but also in the PG-based policy gradient framework, including the MADDPG studied in this paper. From the explanation of the Polyak average update method in the previous section, it is clear that the real stability of the agent in learning optimal policy can be improved by setting the parameters manually, and that the setting of the parameters is constant throughout the training process. This can easily prove that the stability of the whole algorithm is very useful in the early training period, but for the later training, when the Q value of the value function tends to converge locally. Because the τ (usually 0.01) is too small, the parameter θ' of the target network is excessively dependent on the old parameters of the target network, which makes the target network parameters still take a long time to transition to the optimal prediction network parameters when the prediction network parameters. Later experiments show that this phenomenon will greatly delay the convergence speed of the entire algorithm. Although this is a very conservative and safe practice, it will become more obvious for solving the actual complex proxy environment problems because of this conservative operation.

The limitation of using fixed parameter τ to update target network parameters for the Polyak average update method mentioned above. The disadvantage is that the weighted average update of target network parameters using adaptive Polyak is improved. The following formula is used to calculate the value of τ.

$$\tau = 1 - \frac{e^{\text{ratio}} - e^{-\text{ratio}}}{e^{\text{ratio}} + e^{-\text{ratio}}}, \quad \text{where} \quad \text{ratio} = \frac{1}{\text{batch}} \sum_{i=0}^{\text{batch-1}} \left(|Q_i| / \left|Q_i^T\right|\right). \tag{3}$$

In the above equation, we can see that ratio describes the absolute mean difference ratio between the prediction network Q_i and the target network Q_i^T. When the target network is relatively correct, if the prediction network is overestimated, the ratio value will also increase. When both the target network and the prediction network tend to converge, the ratio will approach 1, and when the prediction network are relatively correct. If the predicted network is underestimated, the ratio will decrease by less than 1. So ratios can easily describe the estimated state of the prediction network. Next, the value comes from $1 - tanh(ratio)$, because the tanh function maps any input to any real number between $(-1, 1)$ and ratios are always positive real numbers, so the $tanh(ratio)$ output is always any real number between $(0, 1)$, which satisfies the definition of the Polyak mean update method, $0 \leq \tau \leq 1$.

Of course, all of this is based on the premise of relatively stable estimation of the target network and does not require the estimation state of the target network. Even if overestimation or underestimation occurs, it is obvious that with the update of the Strategic Gradient Method, according to the Policy Improvement Theorem,

Theorem 1 (Policy Improvement Theorem). *For any action taken at any state s, if $q_\pi(s, \pi'(s)) \geq v_\pi(s)$ is true, a larger value function can be obtained, then π' is better than or equivalent to π.*

It can be simply proved that the temporal-difference estimates of both the target networkQ_i^T and the prediction networkQ_i will tend to be optimal. So even if the target network is not an accurate estimation, it will not affect the convergence of the whole proxy policy and the convergence of the value function.

4 Experiments

Baseline Comparison and Experimental Settings. We compare SMPG with MADDPG in two fully cooperative and fully competitive relationship environments in MPE, including simple-spread and simple-tag to make a fair comparison, we follow the same tuning process as SMPG in reimplementing the set of hyperparameters such as learning rate, optimizer and network framework. We also tested various implementation techniques specifically to make the MADDPG implementation match or exceed the performance of the original paper. Full details can be found in our open source code.

Each experiment was conducted on a server configured with 36 GB of RAM, a 32-core CPU, and a single GeForce RTX 3090 GPU for forward propagation and training updates. The results of each experiment were averaged over five separate experiments to obtain the final results.

4.1 Contrast MADDPG

We first tested the simple spread in a scenario where the number of agents was increased from the original 3 to 7. We used DDPG and MADDPG as reference experiments to compare with our SMPG. All network hyperparameters as well as the network model size remain consistent with the benchmark MADDPG, except for three algorithm-specific parameters. We plot the average convergence curves of independent experiments over 50,000 episodes for the various methods in Fig. 2(a).

In the MADDPG citation, the authors analyse that multi-agent reinforcement learning shows an exponentially decreasing trend in the probability of an agent obtaining the correct update direction for a policy gradient when the number of agents is increased significantly. It is therefore not difficult to explain that the algorithm performance of MADDPG in Fig. 2(a) is essentially the same as that of the multi-agent version of DDPG when the number of intelligences is increased significantly, or even shows poorer performance during training. In

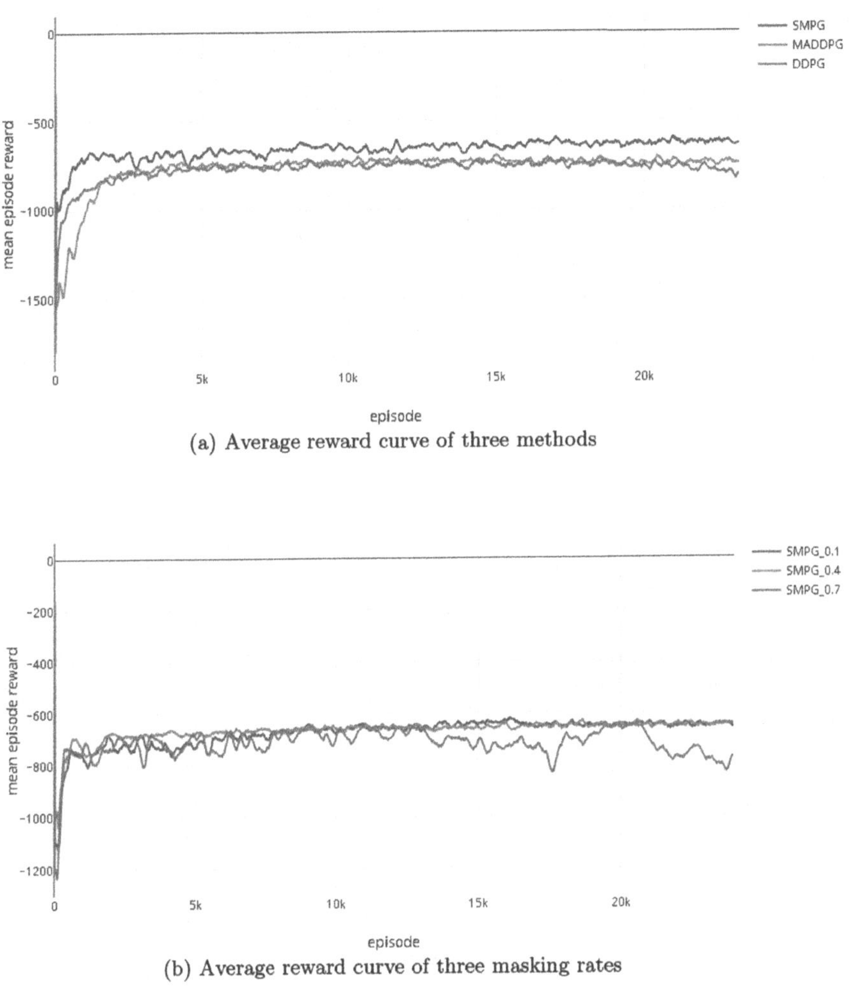

(a) Average reward curve of three methods

(b) Average reward curve of three masking rates

Fig. 2. In (a), we show the average reward convergence curves of three different methods under simple spread. SMPG shows better performance than the other two methods during training, while MADDPG's performance basically drops to the level of DDPG because of the variance accumulation problem. In (b), it can be seen from the reward convergence curve of three SMPGs with different masking rates in simple spread that proper masking can bring better a convergence curve.

contrast, SMPG was able to make the high variance accumulation problem somewhat alleviated after masking certain agent state information, and obtained a better strategy than MADDPG at a later stage. And we also used the benchmark comparison method.

As shown in Table 1, we show the average number of collisions per episode, the average agent distance to the landmark, and the average number of times the agent reaches the landmark for the five independent randomised experiments of

Table 1. In the simple spread environment, the average distance, average collision times and average times of reaching landmarks of each agent in each episode.

Agentπ	Average dist	Collisions	Occupied landmark
SMPG	**9.130**	**4.187**	**1.540**
MADDPG	9.755	4.209	1.380
DDPG	9.761	4.276	1.320

simple spread for the three methods. The lower the average number of collisions, the shorter the average agent distance, and the higher the number of landmarks reached, the better the performance of the algorithm.

Masking Rate. In order to find a better masking ratio, Fig. 2(b) shows the effect of different masking ratios on the agent's exploration strategy. We use 30% as the interval, and start with 10% as the exploratory experiment for three successive masking ratios. 40% is the masking ratio that leads to a better strategy for the agent in our experiment, but there are still better masking ratios, but due to the time and cost constraints of the experiment, we will use 40% masking ratio as the final baseline result in this paper. In Table 2, we can see more intuitively how the data compare with different masking ratios in the simple spread environment.

Table 2. In the simple spread environment, under different masking rates, the average distance, average collision times and average times of reaching landmarks of each agent in each episode.

Agentπ	Average dist	Collisions	Occupied landmark
SMPG01	9.542	**4.130**	1.500
SMPG04	**9.130**	4.187	**1.540**
SMPG07	11.748	4.193	0.954

4.2 Ablation Experiments

Similar conclusions emerged for the simple tag task: in Table 3, we clearly show the average number of successful predations obtained for each agent after five independent random experiments using different strategy algorithms. When we change the number of hunters and prey in the environment from the original 3/1 to 7/4 and 7/7, the SMPG-dominated hunter agent is always more able to catch the MADDPG or DDPG-dominated prey agent. And when the hunter/prey number changes to 4/7, it is easy to conclude that prey agents with SMPG as their main agent are better able to escape hunters with the other two methods

Table 3. In the simple tag environment, different Hunter/prey ratios were compared. SMPG shows excellent strategies both as hunter and prey.

Adversary agentπ	Good agentπ	A/G(4/7)	A/G(7/7)	A/G(7/4)
SMPG	SMPG	2.79	**3.20**	4.58
SMPG	MADDPG	**4.85**	2.61	**6.99**
MADDPG	SMPG	2.52	2.31	3.75
MADDPG	MADDPG	3.33	2.53	4.27

Table 4. The SMPG ablation experiment was conducted in a simple spread environment. The average distance, average collision times, and average times of reaching landmarks of each agent in each episode are displayed below.

Agentπ	Average dist	Collisions	Occupied landmark
SMPG	**9.130**	4.187	**1.540**
SMPG-s	9.274	4.251	1.484
SMPG-m	9.245	**4.157**	1.445

as their main agent. Therefore, using SMPG as a hunter agent or a prey agent is much more successful than the other two methods.

To compare the extent to which the two improvements contribute to SMPG, we conducted ablation experiments for both in the simple spread environment. As Table 4 demonstrates, the MADDPG with only the addition of masking can have a tendency to get a better strategy later on, but the training time is unacceptable. For the MADDPG with only the adaptive Polyak update target network added, it can be of some help in exploring better strategies while speeding up the convergence of the algorithm. In summary, the comparative analysis shows that the masking technique can provide agents with the possibility of better strategy exploration; adaptive Polyak can discard the conservative way of updating the target network in the past, allowing agents to learn more quickly.

5 Conclusions and Future Work

In this paper, we borrow the idea of masked autocoding (MAE) to locally and randomly mask the global state information of the critic network in the original MADDPG algorithm, making it possible for each critic network to be assigned the state information of other agents. In addition, we used the adaptive polyak algorithm to update the target network, and SMPG with adaptive polyak converged nearly 1000 episodes faster on average than the original parameter-fixed polyak update in the MPE environment. Our future work focuses on implementing the SMPG improvements partially in other CTDE-based policy gradient algorithms with adaptive updates of the masking ratio to reduce the adjustment of the masking ratio during migration from different training environments.

Overall, the SMPG improvements yielded robust results that can be optimised by applying them to a wide range of MARL algorithms based on the AC framework, and combined with distributed algorithms to enable the training of large-scale agents.

References

1. Chu, T., Wang, J., Codecà, L., Li, Z.: Multi-agent deep reinforcement learning for large-scale traffic signal control. IEEE Trans. Intell. Transp. Syst. **21**(3), 1086–1095 (2019)
2. Espeholt, L., et al.: Impala: scalable distributed deep-RL with importance weighted actor-learner architectures. In: International Conference on Machine Learning, pp. 1407–1416. PMLR (2018)
3. Foerster, J., Farquhar, G., Afouras, T., Nardelli, N., Whiteson, S.: Counterfactual multi-agent policy gradients. In: Proceedings of the AAAI Conference on Artificial Intelligence, vol. 32 (2018)
4. He, K., Chen, X., Xie, S., Li, Y., Dollár, P., Girshick, R.: Masked autoencoders are scalable vision learners. arXiv preprint arXiv:2111.06377 (2021)
5. Heess, N., et al.: Emergence of locomotion behaviours in rich environments. arXiv preprint arXiv:1707.02286 (2017)
6. Lowe, R., Wu, Y.I., Tamar, A., Harb, J., Pieter Abbeel, O., Mordatch, I.: Multi-agent actor-critic for mixed cooperative-competitive environments. In: Advances in Neural Information Processing Systems, vol. 30 (2017)
7. Mahajan, A., Rashid, T., Samvelyan, M., Whiteson, S.: Maven: multi-agent variational exploration. In: Advances in Neural Information Processing Systems, vol. 32 (2019)
8. Mnih, V., et al.: Playing atari with deep reinforcement learning. arXiv preprint arXiv:1312.5602 (2013)
9. Peng, B., et al.: FACMAC: factored multi-agent centralised policy gradients. In: Advances in Neural Information Processing Systems, vol. 34 (2021)
10. Rashid, T., Samvelyan, M., Schroeder, C., Farquhar, G., Foerster, J., Whiteson, S.: QMIX: monotonic value function factorisation for deep multi-agent reinforcement learning. In: International Conference on Machine Learning, pp. 4295–4304. PMLR (2018)
11. Samvelyan, M., et al.: The starcraft multi-agent challenge. arXiv preprint arXiv:1902.04043 (2019)
12. Schaul, T., Quan, J., Antonoglou, I., Silver, D.: Prioritized experience replay. arXiv preprint arXiv:1511.05952 (2015)
13. Schulman, J., Wolski, F., Dhariwal, P., Radford, A., Klimov, O.: Proximal policy optimization algorithms. arXiv preprint arXiv:1707.06347 (2017)
14. Silver, D., et al.: Mastering chess and shogi by self-play with a general reinforcement learning algorithm. arXiv preprint arXiv:1712.01815 (2017)
15. Son, K., Kim, D., Kang, W.J., Hostallero, D.E., Yi, Y.: QTRAN: learning to factorize with transformation for cooperative multi-agent reinforcement learning. In: International Conference on Machine Learning, pp. 5887–5896. PMLR (2019)
16. Sunehag, P., et al.: Value-decomposition networks for cooperative multi-agent learning. arXiv preprint arXiv:1706.05296 (2017)
17. Vinyals, O., et al.: Grandmaster level in StarCraft II using multi-agent reinforcement learning. Nature **575**(7782), 350–354 (2019)

18. Yang, Y., et al.: Q-value path decomposition for deep multiagent reinforcement learning. In: International Conference on Machine Learning, pp. 10706–10715. PMLR (2020)
19. Yu, C., Velu, A., Vinitsky, E., Wang, Y., Bayen, A., Wu, Y.: The surprising effectiveness of PPO in cooperative, multi-agent games. arXiv preprint arXiv:2103.01955 (2021)
20. Yuan, L., et al.: Multi-agent incentive communication via decentralized teammate modeling (2022)

Attentive Relational State Representation for Intelligent Joint Operation Simulation

Renlong Chen[1], Ling Ye[2], Shaoqiu Zheng[2(✉)], Yabin Wang[2], Peng Cui[2], and Ying Tan[1,3,4,5(✉)]

[1] School of Intelligence Science and Technology, Peking University, Beijing 100871, China
ytan@pku.edu.cn

[2] Nanjing Research Institute of Electronic Engineering, Nanjing 210007, China
zhengshaoqiu1214@foxmail.com

[3] Key Laboratory of Machine Perceptron (MOE), Peking University, Beijing 100871, China

[4] Institute for Artificial Intelligence, Peking University, Beijing 100871, China

[5] Nanjing Kangbo Intelligent Health Academy, Nanjing 211100, China

Abstract. In the multi-agent task, due to the constant changes in the location and state of each agent, the information considered by each agent when making decisions is also constantly changing. This makes it difficult to model cooperatively among agents. Previous methods mainly used average embedding to model feature aggregation. However, this aggregation has the problem of losing permutation invariance or excessive information loss. The feature aggregation method based on attentive relational state representation establishes an insensitive state representation to permutation and problem scale. In our experiments on Intelligent Joint Operation Simulation, experimental results show that attentive relational state representation improves the baseline performance.

Keywords: Multi-agent · Intelligent joint operation simulation · Information aggregation · Attention mechanism

1 Introduction

A lot of real-world robotic tasks involve multiple agents with partial observability and limited communication [2]. Agents have capability to extract useful features from neighboring agents to make optimal decisions and cooperation emerges in the group. Typical examples include the swarm robotics [22], traffic signal control [21], collaborative filter [3], and social network analysis [24].

This work is supported by Science and Technology Innovation 2030 - *New Generation Artificial Intelligence* Major Project (Grant No.: 2018AAA0102301), partially supported by Basic Theory Research Foundation of The Science and Technology Commission of the Central Military Commission and the National Natural Science Foundation of China (Grant No. 62076010 and 62276008).

Y. Tan and Y. Shi (Eds.): DMBD 2022, CCIS 1744, pp. 62–74, 2022.
https://doi.org/10.1007/978-981-19-9297-1_6

For the learning paradigms in multi-agent systems, a centralized controller [5] is theoretically feasible but counters many problems, such as the curse of dimensionality and nonexistence of a possible centralized controller in some real tasks like intelligent transportation systems [10]. Therefore, we focus on a decentralized protocol in multi-agent reinforcement learning (MARL), where agents are connected by a time-varying topology structure, and they aggregate information from all their neighbors. This also promotes the scalability and robustness of multi-agent systems.

However, when decentralized artificial intelligence (AI) agents are trained in an interactive environment, it is tricky to handle the state representation issue because the neighborhoods are highly flexible and scalable. One of the previous approaches to represent the aggregated state is fixing the number of local team members and simply concatenating the information received from neighboring agents, as the input dimension must be invariant in neural-network policies and other machine-learning models. We argue that these formulations lack flexibility. Another popular protocol is pooling embedding, such as max-pooling and mean-pooling. Even though pooling method secures invariant input dimension, it loses much information among neighboring agents.

In this article, we utilize an attention based aggregation method called Attentive Relational State Representation (ARE) to efficiently aggregate information from neighboring agents. By modeling the attention between different neighbors, ARE can actively select relevant information discriminately. By pooling, it constructs a unified state representation for learning policies. With this embedding, we condition the policy and train them simultaneously by deep reinforcement learning (DRL). The compact representation makes the learned policy robust to the changes in the multi-agent system and also reduces the search space for the policy learning method. Enabling learning in this framework opens up the possibility of applying learning-based methods to multi-agent interacting environments where neighbors need to be modeled explicitly and both the quantity and identity are changeable over time.

In our experiments, we apply ARE to Intelligent Joint Operation Simulation, which is a confrontation simulation game. In game setting, the blue side is the defensive side and red side is the offensive side. The blue side relies on the ground, sea and air three-dimensional air defense fire to defend the key targets of the two command posts on your island. While the red side comprehensively uses sea and air assault and supports supporting forces to break through the blue air defense system and destroys the key targets of two command posts of the blue side. Experimental results show that ARE helps decision making progress and outperforms baseline algorithm which indicates that ARE is a more efficient information aggregation method than conventional methods (Fig. 1).

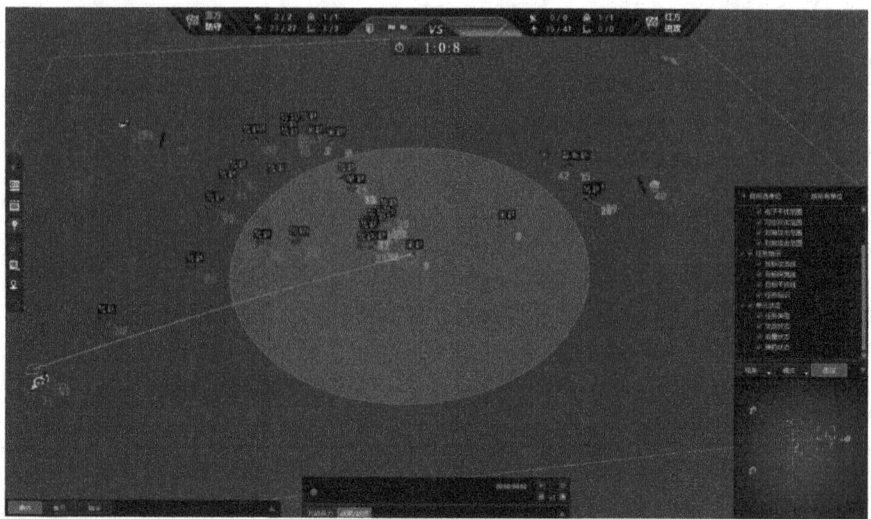

Fig. 1. Joint operation simulation

2 Related Work

2.1 Multi-agent Reinforcement Learning

Learning in the multi-agent system is essentially more difficult than in the single-agent cases, as multiple agents not only interact with the environment but also with each other [1,4,17]. Directly applying the single-agent RL algorithms to the multi-agent system as a whole is a natural approach, which is called the centralized MARL (also called joint action learner [5]). Centralized MARL models the interaction between agents by tightly coupling everything inside the model. Although feasible in execution, it suffers from the curse of dimensionality [4] due to the large-scale joint input space and action space. Thus, decentralized structure has more advantages toward scalability, robustness, and speedup [7,14,18,26].

In the decentralized MARL, a lot of attention has been given to the problem of modeling other agents [1]. In this article, we focus on how to aggregate the information collected from multiple agents, and we make a short survey on the information aggregation approaches in MARL.

2.2 Feature Aggregation in MARL

Concatenation. Concatenation is the simplest and most popular approach in multi-agent RL. By concatenating other features, the augmented state contains all necessary information for decision making. MADDPG [11] constructs the critic for each agent by concatenating other agents' observations and actions, from which the agents can effectively train their actors. A centralized critic is also used in COMA [6], to implement difference reward by comparing with a counterfactual baseline. These methods are under the paradigm of centralized learning with decentralized execution [6,11,12,14,20] which is inspired from DEC-POMDPs [13]. However, concatenation will make the dimension increase linearly, which scales poorly to the large size system. Also, the agent number and identities must be fixed, which is impractical in changeable environments.

Mean Embedding (ME). ME is a workable approach when dealing with a variable dimension problem. By calculating a mean representation, the output has an invariant dimension no matter how many agents are involved. CommNet [19] learns the communication model by rescaling the communication vector by the number of agents to aggregate information. [25] introduced the mean-field theory to MARL. The interactions within the group are approximated by those between a single agent and the average effect from the overall population or neighboring agents. [9] also used the ME method to tackle the representation learning problem in the swarm system. The ME has the advantage of scalability, including dimension and permutation invariance. However, the mean computation is isotropic. The agent has no knowledge of each of its neighbors when pooling averagely around its local view, which may cause ambiguous estimation in many multi-agent tasks where pairwise interactions are important for cooperative decision making.

3 Method

In this section, we first introduce background and give the definition of notations, then introduce ARE structure.

3.1 Background and Notations

We consider multiple agents operating in a partially observable stochastic environment, modeled as a partially observable Markov decision process (POMDP). A stochastic game G is defined by a tuple $< S, U, P, r, Z, O, N, A, \gamma >$, where N agents, $A = \{a_1, a_2, \ldots, a_N\}$, are in an interactive environment. $s \in S$ is the true state of the environment. At each time step, all agents simultaneously execute actions yielding a joint action $\mathbf{u} \in U$ then receive observation $\{o_i\}$ determined by observation function $O(s, u) : S \times U \rightarrow Z$, and rewards $r(s, u) : S \times U \rightarrow \mathbb{R}$ for profits.$P(s' \mid s, u) : S \times U \times S \rightarrow [0, 1]$ is the state transition probability function, and γ is the discount factor. We denote joint quantities over agents in bold, joint quantities other than a specific agent a with the subscript a, i.e., $\mathbf{u} = [u_a, \mathbf{u}_{-a}]$. All agents take the goal of maximizing the discounted reward of r_t.

We consider the parameter-sharing decentralized control [8]. For simplicity and focusing on the representation problem, we assume that each agent can perceive the features of its neighbors in a local sensing range, and there is no other communication protocols.

3.2 Attentive Relational Encoder

An overview of the inference flow is illustrated in Fig. 2. All agents may behave in a possibly time-varying relation network $\mathcal{G}_t = (A, E_t)$, where E_t stands for the set of neighborhood links connecting agents at the time t. In an agent-centric view, we denote the neighboring feature set for the agent i as $\mathcal{N}_i = \{o_j\}_{j \in \mathcal{G}^i}$ where $\mathcal{G}^i$ is the sub-graph of $\mathcal{G}$ induced by all agents adjacent to agent i (we leave out t for brevity). Therefore, our task is to design a function f with trainable weights θ to map the neighborhood feature set to a fixed size of aggregated high-level features, $y : y_i = f(\mathcal{N}_i, \theta)$, where $i \in 1, 2, \ldots, N$.

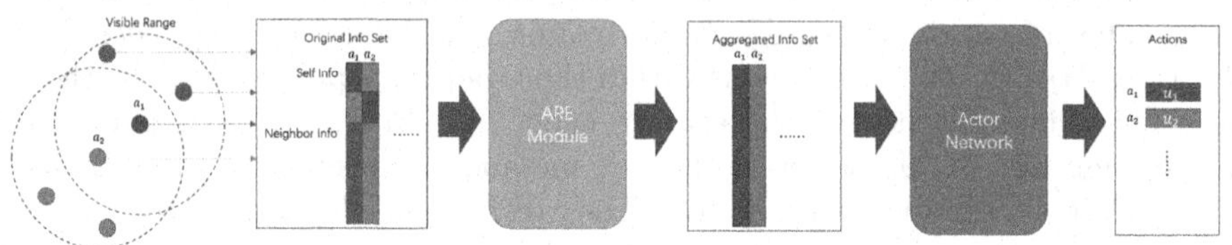

Fig. 2. Overview of the ARE in policy inference.

We utilize a compact neural-network-based architecture, ARE, to aggregate the information from neighboring agents group, whose size is changeable either due to the join or quit of agents. The basic idea of our ARE module is to learn an attention score for each neighbor's feature in the entire neighborhood set. The learnt score can be regarded as a credit that automatically selects useful latent features. For example, within a team of robots moving toward their separate goals, one robot may not care about some neighbors which are behind its moving direction although they are very close. The selected features are then pooled across all elements of the set to aggregate the information and finally served as the state representation for the subject agent.

Figure 3 illustrates the main components of our approach and its execution flow. ARE consists of three encoders, E^f, E^c, and E^a, where $\{f, c, a\}$ stand for feature embedding, communication embedding, and attention embedding. In particular, as shown in Fig. 3, we first feed all the original features (self-feature as well as neighboring features) into two shared encoders E^f and E^c. E^f can be regarded as an intrinsic encoder, which keeps valuable latent features for constructing representation, while E^c is an extrinsic encoder, which reserves the crucial information for interactive relation modeling. Thus, we obtain two streams of latent vectors, e^f and e^c:

$$e_i^f = E^f(o_i) \tag{1}$$

$$e_i^c = E^c(o_i) \tag{2}$$

Second, ARE computes attention scores using the latent vectors e^c for each corresponding neighboring agent through E^a, taking the self feature e_i^c, the cor-

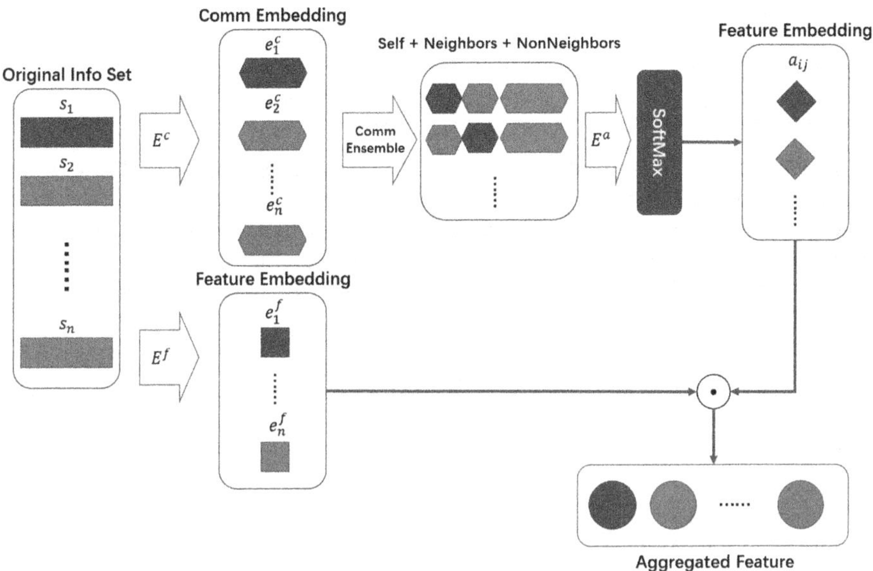

Fig. 3. ARE module on aggregating neighboring features.

responding neighbor's feature e_j^c, as well as an Mean Embedding for other neighboring agents in $\mathcal{G}_i$ other than the agents i and j

$$e_{ij}^a = E^a \left(e_i^c, e_j^c, \overline{e^c}_{-ij}\right) \tag{3}$$

$$\bar{e}_{-ij}^c = \frac{\sum_{k \in \mathcal{G}_i - \{i,j\}} e_k^c}{\|\mathcal{G}_i - \{i,j\}\|} \tag{4}$$

It is worth emphasizing that the self feature is also included in the neighboring feature set in ARE to evaluate the attention score for each agent itself.

We add another channel of ME $\overline{e^c}_{-ij}$ besides pairwise features, in order to model the other neighbors' effect on the pairwise interaction. The output of the function E^a is a set of learnt attention activations $\left\{e_{ij}^a\right\}_{j \in \mathcal{G}_i}$. This procedure is similar to the query-key system [23].

$$e_{ij} \propto \phi\left(e_i^T W_k^T W_q e_j\right) \tag{5}$$

where each sender broadcasts a key transformed by W_k, while the receiver broadcasts a query transformed by W_q. The multiplication of these two parts interprets the relevance or utility of the message. However, we implement this by a neural layer E^a, where the high-level hidden state in neural net can model more abundant interactions between two agents than the query-key system, and generate the attention scores for aggregation.

Third, the learnt attention activations are normalized across the neighborhood set computing a set of attention weights $\overrightarrow{a_i} = \{a_{ij}\}_{j \in \mathcal{G}_i}$. We choose softmax as the normalization operation, so the attention weight for the j-th neighboring feature is

$$a_{ij} = \frac{\exp\left(e_{ij}^a\right)}{\sum_{k \in \mathcal{G}_i} \exp\left(e_{ik}^a\right)} \tag{6}$$

Subsequently, the computed attention weights are multiplied by their corresponding intrinsic latent features in e^f, generating a new set of deep weighted features. Finally, these weighted features are pooled by summing up across the neighborhood set, producing a fixed size of aggregated features which are then fed into a shared decoder to the downstream control policy, as illustrated in Fig. 2.

$$y_i = \sum_j a_{ij} e_j^f \tag{7}$$

$$\pi_i = \text{decoder}\left(y_i\right) \tag{8}$$

In essence, as the weighted features can be parallelly computed and pooled, the output of the ARE module y_i is permutation invariant with regard to the input order.

We here highlight the specific form of the attention weight. In 3, the attention embedding is generated in the scalar value form. To model complex interaction, we can design e_{ij}^a as vector. Therefore, the attention score a_{ij} in 6 is also vector and 7 is revised

$$y_i = \sum_j \left(a_{ij} \cdot W_a\right) \odot e_j^f \tag{9}$$

where we first unify the dimension by multiplying a matrix W_a, then do the Hadamard product with e_j^f. For simplicity, we set the dimension of the attention vector a_{ij} to be the same with e_j^f, thus W_a becomes an identity matrix, and can be ignored.

Design Discussion. In terms of the flexibility in multi-agent state representation learning, the ARE architecture is designed with the following desirable properties and advantages over existing approaches.

- Computational Efficiency: ARE is computationally high efficient since all operations are parallelizable across the neighboring pairs and all modules are shared.
- Quantity Invariance: Although the size of the neighboring feature set can be arbitrary, the output representation is still irrelevant as sum pooling is utilized. This property makes ARE scalable to the changeable and dynamic interactive environments
- Differentiation Ability: Our method is capable of differentiating the utility of multiple neighbors. By feeding each neighbor's feature together with self feature to the attention module and applying the attention mechanism on these features, ARE is able to attach importance to more relevant neighbors' features.

3.3 Training: Proximal Policy Optimization

The ARE module is trained end-to-end by reinforcement learning. The utilized training backend algorithm is Proximal Policy Optimization (PPO) [16].

Proximal Policy Optimization, or PPO, is a policy gradient method for reinforcement learning. The motivation was to have an algorithm with the data efficiency and reliable performance of TRPO [15], while using only first-order optimization.

Let $r_t(\theta)$ denote the probability ratio $r_t(\theta) = \frac{\pi\theta(a_t|s_t)}{\pi_{\theta_{dd}}(a_t|s_t)}$, so $r(\theta_{\text{old}}) = 1$. TRPO maximizes a "surrogate" objective:

$$L^{\mathrm{CPI}}(\theta)=\hat{\mathbb{E}}_t\left[\frac{\pi_\theta\left(a_t \mid s_t\right)}{\pi_{\theta_{dd}}\left(a_t \mid s_t\right)}\right) \hat{A}_t\right]=\hat{\mathbb{E}}_t\left[r_t(\theta) \hat{A}_t\right] \tag{10}$$

where CPI refers to a conservative policy iteration. Without a constraint, maximization of L^{CPI} would lead to an excessively large policy update; hence, PPO modifies the objective, to penalize changes to the policy that move $r_t(\theta)$ away from 1:

$$J^{\mathrm{CLIP}}(\theta)=\hat{\mathbb{E}}_t\left[\min \left(r_t(\theta) \hat{A}_t, \operatorname{clip}\left(r_t(\theta), 1-\epsilon, 1+\epsilon\right) \hat{A}_t\right)\right] \tag{11}$$

where ϵ is a hyperparameter, say, $\epsilon = 0.2$.

4 Experiment

We test our method on Joint Operation Simulation, which is a military operation scenario with red and blue sides which need players to make decisions to achieve intended goals respectively. We will first introduce the task and then give the comparison of our method and baseline algorithm on Joint Operation Simulation.

4.1 Joint Operation Simulation

Scenario Background. The Blue side has long occupied the Red side's islands and recently harassed the Red side's ships for daily operations at sea. In order to swear sovereignty and protect their own interests, joint air and sea combat forces are deployed to strike the Blue side's key targets on the islands to establish a basis for subsequent retaking of the islands. Blue side target (defensive side): rely on ground, sea and air three-dimensional anti-aircraft firepower, guard their own island 2 command post key targets. Red side objective (offensive side): to use a combination of air and sea assault and support forces to break through the blue side's air defense system and destroy the blue side's 2 key command post targets.

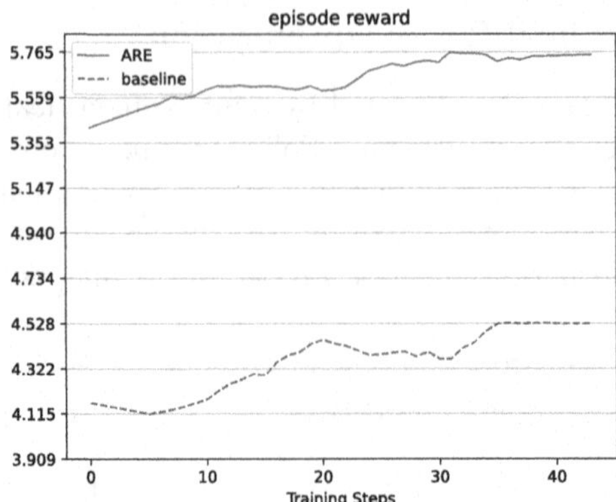

Fig. 4. Comparison of ARE and mean embedding baseline on joint operation simulation.

Scenario Settings. For the characteristics of the two sides, a reasonable set of force composition to confront the idea of rehearsal. Each side has only one airfield, and each airfield has only one runway for the takeoff and landing of combat aircraft. When an aircraft takes off and occupies the runway, no other aircraft can land, and when an aircraft lands, no other aircraft can take off. Through the airport takeoff and landing density to control the speed of force release, to achieve the control of AI available force, consider the tournament against compact, set the minimum interval of aircraft takeoff and landing (by the simulation platform internal control).

Table 1. Comparison of force composition of both sides

	Bomber	AWACS	Jammer	Fighter	Frigate	Radar	Airport	Camp	CC
Red	18	1	1	24	2	1	1	-	-
Blue	10	1	-	20	2	-	1	3	2

Table 1 shows the force composition of both sides. Red side as the offensive side consists of 18 Bombers, 1 AWACS, 1 Jammer, 24 Fighters, 2 Frigates, 1 Radar and 1 Airport. Blue side has a different setting, which consists of 10 Bombers, 1 AWACS, 2 Radars, 20 Fighters, 2 Frigates, 3 Camps, 1 Airport and 2 Command Centers.

For reward settings, all enemy units share 10 points, blue side has a bonus for keeping Command Centers alive, 1 point for each Command Center. Considering the requirement of retaining own units, we also punish unit loss on each side.

Figure 7 gives the composition of entity features, including positions, side, type, speed, direction, damage, alive, weapon, locked. last mission type. ARE aggregates information from each entity, and yields an aggregated and embedded feature containing neighbors' information, which helps a better decision making.

4.2 Results

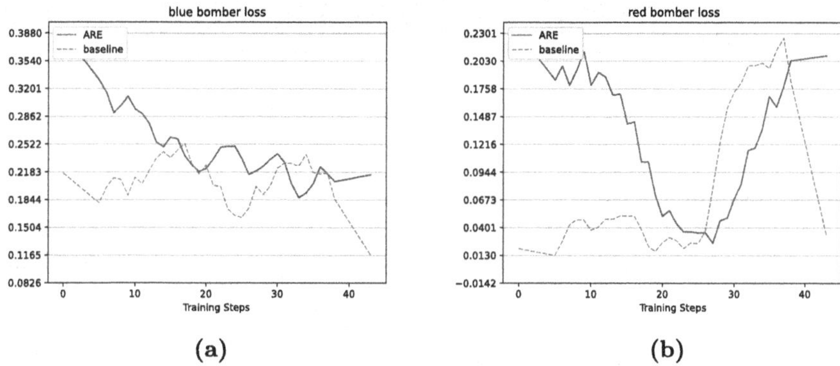

Fig. 5. Comparison of bomber loss of both sides

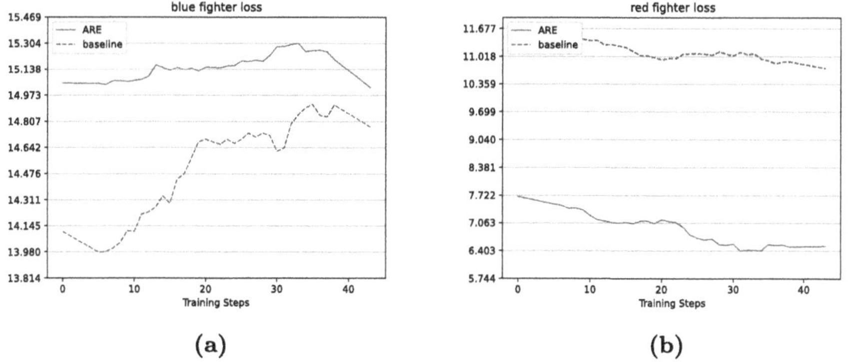

Fig. 6. Comparison of fighter loss of both sides

Both ARE and baseline use PPO as a training backend in our experiments. The red side is set to use RL training algorithms while the blue side is set to use a fixed rule-based method. Figure 4 shows that ARE helps PPO to achieve a higher episode reward throughout the whole training progress. Then more detail comparisons will be given.

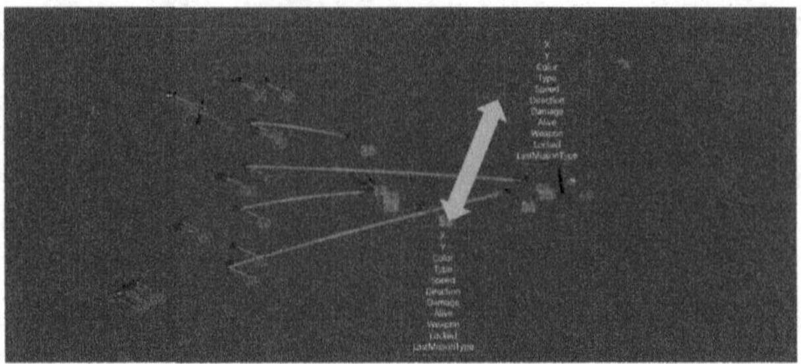

Fig. 7. Composition of entity features.

As is shown in Fig. 5a, ARE based algorithm achieves more average blue side bomber loss during the training progress. The red side bomber loss in Fig. 5b reflects the radical level how a strategy to use bombers, where both ARE and ME baseline vary a lot in different training phases.

Figure 6 shows that ARE outperforms ME baseline by a large margin for a higher damage to blue side and lower red side loss in fighters. It indicates that ARE helps fighters to coordinate with ally units to formulate a more efficient strategy than ME does.

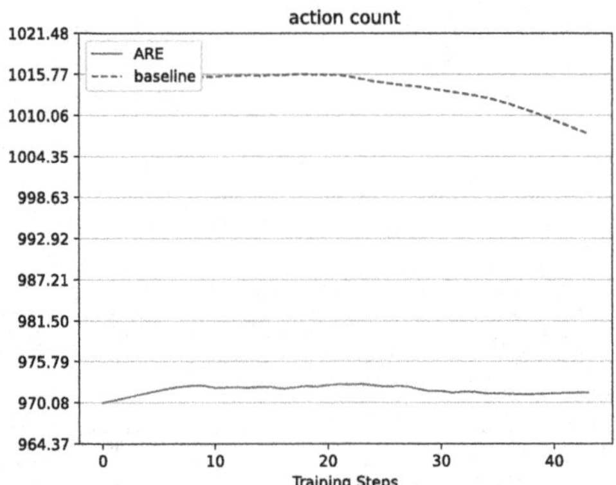

Fig. 8. Comparison of action count per episode.

More actions usually mean more cost in real battles. We also count the action numbers per episode of both methods in Fig. 8. ARE uses significant less actions per episode than ME baseline method, which means ARE helps algorithm learn a much more efficient strategy.

5 Conclusion

In this paper, we analyze the information aggregation problems in multi-agent systems and utilize a computational efficient, quantity invariant and differentiable aggregation method, ARE in a highly simulated joint operation game. Experimental results show that ARE helps decision making progress and outperforms baseline algorithm which indicates that ARE is a more efficient information aggregation method than conventional methods.

References

1. Albrecht, S.V., Stone, P.: Autonomous agents modelling other agents: a comprehensive survey and open problems. Artif. Intell. **258**, 66–95 (2018)
2. Bernstein, D.S., Givan, R., Immerman, N., Zilberstein, S.: The complexity of decentralized control of Markov decision processes. Math. Oper. Res. **27**(4), 819–840 (2002)
3. Breese, J.S., Heckerman, D., Kadie, C.: Empirical analysis of predictive algorithms for collaborative filtering. arXiv preprint arXiv:1301.7363 (2013)
4. Busoniu, L., Babuska, R., De Schutter, B.: A comprehensive survey of multiagent reinforcement learning. IEEE Trans. Syst. Man Cybern. Part C (Appl. Rev.) **38**(2), 156–172 (2008)
5. Claus, C., Boutilier, C.: The dynamics of reinforcement learning in cooperative multiagent systems. AAAI/IAAI **1998**(746–752), 2 (1998)
6. Foerster, J., Farquhar, G., Afouras, T., Nardelli, N., Whiteson, S.: Counterfactual multi-agent policy gradients. In: Proceedings of the AAAI Conference on Artificial Intelligence, vol. 32 (2018)
7. Guestrin, C., Lagoudakis, M., Parr, R.: Coordinated reinforcement learning. In: ICML, vol. 2, pp. 227–234. Citeseer (2002)
8. Gupta, J.K., Egorov, M., Kochenderfer, M.: Cooperative multi-agent control using deep reinforcement learning. In: Sukthankar, G., Rodriguez-Aguilar, J.A. (eds.) AAMAS 2017. LNCS (LNAI), vol. 10642, pp. 66–83. Springer, Cham (2017). https://doi.org/10.1007/978-3-319-71682-4_5
9. Hüttenrauch, M., Adrian, S., Neumann, G., et al.: Deep reinforcement learning for swarm systems. J. Mach. Learn. Res. **20**(54), 1–31 (2019)
10. Li, W.: Notion of control-law module and modular framework of cooperative transportation using multiple nonholonomic robotic agents with physical rigid-formation-motion constraints. IEEE Trans. Cybern. **46**(5), 1242–1248 (2015)
11. Lowe, R., Wu, Y.I., Tamar, A., Harb, J., Pieter Abbeel, O., Mordatch, I.: Multi-agent actor-critic for mixed cooperative-competitive environments. In: Advances in Neural Information Processing Systems, vol. 30 (2017)
12. Mao, H., Gong, Z., Ni, Y., Xiao, Z.: ACCNet: actor-coordinator-critic net for "learning-to-communicate" with deep multi-agent reinforcement learning. arXiv preprint arXiv:1706.03235 (2017)
13. Oliehoek, F.A., Amato, C.: A Concise Introduction to Decentralized POMDPs. Springer, Cham (2016). https://doi.org/10.1007/978-3-319-28929-8
14. Omidshafiei, S., Pazis, J., Amato, C., How, J.P., Vian, J.: Deep decentralized multi-task multi-agent reinforcement learning under partial observability. In: International Conference on Machine Learning, pp. 2681–2690. PMLR (2017)

15. Schulman, J., Levine, S., Abbeel, P., Jordan, M., Moritz, P.: Trust region policy optimization. In: International Conference on Machine Learning, pp. 1889–1897. PMLR (2015)
16. Schulman, J., Wolski, F., Dhariwal, P., Radford, A., Klimov, O.: Proximal policy optimization algorithms. arXiv preprint arXiv:1707.06347 (2017)
17. Shoham, Y., Powers, R., Grenager, T.: If multi-agent learning is the answer, what is the question? Artif. Intell. **171**(7), 365–377 (2007)
18. Su, S., Lin, Z., Garcia, A.: Distributed synchronization control of multiagent systems with unknown nonlinearities. IEEE Trans. Cybern. **46**(1), 325–338 (2015)
19. Sukhbaatar, S., Fergus, R., et al.: Learning multiagent communication with backpropagation. In: Advances in Neural Information Processing Systems, vol. 29 (2016)
20. Sunehag, P., et al.: Value-decomposition networks for cooperative multi-agent learning. arXiv preprint arXiv:1706.05296 (2017)
21. Tan, T., Bao, F., Deng, Y., Jin, A., Dai, Q., Wang, J.: Cooperative deep reinforcement learning for large-scale traffic grid signal control. IEEE Trans. Cybern. **50**(6), 2687–2700 (2019)
22. Tan, Y., Zheng, Z.Y.: Research advance in swarm robotics. Defence Technol. **9**(1), 18–39 (2013)
23. Vaswani, A., et al.: Attention is all you need. In: Advances in Neural Information Processing Systems, vol. 30 (2017)
24. Veličković, P., Cucurull, G., Casanova, A., Romero, A., Lio, P., Bengio, Y.: Graph attention networks. arXiv preprint arXiv:1710.10903 (2017)
25. Yang, Y., Luo, R., Li, M., Zhou, M., Zhang, W., Wang, J.: Mean field multi-agent reinforcement learning. In: International Conference on Machine Learning, pp. 5571–5580. PMLR (2018)
26. Zhang, K., Yang, Z., Liu, H., Zhang, T., Basar, T.: Fully decentralized multi-agent reinforcement learning with networked agents. In: International Conference on Machine Learning, pp. 5872–5881. PMLR (2018)

Graph Neural Networks

Flow Prediction via Multi-view Spatial-Temporal Graph Neural Network

Shan Jiang[1], Qiang Wang[1], Chengjun Wang[1], Kun Liu[1(✉)], Shiqi Ning[1], and Xinrun Xu[2,3]

[1] Advanced Institute of Big Data, Beijing, China
{jiangshan,chenjun110}@alumni.nudt.edu.cn, {wangq,liukun}@aibd.ac.cn, ningshiqi@hit.edu.cn

[2] Institute of Software Chinese Academy of Science, Beijing, China
xuxinrun20@mails.ucas.ac.cn

[3] University of Chines Academy of Sciences, Beijing, China

Abstract. In recent years, the problem of traffic flow prediction in the urban environment has been widely concerned. However, the traffic flow prediction has not been effectively solved for the next period between the origin-destination region pair. In addition, multiple spatial-temporal traffic dependencies exist between the origin-destination area pairs. In this paper, three types of traffic dependencies between origin-destination region pairs were considered: the same origin dependency, same destination dependency, and transfer to dependency. This paper proposed a spatial-temporal forecasting framework for traffic flow prediction between pairs of urban regions with multi-view graphs. This work mainly considered the construction of spatial-temporal deep learning networks under three kinds of multi-view graphs. Finally, the prediction results under the three dependence relationships are fused to get the final prediction results. Comprehensive experiments on two datasets showed that the proposed framework has very high prediction performance, and outperforms the baseline model by more than 6%.

Keywords: Multi-view · Spatial-temporal deep learning · Flow prediction

1 Introduction

Urban region-level traffic flow prediction is one of the hottest topics in recent years [6,7,12,29]. If we can predict the traffic flow between two regions in a city accurately. It can not only help city managers understand regional pedestrian activity and prevent sudden safety problems but also enhance managers' understanding of the relationship between various regions in the city.

The first work was to predict the motion of a single object based on its historical location [5,14,17], which mainly predicted the future location of millions or even billions of mobile users, rather than the population aggregation

Y. Tan and Y. Shi (Eds.): DMBD 2022, CCIS 1744, pp. 77–92, 2022.
https://doi.org/10.1007/978-981-19-9297-1_7

traffic of a region. This requires substantial computing resources and has little significance for the overall study of a region. Other researchers aim to predict driving speed or traffic flow on a single road [1], and study individual or multiple sections of the road rather than city-wide areas. Recently, researchers have focused on the prediction of region flows within cities [6,18,29]. Specifically, they predict the inflow and outflow of each area, which is very helpful to grasp the dynamics of urban public security. To address the complex spatial and temporal dependencies in traffic flow, the ST-ChebNet graph neural network model was proposed for traffic flow prediction to capture the spatial-temporal features, which can ensure accurate traffic flow prediction [24]. Ahmad et al. [2] advised that weather conditions and surrounding point-of-interest (POI) distribution are the most difficult aspect of predicting crowd flows movement and they developed a unified dynamic deep Spatial-temporal neural network model based on convolutional neural networks and long short-term memory, termed as (DHSTNet) to simultaneously predict crowd flows in every region of a city. For the problem of flow prediction in the Internet of Things (IoT) environment, Youcef et al. [4] combined graph optimization and prediction in a single pipeline to investigate an innovative convolutional graph-based neural network for urban traffic flow prediction in an edge IoT environment. However, their research object is the flow of a single area, which is still different from the flow between the area pairs studied in this paper. Another category is origin-destination flow prediction [3,11,21,26], their origin or destination point usually is a certain place, such as a road intersection. In this study, both the origin point and the destination point belong to the regional level, and the flow between the starting and ending points is also a coarse-grained aggregate value, regardless of the specific road flow.

The inter-regional flow prediction problem faces more challenges than the regional inflow/outflow prediction problem, which mainly includes time dependence and spatial flow dependence. Among them, spatial flow dependency mainly includes three types, namely same origin dependency (*sod*), same destination dependency (*sdd*), and transfer to dependency (*ttd*). In this work, *sod*, *sdd*, and *ttd* are regarded as three graphs respectively. The *sod* refers to the mutual influence of flow between the origin and destination regions when the same origin region corresponds to multiple pairs of origin and destination regions. The *sdd* refers to the mutual influence of traffic between origin-destination areas when the same end area corresponds to multiple origin-destination area pairs. The *tdd* refers to that the end area of one origin-destination area pair is the starting area of another origin-destination area pair, and the traffic of the previous origin-destination area pair has an impact on the traffic of the later origin-destination area pair.

In order to solve the above challenges, for time dependence, this paper carries out multi-time scale extraction of datasets and combines the data under different time scales into the overall features. For traffic dependence, three views are designed in this paper to deal with three traffic dependencies respectively. Different dependencies are constructed into different representations in the corresponding views, and different deep learning frameworks are used to deal with them. In this paper, we designed a general multi-view learning framework for traffic prediction between all origin-destination areas in a city.

The previous works of origin-destination flow prediction belong to the intersection level, but in this study, the origin-destination flow prediction task belongs to the grid regional level. In order to solve this new problem, this paper explores the traffic dependence between the origin and destination zones. Based on the three dependencies, a multi-view Spatial-temporal deep learning framework is proposed, and each dependency corresponds to a Graph (or as a graph view). To sum up, the contribution of this work is as follows:

Firstly, in this paper, we proposed the problem of predicting the flow between origin and destination areas in a city. This prediction mission provides a unique analysis perspective for the relationship between regions within a city.

Secondly, a general multi-view learning framework model is proposed for flow prediction between all origin and destination regions in a city to fully address the above challenges. In this framework, three flow dependencies are specifically considered, graphs from three perspectives are constructed for the three dependencies, and a personalized spatial-temporal deep learning network is constructed for them. In the temporal relationship modeling stage of the spatial-temporal deep learning network, this paper uses the attention mechanism to fully explore the contribution degree of different temporal scales to flow prediction.

Lastly, the proposed model is validated on two benchmark datasets. The experimental results show that the prediction accuracy of the proposed model is 6% higher than that of the baseline method, which fully proves the effectiveness of the proposed model.

The rest of the paper is organized as follows: First, we introduce the problem descriptions in Sect. 2. We then present essential preliminaries in Sect. 3. Section 4 presents the overall framework of our multi-view spatial-temporal model followed by the detail on how to generate the dependency graph. Section 5 evaluates the performance of our method. We conclude this paper in the final section.

2 Problem Descriptions

This paper focuses on the problem of interregional flow prediction. Different regions have different static attributes (such as location, size, and shape), dynamic attributes (such as population, weather, and flow), and functional attributes. We believe that the successful prediction of the flow between the origin and destination regions can also indirectly obtain the predicted flow in/out of the region. The origin-destination inter-zone traffic prediction problem can be transformed into the inflow/outflow traffic prediction problem. However, the reverse transformation process is difficult to achieve. Therefore, the origin-destination inter-zone traffic prediction problem faces more challenges than the inflow/outflow traffic prediction problem of a zone, as follows:

A. Time Dependence. In this paper, time dependence mainly refers to time proximity and time periodicity. Time proximity means that the traffic flow between the starting point and the ending point is affected by the adjacent time period. For example, the traffic jam between 8:00 am and 9:00 am will affect the inter-regional traffic flow between 9:00 am and 10:00 am. Time periodicity means that the traffic between the origin-destination area will be affected by the periodicity of different scales, such as the cycle of a day, a week, a year, and so on.

B. Flow Dependency. The flow dependency between different origin-destination region pairs mainly includes the same origin dependency, same destination dependency, and transfer to dependency. The same origin dependency refers to the mutual influence of flows between the origin and destination areas when the same origin area corresponds to multiple origin and destination area pairs. Same destination dependency refers to the mutual influence of traffic between the origin and destination areas when the same destination area corresponds to multiple origin and destination area pairs. Transfer to dependency refers to that when the end area of a origin-destination area pair is the starting area of another origin-destination area pair, the flow of the previous origin-destination area pair will have an influence on the flow of the later origin-destination area pair.

To address the above main challenges, for time dependence, this paper extracts the data set at multiple time scales and combines the data at different time scales into a global feature. For traffic dependency, this paper designs three views to deal with three traffic dependencies respectively, and different dependencies are constructed into different representations in the corresponding views and processed by different deep learning frameworks.

3 Essential Preliminaries

Here we first give some basic definitions as follows:

Definition 2.1 (Grid Region). In this work, along the two directions of longitude and latitude, we set the grid side length as $\ell = 1km$ and divided the city into several grids, each of which represents a region, and all grids constitute the grid map $M(\ell)$ of the city.

Definition 2.2 (Time Slot). Time solt refers to a period of time as a unit of time. The length of each period ϕ is user-defined, and the t-th time solt can be defined as a tuple $t_l = (t_s, t_e)$, where t_s and t_e are the start time and end time of this slot respectively. In this paper, we denote the time slot set of the dataset by $\mathbb{T}$.

Definition 2.3 (Trip). A trip is a journey from one place to another. A trip tr can be defined as a four-tuple: $tr = (o_s, d_s, o_e, d_e)$, where o_s and d_s are the start and end coordinates of tr respectively, o_e and d_e are the start and end time of tr respectively. For simplicity, we use $tr.o$ and $tr.d$ to denote the departure and destination of the trip tr, respectively. The grid of $tr.o_s$ is denoted as $tr(g_o)$. The grid of $tr.d_s$ is denoted as $tr(g_d)$. The time slot of $tr.o_e$ and $tr.d_e$ are respectively denoted as $tr(t_o)$ and $tr(t_d)$. In this paper, we denote the trip set of the dataset by $\mathbb{TR}$.

Definition 2.4 (Origin-destination Region Pairs). For any trip tr, $tr(g_o)$ and $tr(g_d)$ form a origin-destination region pair, denoted as r_p. The origin region and destination region can also be denoted as r_p^o and r_p^d respectively.

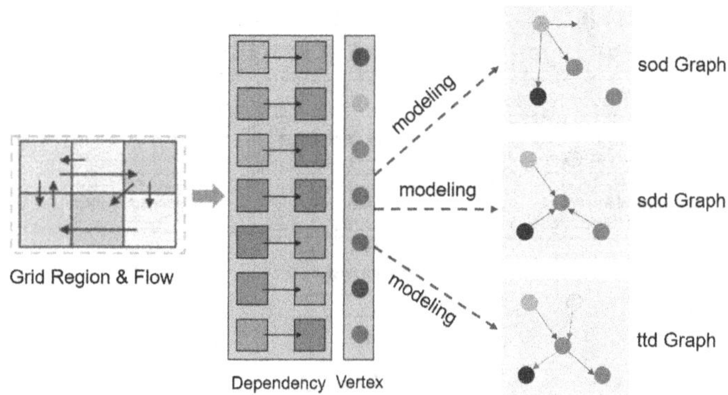

Fig. 1. Transform from a regional grid to a dependency graph.

Definition 2.5 (Flow Dependency Graph). In this paper, the flow dependency between different origin-destination region pairs mainly includes the same origin dependency(denotes as *sod*), same destination dependency(denotes as *sdd*), and transfer to dependency(denotes as *ttd*). In this article, we build topology for each dependency, namely G_{sod}, G_{sdd}, and G_{ttd}. As shown in Fig. 1, these three dependencies are modeled as three dependency graphs. The three dependency features, *sod*, *sdd*, and *ttd*, have a topology at each time slot.

Definition 2.6 (Traffic Flow Between Origin and Destination). The start-destination inter-area traffic flow refers to the number of trips from a starting grid region v_i^o to a destination grid region v_i^d in time slot t. The traffic flow between origin and destination is defined as $f_{v_i^o, v_i^d}^t$ in time slot t.

4 Methodology

In this section, we first present the overall framework of our multi-view spatial-temporal model followed by the detail of how to generate the dependency graph. The framework developed in this article is shown in Fig. 2. At the bottom of the figure, the city is divided into different grid areas, and three types of topological maps are generated according to different dependencies (namely, G_{sod}, G_{sdd}, and G_{ttd}). After the spatial-temporal deep learning network is applied to these three kinds of graphs in parallel, the generated results are fused together, and then the final prediction result is obtained through the action of a multi-layer perceptron. Next, we'll elaborate on the various parts of the framework.

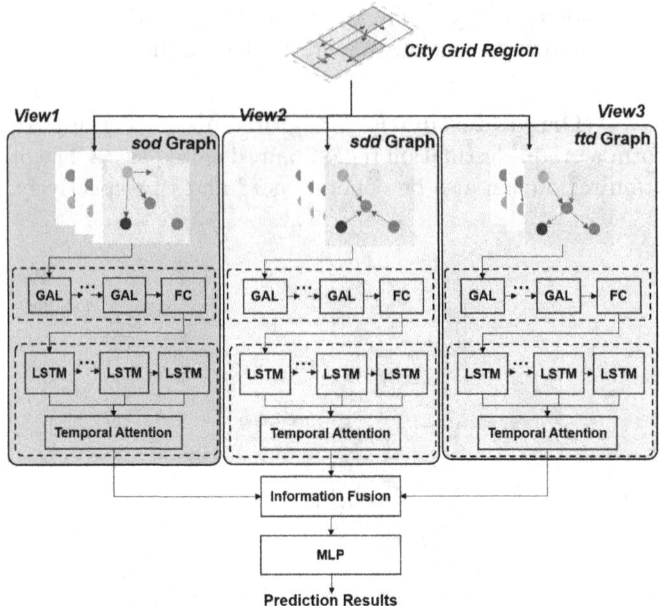

Fig. 2. The overview of multi-view spatial-temporal model.

4.1 Dependency Graph Generation

Vertex Generation. After the city is divided into grid regions, this paper maps the start and end points of the journey to the corresponding grid and obtains all the origin-destination region pairs, and each origin-destination region pair will correspond to a vertex in the topological graph. In order to speed up the calculation performance, this paper only counts once in the whole time range $\mathbb{T}$ of the data set, that is, for a vertex in the graph corresponding to the origin-destination region pair formed by $\forall tr \in \mathbb{TR}$, $tr(g_o)$ and $tr(g_d)$. In this case, the set V of vertices is the same for the graph at any time period and under any dependence.

Edge Generation and Filtering. The edges in the graph are built based on dependencies. That is, at any time period, there are connected edges between vertices satisfying the same dependence relation (*sod*, *sdd*, or *ttd*). Specifically, in time slot t, the adjacency matrix of the dependency graph under the three dependencies is initialized as follows:

$$(A_{\text{sod}})_{ij}^{t} = \begin{cases} 1 & v_i^o = v_j^o, \\ 0 & \text{otherwise} \end{cases} \tag{1}$$

$$(A_{\text{sdd}})_{ij}^{t} = \begin{cases} 1 & v_i^d = v_j^d, \\ 0 & \text{otherwise} \end{cases} \tag{2}$$

$$(A_{\text{ttd}})_{ij}^{t} = \begin{cases} 1 & v_i^d = v_j^o, \\ 0 & \text{otherwise} \end{cases} \tag{3}$$

G_{sod} and G_{sdd} are composed of disjoint directed complete subgraphs. For a grid area of a city, there is almost always a journey between any two areas. Therefore, the total number of edges in the graph can reach $O(K^3)$, where K is the total number of raster regions. It is clear that the computational complexity is very high. Therefore, the edges in the subgraph of G_{sod} and G_{sdd} should be filtered.

The main idea of the filtering method adopted in this paper is to find the vertices with similar but earlier traffic flow waveform patterns as the filtered neighbors for any vertex. The filtering operation can not only reduce the number of edges in the graph and reduce the computation overhead but also find more important neighbor vertices for each vertex in the graph. Due to the generality of origin-destination area pairs within cities, the G_{ttd} graph still tends to converge to a fully directed graph. Therefore, in this paper, the same filtering strategy is used to screen the edges in the G_{ttd} graph.

Vertex Feature Value Mapping. For the initial feature generation of each vertex, the flow data between the origin-destination area pairs is mainly used to generate features. In addition to generating time series features, history records, weighted moving averages, and Fourier transforms amplitude & frequency features, the distance between the region center points between the origin-destination grid region pairs is also considered as a vertex feature. In an effort to G_{sod} for example, in the graph G_{sod} of time slot t, the set of vertex features can be formalized as follows (the same as to G_{sdd} and G_{ttd}).

$$(X_{\text{sod}})^t = \left\{ (x_{\text{sod}})_0^t, \ldots, (x_{\text{sod}})_{N-1}^t \mid (x_{\text{sod}})_n^t \in \mathbb{R}^F, n \in \{0, 1, \ldots, N-1\} \right\} \tag{4}$$

4.2 Multi-view Spatial-Temporal Model

Three graphs can be generated with three dependency views overall time slots. In this subsection, the generated graph will be fed into the spatial-temporal deep learning graph neural network under the respective view to get the preliminary prediction results. The spatial-temporal deep learning network [15] developed in this paper can be divided into two phases: the spatial relation modeling phase and the temporal relation modeling phase.

Spatial Relationship Modeling. In the stage of spatial relationship capture, this paper designs a spatial relationship feature extraction module, which is serially composed of multiple Graph Attention layers (GAL) [25] and a full connection layer, and the number of GAL is a variable parameter. The input of the module is the graph of multiple historical periods, and the output is the same graph, but the vertex features are updated, that is, the adjacency matrix is updated, and the values of the adjacency matrix are replaced by the new weight values. Adjacency matrix updating formula is as follows:

$$e_{ij}^t = \text{leakyReLU}\left(\overrightarrow{\mathbf{a}}^\top \left[\mathbf{W}x_i^t \| \mathbf{W}x_j^t\right]\right) \tag{5}$$

$$A_{ij}^t = \text{softmax}_j\left(e_{ij}^t\right) = \frac{\exp\left(e_{ij}^t\right)}{\sum_{k\in\mathcal{N}_j} \exp\left(e_{kj}^t\right)} \tag{6}$$

where $\mathcal{N}_j$ denotes the set of neighboring vertices of vertex v_j, $\mathbf{W} \in \mathbb{R}^{F\times F}$ represents the weight parameter matrix to be learned, and note $\|$ denotes the concate operation. After the edge weight is updated, we can further obtain the vertex feature update operation, the formula is as follows:

$$\left(x_j^t\right)' = \sigma\left(\sum_{i\in\mathcal{N}_j} A_{ij}^t \mathbb{W} x_j^t\right) \tag{7}$$

where $\mathbb{W}$ denotes the weight parameter matrix to be learned, $\sigma(*)$ represents the activation function.

Temporal Relationship Modeling. In order to capture the temporal relationship, this paper designs a temporal prediction module to complete the prediction of traffic flow. For example, in time slot t, the characteristics of t_{step} historical time periods will be input into the temporal prediction module to predict the traffic flow between the origin-destination area of the whole city in time slot $t+1$.

In this paper, the time distance of proximity, daily degree, weekly degree, monthly degree, and quarterly degree are respectively selected as inputs. For example, we can set the length of the period $\varphi = 1$ h. If we want to predict the traffic of all region pairs between 16:00 and 17:00 this Sunday (September 11, 2022), we also can choose $\gamma_c = 4$ adjacent graphs (i.e., the 15:00–16:00 graph, the 14:00–15:00 graph, the 13:00–14:00 graph, and the 11:00–12:00 graph), and the daily $\gamma_d = 3$ adjacent graphs (i.e., the 16:00–17:00 graph on September 11, 2022, and the graph on 10 September 2022). The adjacent graph from 16:00 to 17:00 on the day, the graph from 16:00 to 17:00 on September 04, 2022), the graph from the weekly $\gamma_w = 2$ adjacent graphs (that is, the graph from 16:00 to 17:00 on September 11, 2022, and the graph from 16:00 to 17:00 on August 28, 2022), and the graph from the monthly $\gamma_m = 1$ adjacent graphs (that is, adjacent graph from 16:00 to 17:00 on August 11, 2022), and the graph from a quarterly $\gamma_q = 1$ adjacent graph (namely the figure from 16:00 to 17:00 on June 11, 2022). In this paper, we set $t_{step} = \gamma_c + \gamma_d + \gamma_w + \gamma_m + \gamma_q$.

The graph, corresponding to time slot t_{step}, will first go through the spatial relationship modeling stage to update the vertex features, and then the feature is input into a time series prediction module respectively. In order to extract the temporal correlation, the time series prediction model selected in this paper is LSTM [27], which is a variant with the strongest expression ability of RNNs [16]. The hidden layer status h_t of LSTM is expressed as follows:

$$h_t = (1 - o_t) * \tanh(C_t), \text{ where } \begin{cases} o_t = \sigma(\mathbf{W}_o [h_{t-1}, x_t] + \mathbf{b}_o) \\ C_t = f_t * C_{t-1} + i_t * \tilde{C}_t \\ \tilde{C}_t = \tanh(\mathbf{W}_C [h_{t-1}, x_t] + \mathbf{b}_C) \\ i_t = \sigma(\mathbf{W}_i [h_{t-1}, x_t] + \mathbf{b}_i) \\ f_t = \sigma(\mathbf{W}_f [h_{t-1}, x_t] + \mathbf{b}_f) \end{cases} \tag{8}$$

where $\mathbf{W}_o$, $\mathbf{W}_C$, $\mathbf{W}_i$, $\mathbf{W}_f$, $\mathbf{b}_o$, $\mathbf{b}_C$, $\mathbf{b}_i$, and $\mathbf{b}_f$ are parameters to be learned. In addition, this paper also calculates the attention weight for each hidden layer state. This will make the feature weight value corresponding to the more important historical slot larger. The weight of the LSTM hidden layer state corresponding to the $h \in \{1, 2, ..., t_{step}\}$ historical time slots is as follows:

$$e_t^h = \mathbf{v}^\top \tanh\left(\mathbf{W}_h h_t^h + \mathbf{b}_h\right) \tag{9}$$

$$\alpha_t^h = \frac{\exp\left(e_t^h\right)}{\sum_{p=1}^{t_{step}} \exp\left(e_t^p\right)} \tag{10}$$

where $\mathbf{W}_h$ and $\mathbf{b}_h$ are parameters to be learned. The final time series prediction results are as follows:

$$y_t = \sum_{p=1}^{t_{step}} \alpha_t^p h_t^p \tag{11}$$

In this paper, the effect of dependency extraction can be adjusted by adjusting the values of parameters such as the number of layers of the attention layer in the figure and the size of hidden states in the attention layer in the graph in the three dependency views. Since the spatiotemporal relationship extraction and prediction results under the three dependent views are independent of each other, the three spatiotemporal deep learning networks can be implemented in parallel.

Information Fusion and Prediction Results. After obtaining the prediction results of spatiotemporal deep learning networks under the three dependencies, it is necessary to fuse the three results. The expression of information fusion is as follows:

$$y = W_{sod} \odot ysod + W_{sdd} \odot y_{sdd} + W_{ttd} \odot y_{ttd} \tag{12}$$

where notion $\odot$ denotes the Hadamard product operation. W_{sod}, W_{sdd}, and W_{ttd} are parameters to be learned. Finally, the predicted values of all origin-destination traffic flow are obtained through a multi-layer perceptron. This paper uses the back-propagation algorithm to train the multi-layer perceptron.

5 Performance Evaluations

This section mainly provides the experimental evaluation of the multi-view spatial-temporal deep learning model for flow prediction developed above.

5.1 Experiment Settings

Datasets and Settings. In our experiments, we choose the most authoritative benchmark datasets, TaxiNYC[1] and BikeDC[2]. The TaxiNYC dataset is a New York City taxi dataset. The TaxiNYC dataset collected data on yellow and green taxis in the borough of Manhattan, New York City, for 91 days from January to March 2016. The field elements of the TaxiNYC dataset include pick-up time, drop-off time, pick-up location, and drop-off location. The BikeDC dataset is the Washington bicycle dataset. The BikeDC dataset contains a total of 472 sites. The field elements in the BikeDC dataset include trip duration, start time, end time, start-stop, and end stop.

We split the TaxiNYC dataset for our experiments with 40,138 samples in the training set, 5,734 samples in the validation set, and 1,1468 samples in the test set. We split the BikeDC dataset for our experiments with 30,300 samples in the training set, 4,328 samples in the validation set, and 8,659 samples in the test set.

All experiments were compiled and tested on Dell Precision 7920 Platform, a Linux Tower Server (CPU: Intel(R) Xeon(R) Gold 5218 CPU @2.30 GHz, GPU: NVIDIA GeForce GTX 2080). Meanwhile, we terminated the training if the validation loss does not decrease for 200 consecutive epochs. Furthermore, we randomly shuffled the dataset to obtain the best training effect.

Metrics and Baselines. The root mean squared errors (RMSE) was used as the evaluation metric. In this work, we compared our traffic flow method with the following baselines:

VAR [8]: Vector Auto-Regressive model. VAR is a traditional time series analysis method.

ARIMA [20]: Auto-Regressive Integrated Moving Average is a time series analysis method for predicting mission. ARIMA is a traditional time series analysis method.

LSTM [22]: Long Short Term Memory network. The LSTM model can learn long temporal dependencies. In this paper, experiments are carried out on six LSTM variants, namely, STM-3, LSTM-6, LSTM-12, LSTM-24, LSTM-48, and LSTM-336.

GRU [19]: The gated recurrent unit (GRU) model can be used to capture long-term temporal dependence. There are also six variants of GRU in this test, namely GRU-3, GRU-6, GRU-12, GRU-24, GRU-48, and GRU-336.

ST-DNN [28]: ST-DNN is a prediction model based on deep neural network acting on spatiotemporal data.

---

[1] https://www1.nyc.gov/site/tlc/about/tlc-triprecord-data.

[2] https://www.capitalbikeshare.com/system-data.

Preprocessing and Hyperparameters. In this paper, we filter the null values and outliers of data sets, and then we segment them in time and space. In the output of the model developed in this paper, *tanh* is used as the final activation function, which ranges between −1 and 1. Therefore, this paper uses the Min-Max normalization method to scale the data to [−1, 1]. In the evaluation, the predicted value is rescaled back to the normal value and compared with the real value. In this article, the parameters to be learned are initialized using the Uniform distribution at the beginning. The size of the hidden layer state output of the graph attention layer is set to 32×32 and the size of the hidden layer state output of the LSTM is set to 64×64. This article uses Adam [9] as the optimizer, with a batch size of 32. In this paper, 90% of the data was selected as the training dataset and the remaining 10% as the test dataset.

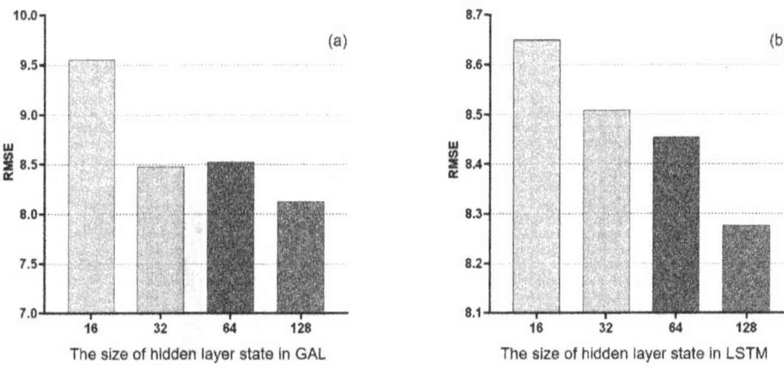

Fig. 3. The size of hidden layer state in GAL and LSTM.

5.2 Results and Analysis

Experiments on Different Variants. In this subsection, we mainly present experimental results of different variants of our developed model, including changing network parameters, using different components, etc. The size of the hidden layer state in GAL and LSTM. On the TaxiNYC dataset, the sizes of hidden layer states in the temporal and spatial submodules are set to 16, 32, 64, and 128, and the results are shown in Fig. 3. It can be seen from Fig. 3(a) that when the size of GAL's hidden layer state is set to 128, the prediction effect is the best. This result shows that the larger the hidden layer is, the better the prediction effect is. Figure 3(b) shows that the prediction error gradually decreases with the increase of the hidden layer state size, which indicates that the larger the hidden layer state is, the more favorable the performance of LSTM is.

Based on the TaxiNYC dataset, this paper conducted experiments on t_{step} size, the side length of grid area, and the number of GAL, and the test results were shown in Fig. 4. It can be seen from Figure Fig. 4(a) that selecting a historical value has the worst effect, which is equivalent to using the characteristics

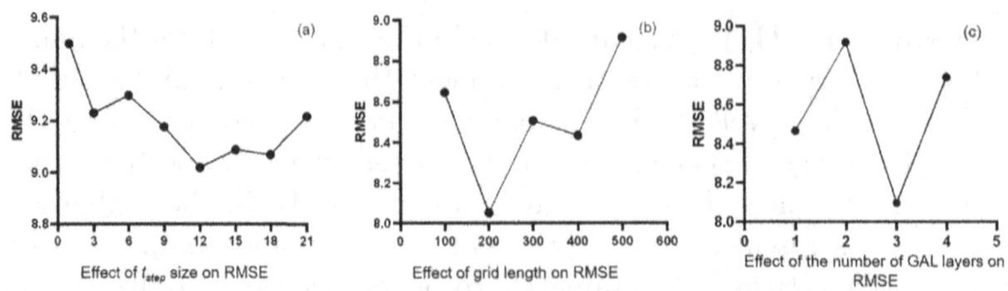

Fig. 4. Effects of different parameter values on the RMSE.

of the current period to predict the flow of the next period. This situation will lead to very little information that can be used.

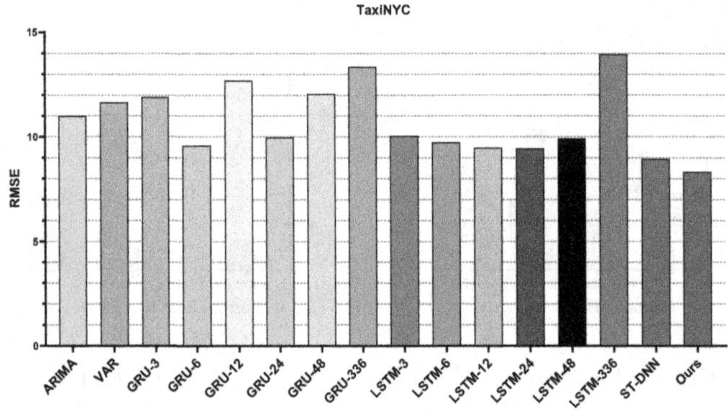

Fig. 5. Performance ranking of the models developed in this paper on the test dataset of TaxiNYC.

As a result, LSTM can not capture any temporal dependencies. However, the prediction error decreases with the increase of t_{step} value, and the best prediction effect is when t_{step} is equal to 12. When t_{step} is greater than 12, the prediction error is on the rise again. Figure 4(b) shows the influence of the side length of the grid region on the performance. As can be seen from the figure, when the side length of the grid is 200 m, the performance is the best, and when the side length is 500 m, the performance is poor. This is because the edge length of the grid area is too large, the number of grids is reduced, and there are too few edges left after filtering in the topological graph, which greatly affects the capture of spatial relations. Figure 4(c) shows the influence of the number of GAL. RMSE does not show a monotonically decreasing or increasing effect with the value on the horizontal axis. When the number of GAL is 2, the prediction error is the lowest.

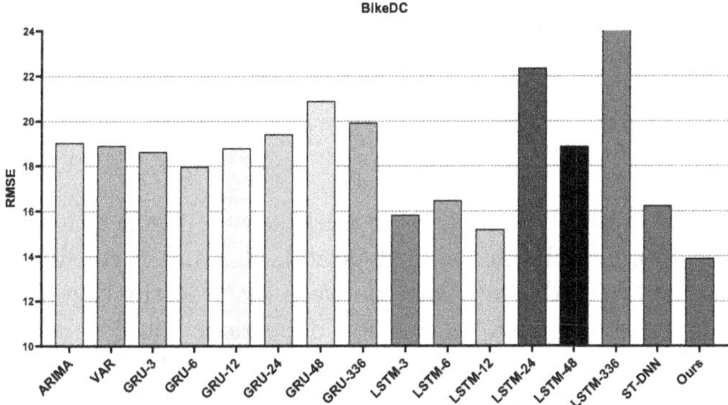

Fig. 6. Performance ranking of the models developed in this paper on the test dataset of BikeDC.

Performance Results. In this subsection, the prediction accuracy of the model is evaluated, that is, s historical observations are used to predict the origin-destination flow at the next moment. Figure 5 and Fig. 6 show the RMSE values on the TaxiNYC and BikeDC datasets, respectively. Specifically, on the dataset TaxiNYC, compared with ARIMA, VAR, ST-DNN, LSTM, and GRU, the accuracy of the model designed in this paper is higher by 24.0%, 28.5%, 6.8%, 11.7%–40.3%, and 13.0%–37.7%, respectively. In all the baseline models, ST-DNN uses spatiotemporal CNNs and performs significantly better than the other baselines. Although VAR uses the relationship between temporal/spatial information and traffic, it is worse than ST-DNN because it only considers the recent temporal information and uses spatial information in a general way without any distinction. In the temporal model, GRU and LSTM have similar RMSE because both GRU and LSTM can capture long-term time dependencies. However, the performance of both GRU-336 and LSTM-336 is very poor, which indicates that RNN-based models cannot capture very long-term dependencies.

Limitations and Outlook. In this work, we only use three types of traffic dependencies between origin-destination region pairs, and future work will investigate more traffic dependencies between area pairs to enrich the current work. For the optimization of convolutional neural networks (CNNs)' architectures, there are no explicit functions to directly calculate the optimal architecture [10]. In order to solve the problems above, the concept of the neural architecture search (NAS) is proposed for the optimization of the deep neural network. The purpose of NAS is to automatically search for parameters such as the optimal architectures of CNNs so that CNNs can outperform those that are hand-crafted [23]. Moreover, the NAS can reduce the high cost of trial-and-error design. In the future work, the NAS will be investigated for the traffic flow prediction mission. Additionally, incorporating recent transformer-based backbones, i.e.,

Spatial-temporal Transformer network [13] could further boost the performance without compromising the simplicity.

6 Conlusion

The target of the traffic flow prediction mission is to predict the flow between origin-destination area pairs in the next period. This paper considers that there are three kinds of traffic dependencies between start-destination area pairs: the same origin dependency, same destination dependency, and transfer to dependency. This paper proposes a spatial-temporal framework for traffic flow prediction, which considers the construction of spatial-temporal deep learning networks under three kinds of dependencies. The final forecast result is obtained by the fusion of the respective forecast results under the three kinds of dependence. Large-scale experiments on two datasets show that the proposed framework achieves very good prediction performance, outperforming the baseline model by more than 6%.

Acknowledgements. This work was supported by the National Natural Science Foundation of China under Grant No. 72201275.

References

1. Abadi, A., Rajabioun, T., Ioannou, P.A.: Traffic flow prediction for road transportation networks with limited traffic data. IEEE Trans. Intell. Transp. Syst. **16**(2), 653–662 (2015). https://doi.org/10.1109/TITS.2014.2337238
2. Ali, A., Zhu, Y., Zakarya, M.: Exploiting dynamic spatio-temporal graph convolutional neural networks for citywide traffic flows prediction. Neural Netw. **145**, 233–247 (2022). https://doi.org/10.1016/j.neunet.2021.10.021
3. Cascetta, E.: Estimation of trip matrices from traffic counts and survey data: a generalized least squares estimator. Transp. Res. Part B Methodol. **18**(4), 289–299 (1984). https://doi.org/10.1016/0191-2615(84)90012-2
4. Djenouri, Y., Belhadi, A., Srivastava, G., Lin, J.C.W.: Hybrid graph convolution neural network and branch-and-bound optimization for traffic flow forecasting. Futur. Gener. Comput. Syst. **139**, 100–108 (2023). https://doi.org/10.1016/j.future.2022.09.018
5. Fan, Z., Song, X., Shibasaki, R., Adachi, R.: Citymomentum: an online approach for crowd behavior prediction at a citywide level. In: Mase, K., Langheinrich, M., Gatica-Perez, D., Gellersen, H., Choudhury, T., Yatani, K. (eds.) Proceedings of the 2015 ACM International Joint Conference on Pervasive and Ubiquitous Computing, UbiComp 2015, Osaka, Japan, 7–11 September 2015, pp. 559–569. ACM (2015). https://doi.org/10.1145/2750858.2804277
6. Hoang, M.X., Zheng, Y., Singh, A.K.: FCCF: forecasting citywide crowd flows based on big data. In: Ravada, S., Ali, M.E., Newsam, S.D., Renz, M., Trajcevski, G. (eds.) Proceedings of the 24th ACM SIGSPATIAL International Conference on Advances in Geographic Information Systems, GIS 2016, Burlingame, California, USA, 31 October–3 November 2016, pp. 6:1–6:10. ACM (2016). https://doi.org/10.1145/2996913.2996934

7. Jiang, W., Luo, J.: Graph neural network for traffic forecasting: a survey. Expert Syst. Appl. **207**, 117921 (2022). https://doi.org/10.1016/j.eswa.2022.117921
8. Kulshreshtha, M., Nag, B., Kulshrestha, M.: A multivariate cointegrating vector auto regressive model of freight transport demand: evidence from Indian railways. Transp. Res. Part A Policy Pract. **35**(1), 29–45 (2001). https://doi.org/10.1016/S0965-8564(99)00046-4
9. Lin, C.H., Lin, Y.C., Tang, P.W.: ADMM-ADAM: a new inverse imaging framework blending the advantages of convex optimization and deep learning. IEEE Trans. Geosci. Remote Sens. **60**(1), 1–16 (2022). https://doi.org/10.1109/TGRS.2021.3111007
10. Liu, Y., Sun, Y., Xue, B., Zhang, M., Yen, G.G., Tan, K.C.: A survey on evolutionary neural architecture search. IEEE Trans. Neural Netw. Learn. Syst. 1–21 (2021). https://doi.org/10.1109/TNNLS.2021.3100554
11. Liu, Z., Liu, Z., Fu, X.: Dynamic origin-destination flow prediction using spatial-temporal graph convolution network with mobile phone data. IEEE Intell. Transp. Syst. Mag. **14**(5), 147–161 (2022). https://doi.org/10.1109/MITS.2021.3082397
12. Liu, Z., Zhang, R., Wang, C., Xiao, Z., Jiang, H.: Spatial-temporal conv-sequence learning with accident encoding for traffic flow prediction. IEEE Trans. Netw. Sci. Eng. **9**(3), 1765–1775 (2022). https://doi.org/10.1109/TNSE.2022.3152983
13. Peng, Z., Huang, X.: Spatial-temporal transformer network with self-supervised learning for traffic flow prediction. In: Sioutis, M., Long, Z., Stell, J.G., Renz, J. (eds.) Proceedings of the 1st International Workshop on Spatio-Temporal Reasoning and Learning (STRL 2022) co-located with the 31st International Joint Conference on Artificial Intelligence and the 25th European Conference on Artificial Intelligence (IJCAI 2022, ECAI 2022), Vienna, Austria, 24 July 2022. CEUR Workshop Proceedings, vol. 3190. CEUR-WS.org (2022). http://ceur-ws.org/Vol-3190/paper1.pdf
14. Scellato, S., Musolesi, M., Mascolo, C., Latora, V., Campbell, A.T.: NextPlace: a spatio-temporal prediction framework for pervasive systems. In: Lyons, K., Hightower, J., Huang, E.M. (eds.) Pervasive 2011. LNCS, vol. 6696, pp. 152–169. Springer, Heidelberg (2011). https://doi.org/10.1007/978-3-642-21726-5_10
15. Shang, P., Liu, X., Yu, C., Yan, G., Xiang, Q., Mi, X.: A new ensemble deep graph reinforcement learning network for spatio-temporal traffic volume forecasting in a freeway network. Digit. Signal Process. **123**, 103419 (2022). https://doi.org/10.1016/j.dsp.2022.103419
16. Singh, N., Nath, R., Singh, D.B.: Splice-site identification for exon prediction using bidirectional LSTM-RNN approach. Biochem. Biophys. Rep. **30**, 101285 (2022). https://doi.org/10.1016/j.bbrep.2022.101285
17. Song, X., Zhang, Q., Sekimoto, Y., Shibasaki, R.: Prediction of human emergency behavior and their mobility following large-scale disaster. In: Macskassy, S.A., Perlich, C., Leskovec, J., Wang, W., Ghani, R. (eds.) The 20th ACM SIGKDD International Conference on Knowledge Discovery and Data Mining, KDD 2014, New York, NY, USA, 24–27 August 2014, pp. 5–14. ACM (2014). https://doi.org/10.1145/2623330.2623628
18. Sun, J., Zhang, J., Li, Q., Yi, X., Liang, Y., Zheng, Y.: Predicting citywide crowd flows in irregular regions using multi-view graph convolutional networks. IEEE Trans. Knowl. Data Eng. **34**(5), 2348–2359 (2022). https://doi.org/10.1109/TKDE.2020.3008774
19. van Maasakkers, L., Fok, D., Donkers, B.: Next-basket prediction in a high-dimensional setting using gated recurrent units. Expert Syst. Appl. 118795 (2022). https://doi.org/10.1016/j.eswa.2022.118795

20. Wang, X., Kang, Y., Hyndman, R.J., Li, F.: Distributed ARIMA models for ultra-long time series. Int. J. Forecast. (2022). https://doi.org/10.1016/j.ijforecast.2022.05.001
21. Wang, Y., Zeng, Z.: Overview of data-driven solutions. In: Wang, Y., Zeng, Z. (eds.) Data-Driven Solutions to Transportation Problems, pp. 1–10. Elsevier (2019). https://doi.org/10.1016/B978-0-12-817026-7.00001-1
22. Wu, P., Li, X., Ling, C., Ding, S., Shen, S.: Sentiment classification using attention mechanism and bidirectional long short-term memory network. Appl. Soft Comput. **112**, 107792 (2021). https://doi.org/10.1016/j.asoc.2021.107792
23. Xue, Y., Wang, Y., Liang, J., Slowik, A.: A self-adaptive mutation neural architecture search algorithm based on blocks. IEEE Comput. Intell. Mag. **16**(3), 67–78 (2021). https://doi.org/10.1109/MCI.2021.3084435
24. Yan, B., Wang, G., Yu, J., Jin, X., Zhang, H.: Spatial-temporal Chebyshev graph neural network for traffic flow prediction in IoT-based its. IEEE Internet Things J. **9**(12), 9266–9279 (2022). https://doi.org/10.1109/JIOT.2021.3105446
25. Yan, Z., Peng, R., Wang, Y., Li, W.: Soft-self and hard-cross graph attention network for knowledge graph entity alignment. Knowl.-Based Syst. **231**, 107415 (2021). https://doi.org/10.1016/j.knosys.2021.107415
26. Yang, H.: Heuristic algorithms for the bilevel origin-destination matrix estimation problem. Transp. Res. Part B Methodol. **29**(4), 231–242 (1995). https://doi.org/10.1016/0191-2615(95)00003-V
27. Zhang, J., Li, S.: Air quality index forecast in Beijing based on CNN-LSTM multi-model. Chemosphere **308**, 136180 (2022). https://doi.org/10.1016/j.chemosphere.2022.136180
28. Zhang, J., Zheng, Y., Qi, D., Li, R., Yi, X.: DNN-based prediction model for spatio-temporal data. In: Proceedings of the 24th ACM SIGSPATIAL International Conference on Advances in Geographic Information Systems, SIGSPACIAL 2016. Association for Computing Machinery, New York (2016). https://doi.org/10.1145/2996913.2997016
29. Zhang, J., Zheng, Y., Sun, J., Qi, D.: Flow prediction in spatio-temporal networks based on multitask deep learning. IEEE Trans. Knowl. Data Eng. **32**(3), 468–478 (2020). https://doi.org/10.1109/TKDE.2019.2891537

RotatSAGE: A Scalable Knowledge Graph Embedding Model Based on Translation Assumptions and Graph Neural Networks

Yubin Ma, Yuxin Ding(✉), and Guangbin Wang

Harbin Institute of Technology (Shenzhen), Shenzhen, China
yxding@hit.edu.cn

Abstract. Knowledge graphs have been widely used in numerous AI applications. In this paper, we propose an efficient knowledge graph embedding model called RotatSAGE by combining the RotatE model and the GraphSAGE model. In the proposed model the RotatE model is used to learn the embedding vectors of heterogeneous entities and relations in a knowledge graph. One problem of the RotatE model is that it only can learn from a single triplet and cannot take advantage of local information to learn embeddings. To solve this issue, we introduce the GraphSAGE model into RotatE. The GraphSAGE model can use neighbor information to improve the embedding of an entity by sampling a small and fixed number of neighbors. We also propose a sampling strategy to further eliminate redundant entity information and simplify the proposed model. In the experiments, the link prediction task is used to evaluate the performance of embedding models. The experiments on four benchmark datasets show the overall performance of RotatSAGE is higher than baseline models.

Keywords: Knowledge graph embedding · Link prediction · Translation · Relational rotation · Complex space · Graph neural network · GraphSAGE

1 Introduction

Knowledge graphs such as is a knowledge base composed of entities and relations, such as WordNet [1], Yago [2] and Freebase [3] have been widely applied in many AI applications, such as relation extraction, link prediction, etc. A knowledge graph usually consists of a large number of triplets. A triplet includes three parts which are head entity, relation and tail entity. The relation defines the relationship between the head entity and the tail entity. In general, a triplet is denoted as (h, r, t). Triplets are structured data, which cannot be easily used in downstream tasks [4]. To solve this problem, knowledge graph embedding (KGE) was proposed. KGE can learn continuous vectors of entities and relations, which can be utilized in many applications, such as link prediction and node classification.

The KGE models can be divided into two categories: a) Translational Distance Models, which use a distance-based scoring function to learn the embeddings of entities and relations, such as TransE [5], TransH [6], TransR [7], TransD [8], TransSparse [9],

Y. Tan and Y. Shi (Eds.): DMBD 2022, CCIS 1744, pp. 93–104, 2022.
https://doi.org/10.1007/978-981-19-9297-1_8

and RotatE [10]. b) Graph Neural Networks (GNNs) [15], which apply neural network techniques to learn the embeddings of nodes and edges in a graph, such as GCN [16], GraphSAGE [17], and R-GCN [19].

Among translational distance models, RotatE has the best representation power, which can model and infer various relation patterns such as symmetry/anti-symmetry, inversion, and composition. In addition, RotatE can be efficiently trained using a novel self-adversarial negative sampling technique. RotatE has achieves state-of-the-art performance in many applications. However, one problem with RotatE is that it learns the embeddings of entities and relations from a single triplet each step, and cannot use more local information in a graph to improve the embeddings. To solve this issue, in this paper we propose an embedding model based on RotatE, called RotatSAGE. RotatSAGE combines RotatE with GraphSAGE. Like RotatE, RotatSAGE uses complex vectors to represent the embeddings of the heterogenous entities and relations, which can represent all the three relation patterns. To utilize the local information for embedding learning, we introduce GraphSAGE into RotatSAGE. GraphSAGE can learn embeddings by aggregating features of nodes in a local neighborhood area. Therefore, compared with RotatE, RotatSAGE can use the local structure information of a graph to learn embeddings, which improves the performance of RotatE. The experimental results show that the overall performance of RotatSAGE is better than the baseline methods on four benchmark datasets, which demonstrates the effectiveness of the proposed model.

The rest of this paper is organized as follow: Sect. 2 introduces basic notations and discusses the related methods on KGE. In Sect. 3, we discuss the proposed knowledge graph embedding model. In Sect. 4, we show the experimental results on four benchmark datasets for link prediction to demonstrate the effectiveness of our model. We conclude our work and suggest future work in Sect. 5.

2 Related Work

2.1 Notations

The entity and relation in a knowledge graph can be regarded as nodes and edges in a graph, and we alternatively use these terms in this paper. We define the following notations. A boldface low-case letter **x** represents a vector. A boldface upper-case letter **X** represents a matrix. The italic low-case letters represent the entity and relation in a knowledge graph, for example h/t is the head/tail entity, and r is the relation between two entities, and each fact is represented as a triplet (h, r, t). $\mathbf{v}_i^{(l)} \in \mathbb{C}^{d^{(l)}}$ denotes the hidden representation of an entity v_i at the l-th layer with dimension $d^{(l)}$ in the complex vector space.

$\mathcal{T}(v_i)$ denotes all the facts associated with v_i. $\mathcal{T}_{in}(v_i)$ is the set containing all the incoming facts and $\mathcal{T}_{out}(v_i)$ is the set containing all the outgoing facts. $\mathcal{T}^k(v_i)$ denotes the subset of $\mathcal{T}(v_i)$, where k is the size of subset, i.e., $|\mathcal{T}^k(v_i)| = k$. The neighbors of an entity v_i can be represented as follows:

$$\mathcal{T}(v_i) = \mathcal{T}_{in}(v_i) \cup \mathcal{T}_{out}(v_i)$$

$$\mathcal{T}_{in}(v_i) = \{(v_j, r_h, v_i) | \forall v_j \; and \; r_h \big(v_j, r_h, v_i\big) \in \mathcal{T}(v_i)\}$$

$$\mathcal{T}_{out}(v_i) = \{(v_i, r_h, v_j)|\forall v_j\, and\, r_h(v_i, r_h, v_j) \in \mathcal{T}(v_i)\}$$

$(\times\mathbb{R}^n \rightarrow \mathbb{R}^n)$ denotes the Hadamard product (element-wise product).

2.2 Translational Distance Models

TransE [5] is the most classical translational distance model. It represents both entities and relations as vectors in the same space, such as $\mathbb{R}^d$. As shown in Fig. 1(a), the basic idea is that each relation is regarded as translation in the embedding space. For a fact (h, r, t), the embedding of h is close to the embedding of t by adding the embedding of r, i.e., $\mathbf{h} + \mathbf{r} \approx \mathbf{t}$. However, this assumption doesn't satisfy 1-to-N, N-to-1, and N-to-N relations. TransH [6] is proposed to solve this problem, which regards a relation as a translating operation on a relation-specific hyperplane. As shown in Fig. 1(b), the embeddings of h and t are first projected onto the hyperplane of relation r to achieve $\boldsymbol{h}_\perp and \boldsymbol{t}_\perp$, then let $\boldsymbol{h}_\perp + \boldsymbol{r}$, equal $\boldsymbol{t}_\perp$. In this way, TransH can distinguish different entities associated with the same relation. The idea of TransR [7] is very similar to TransH, but it projects $\boldsymbol{h}$ and $\boldsymbol{t}$ into the aspects that relation r focuses on through a translation matrix. TransD [8] simplifies TransR and uses two vectors to represent each entity and relation. The first vector represents the meaning of an entity or a relation, and the second one represents how an entity embedding is projected to a relation vector space. TransSparse [9] simplifies TransR by enforcing the projection matrix to be sparse.

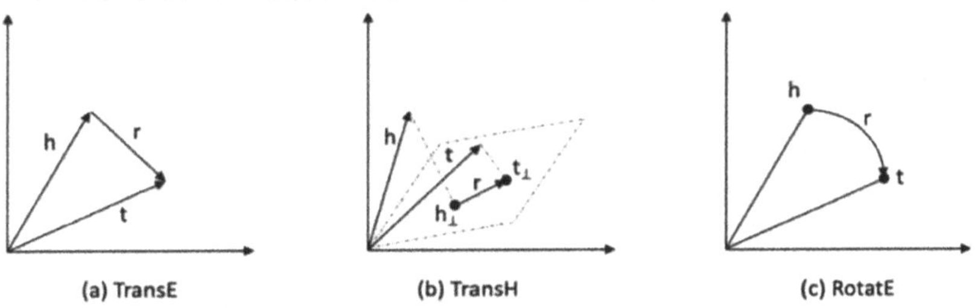

Fig. 1. Illustrations of sTransE, TransH, and RotatE

RotatE [10] represents the entities and relations using complex vectors. From Euler's identity $e^{i\theta} = cos\theta + isin\theta$, a unitary complex number can be seen as a rotation in the complex plane. Given a fact $(h,\ r,\ t)$, RotatE makes $\boldsymbol{h} \circ \boldsymbol{r}$ equal $\boldsymbol{t}$, where $|\boldsymbol{r}| = 1$, as shown in Fig. 1(c). In complex space, RotatE can model and infer various relation patterns including symmetry/anti-symmetry, inversion, and composition. In addition, RotatE can be trained efficiently using self-adversarial negative sampling technique. However, RotatE only learns from single fact, and cannot use local structural information in a graph to improve embedding.

2.3 Graph Neural Networks

Graph Neural Network (GNN) was proposed by Gori et al. (2005) [11], then Scarselli et al. (2009) [12] proposed a generalized model that can directly deal with a more general class of graphs, e.g., cyclic, directed and undirected graphs. GNN consists of an iterative process, which propagates the node states until a state of balance; followed by a neural network, which generates an output for each node based on its state. Li et al. (2016) [13] proposed to use gated recurrent units in the propagation step to further improve the performance of GNN.

Based on the convolutional neural networks (CNNs) [14], Kipf et al. [16] proposed the Graph Convolutional Network (GCN), which applies the convolution operation to learn embeddings of nodes in a graph. GCN can learn the embedding of a node by aggregating its neighbor information. GCN has been applied to different classification tasks, and achieved good performance. The papers [18–20] also discussed how to improve the performance of KGE models by aggregating its neighbor information.

The convolution operation uses an $N \times N$ Laplacian matrix to update the embedding of a node, and N is the number of nodes in a graph. Therefore, the space complexity of GCN is unacceptable when the number of nodes in a graph is large. Besides, GCN is transductive, which uses the information of all nodes to learn entity embeddings. To solve this issue, GraphSAGE [17] was proposed. GraphSAGE is a general inductive framework that can efficiently generate node embedding.Using node feature information. GraphSAGE optimizes GCN from two aspects: First, GraphSAGE learns the embedding of a node only by uniformly sampling a small and fixed number of its neighbors, instead of aggregating all neighbors like GCN. Second, GraphSAGE adopts some new aggregators, such as mean/sum/pooling aggregator, to aggregate the feature information from its neighbors. In this way large-scale graphs can be processed using GraphSAGE.

3 Proposed Model

From above discussion, we can see RotatE can effectively model all the three relation patterns: symmetric/antisymmetric, inversion, and composition. In addition, another advantage of the RotatE model is that it can model heterogeneous graphs. In reality, most graphs are heterogeneous graphs which contains different types of nodes and relations, such as Freebase and WordNet. Compared with RotatE, GraphSAGE can only model heterogeneous graphs. However, the advantage of GraphSAGE is that it can utilize local information in a graph to learn embedding, while RotatE only learn from a single fact.

In our study we introduce GraphSAGE into RotatE, and propose the embedding learning model GraphSAGE. In GraphSAGE, the RotatE model can utilize neighborhood information to improve the embedding representation of a knowledge graph.

3.1 Methodology

WE firstly use RotatE to learn the embeddings of heterogeneous entities and relations. In RoTatE, the entity and relation embeddings are represented as complex vectors. A relation is defined as a rotation from the source entity to the target entity. For each triplet $\left(v_j, r_h, v_i\right) \in \mathcal{T}(v_i)$, the embeddings should satisfy Eq. (1).

$$\mathbf{v}'^{(l)}_i, \mathbf{v}^{(l)}_j \mathbf{r}^{(l)}_h, \left(v_j, r_h, v_i\right) \in \mathcal{T}^k_{in}(v_i) \tag{1}$$

In Eq. (1) $\mathbf{v}_i^{(l)}, \mathbf{v}_j^{(l)}$ *and* $\mathbf{r}_h^{(l)} \in \mathbb{C}^{d^{(l)}}$ are the embeddings of v_j, r_h, and v_i. $|\mathbf{r}_h| = 1$, and $^\circ$ denotes the Hadamard product. In this way, we transform heterogeneous neighbors of a node into homogenous ones.

After getting the embeddings of the homogenous nodes, we introduce GraphSAGE and use neighbors of v_i to update the embedding of node v_i. Usually, we perform a convolution operation on the embeddings of neighbors to obtain the embedding of a center node. The convolution operation is defined as Eq. (2) and (3).

$$\mathbf{m}_i^{(l)} = \sum\nolimits_{(v_j, r_h, v_i) \in \mathcal{T}(v_i)} \left(\mathbf{v}_j^{(l)} \circ \mathbf{r}_h^{(l)}\right) \tag{2}$$

$$\mathbf{v}_i^{(l+1)} = \delta\left(\frac{\mathbf{m}_i^{(l)} + \mathbf{v}_i^{(l)}}{k+1}\right) \tag{3}$$

where $\mathbf{m}_i^{(l)} \in \mathbb{C}^{d^{(l)}}$ is the embedding of convoluted neighbors, which can deem as the overall estimation of center entity embedding $\mathbf{v}_i$. Then, the embedding of v_j at next layer is the average of $\mathbf{m}_i^{(l)}$ and $\mathbf{v}_i^{(l)}$ (see Eq. (3)). In (3), δ is the activation function and k is the number of neighbors of v_i.

To further simplify our model, we only consider the embeddings of incoming neighbors in Eq. (3), which is shown as Eq. (4). A directed graph can be looked as an information network, a center node obtains information from its incoming neighbors and outputs the received information to its outgoing neighbors. Collecting new information from the incoming neighbors can affect the information status of a center node, on the contrary, outputting information from a center node to its outgoing neighbors cannot affect the information status of a center node. The center node still has the same information and its information status does not change. Under this assumption, it is reasonable to only consider incoming neighbors when calculating the embedding of a center node. In this way, the embeddings of entities and relations can be learned more quickly.

Equation (2) is a sum function, therefore, $\mathbf{m}_i^{(l)}$ strongly depends on the number of neighbors of a center node. To solve this issue, for each center node, we randomly sample k samples from its neighbors to calculate the embedding. To handle the problem that some center nodes have no incoming neighbors, we propose a specific relation named self-relation to create incoming neighbors of a center node. A self-relation is a relation connecting the same two nodes. So, we make the following sampling strategy to choose k incoming neighbors. For a given center node v_i, assume it has n incoming neighbors. If $n \geq k$, we sample its neighbors k times without replacement; if $0 \leq n \leq k$, sampling with replacement; if $n = 0$, we create k self-relations for the center node, and choose all neighbors. Figure 2 illustrates the sampling strategy when $k = 3$.

$$\mathbf{m}_i^{(l)} = \sum\nolimits_{(v_j, r_h, v_i) \in \mathcal{T}_{in}^{k}(v_i)} \left(\mathbf{v}_j^{(l)} \circ \mathbf{r}_h^{(l)}\right) \tag{4}$$

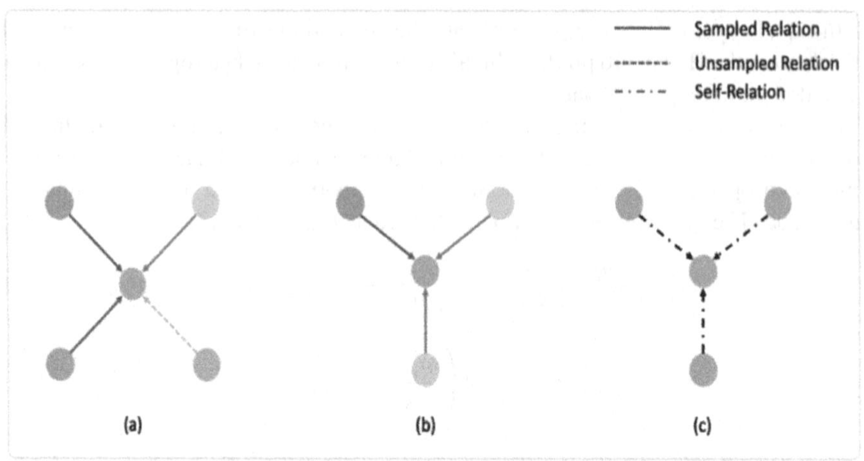

Fig. 2. The sample procedure of our proposed model with $k = 3$

3.2 Loss Function

When training the embedding model, two kinds of training sample are needed, positive samples and negative samples. Usually, a knowledge graph only provides positive samples. Therefore, negative samples have to be produced. In our work, the self-adversarial negative sampling technique [2] is used to generate to generate negative samples. The principle of self-adversarial negative sampling is that the probabilities that different negative samples are drawn as training data should be different, for samples that are obviously false, and cannot provide any meaningful information, a small probability value should be assigned. Therefore, a probability distribution p that a negative sample is drawn as training data is defined as Eq. (5).

$$p\left(h_j', r, t_j'|\{(h_i, r_i, t_i)\}\right) = \frac{\exp\left(-\alpha(d_r\left(\mathbf{h}_j', \mathbf{t}_j'\right)2\right))}{\sum_i \exp(-\alpha(d_r(\mathbf{h}_i', \mathbf{t}_i')2))} \tag{5}$$

In (5) α is the temperature for sampling, $d_r(\mathbf{h}, \mathbf{t}) = |\mathbf{h} \circ \mathbf{r} - \mathbf{t}|$ is the distance function, $\left(h_i', r, t_i'\right)$ is the i th negative triplet. Usually, we define $S_r = -|\mathbf{h} \circ \mathbf{r} - \mathbf{t}|^2$ as the score function.

Then, the above probability can be used as the weight of the negative sample, and the corresponding negative sampling loss function can be written as follows.

$$L = -\log\delta(\gamma - d_r(\mathbf{h}, \mathbf{t})) - \sum_{i=1}^{n} p\left(h_i', r, t_i'\right) log\delta\left(d_r\left(\mathbf{h}_i', \mathbf{t}_i'\right) - \gamma\right) \tag{6}$$

In (6) γ is the fixed margin, and δ is the sigmoid function.

The proposed RotatSAGE algorithm is described as Fig. 3.

Algorithm 1: algorithm of RotatSAGE

Data: Training set $S = (h, r, t)$, incoming neighbors set $\mathcal{T}_{in}^k$
Result: Embeddings of entities and relations

for $P_{batch} \in S$ **do**
  $N_{batch} \leftarrow self\_adv\_neg\_sampling(P_{batch})$
  $T_{batch} = P_{batch} \cup N_{batch}$
  for $(v_i, r_h, v_j) \in T_{batch}$ **do**
    for $x\ in\ \{i, j\}$ **do**
      $\mathbf{m}_x^{(l)} = \sum_{(v_y, r_z, v_x) \in \mathcal{T}_{in}^k(v_x)} (\mathbf{v}_y^{(l)} \circ \mathbf{r}_z^{(l)})$
      $\mathbf{v}_x^{(l+1)} = \delta(\frac{\mathbf{m}_x^{(l)} + \mathbf{v}_x^{(l)}}{k+1})$
    end
    $d_r(\mathbf{v}_i^{(l+1)}, \mathbf{v}_j^{(l+1)}) = |\mathbf{v}_i^{(l+1)} \circ \mathbf{r}_h^{(l+1)} - \mathbf{v}_j^{(l+1)}|$
  end
  update embeddings w.r.t $\sum_{(h,r,t),(h',r,t') \in T_{batch}} \nabla L$
end

Fig. 3. The algorithm of RotatSage

4 Experiment

4.1 Datasets

We evaluate our RotatSAGE model using two kinds of knowledge graphs. One is WordNet and the other is Freebase. For each kind of knowledge graphs, two different datasets are collected. The statistics of each dataset is shown in Table 1. In Table 1 WN18 [5] and WN18RR [23] are collected from WordNet, and FB15k [5] and FB15k-237 [22] are collect from Freebase.

The relation patterns in WN18 contain symmetry/anti-symmetry and inversion, and the relation patterns in WIN18RR mainly include symmetry/anti-symmetry and composition patterns. The relations in FB15k contain symmetry/anti-symmetry and inversion patterns, and the relations in FB15k-237 mainly include the symmetry/anti-symmetry and composition patterns. In FB15k and WN18, many relation patterns are inverse patterns.

In our work, we perform link prediction on these four datasets. Link prediction aims to predict the missing head entity or tail entity in a triplet (h, r, t). In this task, we need to rank a set of candidate entities from the knowledge graph, instead of only giving the best prediction result.

In our work the performance measures we use are Mean Rank (MR) of the correct triplets, Mean Reciprocal Rank (MRR) of the correct triples, and Hits at N (Hit@N) which measures the proportion of the correct triples in top-n candidate triplets. A good link prediction model should has lower MR value or higher MRR and Hit@N values. The best parameters for each prediction model are selected when Hit@10 achieves the best value on the validation sets.

We follow the experiment setting in [5]. In testing phase, for each test triplet (h, r, t), we replace the head/tail entity by all entities in the knowledge graph, and rank these entities in descending order of similarity scores computed by score function.

In the proposed method Adam [24] is used to optimize the hyperparameters, and these parameters include the dimension of entity and relation embedding d, the number of sampled neighbors k, and α, γ in RotatE. The best parameters are also selected when H@10 achieves the best values on the validation sets.

Table 1. Statistics of FB15k, WN18, FB15k-237, and WN18RR

Dataset	#entity	#relation	#training	#validation	#test
FB15k	14,951	1,345	483,142	50,000	59,071
WN18	40,943	18	141,442	5,000	5,000
FB15k-237	14,541	237	272,115	17,535	20,466
WN18RR	40,943	11	86,835	3,034	3,134

4.2 Experimental Results

We make explements on four datasets. To fully evaluate the performance of the proposed method, we compare it with the following baseline methods, TransE, RotatE, HRAN [28], M-DCN [29],AutoKGE [25], Inverse Model [23], GAATs [26], and StAR [27].

Tables 2 and 3 show the evaluation results of different models on FB15kand WN18. From the table we observe that RotatSAGE outperforms all the baseline models on WN18 datasets. On the FB15k dataset, RotatSAGE also performs well. It has the greatest Hit@3 value and the smallest MR value, and its performance values on other metrics are also comparable to other methods.

Table 2. Results of embedding models evaluated on FB15k (All results are cited from the corresponding papers. Bolded means the best performance, underlined means the second place)

	MRR	MR	HIT@1	HIT@3	HIT@10
TransE	-	125	-	-	0.471
RotatE	<u>0.797</u>	<u>40</u>	**0.746**	<u>0.830</u>	0.884
HRAN	-	-	-	-	-
M-DCN	0.762	-	0.701	0.820	0.879
R-GCN	0.262	-	0.601	0.760	0.842
AuokKGE	**0.861**	-	-	-	**0.914**
Inverse Model	0.660	2501	0.658	0.659	0.660
RotatSAGE	0.779	**29**	<u>0.701</u>	**0.841**	<u>0.897</u>

Table 3. Results of embedding models evaluated on WN18 (All results are cited from the corresponding papers. Bolded means the best performance, underlined means the second place)

	MRR	MR	HIT@1	HIT@3	HIT@10
TransE	-	<u>263</u>	-	-	0.892
RotatE	0.949	309	0.944	0.952	0.959
HRAN	-	-	-	-	-
M-DCN	0.950	-	0.946	0.954	0.958
R-GCN	0.561	-	0.697	0.929	0.964
AuokKGE	0.952	-	-	-	0.961
Inverse Model	<u>0.963</u>	740	<u>0.953</u>	<u>0.964</u>	<u>0.964</u>
RotatSAGE	**0.968**	**170**	**0.954**	**0.981**	**0.989**

Tables 4 and 5 give the experimental results on FB15k-237 and WN18RR. From the table, we can see our model outperforms almost all the baseline models on WN18RR for all metrics except MR, and also achieves better performance on FB15k-237.

From Tables 2, 3, 4, and 5, we can see our model outperforms RotatE on three evaluation sets WN18, WN18RR and FB15k-237, and achieves similar performance as RotatE on FB15k. Therefore, the overall performance of our model is significantly higher than that of RotatE. It shows that by introducing GraphSAGE into RotatE, RotatE can aggregate neighbor features to learn the embedding of an entity, which can significantly improve the representation ability of the embedding vector. The original GraphSAGE model cannot learn the embeddings of relations. By combining RotatE with GraphSAGE, the function of the original GraphSAGE is enhanced, which can learn both entity and relation embeddings in a graph. Moreover, different form GrapgSAGE, the entities and relations in RotatSAGE can be heterogeneous.

Table 4. Results of embedding models evaluated on FB15k-237. (All results are cited from the corresponding papers. Bolded means the best performance, underlined means the second place)

	MRR	MR	HIT@1	HIT@3	HIT@10
TransE	0.294	-	-	-	0.465
RotatE	0.338	177	0.241	0.375	0.533
HRAN	0.355	156	0.263	0.390	0.541
M-DCN	0.345	-	0.255	0.380	0.528
R-GCN	0.249	-	0.151	0.264	0.417
GAATs	**0.547**	187	**0.512**	**0.572**	**0.650**
StAR	0.365	**117**	0.366	0.404	0.562
RotatSAGE	0.377	144	0.276	0.420	0.575

Table 5. Results of embedding models evaluated on WN18RR. All results are cited from the corresponding papers. Bolded means the best performance, underlined means the second place.

	MRR	MR	HIT@1	HIT@3	HIT@10
TransE	0.226	-	-	-	0.501
RotatE	0.476	3340	0.428	0.492	0.571
HRAN	0.479	2113	0.450	0.494	0.542
M-DCN	0.475	-	0.440	0.485	0.540
R-GCN	-	-	-	-	-
GAATs	0.467	1270	0.424	0.525	0.604
StAR	0.401	**51**	0.243	0.491	0.709
RotatSAGE	**0.631**	2044	**0.577**	**0.657**	**0.737**

Compared with other baseline models, our model achieves the best performance on WN18 for all the evaluation metrics, and also achieves the best performance on WN18RR for all metrics except MR. On FB15k and FB15k-237, our model also achieves better performance and is comparable to the best models, such as GAATs. Therefore, the overall performance of our model is also higher than that of the baseline models. The R-GCN, GAATs, AutoKEG and StAR models all can utilize neighborhood information to learn embedding vectors of entities and relations. Different from these models, our model represents the embeddings of entities and relations in the complex space, which can effectively model all the three relation patterns: symmetric/antisymmetric, inversion, and composition. Therefore, the representation ability of our model is relatively better than that of other models.

The performance of the RotatSAGE model on WN18 and WN18RR is better than that on FB15k and FB15k-237. We interpret it as follows.

1. The number of relations in WN18 and WN18RR is significantly smaller than that in FB15k and FB15k-237. The relationships between entities are not complex. Therefore, it is relatively easy for our model to learn better embeddings from simple relations.
2. The number of entities in WN18 and WN18RR is significantly bigger than that in FB15k and FB15k-237. This results the entities in WN18 and WN18RR has more neighbors. Compare with FB15k and FB15k-237, the neighbor entities in WN18 and WN18RR can provide more local information to learn the embedding of an entity, which can improve the representation ability of the embedding vector.

5 Conclusion

In this paper, we introduce GraphSage into RotatE and propose a novel knowledge graph embedding model, called RotatSAGE. In RotatSAGE we use RotatE to learn embeddings of the heterogeneous entities and relations, and use GraphSAGE to aggregate the features of local neighbors for embedding learning. We also propose a sampling strategy to further remove redundancy information from local neighbors and improve model performance. To evaluate the performance of the proposed model, we apply it to predict links in two knowledge graphs. The experimental results show that the overall performance of RotatSAGE is better than the baseline models, which shows that RotatSAGE can effectively learn the embeddings of entities and relations in a knowledge graph.

Acknowledgement. This work was supported by the National Natural Science Foundation of China (Grant No. 61872107).

References

1. Miller, G.A.: WordNet: a lexical database for English. Commun. ACM **38**(11), 39–41 (1995)
2. Fabian, M., Suchanek, K.G., Weikum, G.: YAGO: A core of semantic knowledge unifying WordNet and Wikipedia. In: Proceedings of the 16th International Conference on World Wide Web (2007)
3. Bollacker, K., et al.: Freebase: a collaboratively created graph database for structuring human knowledge. In: Proceedings of the 2008 ACM SIGMOD International Conference on Management of Data (2008)
4. Wang, Q., Mao, Z., Wang, B., Guo, L.: Knowledge graph embedding: a survey of approaches and applications. IEEE Trans. Knowl. Data Eng. **29**(12), 2724–2743 (2017). https://doi.org/10.1109/TKDE.2017.2754499
5. Bordes, A., et al.: Translating embeddings for modeling multi-relational data. In: Neural Information Processing Systems (NIPS) (2013)
6. Wang, Z., et al.: Knowledge graph embedding by translating on hyperplanes. Proc. AAAI Conf. Artif. Intell. **28**(1) (2014)
7. Lin, Y., et al.: Learning entity and relation embeddings for knowledge graph completion. Proc. AAAI Conf. Artif. Intell. **29**(1) (2015)
8. Ji, G., et al.: Knowledge graph embedding via dynamic mapping matrix. In: Proceedings of the 53rd Annual Meeting of the Association for Computational Linguistics and the 7th International Joint Conference on Natural Language Processing (volume 1: Long papers) (2015)

9. Ji, G., et al.: Knowledge graph completion with adaptive sparse transfer matrix. Proc. AAAI Conf. Artif. Intell. **30**(1) (2016)
10. Sun, Z., et al.: Rotate: Knowledge graph embedding by relational rotation in complex space. arXiv preprint arXiv:1902.10197 (2019)
11. Gori, M., Monfardini, G., Scarselli, F.: A new model for learning in graph domains. In: IEEE International Joint Conference on Neural Networks, pp. 729–734 (2005)
12. Scarselli, F., Gori, M., Tsoi, A.C., Hagenbuchner, M., Monfardini, G.: The graph neural network model. IEEE Trans. Neural Netw. **20**(1), 61–80 (2009)
13. Li, Y., Tarlow, D., Brockschmidt, M., Zemel, R.: Gated graph sequence neural networks. In: International Conference on Learning Representations (ICLR) (2016)
14. LeCun, Y., et al.: Gradient-based learning applied to document recognition. Proc. IEEE **86**(11), 2278–2324 (1998)
15. Wu, Z., et al.: A comprehensive survey on graph neural networks. IEEE Trans. Neural Netw. Learn. Syst. **32**, 4–24 (2020)
16. Kipf, TN., Welling, M.: Semi-supervised classification with graph convolutional networks. arXiv preprint arXiv:1609.02907 (2016)
17. Hamilton, W.L., Ying, R., Leskovec, J.: Inductive representation learning on large graphs. arXiv preprint arXiv:1706.02216 (2017)
18. Wang, X., et al.: Heterogeneous graph attention network. In: The World Wide Web Conference (2019)
19. Schlichtkrull, M., Kipf, T.N., Bloem, P., van den Berg, R., Titov, I., Welling, M.: Modeling relational data with graph convolutional networks. In: Gangemi, A., Navigli, R., Vidal, M.-E., Hitzler, P., Troncy, R., Hollink, L. (eds.) ESWC 2018. LNCS, vol. 10843, pp. 593–607. Springer, Cham (2018). https://doi.org/10.1007/978-3-319-93417-4_38
20. Yang, B., et al.: Embedding entities and relations for learning and inference in knowledge bases. arXiv preprint arXiv:1412.6575 (2014)
21. Cai, L., Wang, Y.W.: Kbgan: adversarial learning for knowledge graph embeddings. arXiv preprint arXiv:1711.04071 (2017)
22. Toutanova, K., Chen, D.: Observed versus latent features for knowledge base and text inference. In: Proceedings of the 3rd Workshop on Continuous Vector Space Models and Their Compositionality (2015)
23. Dettmers, T., et al.: Convolutional 2d knowledge graph embeddings. Proc. AAAI Conf. Artif. Intell. 32(1) (2018)
24. Kingma, D.P., Ba, J.B.: Adam: a method for stochastic optimization. arXiv preprint arXiv: 1412.6980 (2014)
25. Zhang, Y., et al.: AutoSF: searching scoring functions for knowledge graph embedding. In: 2020 IEEE 36th International Conference on Data Engineering (ICDE). IEEE (2020)
26. Wang, R., et al.: Knowledge graph embedding via graph attenuated attention networks. IEEE Access **8,** 5212–5224 (2019)
27. Wang, B., et al.: Structure-augmented text representation learning for efficient knowledge graph completion. In: International World Wide Web Conference (2021)
28. Li, Z., et al.: Learning knowledge graph embedding with heterogeneous relation attention networks. IEEE Trans. Neural Netw. Learn. Syst. **33**, 3961–3973 (2021)
29. Zhang, Z., et al.: Multi-scale dynamic convolutional network for knowledge graph embedding. IEEE Trans. Knowl. Data Eng. **34**, 2335–2347 (2020)

Denoise Network Structure for User Alignment Across Networks via Graph Structure Learning

Li Liu, Chongyang Wang, Youmin Zhang(✉), Ye Wang, Qun Liu, and Guoyin Wang

Chongqing Key Laboratory of Computational Intelligence, Chongqing University of Posts and Telecommunications, Chongqing 400065, China
ymzhang0103@hotmail.com

Abstract. User alignment aims to identify accounts of one natural person across networks. Nevertheless, different social purposes in multiple networks and randomness of following friends form the diverse local structures of the same person, leading to a high degree of non-isomorphism across networks. The edges resulting in non-isomorphism are harmful to learn consistent representations of one natural person across networks, i.e., the structural "noisy data" for user alignment. Furthermore, these edges increase the time complexity, compromising the model's efficiency. To this end, we propose a network structure denoising framework to learn an alignment driven structure heuristically. Specifically, under the guidance of alignment driven loss, parameter sharing encoder and graph neural network for structure denoising are learned using an iterative learning schema. Experiments on real-world datasets demonstrate the outperformance of the proposed framework in terms of efficiency and transferability.

Keywords: User alignment · Graph neural networks · Graph structure learning · Structure denoise

1 Introduction

Social network alignment aims to identify accounts of one natural person across multiple online social platforms. Aligning users across networks benefits the data transfer between standalone social networks and alleviates the "data isolation" issue in several data mining tasks, including information diffusion, recommendation, etc. Recently, graph representation learning (GRL) algorithms have demonstrated their superior performance on this task attributed to their ability to represent users without manual efforts.

Generally speaking, graph representation learning algorithms attempt to represent nodes by preserving the structural proximity. Specifically, according to the structure across networks, several studies [16,17,30–32,34] are proposed to learn the representations of users by aggregating and combing features of their

Y. Tan and Y. Shi (Eds.): DMBD 2022, CCIS 1744, pp. 105–119, 2022.
https://doi.org/10.1007/978-981-19-9297-1_9

neighbors. Based on the learned representations, nodes across networks can be aligned using the similarity of representations [28,35]. The aforementioned processes indicate that the network structure plays a critical role in user representation, and thus influences the precision of downstream alignment.

Nevertheless, people usually join multiple platforms for different social purposes. Therefore, the random nature of users' behavior in following friends is unavoidable across social networks. These factors result in the diverse local structure topologies across social networks for the same person, i.e., a high degree of non-isomorphism between multiple networks. Different from representing users within a single network, the non-isomorphism between the network structure brings structural "noisy data" for representing users across networks, compromising the effectiveness of the user alignment task. For the GRL algorithms, these "noisy data" will trigger a cascade of negative influences in their aggregation and combination process. Moreover, due to the presence of the "noisy data", high time and space complexities are unavoidable as many GRL algorithms are exponential growth with the increase in the scale of the network.

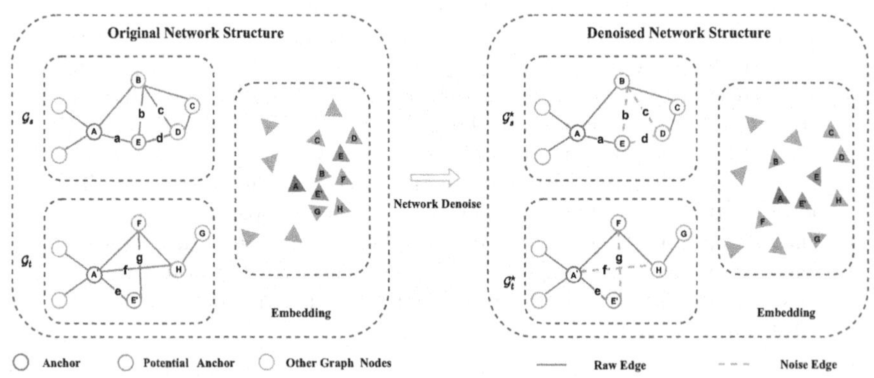

Fig. 1. A toy example for explaining why structural "noisy data" compromises the representation learning across networks.

Figure 1 illustrates an example to illustrate the key ideas of why the structural "noisy data" compromises the GRL across social networks. In Fig. 1, $\mathcal{G}_s$ and $\mathcal{G}_t$ are two networks. A and A' are labeled anchor (accounts belonging to the same person). E and E' are the potential anchors (nodes to be aligned). Due to the diverse social purposes in multiple networks, E' and E' may follow different users in separated networks such as B, D in $\mathcal{G}_s$ and F in $\mathcal{G}_t$. This phenomenon results in a really dense but non-isomorphism local structure around E and E', such as edges $\{a, b, c, d\}$ in $\mathcal{G}_s$ and edges $\{e, f, g\}$ in $\mathcal{G}_s$. According to the structure preserving objective of GRL [14,23,24,26], nodes with dense connectivity will be close in the embedding space. Therefore, B, E, and D will be close due to the existence of edges $\{b, c, d\}$ and F, E' and H will be close due to the existence of edges $\{f, g\}$. Nevertheless, the "overly-close" embedding space compromises the alignment task as potential anchors are hard to be aligned preciously, especially with many non-anchor nodes (such as F and B) around them. Therefore, we name the edges $\{b, c, d, g, f\}$ as alignment task oriented "structural noisy data". To address this issue, we attempt to design a strategy that can denoise the structure heuristically. As shown in the right part of Fig. 1, we hope the structures $\mathcal{G}_t^\star$ and $\mathcal{G}_s^\star$ can be learned. Compared to the original network structure, E and E' can be close due to their connectivity to anchor A. Meanwhile, B and D can be far away from them due to the absence of edge $\{b, c, d, f, g\}$, facilitating the downstream user aligning module.

To this end, we first leverage a parameter sharing graph encoder to obtain the primary embedding of every node. To further denoise the original network structure, a graph neural network is adopted for determining which edges can be removed. Under the guidance of the designed alignment-oriented loss and structure regularization, we perform the aforementioned process iteratively for parameter learning. Finally, the denoised networks can be obtained via the learned graph neural networks. The denoised networks also can be transferred to other state-of-the-art (SOTA) alignment models for efficient learning.

Our main contributions are summarized as follows:

- We propose a network structure denoising framework for the user alignment task. With the guidance of the alignment-oriented loss, a parameterized graph neural network is learned to denoise the network structure.
- We investigate the transferability of the learned network structure. We provide evidence that, beyond the graph encoder adopted in the framework, the denoised structure can boost several SOTA network alignment algorithms.
- We evaluate the proposed framework by applying it to several state-of-the-art models. The experimental results on three real-world datasets demonstrate the effectiveness of the proposed framework.

2 Related Work

2.1 Network Alignment

Network alignment aims to identify different accounts of one natural person. Recently, graph representation learning algorithms demonstrate their superior performance. Compared to classification based [15] and matrix factorization based algorithm [22], it learns user representations via preserving structural proximity without manual efforts, and the Stochastic Gradient Descent and sampling strategy adopted in the learning process guarantees its effectiveness. Generally speaking, the related studies can be categorized into *supervised* and *unsupervised* according to the existence of labeled anchors.

For supervised algorithms, IONE [17] learns representations of users via preserving second order structure proximity and leverages cosine similarity to identify the potential anchors. PALE [20] learns node embedding in the separated network and further leverage a shallow neural network to conduct the user alignment. DeepLink [35] and DCIM [21] further adopt deep neural networks for constructing the mapping function. Besides, SNNA [16] leverages a generate adversarial network to train a mapping function. Different from the above studies that focus on constructing mapping functions, some works investigate the structure consistency across networks. NextAlign [31] studies the correlation between graph convolutional networks and the assumption of network consistency adopted in the traditional alignment model. cM^{2}NE [28] proposes an end-to-end contrastive learning framework to model the inconsistency across social networks. Also, several studies attempt to learn better representation to facilitate the mapping functions. MGCN [2] uses convolution on both local and hypergraph network structure to learn network embedding. iMap [27] iteratively constructs sub-graphs and adopts graph neural network to learn the representations.

Under the condition of the absence of the labeled anchors, the unsupervised models are designed based on the consistency assumption across networks [3]. In general, structural and attributes representations are learned simultaneously to complement each other [10,34]. To align users from the distribution perspective, UAGA [1] and WAlign [7] try to perform the alignment according to the distributions of the entire embedding space. After learning the embeddings across networks, they adopt Wasserstein distance to measure the discrepancy of nodes' distributions to identify potential anchors.

The aforementioned methods demonstrate their outperformance in the network alignment task. However, these methods are learned using networks that may contain structural "noisy data" for the alignment task. As we introduced in Fig. 1, structural "noisy data" will compromise the learning efficiency and performance, which motivates our proposed denoising framework.

2.2 Graph Structure Learning

As the network grows in size, the graph representation learning algorithms faced several challenges, including noisy data, training efficiency, etc. To this end, graph structure learning algorithms are proposed to learn a proper network structure for representation learning. Primary studies attempt to learn network structure based on the similarities between nodes. Gidaris et al. [8] construct K nearest neighbor graph based on structure similarity via setting a threshold. Wang et al. [25] adopt graph neural network learn node representations. They further calculate the similarity between nodes to construct the network structure. Rather than the single similarity mentioned above, Jonathan et al. [9] leverages the multiple similarities to learn the network structure, where weak similarities between nodes are also incorporated into the network construction. Chen et al. [4] propose an iterative learning schema for learning graph networks. They learn the network structure using a parameterized adjacency matrix.

Rather than learning network structure only, some studies are proposed to learn network structure and model of the target task simultaneously. AneesKazi et al. [13] learn node representations using a graph neural network. They further construct a graph generator to learn a proper network structure under the guidance of the predictions of a downstream GNN. Zheng et al. [33] propose a graph structure learning algorithm to sparse the network structure, where a deep neural network is adopted to model the network sparsing process. Luca et al. [6] propose a probabilistic graph generator where edges are learnable parameters. The generator is optimized with the task driven graph neural networks simultaneously.

Jiang et al. [11] proposed a framework consisting of two components, the first one to learn graph structure, and the second one is a graph convolutional network. Jin et al. [12] learn network structure under the principle that the learned network has certain characteristics, including sparsity and low rank.

Different from the aforementioned studies which may add and remove edges for optimizing graph structure, we focus on denoising (only removing) the network structure for efficient graph representation learning across networks. Furthermore, rather than learning structure within the single network, we specifically design an alignment-oriented loss for network denoising.

3 Preliminaries

In this section, we provide brief descriptions of the notions and definitions.

Network: We use $\mathcal{G} = (V, A)$ to denote the network, where V is the set of the nodes. Every node $v_i \in V$ represents one user. A is the adjacency matrix of $\mathcal{G}$. $a_{i,j} = 1$ when there is a relationship between v_i and v_j, $a_{i,j} = 0$ otherwise.

Anchors: The anchors denote the identities across networks of one natural person. Given two networks $\mathcal{G}_s$ and $\mathcal{G}_t$. $v_s \in V_s, v_t \in V_t$ are one anchor if they belong to one person.

Network Alignment: Given two networks $\mathcal{G}_s$ and $\mathcal{G}_t$, the network alignment aims to learn a function $f(\boldsymbol{u}_s, \boldsymbol{u}_t) \in \{0, 1\}$ to determine whether v_s and v_t are the anchor pair, where $\boldsymbol{u}_s$ and $\boldsymbol{u}_t$ are the embeddings/features that can be learned by graph representation learning algorithms.

Network Denoise: Given one network $\mathcal{G} = (V, A)$, network denoise aims to learn a mask generator $Mask = g(V, A)$ that determines which edges can be removed for the user alignment. Based on the $Mask$, we can obtain the denoised network $\mathcal{G}^\star = (V, A^\star)$. Rather than removing nodes, we only remove edges as removing nodes may exclude potential anchors in the network, which is inadvisable for the network alignment task.

4 Model Framework

To design a structure denoising framework for the network alignment task, we propose to learn a parameterized mask generator based on the network representations across networks. As shown in Fig. 2, our proposed framework consists of three components. The first is a graph encoder across networks that learns the initial representations according to the network structure. The second is the parameterized graph neural network that acts as the mask generator. The third is the network regularizer and the alignment loss calculated by the graph encoder.

4.1 Graph Encoder Across Networks

The graph encoder in this paper serves two purposes. The first is to learn initial embeddings for nodes across networks. The second is to learn embeddings

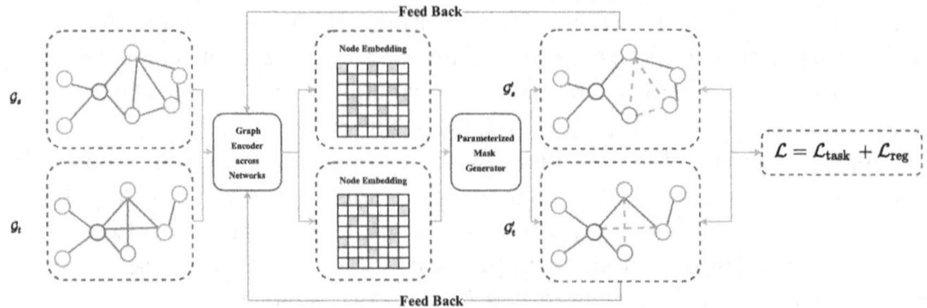

Fig. 2. Model framework

of denoised networks for calculating the alignment loss. Rather than designing a graph representation learning algorithm, our goal is to design a denoising framework for networks. To this end, we adopt IONE [17] as our graph encoder attributed to its learning efficiency in the iterative learning process. First, we denote the learned initial embedding as $X_{s/t}^{Init} \in \mathbb{R}^{n_{s/t} \times d}$

$$X_s^{Init}, X_t^{Init} = Encoder(\mathcal{G}_s, \mathcal{G}_t) \tag{1}$$

where $n_{s/t}$ are the number of nodes in $\mathcal{G}_{s/t}$, d is the dimension of learned embeddings. We believe that the learned embeddings contain structural features of nodes across networks, and properly utilizing them can benefit the learning of the mask generator.

4.2 Parameterized Mask Generator

Given the initial embeddings learned by the graph encoder, we further leverage a graph neural network to determine which edges to remove for the alignment task. Here we use GAT [23] for this task attributed to its powerful ability in modeling the structure and features simultaneously, shown as Eq. (2).

$$Z = GAT(X, A; \Theta) \tag{2}$$

where A is the adjacency matrix for one network and X is the corresponding learned initial embedding. Z is the latent representation learned by GAT and Θ is the learnable parameter.

After obtaining the latent representation Z, we try to norm the representation Z_{norm} to avoid the influence of the value scale, shown in Eq. (3).

$$Z_{norm} = \frac{v_i}{\max(||v_i||_2, \epsilon)}, [v_0, v_1, v_2, ..., v_i] \in Z^T \tag{3}$$

where $||\ ||_2$ is the L_2 norm. And we set $\epsilon = 1e-12$ to avoid the zero values in the denominator.

Algorithm 1. The Learning Algorithm of the Proposed Framework

Input: A training set of anchors V_a, the network alignment encoder $Encoder$, The original networks $\mathcal{G}_s = (V_s, A_s)$ and $\mathcal{G}_t = (V_t, A_t)$. The number of negative samples N_{neg}. The number of iterations $Iter$

Output: Learned parameters for mask generator Θ. Denoised network $\mathcal{G}_s^\star$, $\mathcal{G}_t^\star$

Sample N_{neg} negative nodes from all nodes as S_{neg}
Calculate node embedding using encoder $X_s^{Init}, X_t^{Init} = Encoder(\mathcal{G}_s, \mathcal{G}_t)$
for $i = 0; i < Iter; i = i + 1$ **do**
  if $i == 0$ **then** $X_s = X_s^{Init}, X_t = X_t^{Init}$
  end if
  Calculate Z_{norm} according to Eqs. (2) and (3).
  Calculate $A_s^{'}$ and $A_t^{'}$ according to Eqs. (4) and (5). Then get the structure $\mathcal{G}_s^{'}, \mathcal{G}_t^{'}$
  Calculate node embedding matrix using encoder $X_s, X_t = Encoder(\mathcal{G}_s^{'}, \mathcal{G}_t^{'})$
  Calculate $\mathcal{L}_{reg}$ and $\mathcal{L}_{task}$ according to Eqs. (6) and (7).
  Update Θ using the Adam optimizer
end for
$\mathcal{G}_s^\star$, $\mathcal{G}_t^\star = \mathcal{G}_s^{'}, \mathcal{G}_t^{'}$

Based on the normalized representation, we try to learn the mask of the adjacency matrix, shown in Eq. (4).

$$Mask = \sigma(Z_{norm} \times Z_{norm}^T) \odot A \tag{4}$$

where σ is the sigmoid activation function, and $\odot$ is the Hadamard product. Then the values in $\sigma(Z_{norm} \times Z_{norm}^T)$ denote the importance scores of all node pairs. We further use the adjacency matrix A to filter the $m_{i,j} \in Mask$ to ensure the corresponding users v_i and v_j have an edge. After that, we can select denoised network A' based on a hyper-parameter R, given as Eq. (5).

$$A^{'} = top(Mask; R) \tag{5}$$

where $top(Mask; R)$ means ranking all elements in the $Mask$ matrix and then retaining the top R largest elements. We performs the above processes on $\mathcal{G}_s = (V_s, A_s), \mathcal{G}_t = (V_t, A_t)$ separately to obtain $A_s^{'}$ and $A_t^{'}$. Then we feed them to the graph encoder across networks to calculate the loss. We repeat it for the parameter learning of the mask generator until a stable performance is achieved.

4.3 Design of the Loss Function

To guide the learning of the parameter Θ in the mask generator, we design an alignment-oriented loss function. Specifically, we try to achieve two objectives.

Objective 1: Given the denoised networks, we hope the embedding of anchors should be as close as possible. Meanwhile, the anchor node should be apart from other nodes as far as possible. We define the loss function $\mathcal{L}_{task}$ as Eq. (6).

$$\mathcal{L}_{task}(v_s, v_t) = |cos(X_s, X_t)| - |cos(X_{s/t}, X_{t/s}^{neg})| \tag{6}$$

where $X_{s/t}$ is the embedding learned by the graph encoder when feeding the denoised network to it in each iteration. The $X_{t/s}^{neg}$ is the embeddings of the nodes in the opposite network sampled according to the degree distribution.

Objective 2: In addition to objective 1, to ensure the robustness of the denoised network, we hope the denoised network retains some characteristics of the original network. We use line-wise cosine similarities of embeddings learned from the denoised and the original networks, shown in Eq. (7).

$$\mathcal{L}_{reg}(X^{\star}, X^{Init}) = cos(X^{\star}, X^{Init}) \tag{7}$$

Finally, we combine the above objective functions $\mathcal{L} = \mathcal{L}_{task} + L_{reg}$ to guide the optimization of the parameters in the proposed framework. Algorithm 1 provides a detailed description of the learning process.

5 Experiment and Analysis

5.1 Datasets and Evaluation Metrics

To evaluate the performance of the proposed framework, we conduct extensive experiments on three public datasets. The first Foursquare-Twitter [17,29,35], the second is ACM-DBLP [31,35] and the third is DBLP [18]. Foursquare and Twitter are two social networks. The labeled anchors are obtained by finding users who provide their Twitter accounts in Foursquare profiles. ACM and DBLP are two academic social networks, where identical authors in both ACM and DBLP are the anchors. DBLP are two academic social networks, where authors are split into different co-author networks by filtering publication venues of their papers.Table 1 lists out the statistics of the datasets.Table 1 lists out the statistics of the datasets.

Table 1. Statistics of datasets.

Networks	#Nodes	#Edges	#Anchors
Foursquare	5313	54233	1609
Twitter	5120	130575	
ACM	9872	39561	6325
DBLP	9916	44808	
DBLP_DM	11526	47326	1295
DBLP_ML	12311	43948	

We use a widely adopted metric *Precison@N* [5,17,19,35–37] to evaluate the performances of the above three datasets, shown in Eq. (8).

$$Precision@N = \frac{|CorrUser@N|^{X} + |CorrUser@N|^{Y}}{|UnMappedAnchors| \times 2} \tag{8}$$

where $|CorrUser@N|$ is the number of anchors that can be identified among the top-N candidate list defined by the cosine similarity. $|UnMappedAnchors|$ is the number of all testing anchors. We report the averaged $Precison@N$ by considering one network as the source and the target network respectively. For the configurations of the baseline models, the default settings of the open source codes provided by the authors are utilized.

5.2 Baseline Methods

We evaluate our framework based on three state-of-the-art models.

- **IONE** [17] is an embedding sharing based algorithm. It learns a unified latent space for the alignment via preserving the second-order proximity.
- **DEEPLINK** [35] is an embedding mapping based algorithm. It learns representation learned using random walk and skip-gram algorithms, deep neural networks and dual learning are leveraged to align users.
- **NeXtAlign** [31] proposes a RelGCN-U model and a scoring function to learn user embeddings. This model achieves a good trade-off between alignment consistency and alignment disparity,

5.3 Performance Comparison

We first investigate the performance when deleting different ratios of edges. Figure 3 and Fig. 4 illustrate the $Precision@1-30$ performance under training ratio 50% and 60%, where the network encoder is IONE [17] attributed to its training efficiency. And the ratios (the parameter R in Eq. (5) of deleted edges are set as [5%, 15%, 30%, 50%]. We observed that even if we delete 15% edges of the original network, the performance of the proposed framework does not decrease on all datasets, indicating the effectiveness of the proposed framework. Under the training ratio of 60% of the ACM-DBLP dataset, the model on the denoised network still shows comparable performance when we deleted 30% edges.

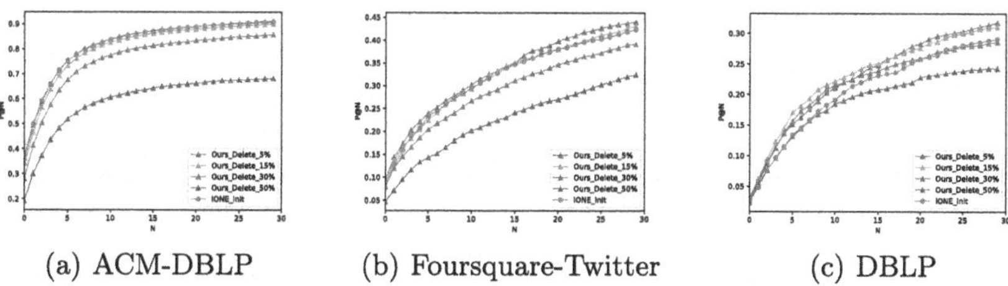

(a) ACM-DBLP (b) Foursquare-Twitter (c) DBLP

Fig. 3. Precision@1-30 performance under training ratio of 50%.

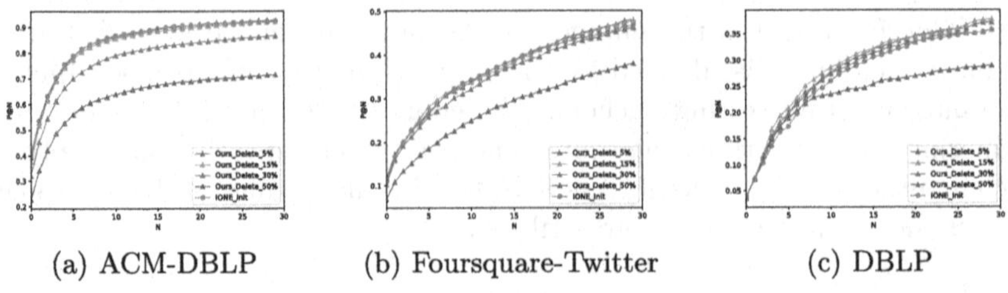

(a) ACM-DBLP (b) Foursquare-Twitter (c) DBLP

Fig. 4. P@1-30 performance under training ratio of 60%.

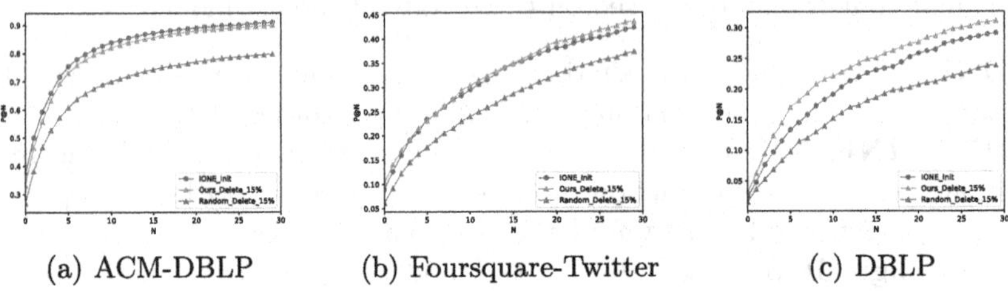

(a) ACM-DBLP (b) Foursquare-Twitter (c) DBLP

Fig. 5. Comparison with randomly deleting edges under training ratio of 50%.

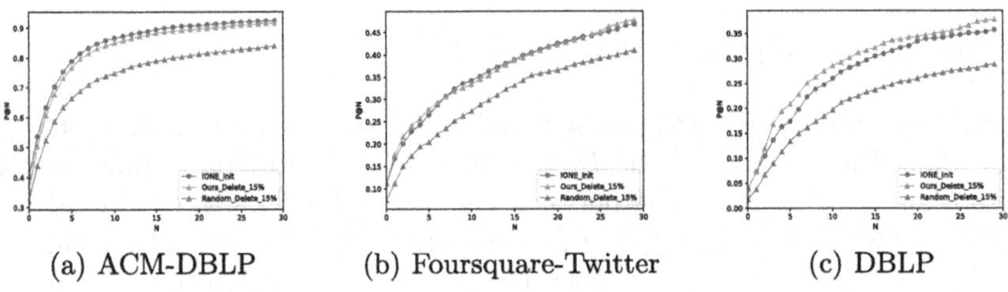

(a) ACM-DBLP (b) Foursquare-Twitter (c) DBLP

Fig. 6. Comparison with randomly deleting edges under training ratio of 60%.

To prove the effectiveness of the mask generator for the alignment task, we compare our framework with a method that randomly deletes 15% edges, illustrated in Fig. 5 and Fig. 6. Compared with randomly deleting 15% edges, our framework shows a significant increment under the $Precision@1-30$ metric. This phenomenon means that heuristically selecting edges for the alignment task is crucial, randomly removing edges may break the characteristics of the original network, compromising the performance of alignment. The increment indicates that our proposed framework can heuristically remove the edges for the network alignment task.

Further, to demonstrate that the mask generator can perform masking operations using all the commonly used graph convolution networks, we replace the GAT [23] in the mask generator with GCN [14], which also achieves the similar results. Figure 9 shows that using any GNN as the mask generator can be obtained similar results.

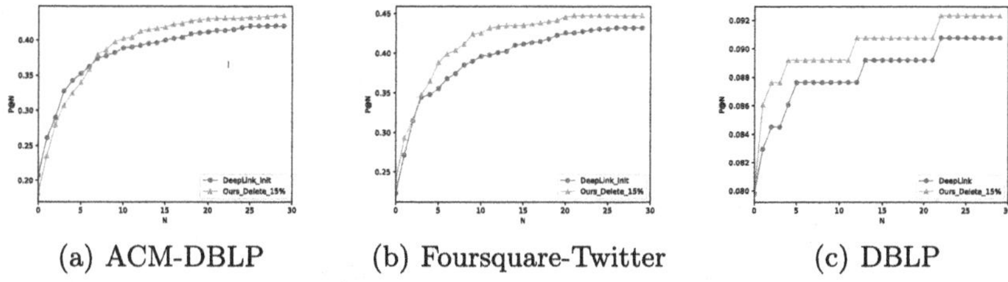

(a) ACM-DBLP (b) Foursquare-Twitter (c) DBLP

Fig. 7. Performance comparison when feeding the denosied network to DeepLink.

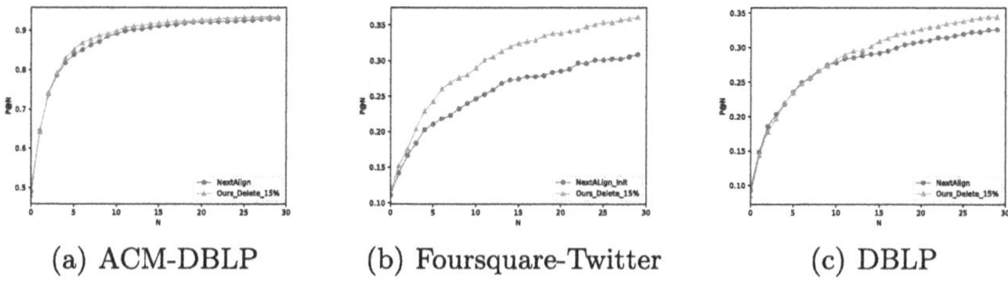

(a) ACM-DBLP (b) Foursquare-Twitter (c) DBLP

Fig. 8. Performance comparison when feeding the denosied network to NeXtAlign.

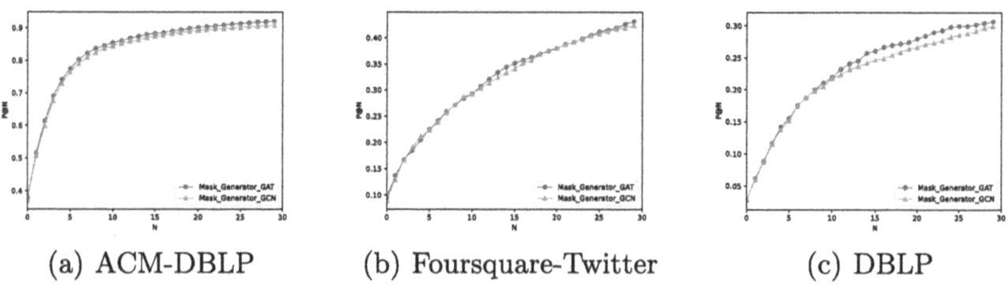

(a) ACM-DBLP (b) Foursquare-Twitter (c) DBLP

Fig. 9. Performance comparison when feeding the denosied network to NeXtAlign.

To further investigate the transferability of the denoised network, we feed the learned networks with 15% edges removed to two STOA models, including the DeepLink [35] and the NeXtAlign [31]. The performance are shown in Fig. 7 and Fig. 8. We observe that, compared with using the original network structure, there is an increment when we feed the denoised network learned by IONE to the DeepLink model. One possible reason for this is the powerful ability of the deep neural networks in the DeepLink model. For the NeXtAlign model, we observe a similar performance on the ACM-DBLP dataset compared with the original network, while there is a significant increment on the Foursquare-Twitter dataset. We notice that the ratio of anchors of ACM-DBLP is higher than it of Foursquare-Twitter. It indicates that the denoising structure will benefit the alignment model more when there are few anchors for supervision.

As illustrated in Table 2, we investigate the time consumption when feeding the denoised network with 15% edges removed to the IONE model. We implement our model using PyTorch and run it on GeForce RTX 3090 GPU and

Table 2. Time consumption on different datasets when deleted 15% edges

Dataset	The original network	The denosied network	Time saving (%)
ACM-DBLP	698 s	561 s	19.6%
Foursquare-Twitter	569 s	462 s	18.8%
DBLP	675 s	807 s	16.3%

Intel(R) Xeon(R) Silver 4210R CPU. We observe that the denoised network can same time more than 15% on both the networks. The percentages of the time saving are 19.6%,18.8% and 16.3% for ACM-DBLP, Foursquare-Twitter and DBLP, respectively. It provides evidence that denoising the network structure can benefit the alignment model for efficient learning.

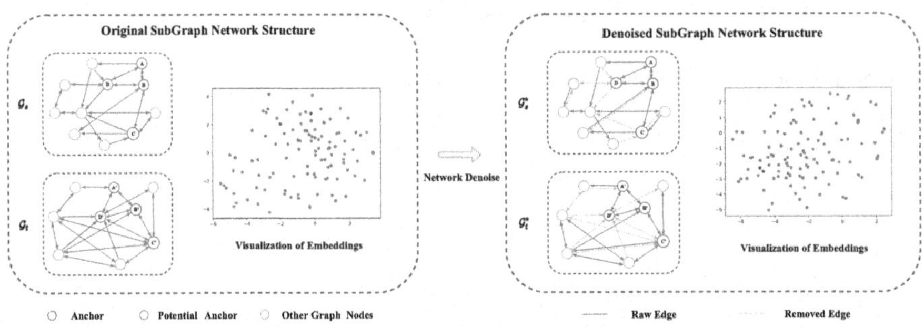

Fig. 10. Case study of the real-world dataset

5.4 Case Study

Figure 10 illustrates the structure of two subgraphs and the corresponding visualization of embeddings in the Foursqure-Twitter dataset. We notice that the potential anchor $((D, D^{'})$ has different local connectivities in the original network, such as D' connects to the anchor C' in $\mathcal{G}_t$ while D is not in $\mathcal{G}_s$. Meanwhile, D and D' connect several other nodes in separate networks, which are the structural "noisy data" for the alignment. Thus we observe that the potential anchors are far from each other in the embedding space, compromising the alignment task. After deleting 15% edges of the original network structure by our proposed framework, illustrated in the right part of Fig. 10, we obtain a more isomorphic local structure around the D and D', i.e., the structural "noisy data" are denoised. It results in a more properly distributed embedding space, where the D and D' are close in this space, making them easy to align.

6 Conclusion

In this paper, we study the problem of denoising network structure for the user alignment task. We proposed a framework based on graph structure learning. Specifically, under the guidance of the specially designed alignment loss and structure regularization, a graph encoder across networks and a parameterized mask generator are learned in an iterative learning schema. Then whether one certain edge can be removed is determined by the mask generator. We conduct experiments from several perspectives, including performance, transferability, and running time, and the visualization of learned space. Results demonstrate the effectiveness of the proposed model. We hope this framework can provide a way to deploy an alignment model in practice attributed to its ability to denoise the structural "noisy data" and reduce the training complexity. Further studies will include denoising network structure in dynamic environments and ingenious GNNs for the mask generator.

Acknowledgements. The work is partially supported by National Natural Science Foundation of China (61936001, 61806031), and in part by the Natural Science Foundation of Chongqing (cstc2019jcyj-cxttX0002, cstc2020jcyj-msxmX0943), and in part by the key cooperation project of Chongqing Municipal Education Commission (HZ2021008), and in part by Science and Technology Research Program of Chongqing Municipal Education Commission (KJQN202100629, KJQN202001901, KJQN201901901), and in part by Doctoral Innovation Talent Program of Chongqing University of Posts and Telecommunications (BYJS202118). This work is partially done when Li Liu works at Hong Kong Baptist University supported by the Hong Kong Scholars program (XJ2020054).

References

1. Chen, C., et al.: Unsupervised adversarial graph alignment with graph embedding. arXiv preprint arXiv:1907.00544 (2019)
2. Chen, H., Yin, H., Sun, X., Chen, T., Gabrys, B., Musial, K.: Multi-level graph convolutional networks for cross-platform anchor link prediction. In: The 26th ACM SIGKDD Conference on Knowledge Discovery and Data Mining, CA, USA, 23–27 August 2020, pp. 1503–1511 (2020)
3. Chen, X., Heimann, M., Vahedian, F., Koutra, D.: Cone-align: consistent network alignment with proximity-preserving node embedding. In: The 29th ACM International Conference on Information and Knowledge Management, Ireland, 19–23 October 2020, pp. 1985–1988 (2020)
4. Chen, Y., Wu, L., Zaki, M.J.: Deep iterative and adaptive learning for graph neural networks. arXiv preprint arXiv:1912.07832 (2019)
5. Chu, X., Fan, X., Zhu, Z., Bi, J.: Variational cross-network embedding for anonymized user identity linkage. In: The 30th ACM International Conference on Information and Knowledge Management, Queensland, Australia, 1–5 November 2021, pp. 2955–2959 (2021)
6. Franceschi, L., Niepert, M., Pontil, M., He, X.: Learning discrete structures for graph neural networks. In: Proceedings of the 36th International Conference on Machine Learning, ICML 2019, 9–15 June 2019, Long Beach, California, USA. Proceedings of Machine Learning Research, vol. 97, pp. 1972–1982. PMLR (2019)

7. Gao, J., Huang, X., Li, J.: Unsupervised graph alignment with wasserstein distance discriminator. In: The 27th ACM SIGKDD Conference on Knowledge Discovery and Data Mining, Singapore, 14–18 August 2021, pp. 426–435 (2021)
8. Gidaris, S., Komodakis, N.: Generating classification weights with gnn denoising autoencoders for few-shot learning. In: Proceedings of the IEEE/CVF Conference on Computer Vision and Pattern Recognition, pp. 21–30 (2019)
9. Halcrow, J., Mosoi, A., Ruth, S., Perozzi, B.: Grale: designing networks for graph learning. In: The 26th ACM SIGKDD Conference on Knowledge Discovery and Data Mining, CA, USA, 23–27 August 2020, pp. 2523–2532. ACM (2020)
10. Heimann, M., Shen, H., Safavi, T., Koutra, D.: Regal: representation learning-based graph alignment. In: Proceedings of the 27th ACM International Conference on Information and Knowledge Management, pp. 117–126. ACM (2018)
11. Jiang, B., Zhang, Z., Lin, D., Tang, J., Luo, B.: Semi-supervised learning with graph learning-convolutional networks. In: IEEE Conference on Computer Vision and Pattern Recognition, CVPR 2019, Long Beach, CA, USA, 16–20 June 2019, pp. 11313–11320. Computer Vision Foundation/IEEE (2019)
12. Jin, W., Ma, Y., Liu, X., Tang, X., Wang, S., Tang, J.: Graph structure learning for robust graph neural networks. In: KDD 2020: The 26th ACM SIGKDD Conference on Knowledge Discovery and Data Mining, Virtual Event, CA, USA, 23–27 August 2020, pp. 66–74. ACM (2020)
13. Kazi, A., Cosmo, L., Ahmadi, S.A., Navab, N., Bronstein, M.: Differentiable graph module (DGM) for graph convolutional networks. IEEE Trans. Pattern Anal. Mach. Intell. (Early Access) (2022)
14. Kipf, T.N., Welling, M.: Semi-supervised classification with graph convolutional networks. In: 5th International Conference on Learning Representations, ICLR 2017, Toulon, France, 24–26 April 2017. OpenReview.net (2017)
15. Kong, X., Zhang, J., Yu, P.S.: Inferring anchor links across multiple heterogeneous social networks. In: 22nd ACM International Conference on Information and Knowledge Management, CIKM 2013, San Francisco, CA, USA, 27 October–1 November 2013, pp. 179–188. ACM (2013)
16. Li, C., et al.: Adversarial learning for weakly-supervised social network alignment. In: Proceedings of the AAAI Conference on Artificial Intelligence, vol. 33, pp. 996–1003 (2019)
17. Liu, L., Cheung, W.K., Li, X., Liao, L.: Aligning users across social networks using network embedding. In: Proceedings of the Twenty-Fifth International Joint Conference on Artificial Intelligence, IJCAI 2016, New York, NY, USA, 9–15 July 2016, pp. 1774–1780. IJCAI/AAAI Press (2016)
18. Liu, L., Li, X., Cheung, W.K., Liao, L.: Structural representation learning for user alignment across social networks. IEEE Trans. Knowl. Data Eng. **32**(9), 1824–1837 (2020)
19. Liu, L., Zhang, Y., Fu, S., Zhong, F., Hu, J., Zhang, P.: ABNE: an attention-based network embedding for user alignment across social networks. IEEE Access **7**, 23595–23605 (2019)
20. Man, T., Shen, H., Liu, S., Jin, X., Cheng, X.: Predict anchor links across social networks via an embedding approach. In: Proceedings of the Twenty-Fifth International Joint Conference on Artificial Intelligence, IJCAI 2016, New York, NY, USA, 9–15 July 2016, pp. 1823–1829. IJCAI/AAAI Press (2016)
21. Nie, Y., Jia, Y., Li, S., Zhu, X., Li, A., Zhou, B.: Identifying users across social networks based on dynamic core interests. Neurocomputing **210**, 107–115 (2016)

22. Tang, R., Jiang, S., Chen, X., Wang, H., Wang, W., Wang, W.: Interlayer link prediction in multiplex social networks: an iterative degree penalty algorithm. Knowl. Based Syst. **194**, 105598 (2020)
23. Veličković, P., Cucurull, G., Casanova, A., Romero, A., Liò, P., Bengio, Y.: Graph attention networks. In: International Conference on Learning Representations (2018)
24. Wang, D., Cui, P., Zhu, W.: Structural deep network embedding. In: Proceedings of the 22nd ACM SIGKDD International Conference on Knowledge Discovery and Data Mining, CA, USA, 13–17 August 2016, pp. 1225–1234. ACM (2016)
25. Wang, Y., Sun, Y., Liu, Z., Sarma, S.E., Bronstein, M.M., Solomon, J.M.: Dynamic graph CNN for learning on point clouds. ACM Trans. Graph. **38**(5), 1–12 (2019)
26. Wu, Z., Pan, S., Chen, F., Long, G., Zhang, C., Yu, P.S.: A comprehensive survey on graph neural networks. IEEE Trans. Neural Netw. Learn. Syst. **32**, 4–24 (2019)
27. Xia, Y., Gao, J., Cui, B.: iMap: incremental node mapping between large graphs using GNN. In: The 30th ACM International Conference on Information and Knowledge Management, Australia, 1–5 November 2021, pp. 2191–2200 (2021)
28. Xiong, H., Yan, J., Pan, L.: Contrastive multi-view multiplex network embedding with applications to robust network alignment. In: Proceedings of the 27th ACM SIGKDD Conference on Knowledge Discovery and Data Mining, pp. 1913–1923 (2021)
29. Zhang, J., Yu, P.S.: Integrated anchor and social link predictions across social networks. In: Proceedings of the Twenty-Fourth International Joint Conference on Artificial Intelligence, IJCAI 2015, Buenos Aires, Argentina, 25–31 July 2015, pp. 2125–2132. AAAI Press (2015)
30. Zhang, J., et al.: Mego2vec: embedding matched ego networks for user alignment across social networks. In: Proceedings of the 27th ACM International Conference on Information and Knowledge Management, pp. 327–336 (2018)
31. Zhang, S., Tong, H., Jin, L., Xia, Y., Guo, Y.: Balancing consistency and disparity in network alignment. In: Proceedings of the 27th ACM SIGKDD Conference on Knowledge Discovery and Data Mining, pp. 2212–2222 (2021)
32. Zhang, S., Tong, H., Xia, Y., Xiong, L., Xu, J.: NetTrans: neural cross-network transformation. In: KDD 2020: The 26th ACM SIGKDD Conference on Knowledge Discovery and Data Mining, CA, USA, 23–27 August 2020, pp. 986–996 (2020)
33. Zheng, C., et al.: Robust graph representation learning via neural sparsification. In: International Conference on Machine Learning, pp. 11458–11468. PMLR (2020)
34. Zhong, Z., Cao, Y., Guo, M., Nie, Z.: Colink: an unsupervised framework for user identity linkage. In: Proceedings of the Thirty-Second AAAI Conference on Artificial Intelligence (AAAI 2018), pp. 5714–5721. AAAI Press (2018)
35. Zhou, F., Liu, L., Zhang, K., Trajcevski, G., Wu, J., Zhong, T.: Deeplink: a deep learning approach for user identity linkage. In: IEEE INFOCOM 2018-IEEE Conference on Computer Communications, pp. 1313–1321. IEEE (2018)
36. Zhou, F., Wen, Z., Trajcevski, G., Zhang, K., Zhong, T., Liu, F.: Disentangled network alignment with matching explainability. IEEE INFOCOM 2019 - IEEE Conference on Computer Communications, pp. 1360–1368 (2019)
37. Zhou, F., Wen, Z., Zhong, T., Trajcevski, G., Xu, X., Liu, L.: Unsupervised user identity linkage via graph neural networks. In: IEEE Global Communications Conference, GLOBECOM 2020, 7–11 December 2020, pp. 1–6. IEEE (2020)

OLPGP: An Optimized Label Propagation-Based Distributed Graph Partitioning Algorithm

Haoqing Ren[1] and Bin Wu[1,2(✉)]

[1] Beijing University of Posts and Telecommunications, Beijing, China
{bycsrhqq,wubin}@bupt.edu.cn

[2] Beijing Key Laboratory of Intelligent Telecommunications Software and Multimedia, Beijing, China

Abstract. One of the concepts that have attracted attention since entering the big data era is graph-structured data. Distributed systems for graph analysis are widely used to process large graphs. Graph partitioning is critical in parallel and distributed graph processing systems because it can balance the computational load and reduce communication load. An efficient graph partitioning algorithm can significantly improve the performance of large-scale graph data analysis and processing. In this paper, we propose a new Optimized Label Propagation-based distributed Graph Partitioning algorithm (OLPGP). OLPGP optimizes the label propagation algorithm and considers the differences between nodes. To improve computational efficiency, we implement OLPGP on the open-source distributed graph processing framework Spark GraphX. Conducted experiments on real-world networks indicate that OLPGP is scalable and achieves higher partition quality than the state-of-the-art label propagation-based graph partitioning algorithms.

Keywords: Graph partitioning · Label propagation · Distributed computing · Spark GraphX

1 Introduction

With the rapid development of the information age, more and more big graph datasets are generated from various domains, such as communication networks, urban transportation, biological data, and social networks. Due to these graph data's huge scale and complex structure, it is hard to process and analyze them in a single machine environment. Many research works focus on graph-parallel computation in distributed systems, e.g., Giraph [1], PowerGraph [11], GraphLab [23], Powerlyra [7] and GraphX [12]. Most graph processing systems are developed based on a vertex-centric programming model called Think Like A Vertex (TLAV) [24]. In this model, the graph structure is partitioned and distributed over a cluster of workers. Each worker runs a user-defined function recursively for its active vertices.

Y. Tan and Y. Shi (Eds.): DMBD 2022, CCIS 1744, pp. 120–133, 2022.
https://doi.org/10.1007/978-981-19-9297-1_10

The critical prerequisite for efficient computing in vertex-centric systems is graph partitioning (GP). In general, a large graph should be split into k partitions. Each partition is assigned to one of the k workers. The amount of communication between workers depends on the number of edges across partitions. Furthermore, the load of workers depends on the size (e.g., the number of vertices or the number of edges) of the partition assigned to them. The aim of graph partitioning is to balance the load of each worker and minimize their internal communication.

The graph partitioning problem is NP-complete [10], and there is no approximation algorithm with a constant ratio factor for general graphs [6]. In recent decades there have been many heuristic algorithms proposed. The most classic approaches are multilevel algorithms like Metis [16]. These algorithms can get high-quality partitions, but they consume a large number of resources and do not scale with large graphs. Another approach of graph partitioning is streaming graph partitioning algorithms [11,38,39], in which vertices or edges of the graph are processed in a stream successively. These algorithms have low space complexity, but the results are of less quality and depend on the order of vertices or edges in the stream.

In recent works, Label Propagation (LP) has been adopted for graph partitioning due to its high computational efficiency [9,25,28]. In this approach, changes in vertex labels represent partition migrations. LP-based partition algorithms can achieve great results and are usually easy to parallelize, but there are also some shortcomings: (1) Partitioning quality depends on the initial partitioning. If the initial partitioning has good locality, the subsequent algorithm can converge faster and get better results, and vice versa. (2) The local optimum problem of label propagation algorithm still exists, which may lead to lower partitioning quality. (3) These algorithms do not take into account the differences between vertices. While in complex network theory, vertices have their unique characteristics(e.g., node importance). Considering the uniqueness of these vertices may bring more information to the choice of partitions.

To solve the above problems, we propose a new distributed graph partitioning algorithm based on optimized label propagation (OLPGP) to producing high-quality graph partitions. Our contributions in this paper can be listed as follows:

- An effective method for initial partitioning, which has good locality and can improve the efficiency of label propagation algorithms.
- A label propagation-based graph partitioning algorithm, which can jump out of local optima and adapt to synchronous parallel models.
- We implemented our algorithm on Apache Spark GraphX [12] so that it can run in parallel in distributed systems.
- We conducted sufficient experiments on real-world large-scale graph datasets. The experimental results demonstrates that our algorithm can get higher partitioning quality and competitive time consumption than exist algorithms.

The rest of this paper is organized as follows: Related works on graph partitioning are discussed in Sect. 2. The definitions and notations used in this paper are presented in Sect. 3. Section 4 describes the proposed algorithm. The experimental results are presented in Sect. 5. Finally, we draw our conclusions and future perspectives in Sect. 6.

2 Related Works

In the last decade, many researches have been devoted to developing efficient graph partitioning algorithms. In this section, we classify graph partitioning algorithms according to their properties and present recent work.

Multilevel partitioning is a classic partitioning strategy. It allows at any given level to partition each partition into sub-partitions. The basic idea consists of first reducing the size of the original graph by recursively collapsing vertices and edges until a smaller graph is obtained. Then, it performs partitioning on the smaller graph. During the refinement phase, the partition results are projected onto a larger graph until the entire graph is covered.

A widely used algorithm for this approach is Metis [15,16]. In the coarsening phase, the authors introduced the heavy edge matching strategy to collapse the edges. In the partitioning phase, the authors used the Kernighan-Lin(KL) Algorithm [18]. Finally, in the refinement phase, the result is projected back through the graph by refining it with respect to each partition border. Other well-known multi-level partitioning algorithms are KaHIP [33] and Scotch [30]. These algorithms can get high-quality partitions, but are limited by high computation time and are not suitable for large graphs. Their parallel versions ParMetis [17], PT-Scotch [8] also face the problem of unbalance and poor partition quality [3].

The authors of [3] proposed a shared-memory parallel multilevel graph partitioning algorithm, which adopted parallel localized local search to ensure high quality and balanced partitions. Cache-aware hash tables are used to reduce memory consumption.

Another well-known approach is Stream-based partitioning [5,11,26,38,39]. These methods visit vertices of the graph in a stream successively. Each vertex is assigned to a partition as soon as it is visited in the stream and will not be changed afterward. The performance of this approach is high but has some disadvantages: (1) The resulting graph partitioning depends on the order of the vertices or edges in the stream [37]. The sensitivity to stream order leads to lower partition quality. (2) These approach is usually difficult to parallelize [11,32]. (3) There is no heuristic that approximates one-pass balanced graph partitioning in $o(n)$ [37].

Some works combine multiple graph partitioning strategies. The authors of [14] attempted to use streaming graph partitioning algorithms within the multilevel framework. The authors adapted and parallelized LDG algorithm [38] for both coarsening and refinement phases. And ultimately, a competitive partition quality can be produced.

The label propagation algorithm was initially used in the field of community detection. In recent years, it has been applied to graph partitioning due to its lightweight mechanism. Compared to multilevel algorithms, it has lower complexity and produces fewer intermediate results. Furthermore, LP method is semantic-aware, given the existence of local closely connected substructures, a label tends to propagate within such structures [9].

The Spinner algorithm [25] is one of the most successful of these algorithms. It uses penalty function to ensure balanced partitioning and is implemented on

Giraph [1] for parallel execution. However, it does not take into account the differences of nodes and depends on the initial random partitioning of vertices. The authors of [9] adopted a new initial partitioning method, and proposed two partitioning algorithms considering vertex balance and edge balance, respectively.

The authors of [35] proposed PuLP, which presents a three-phase partitioning method. All of them are based on the label propagation algorithm. The output of each phase is the initial partitioning of the next phase. Some of these constraints and objectives are considered in each phase. The authors of [36] extend and parallelize PuLP to handle large graphs.

The authors of [29] apply reinforcement learning for distributed graph partitioning. Their algorithm, named Revolver, assigns an agent to each vertex. The agent selects partitions for vertices in each round according to the probability distribution and evaluates these choices through label propagation.

In this paper, we present a new distributed algorithm for graph partitioning based on the label propagation algorithm and implement it on Spark GraphX. Compared with existing algorithms, our method considers the differences of nodes and optimizes the label propagation process. Moreover, we propose an initialization algorithm to speed up convergence and improve partition quality.

3 Preliminaries

We first introduce the necessary notations. Assume that $G = (V, E)$ is a graph where V is the set of vertices and E is the set of edges such that an edge $e \in E$ is a pair (u, v) with $u, v \in V$. We denote the neighborhood of a vertex v by $N(v) = \{u \mid u \in V, (u, v) \in E\}$, and the degree of v by $deg(v) = |N(v)|$. In a k-way partitioning, we define L as a set of labels $L = \{l_1, ..., l_k\}$ that essentially correspond to the k partitions. ϕ is the labeling function $\phi : V \rightarrow L$ such that $\phi(v) = l_i \, (i \in [1, k])$ if label l_i is assigned to vertex v.

3.1 Balanced K-Way Graph Partitioning

The purpose of balanced k-way graph partitioning is to find the set of partitions $P = \{P_1, P_2, ..., P_k\}$ on the vertices V that are pairwise disjoint and the union of which is equal to V. These partitions are subject to two constraints:

The Cut-Edge. The first constraint is the cut-edge, which means minimizing the number of edges between different partitions. Minimizing cut edges helps reduce communication overhead in distributed systems. The constraint can be formulated as:

$$\min_{P} |\{e \mid e = (v_i, v_j) \in E, v_i \in P_x, v_j \in P_y, x \neq y\}| \tag{1}$$

The Partition Load. Another constraint takes into account load balancing in distributed computing. Precisely speaking, the load of each partition is defined as the sum of the degrees of all vertices in the partition, i.e.,

$$load(P_i) = \sum_{v \in P_i} deg\,(v)\,, i \in [1, k] \tag{2}$$

Our goal is to limit the ratio of maximum load to average load to a certain range, which is formalized as follows:

$$\frac{\max\{load\,(P_i)\}}{\frac{1}{k}\sum_{i=1}^{k} load(P_i)} \leq \epsilon \tag{3}$$

where $\epsilon \geq 1$ is a constant number that identifies the acceptable imbalance.

3.2 Label Propagation Algorithm

The label propagation algorithm is a classical method in community discovery [13,31]. It is widely used in the field of graph partitioning due to its lightweight and intuitive mechanism. The original LP algorithm first randomly assigns an initial label l to each vertex in the graph, where $l \in [1, k]$. Subsequently, every vertex iteratively propagates its label to its neighbors. During this iterative process, a vertex acquires the label that is more frequent among its neighbors. Specifically, every vertex v assigns a different score for a particular label l which is equal to the number of neighbors assigned to label l

$$score\,(v, l) = \sum_{u \in N(v)} \delta\,(\phi\,(u)\,, l) \tag{4}$$

where δ is Kronecker delta. Vertices prefer to choose labels with high score. More formally, a vertex updates its label to label l_v according to the following update function

$$l_v = \operatorname*{argmax}_{l}\, score(v, l) \tag{5}$$

We call such an update a migration as it represents a logical vertex migration between two partitions. If multiple labels satisfy the update function, we will randomly select a label. The algorithm halts when no vertex updates its label.

3.3 Spark GraphX

Spark [44] is a parallel and distributed computing framework that enables the processing of big data very efficiently and fast through a cluster of computers by utilizing its in-memory programming model and its data abstraction called RDD. GraphX [12] is a Resilient Distributed Graph (RDG) system based on Spark and was inspired from Pregel [24] and Bulk Synchronous Parallel (BSP) programming model. GraphX extends Spark's Resilient Distributed Dataset (RDD) to RDG. This RDG is composed of two record files, one for the vertices and the other containing the edges. GraphX provides a complete API that simplifies graph ETL and computations. Since GraphX is based on Spark, it provides streaming algorithms for dynamic graphs [2].

4 The Proposed Algorithm

4.1 Initialization

Most existing GP algorithms and graph processing frameworks use random or hash algorithm for initial partitioning, which do not take into account the topology of the graph. It incurs many subsequent calculations, and even leads to a poor partitioning quality. To solve this problem, we take into consideration that the degree distribution of vertices in natural graphs follows a power law [4]. In power-law graphs, a large fraction of vertices in the graph is connected to only a few vertices that have a very high degree. If a high degree vertex and its neighbors are assigned to the same initial partition, the initial partitioning will get higher locality and fewer cut edges. For this purpose, we employ degree-weighted label propagation for the initial partitioning. First, randomly assign labels to each vertex. Then change the label's score to Eq. (6)

$$score_{degree}\left(v,l\right)=\sum_{u\in N(v)}deg(u)\delta\left(\phi\left(u\right),l\right) \tag{6}$$

Unlike conventional convergence judgments, we fix the number of iterations to 2; that is, the labels of the high degree vertices are diffused to the two-level neighborhood. Note that we do not impose any restrictions on partition size during this process, which means that the initial partitioning may be very unbalanced. We will deal with it in subsequent algorithms.

4.2 Balanced and Optimized Label Propagation

Since the original label propagation algorithm did not care about the partition size. We add a penalty function to penalize overly large partitions and integrate it into the score function

$$score_{balance}\left(v,l\right)=\frac{\sum_{u\in N(v)}\delta\left(\phi\left(u\right),l\right)}{deg(v)}-\frac{load(P_l)}{C} \tag{7}$$

where C is is the ideal load of each partition, defined as

$$C=\epsilon\cdot\frac{\sum_{v\in V}deg(v)}{k} \tag{8}$$

In Eq. (7), we first normalize Eq. (4), and then add the penalty function. The larger the load of the partition, the lower the corresponding score. Partitions that are too large will get low scores and harder to be selected. The parameter ϵ controls the tradeoff between convergence speed and partition unbalance. The larger the value of ϵ, the more vertices are migrated to the large partition at each iteration. This possibly speeds up convergence, but may also increase unbalance as more vertices are allowed to be assigned to each partition that exceeds the ideal load $\sum_{v \in V} deg(v)/k$.

Another problem with original label propagation is that it is easy to fall into local optima. In each iteration, the prevailing labels are always adopted, which may trap the algorithm in a local optimum and never find the best solution. To solve this problem, we draw on the idea of simulated annealing algorithm [40]. We allow vertices to adopt suboptimal labels instead of optimal labels with the following probability p_s to encourage the algorithm to jump out of local optima.

$$p_s = \exp(\frac{score_s - score_o}{T \cdot score_o}) \tag{9}$$

where $score_o$ represents the highest score, $score_s$ represents the second-highest score. The closer $score_s$ is to $score_o$, the greater the probability of adopting a suboptimal solution. T represents the initial temperature, which is a constant and set to 1. After each iteration, T should be multiplied by a constant λ that is less than 1 so that p_s decreases and the process tends to stabilize.

$$T = \lambda \cdot T \tag{10}$$

After extensive experimentation, we recommend setting λ to 0.8.

4.3 Parallelization

After the above process, each vertex has selected the label that it should change, which we call candidate label. Since each vertex changes its label independently, in a synchronous parallel model, a situation arises where at a given time, a partition with low load will attract a large number of vertices to migrate at the same time, thus exceeding its load limit. To avoid this, vertices need to coordinate after calculating their candidate labels. To make the solution independent, we used a probabilistic approach. The probability of a vertex changing to its candidate label depends on the following factors:

Global Status. The global state takes into account the current partition load and the total number of candidate vertices for each partition. More specifically, suppose that at iteration t partition l has a remaining capacity $r(l)$ such that

$$r(l) = C - load(P_l) \tag{11}$$

Suppose that $c(l)$ is the set of candidate vertices that want to migrate to partition l. If all candidate vertices of partition l are migrated, the added load is $\sum_{v \in c(l)} deg(v)$, which may exceed the remaining load $r(l)$. So we set the migration probability p_{global} as

$$p_{global}(l) = \frac{r(l)}{\sum_{v \in c(l)} deg(v)} \tag{12}$$

Vertex Attribute. The above probability p_{global} is shared by all vertices with candidate label l, it ignores the difference between nodes. In power-law graphs, most of the edges are related to only a few vertices with a very high degree. This property can be exploited by assigning vertices to partitions in such a way that the replication of a low-degree vertex is preferred to the replication of a high-degree vertex. The rationale for this is that high-degree vertices are incident to so many edges that they are likely to produce a large number of cut edges anyway. By focusing on placing low-degree vertices with low cut edges, the overall cut edges can be decreased [27].

Limited by the synchronous parallel model, we still use probability to implement this idea. Specifically, high-degree vertices are more likely to migrate to other partitions, while low-degree vertices tend to be fixed to the original partition. The migration probability p_{degree} of vertex v is

$$p_{degree}(v) = \frac{deg(v)}{deg_{max}} \tag{13}$$

The final migration probability $p_{migration}$ combines the above two factors, which is

$$p_{migration}(v) = \alpha \cdot p_{degree}(v) + (1 - \alpha) \cdot p_{global}(\phi(v)) \tag{14}$$

where $\alpha \in [0, 1]$ is a constant and represents the trade-off between global status and node attribute. A larger value of α can achieve better partition quality, but will result in unbalanced partitions, and vice versa. We recommend setting α to 0.2.

4.4 Convergence and Halting

In the original label propagation algorithm, convergence is detected by no vertices changing labels, called halting conditions. While in graph partitioning, we need to optimize both locality and partition balance, which makes this strategy inapplicable. It is a natural idea to judge the convergence according to the cut-edge rate and partition balance. Specifically, at iteration t, when the algorithm satisfies both of the following conditions, it is considered to be convergent: 1) The increment of the cut-edge rate is less than the given threshold, that is

$$\triangle\, \mu = \left| 1 - \frac{\mu(P_t)}{\mu_{max}} \right| \leq \beta \tag{15}$$

where $\mu(P_t)$ represents the current cut-edge rate of iteration t, μ_{max} represents the maximum cut-edge rate achieved before t iterations. 2) The current partition load meets the conditions in Formula (3).

5 Experiments

In this section, comprehensive experiments are applied on different real-world datasets to evaluate the effectiveness and performance of the proposed algorithm with other state-of-the-art algorithms. We compare our algorithm with

Spinner [25] and B-GRAP [9] because they are also LP-based graph partitioning algorithms. Furthermore, like our algorithm, both of the two algorithms are developed on a distributed system. After extensive experimentation, we set the algorithm parameters as follows: additional capacity $\epsilon = 1.05$, $\lambda = 0.8$, $\beta = 0.0025$ and $\alpha = 0.2$. For baselines, we set $\epsilon = 1.05$, other parameters follow the default settings.

All of the experiments are conducted on a cluster with 9 computing nodes. Each node has 32 GB of RAM and Intel(R) Xeon(R) CPU E5-2620 with 8 cores. One node acts as the master, and the remaining 8 nodes act as workers. Evaluations are done with Spark version 2.4.0-cdh6.2.1, Scala programing language version 2.11.12, Hadoop version 3.0 and Giraph version 1.1.0 for baselines.

5.1 Real-World Datasets

We adopt five real-world datasets to examine our algorithm and compared algorithms whose details are summarized in Table 1. We got these datasets from Stanford large network dataset collection [22] and Social Computing Data Repository at Arizona State University [42]. The properties of GraphX make it unnecessary to add edges to directed graphs.

Table 1. Datasets description

Dataset	$\lvert V\rvert$	$\lvert E\rvert$	Directed	Source
Youtube	1,134,890	2,987,624	False	[41]
RoadNet-CA	1,965,206	2,766,607	False	[21]
Hyves	1,402,611	2,777,419	False	[43]
Wikitalk	2,394,385	5,021,410	True	[19]
Skitter	1,696,415	11,095,298	False	[20]

5.2 Partitioning Quality

We first evaluate the partitioning quality. We use two metrics shown in Eq. (16) and (17) for evaluation of the cut-edge rate μ and the balance of the sizes of partitions θ. These two metrics are the smaller the better.

$$\mu = \frac{\#cutedges}{\#totaledges} \tag{16}$$

$$\theta = \frac{\max\{load(P_i)\}}{\frac{1}{k}\sum_{i=1}^{k} load(P_i)} \tag{17}$$

Table 2 shows the partition quality of all algorithms when k is from 8 to 64. It can be seen that OLPGP achieves the best cut-edge rate and balance at the same time in most cases. In Skitter dataset, OLPGP does not achieve the best balance, but the cutting edge rate is much higher than baselines. Furthermore, OLPGP is not affected by k, which indicates it is scalable.

In Fig. 2, we show the evolution of metrics μ, θ over iterations. Due to space limitations, we only show the results on the WikiTalk dataset when $k = 64$, the results on other datasets are similar. It can be seen that although the initial partitioning process produces extremely unbalanced partitions, our algorithm can still reach balance after a few iterations and continuously improve the cut-edge rate, which shows that our initialization strategy can be well combined with the strategy of maintaining balance.

Table 2. Partitioning quality on all datasets.

k	8		16		32		64	
	μ	θ	μ	θ	μ	θ	μ	θ
Youtube								
Spinner	0.44	1.049	0.50	1.045	0.58	1.051	0.63	1.276
BGRAP	0.42	1.043	**0.45**	1.038	0.52	1.054	0.56	1.532
OLPGP	**0.39**	**1.021**	**0.45**	**1.030**	**0.50**	**1.037**	**0.53**	**1.045**
WikiTalk								
Spinner	0.68	1.037	0.66	1.146?	0.73	1.031	0.76	1.101
BGRAP	0.49	1.037	0.52	1.048	0.53	1.162	0.54	1.790
OLPGP	**0.44**	**1.005**	**0.47**	**1.012**	**0.50**	**1.022**	**0.49**	**1.049**
Skitter								
Spinner	0.27	1.048	0.30	1.036	0.39	1.068	0.41	**1.133**
BGRAP	0.26	1.298	0.31	1.494	0.36	1.329	0.39	1.535
OLPGP	**0.24**	**1.008**	**0.28**	**1.029**	**0.32**	**1.040**	**0.38**	1.212
RoadNet-CA								
Spinner	0.46	**1.009**	0.47	1.017	0.48	1.022	0.48	1.023
BGRAP	0.45	1.011	0.47	**1.014**	0.49	**1.016**	0.49	**1.021**
OLPGP	**0.20**	1.014	**0.23**	1.019	**0.28**	1.017	**0.25**	1.025
Hyves								
Spinner	0.53	1.017	0.57	1.026	0.59	1.045	0.61	1.048
BGRAP	**0.37**	1.190	0.42	1.930	0.45	2.015	0.48	2.066
OLPGP	0.39	**1.002**	**0.41**	**1.022**	**0.42**	**1.030**	**0.43**	**1.043**

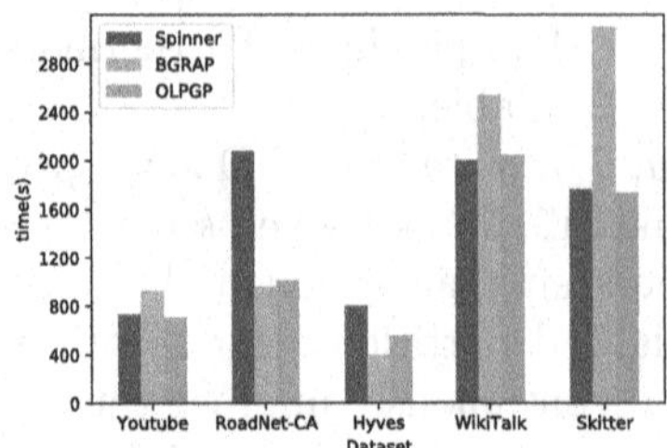

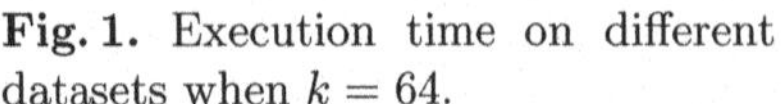
Fig. 1. Execution time on different datasets when $k = 64$.

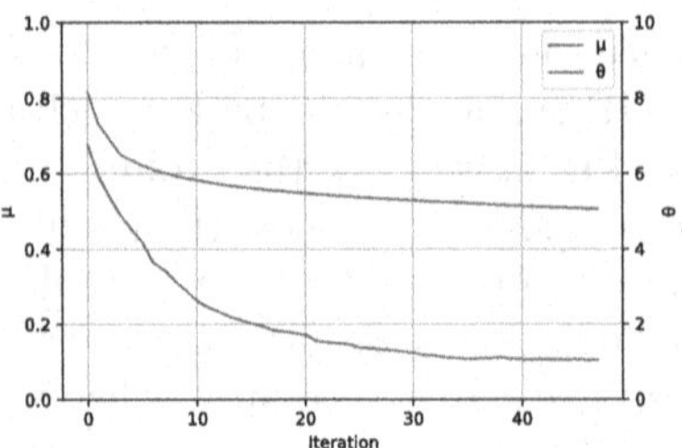

Fig. 2. Metrics over iterations on WikiTalk dataset ($k = 64$).

5.3 Execution Time

Execution time is also an important metric for graph partitioning algorithms. In this section, we compare the execution time of all algorithms when $k = 64$, and the results are shown in Fig. 1. Obtained results show that the performance of OLPGP is competitive, the execution time is always close to the best baseline.

6 Conclusion

In this paper we proposed OLPGP, a distributed graph partitioning algorithm based on label propagation. We first initialize the partitions with a strategy of degree-weighted label propagation, which provides good locality and allows to speed up the convergence. Next, we add a penalty function to label propagation to ensure balanced partitions and optimize the algorithm to avoid local optima. In order to adapt the algorithm to the synchronous parallel model, we comprehensively consider the global state and the characteristics of vertices to avoid partition overload. Our experiments show that OLPGP is scalable and can achieve better cut-edge ratio and balance than other popular and state-of-the-art algorithms. Moreover, the performance of OLPGP is competitive, indicating its availability. Nowadays, the scale of complex networks is developing rapidly. Most popular social networks will have new users joining every moment. As future work, we plan to adapt our algorithm to graph changes in dynamic graphs.

References

1. Apache Giraph Project. https://giraph.apache.org/. Accessed 6 Jan 2022
2. Adoni, H.W.Y., Nahhal, T., Krichen, M., Aghezzaf, B., Elbyed, A.: A survey of current challenges in partitioning and processing of graph-structured data in parallel and distributed systems. Distrib. Parallel Databases **38**(2), 495–530 (2020)
3. Akhremtsev, Y., Sanders, P., Schulz, C.: High-quality shared-memory graph partitioning. IEEE Trans. Parallel Distrib. Syst. **31**(11), 2710–2722 (2020)
4. Albert, R., Barabási, A.L.: Statistical mechanics of complex networks. Rev. Mod. Phys. **74**(1), 47 (2002)

5. Awadelkarim, A., Ugander, J.: Prioritized restreaming algorithms for balanced graph partitioning. In: Proceedings of the 26th ACM SIGKDD International Conference on Knowledge Discovery & Data Mining, pp. 1877–1887 (2020)
6. Bui, T.N., Jones, C.: Finding good approximate vertex and edge partitions is NP-hard. Inf. Process. Lett. **42**(3), 153–159 (1992)
7. Chen, R., Shi, J., Chen, Y., Zang, B., Guan, H., Chen, H.: PowerLyra: differentiated graph computation and partitioning on skewed graphs. ACM Trans. Parallel Comput. (TOPC) **5**(3), 1–39 (2019)
8. Chevalier, C., Pellegrini, F.: PT-scotch: a tool for efficient parallel graph ordering. Parallel Comput. **34**(6–8), 318–331 (2008)
9. El Moussawi, A., Seghouani, N.B., Bugiotti, F.: B-GRAP: balanced graph partitioning algorithm for large graphs. J. Data Intell. **2**(2), 116–135 (2021)
10. Garey, M.R., Johnson, D.S., Stockmeyer, L.: Some simplified NP-complete problems. In: Proceedings of the Sixth Annual ACM Symposium on Theory of Computing, pp. 47–63 (1974)
11. Gonzalez, J.E., Low, Y., Gu, H., Bickson, D., Guestrin, C.: Powergraph: distributed graph-parallel computation on natural graphs. In: 10th {USENIX} Symposium on Operating Systems Design and Implementation ({OSDI} 2012), pp. 17–30 (2012)
12. Gonzalez, J.E., Xin, R.S., Dave, A., Crankshaw, D., Franklin, M.J., Stoica, I.: Graphx: graph processing in a distributed dataflow framework. In: 11th {USENIX} Symposium on Operating Systems Design and Implementation ({OSDI} 2014), pp. 599–613 (2014)
13. Gregory, S.: Finding overlapping communities in networks by label propagation. New J. Phys. **12**(10), 103018 (2010)
14. Jafari, N., Selvitopi, O., Aykanat, C.: Fast shared-memory streaming multilevel graph partitioning. J. Parallel Distrib. Comput. **147**, 140–151 (2021)
15. Karypis, G., Kumar, V.: Multilevel graph partitioning schemes. In: ICPP (3), pp. 113–122 (1995)
16. Karypis, G., Kumar, V.: A fast and high quality multilevel scheme for partitioning irregular graphs. SIAM J. Sci. Comput. **20**(1), 359–392 (1998)
17. Karypis, G., Kumar, V.: A parallel algorithm for multilevel graph partitioning and sparse matrix ordering. J. Parallel Distrib. Comput. **48**(1), 71–95 (1998)
18. Kernighan, B.W., Lin, S.: An efficient heuristic procedure for partitioning graphs. Bell Syst. Tech. J. **49**(2), 291–307 (1970)
19. Leskovec, J., Huttenlocher, D., Kleinberg, J.: Signed networks in social media. In: Proceedings of the SIGCHI Conference on Human Factors in Computing Systems, pp. 1361–1370 (2010)
20. Leskovec, J., Kleinberg, J., Faloutsos, C.: Graphs over time: densification laws, shrinking diameters and possible explanations. In: Proceedings of the Eleventh ACM SIGKDD International Conference on Knowledge Discovery in Data Mining, pp. 177–187 (2005)
21. Leskovec, J., Lang, K.J., Dasgupta, A., Mahoney, M.W.: Community structure in large networks: natural cluster sizes and the absence of large well-defined clusters. Internet Math. **6**(1), 29–123 (2009)
22. Leskovec, J., Sosič, R.: SNAP: a general-purpose network analysis and graph-mining library. ACM Trans. Intell. Syst. Technol. (TIST) **8**(1), 1 (2016)
23. Low, Y., Gonzalez, J.E., Kyrola, A., Bickson, D., Guestrin, C.E., Hellerstein, J.: Graphlab: a new framework for parallel machine learning. arXiv preprint arXiv:1408.2041 (2014)

24. Malewicz, G., et al.: Pregel: a system for large-scale graph processing. In: Proceedings of the 2010 ACM SIGMOD International Conference on Management of Data, pp. 135–146 (2010)
25. Martella, C., Logothetis, D., Loukas, A., Siganos, G.: Spinner: scalable graph partitioning in the cloud. In: 2017 IEEE 33rd International Conference on Data Engineering (ICDE), pp. 1083–1094. IEEE (2017)
26. Mayer, C., et al.: Adwise: adaptive window-based streaming edge partitioning for high-speed graph processing. In: 2018 IEEE 38th International Conference on Distributed Computing Systems (ICDCS), pp. 685–695. IEEE (2018)
27. Mayer, R., Jacobsen, H.A.: Hybrid edge partitioner: partitioning large power-law graphs under memory constraints. In: Proceedings of the 2021 International Conference on Management of Data, pp. 1289–1302 (2021)
28. Meyerhenke, H., Sanders, P., Schulz, C.: Parallel graph partitioning for complex networks. IEEE Trans. Parallel Distrib. Syst. **28**(9), 2625–2638 (2017)
29. Mofrad, M.H., Melhem, R., Hammoud, M.: Revolver: vertex-centric graph partitioning using reinforcement learning. In: 2018 IEEE 11th International Conference on Cloud Computing (CLOUD), pp. 818–821. IEEE (2018)
30. Pellegrini, F., Roman, J.: Scotch: a software package for static mapping by dual recursive bipartitioning of process and architecture graphs. In: Liddell, H., Colbrook, A., Hertzberger, B., Sloot, P. (eds.) HPCN-Europe 1996. LNCS, vol. 1067, pp. 493–498. Springer, Heidelberg (1996). https://doi.org/10.1007/3-540-61142-8_588
31. Raghavan, U.N., Albert, R., Kumara, S.: Near linear time algorithm to detect community structures in large-scale networks. Phys. Rev. E **76**(3), 036106 (2007)
32. Sajjad, H.P., Payberah, A.H., Rahimian, F., Vlassov, V., Haridi, S.: Boosting vertex-cut partitioning for streaming graphs. In: 2016 IEEE International Congress on Big Data (BigData Congress), pp. 1–8. IEEE (2016)
33. Sanders, P., Schulz, C.: Engineering multilevel graph partitioning algorithms. In: Demetrescu, C., Halldórsson, M.M. (eds.) ESA 2011. LNCS, vol. 6942, pp. 469–480. Springer, Heidelberg (2011). https://doi.org/10.1007/978-3-642-23719-5_40
34. Sanders, P., Schulz, C.: Distributed evolutionary graph partitioning. In: 2012 Proceedings of the Fourteenth Workshop on Algorithm Engineering and Experiments (ALENEX), pp. 16–29. SIAM (2012)
35. Slota, G.M., Madduri, K., Rajamanickam, S.: PuLP: scalable multi-objective multi-constraint partitioning for small-world networks. In: 2014 IEEE International Conference on Big Data (Big Data), pp. 481–490. IEEE (2014)
36. Slota, G.M., Rajamanickam, S., Devine, K., Madduri, K.: Partitioning trillion-edge graphs in minutes. In: 2017 IEEE International Parallel and Distributed Processing Symposium (IPDPS), pp. 646–655. IEEE (2017)
37. Stanton, I.: Streaming balanced graph partitioning algorithms for random graphs. In: Proceedings of the Twenty-Fifth Annual ACM-SIAM Symposium on Discrete Algorithms, pp. 1287–1301. SIAM (2014)
38. Stanton, I., Kliot, G.: Streaming graph partitioning for large distributed graphs. In: Proceedings of the 18th ACM SIGKDD International Conference on Knowledge Discovery and Data Mining, pp. 1222–1230 (2012)
39. Tsourakakis, C., Gkantsidis, C., Radunovic, B., Vojnovic, M.: Fennel: streaming graph partitioning for massive scale graphs. In: Proceedings of the 7th ACM International Conference on Web Search and Data Mining, pp. 333–342 (2014)
40. Van Laarhoven, P.J., Aarts, E.H.: Simulated annealing. In: Van Laarhoven, P.J., Aarts, E.H (eds.) Simulated Annealing: Theory and Applications, pp. 7–15. Springer, Dordrecht (1987). https://doi.org/10.1007/978-94-015-7744-1_2

41. Yang, J., Leskovec, J.: Defining and evaluating network communities based on ground-truth. Knowl. Inf. Syst. **42**(1), 181–213 (2015)
42. Zafarani, R., Liu, H.: Social computing data repository at ASU (2009). http://socialcomputing.asu.edu
43. Zafarani, R., Liu, H.: Social computing data repository at ASU (2009)
44. Zaharia, M., Chowdhury, M., Franklin, M.J., Shenker, S., Stoica, I.: Spark: cluster computing with working sets. In: 2nd USENIX Workshop on Hot Topics in Cloud Computing (HotCloud 2010) (2010)

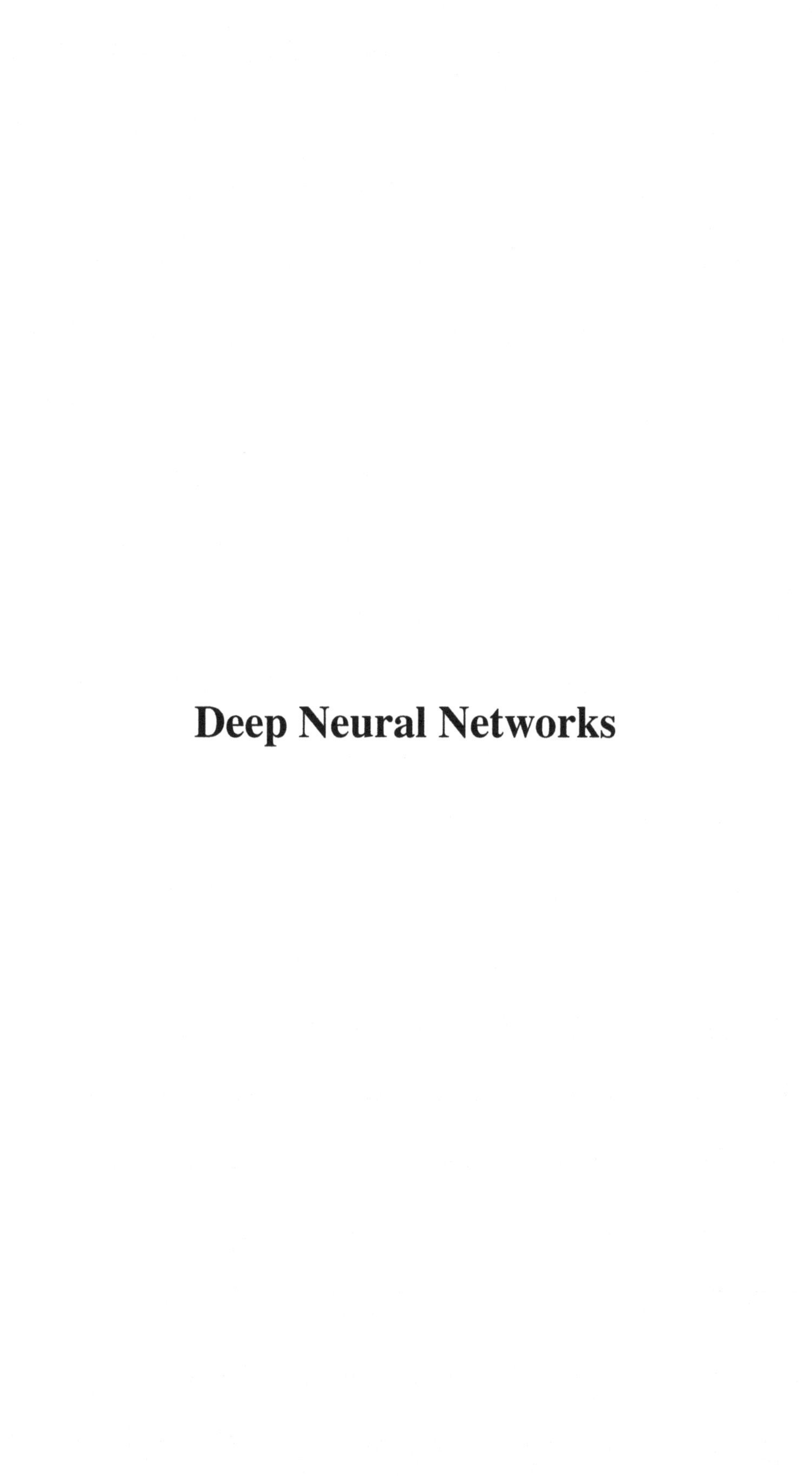

Deep Neural Networks

DRGS: Low-Precision Full Quantization of Deep Neural Network with Dynamic Rounding and Gradient Scaling for Object Detection

Qiaojun Wu[1], Yuan Li[2], Song Chen[1,2], and Yi Kang[1,2](✉)

[1] Institute of Advanced Technology, University of Science and Technology of China, Hefei, China
qjwu@mail.ustc.edu.cn
[2] School of Microelectronics, University of Science and Technology of China, Hefei, China
ly549826@mail.ustc.edu.cn, {songch,ykang}@ustc.edu.cn

Abstract. To improve the inference accuracy of neural networks, their size and complexity are growing rapidly, making the deployment of complex task models on mobile devices with efficient inference a major challenge for industry today. Low-precision quantization is one of the key methods to achieve efficient inference on complex networks, but previous works often quantize partial layers because severe accuracy degradation occurs when quantizing is applied to the entire network. In order to improve the stability and accuracy of low-precision quantization-fine-tuning, we propose a hardware-friendly low-precision full quantization method, called DRGS, which dynamically selects rounding mode for weights according to the direction of weight updates during the training forward and scales the corresponding gradient, finally completing the quantization of all layers of the complex network to achieve floating-free-inference. To validate the effectiveness of DRGS, we apply it to RetinaNet with full 4-bit quantization, and the result of the MS-COCO dataset shows that DRGS has a 2.1% improvement in mAP or at least 2X less quantization loss compared to the state of art implementation. This improvement is also significant even on the YOLO, an object detection model family known for run-time low latency and efficiency. In the latest version of YOLO-v5s, the 4-bit fully quantized network reaches mAP 33.4 which to our knowledge is the best mAP achieved at this category.

Keywords: Low-precision · Full quantization · Dynamic rounding · Gradient scaling · YOLO

1 Introduction

Deep neural networks (DNNs) have been a promising technology in recent years and achieved excellent performance in areas such as computer vision and natural language processing. However, the deeper and more complex DNN models make

Y. Tan and Y. Shi (Eds.): DMBD 2022, CCIS 1744, pp. 137–151, 2022.
https://doi.org/10.1007/978-981-19-9297-1_11

Table 1. Comparison between different quantizers. **AL**: Quantifying the parameters of all layers, including weights, biases, and activations. **BN**: BN layers [8] exist only during the training phase and are incorporated into the Conv layers during inference. **CT**: Complex tasks other than classification, such as object detection. **LS**: Weights are linearly symmetrically quantized. **SI**: No modification of the original network, maintaining structural integrity. ✓ means the condition is met.

Methods	AL	BN	CT	LS	SI
LQ-Nets [22]					✓
DSQ [6]				✓	✓
LSQ+ [2]				✓	✓
HPAQ [4]			✓	✓	✓
Log-scale [5]			✓		✓
AQD [3]	✓		✓	✓	
LLSQ [23]	✓	✓		✓	✓
DRGS(Ours)	✓	✓	✓	✓	✓

efficient deployment on mobile devices with limited computing resources and memory bandwidth a challenge [19]. Therefore, how to achieve efficient inference on resource-limited devices with as little accuracy loss as possible through model compression has become a research focus.

Quantization, as a compression method, maps a large number of continuous high-precision floating-point values into a finite number of discrete values. In this way, the memory footprint during inference is reduced while expensive floating-point operations are replaced with efficient fixed-point operations. Therefore, model quantization is a key to deploy complex networks on resource-limited or integer-only devices, and this work focuses on efficient network quantization schemes.

An effective quantizer is able to perform hardware-friendly end-to-end quantization of DNNs, where the conditions [12,23] to be satisfied are extended as shown in Table 1. Most quantization schemes only deal with convolution (Conv) layers, and compute those non-convolutional layer in floating point format. LQ-Nets [22] and Log-scale [5] use nonlinear quantizer, which requires special hardware support and cannot be applied to most off-the-shelf DNN accelerators. LLSQ [23] and AQD [3] quantize all layers, but LLSQ only targets on the classification task, and AQD modifies the network structure, can not fold the BN layer, increases resource requirements and adds inference latency. Although DSQ [6], LSQ+ [2] and HPAQ [4] use linear quantizers, quantization is performed only for Conv and fully connected layers. Since non-convolutional parts are significant in object detection schemes, computations in those parts not only require a large number of floating-point units in hardware, but also require frequent switching of data types that would reduces the acceleration gain by quantization.

To address these issues, we propose a hardware-friendly full quantization scheme that can be used for complex tasks, which will quantize the parameters

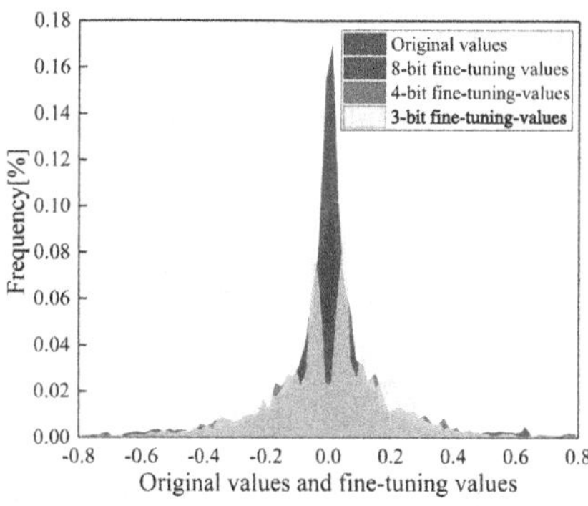

(a) Comparison of the distribution between the original and fine-tuned values.

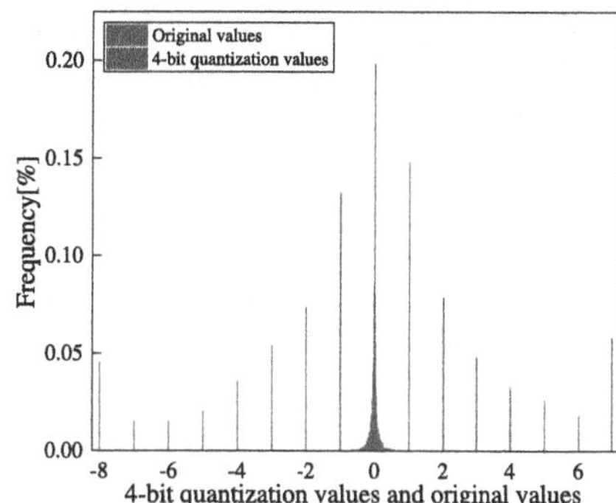

(b) Comparison of the distribution between the original and 4-bit quantization values.

Fig. 1. Comparison of the distribution between original values, fine-tuned values, and quantified values, based on the 2nd Conv weights of YOLO-v5n [20].

of all layers in the network, including Conv layers, BN layers, Skip-connection, and Concat layers, resulting in that all learned quantization parameters are represented by fixed-point numbers, thus enabling floating-point free inference.

When a complex object detection network is quantized to a low bit precision, we observed a large variation in accuracy during quantization-fine-tuning. Figure 1(a) shows the changes in the distribution of weights before and after quantization-fine-tuning. It can be seen that low precision quantization usually leads to a large deviation in distribution of the pre-quantization weights. Obviously, the lower quantization precision is, the larger updates are needed for the pre-quantization weights to approach target quantization points, as shown in Fig. 1(b), and this needs to be done by a rounding function. Nagel et al. [15] pointed out that rounding to the nearest may not be the best rounding mode, and proposed a rounding mode selection method for post-training-quantization [16]. Inspired by the work, we propose a dynamic rounding mode selection method for quantization-aware-training. In the training forward, the rounding mode is dynamically selected according to the direction of weight change in the critical rounding interval(CRI). At the same time, the corresponding gradient is also scaled in order to locate the weights in the CRI out of the interval as soon as possible. In this way we have a stable rounding mode the convergence is fast. We refer to the above quantization method as DRGS(Dynamic Rounding and Gradient Scaling). Our specific contributions are summarized as follows:

- We propose a hardware-friendly end-to-end full quantization method that enables floating-point-free inference.
- We show that one reason for low stability in quantization-fine-tuning training of a object detection model in low-precision is the rounding to the nearest for all parameters, and propose a method to dynamically select the rounding mode to improve the stability and accuracy of the fine-tuning.

- We propose a gradient scaling mechanism that can train the weights to converge to a stable rounding mode faster.
- To the best of our knowledge, we are the first to fully quantize the YOLO model, a widely used detection model known for its run-time low latency and efficiency, to 4bit or below.

2 Related Work

2.1 Network Quantization

Quantization can be divided into two categories from the perspective of whether training is required [16], post-training-quantization(PTQ) [15] and quantization-aware-training(QAT) [2–6,12,22,23]. PTQ suffers from severe accuracy loss when quantizing models to 4-bit or below, while QAT can partially recover this accuracy loss by fine-tuning the pre-trained models. In recent work, LLSQ [23], TQT [10] and LSQ+ [2] propose learnable quantization parameters. Motivated by these, we propose DRGS and implement low-precision full quantization on detection model.

Aside from quantization methods, some works improve the quantization accuracy by overlaying other methods. For example, knowledge distillation is used in QKD [11] to improve the quantization accuracy. Unlike these methods, DRGS focuses on fine-tuning the forward and backward propagation without bells and whistles, and DRGS is orthogonal to these methods.

2.2 Quantization on Modern Detectors

In recent years, the mainstream object detection algorithms are anchor-based deep detection networks [24], which mainly contain two categories of two-stage object detection and one-stage object detection, such as one-stage RetinaNet [13], YOLO [17,20] and two-stage Faster RCNN [18] have received wide attention. The main efforts to quantize such detection models are [3–5,12], none of which can satisfy all the conditions listed in Table 1. FQN [12] has a severe accuracy loss in the case of low bit width quantization at 4-bit and below. Chin et al. [4] and Choi et al. [5] quantize only the Conv layers, and Choi et al. [5] uses a nonlinear quantization method, and this requires special hardware design to support it. Chen et al. [3] proposes Multi-BN blocks to improve the network accuracy, which makes the original network cannot fold the BN layer, which will not only increase the hardware resources required for deployment, but also increase the inference latency, and the method is difficult to be extended to other structures. Furthermore, Wei et al. [21] use quantization and knowledge distillation to train very tiny CNNs for object detection, and this work also has only quantized Conv layers. In contrast, DRGS has no special requirements for network structure, and no special hardware design is required, more versatile and flexible. All these will facilitate us to get better performance directly on more object detection models.

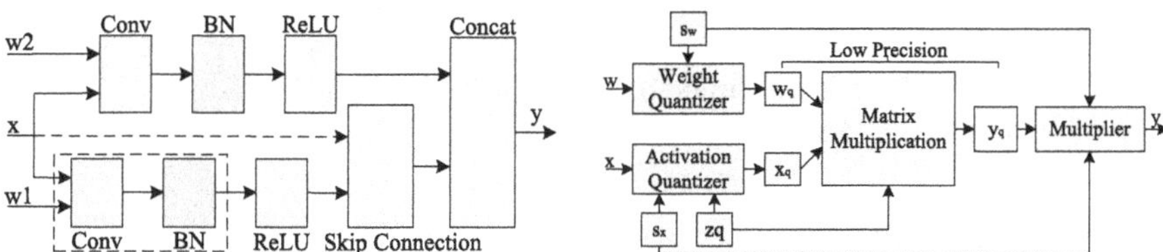

(a) Illustration of a typical block in the object detection network.

(b) Low-precision calculation of a Conv layer.

Fig. 2. Typical block in the detection network and low-precision calculation of a Conv layer. Dotted line indicate optional, and dotted box indicates that the fusion of the Conv and BN layer will be implemented during inference.

3 Methods

In this section, we present the proposed DRGS method in detail. As shown in Fig. 2(a), the combination of Conv, BN, and activation function layers is repeated in object detection models, and other layers that also need to be quantified include Skip Connection, Concat layer, etc. DRGS is able to fully quantize the modules in modern detection networks, allowing dense matrix multiplication to be implemented at low-precision, as shown in Fig. 2(b).

3.1 Weight Quantization

It is observed that the distribution range of the weight tensor varies greatly along the direction of the output channel, and the weights of each layer are mostly symmetrically distributed around zero [12]. In order to achieve fine quantization in each channel, per-channel symmetric quantization should be used for the weights. The formula is as follows.

$$\begin{aligned} w_q &= \left\lfloor clip\left(\frac{w}{s_w}, -2^{b-1}, 2^{b-1}-1\right)\right\rceil \\ \bar{w} &= w_q \cdot s_w \end{aligned} \tag{1}$$

where $\lfloor \cdot \rceil$ represents the rounding function, and the $clip\,(a, b, c)$ function clamps the input a to the range $[b, c]$. w denotes the weights in the weight tensor, and b represents the quantization bit width. w_q, an integer scaled representation of the quantized weight, and $\bar{w}$, a quantized representation of the w at the same scale as origin weight data. There is only one quantization parameter in the weight quantizer, s_w, which is a scaling factor and also a learnable parameter based on the training loss. The calculation of its gradient will be introduced in Sect. 3.4. He et al. [7] argued that the weights approximate the Gaussian distribution, and inspired by this argument, we propose an initialization scheme for s_w with practical value.

$$
\begin{aligned}
s_{w_{init}} &= \frac{\max(|\mu - 3\sigma|, |\mu + 3\sigma|)}{2^{b-1} - 1} \\
s_{w_{\text{init}}}{}^{t} &= \beta \cdot s_{w_{\text{init}}}{}^{t-1} + (1 - \beta) \cdot s_{w_{\text{init}}}{}^{t}
\end{aligned} \tag{2}
$$

where μ and σ denote the mean and standard deviation of the weights, respectively. Equation(2) indicates that the initial value will be determined after a few iterations by exponential moving average(EMA), where the β is set to 0.9. t is the time step.

3.2 Activation Quantization and Floating-Point Free Inference

Activation Quantization. To avoid introducing more computations by quantization, we use per-layer asymmetric quantization of the activation. And unlike most of previous works about quantization, we propose DRGS to quantize the detect model from the input to the output of the final detection head, as well as the input of the sigmoid function in the post-processing. This allows us to replace the hardware-unfriendly exponential operations with table lookups. The formula is as follows.

$$
\begin{aligned}
x_q &= \left\lfloor clip\left(\frac{x}{s_x} + zp, 0, 2^b - 1\right)\right\rceil, zp = \left\lfloor clip\left(\frac{-zf}{s_x}, 0, 2^b - 1\right)\right\rceil \\
\bar{x} &= (x_q - zp) \cdot s_x
\end{aligned} \tag{3}
$$

x denotes the input activation, x_q and $\bar{x}$ are the same as the weight quantization. The difference is that since the activation are quantized asymmetrically, each quantizer has two quantization parameters, zp and s_x. zp denotes the zero point, which has the same data type as the values x_q, and is in fact the quantized x_q corresponding to the real value 0, this enables us to automatically satisfy the requirement that the real value $x = 0$ can be accurately represented by a quantized value. These two quantization parameters are also learnable parameters, and for this purpose it is necessary to update zp with a real domain value instead of zp, which is represented by zf in Eq. (3). These two parameters are initialized as follows.

$$
s_{x_{\text{init}}} = \frac{x_{\max} - x_{\min}}{2^b - 1}, zf_{\text{init}} = x_{\min} \tag{4}
$$

We still initialize via EMA, but note that to eliminate the effect of outliers in the activation, $x_{\min}$ and $x_{\max}$ are taken from the activation according to the percentage $(1 - \gamma)$ and γ, here $\gamma = 0.999$.

Floating-Point Free Inference. After quantizing the weights and activation, as shown in Fig. 2(b), the expensive floating-point operations can be replaced with efficient low-precision operations, as follows.

$$
\begin{aligned}
s_{x_{\text{out}}}(x_{q_{\text{out}}} - zp_{\text{out}}) &= (w_q \cdot s_w) \cdot (x_{q_{\text{in}}} - zp_{\text{in}}) \cdot s_{x_{\text{in}}} \\
x_{q_{\text{out}}} &= \frac{s_w \cdot s_{x_{\text{in}}}}{s_{x_{\text{out}}}}(w_q \cdot x_{q_{\text{in}}} - w_q \cdot zp_{\text{in}}) + zp_{\text{out}}
\end{aligned} \tag{5}
$$

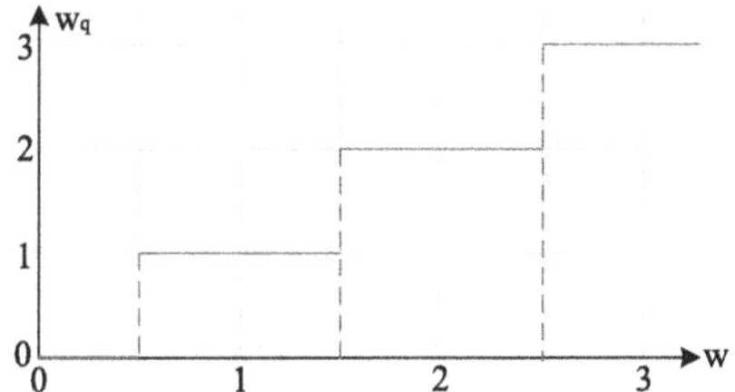

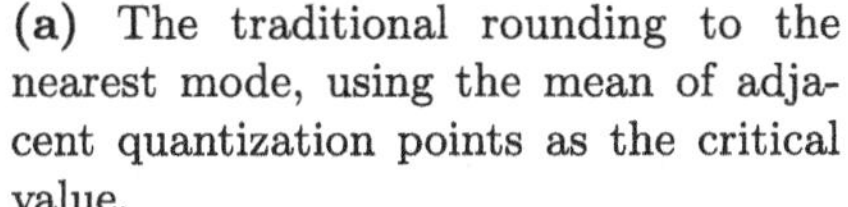

(a) The traditional rounding to the nearest mode, using the mean of adjacent quantization points as the critical value.

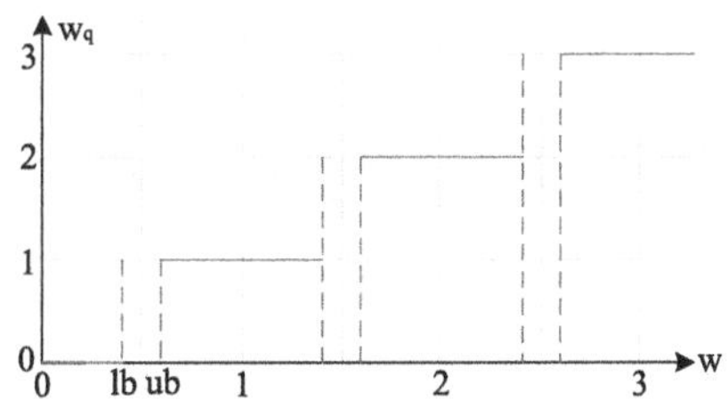

(b) Dynamic rounding with critical rounding intervals, *lb* and *ub* are both critical values of CRI, distributed around the mean of adjacent quantization points.

Fig. 3. Traditional rounding to the nearest and dynamic rounding with CRI.

Although the activation are asymmetrically quantized, the $w_q \cdot zp_{\text{in}}$ term can be precomputed, which does not cause additional computation in inference; meanwhile, $\frac{s_w \cdot s_{x_{\text{in}}}}{s_{x_{\text{out}}}}$ can be converted to fixed-point multiplications, therefore complete floating-point-free inference is realized.

3.3 Dynamic Rounding

As mentioned above, rounding to the nearest is not the best way to round for each weight. Therefore we propose a method of dynamically selecting the rounding mode. Observing Fig. 3(b), the weights located in the (lb, ub) interval are often extremely prone to changing between the two rounding modes even for a very small update, thus making the corresponding quantization values alternating between two adjacent values, causing instability in the quantization-fine-tuning. To solve this problem, we introduce a new concept of critical rounding interval(CRI), the corresponding interval range is (lb, ub). For the weights in CRI, the corresponding rounding mode will be selected based on the direction of the weight update. The quantification scheme of the weights in CRI is as follows.

$$w_q^t = \begin{cases} \lceil w^t \rceil, & \text{if } w^t > w^{t-1} \\ \lfloor w^t \rfloor, & \text{if } w^t < w^{t-1} \end{cases} \tag{6}$$

w^t is the current weight, and w^{t-1} represents the last weight. The proposed dynamic rounding method in DRGS reduces fluctuation of weights in CRI, stabilizing the process of quantization-fine-tuning. Specially, the nearest rounding is a special case of dynamic rounding in DRGS when lb equals to ub in CRI.

3.4 Gradient Scaling

Gradient Calculation of Quantization Parameter. Since the rounding function is not derivable, Straight Though Estimator (STE) [1] is needed to

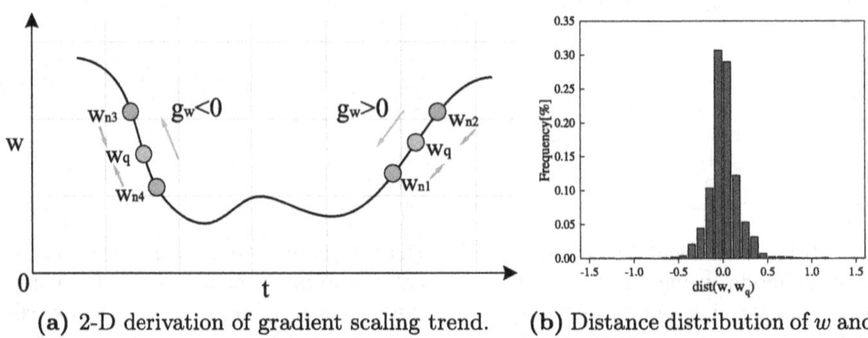

(a) 2-D derivation of gradient scaling trend.

(b) Distance distribution of w and w_q in CRI.

Fig. 4. 2-D derivation of gradient scaling trend and distance distribution of w and w_q in CRI. The distance shown is calculated at the first iteration before fine-tuning and is based on YOLO-v5n [20].

approximate the gradient through the round function. The gradient of the three quantization parameters in DRGS is calculated as follows.

$$\frac{\partial \bar{w}}{\partial s_w} = \begin{cases} \frac{-w}{s_w} + DR\left(\frac{w}{s_w}\right), & \text{if } -2^{b-1} < \frac{w}{s_w} < 2^{b-1} - 1 \\ -2^{b-1} \text{ or } 2^{b-1} - 1, & \text{otherwise} \end{cases}$$
$$\frac{\partial \bar{x}}{\partial s_x} = \begin{cases} -\left(\frac{x}{s_x} + zp\right) + \left\lfloor \frac{x}{s_x} + zp \right\rceil, & \text{if } 0 < \frac{x}{s_x} + zp < 2^b - 1 \\ 0 \text{ or } 2^b - 1, & \text{otherwise} \end{cases} \quad (7)$$
$$\frac{\partial \bar{x}}{\partial zf} = \begin{cases} 0, & \text{if } 0 < \frac{x}{s_x} + zp < 2^b - 1 \\ 1, & \text{otherwise} \end{cases}$$

Where the $DR(\cdot)$ function indicates that each weight will be rounded using the rounding mode chosen at its forward inference.

Gradient Scaling for Weights. The gradient of the quantization parameters requires STE, which propagates the same gradient, $g_w = g_{w_q}$, without considering the value of the weights. This results in that the weights located in the CRI are extremely prone to change of the rounding mode due to an approximate inaccurate gradient falling into a state of frequent alternation between two neighboring quantization points. In order to solve this problem to enable that the weights in CRI can be updated more quickly toward the target quantization points and then be out of this critical interval to obtain a stable rounding mode, the gradient needs to be scaled according to the distance between the weights and the corresponding target quantization points. Based on weight update formula in the gradient descent method, we can obtain the following equation.

$$w^{t+1} = w^t - \eta \cdot g_w \cdot s_g \quad (8)$$

Table 2. RetinaNet 4-bit quantization based on the MS-COCO dataset. FP32 means no quantization.

Model	Method	mAP	$\text{mAP}^{0.5}$	$\text{mAP}^{0.75}$	mAP^{S}	mAP^{M}	mAP^{L}
RetinaNet50	FP32	35.7	52.8	38.3	19	39.8	46.9
RetinaNet50	FQN [12]	32.5	51.5	34.7	17.3	35.6	42.6
RetinaNet50	DRGS	34.6	51.7	37.1	18.2	38.5	46.1
RetianNet18	FP32	31.7	49.9	33.2	16.4	34.8	42.3
RetianNet18	FQN [12]	28.6	46.9	29.9	14.9	31.2	38.7
RetinaNet18	DRGS	30.1	48.2	31.7	15.5	32.8	40.4

Where η denotes the learning rate, w^t represents the current weight, and g_w and s_g are the gradient and gradient scaling factor corresponding to that weight, respectively. Combining with Fig. 4(a), when $g_w > 0$ and $w_{n1} < w_q$, although we want w^{t+1} to increase, we can only retard its decreasing trend because of $g_w > 0$, so we need $s_g < 1$. Similarly, when $g_w > 0$ and $w_{n2} > w_q$, $s_g > 1$ is needed to reduce w^{t+1}. And for $g_w < 0$, $w_{n4} < w_q$, we need $s_g > 1$ to increase w^{t+1}, but for $g_w < 0$ and $w_{n3} > w_q$, although we want w^{t+1} to decrease to approach w_q, since $g_w < 0$, we can only retard its increasing trend, so $s_g < 1$.

Meanwhile it can be seen from Fig. 4(b) that distances between w and w_q in CRI are mostly close to zero, but there are still a few larger values, so we need to reduce this distance appropriately. Heuristically we propose the formula for s_g as follows.

$$\begin{gathered}\operatorname{dist}(w, w_q) = w - w_q \\ s_g = 1 + s_d \cdot \operatorname{sign}(g_w) \cdot \operatorname{dist}(w, w_q) \cdot CRI_{addr}\end{gathered} \tag{9}$$

s_d is the scaling factor of $\operatorname{dist}(w, w_q)$, which is used to scale the distances between w and w_q. In all experiments of this paper, $s_d = 0.2$ is set empirically. $sign(g_w)$ is the sign function, and CRI_{addr} is used to indicate that only the gradient of the weight in the CRI is scaled.

3.5 Other Layers

As shown in Fig. 2(a), the Conv layer is often followed by a BN layer [8], which normalize the input in batch using minibatch statistics μ_{BN} and σ_{BN} to eliminate covariance shifting. When only inference is performed, the computation overhead can be reduced by folding the BN layer into the Conv layer. The fused weights and biases are as follows.

$$\begin{aligned} w_{\text{fold}} &= \frac{w}{\sqrt{\sigma_{BN}^2 + \epsilon}} \cdot \gamma_{BN} \\ b_{\text{fold}} &= \frac{b - \mu_{BN}}{\sqrt{\sigma_{BN}^2 + \epsilon}} \cdot \gamma_{BN} + \beta_{BN} \end{aligned} \tag{10}$$

Table 3. 4-bit quantization of RetinaNet18 with different methods.

Model	Quantizationn method	Activation calibration	mAP
RetinaNet18	FP32 baseline	—	31.7
RetinaNet18	Integer-only [9]	Moving Average	19.7
RetinaNet18	Quant whitepaper [16]	Moving Average	22.6
RetinaNet18	FQN [12]	Percentile	28.6
RetinaNet18	DRGS	Percentile	30.1

where γ_{BN} and β_{BN} parameters are learnable parameters in the quantization fine-tuning. For the max-pooling layer and the upsampling layer using the nearest interpolation, no floating-point operation is introduced and the zp and s_x are not changed. Thus, no special modifications are needed. For the Skip-connection and Concat layer, the quantization is performed by referring to the method in activation quantization [9].

4 Experiments and Results

4.1 Experimental Settings

Datasets. To validate the effectiveness of the DRGS, we carried out extensive experiments on the MS-COCO dataset [14]. The MS-COCO dataset contains 80 object categories of over 200K images and is widely used to benchmark SOTA object detectors because of its rich annotations and challenging scenarios.

Detectors. The detectors we selected include RetinaNet [13] and YOLO [20]. Note that we choose two models with different parameter sizes in the latest version, YOLO-v5nano and YOLO-v5small (YOLO-v5n and YOLO-v5s for short). We do not modify any structure of the network, and all activation functions use ReLU. All detectors were trained based on MS-COCO.

Full-Precision Training Details. For RetinaNet, the total batchsize is 8 with 4 workers, the initial learning rate is 1e–4, at the 8th and 12th epoch multiplied by 0.1. For fair comparison [12], the short edges of all images are adjusted to 800 in training and evaluation. For YOLO-v5, all training settings are officially consistent.

Quantization-Fine-Tuning. Quantization-fine-tuning is initialized by a full-precision model, the weights and activations of all layers are quantized to 4-bit or below except for the first and last layer, which are quantized to 8-bit [9,12,23]. Without loss of generality, we empirically set the CRI with $lb = 0.45$, $ub = 0.55$. With RetinaNet, the initial learning rate drops 10x, the batchsize is halved, and other settings remain unchanged. For YOLO-v5, the quantization parameters are trained using the Adam optimizer, and the batchsize is set to 32 which is half of the full precision. The initial learning rate also differs for different quantization

Table 4. Results of YOLO-v5n and YOLO-v5s at different bit widths. W/A denotes the quantization bit width of weight and activation.

Model	W/A				
	32/32	2/2	3/3	4/4	8/8
YOLO-v5n	26.5 mAP	8.6 mAP	17.9 mAP	22.9 mAP	27.1 mAP
YOLO-v5s	36.5 mAP	18.7 mAP	29.7 mAP	33.4 mAP	36.3 mAP

bit widths of the two models. For YOLO-v5n, the initial learning rate is 3e–4, 3.5e–4, 4e–4 corresponding to 4-bit, 3-bit and 2-bit quantization respectively. For YOLO-v5s, the learning rate is 1.5e–4, 2e–4, 3e–4 respectively. In addition, we use only 100 epochs (1/3 of baseline) for fine-tuning.

4.2 Results on RetinaNet and YOLO-v5

Results on RetinaNet. We first apply DRGS to RetinaNet using 4bit quantization, the results are shown in Table 2. For 4-bit RetinaNet with ResNet50 backbone, DRGS only suffers a 1.1% mAP loss while the references suffers 3.2% lost compared to full-precision floating point 32bit baseline. Table 2 shows that DRGS has about 2× less quantization loss with different backbones compared to FQN [12].

As shown in Table 3, we compared DRGS method with several existing full quantization algorithms, among which there are two different activation calibration methods, namely Moving Average and Percentile method. It can be seen that our proposed DRGS clearly exceeds these references in mAP loss, our method has quantization loss 1.6% while references have 3.1%, 9.1%, 12%.

Results on YOLO-v5. We carry out quantization experiments applying DRGS with a wide range of quantization bit widths to YOLO-v5n and YOLO-v5s, in order to explore the impact of quantization width and model size. As shown in Table 4, the 8-bit full quantization result of YOLO-v5n is actually 0.6% mAP higher than FP32 baseline, which reflects the excellent results of DRGS on small

Table 5. Quantization results of different methods on YOLO-v5. [a] represents non-full-quantization. [b] indicates that YOLO-v5m uses 8-bit quantization.

Method	Model	W/A	FP32 Baseline	Accuracy
Integer-only [9]	YOLO-v5n	4/4	26.5 mAP	12.5 mAP
FQN [12]	YOLO-v5n	4/4	26.5 mAP	19.4 mAP
DRGS	YOLO-v5n	4/4	26.5 mAP	22.9 mAP
Log-scale [5][ab]	YOLO-v5m	8/8	62.5 $mAP^{0.5}$	61.7 $mAP^{0.5}$
DRGS[b]	YOLO-v5m	8/8	62.5 $mAP^{0.5}$	62.4 $mAP^{0.5}$

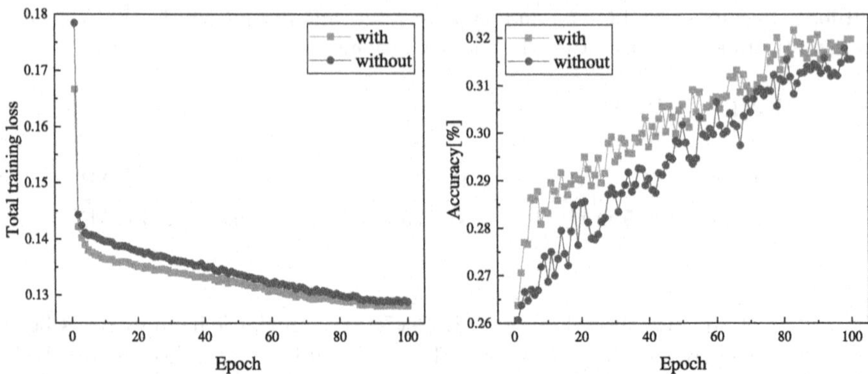

Fig. 5. The total loss and accuracy during training with and without DRGS(the first two cases in Table 6). In YOLO-v5s, the losses include *cls* loss, *box* loss, and *obj* loss, and the inference accuracy during training is 1–2% lower than that during validation [20].

models. Table 4 also shows that quantization less than 4-bit input/4-bit weight might not be useful due to heavy loss suffered in detection accuracy. Interestingly at 4-bit input/4-bit weight or lower, the accuracy loss caused by quantization is smaller for YOLO-v5s than for YOLO-v5n in all quantization experiments. We speculate that this is caused by the higher redundancy of YOLO-v5s, which has four times more parameters than YOLO-v5n's about 1.9 million parameters.

Table 5 shows the comparison of different quantization methods. We can see that our proposed DRGS quantizes significantly better than the other two full quantization algorithms for the 4-bit quantization of YOLO-v5n. We can also see that the nonlinear logarithmic quantization algorithm [5], although it quantizes only the Conv layers with complex logarithm method, has accuracy loss 8X higher than DRGS (0.8% vs 0.1% loss).

4.3 Discussion

Analysis on Dynamic Rounding and Gradient Scaling. To verify the effect of Dynamic Rounding and Gradient Scaling in DRGS, we carried out

Table 6. YOLO-v5s 4-bit and 8-bit quantization *with* or *without* Dynamic Rounding and Gradient Scaling.

Model	W/A	Dynamic rounding & gradient scaling	mAP
YOLO-v5s	4/4	*with*	33.4 mAP
YOLO-v5s	4/4	*without*	33.0 mAP
YOLO-v5s	8/8	*with*	36.3 mAP
YOLO-v5s	8/8	*without*	36.1 mAP

Table 7. YOLO-v5s 4-bit quantization experiment under different CRI Settings. *lb* and *ub* denote the boundaries of CRI.

Model	W/A	*lb*	*ub*	mAP
YOLO-v5s	4/4	0.35	0.65	32.7 mAP
YOLO-v5s	4/4	0.45	0.55	33.4 mAP
YOLO-v5s	4/4	0.50	0.50	33.0 mAP

experiments based on YOLO-v5s, and the results are shown in Table 6. It can be seen that Dynamic Rounding and Gradient Scaling have more significant optimization effects at lower precision quantization. Figure 5 shows the total loss and accuracy during training with and without DRGS(the first two cases in Table 6). It can be seen from Fig. 5 that the training with DRGS yields higher accuracy and has faster convergence speed compared to the training without DRGS. Also, we believe that DRGS can benefit object detection schemes in similar ways.

Analysis on Lb and Ub of CRI. As mentioned in the previous experimental settings, we empirically chose lb and ub in CRI, and to verify the effect of this setting, we carried out three sets of quantization experiments, as shown in Table 7. Obviously, the second setting is significantly better than the other two. Also, it should be noted that $lb = ub = 0.5$ in the third setting, which means that there is no effect of DRGS since we only perform gradient scaling for the weights located in the CRI.

5 Conclusion

In this paper, we propose DRGS, a low-precision full quantization method with BN folding, which combines dynamic rounding and gradient scaling to obtain higher accuracy and stability, and finally achieve floating-point-free inference. We carried out extensive experiments on two complex object detection tasks and achieved SOTA quantization results, even on YOLO-v5, which is widely used and known for its run-time low latency and efficiency. We believe that DRGS can be an effective alternative for low-precision full quantization of complex tasks, and we will explore hybrid-precision quantization on complex tasks to further improve quantization performance.

Acknowledgement. This work was partly supported by the National Key R&D Program of China under grant No. 2019YFB2204800.

References

1. Bengio, Y., Léonard, N., Courville, A.: Estimating or propagating gradients through stochastic neurons for conditional computation. arXiv preprint arXiv:1308.3432 (2013)

2. Bhalgat, Y., Lee, J., Nagel, M., Blankevoort, T., Kwak, N.: LSQ+: improving low-bit quantization through learnable offsets and better initialization. In: Proceedings of the IEEE/CVF Conference on Computer Vision and Pattern Recognition Workshops, pp. 696–697 (2020)
3. Chen, P., Liu, J., Zhuang, B., Tan, M., Shen, C.: AQD: towards accurate quantized object detection. In: Proceedings of the IEEE/CVF Conference on Computer Vision and Pattern Recognition, pp. 104–113 (2021)
4. Chin, H.H., Tsay, R.S., Wu, H.I.: A high-performance adaptive quantization approach for edge CNN applications. arXiv preprint arXiv:2107.08382 (2021)
5. Choi, D., Kim, H.: Hardware-friendly log-scale quantization for CNNs with activation functions containing negative values. In: 2021 18th International SoC Design Conference (ISOCC), pp. 415–416. IEEE (2021)
6. Gong, R., et al.: Differentiable soft quantization: Bridging full-precision and low-bit neural networks. In: Proceedings of the IEEE/CVF International Conference on Computer Vision, pp. 4852–4861 (2019)
7. He, Z., Fan, D.: Simultaneously optimizing weight and quantizer of ternary neural network using truncated gaussian approximation. In: Proceedings of the IEEE/CVF Conference on Computer Vision and Pattern Recognition, pp. 11438–11446 (2019)
8. Ioffe, S., Szegedy, C.: Batch normalization: Accelerating deep network training by reducing internal covariate shift. In: International Conference on Machine Learning, pp. 448–456. PMLR (2015)
9. Jacob, B., et al.: Quantization and training of neural networks for efficient integer-arithmetic-only inference. In: Proceedings of the IEEE Conference on Computer Vision and Pattern Recognition, pp. 2704–2713 (2018)
10. Jain, S., Gural, A., Wu, M., Dick, C.: Trained quantization thresholds for accurate and efficient fixed-point inference of deep neural networks. In: Proceedings of Machine Learning and Systems, vol. 2, pp. 112–128 (2020)
11. Kim, J., Bhalgat, Y., Lee, J., Patel, C., Kwak, N.: QKD: quantization-aware knowledge distillation. arXiv preprint arXiv:1911.12491 (2019)
12. Li, R., Wang, Y., Liang, F., Qin, H., Yan, J., Fan, R.: Fully quantized network for object detection. In: Proceedings of the IEEE/CVF Conference on Computer Vision and Pattern Recognition, pp. 2810–2819 (2019)
13. Lin, T.Y., Goyal, P., Girshick, R., He, K., Dollár, P.: Focal loss for dense object detection. In: Proceedings of the IEEE International Conference on Computer Vision, pp. 2980–2988 (2017)
14. Lin, T., et al.: Microsoft COCO: common objects in context. In: Fleet, D., Pajdla, T., Schiele, B., Tuytelaars, T. (eds.) ECCV 2014. LNCS, vol. 8693, pp. 740–755. Springer, Cham (2014). https://doi.org/10.1007/978-3-319-10602-1_48
15. Nagel, M., Amjad, R.A., Van Baalen, M., Louizos, C., Blankevoort, T.: Up or down? Adaptive rounding for post-training quantization. In: International Conference on Machine Learning, pp. 7197–7206. PMLR (2020)
16. Nagel, M., Fournarakis, M., Amjad, R.A., Bondarenko, Y., van Baalen, M., Blankevoort, T.: A white paper on neural network quantization. arXiv preprint arXiv:2106.08295 (2021)
17. Redmon, J., Divvala, S., Girshick, R., Farhadi, A.: You only look once: Unified, real-time object detection. In: Proceedings of the IEEE Conference on Computer Vision and Pattern Recognition, pp. 779–788 (2016)
18. Ren, S., He, K., Girshick, R., Sun, J.: Faster r-CNN: towards real-time object detection with region proposal networks. In: 28th Proceedings of Conference on Advances in Neural Information Processing Systems (2015)

19. Wang, E., et al.: Deep neural network approximation for custom hardware: where we've been, where we're going. ACM Comput. Surv. **52**(2), 1–39 (2019)
20. YOLO-v5. https://doi.org/10.5281/zenodo.5563715.. Accessed 16 Dec 2020
21. Wei, Y., Pan, X., Qin, H., Ouyang, W., Yan, J.: Quantization mimic: towards very tiny CNN for object detection. In: Proceedings of the European conference on computer vision (ECCV), pp. 267–283 (2018)
22. Zhang, D., Yang, J., Ye, D., Hua, G.: LQ-nets: learned quantization for highly accurate and compact deep neural networks. In: Ferrari, V., Hebert, M., Sminchisescu, C., Weiss, Y. (eds.) ECCV 2018. LNCS, vol. 11212, pp. 373–390. Springer, Cham (2018). https://doi.org/10.1007/978-3-030-01237-3_23
23. Zhao, X., Wang, Y., Cai, X., Liu, C., Zhang, L.: Linear symmetric quantization of neural networks for low-precision integer hardware. In: ICLR (2020)
24. Zou, Z., Shi, Z., Guo, Y., Ye, J.: Object detection in 20 years: a survey. arXiv preprint arXiv:1905.05055 (2019)

Emotion Recognition Based on Multi-scale Convolutional Neural Network

Zeen Wang(✉)

Xiamen No. 1 High School of Fujian, Xiamen, China
zayn71ie.blazender@gmail.com

Abstract. The Convolutional neural network is one of the most mature models used in deep learning technology and have achieved a series of remarkable results in cross-domain research. It has become a hot research topic to apply Convolutional neural network (CNN) to emotion recognition based on EEG signals. Although many researchers have used experiments showing that CNNs have good results for emotion recognition, they ignore the individual differences of subjects and the time differences of the same subject. Then we propose the 1D multi-scale CNN in this paper that can effectively solve individual differences and temporal differences with optimal scale convolution, which solves restrictions of the results when classifying. The experiments on public DEAP dataset show that the 1D multi-scale CNN proposed outperforms other existing models.

Keywords: Emotion recognition · Multi-scale Kernels · EEG · Convolutional neural network

1 Introduction

Emotion is the corresponding behavioral responses following the experience of human attitudes towards objective things, affecting human perceptions, decision making and interpersonal interactions, and play an important role in daily life [7]. Therefore, research on the recognition of emotion has been triggered in computer science, healthcare, and human-computer interaction [5,23]. As an important research direction in cross-cutting areas, several researchers have classified different emotions through human-computer interaction based on emotional artificial intelligence [17,24,31]. Especially, based on EEG signals, the methods of recognizing emotion have turned into a hot research direction because they can objectively and accurately respond to the real emotion of the subjects.

With the great success of deep learning in many fields such as speech recognition, computer vision, and natural language processing, many researchers have also applied deep learning to emotion recognition based on EEG signals. For example, some researchers based on deep learning have shown experimentally that emotion recognition gives good results in the field of brain-computer

Y. Tan and Y. Shi (Eds.): DMBD 2022, CCIS 1744, pp. 152–164, 2022.
https://doi.org/10.1007/978-981-19-9297-1_12

interface [35,36]. Convolutional neural networks, the most widely used of deep learning methods, have the ability to learn directly from EEG data. It has shown excellent results in brain-computer interface systems [15,20,25]. Specifically, both Schirrmeister and Lawhern et al. used 1D single-scale convolution kernels to extract temporal and spatial information from the EEG [15,27]. Considering the need to address the problem of capturing temporal dynamics and spatial asymmetry in EEG due to its non-stationary and dynamic nature, Ding et al., proposed a one-dimensional multi-scale TSception model for convolutional neural networks (CNNs) to achieve more accurate emotion classification [6]. It is now shown that there are temporal differences and individual differences in EEG [13]. There is a lack of research in CNN model-based emotion recognition for the problem of individual differences and temporal differences. Since it is difficult to determine the optimal scale convolution for individual differences and temporal differences for emotion recognition classification, it makes the accuracy of emotion recognition classification challenging.

To solve the above challenges, this paper proposes a new end-to-end deep learning model: 1D multi-scale Emotion Convolutional Neural Network (ECNN). Our ECNN has 5 parallel EEG's Emotional Networks (EENs), consisting of multi-scale convolutional kernel sizes. The main contributions of this paper are summarized in three aspects as follows:

(1) Based on parallel processing, we propose a 1D multi-scale convolutional model, which is able to deal with individual differences of subjects and the time differences of the same subject problems of emotion classification.
(2) We design an end-to-end ECNN model, which can effectively decode the original EEG signal without any preprocessing (including filtering) and can be transfer to other disciplines for research with broad practical application prospects.
(3) We conduct experiments on the publicly available DEAP dataset, and the experimental results show that our model outperforms other baseline models.

2 Related Work

In the field of affective computing, a lot of research has been conducted on emotion recognition based on different data. Since physiological signals can accurately and objectively reflect the real emotion of the subject, while EEG signals because the subject cannot be subjectively controlled. Therefore, it can more accurately represent the inner emotional state than signals such as voice facial expressions, thus becoming a research hotspot for emotion recognition.

Earlier, Bahari et al., used a recursive graph-based nearest neighbor classification algorithm (kNN) with a nonlinear model k to identify different emotions [4]. Wang et al., used a support vector machine (SVM) classification algorithm based on frequency features for emotion classification [30]. However, traditional machine learning techniques have feature design and feature selection limitations.

With the rapid development of deep learning, some researchers have found that deep learning can address the deficiencies in traditional machine learning techniques, thus applying deep learning to EEG emotion recognition. For example, Alarcao and Mahmud et al., used deep learning methods in emotion recognition tasks [1,19]. Song et al., proposed a multi-channel EEG based on a new dynamic graph convolution neural network (DGCNN) in order to improve the emotion recognition performance of EEG. The model used the learned adjacency matrix to improve the ability of more discriminating features [28]. Kim et al., summarized the computational method of EEG-based emotion estimation by a related previous study, and showed the EEG-based emotion recognition computational model is valid and feasible [22].

Research based on deep learning models from EEG signals for emotion recognition has been mainly through the following three dimensions of feature extraction: (1) Frequency feature extraction dimension: Zheng et al., proposed the deep belief network (DBN), which used differential entropy (DE) features to identify emotion. The research showed that the DE feature extracted from EEG signals is a stable and accurate classification method [38]. Yang et al., proposed a hierarchical network using DE features of five frequency bands to identify different emotions [33]. (2) Temporal feature extraction dimension: Alhagry et al., showed experimentally that good results were obtained by using two-layer LSTM with EEG signals as input [2]. Ma et al., proposed a multi-modal residual LSTM model (MMResLSTM) with temporal weights shared across multiple modalities [18]. (3) Spatial feature extraction dimension: Li et al., designed EEG-based 2D images, a layered CNN for extracting spatial information between different channels [16]. Mei and Kwon et al., used a 2D CNN model for extracting and classifying features [21,34]. Yang et al., research showed that 2D CNN module and LSTM module extract spatial and temporal features respectively. In addition, it also combined the corresponding features for classification, it achieved a relatively high accuracy in the emotion recognition task [32]. However, the 2D conventional method ignores the spatial characteristics of the EEG signal. Therefore, Jia et al., proposed HetEmotionNet, a dual-stream heterogeneous graph recurrent neural network fusing multi-modal physiological signals, to exploit the complementarity between spatio-temporal domain features for emotion recognition [12]. Salama et al., also proposed a 3D CNN model considering that the model of 2D CNN ignores the spatial features of EEG signals. This model added a spatio-temporal feature extraction method for EEG signal spatio-temporal feature extraction and classification. The 3D CNN model was shown to be superior to other methods for emotion recognition by experimental data [26]. Jia et al., designed a model that integrates spatial-spectral-temporal features simultaneously into a unified network framework that leverages discriminative local patterns between different EEG features and features targeting different emotions to pair recognize emotion, a novel SST-EmotionNet based on a 3D dense network of spatio-temporal attention [8]. Zhao et al., also proposed a 3D CNN model for automatic extraction of spatio-temporal features of EEG signals, preprocessed by relocating the electrode topology and baseline signals, which has a high accuracy for emotion recognition [37].

So far, although existing emotion recognition methods have achieved high accuracy, the importance of addressing is temporal differences and individual differences has been overlooked. To fill this research gap, in this paper we design a 1D multi-scale CNN with the main purpose of using to study emotion recognition by 1D CNNs and thus compare the accuracy of emotion recognition.

3 One-dimensional Multi-scale Emotional CNN Model

CNN is a deep neural network model consisting of three network layers: convolutional layer, downsampling layer, and fully connected layer. Each EEN consists of an Emotion Multi-scale module and a Residual module. Overall framework of the proposed ECNN model as shown in Fig. 1.

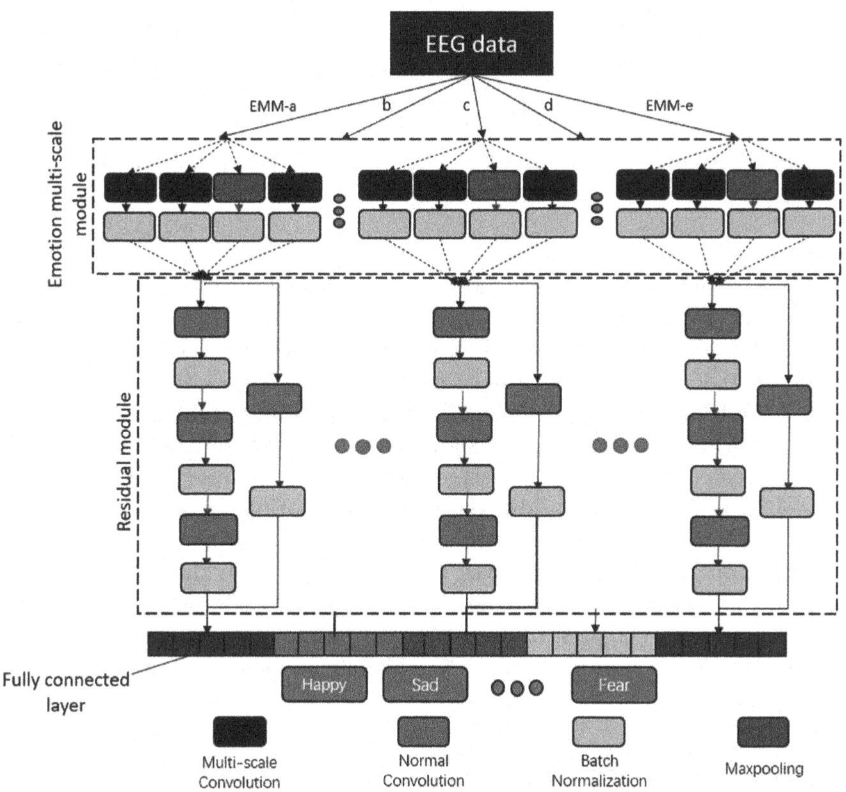

Fig. 1. General framework of the proposed ECNN model. To be more specific, our ECNN includes 5 parallel EENs

As shown in Fig. 2. and Fig. 3: the horizontal axis indicates the size of different convolution kernels, and the vertical axis is the degree of accuracy. Figure 2: Individual A has the highest degree of accuracy of 0.84 at a convolution kernel size of 45. As for individual B, the accuracy was 0.93 at a convolution kernel

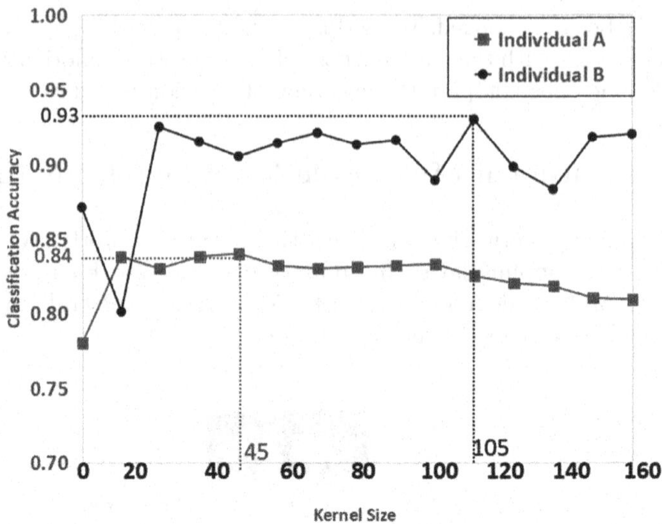

Fig. 2. Subject difference: classification accuracy of two different subjects with different kernel size.

size of 105, which reached the highest degree. This shows that the classification results of different individuals are influenced by the size of the convolution kernel. Figure 3: The same individual with a convolutional kernel size of 15 and a precision of 0.86 within time period 1 to the highest degree, and a convolutional kernel size of 55 and a precision of 0.88 within time period 2 to the highest degree. Figure 2 and Fig. 3 further show that the results of emotion recognition using different convolutional kernels are different. In summary, there is temporal differences and individual differences in the emotion recognition task. Since the optimal scale convolution varies with individual differences and temporal differences, our ECNN model solves the problem of individual differences and temporal differences by multi-scale convolution: all EEN branches use different convolution kernel sizes (different scales). To improve the noise immunity, ELU function is adopted in our ECNN, which avoid using the traditional RELU function [13].

3.1 Emotional Multi-scale Module

To increase the convolutional kernel size in parallel, our ECNN model utilizes Emotion Multi-scale modules (EMM) a-e EEN in order to achieve multi-scale convolution. We devise the Emotion Multi-scale module, mainly derived from the classical inception network [29]. Each Emotion Multi-scale module has 4 parts, where have multi-scale 1D convolution and pooling operations. Figure 4

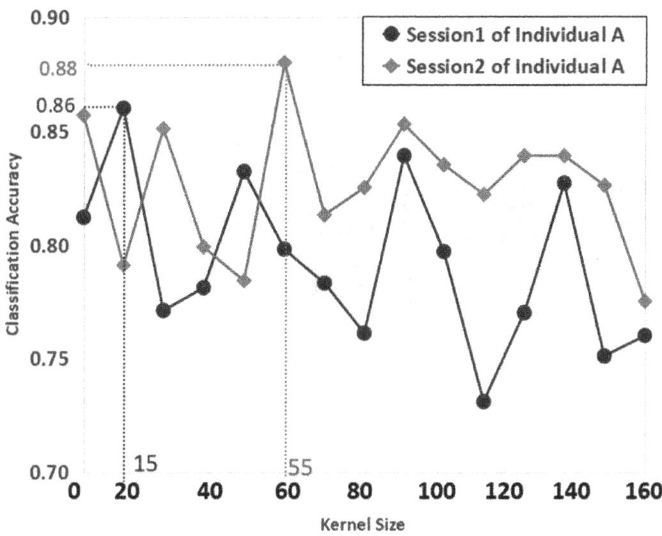

Fig. 3. Time difference: classification accuracy of two different sessions of Subject A with different kernel size.

shows the structure of Emotion Multi-scale module-a. The specific data of each convolution kernel is shown in Table 1.

Table 1. Summary of relevant information of convolution kernel data.

EMM	Kernel size
a	1 ∗ 10 1 ∗ 15 1 ∗ 20
b	1 ∗ 45 1 ∗ 50 1 ∗ 55
c	1 ∗ 65 1 ∗ 70 1 ∗ 75
d	1 ∗ 85 1 ∗ 90 1 ∗ 95
e	1 ∗ 100 1 ∗ 105 1 ∗ 110

The kernel size increases gradually in all Emotion Multi-scale modules. The Emotion Multi-scale module process is defined as:

$$Y = [q^p_{j=1,k} * x; Y = q^p_{j=2,k} * x; Y = q^p_{j=3,k} * x; F_{maxpooling}(x)] \tag{1}$$

where Y is the output of the Emotion Multi-scale module in different EENs. $Y \in R^{T' \times C'}, p \in [a, b, c, d, e]$ in the Emotion Multi-scale module, with five branches in q_j. $q^p_{j,k}*$ denotes the convolution operation, x denotes the input sample.

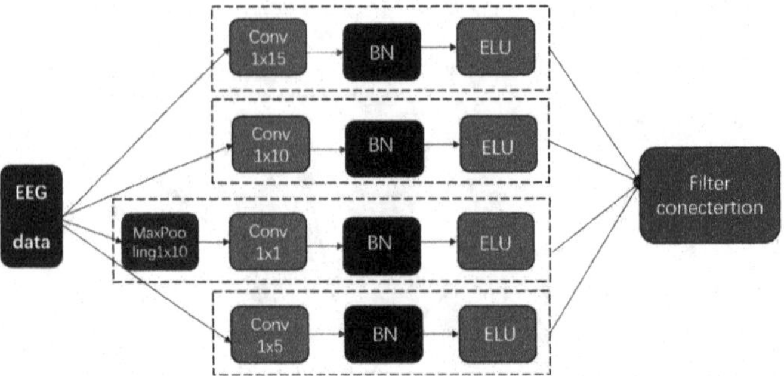

Fig. 4. Structure of emotion multi-scale module-a (EMM-a). Emotion multi-scale module-a has four parts, three of which are multi-scale convolutional layers, and one is a pooling layer.

3.2 Residual Module

Network degradation might happen when the network layers number is increasing [25]. In order to solve such a problem, a Residual module is used as shown in Fig. 5.

Every Residual module includes two branches: first branch performs a series of layers interleaved with 1D convolutional and batch normalization (BN) layers, and obtains the output $F_{res}(X)$; second branch inserts a shortcut connection. Final output are able to be formed after that these branches are combined, which can be defined as:

$$U_p = F_{res}(X) + X \tag{2}$$

where U_p represents outputs of Residual modules and X represents inputs. We can extract these features from shallow layers, and then transfer them to layers that are deeper. As a result, the Residual module solves the problem of degrading to a large extent.

4 Experiment

4.1 Dataset

The DEAP dataset used physiological signals for the analysis of human emotional states. There were 32 subjects who watched music videos while their physiological signals of EEG, facial expressions, and skin current response (GSR) were recorded. Each subject participated in a total of 40 trials. The duration of each trial was 1 min, with a pre-trial baseline of 3 s (each signal recording was preceded by a 3-s silent period). After each trial, subjects promptly self-assessed their own emotional state on the self-assessment manikins (SAM) questionnaire on 4 dimensions of potency, arousal, dominance, and liking, with 9 scales for each dimension. The EEG is acquired using a 32-channel device with a sampling rate 512 Hz 128 Hz resampling (official pre-processed resampling data is provided).

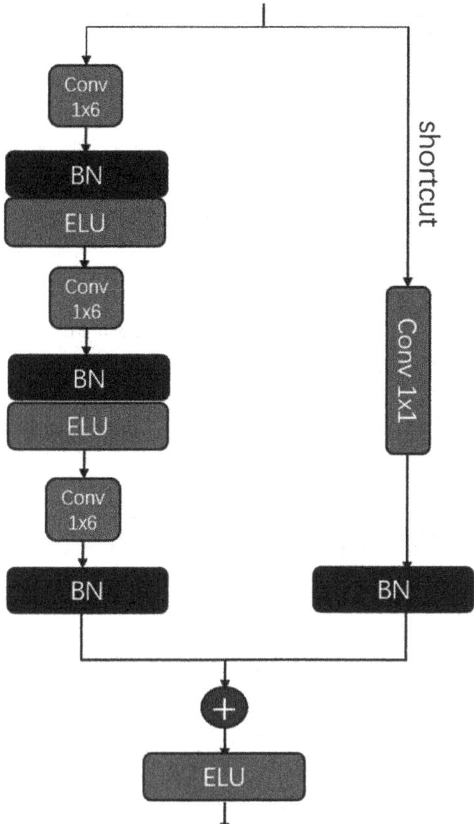

Fig. 5. Structure of the residual module.

4.2 Pre-processing

For DEAP, because each segment of signal recording was preceded by 3 s of silence, a 3 s pre-test baseline is removed for each trial. Next, the data is down sampled 512 Hz 128 Hz, and then the electrooculogram is removed with a blind source separation method as in the experimental method of Koelstra et al. A bandpass filter of 4.0–45 Hz is then applied to the raw EEG in order to remove low and high frequency noise [14].

Finally, the EEG channels are averaged to the open reference. In this study, only arousal and valence dimensions are used, with class labels from 1 to 9 for each dimension, and 5 is chosen as the threshold to project the 9 discrete values into the low and high classes of each dimension [3,14]. Deep neural networks have more trainable parameters and therefore a large sample of labeled data is required in order to optimally learn the emotional state representation in the EEG. However, as shown in Table 2, the number of trials in the selected dataset is very small. To overcome this challenge, the data needs to be augmented by

Table 2. Summary of information related to the datasets used in the experiments.

Factor	Value
Subjects	32
Stimuli	Music videos
Trials	40
Trials duration	1 min
EEG channels	32
Sampling rate	512 Hz
Label	Valence/Arousal

dividing each trial into smaller non-overlapping 4s segments. These segments are then used to train the deep neural network.

4.3 Performance Evaluation Indicators

Accuracy is one of the most commonly used evaluation indicators in classification problems [3]. It is the ratio of correctly predicted samples to the total number of samples. For binary classification problems, accuracy can also be defined as:

$$Accuracy = \frac{TP + TN}{TP + FP + TN + FN}$$

where TP is true positive, TN is true negative, FP is false positive, and FN is false negative.

4.4 Baseline Models

We use following baselines:

MLP [9]: This is a general function approximation method that can be used to solve classification problems.

SVM [30]: The least squares support vector machine classification analysis that uses frequency features for emotion classification.

DGCNN [28]: This model multi-channel EEG features based on dynamic graph CNNs performs EEG emotion classification.

SST-EmotionNet [8]: A 3D attention mechanism is designed to adaptively explore discriminative local patterns for EEG emotion recognition by simultaneously integrating spatial-spectral-temporal features into a unified network framework.

HetEmotionNet [12]: Modeling the heterogeneity and correlation between multi-modal signals is a two-stream heterogeneous graph recurrent neural network that incorporates multi-modal physiological signals for emotion recognition.

Table 3. Comparison of the accuracy effects of our ECNN and other baseline models on the DEAP dataset.

Model	Valance (%)	Arousal (%)
MLP	62.31 ± 4.26	65.23 ± 5.02
SVM	71.14 ± 3.36	73.60 ± 4.23
DGCNN	80.14 ± 3.01	81.70 ± 3.46
SST-EmotionNet	81.30 ± 1.55	82.87 ± 2.11
HetEmotionNet	82.72 ± 3.21	82.38 ± 3.73
ECNN (Our method)	83.97 ± 4.13	83.72 ± 3.05

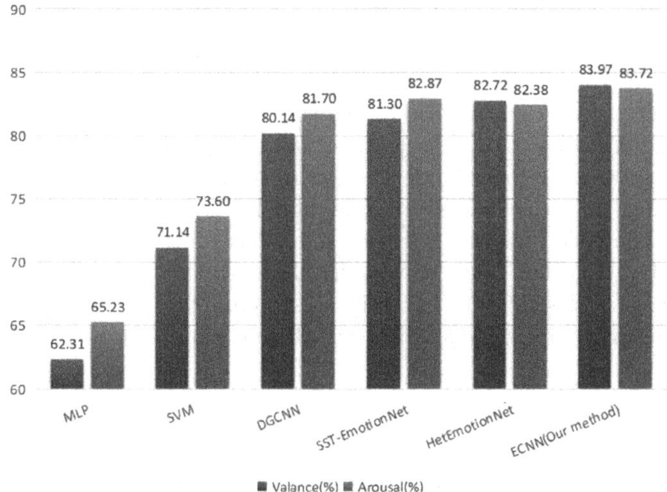

Fig. 6. Comparison of the most accurate results of our ECNN and other baseline models on the DEAP dataset.

4.5 Analysis and Comparison of Results

In this paper, our model is compared with other baseline models based on the DEAP dataset. Table 3 and Fig. 6 show the average precision and standard deviation of these models for the valance and arousal dimensions in EEG-based emotion recognition. The proposed ECNN model achieves the best results on the DEAP dataset. Experimental results show that the deep learning model outperforms the MLP and SVM models. DGCNN considers spatial information of EEG signals collected from different channels and uses graph convolution to extract spatial information with 82.72% and 82.38% accuracy in valance and arousal dimensions. SST-EmotionNet considers spatial, spectral, and temporal features simultaneously and is designed to explore discriminative local patterns adaptively, with the accuracy of valance and arousal dimensions reaching 81.30% and 82.87%, separately. HetEmotionNet models the heterogeneity and correlation between multi-modal signals and makes full use of the different domain between features for emotion recognition. Valance and arousal dimensional accuracies of 82.72% and 82.38% are achieved. ECNN(Our model) takes into account both individual differences and temporal differences. Compared with all the baseline models, the accuracy of our model is further improved, reaching 83.97% and 83.72% accuracy in the valance and arousal dimensions, reaching the optimal level.

5 Conclusion

In this paper, we propose an end-to-end 1D multi-scale CNN as a simple and effective method for emotion recognition based on EEG signals. Our model takes into account the factors of individual difference and time evolution, and successfully overcomes the challenge of the individual differences of subjects and the time differences of the same subject with the optimal convolution scale. We use the public DEAP dataset for systematic evaluation of emotion recognition. From the experimental results, our model is superior to the most advanced model, with good reliability and excellent effect. The model is a general framework for classification of multiple physiological time series based on EEG signals, so we can further apply it to other fields, such as EEG based sleep stage classification and driving fatigue analysis [9–11]. In addition, some popular deep learning methods such as transformer could be applied into the emotion recognition.

References

1. Alarcão, S., Fonseca, M.J.: Emotions recognition using EEG signals: a survey. Affective Computing, IEEE Trans. Affct. Comput. **10**, 374–393 (2017)
2. Alhagry, S., Aly, A., Reda, A.: Emotion recognition based on EEG using LSTM recurrent neural network. Int. J. Adv. Comput. Sci. Appl. **8**(10) (2017)
3. Appriou, A., Cichocki, A., Lotte, F.: Modern machine learning algorithms to classify cognitive and affective states from electroencephalography signals. IEEE Syst. Man Cybern. Mag. **6**(3), 29–38 (2020)
4. Bahari, F., Janghorbani, A.: EEG-based emotion recognition using recurrence plot analysis and k nearest neighbor classifier. In: 2013 20th Iranian Conference on Biomedical Engineering (ICBME), pp. 228–233. IEEE (2013)
5. Christian, M., Brendan, A., Anton, N., Guillaume, C.: A survey of affective brain computer interfaces: principles, state-of-the-art, and challenges: Brain-Comput. Interfaces **1**(2), 66–84 (2014)
6. Ding, Y., Robinson, N., Zhang, S., Zeng, Q., Guan, C.: Tsception: capturing temporal dynamics and spatial asymmetry from EEG for emotion recognition. arXiv preprint arXiv:2104.02935 (2021)
7. Dolan, R.J.: Emotion, cognition, and behavior. Science **298**(5596), 1191–1194 (2002)
8. Jia, Z., Lin, Y., Cai, X., Chen, H., Gou, H., Wang, J.: SST-emotionnet: spatial-spectral-temporal based attention 3d dense network for EEG emotion recognition. In: MM '20: The 28th ACM International Conference on Multimedia (2020)

9. Jia, Z., et al.: Multi-view spatial-temporal graph convolutional networks with domain generalization for sleep stage classification. In: International Conference of the IEEE Engineering in Medicine and Biology Society (2021)
10. Jia, Z., Cai, X., Jiao, Z.: Multi-modal physiological signals based squeeze-and-excitation network with domain adversarial learning for sleep staging. IEEE Sens. J. **22**(4), 3464–3471 (2022)
11. Jia, Z., Ji, J., Zhou, X., Zhou, Y.: Hybrid spiking neural network for sleep electroencephalogram signals. Sci. China Inf. Sci. **65**(4), 1–10 (2022)
12. Jia, Z., Lin, Y., Wang, J., Feng, Z., Xie, X., Chen, C.: Hetemotionnet: two-stream heterogeneous graph recurrent neural network for multi-modal emotion recognition. In: Proceedings of the 29th ACM International Conference on Multimedia, pp. 1047–1056 (2021)
13. Jia, Z., Lin, Y., Wang, J., Yang, K., Liu, T., Zhang, X.: MMCNN: a multi-branch multi-scale convolutional neural network for motor imagery classification. In: Hutter, F., Kersting, K., Lijffijt, J., Valera, I. (eds.) ECML PKDD 2020. LNCS (LNAI), vol. 12459, pp. 736–751. Springer, Cham (2021). https://doi.org/10.1007/978-3-030-67664-3_44
14. Koelstra, S.: Deap: A database for emotion analysis; using physiological signals. IEEE Trans. Affect. Comput. **3**, 18–31 (2012)
15. Lawhern, V.J., Solon, A.J., Waytowich, N.R., Gordon, S.M., Hung, C.P., Lance, B.J.: EegNet: a compact convolutional network for eeg-based brain-computer interfaces. J. Neural Eng. **15**(5), 056013.1-056013.17 (2018)
16. Li, J., Zhang, Z., He, H.: Hierarchical convolutional neural networks for EEG-based emotion recognition. Cogn. Comput. **10**(2), 368–380 (2018)
17. Liu, W., Qiu, J.L., Zheng, W.L., Lu, B.L.: Multimodal emotion recognition using deep canonical correlation analysis. arXiv preprint arXiv:1908.05349 (2019)
18. Ma, J., Tang, H., Zheng, W., Lu, B.: Emotion recognition using multimodal residual LSTM network. In: the 27th ACM International Conference (2019)
19. Mahmud, M., Kaiser, M.S., McGinnity, T.M., Hussain, A.: Deep learning in mining biological data. Cogn. Comput. **13**(1), 1–33 (2021)
20. Mane, R., Robinson, N., Vinod, A., Lee, S., Guan, C.: A multi-view CNN with novel variance layer for motor imagery brain computer interface. In: Annual International Conference of the IEEE Engineering in Medicine and Biology Society. IEEE Engineering in Medicine and Biology Society. Annual International Conference 2020, pp. 2950–2953 (2020)
21. Mei, H., Xu, X.: EEG-based emotion classification using convolutional neural network. In: 2017 International Conference on Security, Pattern Analysis, and Cybernetics (SPAC), pp. 130–135. IEEE (2017)
22. Min-Ki, K., Miyoung, K., Eunmi, O., Sung-Phil, K.: A review on the computational methods for emotional state estimation from the human EEG. Comput. Math. Methods Med. **2013**, 573734 (2013)
23. Nijboer, F., Morin, F.O., Carmien, S.P., Koene, R.A., Leon, E., Hoffmann, U.: Affective brain-computer interfaces: psychophysiological markers of emotion in healthy persons and in persons with amyotrophic lateral sclerosis. In: 2009 3rd International Conference on Affective Computing and Intelligent Interaction and Workshops, pp. 1–11. IEEE (2009)
24. Qiu, J.L., Li, X.Y., Hu, K.: Correlated attention networks for multimodal emotion recognition. In: 2018 IEEE International Conference on Bioinformatics and Biomedicine (BIBM), pp. 2656–2660. IEEE (2018)

25. Robinson, N., Lee, S.W., Guan, C.: EEG representation in deep convolutional neural networks for classification of motor imagery. In: 2019 IEEE International Conference on Systems, Man and Cybernetics (SMC), pp. 1322–1326. IEEE (2019)
26. Salama, E.S., El-Khoribi, R.A., Shoman, M.E., Shalaby, M.A.W.: EEG-based emotion recognition using 3d convolutional neural networks. Int. J. Adv. Comput. Sci. Appl. **9**(8) (2018)
27. Schirrmeister, R.I., et al.: Deep learning with convolutional neural networks for EEG decoding and visualization. Hum. Brain Mapp. **38**(11), 5391–5420 (2017)
28. Song, T., Zheng, W., Song, P., Cui, Z.: EEG emotion recognition using dynamical graph convolutional neural networks. IEEE Trans. Affect. Comput. **11**(3), 532–541 (2018)
29. Szegedy, C., et al.: Going deeper with convolutions. In: Proceedings of the IEEE Conference on Computer Vision and Pattern Recognition, pp. 1–9 (2015)
30. Wang, X., Nie, D., Lu, B.: EEG-based emotion recognition using frequency domain features and support vector machines. Lect. Notes Comput. Sci. **7062**, 734–743 (2011)
31. Wu, Y., Xia, M., Nie, L., Zhang, Y., Fan, A.: Simultaneously exploring multi-scale and asymmetric EEG features for emotion recognition. Comput. Biol. Med. **149**, 106002 (2022)
32. Yang, Y., Wu, Q., Ming, Q., Wang, Y., Chen, X.: Emotion recognition from multichannel EEG through parallel convolutional recurrent neural network. In: 2018 International Joint Conference on Neural Networks (IJCNN) (2018)
33. Yang, Y., Wu, Q.J., Zheng, W.L., Lu, B.L.: EEG-based emotion recognition using hierarchical network with subnetwork nodes. IEEE Trans. Cogn. Dev. Syst. **10**(2), 408–419 (2017)
34. Yea-Hoon, K., Sae-Byuk, S., Shin-Dug, K.: Electroencephalography based fusion two-dimensional (2D)-convolution neural networks (CNN) model for emotion recognition system. Sensors **18**(5), 1383– (2018)
35. Zhang, T., Zheng, W., Cui, Z., Zong, Y.: Spatial-temporal recurrent neural network for emotion recognition. IEEE Trans. Cybern. **49**, 839– 847 (2019)
36. Zhang, T., Cui, Z., Xu, C., Zheng, W., Yang, J.: Variational pathway reasoning for EEG emotion recognition. In: Proceedings of the AAAI Conference on Artificial Intelligence, vol. 34, pp. 2709–2716 (2020)
37. Zhao, Y., Yang, J., Lin, J., Yu, D., Cao, X.: A 3D convolutional neural network for emotion recognition based on EEG signals. In: 2020 International Joint Conference on Neural Networks (IJCNN) (2020)
38. Zheng, W.L., Zhu, J.Y., Peng, Y., Lu, B.L.: EEG-based emotion classification using deep belief networks. In: 2014 IEEE International Conference on Multimedia and Expo (ICME), pp. 1–6. IEEE (2014)

Pose Sequence Model Using the Encoder-Decoder Structure for 3D Pose Estimation

Jiwei Zhang[1](✉), Lian Yang[1], Tianbo Ye[1], Jiaen Zhou[1], Wendong Wang[1], and Ying Tan[2]

[1] Beijing University of Posts and Telecommunications, Beijing 100876, China
jwzhang666@bupt.edu.cn
[2] Peking University, Beijing 100091, China

Abstract. Human pose estimation is a hot research problem in computer vision, it has a certain application prospect in the automatic driving industry, security field, film and television industry, and specific action monitoring of special scenes. Because a 2D skeleton usually corresponds to multiple 3D skeletons, the mapping from 2D to 3D in the monocular video has inherent depth ambiguity and is ill-posed, which makes the research on the technology of 3D human pose estimation in monocular video challenging. In this paper, a Pose Sequence Model (PSM) for 3D human pose estimation in the monocular video is proposed, which combines the full convolution neural network based on extended convolution with the Long Short-Term Memory (LSTM) network. We make full use of convolution to extract spatial features and use LSTM to obtain temporal features. With this model, we can predict 3D human posture through 2D sequences. Compared with the previous work on classical data sets, our method has good detection results.

Keywords: 3D human pose estimation · PSM · Monocular video

1 Introduction

The research on 2D pose estimation has 2 main methods: top-down and bottom-up methods. The top-down method [19,25,28,30] takes the result from human detection, generally a bounding box, and performs the single human pose estimation on each human block diagram. The bottom-up method [18], oppositely, starts by detecting the human body key points in the image and then groups the key points into a human body. Toshev et al. [26] transformed the 2D human pose estimation problem from the original image processing and template matching problem into CNN image feature extraction and keypoint coordinate regression problem, and used DNN-based regression criteria to estimate the occludes/missing human joint nodes, which brings great influence. Until now, the 2D pose estimation has reached relatively high accuracy and high resolution

Y. Tan and Y. Shi (Eds.): DMBD 2022, CCIS 1744, pp. 165–177, 2022.
https://doi.org/10.1007/978-981-19-9297-1_13

[23]. Combining the 2D and 3D human pose estimation, Chen et al. [4] conveyed that rather than directly measure 3D pose from images, the procedure of 3D pose estimation can be divided into 2D pose estimating using Mature deep neural networks, and 3D mocap data matching, this has been the main idea of posture estimating.

In recent years, there has been vast research on 3D posture estimating. Some focus on estimating 3D pose from 2D pose of a single image, Martinez et al. [16] conducted an efficient neural network to infer from 2D projections to 3D joints, which focuses on the visual parsing of human bodies in 2d images. To solve the problem of unknown motions and camera positions, Wandt et al. [27] proposed an extra camera network to infer camera parameters, followed by a reprojection layer to reproject the 3D pose back to 2D. Li et al. [14] designed a dataset evolution framework to address the problem of the biased dataset, along with a cascaded network: TAGNet to predict the final 3D skeleton from the enhanced data. Based on the part-guided novel image synthesis, Kundu et al. [10] proposed a self-supervised learning framework to disentangle the inherent factors of variations: shape and appearance. Some research may get 3D pose from explicit middle representations, Pavlakos et al. [20] proposed volumetric representation for 3D human pose(3D heatmap) and coarse-to-fine prediction technique to validate the value of end-to-end learning for the representation of 3D pose, which addresses the challenge of estimating 3D human poses from a single color image. Li et al. [12] introduced the mixture density networks (MDN) [1,32] into the 3D joint estimation to verify the hypotheses that multiple feasible poses can be inferred from a monocular input. Li et al. [13] designed HybrIK reconstructing 3D body mesh by twist-and-swing decomposition to bridge the gap between volume grid estimation and 3D keypoint estimation, which both preserve the accuracy of the 3D pose and the real body structure of the parameterized human body model, to obtain a pixel-aligned 3D body grid and a more accurate 3D pose.

CNN can fully learn images or videos' high-level semantic information and has excellent spatial information extraction capabilities. However, the 3D human pose recognition task based on the human skeleton sequence is a significant time-dependent problem for monocular video. So, balancing and making better use of spatial and temporal information is an extremely difficult task. An additional issue that needs to be addressed is raising the model's generalizability for outdoor datasets. As a result, we propose a multi-stage framework for estimating the 3D human pose that begins by estimating the 2D human pose from the image, then from the result to estimate the 3D human pose. Some 2D outdoor datasets can be used to provide the model with generalization capabilities by making use of the model's revolutionized 2D human pose detector. After that, the mapping relationship sequence from the 2D human pose to the 3D human pose is modeled, transforming the issue into a time-based sequence modeling task. The encoder-decoder structure PSM makes use of the LSTM as an encoder and the fully convolutional neural network as a decoder. The use of LSTM as an encoder makes it possible to first encode the video frame's correlation into a vector of fixed size and then decode it using a fully convolutional neural network. The CNN network's spatial information processing capability and the RNN network's temporal information acquisition capability can be combined and fully utilized in this manner. Additionally, the jitter of 3D human motion between video frames frequently presents a challenge when estimating the 3D human pose from monocular video. Since the polynomial order can be modeled using motion refinement and used as an optional branch to optimize the prediction results, motion refinement is used to reduce bounce and increase accuracy. Consequently, the performance of 3D human pose estimation can be improved by the proposed framework. In Fig. 1, the first row contains the images, and the second row corresponds to the estimation results of the 3D pose.

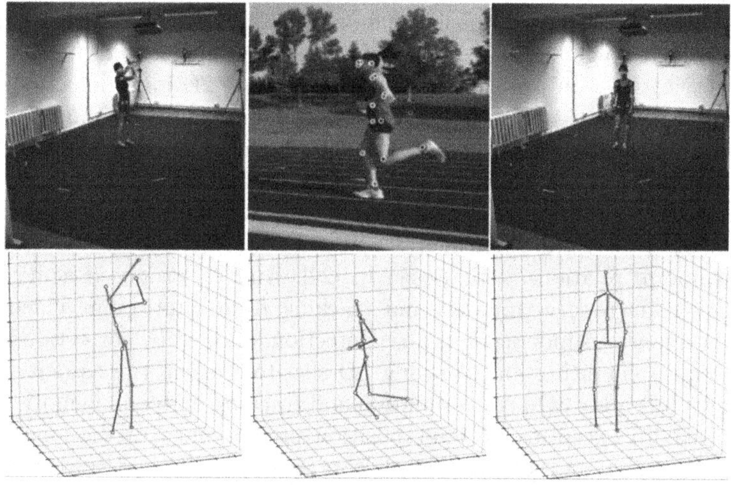

Fig. 1. The effect of the 3D human pose estimation.

The contribution is reflected in the following points:

1. The structure of encode-decode is formed by CNN and RNN, which can utilize spatial and temporal information by encoder-decoder structure.
2. We propose a PSM that combines LSTM with a fully convolutional neural network, which can be used for the estimation of 3D pose.
3. Our framework is implemented in the 3D datasets and good results can also be obtained for wild web videos.

2 Related Work

In recent years, the field of 3D pose recognition has developed rapidly, mainly in two directions: picture recognition and video recognition. A method for multi-person 3D pose recognition using a single image is proposed in [7], which allows the recognition of single or multi-person poses using constant time. They designed a simple and effective compression method using high-resolution body heat maps and decoded them using an auto-encoder. [6] addressed the problem of 3D pose estimation for multiple people in a few calibrated camera views. A multi-way matching algorithm is used to cluster the detected 2D poses in all views. Each cluster encodes the correspondence between the pose and key points of the same person in different 2D views to efficiently infer the 3D pose of the person. A feature-enhanced network is proposed in [15] to estimate 3D hand pose and 3D body pose using a single RGB image. To address the effects arising from texture, illumination changes, and occlusion in real applications, a long and short-term dependent perception module is used for enhancement. A contextual consistency gate is also introduced to modulate based on contextual consistency. A graph-based approach is proposed in [3] for the problems of depth ambiguity and severe self-obscuration, considering spatial dependence and temporal consistency. A local-to-global network structure is also implemented to solve the 3D human pose estimation problem from short sequence 2D joint detection.

Although it is possible to divide the video into multiple frames for pose recognition, there are often different problems in the video. Graph convolutional networks are often built on fixed human-joint affinities, which can reduce the adaptive ability of GCNs to handle complex Spatio-temporal pose changes in videos. A 3D pose estimation neural network that can adaptively learn video Spatio-temporal relations is proposed in [22]. And [2] proposed a method for multi-person 3D pose estimation and tracking from multi-point video, where each point undergoes independent pose detection followed by correction and correlation, thus generating and tracking 3D skeletons using the associated pose. Multiplayer full-body 3D pose estimation and tracking in dynamic motion scenes are achieved. In exception to joint position prediction, a prediction based on skeletal orientation and skeletal length is proposed in [5], and since the human skeletal length is constant, a full convolutional propagation architecture with long jump connections that can effectively use the information in the video for prediction is proposed. To address the accurate recognition of depth ambiguity, self-obscuration, or other uncommon poses, [33] proposed a new skeletal GNN solution using a hop-count-aware hierarchical channel squeezing fusion layer that effectively extracts information from neighboring nodes while suppressing undesired noise in the GNN, thus effectively improving the prediction accuracy.

3 Method

3D human pose detection methods which are end-to-end must simultaneously complete feature extraction and 3D joint prediction. In addition, since 2D human posture corresponds to multiple 3D human postures, there are inherent fuzziness and discomfort in using end-to-end methods to estimate 3D human posture using monocular images. In this paper, the framework we propose is multi-stage. First, we convert the image into 2D human pose through a 2D detector, and then establish the mapping relationship between 2D and 3D human pose through depth learning method. The prediction framework is shown in Fig. 2.

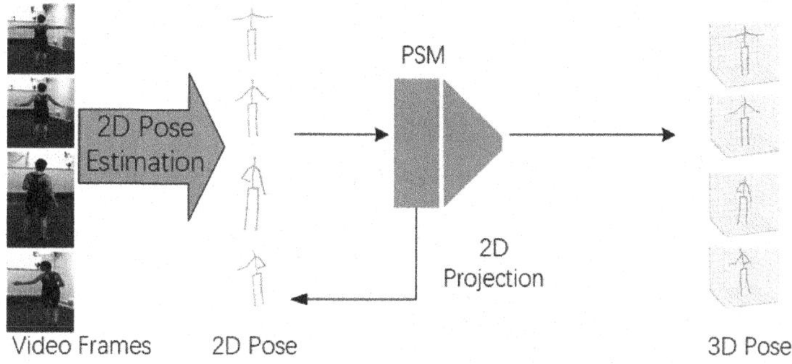

Fig. 2. The prediction framework for the estimation of 3D human pose.

It can be seen from Fig. 2 that our framework is a multi-stage 3D human posture, and different 2D human posture detectors can be used to improve the generalization performance of the model. At the same time, a PSM composed of LSTM and a complete convolution model is proposed to predict 3D human pose through 2D human pose sequence.

3.1 Time-Series Modeling

The input sequence can supposed as $x_0 \ldots, x_t \ldots, x_T$, where x_t is the 2D human poses. Then, we estimate the output $y_0, \ldots, y_t \ldots, y_T$, where y_t is the 3D human poses. In the case of non-causality, for the given time t, the output y_t can be got by passing any subset of x_T. For the causal cases, the data $x_0, \ldots, x_t$ is observed before the t state can only be used. So the time series modeling can be as a function $f : X^\tau \rightarrow Y^\tau$ that can produce a mapping relationship:

$$y'_0, \ldots, y'_T = f(x_0, \ldots, x_T) \tag{1}$$

For the causal situation, y_t should be obtained only from $x_0, \ldots, x_t$ instead of the subsequent input $x_{t+1}, \ldots, x_T$.

3.2 The Proposed Pose Sequence Model

The encoder-decoder model is a common scheme in time series modeling. The encoding can convert the input time series into vectors, and the decoding can convert the vectors into output sequences. The combination of CNN and RNN can form an encoder and decoder structure. The encoder part of the PSM model we use is the LSTM structure, and the decoder part is a fully convolutional network, forming the RNN-CNN structure. It can effectively use the ability of LSTM to extract time information in time series modeling and the advantages of CNN in processing spatial information. The PSM model is shown in Fig. 3.

Because LSTM can be used to deal with the long-term dependence in time series modeling, its structure is relatively simple and its parameters are few,

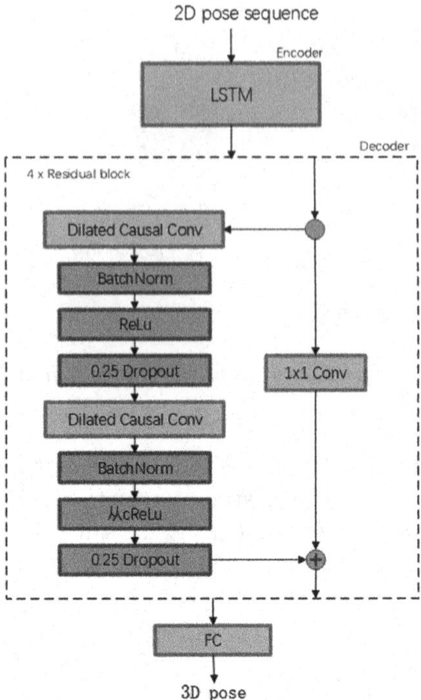

Fig. 3. The proposed PSM for 3D pose estimation.

so it is used as the encoder of the model in this paper. In addition, a dilated convolution is used to decode the LSTM encoding. When causal PSM is used for training, the encoder uses LSTM, while noncausal PSM uses bidirectional LSTM. There are some differences between bidirectional LSTM and LSTM. The current state $t$is not only related to the previous state $t-1$, but also related to the next state $t+1$.

The PSM decoder consists of the full convolution model of the dilated convolution, and the dilated convolution refers to the standard convolution with holes. The reception field of each convolution kernel can be changed by adjusting the kernel spacing, and the dilated convolution obtains multi-scale information by setting different dilation rates. We set different expansion rates for different blocks. This strategy can play the advantages of parallel processing and reduce the loss of information at the hole. For a 2D sequence x $\in \mathfrak{R}^2$ and a function $f:\{0,\ldots,k-1\} \Rightarrow \mathfrak{R}$, operation of dilated convolution F acting on any element e of the sequence x is expressed as follow.

$$F(e) = (x *_D f)(e) = \sum_{i=0}^{k-1} f(i) \cdot X_{s-D \cdot i} \tag{2}$$

k is the size of the convolution kernel and D is the expansion factor. The fully convolutional neural network includes the Batch Norm (BN), Relu, and dropout. The BN layer is to normalize the batch of data, a BN layer is after the fully connected layer to ensure each layer remains uniformly distributed. Moreover, the Relu function is chosen as the activation function. For the dropout, each neuron stops with a probability of p. Moreover, a residual connection is used to superimpose the input and the output, which solves the problem of gradient disappearance caused by deep networks. After obtaining the 2D joints J in each image, LSTM is used to perform encoding, and a fully convolutional neural network is used to complete the decoding of temporal convolution. For the LSTM, the number of hidden layers is set to $J * 2$. For the decoder, kernel with size K is set to 3, the output is dilated convolution with a size C=1024 and an expansion factor $D = K^N$, where N are the n-th residual modules. The next part is BatchNorm, Relu, and dropout layers.

3.3 Training Details

The training process is shown in Fig. 4.

Here, the 2D pose represents the 2D sequences. The branch of the 3D pose prediction learns the mapping relationship from 2D to 3D pose using PSM. The $y^{(j)}_{f_{3d,t}}(i)$ is the joint j in the t-th frame predicted by the model, and $y^{(j)}_{f_{gt,t}}(i)$ is the ground truth for the t-th frame. The loss function of Mean Per Joint Position Error (MPJPE) can be defined as:

$$L_{3d}=\frac{1}{N_T}\frac{1}{N_S}\sum_{j=1}^{N_T}\sum_{i=1}^{N_S}\left\|y^{(j)}_{f_{3d,t}}(i)-y^{(j)}_{gt,t}(i)\right\|_2 \tag{3}$$

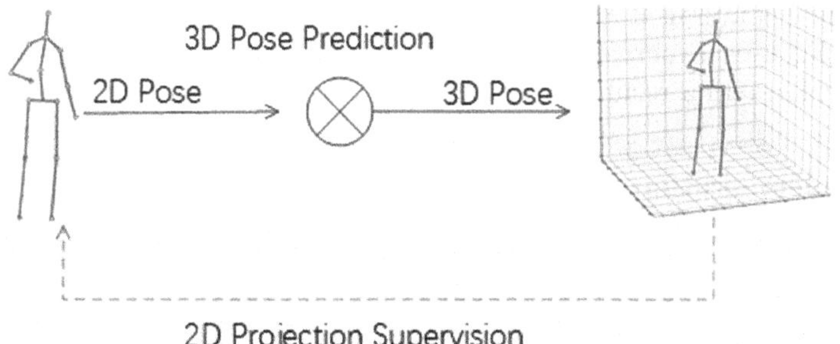

Fig. 4. The training process.

N_T is the number of video frames, and N_S is the number of joints.

Simultaneously, weak supervision of 2D projection is used. We project the estimated 3D pose to the 2D space and get the MPJPE loss L_{proj}, then the loss of the overall task is :

$$L = L_{3d} + L_{proj} \tag{4}$$

Where L_{3d} is 3D loss, L_{proj} is 2D loss.

During training, each step represents as N. The framework consists of the below steps. First, the 2D joints J^{2D} are normalized, and then the 3D joint $\widehat{J^{3D}}$ are predicted through the PSM. $\widehat{J^{3D}}$ can be calculated with the ground truth to obtain L_{3d}. The projected 2D joint can be obtained through projection, and then we calculated with the ground truth to obtain L_{proj}, where the camera parameter is C.

4 Experimental Verifications

First, the data sets used for training and testing and the overall evaluation indicators are introduced, and the proposed framework is compared with the baselines method in different data sets. After verification, our framework has achieved good results.

4.1 Datasets and Evaluation

In the experiment, we mainly used two data sets, HumanEVA and Human3.6m. Hman3.6M is a general data set in the field of 3D human pose estimation. It includes 15 groups of actions completed by motion capture, and a total of 3.6 million videos are provided in 50 HZ format. 17 joint point models are used, 5 object groups (S1, S5, S6, S7, S8) are used as training sets, and (S9, S11) are used as test sets. HumanEVA is another data set used in the experiment, with a total of 4 test objects. According to actions, it can be divided into single-action SA protocol and multi-action MA protocol.

In the evaluation process, we used two protocols: P1 is used to calculate the Euclidean distance between the predicted 3D coordinates and the ground truth, which is averaged according to the number of joints and frames, namely MPJPE. P2 uses Procrustes analysis to evaluate the error between the rigid body transformation result and the ground truth, which is P-MPJPE.

4.2 Implementation Details

Our 2D detector can use different networks, including Mask R-CNN [9] and HRNet [24]. For Mask R-CNN, the ResNet-101 backbone network can be used. The learning rate starts from 1e–3, the attenuation rate is 0.995, and 80k iterations of training have been conducted. For HRNet, starting from 1e–4, it was reduced to 1e–6 in the 15th iteration, and a total of 20k iteration trainings were conducted.

In addition, the Human3.6m dataset has been translated and rotated. The receptive field of the PSM model is set to 243 and the attenuation factor is 0.95. For the HumanEVA dataset, the attenuation factor is 0.99, and 800 cycles of training were conducted.

4.3 Experiment on 3D Datasets

Comparison Results on Human3.6m Dataset. Comparative experiments are carried out on the Human3.6m dataset and the results are as follows.

Table 1. The value of P1 on Human3.6m dataset

	Dir	Disc	Eat	Greet	Phone	Photo	Pose	Purch	Sit	Smoke	Wait	Walk	Avg
Fang et al. AAAI (2018) [8]	50.1	54.3	57.0	57.1	66.6	73.3	53.4	55.7	72.8	60.3	57.7	47.5	60.4
Yang et al. CVPR (2018) [31]	51.5	58.9	50.4	57.0	62.1	65.4	49.8	52.7	69.2	57.4	58.4	60.1	58.6
Pavllo et al. CVPR (2019) [21]	45.2	46.7	43.3	45.6	48.1	55.1	44.6	44.3	57.3	47.1	**44.0**	32.8	46.8
Wu et al. AAAI (2020) [29]	**36.9**	43.9	39.5	60.4	45.3	**51.6**	**38.1**	41.9	54.1	44.4	57.6	32.2	47.3
Ours, causal	41.7	44.1	41.4	43.1	46.0	52.4	44.9	43.2	54.4	44.2	45.1	32.8	44.7
Ours, non-causal	41.3	**43.8**	**39.1**	**42.5**	**45.1**	51.8	44.7	**41.5**	**52.8**	**43.9**	44.8	**32.0**	**43.9**

Table 1 and Table 2 show the results on the Human3.6m dataset under the evaluation indicators P1 and P2. The model uses HRNet as a two-dimensional attitude detector, and the data in the table contains the results of multiple actions. The smaller the value of the evaluation index P1 and P2, the better. The last column of the table is the average value of multiple groups of actions. Cause and effect represent cause and effect PSM, which takes the previous frame as input, rather than cause and effect represents PSM, and the input data includes future frames. The best result in the table is shown in bold, and the second-best result is shown in the underline. It can be seen from the table that non-causal PSM achieves better results than causal PSM. Our method ranks first in most actions and second in some actions.

Table 2. The value of P2 on Human3.6m dataset

	Dir	Disc	Eat	Greet	Phone	Photo	Pose	Purch	Sit	Smoke	Wait	Walk	Avg
Fang et al. AAAI (2018) [8]	38.2	41.7	43.7	44.9	48.5	55.3	40.2	38.2	54.5	47.2	44.3	36.7	45.7
Yang et al. CVPR (2018) [31]	**26.9**	**30.9**	36.3	39.9	43.9	47.4	38.8	**29.4**	**36.9**	41.5	30.5	42.5	37.7
Pavllo et al. CVPR (2019) [21]	45.2	46.7	43.3	45.6	48.1	55.1	44.6	44.3	57.3	47.1	44.0	32.8	46.8
Wu et al. AAAI (2020) [29]	32.1	36.2	33.9	41.2	**37.4**	**40.6**	**30.7**	33.4	45.0	37.4	38.8	**25.7**	37.3
Ours, causal	33.1	39.0	33.2	36.8	39.9	40.9	31.2	32.3	43.7	37.0	35.9	26.1	35.7
Ours, non-causal	32.7	38.6	**32.9**	**35.3**	39.8	39.5	30.9	31.9	42.2	**36.8**	**35.2**	**25.7**	**35.2**

Comparison Results on HumanEVA Dataset. We conducted experiments in the HumanEVA dataset to prove the effectiveness of our framework on small-scale datasets. Three participants were selected as test subjects, S1, S2, and S3. Then, using the two-dimensional attitude detector HRNet, multiple actions (MA) and single action (SA) strategies are selected for experiments. As can be seen from Table 3, our framework has generally achieved good results on P2. Especially in the case of MA, the best results are obtained.

Table 3. Comparative experiments on the HumanEVA dataset

Subjects	Walk(S1)	Walk(S2)	Jog(S1)	Jog(S2)	Box(S1)	Box(S2)
Martinez et al. (SA) [17]	19.7	17.4	26.9	18.2	-	-
Lee et al. [11]	18.6	19.9	25.7	16.8	42.8	48.1
Pavllo et al. (SA)	14.5	10.5	21.9	13.4	24.3	34.9
Pavllo et al. (MA)	13.9	10.2	20.9	<u>13.1</u>	<u>23.8</u>	33.7
ours(SA)	<u>12.6</u>	<u>10.0</u>	<u>18.6</u>	13.4	24.1	30.4
ours(MA)	**12.4**	**9.8**	**18.2**	**11.4**	**21.8**	**29.4**

5 Conclusion

The framework proposed in this paper is multi-stage, which is used to realize 3D human pose estimation in monocular video. First, obtain the 2d pose of the human body from the video, and then use the 2d pose to predict the 3d pose. Our model adopts PSM, which can realize the sequence modeling of 2d to 3d pose. PSM is an encoded second structure, which makes full use of the multi-level features extracted by a fully convolutional neural network and LSTM. In addition, since our framework is multi-stage, we can use different 2D detectors to improve performance. Compared with the corresponding baseline methods, our method has achieved good results on HumanEVA and Human3.6m datasets.

Acknowledgements. This work is supported by Key Research and Development Projects of Hebei Province under Grant 21310102D.

References

1. Bishop, C.M.: Mixture Density Networks. IEEE Computer Society, Washington, DC (1994)
2. Bridgeman, L., Volino, M., Guillemaut, J.Y., Hilton, A.: Multi-person 3D pose estimation and tracking in sports. In: 2019 IEEE/CVF Conference on Computer Vision and Pattern Recognition Workshops (CVPRW), pp. 2487–2496. IEEE, Long Beach, CA, USA, June 2019. https://doi.org/10.1109/CVPRW.2019.00304, https://ieeexplore.ieee.org/document/9025555/

3. Cai, Y., et al.: Exploiting Spatial-Temporal Relationships for 3D pose estimation via graph convolutional networks. In: 2019 IEEE/CVF International Conference on Computer Vision (ICCV). pp. 2272–2281. IEEE, Seoul, Korea (South), October 2019. https://doi.org/10.1109/ICCV.2019.00236, https://ieeexplore.ieee.org/document/9009459/
4. Chen, C.H., Ramanan, D.: 3D human pose estimation = 2D pose estimation + matching. In: Proceedings of the IEEE Conference on Computer Vision and Pattern Recognition (CVPR), pp. 7035–7043, July 2017
5. Chen, T., Fang, C., Shen, X., Zhu, Y., Chen, Z., Luo, J.: Anatomy-aware 3D human pose estimation with bone-based pose decomposition. IEEE Trans. Circ. Syst. Video Technol. **32**(1), 198–209 (2022). https://doi.org/10.1109/TCSVT.2021.3057267, https://ieeexplore.ieee.org/document/9347537/
6. Dong, J., Jiang, W., Huang, Q., Bao, H., Zhou, X.: Fast and robust multi-person 3D pose estimation from multiple views. In: 2019 IEEE/CVF Conference on Computer Vision and Pattern Recognition (CVPR). pp. 7784–7793. IEEE, Long Beach, CA, USA, June 2019. https://doi.org/10.1109/CVPR.2019.00798, https://ieeexplore.ieee.org/document/8953350/
7. Fabbri, M., Lanzi, F., Calderara, S., Alletto, S., Cucchiara, R.: Compressed volumetric heatmaps for multi-person 3D pose estimation. In: 2020 IEEE/CVF Conference on Computer Vision and Pattern Recognition (CVPR), pp. 7202–7211. IEEE, Seattle, WA, USA, June 2020. https://doi.org/10.1109/CVPR42600.2020.00723, https://ieeexplore.ieee.org/document/9156316/
8. Fang, H., Xu, Y., Wang, W., Liu, X., Zhu, S.: Learning pose grammar to encode human body configuration for 3D pose estimation. In: Proceedings of AAAI Conference on Artificial Intelligence, New Orleans, Louisiana, USA, pp. 6821–6828 (Feb2018)
9. He, K., Gkioxari, G., Dollár, P., Girshick, R.B.: Mask R-CNN (2017). http://arxiv.org/abs/1703.06870
10. Kundu, J.N., Seth, S., Jampani, V., Rakesh, M., Babu, R.V., Chakraborty, A.: Self-supervised 3d human pose estimation via part guided novel image synthesis. In: Proceedings of the IEEE/CVF Conference on Computer Vision and Pattern Recognition (CVPR), pp. 6152–6162, June 2020
11. Lee, K., Lee, I., Lee, S.: Propagating LSTM: 3D pose estimation based on joint interdependency. In: Ferrari, V., Hebert, M., Sminchisescu, C., Weiss, Y. (eds.) ECCV 2018. LNCS, vol. 11211, pp. 123–141. Springer, Cham (2018). https://doi.org/10.1007/978-3-030-01234-2_8
12. Li, C., Lee, G.H.: Generating multiple hypotheses for 3D human pose estimation with mixture density network. In: Proceedings of the IEEE/CVF Conference on Computer Vision and Pattern Recognition (CVPR), pp. 9887–9895, June 2019
13. Li, J., Xu, C., Chen, Z., Bian, S., Yang, L., Lu, C.: Hybrik: a hybrid analytical-neural inverse kinematics solution for 3d human pose and shape estimation. In: Proceedings of the IEEE/CVF Conference on Computer Vision and Pattern Recognition (CVPR), pp. 3383–3393, June 2021
14. Li, S., Ke, L., Pratama, K., Tai, Y.W., Tang, C.K., Cheng, K.T.: Cascaded deep monocular 3D human pose estimation with evolutionary training data. In: Proceedings of the IEEE/CVF Conference on Computer Vision and Pattern Recognition (CVPR), pp. 6173–6183, June 2020
15. Liu, J., et al.: Feature Boosting Network For 3D Pose Estimation. IEEE Trans. Pattern Anal. Mach. Intell. **42**(2), 494–501 (2020). https://doi.org/10.1109/TPAMI.2019.2894422, https://ieeexplore.ieee.org/document/8621059/

16. Martinez, J., Hossain, R., Romero, J., Little, J.J.: A simple yet effective baseline for 3D human pose estimation. In: Proceedings of the IEEE International Conference on Computer Vision (ICCV), pp. 2640–2649, October 2017
17. Martinez, J., Hossain, R., Romero, J., Little, J.J.: A simple yet effective baseline for 3D human pose estimation. In: Proceedings of IEEE International Conference on Computer Vision (ICCV), Venice, Italy. pp. 2659–2668 (Oct2017)
18. Newell, A., Huang, Z., Deng, J.: Associative embedding: End-to-end learning for joint detection and grouping. In: Guyon, I., Luxburg, U.V., Bengio, S., Wallach, H., Fergus, R., Vishwanathan, S., Garnett, R. (eds.) Advances in Neural Information Processing Systems. vol. 30. Curran Associates, Inc. (2017). https://proceedings.neurips.cc/paper/2017/file/8edd72158ccd2a879f79cb2538568fdc-Paper.pdf
19. Papandreou, G., Zhu, T., Kanazawa, N., Toshev, A., Tompson, J., Bregler, C., Murphy, K.: Towards accurate multi-person pose estimation in the wild. In: Proceedings of the IEEE Conference on Computer Vision and Pattern Recognition (CVPR), pp. 4903–4911, July 2017
20. Pavlakos, G., Zhou, X., Derpanis, K.G., Daniilidis, K.: Coarse-to-fine volumetric prediction for single-image 3d human pose. In: Proceedings of the IEEE Conference on Computer Vision and Pattern Recognition (CVPR). pp. 7025–7034, July 2017
21. Pavllo, D., Feichtenhofer, C., Grangier, D., Auli, M.: 3D human pose estimation in video with temporal convolutions and semi-supervised training. In: Proceedings of IEEE Conference on Computer Vision and Pattern Recognition (CVPR), Long Beach, CA, USA, pp. 7753–7762, June 2019
22. Sengupta, A., Budvytis, I., Cipolla, R.: Hierarchical kinematic probability distributions for 3d human shape and pose estimation from images in the wild. In: 2021 IEEE/CVF International Conference on Computer Vision (ICCV). pp. 11199–11209. IEEE, Montreal, QC, Canada, October 2021. https://doi.org/10.1109/ICCV48922.2021.01103, https://ieeexplore.ieee.org/document/9709969/
23. Sun, K., Xiao, B., Liu, D., Wang, J.: Deep high-resolution representation learning for human pose estimation. In: Proceedings of the IEEE/CVF Conference on Computer Vision and Pattern Recognition (CVPR), pp. 5693–5703, June 2019
24. Sun, K., Xiao, B., Liu, D., Wang, J.: Deep high-resolution representation learning for human pose estimation. In: Proceedings of the IEEE Conference on Computer Vision and Pattern Recognition (CVPR), Long Beach, CA, USA, pp. 5693–5703, June 2019
25. Sun, X., Shang, J., Liang, S., Wei, Y.: Compositional human pose regression. In: Proceedings of the IEEE International Conference on Computer Vision (ICCV), pp. 2602–2611, October 2017
26. Toshev, A., Szegedy, C.: Deeppose: human pose estimation via deep neural networks. In: Proceedings of the IEEE Conference on Computer Vision and Pattern Recognition (CVPR), pp. 1653–1660, June 2014
27. Wandt, B., Rosenhahn, B.: RepNet: weakly supervised training of an adversarial reprojection network for 3D human pose estimation. In: Proceedings of the IEEE/CVF Conference on Computer Vision and Pattern Recognition (CVPR), pp. 7782–7791, June 2019
28. Wang, J., Sun, K., Cheng, T., Jiang, B., Deng, C., Zhao, Y., Liu, D., Mu, Y., Tan, M., Wang, X., Liu, W., Xiao, B.: Deep high-resolution representation learning for visual recognition. IEEE Trans. Pattern Anal. Mach. Intell. **43**(10), 3349–3364 (2021). https://doi.org/10.1109/TPAMI.2020.2983686
29. Wu, H., Xiao, B.: 3D human pose estimation via explicit compositional depth maps. In: Proceedings of AAAI Conference on Artificial Intelligence New York, NY, USA, 7–12 February 2020, pp. 12378–12385, Feb 2020

30. Xiao, B., Wu, H., Wei, Y.: Simple baselines for human pose estimation and tracking. In: Ferrari, V., Hebert, M., Sminchisescu, C., Weiss, Y. (eds.) ECCV 2018. LNCS, vol. 11210, pp. 472–487. Springer, Cham (2018). https://doi.org/10.1007/978-3-030-01231-1_29
31. Yang, W., Ouyang, W., Wang, X., Ren, J.S.J., Li, H., Wang, X.: 3D human pose estimation in the wild by adversarial learning. In: Proceedings of the IEEE Conference on Computer Vision and Pattern Recognition (CVPR), Salt Lake City, UT, USA. pp. 5255–5264, June 2018
32. Ye, Q., Kim, T.K.: Occlusion-aware hand pose estimation using hierarchical mixture density network. In: Proceedings of the European Conference on Computer Vision (ECCV), pp. 801–817, September 2018
33. Zhang, J., Wang, Y., Zhou, Z., Luan, T., Wang, Z., Qiao, Y.: Learning dynamical human-joint affinity for 3d pose estimation in videos. IEEE Trans. Image Process. **30**, 7914–7925 (2021). https://doi.org/10.1109/TIP.2021.3109517, https://ieeexplore.ieee.org/document/9531423/

Research and Analysis of Video-Based Human Pose Estimation

Zheng Wang[1], Jing Sun[1], Qingxiao Xu[2], and Kun Liu[3](✉)

[1] School of Information Science and Technology, North China University of Technology, Beijing, China
[2] School of Artificial Intelligence, Beijing Normal University, Beijing, China
[3] Advanced Institute of Big Data, Beijing, China
liukun@aibd.ac.cn

Abstract. With the rapid development of computer vision and artificial intelligence, human pose estimation has become the subject of intense scholarly debate. In addition, ubiquitous video software and monitoring machines provide sufficient video data, and all kinds of key elements can be found in the visual information. However, due to different task subdivision scenarios as well as the confusing nature of the human actions, the scenario-oriented video detection techniques aim to establish standard libraries for distinct application scenarios, aggregating both original joint coordinates and composite features. In this paper, we present an innovative framework for detecting possible actions in various scenarios, table tennis training, pilot running planes and boot camp scenes, which covers vast range of social scenes. First, we call OpenPose for accurate and robust skeleton information. Then, manually constructed features of pose angles, relative displacements, moving pattern sequences and etc. are calculated. These informative features enlighten people of latent motion rules. Finally, we report how our framework is applied to realistic classification datasets. Through our work, an overall sketch for skeleton-based human pose estimation and a framework with practical application value is proposed, where people can gain a deep theoretical and practical understanding of a front field of computer vision.

Keywords: Action recognition · Pattern matching · Data analysis

1 Introduction

1.1 Technical Background

Computer vision helps the machine to learn through observation. Deep learning techniques have facilitated the precise image and video recognition. Two main research directions are object recognition and human motion recognition [1]. For human motion recognition, the object is to identify the human moving pattern and analyze the purpose and intent driving the movements. However, the identification is always scenario-oriented, that is, if we draw conclusions simply base on the actions and neglect the item

Y. Tan and Y. Shi (Eds.): DMBD 2022, CCIS 1744, pp. 178–191, 2022.
https://doi.org/10.1007/978-981-19-9297-1_14

and background information, tapping the keys without the piano will seem very confusing. Another challenge arises when the human target performs delicate maneuvers. Elaborate finger movements are either inconspicuous or hidden from the camera angle.

The exciting technological trend has been upward with an explosion of video data and software. Also, the people demand upbeat calls for a more accurate and interpretable result for image detection and image recognition. Both RGB images and joint coordinates provide informative insights on body postures, while coordinates information is more popular for its data size and final accuracy. OpenPose [2] has offered to jointly detect human body, hand, facial, and foot keypoints for images and videos. With keypoint coordinates, it is easy to recover the skeleton information that suits for transformation and calculation. In addition, the skeleton information is robust to confounding factors in the background and mainly records the bearing and angle of the actions.

Carreira et al. [3] proposed a general regression framework leveraging GoogleNet that jointly learns the input and output features. A feedback mechanism in the framework uses the current estimating deviations to iteratively modify the prediction results. Shuang et al. [4] transforms the joints information through skeleton parameterization, thus achieving better human posture structure representation. Wang et al. [5] proposed the HR-ARNet, using attention mechanism to reinforce multi-scale feature fusion. The informative features are distinct from those unwanted ones, and the inconsistency problem of keypoints are solved.

Videos records what happens in vast, unbroken slabs of time sequences. A common way to process video data is through capturing the time sequence information and reconstructing the continuously dynamic moving patterns, which are useful in dealing with blurring, occlusion, and changing appearance problems. The pattern recognition methods will be integrated with specific posture estimation missions. The FAMI-Pose framework [6], like all other methods, combining additional visual evidence from neighboring frames to facilitate pose estimation of the target frame. FAMI-Pose framework hands extracted features to its global transformation module and its local calibration module for temporal alignment. In addition, the framework provides a feature level supervision for the target frame from calculating the maximal complementary information in the supporting frames.

1.2 Application Scenarios

Skeleton coordinates information records human acts in all kinds of scenarios, life, work, entertainment scenes, and etc. Studying different scenario cases and their corresponding latent human pose patterns greatly promotes progress in technology, and facilitates people's social life. In point of fact, this paper will expose the people to three typical application scenarios of human pose estimation, including table tennis training, pilot running planes and boot camp scenes.

Table tennis sport is a hold bat net separated competition that calls for physical fitness and mental preparation in players. And winning such competitive sport requires mainly techniques and strategies. Table tennis action shots are of distinct characteristics. In beginner and player training, the most common shots are forehand hits and backhand hits. Normally, it is best for players to use balanced forehand and backhand skills. However, the choice of different bat swings actually indicate possible movements in that the standing of forehand and backhand hits constrains the players' waist rotation angles. Classification for Table tennis actions are of significant value in technical analysis and tactical arrangement for players.

A number of civil aviation accidents have aroused people's attention. It is pilots' first priority to ensure the safety of every flight. Flight surveillance videos records pilots' actions during take-off and landing. However, videos of surviving a failed takeoff, emergency landing, crash landing or runway collision are inaccessible, either damaged or too rare. So, the task in this scenario is to identify features of the only kind action in available surveillance videos. And by doing this, we perform a rough screening test for pilots driving safety assurance, without accounts of planes crashing records.

For every action in boot camps, there are standard evaluate criteria. And new recruits undergoing training are imposed of strict orders requesting accurate and repetitive actions. This adaptive training process is a comprehensive observation at recruits' physical quality and ideological foundation. Nevertheless, it is heavy work training the recruits, since there just aren't a lot of instructors relative to the number of recruits. To attention, salute and squat are three basic actions for every recruit enlisted. The recruit movements should be standard and elaborate, so that paradigms of the different actions can be in a standard library. Video detection techniques in this scenario helps to facilitate automatic training, regulating and constant supervision.

1.3 Problems and Algorithm Innovation

For the type behavior recognition of the current three application scenarios (table tennis training, pilot driving, and boot camp), most of them use video decoding technology to decode the video frame by frame into pictures, and use machine learning, depth learning and other related technologies for training to obtain the classification model after training, and then use the model to achieve the effect of action classification.

In the process of our constant experiments, we found that there are two major problems. First, using the trained classification model can only achieve the purpose of recognition results, but cannot achieve the purpose of calculating times. For example, in the process of table tennis training, the same action of an athlete needs to be repeated 500 times, but at this time this classification model cannot achieve the purpose of calculating the number of times, and can only simply continue to classify the action. Second, in the process of using deep learning or machine learning, when the data reaches the fitting point is the most difficult problem for designers. Over fitting and under fitting will lead to errors in the identification results. The cost of time and energy spent in searching for appropriate training times and iterations of a certain type of data cannot be estimated.

For the two problems found above, we propose a new behavior recognition algorithm based on user-defined rules. For different application scenarios, we design a unique algorithm for classification. We use Openpose technology to extract the skeleton frame coordinates of each frame in the video, use it to calculate the relevant angle and distance, as well as the angle change curve, and use the most original pattern matching method to achieve the function of action classification and counting, which effectively solves the above problems. The two are the highlights of our algorithm.

The paper is organized as follows. Section 2 introduces the core algorithm and methodology. Section 3 presents and analyzes the influencing factors for each application scenario based on experiments. Section 4 discusses plausible suggestions for future use of the pose recognition system, and concludes the paper. Section 5 discusses the next research direction and relevant assumptions.

2 Algorithm Design

2.1 Methodology of Pose Recognition

Openpose is a technique used in mainstream research on human pose recognition, which transforms the person in the video into a skeleton map or skeleton point coordinates. The coco model used in this paper uses opepose to extract the 25 pairs of coordinates of the person, as shown in Fig. 1. The current mainstream research method for pose recognition is roughly divided into three steps, the first step is to transform the video into a skeleton map, the second step is to combine the skeleton map with a deep learning and machine learning model framework, and the third part uses the classification model trained in the previous step to perform classification operations so as to achieve the effect of pose recognition.

However, there are two main problems. First, for the pose, the image does not directly represent the relative position of each point, but only an approximate orientation, and cannot clearly represent the characteristics of the pose. Second, when training the model, researchers need to spend a lot of time and effort, first of all, to have a sufficiently complete training set, the amount of data needs to be large enough to get more relevant parameters of the pose, and in the design of the learning network, the number of layers, size of the convolutional layer, pooling layer, and the threshold value are required a lot of tests to get a suitable range, and not an accurate value. It will also change in different application scenarios.

For the first problem, we chose to further extract the human posture characteristics to get the skeleton coordinates, and the coordinate points more clearly show the position relationship and specific angles and distances of the limbs. The characteristics of the action can be shown more directly.

For the second problem, we choose the original idea of pattern matching which is gradually forgotten, and use the extracted skeleton coordinates to calculate the relevant angle and distance ratios as the basis of determination to identify the posture of the person in the video, which greatly reduces the time and effort to get the posture results in a short time.

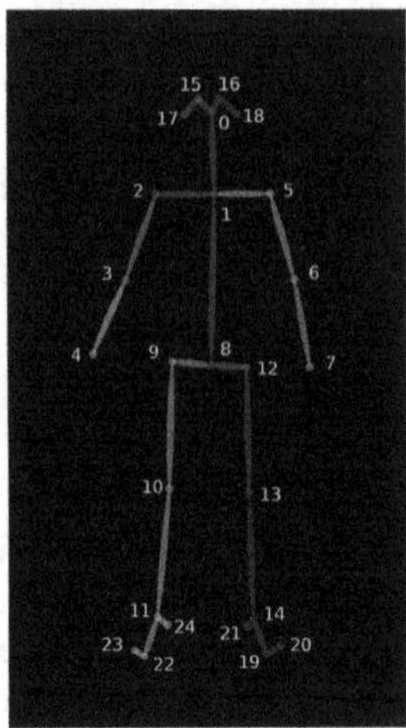

Fig. 1. Sequence diagram of 25 human body points extracted

For the three application scenarios, we initially calculated Angle-A, Angle-B, Distance-D1 and Distance-D2 based on the overall state of the action as the rules data for determining the pose. Detailed descriptions of the angles and distances are shown in Table 1.

Table 1. Angle distance description table

Name	Explanation
Angle A	Take (2, 3) and (4, 3) as edges and 3 as angles
Angle B	Take (9, 10) and (11, 10) as edges and 10 as angles
Distance-D1	Linear distance from point 4 to point 8
Distance-D2	Linear distance from point 4 to point 17

In the table tennis training scene, the recognition posture is preset for forehand attack (Fig. 2(1)) and backhand attack (Fig. 2(2)), as shown in the Fig. 2. Through a large amount of data analysis, it can be concluded that there are more frames with the ratio of Distance-D1 to Distance-D2 less than 1 in forehand attack, and more frames with the ratio of Distance-D1 to Distance-D2 greater than 1 in backhand attack.

Fig. 2. Forehand attack and backhand attack

According to the above steps, convert the video into 25 pairs of human skeleton frame coordinates, calculate the required values of Distance-D1 and Distance-D2, and divide the Distance-D1 and Distance-D2 of each frame to obtain their ratio L; when L is less than 1, it is judged as a forehand shot; when L is greater than 1, it is judged as a backhand shot. An example results is shown in Fig. 2.

The coordinates of all frames in the current video are operated in this way, and two parameters a and b are set using the statistical method. When the frame is determined as a forehand attack, a is added with 1, and when the frame is determined as a backhand attack, b is added with 1. In the final judgment, the sizes of a and b are compared. When a is greater than b, the video is judged as forehand attack; When a is less than b, the video is judged as backhand attack.

As shown in Fig. 3, the Fig. 3(1) is the distribution diagram of the decision points of the forehand attack video, and Fig. 3(2) is the distribution diagram of the decision points of the backhand attack video.

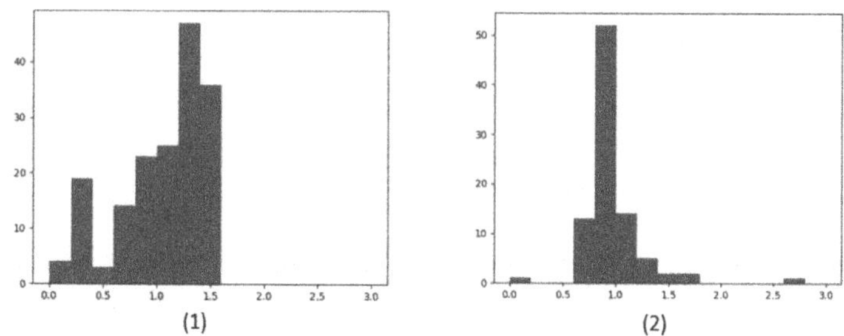

Fig. 3. The impact point of the ratio L of forehand attack and backhand attack

In the boot camp scene, the preset recognition poses is squat, salute and attention, as shown in Fig. 4.

Fig. 4. Squat, salute and attention

After pre-processing and analysis of data, it is concluded that the key characteristics to determine poses in this scene is angle A and angle B, as shown in Fig. 5.

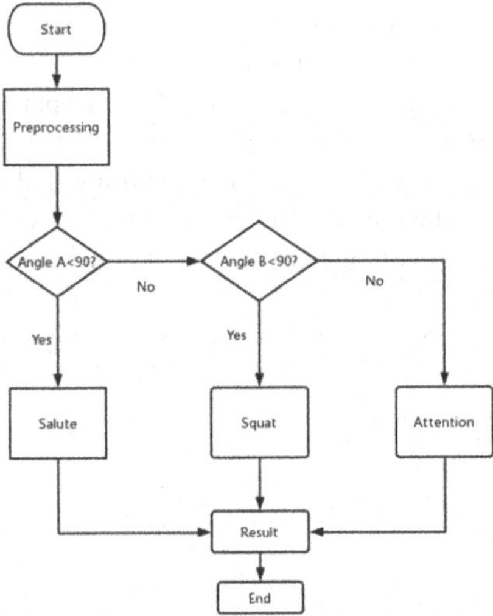

Fig. 5. Decision flow chart

In the pilot driving application scenario, a SVM model are trained for calculating the specific values in the above table. Normal frames can be identified as normal driving, and the others can be identified as abnormal driving. Abnormal driving is shown in Fig. 6. Perform this operation on the coordinates of all frames in the current video, and use the statistical method to set two parameters a and b. When the frame is determined as normal driving, a is added by 1, and when the frame is determined as abnormal driving, b is added by 1. In the final determination, the sizes of a and b are compared. When a is greater than b, the video is determined as normal driving; when a is less than b, the video is seen as abnormal driving.

(1)

(2)

Fig. 6. Diagram driving

2.2 Counting Algorithm in Table Tennis Training

In the application scenario of table tennis training, this paper proposes an algorithm to calculate the number of times of a same pose. When the forehand attack or backhand attack move is carried out continuously, the angle transformation of angle A presents a circular state. Here, the angle is binarized. First, calculate the average value Avg of angle A in the video, and then traverse the entire video. When angle A is greater than Avg, it is recorded as 1, otherwise it is recorded as 0, and then connect it. As shown in the Fig. 7, after binarization, it is a scatter plot of angle change, Fig. 7(1) is a backhand shot plot, Fig. 7(2) is a forehand shot plot, and it is recorded as one shot from the crest to the trough, and to the crest. Thus, the number of times of this action in the video can be obtained.

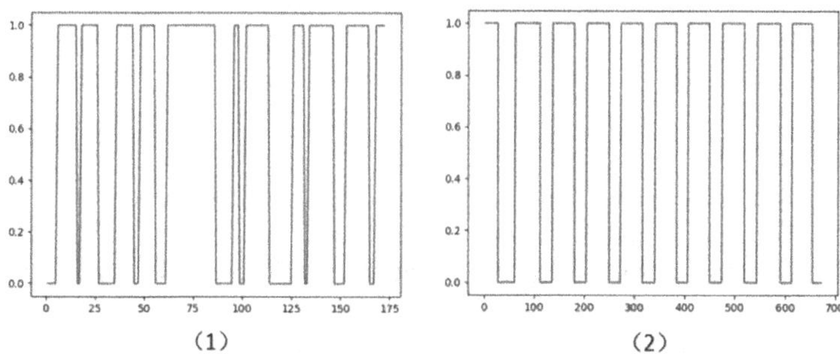

Fig. 7. Scatter diagram of angle change after binary processing

3 Experiment Results

3.1 Table Tennis Training Test

In the video test of table tennis training, there are 30 test videos, the time is about 60 seconds to 100 seconds, and the average frame number is 25 f/s. Using Openpose to decode the video, the data obtained is about 2500 groups. The following Table 2 shows the recognition accuracy of the table tennis training posture.

Table 2. Table tennis training test results

Class	Quantity (Number of frame groups)	Recognition accuracy
Forehand attack	1343	85%
Backhand attack	1148	87%

In order to reflect the availability of this algorithm, a control group using CNN for pose classification is set. However, since this algorithm only uses one ratio as the basis for judgment, if a parameter is directly used for training in the depth learning network, the effect is poor, so 70% of the data set obtained by combining the skeleton coordinates extracted from the above data video with the calculated Distance D1, Distance D2 and their ratio L is put into the 1D CNN, As a training set, it is used for model training, and 30% as a test set, it is used for model testing. The number of layers of CNN model is 4. Each layer includes convolution layer, pooling layer and full connection layer. The number of convolution cores is 16, 32, 64 and 128, respectively. The length of convolution cores is 6. Test results are shown in the following Table 3.

Table 3. CNN classification and testing (table tennis training)

Class	Number of training sets	Number of test sets	Training accuracy	Accuracy of test
Forehand attack	941	402	80%	69%
Backhand attack	1148	344	82%	71%

According to Table 2 and Table 3, the test accuracy of the classification algorithm proposed in this paper is better than that of CNN model classification. Secondly, when using CNN, the data needs to be transferred into the CNN model for parameter calculation, and then compared with the parameters in the pre trained model, and then output the results. The classification algorithm proposed in this paper does not need parameter calculation, and directly classifies according to the set rules. The output results greatly reduce the user's waiting time.

There are 6 counting algorithm test videos, the time is about 60 s to 100 s, and the average frame number is 25 f/s. The test results are shown in the following Table 4. The test data is basically correct, and the error is within ± 1. In addition, counting algorithm is not provided by deep learning and machine learning model classification.

Table 4. Counting test

Id	Actual times	Number of tests	Correctness
Test-1	13	13	YES
Test-2	6	6	YES
Test-3	6	6	YES
Test-4	7	7	YES
Test-5	9	8	NO
Test-6	5	5	YES

3.2 Boot Camp Test

In the video test of boot camp test, there are 33 test videos, with the time between 60 s and 100 s, and the average number of frames is 25 f/s. Using Openpose to decode the video, the data obtained is about 2300 groups. The following Table 5 shows the recognition accuracy of recruits poses.

Table 5. Test results of recruits poses

Class	Quantity (Number of frame groups)	Recognition accuracy
Squat	953	90%
Salute	758	89%
Attention	637	95%

In order to reflect the availability of this algorithm, a group of control groups using CNN for pose classification is set. The specific model is consistent with the field of table tennis training. The training data is the combination of skeleton coordinates extracted from the video and calculated Angle A and Angle B to obtain a data set. 70% of the data is put into 1D CNN as a training set for model training, 30% as a test set for model testing. The test results are shown in the following Table 6.

Table 6. CNN classification and testing (boot camp)

Class	Number of training sets	Number of test sets	Training accuracy	Accuracy of test
Squat	667	286	81%	70%
Salute	530	228	78%	71%
Attention	445	192	82%	68%

According to Table 5 and Table 6, the test accuracy of the classification algorithm proposed in this paper is better than that of CNN model classification. It shows that the classification effect of this innovative algorithm is ideal.

3.3 Pilot Driving Test

In the video test of pilot driving test, there are 30 test videos, the time is about 60 s to 100 s, and the average frame number is 25 f/s. Using Openpose to decode the video, the data obtained is about 2200 groups. The following Table 7 shows the recognition accuracy of pilot driving poses.

Table 7. Test results of pilots driving poses

Class	Quantity (Number of frame groups)	Recognition accuracy
Normal driving	1593	90%
Abnormal driving	636	85%

In order to reflect the availability of ideas, set up a control group that uses CNN for posture classification. The specific model is consistent with the field of table tennis training. The training data is the combination of skeleton coordinates extracted from the video and calculated Angle A, Angle B, Distance D1 and Distance D2 to obtain a data set. 70% of the data is put into 1D CNN as a training set for model training, and 30% is used as a test set for model testing. The test results are shown in the following Table 8.

Table 8. CNN classification and testing (pilot driving)

Class	Number of training sets	Number of test sets	Training accuracy	Accuracy of test
Normal driving	1115	478	78%	70%
Abnormal driving	445	191	81%	72%

According to Table 7 and Table 8, the test accuracy of the classification algorithm proposed in this paper is better than that of CNN model classification. The training effect of CNN model for one-dimensional data is weaker than that of svm model. The advantage of CNN model is that it is more sensitive to RGB type images, while the advantage of svm model is that it is more sensitive to one-dimensional data. In the case of fewer categories and one-dimensional data, the effect of svm is more prominent.

3.4 Algorithm Analysis

First of all, based on the above experimental results, it can be seen that the experimental results of the human pose recognition algorithm based on rule matching are better than those of the human pose recognition algorithm based on CNN. The advantage of rule matching based human pose recognition algorithm is that when the angle in the video is positive and the picture is clear and the skeleton is intact, it is less difficult to analyze the human pose rules; when recognizing the human pose, there are better results and it takes relatively less time and effort. The accuracy rate of single pose recognition is above 85%. When there are more angles in the video, the screen angle switches frequently or the screen is not clear and the skeleton is not complete, the difficulty of analyzing the human pose rules increases subsequently and fluctuates when recognizing the human pose. This is a more testing data set, whether there is the same action of different angles and orientation of the pose data. When there is enough variety of data, the results are relatively stable, otherwise there will be fluctuations.

Secondly, the pose counting is a brand new proposed algorithm, currently its recorded times, the error is within ± 1, the main original, the current algorithm is not able to determine what state the character pose is in at the beginning of the video. A complete pose of the character is divided into a start state, an intermediate state and an end state. When the video starts in the middle state, the pose counting algorithm will have errors. When the video starts in the other two states, the pose counting algorithm does not make errors.

Finally, although the algorithm still needs to be improved, it still has a relatively large advantage over CNN-based human pose recognition algorithms. First, the algorithm is simpler in terms of implementation difficulty. The algorithm is more targeted and oriented to individual application scenarios and practical needs. It is not just pursuing to increase the variety of recognized postures. Second, the problem of fitting in machine learning algorithms such as CNN networks has always existed, and it is not easy to train when to reach the best fit.

4 Conclusion

In this paper, the original idea of pattern matching is used, and a user-defined rule-based pose classification algorithm is proposed, which greatly reduces the time and energy spent in training models and selecting process of the optimal model in machine learning or deep learning. The algorithm also provides the function of calculating the number of actions that the mainstream deep learning and machine learning models do not support. It can get the classification results and number of times in a very short time, effectively solving its shortcomings, and also help users get the required information more quickly and accurately. The research and proposal of this algorithm also provides a new idea for attitude estimation research, and does not blindly use depth learning or machine learning framework. We can start from the most fundamental of the data, mining its internal relationship from its most original geometric relationship, and apply it to the algorithm, that is, the idea of pattern matching, to solve practical problems more quickly.

5 Future Work

We will continue to further analyze the attitude of the above three application scenarios, introduce more attitudes, enrich the categories identified in the scene, and further improve the two algorithms (attitude estimation algorithm and counting algorithm).

There are two points in the research of attitude estimation algorithm. First, the currently set decision rules are mainly used to classify and recognize the pose with a clear face and a more accurate skeleton coordinate recognition. Later, multi angle recognition will be introduced, and different angle projections will be introduced for the same pose. Analyze the relevant features of the same action at different angles to further improve the accuracy of recognition. Second, for the motion process of two types of poses in the same application scenario, there are similar fragments or confusing features. Later, time series will be introduced to further describe the motion process of the pose and further improve the accuracy of recognition.

For the counting algorithm, after introducing the dimension of time sequence, we can more accurately find the starting and ending states of the attitude, calculate the changes of its coordinates and angles in this short time, seek its internal laws, and obtain more accurate times information.

Provide a new algorithm with higher recognition rate and better robustness for the research field of attitude estimation.

References

1. Lei, Q., Chen, D.S., Li, S.Z.: Advances on human action recognition in realistic scenes. Comput. Sci. **41**(12), 1–7 (2014)
2. Cao, Z., Gines, H.M., Tomas, S., Wei, S.-E., Sheikh Yaser, A.: OpenPose: realtime multi-person 2D pose estimation using part affinity fields. IEEE Trans. Pattern Anal. Mach. Intell. **2021,** 172–186 (2021)
3. Liang, S., Sun, X., Wei, Y.: Compositional human pose regression. Comput. Vis. Image Underst. 176–177 (2018)
4. Wang, X., Tong, J., Wang, R.: Attention refined network for human pose estimation. Neural Process. Lett. **53**, 2853–2872 (2021)
5. Liu, Z., et al.: Temporal feature alignment and mutual information maximization for video-based human pose estimation. In: Proceedings of the IEEE/CVF Conference on Computer Vision and Pattern Recognition, pp. 11006–11016 (2022)
6. Jianrong, C., Yaqin, Z., Zhang, Y., Lv, J., Yang, H.: Fall detection algorithm based on joint features. Comput. Appl. **42**(02), 622–630 (2022)
7. Haozu, J.: Abnormal behavior recognition based on human joint points. Dalian University of Technology (2021)
8. Baraldi, L., et al.: Gesture recognition in ego-centric videos using dense trajectories and hand segmentation. In: Computer Society Conference on Computer Vision and Pattern Recognition Workshops, OH, pp. 702–707. IEEE (2014)
9. Guo, G., Lai, A.: A survey on still image based human action recognition. Pattern Recogn. **47**(10), 3343–3361 (2014)
10. Poppe, R.: A survey on vision-based human action recognition. Image Vis. Comput. **28**(6), 976–990 (2010)
11. Herath, S., Harandi, M., Porikli, F.J.: Going deeper into action recognition: a survey. Image Vis. Comput. **2017**(60), 4–21 (2017)
12. Kutschbach, T., et al.: Sequential sensor fusion combining probability hypothesis density and kernelized correlation filters for multi-object tracking in video data. In: 2017 14th IEEE International Conference on Advanced Video and Signal Based Surveillance (AVSS). IEEE, USA (2017)

13. Ellis, C., et al.: Exploring the trade-off between accuracy and observational latency in action recognition. Int. J. Comput. Vis. **101**(3), 420–436 (2013)
14. Eweiwi, A., Cheema, M.S., Bauckhage, C., Gall, J.: Efficient pose-based action recognition. In: Cremers, D., Reid, I., Saito, H., Yang, M.-H. (eds.) ACCV 2014. LNCS, vol. 9007, pp. 428–443. Springer, Cham (2015). https://doi.org/10.1007/978-3-319-16814-2_28
15. Yang, X., Tian, Y. L.: Eigenjoints-based action recognition using naive-Bayes-nearest-neighbor. In: 2012 IEEE Computer Society Conference on Computer Vision and Pattern Recognition Workshops. RI, pp. 14–19. IEEE (2012)
16. Seidenari, L., et al.: Recognizing actions from depth cameras as weakly aligned multi-part bag-of-poses. Proceedings of the IEEE Conference on Computer Vision and Pattern Recognition Workshops 2013, pp. 479–485. IEEE, OR (2013)
17. Du, Y., Wang, W., Wang, L.: In: Proceedings of the IEEE Conference on Computer Vision and Pattern Recognition, pp. 1110–1118. IEEE, MA (2015)
18. Song, S., et al.: An end-to-end spatio-temporal attention model for human action recognition from skeleton data. In: Proceedings of AAAI Conference on Artificial Intelligence, vol. 31(1), pp. 4263–4270. AAAI, CA (2017)
19. Li. S., et al.: Independently recurrent neural network (INDRNN): Building a longer and deeper RNN. In: Proceedings of the IEEE Conference on Computer Vision and Pattern Recognition, pp. 5457–5466. IEEE, UT (2018)
20. Lipton, Z.C.: A critical review of recurrent neural networks for sequence learning. Comput. Sci. **2015**, 1–35 (2015)
21. Tang, W., Yu, P., Wu, Y.: Deeply learned compositional models for human pose estimation. In: Ferrari, V., Hebert, M., Sminchisescu, C., Weiss, Ys. (eds.) ECCV 2018. LNCS, vol. 11207, pp. 197–214. Springer, Cham (2018). https://doi.org/10.1007/978-3-030-01219-9_12
22. Papandreou, G., et al.: Towards accurate multi-person pose estimation in the wild. In: Proceedings - 30th IEEE Conference on Computer Vision and Pattern Recognition 2017, pp. 3711–3719. IEEE, HI (2017)
23. Xing, J., Zhang, J., Xue, C.: Multi person pose estimation based on improved openpose model. IOP Conf. Ser. Mater. Sci. Eng. **768**(7) (2020)
24. Zhu, H., Zhu, C., Xu, Z.: Research progress of human behavior recognition dataset. Acta Automatica Sinica **44**(06), 978–1004 (2018)
25. Xu, G., et al.: Action recognition and behavior understanding. J. Image Graphics **14**(2), 7–13 (2009)

Action Recognition for Solo-Militant Based on ResNet and Rule Matching

Lijing Tong[1], Jinzhi Feng[1], Huiqun Zhao[2], and Kun Liu[2](✉)

[1] School of Information Science and Technology, North China University of Technology, Beingjing 100144, China
ljtong@ncut.edu.cn, fengjinzhi@mail.ncut.edu.cn
[2] Advanced Institute of Big Data, Beijing 100195, China
Zhaohq6625@sina.com, liukun@aibd.ac.cn

Abstract. To solve the problem of low accuracy of solo-militant action recognition under small sample data set, a new method of solo-militant behavior analysis based on ResNet and rule matching is proposed in this paper. The militant's action classification is done by 2 levels of classification. Firstly, the skeleton key points are extracted from the militant's combat video frames by OpenPose. Then, the first level classification of militant's action is performed by the ResNet deep learning network based on RGB images and combined with the skeleton key point rule set of militant's action. Next, the second level classification of militant's action is performed by the CNN network based on skeleton map. At last, the final classification of militant's action is output according to the 2 levels of classification. The experimental results show that the proposed method in this paper can achieve more effective recognition rate of solo-militant action under small sample data set.

Keywords: ResNet Network · Rule matching · Action recognition

1 Introduction

With the rapid spread and development of video acquisition equipment and broadband networks, video has become the main carrier of information. The massive emergence of video data contains a wealth of information, providing a basis for information mining. Deeper mining of media information to provide users of media videos with information to assist in decision making has gradually become a widespread demand among video users, but it also poses a greater challenge. If the massive amount of videos are analyzed and labeled manually, the workload is huge, which will not only consume a lot of energy and financial resources, but also there will certainly be delays, and timeliness and efficiency cannot be guaranteed. Video behavior recognition is an important research area of computer vision, which refers to the automatic recognition of actions and behaviors from videos, and has a very wide application value. And analyzing foreign war videos has an important research value for one country to understand other countries' combat methods, weapons, etc.

Y. Tan and Y. Shi (Eds.): DMBD 2022, CCIS 1744, pp. 192–208, 2022.
https://doi.org/10.1007/978-981-19-9297-1_15

This paper introduces the traditional rule matching method into the solo-militant behavioral action classification and proposes a behavioral analysis algorithm combined with ResNet, aiming to identify the combat behaviors of solo-militant including marching, equipment use, standing shooting aiming behavior, kneeling shooting aiming behavior, ambush shooting aiming behavior and other behaviors in domestic and foreign media videos of Russian and Ukrainian war reports, starting from video big data analysis technology. The method extracts the information of the key point location of the militant's skeleton by OpenPose model, calculates the angle and distance to give the classification labels for the action design features, and combines the ResNet classification results to give the final classification results.

2 Related Works

Despite the importance of militant action recognition for battlefield awareness, intelligence analysis, and video retrieval in the military domain, very limited research work has been conducted in this specific area, and the research interests of some experts are currently focused on the broader field of action recognition.

As far as the field of action recognition is concerned, human action recognition is mainly divided into two categories: action recognition based on 2-dimensional image data and action recognition based on 3-dimensional image data.

Action recognition based on 2-dimensional image data is used to obtain the action category of the human body by analyzing 2-dimensional image RGB data or by analyzing the RGB image frame data decoded from the video. It can be further divided into two main categories: traditional feature extraction methods and deep learning-based feature extraction methods [1].

Traditional feature extraction methods include two types: feature extraction methods based on human geometric features or motion information and feature extraction methods based on spatio-temporal interest points. Fujiyoshi et al. [2] is a human action recognition method based on human geometric features, which uses a star-like diagram represented by five vertices of the limbs and head to represent the human pose in the current frame, and uses a vector of five feature points and the center of gravity as the feature vector of the action. Bobick et al.'s work is a motion information-based feature extraction method, which extracts different features from motion energy images (MEI) and motion history images (MHI) [3] to interpret the motion category of human body [4]. The feature extraction method based on spatio-temporal interest points is based on detecting the interest points in the video, which are the most dramatically changing locations in the spatio-temporal dimension [5], and then extracting the relevant regional features based on the interest point locations and analyzing the human motion classes. Wang et al. [6] compared various local feature descriptors (HOG3D, HOG/HOF [7], Extended SURF), in the literature. Among these descriptors, it was found that the descriptors integrating gradient and optical flow information had better effect on human motion recognition, while HOG3D had the best effect on human motion recognition. To automatically recognize actions in realistic and complex scenes, Nazir et al. [8] combined Har-ris 3D spatio-temporal features and 3D scale-invariant feature transformation detection methods to extract key regions and represented actions with traditional visual word histograms, which greatly improved the accuracy of action recognition. Wang et al. [9] made full use of valid pose information in still image action recognition. By computing key points to generate an explicitly action inclusive scalable posture-enhanced relationship module is used to extract the implicit relationship between posture and human body, and output posture-enhanced relationship features with powerful representation capability. Sima et al. [10] proposed to first fuse motion and static information of human action into features, and construct a motion model using skeleton vectors to describe the changes of human action after feature extraction. The model is then introduced into an adaptive time pyramid to obtain global and local information.

Deep learning-based feature extraction methods, mainly through supervised convolutional neural networks, Au-to Encoder-based deep neural networks, Restricted Boltzmann machine (RBM)-based deep belief networks (DBN) [11, 12] and Recurrent neural network (RNN)-based deep neural networks, are used to recognize human action types. Russel et al. [13] used single-frame data and optical flow data to capture human motion information using convolutional neural networks for human behavior recognition. Karpathy et al. [14] used a multi-resolution convolutional neural network for video feature extraction, where the input video was divided into two separate data streams: the low-resolution stream and the original-resolution stream. Song et al. [15] constructed an action recognition model based on RNN using LSTM, which uses different levels of attention to learn the recognizable joints of skeleton in each input frame. Donahue et al. [16] explored the application of LSTM in two-dimensional convolutional network time series modeling and proposed a long-term recurrent convolutional network that maps variable-length video frames to variable-length outputs instead of simple action classification. Shen et al. [17] proposed to combine complex network coding and LSTM for human action recognition by using network topological attributes as feature vectors. Shi et al. [18] encoded body part features into a human body based spatio-temporal graph and used a lightweight graph convolution module to explicitly model the dependencies between body parts. Xu et al. [19] proposed a fast network for human action recognition to improve the efficiency of optical flow feature extraction, using CNN instead of VGG16 to process optical flow features to obtain rich features. Qin et al. [20], to improve the recognition of similar action accuracy, higher-order features in the form of human motion skeletal angle coding (AGE) were fused into a modern architecture to robustly capture the relationship between joints and body parts. Yang et al. [21] extracted and fused temporal and spatial information through two networks consisting of CNN and LSTM with multiple inputs for processing large-scale video frames, which has solved the problem of long-term dependency.

Action recognition based on 3-dimensional image data is to obtain the classification of human body's action by analyzing the depth data of each point on the 2-dimensional image RGB data composite to form RGB-D data, or by analyzing the sequence of 3-dimensional RGB-D image data captured by 3-dimensional cameras. The methods can be divided into three categories: depth sequence-based methods, skeletal data-based methods, and multi-feature fusion methods. The typical research results are as follows. Chen et al. [22] gave a depth sequence-based action recognition method, which used local binary pattern features based on DMM to represent actions, analyzed the spatio-temporal depth structure in forward, lateral and upward directions [23], extracted the motion trajectory shape and boundary histogram features of spatio-temporal interest points, and used dense sample points and joints in each view to represent the action and improve the accuracy of action recognition. Li et al. [24] proposed a human action recognition method based on skeletal data, which uses CNN deep learning to represent skeletal sequences as images, encodes temporal dynamics and skeletal joints as rows and columns, respectively, and then feeds them into CNN to recognize human action classification just like image classification. Shahroudy et al. [25] proposed a new human action recognition method based on multi-feature fusion. It is based on a depth self-encoding nonlinear co-component analysis network that fuses multiple dynamic features extracted from RGB, depth video, and 3D skeleton sequences for human action recognition. Alsarhan et al. [26] focused on adaptive feature extraction of high-resolution information in spatial and temporal dimensions, and proposed an enhanced discriminative graph convolutional network based on the skeleton data recognition attention mechanism (ED-GCN), for the temporal dimension motivated by temporal modeling in video. They introduced the adaptive time building block (ATB), which is able to capture temporal structure flexibly. Li et al. [27] proposed a new dual-stream spatial Graphormer network that uses structural encoding combined with attention to construct joint and skeletal information. Jacek et al. [28] proposed to build a network on the original depth map for action recognition. Frame features are extracted using a convolutional autoencoder on the depth mapping sequence, and features are extracted in a CNN sent to a 1D CNN. Xu et al. [29] used an effective data preprocessing method for RGB and skeleton, and proposed a multimodal fusion network BPAN combining RGB and skeleton sequences, which can effectively compress RGB and skeletal features and project them into the latent subspace to obtain fusion features.

The action recognition based on traditional feature extraction method for 2-dimensional image data has achieved good recognition effect in certain application scenarios, but it lacks flexible adaptability and robustness for complex action classification in complex scenarios. The action recognition based on deep learning feature extraction method for 2-dimensional image data, although incorporating artificial intelligence method, has good action recognition effect for large data samples, but the recognition accuracy for small sample data is not high. For the various action recognition methods for 3-dimensional image data, although the combination of image depth data improves the accuracy of action recognition, but the complexity of the algorithm, the acquisition results of image depth data are often not accurate enough, the cost of 3-dimensional capture equipment is expensive, and other reasons, and limit the application of action recognition algorithms.

Aiming at the problems of poor robustness, low accuracy of small sample data and difficulty of 3-dimensional data acquisition in some current research works in the field of human action recognition, this paper proposes a solo-militant action recognition method based on ResNet and rule matching under the premise of small sample for 2-dimensional video data.

This paper is organized as follows: Sect. 3 gives a ResNet and CNN based approach for solo-militant action recognition. In this section, two-level heterogeneous hybrid deep learning network architectures, ResNet-based recognition method, and CNN-based recognition method are given respectively. Section 4 gives a rule-set based action discrimination method for solo-militant. In this section, the rule matching based action recognition processing method and its hybrid inference mechanism combined with ResNet and CNN recognition methods are introduced. Section 5 gives the experimental results and analysis. In this section, the experimental setting, the data set, and the comparison of our method with other methods are presented. Section 6 gives a summary of the content and methods of this paper.

3 Action Recognition Based on ResNet and CNN

3.1 Two Level Heterogeneous Hybrid Deep Learning Network Architecture

In using deep learning network for analysis of marching, apparatus use, other, standing shooting aiming behavior, kneeling shooting aiming behavior, ambush shooting aiming behavior of solo-militant, in order to improve the accuracy of deep learning network analysis and reduce the influence of video angle, color, illumination and other factors, the traditional means of analysis of single neural network is improved and deep learning and analysis method of two-stage neural network is used. The first level uses ResNet18 network model to learn and analyze marching, instrument use, shooting-like aiming behavior, and other behaviors; the second level uses CNN deep learning network to learn and analyze standing shooting aiming behavior, kneeling shooting aiming behavior, and ambling shooting aiming behavior.

According to the different task characteristics of the two-layer deep learning network, the input of the first-level deep learning network model is the original scene picture, and the first-level classification is performed by the information of environment, militant behavior, and weaponry; the second-level deep learning network model uses pseudo-images of extracted militant skeleton maps for the input of the network model since it only needs to identify specific shooting aiming actions for classification based on the militant's action posture without redundant scene information judgment. A combination of original image and skeleton map is used for hierarchical training to achieve better behavioral analysis.

The flowchart of the two-level heterogeneous hybrid deep learning network system is shown in Fig. 1.

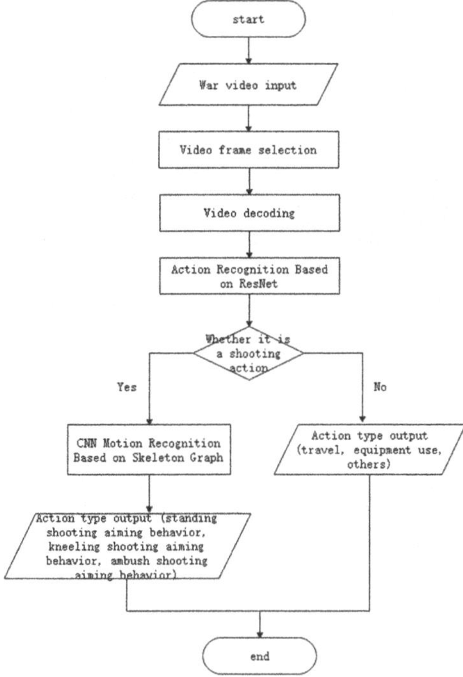

Fig. 1. Flow chart of two-level heterogeneous hybrid deep learning network system

The input of the second layer of the deep learning network is a pseudo-image of the human skeleton map based on the location information of 25 skeletal points of the human body extracted from the OpenPose human pose model. The original image and the pseudo-image of skeleton are shown in Fig. 2.

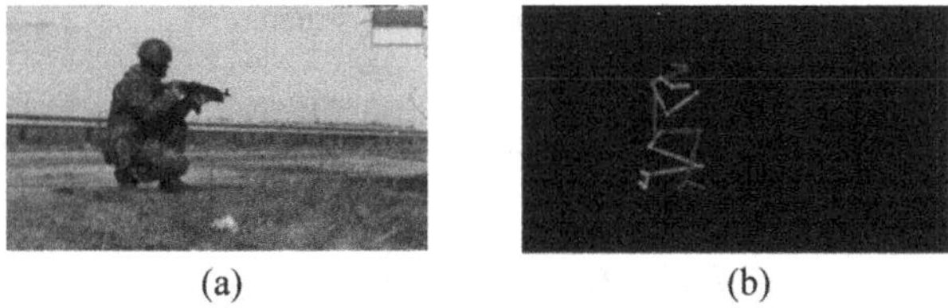

(a) (b)

Fig. 2. Original image and its pseudo-images of skeleton: (a) original image; (b) pseudo-images of skeleton.

3.2 Recognition Based on ResNet Network

For regular networks, the model accuracy is continuously improved with the increasing number of network layers, while the training accuracy and testing accuracy decrease rapidly after the network layers increase to a certain number. ResNet introduces a residual network structure, in which the data output of a layer in the first few layers is directly skipped and introduced into the input part of the later data layers. By this residual network structure, the network layers can be designed to be very deep and the final classification results are very good. Therefore, in this paper, ResNet18 is used for the first layer of action classification, and the structure is shown in Fig. 3. The data is first input through a 7 * 7 convolution, and then input to a residual block after a maximum pooling layer. This residual block consists of two convolutional layers with 64 3 * 3 convolutional kernels. The residual blocks of different dimensions are stacked and the data are downscaled with 1 * 1 convolution for each doubling of the number of convolution kernels. Finally, the image is predicted by a fully connected classification layer.

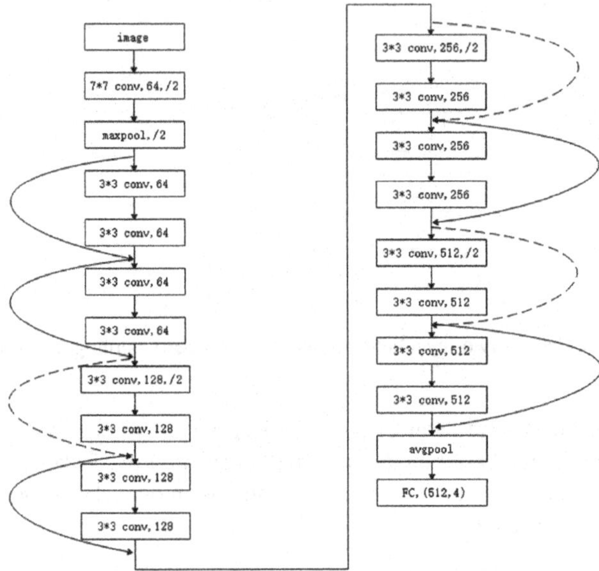

Fig. 3. ResNet18 network structure

A residual network is composed of a series of residual blocks. A residual block can be expressed as:

$$H(x) = x + F(x) \tag{1}$$

In the unit mapping, $y = x$ is the observed value, i.e., the input of the model is the original video frame picture, *H(x)* is the predicted value, i.e., the output of the model, and *F(x)* is the corresponding residual.

The residual block is divided into two parts: the direct mapping part and the residual part. $h(x_l)$ is the direct mapping, and is shown on the left in the Fig. 4; $F(x_l, W_l)$ is the residual part, which generally consists of two or three convolution operations, i.e., the part containing the convolution on the right in Fig. 4.

Weight in Fig. 4 here refers to the convolution operation, addition refers to the unit addition operation. BN is batch normalization, which is a structure that approximates the output of the convolutional layer as a Gaussian distribution, making the network more stable during training and effectively avoiding gradient disappearance and gradient explosion. Using BN together with the activation function can effectively improve the performance of the network, and the batch normalization formula is:

$$y(k) = \gamma(k)\frac{x^k - \mu^k}{\sqrt{\left(\sigma^k\right)^2 + \varepsilon}} + \beta^2 \tag{2}$$

where $x(k)$ and $y(k)$ are the original data and the output data after normalization, respectively, $\mu(k)$ and $\sigma(k)$ are the mean and standard deviation of the data, respectively, ε is a quantity to prevent the denominator from being zero, $\beta(k)$ and $\gamma(k)$ are the learnable translation and scaling parameters, respectively. The role of β and γ in batch normalization is mainly to preserve the parameters during the training of the network, making the neurons adaptive to learn the mean and variance of a batch.

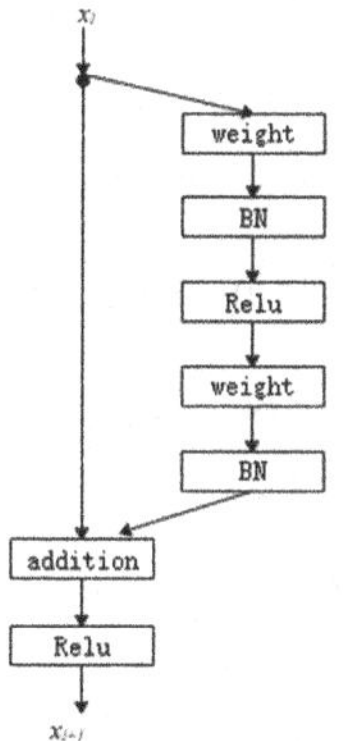

Fig. 4. Residual blocks

In a convolutional network, x_l may not have the same number of feature map as x_{l+1}, and it is then necessary to use 1×1 convolution for dimensionality up or down. At this point, the residual block is expressed as:

$$x_{l+1} = h(x_l) + F(x_l, W_l) \tag{3}$$

where $h(x_l) = W_l^{'}x$. $W_l^{'}$ is the 1×1 convolution operation.

3.3 Identification Based on CNN Network

The design of CNN-based deep learning network architecture for solo-militant behavior analysis is shown in Fig. 5.

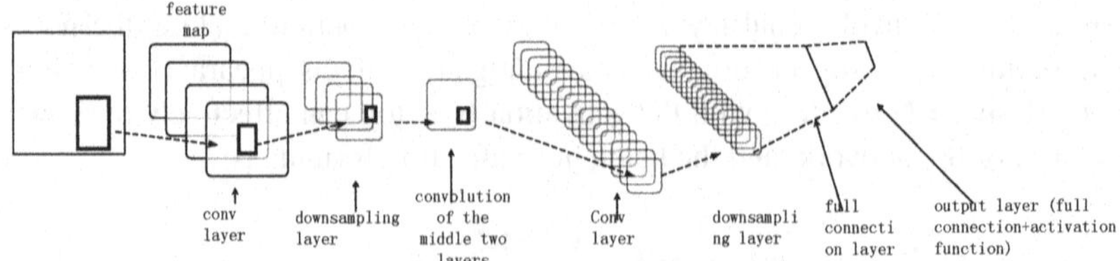

Fig. 5. CNN-based deep learning network for warfighter action recognition

(1) A CNN based deep learning network is established through the deep learning framework Tensorflow, which is divided into input layer, convolution layer, incentive layer, pooling layer, full connection layer and output layer.
(2) For the standing shot aiming behavior, kneeling shot aiming behavior, and ambush shot aiming behavior, the input layer is fed with a 150 * 150 pseudo-militant skeleton image generated based on 25 key point coordinate data.
(3) The convolution layer uses a 6 * 6 convolution kernel, and the convolution operation uses a template operation
(4) The convolution layer is followed by the excitation layer, which is a mapping of the output of the convolution layer, and the excitation function used is ReLu function.

$$f(x) = max(x, 0) \tag{4}$$

The function is shown in Fig. 6:

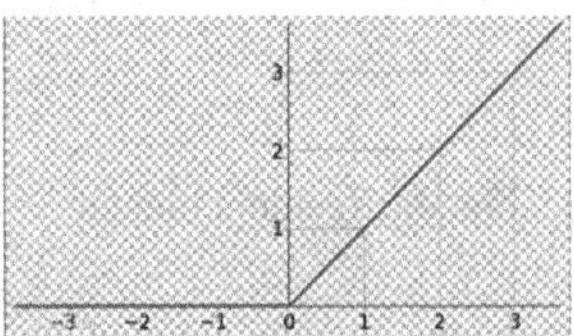

Fig. 6. ReLu function image

(5) The pooling layer scales down the width and height of the feature image from *(W, H)* to *(W/2, H/2)*, using a maximum pooling operation of 2 * 2 for down sampling.
(6) The full connection layer performs weight-based combination operations on image features, as shown in Fig. 7.

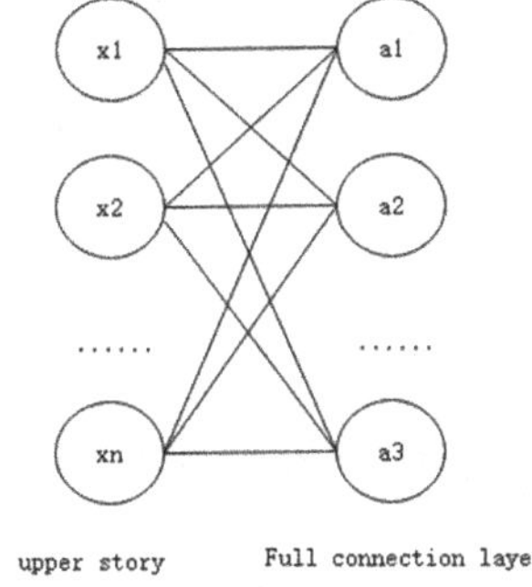

Fig. 7. Schematic diagram of the fully connected layer

The output of the full connection layer is:

$$\begin{cases} a1 = W_{11} * x1 + W_{12} * x2 + \cdots + W_{1n} * xn + b_1 \\ a2 = W_{21} * x1 + W_{22} * x2 + \cdots + W_{2n} * x3 + b_2 \\ a3 = W_{31} * x1 + W_{32} * x2 + \cdots + W_{3n} * x3 + b_3 \\ \cdots\cdots\cdots\cdots\cdots\cdots\cdots\cdots\cdots\cdots\cdots\cdots\cdots \\ an = W_{n1} * x1 + W_{n2} * x2 + \cdots + W_{nn} * x3 + b_3 \end{cases} \tag{5}$$

where *x1, x2, x3... xn* are the inputs of the fully connected layer and *a1, a2, a3... an* are the outputs.

(7) The output layer finally completes the output of the final target result, the excitation function used is the softmax function, the softmax function is accessed behind the fully connected layer, the output result is the probability of a specific kind of shooting aiming action, the softmax function can be expressed as:

$$Softmax_i = \frac{e^{v_i}}{\sum_{j=1}^{k} e^{v_j}} \tag{6}$$

where $k = 3$ denotes the three categories of standing shot aiming bahavior, kneeling shot aiming behavior, and ambush shot aiming behavior output by the deep learning network, v is the output vector, v_j is the value of the *jth* output or category in v, and i denotes the current category to be calculated between 0 and 1, and the softmax value of all categories sums to 1.

The softmax function of a militant's skeletal image for different values of v_i is shown in Fig. 8.

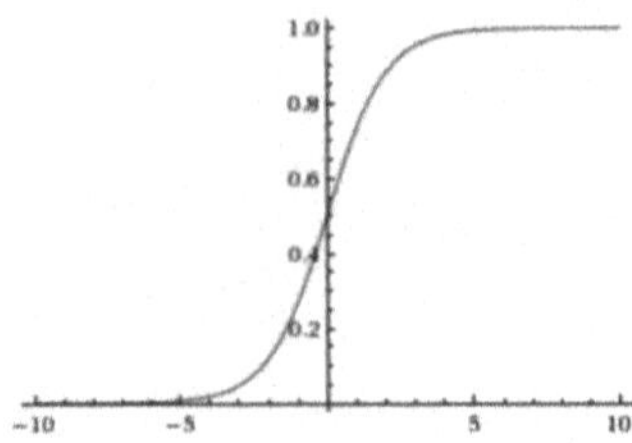

Fig. 8. Softmax function image

(8) The loss function is proposed to be a cross-entropy loss function with multiple classifications.

$$L = \frac{1}{N}\sum_i L_i = -\frac{1}{N}\sum_i \sum_{c=1}^{M} y_{ic}\log(p_{ic}) \tag{7}$$

where M = 3 denotes the number of categories, y_{ic} symbolic function, and p_{ic} predicted probability of observing sample i belonging to category c (standing shot aiming behavior, kneeling shot aiming behavior, and ambulatory shot aiming behavior).

4 Individual Action Discrimination Based on Rule Set

Although deep learning networks have a certain learning capability, they require a large amount of sample data and sometimes under or over-fit, so a geometric logic relationship based on skeletal joint points is used to construct a rule set for solo-militant behavior analysis for marching, equipment use, shooting-like aiming actions, and other classifications. For a given solo-militant behavior category, the position relationship between its corresponding skeletal joint points is constructed, and the spatial position relationship between the skeletal joint points is used to analyze the behavior categories such as marching, instrument use, shooting class aiming action, and others.

This part mainly addresses the problem that the recognition of deep learning network is sometimes not accurate enough, and gives specific rules for determining the type of action based on the skeletal coordinate points extracted by OpenPose according to the actual situation of solo-militant action. For the specific geometric position of the current skeletal joint point, the determination result of the rule set is used if the preconditions of rule inference are satisfied, otherwise the determination result of the deep learning network is used.

The flow chart of action recognition based on rule set is shown in Fig. 9.

Fig. 9. Flow chart of action recognition based on rule set

The information of skeleton key point location extracted by OpenPose is shown in Fig. 10.

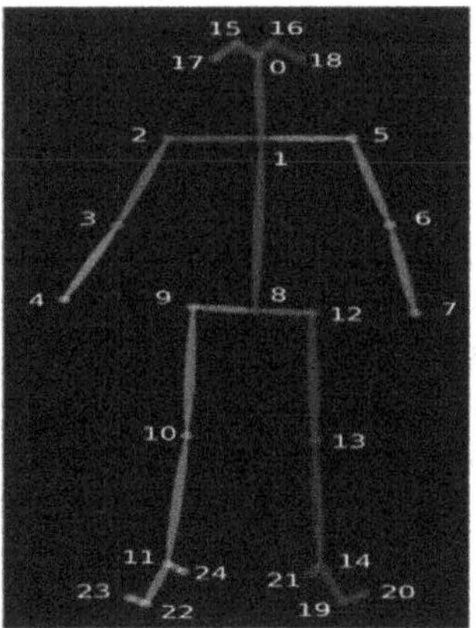

Fig. 10. Position information of skeleton key points

For the classification of equipment use, marching, shooting-like aiming behavior, and other behaviors, the distance, angle, and height difference were calculated from the extracted skeletal key point coordinate data according to the difference between action types, as the basis for action classification. The distance is chosen as the relative distance based on the spine height, and the angle is based on the cosine theorem. The specific calculated angles and distances are shown in Table 1.

Table 1. Distance and angle calculated by rule set

Name	Explaining
Distance0	a0 to a4
Distance1	a0 to a7
Distance2	a2 to a4
Distance3	a5 to a7
Distance4	a4 to a11
Distance5	a7 to a14
altitude_differ1	a20 to a23
altitude_differ2	a3 to a4
altitude_differ3	a6 to a7
angle0	Inner angle with a3 as vertex a2 and a4 as edge
angle1	Inner angle with a6 as vertex a5 and a7 as edge
angle2	Inner angle with a10 as vertex a9 and a11 as edge
angle3	Inner angle with a13 as vertex a12 and a14 as edge

5 Experimental Results and Analysis

5.1 Experimental Data Set

There are already many datasets related to action classification, but they are not highly targeted, so the experimental datasets used in this paper are all from video clips and pictures about the behavior of militants in the Russian-Ukrainian war collected from the Internet, including equipment use, marching, standing shooting aiming behavior, kneeling shooting aiming behavior, ambling shooting aiming behavior, and other behaviors. The overall dataset contains different light and darkness, background, shooting distance and shooting angle. 41 video datasets are in MP4 format with an average frame rate of 26 fps and video duration of 4 s–96 s, and the number of training, validation and test sets are divided according to 6:2:2.

5.2 Analysis of Experimental Results

The experimental environment used is Windows 10, python programming language, AMD Ryzen7 5800H processor, NVIDIA GeForce RTX 3050Ti, 16G video memory. The experimental data were classified using the method in this paper, and the experimental results are shown in Table 2.

The proposed method in this paper is compared with CNN deep learning network with raw images as input data, ResNet50 network with raw images as input data, and CNN deep learning network with pseudo images of skeletal key points as input data. The experimental comparison with the result is shown in Fig. 11. The experimental results show that the accuracy of the proposed method in this paper is improved by about 8% relative to ResNet50 of the input original image, so the proposed solo-militant action recognition method in this paper has better performance for solo-militant action recognition in war video under small data set.

Table 2. Experimental results

Video_id	Frames	Actions	Accuracy
Video1	1175	Marching, standing shooting aiming behavior	85%
Video2	700	standing shooting aiming behavior, kneeling Shooting aiming behavior, ambush shooting aiming behavior, use of equipment	80%
Video3	1020	Standing shot aiming behavior, kneeling shot Aiming behavior, ambush shot aiming behavior, other behavior	83%
Video4	200	Ambush firing aiming behavior, standing firing aiming behavior, kneeling firing aiming behavior	76.2%
Video5	350	Kneeling shooting aiming behavior, standing shooting aiming behavior	78.6%
Video6	377	marching, standing shooting aiming behavior	84.2%
Video7	2784	standing shot aiming behavior, kneeling shot aiming behavior, ambush shot aiming behavior, marching, other behavior	70.6%
Video8	210	standing shooting aiming behavior, kneeling Shooting aiming behavior, marching, use of equipment	79.2%

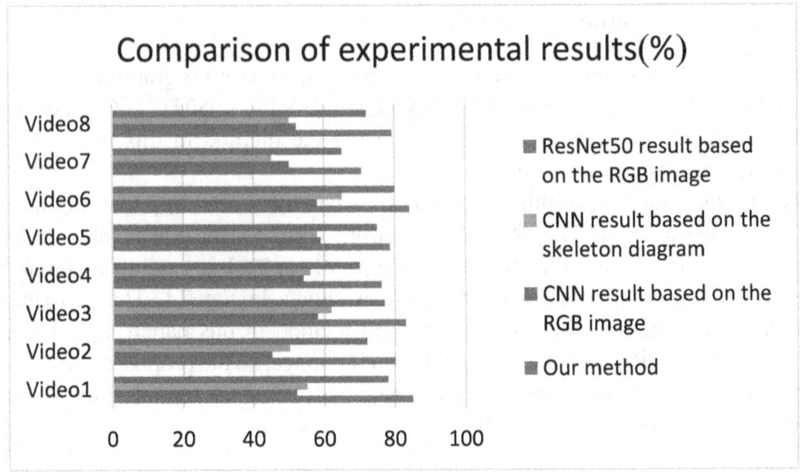

Fig. 11. Comparison of experimental results

6 Conclusion

In this paper, a ResNet and rule matching based solo-militant action recognition classification method is proposed, which can effectively recognize solo-militant actions in war videos. Firstly, the first stage original image is input to the ResNet18 network for classifying equipment use, marching, shooting class aiming behavior, and other behaviors. Then the network recognition results are combined with the rule set established by the skeleton point coordinates extracted by OpenPose for final judgment. If it is shooting class, the second stage skeleton pseudo-image extracted by OpenPose is input to the CNN network for classifying standing shooting aiming behavior, kneeling shooting aiming behavior, and ambush shooting aiming behavior. The experiments and the comparison of the result analysis show that the proposed method is robust and effective.

References

1. Hong-Bo, Z., et al.: A comprehensive survey of vision-based human action recognition methods. Sensors **19**(5), 1005 (2019)
2. Fujiyoshi, H., Lipton, A.J., Kanade T.: Real-time human motion analysis by image skeletonization. IEICE Trans. Inf. Syst. **87-D**(1), 113–120 (2004)
3. Weinland, D., Ronfard, R., Boyer, E.: Free viewpoint action recognition using motion history volumes. Comput. Vis. Image Underst. **104**(2–3), 249–257 (2006)
4. Bobick, A.F., Davis, J.W.: The recognition of human movement using temporal templates. IEEE Trans. Pattern Anal. Mach. Intell. **23**(3), 257–267 (2001)
5. Das Dawn, D., Shaikh, S.H.: A comprehensive survey of human action recognition with spatio-temporal interest point(STIP) detector. The Vis, Comput. **32**(3), 289–306 (2016)
6. Wang, H., et al.: Evaluation of local spatio-temporal features for action recognition. In: Proceedings of the 2009 British Machine Vision Conference, pp. 124.1–124.11. BMVA Press, London, UK (2009)

7. Wang, H., et al.: Action recognition by dense trajectories. In: Proeedings of the 2011 IEEE Conference on Computer Vision and Pattern Recognition (CVPR). Providence, pp. 3169–3176. IEEE, RI (2011)
8. Jie, X., et al.: A fast human action recogntion network based on spatio-temporal features. Neurocomputing **441**, 350–358 (2021)
9. Wang, J., Liang, S.: Pose-enhanced relation feature for action recognition in still images. In: Þór Jónsson, B. et al. (eds.) Multi-media Modeling. MMM 2022. LNCS, vol. 13141, pp. 154–165. Springer, Cham (2022). https://doi.org/10.1007/978-3-030-98358-1_13
10. Sima, M., et al.: Action recognition algorithm based on skeletal joint data and adaptive time pyramid. Signal Image Video Process. **16**, 1615–1622 (2022)
11. Sarikaya, R., Hinton, G.E., Deoras, A.: Application of deep belief networks for natural language understanding. IEEE/ACM Trans. Audio Speech Lang. Process. **22**(4), 778–784 (2014)
12. Yuanfang, R., Yan, W.: Convolutional deep belief networks for feature extraction of EEG signal. In: Proceedings of the 2014 International Joint Conference on Neural Networks (IJCNN), pp. 2850–2853, IEEE, Beijing, China: (2014)
13. Russel, N.S., Selvaraj, A.: Fusion of spatial and dynamic CNN streams for action recognition. Multim. Syst. **27**(5), 969–984 (2021). https://doi.org/10.1007/s00530-021-00773-x
14. Yixue, L., et al.: Human action recognition algorithm based on improved ResNet and skeletal key points in single image. Math. Probl. Eng. **2020** (2020)
15. Sijie, S., Cuiling, L., Junliang, X., et al.: Spatio-temporal attention based LSTM networks for 3D action recognition and detection. IEEE Trans. Image Process. **27**(7), 3459–3471 (2018)
16. Donahue, J., Hendrcks, A.L., Rohrbach, M., et al.: Long-term recurrent convolutional networks for visual recognition and description. IEEE Trans. Pattern Anal. Mach. Intell. **39**(4), 677–691 (2017)
17. Xiangpei, S., Yanrui, D.: Human skeleton representation for 3D action recognition based on complex network coding and LSTM. J. Vis. Commun. Image Represent. **82** (2022)
18. Lei, S., Yifan, Z.: Action recognition via pose-based graph convolutional networks with intermediate dense supervision. Pattern Recogn. **121** (2022)
19. Jie, X., et al.: A fast human action recognition network based on spatio-temporal features. Nerucomputing **41**, 350–358 (2021)
20. Zhenyue, Q., et al.: Fusing higher-order features in graph neural networks for skeleton-based action recognition. IEEE Trans. Neural Netw. Learn. Syst.: 1–15 (2022)
21. Yang, G., Zou, W.-X.: Deep learning network model based on fusion of spatiotemporal features for action recognition. Multim. Tools Appl. **81**(7), 9875–9896 (2022). https://doi.org/10.1007/s11042-022-11937-w
22. Chen, C., Jafari, R., Kehtarnavaz, N.: Action recognition from depth sequences using depth motion maps-based local binary patterns. In: Proceedings of IEEE Winter Conference on Applications of Computer Vision, pp. 1092–1099. IEEE Press, Piscataway, NJ: (2015)
23. Wenbin, C., Guodong, G., TriViews.: A general framework to use 3D depth data effectively for action recognition. J. Vis. Commun. Image Represent. **26**(1), 182–191 (2015)
24. Alsawadi, M.S., Rio, M.: Skeleton-split framework using spatial temporal graph convolutional networks for action recogntion. arXiv Accession number: 20210391100, E-ISSN: 23318422, 4 November 2021
25. Shahroudy, A., et al.: Deep multimodal feature analysis for action recognition in RGB + D videos. IEEE Trans Pattern Anal. Mach. Intell. **40**(5), 1045–1058 (2017)
26. Tamam, A., Usman, A., Hongtao, L.: Enhanced discriminative graph convolutional network with adaptive temporal modelling for skeleton-based action recognition. Comput. Vis. Image Underst. **216** (2022)
27. Xiaolei, L., et al.: Two-stream spatial graphormer networks for skeleton-based action recognition. IEEE Access. **10**, 100426–100437 (2022)

28. Jacek, T., Bogdan, K.: Human action recognition on raw depth maps. In: 2021 International Conference on Visual Communications and Image Processing, pp. 1–4 (2021)
29. Weiyao, X., et al.: Multimodal feature fusion model for RGB-D action recognition. In: 2021 IEEE International Conference on Multimedia & Expo Workshops, pp. 1–15 (2021)

Multiple Residual Quantization of Pruning

Yee Zhou[1], HaiDong Kang[1], Tian Zhang[1], LianBo Ma[1,2(✉)], and TieJun Xing[3]

[1] College of Software, Northeastern University, Shenyang, China
malb@swc.neu.edu.cn
[2] Key Laboratory of Smart Manufacturing in Energy Chemical Process, Ministry of Education, East China University of Science and Technology, Shanghai, China
[3] Neusoft Corporation, Shenyang, China

Abstract. Model compression technology investigates the compression of deep neural networks by quantizing the full-precision weights of the network into low-bit ones, to achieve network acceleration. However, most of the existing quantization operations are calculated by simple thresholding operations, which will lead to serious precision loss. In this paper, we propose a new quantization framework combined with pruning, called Multiple Residual Quantization of Pruning (MRQP), to achieve higher precision quantization neural network (QNN). MRQP recursively performs quantization of the full-precision weights by combining the low-bit weights stem and residual parts many times, to minimize the error between the quantized weights and the full-precision weights, and to ensure higher precision quantization. At the same time, MRQP prunes some weights that have less impact on loss function to further reduce model size.

Keywords: Quantization neural networks · Quantization · Model compression · Pruning

1 Introduction

In the past few years, deep neural networks (DNNs) have improved their performance in a wide range of applications, including computer vision [1–3], speech recognition [4–6], natural language processing [7,8], robots [9], and optimization [10–14] which have widely used deep neural networks. DNNs has shown the best accuracy in many AI tasks, but when applied to computing-constrained environments, such as mobile devices, there are problems such as large model size and high computing costs. At the same time, as the increase in computing and storage consumption in various cloud/edge computing applications, people are increasingly interested in deploying deep neural networks on resource-constrained devices. To improve the efficiency of neural networks, it is very important to compress neural networks without or with little performance degradation. To solve the above problems, many methods of model compression have

Y. Tan and Y. Shi (Eds.): DMBD 2022, CCIS 1744, pp. 209–219, 2022.
https://doi.org/10.1007/978-981-19-9297-1_16

been proposed, such as pruning [15], distillation [16,17], and quantization [18–21]. In this paper, we focus on quantization, especially ternary quantization, which quantizes full-precision weights while still maintaining considerable performance. Pruning and distillation are representative technologies of network compression. Pruning removes redundant weights in the network, and the distillation aims to train a smaller model to replicate the behavior of the original model. The networks compressed by these technologies still use floating-point computing, so they are not suitable for fixed-point edge devices to improve energy efficiency. Network quantization is an alternative method that converts full precision weights to low-bit counterpart, supports fixed-point reasoning, and reduces memory and computing costs.

Because the weight in quantization neural networks (QNNs) is low-bit, it will inevitably cause the accuracy of the neural network to decline. For QNNs, to mitigate the performance degradation caused by quantization, it is very important to have a quantizer that can accurately map the full-precision value to the quantized value. Many approaches have been explored for quantizer optimization. First, BinaryConnect [22] and BWN [23] perform binarization by using a symbolic function: convert each element of the weight w to -1 or $+1$. Thus, multiplication operation is eliminated, operation speed and resource efficiency are improved, and model size is reduced. Then TTQ [24] optimizes the weight quantizer by learning different scale factors under different weight states, achieving higher performance in recognition tasks. Besides, Nahshan Y, Chmiel B, and Baskin C, et al. [25] study the effect of quantization on the structure of the loss landscape. In fact, although the above literature has improved the quantizer, it always uses simple threshold operation training (for example Fig. 1), resulting in a large approximation error to the full precision weight, and there is still a large performance gap.

The goal of this paper is to design a more accurate and flexible quantizer to improve the performance of the quantization neural network. Specifically, we propose a quantized neural network with a multiple residual quantization with pruning process, which first prunes the network model to reduce the model size. Then, by introducing the multiple dry residuals framework, the quantization process is implemented, which will further reduce the size of the model at the same time. Instead of directly performing threshold operation, we perform quantization weight through the combination of binary stems and residuals. These weights are obtained by recursive quantization of full precision weights. This method can accurately reconstruct quantization weight, with small quantization errors and accurate mapping. The experimental results show that MRQP has good performance on CIFAR-10 and MNIST. Our contributions are summarized as follows:

1) We propose a quantized neural network (MRQP) based on a multiple residuals framework, which computes quantized weights recursively, and significantly improves the performance of threshold-based methods.
2) Our method combines pruning and quantification processes, significantly reducing model size.

3) We evaluated MRQP on different categorical datasets and proved that our method performs better than the base method.

The rest of this paper is organized as follows: Sect. 2 reviews prior work, Sect. 3 describes the nature of quantization and then describes a proposed method. Section 4 provides experimental results, and Sect. 5 summarizes this paper.

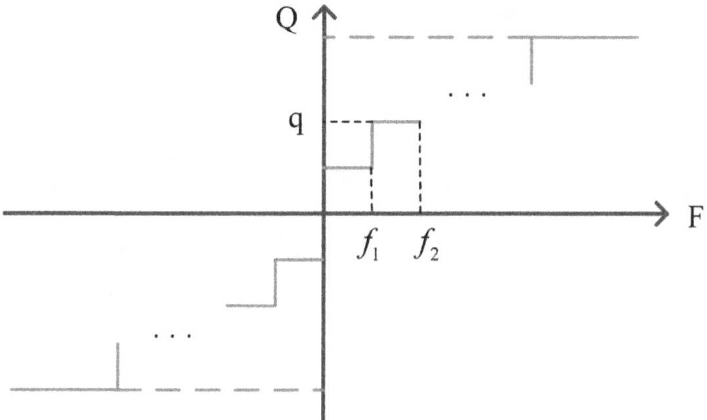

Fig. 1. Simple principle of threshold operation. (F represents the floating-point number before quantization, and Q represents the integer after quantization. Numbers between f_1 and f_2 are all quantized as q.)

2 Prior Work

Modern large-scale networks usually have a large number of parameters and huge computing costs. Compressing large networks facilitates the evaluation of these networks on devices with limited resources. The basic idea of model quantization is to replace the original floating-point precision with lower precision. It aims to reduce the weight value and active bit width, but it can still produce high performance. The core challenge of quantification is how to reduce the accuracy of representation without dropping the accuracy of the model, that is, to balance the loss of compression rate and accuracy rate [23,26–29].

Early research used 8-bit fixed-point representation to quantify the network and achieved the most advanced performance on ILSVRC-12 [23]. Later, people explored the DDN compression method of very low-bit quantization. For example, the activation and weight of DNN are discretized into binary or ternary values (for example, $\{-1,+1\}$ or $\{-1,0,+1\}$) [18,22,24,30–32]. However, these methods only use bit operations to approximate the convolution operations of DNN, which easily leads to performance degradation. To narrow the accuracy gap, some improvements have been made to the quantization methods, such as distance sensing quantization [33] and loss-aware quantization [34]. These methods enable the network to have more powerful capabilities, thus further narrowing the accuracy gap. Zhang et al. LQ-Net [35] and Lou et al. RQDNN [36] proposed a learnable quantizer to improve the performance of quantitative models. Miyashita et al. [37] proposed using non-uniform logarithmic representations to approximate weights and activation without significantly degrading performance. In this paper, we propose that MRQP introduces a multiple residual quantization network with pruning, which realizes the quantization process in a novel recursive way, further reduces the size of the model and improves the performance of the network.

3 Method

This section introduces our ternary neural networks with multiple residual quantizations, which are designed to reduce the quantization error recursively. In the following, we first give some preliminaries about ternarization. Then we propose our ternary quantization method, including the details on the forward and backward propagation.

3.1 Overview

The main operation in deep neural networks is expressed as

$$z = w^T a, \tag{1}$$

where $w \in R^{n*n}$ is the weight vector, $a \in R^{n*n}$ is the activition vector. The ternary neural network refers to the use of ternary values to represent floating point weights and/or activities. Formally, quantization can be expressed as(we uniformly use ternary quantization)

$$Q(x) = c_x T_x, \tag{2}$$

where x is the full-precision parameters including full-precision weights w and full-precision activations a, $Q(x)$ is the quantized full-precision parameters, T_x denotes ternary values after the quantization on x, c is a scalar used to scale the ternary values, which can be computed from the full-precision parameters or learned via backpropagation. T_x is usually obtained by thresholding function

$$T_x = \begin{cases} +1 \quad if \quad x > \Delta \\ 0 \quad if \quad |x| \leq \Delta \\ -1 \quad if \quad x < -\Delta, \end{cases} \tag{3}$$

where Δ denotes a fixed threshold used for quantization. With the ternary weights and activitions, the vector multiplications in the forward propagation can be reformulated as

$$z = Q(w)Q(a) = c_w c_a (T_w \odot T_a), \tag{4}$$

where $\odot$ represents the inner product for vectors with bitwise operations.

In general, the derivative of quantization function $Q(x)$ is non-differentiable and thus unpractical to directly apply the backpropagation to perform the training phase. For this issue, we follow the now widely adopted "Straight-Through Estimator (STE)" [26] to approximate the partial gradient calculation, which is formally expressed as

$$\frac{\partial Q(x)}{\partial x} \approx c1_{|x|\leq 1}. \tag{5}$$

3.2 MRQP

As can be seen, existing quantization methods simply find the closest quantized value approximation of w [22,23], inevitably causing performance degradation due to an inaccurate mapping of full-precision parameters to low-bit counterparts. In this paper, we consider multiple residual quantizations. After pruning the weights, MRQP extracts binary stems and residuals repeatedly by recursively quantizing the full-precision weights, and combining them to generate a refined ternary representation, thus obtaining the multi-stem-residual framework of QNNs.

Pruning Weights. In this step, we gradually reduce the size of the model by pruning the least important weights. We only set some elements of w to zero (that is, they are removed from weights domain, resulting in a decrease in model size) without changing the others. We first find the impact of each weight on the final loss function, and rank them according to the impact. Then, according to the weights proportion we need to prune, set the weights within this proportion to 0. (In this way, the sparse tensor is not introduced. Sparse tensors can lead to harmful irregular calculations.)

Multi-stem-Residual Quantization. We first need to have an acceptable error range ϵ (ϵ is a small positive number, to ensure that residual quantization can be performed repeated), then extract stems as rough fitting of full-precision weight w, which is calculated by performing sign $(\cdot)$ on w as

$$Q_w = csign(w), \tag{6}$$

where c is a learnable coefficient. Then, we further calculate the quantization error as

$$R = w - Q_w. \tag{7}$$

If condition $R \geq \epsilon$ is met, we continue to extract the residual, calculate the residual R_w from R by performing sign $(\cdot)$ on the quantization error R

$$R_w = csign(R). \tag{8}$$

By combining Eq. 6 and Eq. 8, we can obtain the more accurate ternary weight approximation (new Q_w)

$$Q_w = Q_w + R_w. \tag{9}$$

Then we repeat the process from Eq. 7 to Eq. 9 for the new Q_w until condition $R < \epsilon$ is satisfied.

Up to now, we achieve the quantization in our framework, with the full-precision weights quantized to multi values, i.e.,

$$\{-nc, -(n-1)c, \cdots, -c, 0, c, \cdots, (n-1)c, nc\}.$$

where n refers to the number of residual quantization (Eq. 7 to Eq. 9).

Obviously, seeking a better coefficient c is significantly important for the effectiveness of quantizer, which would be detailed in the following section.

3.3 Backward Propogation of MRQP

In the backward propagation, We need to learn and update the full-precision weight w and the learnable coefficient c. In multi-stem-residual framework, the two kinds of parameters are jointly learned. And in each layer, MRQP updates the w first and then the c.

Update w**.** For W updating, the gradient through the quantizer to weights are estimated by a STE that pass the gradient whose weight value is in the range of $(-nc, nc)$:

$$\frac{\partial Q_w}{\partial w} = 1_{|x| \leq nc}. \tag{10}$$

Then we can obtain the updating process of w

$$\delta_w = \frac{\partial L}{\partial Q_w}\frac{\partial Q_w}{\partial w}, \tag{11}$$

$$w = w - \eta\delta_w, \tag{12}$$

where L is the loss function and η is learning rate.

Update c**.** The coefficient c determines the scale of binary stems and residuals, which is directly related to the quality of ternary weights. Therefore, unlike the way to obtain the gradient of w, we decompose the quantizer to calculate the more refined gradient of c.

It is worth mentioning that we find that the derivatives of Q_x and c times Q_x with respect to c are almost equal, The difference between them is c^2 or 0. Since c is a small positive number, we ignore this error term without losing generality, so we calculate the derivative of Q_x with respect to c as follows

$$\frac{\partial Q_w}{\partial c} = sign(w), \tag{13}$$

$$\frac{\partial Q_w}{\partial c}_{new} = \frac{\partial Q_w}{\partial c}_{old} + sign(w - c\frac{\partial Q_w}{\partial c}_{old}) - c\frac{\partial Q_w}{\partial c}_{old} 1_{|w - c\frac{\partial Q_w}{\partial c}_{old}| \leq 1}. \tag{14}$$

If condition $|\frac{\partial Q_w}{\partial c}_{new} - \frac{\partial Q_w}{\partial c}_{old}| \geq \zeta$ is met, we have

$$\frac{\partial Q_w}{\partial c}_{old} = \frac{\partial Q_w}{\partial c}_{new}, \tag{15}$$

where ζ is a small positive number, which can be set freely according to different needs.

Then continue to execute Eq. 14 and judge whether condition $|\frac{\partial Q_w}{\partial c}_{new} - \frac{\partial Q_w}{\partial c}_{old}| \geq \zeta$ is met, and cycle the process until condition $|\frac{\partial Q_w}{\partial c}_{new} - \frac{\partial Q_w}{\partial c}_{old}| \geq \zeta$ is not met.

Then we can obtain the updating process of c

$$\delta_c = \frac{\partial L}{\partial Q_w}\frac{\partial Q_w}{\partial c}, \tag{16}$$

$$c = c - \eta\delta_c. \tag{17}$$

4 Experiments

In this section, in order to demonstrate the performance of our MRQP, we conducted different experiments on two classification datasets: MNIST and CIFAR-10. Note that in the following, unless otherwise stated, we refer to the baseline as a quantitative network with the same architecture as MRQP, and use the conventional quantization method described in Sect. 3.1.

This setting is similar to that of Courbariaux [22]. We do not conduct data expansion or unsupervised pre-training. The experiment was conducted on two commonly used data sets:

1) MNIST: This data set is a very classic data set in the field of machine learning. It consists of 60000 training samples and 10000 test samples, including 28×28 grayscale images. We used 50000 images for training, another 10000 for validation, and the remaining 10000 for testing. We use the 5-layer model:

$$784FC - 1024FC - 1024FC - 1024FC - 10SVM$$

where FC is a fully-connected layer, and SVM is a L2-SVM output layer using the square hinge loss. We run the training algorithm for 100 epochs with a batch size of 200. The learning rate of the weighted quantization network starts from 0.005 and decays 0.1 every 15 epochs. For all settings, Adam with momentum of 0.9 is adopted as the optimizer.
2) CIFAR-10: This contains 32×32 color images from ten object classes. We use 45000 images for training, another 5000 for validation, and the remaining 10000 for testing. The images are preprocessed with global contrast normalization and ZCA whitening. We use the VGG-like architecture [34]:

$$(2*128C3) - MP2 - (2*256C3) - MP2 - (2*512C3) - MP2 - (2*1024FC) - 10SVM$$

where C3 is a 3*3 ReLU convolution layer, and MP2 is a 2*2 max-pooling layer. Batch normalization, with a minibatch size of 256, is used. The maximum number of epochs is 200. The learning rate of the weighted quantization network starts from 0.01 and decays 0.5 every 15 epochs. For all settings, Adam with momentum of 0.9 is adopted as the optimizer.

For these two models, we conducted three kinds of pruning ratios, pruning 0% (no prune), 30%, and 50% weights respectively. The experimental results are as follows (It is worth mentioning that, in order to ensure accuracy, we didn't quantize the first and last layers of the network, nor did we prune them.):

Table 1. Top-1 accuracy (5-layer Model network on MNIST)

	Pruning rate	Top-1 accuracy
Full-precision	(no prune)	98.52%
Baseline	(no prune)	97.63%
MRQP	(no prune)	98.01%
	30%	98.15%
	50%	97.8%

Table 2. Top-1 accuracy (VGG-like Model network on CIFAR-10)

	Pruning rate	Top-1 accuracy
Full-precision	(no prune)	92.3%
Baseline	(no prune)	88.9%
MRQP	(no prune)	90.5%
	30%	89.6%
	50%	89.4%

Table 1 and Table 2 shows the accuracy comparison between our method and the baseline method on MNIST (where implements a 5-layer full-connected network) and CIFAR-10 (where VGG-like network is implemented). From the table, we can see that our method is superior to the baseline, and the Top-1 accuracy is improved by at least 0.17% (MNIST) and 0.5% (CIFAR-10).

5 Conclusion

In this paper, we propose an efficient and accurate MRQP neural network with pruning. Different from the previous work of directly applying threshold quantization, our MRQP realizes quantization from the perspective of stem residual. In particular, MRQP reconsiders the ternary quantization weight as a combination of binary stems and residuals, thus giving the quantizer more accurate mapping between full-precision weights and quantization weight. Furthermore, experiments on two datasets show that the accuracy of the quantization neural network is improved by using our MRQP method. And our method does not need any special hardware support, such as channel or filter quantization.

Acknowledgments. This work is partially suported by NSFC under grant No. 62172083 and the Fundamental Research Funds for the Central Universities.

References

1. Pradhyumna, P., Shreya, G.P.: Graph neural network (GNN) in image and video understanding using deep learning for computer vision applications. In: International Conference on Electronics and Sustainable Communication Systems (ICESC), pp. 1183–1189 (2021). https://doi.org/10.1109/ICESC51422.2021.9532631
2. Zhang, X., Yi, W.J., Saniie, J.: Home surveillance system using computer vision and convolutional neural network. In: International Conference on Electro Information Technology (EIT), pp. 266–270 (2019). https://doi.org/10.1109/EIT.2019.8833773
3. Bantupalli, K., Xie, Y.: American sign language recognition using deep learning and computer vision. IEEE International Conference on Big Data (Big Data), pp. 4896–4899 (2018). https://doi.org/10.1109/BigData.2018.8622141
4. Nassif, A.B., Shahin, I., Attili, I., et al.: Speech recognition using deep neural networks: a systematic review[J]. IEEE ACCESS **7**, 19143–19165 (2019)
5. Shewalkar, A.: Performance evaluation of deep neural networks applied to speech recognition: RNN, LSTM and GRU. J. Artif Intell. Soft Comput. Res. **9**(4), 235–245 (2019)
6. Lokesh, S., Malarvizhi Kumar, P., Ramya Devi, M., et al.: An automatic Tamil speech recognition system by using bidirectional recurrent neural network with self-organizing map[J]. Neural Comput. Appl. **31**(5), 1521–1531 (2019)
7. Giménez, M., Palanca, J., Botti, V.: Semantic-based padding in convolutional neural networks for improving the performance in natural language processing. a case of study in sentiment analysis. Neurocomputing **378**, 315–323 (2020)
8. Galassi, A., Lippi, M., Torroni, P.: Attention in natural language processing. IEEE Trans. Neural Netw. Learn. Syst. **32**(10), 4291–4308 (2020)
9. Moon, J., Kim, H., Lee, B.: View-point invariant 3D classification for mobile robots using a convolutional neural network. Int. J. Control Autom. Syst. **16**(6), 2888–2895 (2018)
10. Zeng, R., Zeng, C., Wang, X., Li, B., Chu, X.: Incentive mechanism for federated learning and game-theoretical approach. IEEE Netw. (Early Access), 1–7 (2022)
11. Zhang, T., Ma, L., Liu, Q., et al.: Genetic programming for ensemble learning in face recognition. In: International Conference on Sensing and Imaging. Springer, Cham, pp. 209–218 (2022) https://doi.org/10.1007/978-3-031-09726-319
12. Ma, L., Wang, X., Huang, M., Lin, Z., Tian, L., Chen, H.: Two-level master-slave rfid networks planning via hybrid multi-objective artificial bee colony optimizer. IEEE Trans. Syst. Man Cybernet. Syst. **49**(5), 861–880 (2019)
13. Lianbo. M., Cheng, S., Shi, M.: Enhancing learning efficiency of brain storm optimization via orthogonal learning design. IEEE Trans. Syst. Man Cybernet.: Syst. **51**(11), 6723–6742 (2021)
14. Ma, L., Huang, M., Yang, S., Wang, R., Wang, X.: An adaptive localized decision variable analysis approach to large-scale multiobjective and many-objective optimization. IEEE Trans. Cybern. **52**(7) (2022)
15. Molchanov, P., Mallya, A., Tyree, S., et al.: Importance estimation for neural network pruning. In: Proceedings of the IEEE/CVF Conference on Computer Vision and Pattern Recognition, pp. 11264–11272 (2019). https://doi.org/10.1109/CVPR.2019.01152

16. Yang, Y., Qiu, J., Song, M., et al.: Distilling knowledge from graph convolutional networks. In: Proceedings of the IEEE/CVF Conference on Computer Vision and Pattern Recognition, pp. 7074–7083 (2020). https://doi.org/10.1109/CVPR42600.2020.00710
17. Liu, F., Wu, X., Ge, S., et al.: Exploring and distilling posterior and prior knowledge for radiology report generation. In: Proceedings of the IEEE/CVF Conference on Computer Vision and Pattern Recognition, pp. 13753–13762 (2021). https://doi.org/10.1109/CVPR46437.2021.01354
18. Li, Y., Ding, W., Liu, C., et al.: TRQ: Ternary neural networks with residual quantization. Proc. AAAI Conf. Artif. Intell. **35**(10), 8538–8546 (2021). https://doi.org/10.1609/aaai.v35i10.17036
19. Qu, Z., Zhou, Z., Cheng, Y., et al.: Adaptive loss-aware quantization for multi-bit networks. In: Proceedings of the IEEE/CVF Conference on Computer Vision and Pattern Recognition, pp. 7988–7997 (2020). https://doi.org/10.1109/CVPR42600.2020.00801
20. Peng, H., Wu, J., Zhang, Z., et al.: Deep network quantization via error compensation. IEEE Trans. Neural Netw. Learn. Syst. **33**(9), 4960–4970 (2021)
21. Chen, P., Zhuang, B., Shen, C.: FATNN: fast and accurate ternary neural networks. In: Proceedings of the IEEE/CVF International Conference on Computer Vision, pp. 5219–5228 (2021). https://doi.org/10.1109/ICCV48922.2021.00517
22. Courbariaux, M., Bengio, Y., David, J.P.: BinaryConnect: training deep neural networks with binary weights during propagations. Adv. Neural. Inf. Process. Syst. **2**, 3123–3131 (2015)
23. Rastegari, M., Ordonez, V., Redmon, J., Farhadi, A.: XNOR-Net: ImageNet classification using binary convolutional neural networks. In: Leibe, B., Matas, J., Sebe, N., Welling, M. (eds.) ECCV 2016. LNCS, vol. 9908, pp. 525–542. Springer, Cham (2016). https://doi.org/10.1007/978-3-319-46493-0_32
24. Zhu, C., Han, S., Mao, H., et al.: Trained ternary quantization (2016). https://arxiv.org/abs/1612.01064
25. Nahshan, Y., Chmiel, B., Baskin, C., et al.: Loss aware post-training quantization. Mach. Learn. **10**(11), 3245–3262 (2021)
26. Yin, P., Lyu, J., Zhang, S,. et al.: Understanding straight-through estimator in training activation quantized neural nets (2019). https://arxiv.org/abs/1903.05662
27. Yang, J., Shen, X., Xing, J., et al.: Quantization networks. In: Proceedings of the IEEE/CVF Conference on Computer Vision and Pattern Recognition, pp. 7308–7316 (2019). https://doi.org/10.1109/CVPR.2019.00748
28. Liu, Z., Wang, Y., Han, K., et al.: Post-training quantization for vision transformer. Adv. Neural. Inf. Process. Syst. **34**, 28092–28103 (2021)
29. Nedic, A., Olshevsky, A., Ozdaglar, A., et al.: On distributed averaging algorithms and quantization effects. IEEE Trans. Autom. Control **54**(11), 2506–2517 (2009)
30. Deng, L., Jiao, P., Pei, J., et al.: GXNOR-Net: training deep neural networks with ternary weights and activations without full-precision memory under a unified discretization framework[J]. Neural Netw. **100**, 49–58 (2018)
31. Bulat, A., Tzimiropoulos, G.: XNOR-Net++: improved Binary Neural Networks (2019). https://arxiv.org/abs/1909.13863
32. Kim, H., Kim, K., Kim, J., et al.: BinaryDuo: reducing gradient mismatch in binary activation network by coupling binary activations. In: International Conference on Learning Representations (2019). https://doi.org/10.48550/arXiv.2002.06517
33. Kim, D., Lee, J., Ham, B.: Distance-aware quantization. In: Proceedings of the IEEE/CVF International Conference on Computer Vision, pp. 5271–5280 (2021). https://doi.org/10.1109/ICCV48922.2021.00522

34. Hou, L., Yao, Q., Kwok, J.T.Y.: Loss-aware binarization of deep networks. In: International Conference on Learning Representations (2017). https://ui.adsabs.harvard.edu/abs/2016arXiv161101600H
35. Zhang, D., Yang, J., Ye, D., Hua, G.: LQ-Nets: learned quantization for highly accurate and compact deep neural networks. In: Ferrari, V., Hebert, M., Sminchisescu, C., Weiss, Y. (eds.) ECCV 2018. LNCS, vol. 11212, pp. 373–390. Springer, Cham (2018). https://doi.org/10.1007/978-3-030-01237-3_23
36. Louizos, C., Reisser, M., Blankevoort, T., et al.: Relaxed quantization for discretized neural networks. In: International Conference on Learning Representations (2018). https://doi.org/10.48550/arXiv.1810.01875
37. Miyashita, D., Lee, E.H., Murmann, B.: Convolutional neural networks using logarithmic data representation (2016). https://arxiv.org/abs/1603.01025v1

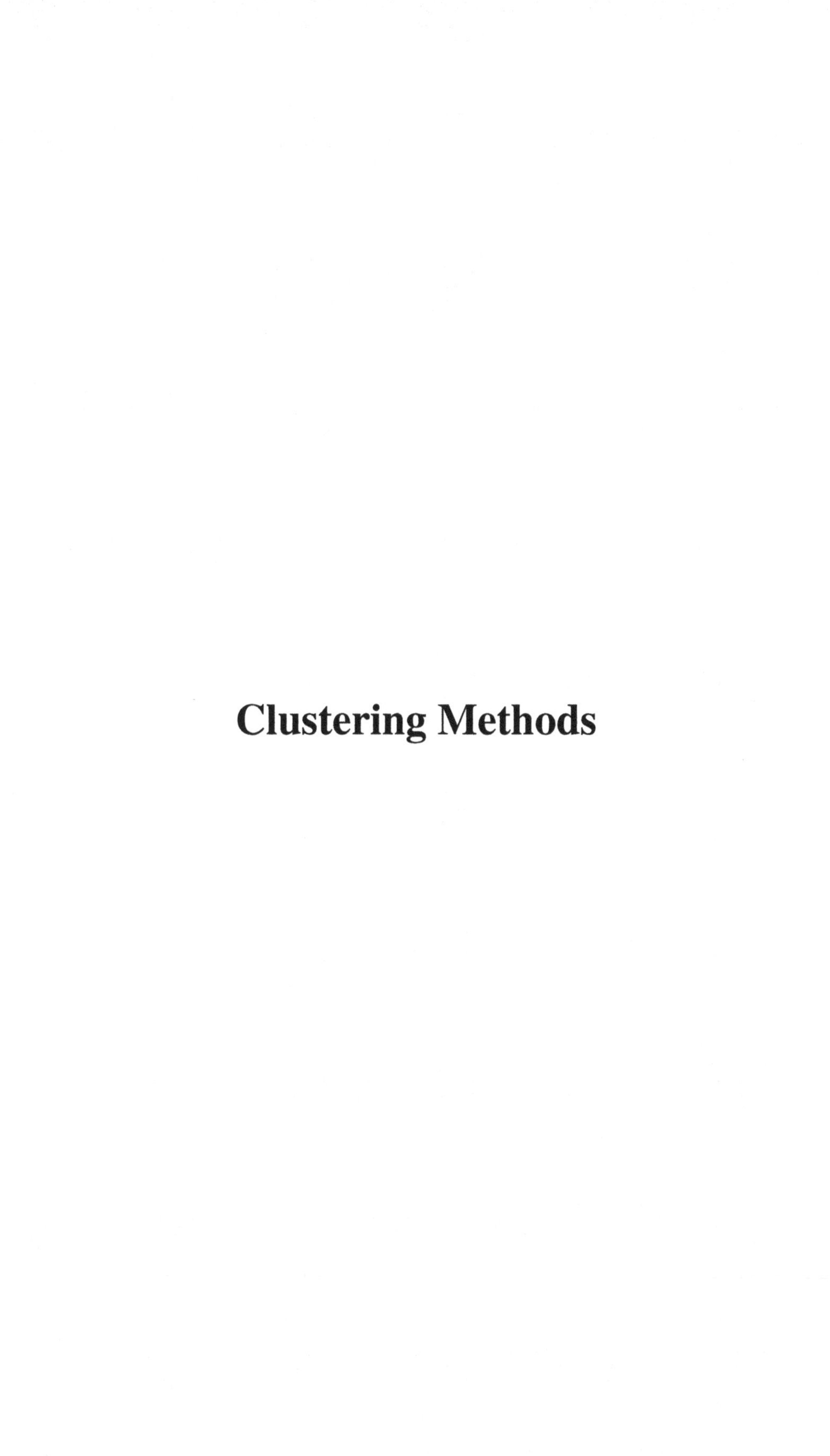

Clustering Methods

Deep Structured Graph Clustering Network

Sun Li[1], Zihan Wang[2], Yong Li[1], Yang Yu[3], Wenbo Li[1], Hongliang Liu[3], Rong Song[3], and Lei Zhu[2](✉)

[1] State Grid Shandong Electric Power Company, Jinan, China
[2] Shandong Normal University, Jinan, China
leizhu0608@gmail.com
[3] State Grid Zibo Power Supply Company, Zibo, China

Abstract. Shallow clustering methods adopt linear or simple nonlinear projections to reduce the feature dimensions, which may suffer from the weak representation capability. Contrastively, deep clustering methods have the advantages on representing the sample characteristics. However, most deep clustering models focus on preserving feature information of samples and ignore the important intrinsic structures of samples. Besides, large amounts of neural network parameters should be optimized in deep clustering models, but no proper semantic supervision can be used in the unsupervised clustering process. To alleviate these problems, in this paper, we propose a unified deep structured graph clustering network to guide the unsupervised deep clustering process with a theoretically ideal cluster structure. Specifically, we simultaneously learn the discriminative feature representation of samples, and the similarity graph of samples with well clustering structure by automatically assigning proper neighbors to each sample. Experiments on several public testing datasets demonstrate the effects of the proposed method.

Keywords: Clustering · Deep learning · Structured graph · Joint learning

1 Introduction

Clustering is one of the most important research topics in data science and machine learning. A large number of clustering methods are proposed over the past decades such as k-means [19], support vector clustering [2], hierarchical clustering [14] and multi-view clustering [36].

Traditional shallow clustering methods like k-means or spectral clustering [17], adopt the original features and space manifold information of samples to compute the clustering results when the dimension of samples is small. However, when the dimension of the input sample features becomes high, the traditional clustering method will become unreliable due to the complexity of the manifold structure [26]. Thus, how to effectively realize the dimensionality reduction

S. Li and Z. Wang—Contributed equally to this paper.

Y. Tan and Y. Shi (Eds.): DMBD 2022, CCIS 1744, pp. 223–239, 2022.
https://doi.org/10.1007/978-981-19-9297-1_17

during the clustering process is important. Recent clustering methods Projected Clustering with Adaptive Neighbors (PCAN) [21] and Robust Structured Graph Clustering (RSGC) [28] learn a structured graph with dimension reduction methods Principal Components Analysis (PCA) [23] and Sparse Matrix Factorization (SMF) [16] respectively to retrain the manifold structure and perform the clustering process. However, due to the limited feature representation capability of dimension reduction (linear or simple nonlinear projection) and the complex manifold structure hidden in the high-dimensional feature, these methods still cannot achieve satisfactory results.

With the development of deep learning, deep neural networks are introduced to the clustering research area in recent literature. Stacked AutoEncoder (SAE) [30] makes use of Deep Neural Networks (DNNs) [11] to learn a nonlinear mapping to convert samples to low dimensions. Deep learning with nonparametric clustering (DNMC) [10] trains a Deep Belief Network (DBN) [35] for dimension reduction, then learns clustering results with nonparametric maximum margin clustering. These methods aim at learning a low-dimensional subspace, where the traditional clustering methods can achieve better results. However, they basically treat their DNNs as a preprocessing stage. The feature extraction process is separate from the subsequent clustering process. Under such circumstances, sub-optimal performance may be brought due to the two-step learning.

In recent years, several models like Deep Clustering Network (DCN) [34], Deep Embedded Clustering (DEC) [33], and Deep Subspace Clustering Networks (DSC) [13] are proposed to jointly optimize the feature learning and clustering. Due to the joint learning, these methods generally achieve better clustering performance. However, incorporating the deep neural networks into the clustering process will bring large amounts of parameters. It is contradictory to the fact that no semantic guidance can be used to train these parameters in the unsupervised clustering process. Under such circumstances, insufficient semantic guidance will lead to weak deep neural networks. Besides, the manifold structure of samples is important for the clustering task [28]. Nevertheless, existing deep clustering methods focus on preserving the original information of samples, ignoring the similarity relationship of samples. Moreover, existing methods separate the similarity measurement from the clustering process, which may make the acquisition of similarity matrix inaccurate and thus deteriorate the clustering performance.

To address these problems, in this paper, we propose an effective Deep Structured Graph Clustering (DSGC) method. The basic learning framework is shown in Fig. 1. Our unified learning framework jointly performs deep representation and structured graph learning, and simultaneously employs the learned structured graph to guide the deep neural network learning. Different from the existing clustering method, the guidance of the structured graph enables the deep neural network to retain the manifold structure of samples during the training process and thus achieve better clustering effects. Besides, we build the model based on the AutoEncoder [20] with similarity constraint, so that the original manifold structure can be retained more accurately in the projection process. The main contributions of this paper can be summarized as follows:

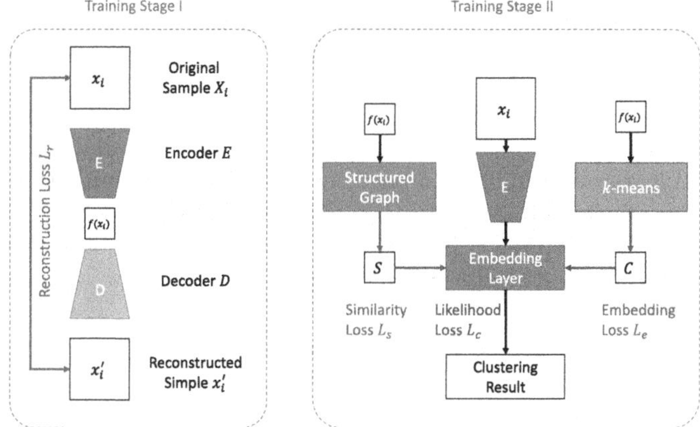

Fig. 1. The basic framework of the proposed DSGC. The original sample x_i is encoded by encoder E to obtain the embedded sample $f(x_i)$. The similarity matrix S and clustering center C are trained by optimizing the similarity Loss L_s and the embedding loss L_e, and the final model is obtained by using C and S to construct the embedded layer and encoder E with likelihood Loss L_c.

1. We propose a deep structured graph clustering network, which simultaneously performs deep feature representation learning, structured graph learning, and clustering. The deep embedding processing can retain the manifold structure of samples more accurately to pursue an ideal clustering structure. To the best of our knowledge, there is still no similar work.
2. We propose a deep neural network to perform feature learning by optimizing the loss function of KL divergence based on the clustering objective with a self-training target distribution. In this network, the deep feature learning, structured graph learning as well as data clustering are jointly optimized and can enhance each other. The feature information of the samples and the similarity relations of the pair-wise samples are preserved in the whole learning processing.
3. We evaluate our model on widely tested clustering benchmarks, and extensive experiments on public datasets demonstrate that our method significantly outperforms the state-of-the-art deep clustering approaches.

2 Related Work

Shallow Clustering. Clustering algorithms have been extensively studied in machine learning. k-means [19] is a classic clustering method that aims to learn k cluster centroids by minimizing the distances from samples to the cluster centroids. Spectral clustering (SC) [17] is based on graph theory, which clusters data by the spectral embedding with the eigenvectors of the graph Laplacian matrix. Despite the success of these methods in a wide range, their effects are limited on handling the low-dimensional samples. As the sample feature dimension rises, these methods will suffer from the curse of dimensionality and lead to unsatisfactory results.

In recent years, optimal graph-based clustering methods are proposed to improve clustering performance. Projected Clustering with Adaptive Neighbors (PCAN) [21] learns the similarity matrix by adaptively assigning the neighbors for each data point based on the local distance. Robust Structured Graph Clustering (RSGC) [28] proposes a framework to simultaneously perform the structured graph learning and clustering, and learns a robust latent representation to resist the noises.

The shallow clustering methods have achieved promising performance on many datasets. However, when datasets contain more semantics, linear and simple nonlinear projection in existing shallow clustering methods cannot preserve the sample information well. With the development of deep learning, various deep clustering methods based on deep neural networks are proposed.

Deep Clustering. Deep clustering has received broad attention recently. Existing deep clustering methods can be classified into two categories: two-step learning approaches that get clustering results after learning deep embedded features [4,24], and the joint learning approaches that simultaneously optimize the feature learning and clustering [33,34].

The former combines existing deep learning with clustering methods. Deep Representations for Graph Clustering (DRGC) [29] uses AutoEncoder to learn low dimensional features from the original sample, then use k-means algorithm to get clustering results. Nonparametric Maximum Margin Clustering (NMMC) [4] currently use Deep Belief Network (DBN) [35] instead of AutoEncoder for fast feature learning and then use non-parametric maximum-margin clustering to learn sample representations.

The other category of deep clustering approaches try to define a loss that can simulate classification error in supervised deep learning. Typical examples include Deep Clustering Network (DCN) [34], Deep Embedded Clustering (DEC) [33] and Improved Deep Embedded Clustering (IDEC) [9]. DCN proposes a recurrent framework in deep feature representation and clusters. It combines two processes into one model and performs the optimization. DEC learns a mapping from the data space to a lower-dimensional feature space in which a clustering objective is iteratively optimized. Based on DEC, IDEC manipulates feature space with the guidance of clustering loss to scatter data points. Because of the introduction of the DNNs, the deep clustering method can retain the original features of the samples better. However, the existing deep clustering methods focus on preserving the features inside the samples but ignore the sample relations, which limits the clustering performance.

Different from existing methods, in this paper, we propose a deep structured graph clustering method that integrates feature representation and structured graph learning into a unified learning framework. Our model performs well on the high-dimension feature and is superior to other models on the clustering performance due to the supervision of a well clustering structure.

3 Deep Structured Graph Clustering Network

3.1 Notations and Definitions

Throughout this paper, matrices are marked as uppercase letters and vectors are marked as lowercase letters. For matrix H, the i_{th} row and the $(i,j)_{th}$ element are denoted by h_i and h_{ij}, respectively. The trace of matrix H and the transpose of H are denoted by $Tr(H)$ and H^T, respectively. The Frobenius norm of H is denoted by $\parallel H \parallel_F$. An identity matrix is denoted by I and an all-one vector is denoted by $\mathbf{1}$. The main notations used in the paper are listed in Table 1.

Table 1. Summary of the main notations in this paper.

Symbols	Explanations
X	Original data matrix
Z	Latent feature space
S	Similarity matrix
L_S	Laplacian matrix
θ	Parameters of AutoEncoder
c	Number of clusters
u	Clustering center
η	Similarity threshold
q_{ij}	Similarity between embedding sample $f(x_i)$ and clustering center u_j
p	Auxiliary variable
h_{ij}	Likelihood between x_i and x_j
ω_{ij}	Distance between x_i and x_j

3.2 Deep Embedded Network

Consider the problem of clustering a set of n samples $\{x_i\}_{i=1,...,N}$ in to c cluster, each sample is represented by a clustering center u_j, $j = 1, \cdots, n$. instead of performing clustering in the high-dimensional space X, we propose a multi-layer non-linear mapping $f_\theta : X \rightarrow Z$, where θ are learnable parameters of AutoEncoder and Z is the latent feature space. The dimension of Z is much smaller than X to avoid the curse of dimensionality [1]. For parameters f_θ, we choice the AutoEncoder and θ denotes its parameters. So we introduce the reconstruction loss defined as follows:

$$L_r = \parallel X - f_{\theta_d}(f_{\theta_e}(X)) \parallel_F^2 . \tag{1}$$

In addition to preserve the original features of samples, we want the projected low-dimensional space to have a well cluster structure. It is promising to measure the soft distribution between the embedded samples and cluster centers, and then use it to optimize network parameters f_θ and cluster centers u. Therefore, inspired by t-Stochastic Neighbor Embedding (t-SNE) [18], we use q_{ij} to measure the similarity between embedded point $f_{\theta_e}(x_i)$ and cluster center u_j.

$$q_{ij} = \frac{(1+ \| f_{\theta_e}(x_i) - u_j \|^2 /\alpha)^{-\frac{\alpha+1}{2}}}{\sum_{j'}(1+ \| f_{\theta_e}(x_i) - u_j \|^2 /\alpha)^{-\frac{\alpha+1}{2}}}, \tag{2}$$

where α is the degree of freedom. q_{ij} can be interpreted as the probability of assigning sample i to clustering center j, and we define q_{ij} is the soft assignment betwen z_i and u_j.

We define an auxiliary distribution as:

$$p_{ij} = \frac{q_{ij}^2/f_j}{\sum_{j'} q_{ij}^2/f_{j'}}, \tag{3}$$

where $f_j = \sum_i q_{ij}$ is the soft clustering frequency. Then, we adopt the KL divergence loss [25] between the soft assignments q_i and the auxiliary distribution p_i to iteratively refine the clusters. The embedding loss is as follows:

$$L_e = \sum_i \sum_j p_{ij} log \frac{p_{ij}}{q_{ij}}. \tag{4}$$

3.3 Structured Graph with Adaptive Neighbors

In this paper, to retain the manifold structure between the samples, we adopt the structured graph to guide the training of DNNs. Obviously, closer samples are connected with larger probability. Hence, the probability of two data to be neighbors can be regarded as the similarity between them. In this paper, we define $s_{ij} \in S$ as the probability that x_i is connected to x_j. s_{ij} is inversely proportional to the distance between x_i and x_j. Specifically, we calculate the similarity matrix S by solving

$$\min_{s_i^T 1=1, 0 \le s_{ij} \le 1} \sum_{i,j} \| x_i - x_j \|_2^2 \, s_{ij} + \gamma s_{ij}^2, \tag{5}$$

where γ is the regularization parameter to avoid the trivial solution.

We can get the loss function as follows:

$$L = \min_{s_i^T 1=1, 0 \le s_{ij} \le 1} \sum_{i,j} \| x_i - x_j \|_2^2 \, s_{ij} + \gamma s_{ij}^2 + L_e + L_r. \tag{6}$$

For the similarity matrix S in Eq. (5), it is noisy if we directly use it to guide the clustering process. Thus, we further process S as follows:

$$s_{ij} = \begin{cases} 1 & s_{ij} > 0 \ or \ sim(x_i, x_j) > \eta \\ 0 & otherwise, \end{cases} \tag{7}$$

where $sim(\cdot)$ is the similarity function which measures the similarity between x_i and x_j, and η is hyper-parameter. After obtaining the updated similarity S, we can define the likelihood of the pairwise samples as follows:

$$h(s_{ij}) = \begin{cases} \delta(\omega_{ij}) & s_{ij} = 1 \\ 1 - \delta(\omega_{ij}) & s_{ij} = 0, \end{cases} \tag{8}$$

where $\delta(\omega_{ij}) = \frac{1}{1+e^{\omega_{ij}}}$, and ω_{ij} is the distance between x_j and x_i, it is defined as follows:

$$\omega_{ij} = (x_i - x_j)^2, \tag{9}$$

It is difficult to calculate the distance between two samples directly in the training process, so we rewrite Eq. (9) as follows:

$$\Omega = 2(H - XX^T), \tag{10}$$

where $h_{ij} \in H, \forall h_{ij} = x_i^2$. Note that, $\Omega_{ij} = \omega_{ij}$.

Therefore, we can get optimization loss function L_c as follows:

$$\min L_c = -\log h(S|X) = -\sum_{s_{ij} \in S} (s_{ij}\omega_{ij} - \log(1 + e^{\omega_{ij}})) = S\Omega - \log(1 + e^{\Omega}). \tag{11}$$

Thus, we rewrite the loss function as:

$$L = \min_{s_i^T \mathbf{1}=1, 0 \le s_{ij} \le 1} \sum_{i,j} \| x_i - x_j \|_2^2 \, s_{ij} + \gamma s_{ij}^2 + L_c + L_e + L_r. \tag{12}$$

For deep clustering, fewer parameters usually indicate stronger robustness. Following CAN [21], we can get S with stable training by setting fewer parameters. The matrix S can be seen as a similarity matrix of the graph with n data points as the nodes. The ideal state of S is that it contains c connected components, which is beneficial for the subsequent processing. Suppose each node i is assigned a function value as f_i, then it can be verified as follows:

$$\sum_{i,j=1}^{n} \| f_i - f_j \|_2^2 \, s_{ij} = 2Tr(F^T L_S F), \tag{13}$$

where F with i row arranged by f_i, and $L_S = D_S - \frac{S^T+S}{2}$ is called Laplacian matrix, D_S is degree matrix and the i-th entry is defined as $\sum_j \frac{(s_{ij}+s_{ji})}{2}$. It can be proved that similarity matrix S will have c components connected if $rank(L_S) = n - c$. Then we can get S by solve:

$$\min \sum_{i,j} \| f_{\theta_e}(x_i) - f_{\theta_e}(x_j) \|_2^2 \, s_{ij} + \gamma s_{ij}^2, s.t. \forall i, s_i^T \mathbf{1} = 1, 0 \le s_{ij} \le 1, rank(L_S) = n - c. \tag{14}$$

It is difficult to solve with constraint $rank(L_S) = n - c$. Consider L_S is positive semi-definite, we suppose $\epsilon_i(L_S)$ is the i-th smallest eigenvalue of L_S, we know $\epsilon_i(L_S) \geq 0$. According to the Ky Fan Theorem [8], we can rewrite Eq. (14) as follows:

$$\begin{aligned} &\min \sum_{i,j} (\| f_{\theta_e}(x_i) - f_{\theta_e}(x_j) \|_2^2 s_{ij} + \gamma s_{ij}^2) + \lambda Tr(F^T L_S F) \\ &s.t. \quad \forall i, s_i^T \mathbf{1} = 1, 0 \leq s_{ij} \leq 1, F^T F = I, \end{aligned} \tag{15}$$

where λ is the parameter to ensure $Tr(F^T L_S F)$ close to zero.

By comprehensively considering the above factors, we derive our overall objective formulation as

$$\begin{aligned} L_{fin} = &\min \sum_{i,j} (\| f_{\theta_e}(x_i) - f_{\theta_e}(x_j) \|_2^2 s_{ij} + \gamma s_{ij}^2) + \lambda Tr(F^T L_S F) + L_r + L_e + L_c \\ &s.t. \quad \forall i, s_i^T \mathbf{1} = 1, 0 \leq s_{ij} \leq 1, F^T F = I. \end{aligned} \tag{16}$$

3.4 Optimization

–***Update structured graph.*** According to CAN [21], we can solve the problem (15) by applying the alternative optimization approach.

When S is fixed, the problem (15) becomes:

$$\min_{F^T F = I} Tr(F^T L_S F). \tag{17}$$

The optimal solution F is formed by the c eigenvectors of L_S corresponding to the c smallest eigenvalues.

When F is fixed, according to Eq. (13), we can rewrite the problem (15) as:

$$\begin{aligned} &\min \sum_{i,j} (\| f_{\theta_e}(x_i) - f_{\theta_e}(x_j) \|_2^2 s_{ij} + \gamma s_{ij}^2 + \lambda \| f_i - f_j \|_2^2 s_{ij}) \\ &s.t. \quad \forall i, s_i^T \mathbf{1} = 1, 0 \leq s_{ij} \leq 1. \end{aligned} \tag{18}$$

We denote $d_{ij}^x = \| f_{\theta_e}(x_i) - f_{\theta_e}(x_j) \|_2^2$, $d_{ij}^f = \| f_i - f_j \|_2^2$, and $d_{ij} = d_{ij}^x + d_{ij}^f$. Then we can get structure graph S by optimizing the following formula:

$$\min_{s_i^T \mathbf{1} = 1, 0 \leq s_{ij} \leq 1} \left\| s_i + \frac{1}{2\gamma} d_i \right\|_2^2. \tag{19}$$

The Lagrangian function of the problem (19) is

$$\mathcal{L}(s_i, \phi, \beta) = \frac{1}{2} \left\| s_i + \frac{d_i^x}{2\gamma_i} \right\|_2^2 - \phi(s_i^T \mathbf{1} - 1) - \beta_i^T s_i, \tag{20}$$

where ϕ and $\beta_i \geq 0$ is the Lagrangian multipliers.

According to the KKT condition [12], the optimal solution s_i can be calculated as

$$s_{ij} = \left(-\frac{d_{ij}^x}{2\gamma_i} + \phi \right)_+. \tag{21}$$

–***Update AutoEncoders weights and clustering centers.*** We optimize θ and u using Stochastic Gradient Descent (SGD) and Back Propagation (BP) [3]. Fixing the structured graph S, the gradients of L_{fin} with respect to clustering center u_j and embedded point $z_i = f_{\theta_e}(x_i)$ can be computed as:

$$\frac{\partial L_{fin}}{\partial u_j} = \frac{\partial L_e}{\partial u_j} = 2\sum_{j=1}^{n}(1+ \parallel z_i - u_j \parallel^2)^{-1}(q_{ij} - p_{ij})(z_i - u_j) \tag{22}$$

$$\begin{aligned}\frac{\partial L_{fin}}{\partial z_i} = \frac{\partial L_e}{\partial z_i} + \frac{\partial L_c}{\partial z_i} =& 2\sum_{j=1}^{c}(1+ \parallel z_i - u_j \parallel^2)^{-1}(p_{ij} - q_{ij})(z_i - u_j) \\ &+ \frac{1}{2}\sum_{j:s_{ij}\in S}(a_{ij} - s_{ij})z_j + \frac{1}{2}\sum_{j:s_{ij}\in S}(a_{ji} - s_{ji})z_j,\end{aligned} \tag{23}$$

where $a_{ij} = \delta(\omega_{ij})$.

The whole algorithm is summarized in Algorithm 1.

Algorithm 1: Learning algorithm for DSGC

Input: The original sample X, the number of pertrain iterations $PreIter$, similarity threshold η, hyper-parameter λ

Output: AutoEncoder weight θ, cluster center c, and label y

```
for iter ∈ {0, 1, ..., PreIter} do
    Calculate parameter θ of the AutoEncoder by optimizing Eq.(1).
end
Get the structured graph S using (21).
Improve the structured graph S according to Eq. (8).
while not convergence do
    Calculate parameters p and q by Eq. (2) and Eq.(3).
    Update θ and c via Eq. (23) and Eq. (22) with p, q, and S.
end
```

4 Experimental Configuration

4.1 Experimental Datasets

1. **MNIST** [7] is provided by NIST, and consists of 70,000 handwritten digits in 28*28 pixel from 0 to 9. It contains 60,000 training samples and 10,000 test samples, and has been widely used to test character recognition method.
2. **USPS** [27] is the handwritten digital image dataset provided by the United States postal service. It consists of 9,298 handwritten digits (0–9) in 16*16 grayscale pixel. USPS is also one of the datasets widely used in handwritten numeral recognition.
3. **Fashion MNIST (FMNIST)** [37] is an image dataset provided by Zalando that replaces the MNIST dataset. It includes 70,000 positive digits in 10 classes with different fashion items.

4. **STL-10** [5] is an image recognition dataset that contains 10,000 96*96 pixel color images. In this paper, we use the VGG16 network to convert these images into 4096-dimensional vectors for the convenience of later training.
5. **CIFAR-10** [32] consists of 60,000 32*32 colour images in 10 classes, with 6,000 images per class. We select 50,000 images for training, and 10,000 images for testing.
6. **REUTERS10K** [15] is based on 11,228 Reuters news texts and divided into 46 topics. In this paper, according to DEC [33], we use root categories: corporate/industrial, government/social, markets, and economics as labels for training, all documents with multiple labels. Then we use the text feature extraction method to transform the text data into the 2,000-dimensional vector by word frequency.

4.2 Evaluation Baselines

1. **AE+k-means** [19], **AE+SC** [17] and **AE+CAN** [21] are two-step deep clustering approaches. The features are first extracted by the AutoEncoder. Then, k-menas, SC and CAN are performed on the embedding features.
2. **DCN** [34] is a joint deep neural network and k-means clustering approach to train a model that can project samples into a k-means-friendly Spaces.
3. **DEC** [33] simultaneously learns feature representations and cluster assignments by using deep neural networks. It clusters data into a jointly optimized feature space by optimizing the KL divergence between the samples and the cluster center.
4. **IDEC** [9] is based on DEC, which manipulate feature space to scatter data points by using a clustering loss as guidance.
5. **DCCM** [32] learns feature representation by mining a comprehensive correlation and using mutual information between corresponding features.

Table 2. ACC of all methods on six public datasets. The best result in each line is marked with bold.

Methods	MNIST	USPS	FMNIST	STL-10	CIFAR-10	REUTERS10K
AE+k-means	0.8050	0.6278	0.4918	0.6163	0.4596	0.4842
AE+SC	0.7536	0.6345	0.5777	0.6142	0.4668	0.6134
AE+CAN	0.6497	0.7113	0.5112	0.2217	0.2336	0.3873
DCN	0.8400	0.6900	0.5600	0.6400	0.5500	0.5300
DEC	0.7486	0.7399	0.6056	0.8894	0.5126	0.7221
IDEC	0.7730	0.7384	0.5904	0.9017	0.5731	0.7478
DCCM	0.7510	0.4918	0.3609	0.4820	0.6230	-
Ours	**0.9549**	**0.7662**	**0.6162**	**0.9202**	**0.6489**	**0.7920**

4.3 Evaluation Metrics

We adopt three evaluation metrics widely used in clustering task: Accuracy (ACC) [31], Normalized Mutual Information (NMI) [22], and Adjusted Rand Index (ARI) [6] to evaluate the performance of clustering methods.

4.4 Parameter Setting

Following setting in DEC, we construct an AutoEncoder network as a fully connected Multi-Layer Perception (MLP) with dimensions d - 500 - 500 - 2000 - c for all datasets, where d is the dimensions of samples and c is the number of clusters. Except for the input layer, output layer, and embedding layer, all other layers in the AutoEncoder model are activated by the ReLU nonlinearity function. For AE+k-means, AE+SC, and AE+CAN, we set the number of pre-training iterations of AutoEncode for each dataset to 200. For DEC and IDEC, we set the pre-training iteration of MNIST data to 300, the pre-training iteration of USPS to 50, and for the other datasets, we set the number of pre-training sessions to 10. For our method, we set the similarity threshold η to 0.85.

5 Experiment Results

5.1 Performance Comparison

This subsection evaluates the clustering performance of DSGC with seven clustering methods on six datasets. The results are reported in Tables 2, 3, and 4. From the results, we can find that DSGC dramatically outperforms other baselines, include the two-step clustering method, embedded methods like DEC, IDEC and others. For example, on STL10 dataset, DSGC achieved the ACC value of 0.9202, and 0.02 improvement than the second-best method IDEC. Moreover, DSGC obtains the NMI value of 0.8480 on STL-10 dataset, 0.6489 on CIFAR-10 dataset, better than the other baseline. Both DSGC and DEC are deep clustering methods that project samples into a clustered friendly space. By comparing DSGC and DEC, we can find that DSGC can significantly improve the clustering effect with the guidance of the structured graph.

The superior performance of our model is attributed to the following reasons. First, we used embedded deep neural networks to joint optimization feature learning and clustering, the results of the embedding clustering methods like DEC or IDEC demonstrate the effectiveness of jointly optimize. Then, we add the structured graph constraints between samples to the process of feature learning, which enables the manifold information between samples to be introduced into feature learning. Through joint optimization of feature learning, clustering, and similarity constraint between samples, our method achieves superior performance compared with the previous methods.

Table 3. NMI of all methods on six public datasets.

Methods	MNIST	USPS	FMNIST	STL-10	CIFAR-10	REUTERS10K
AE+k-means	0.7384	0.6198	0.4874	0.5797	0.3842	0.1932
AE+SC	0.6346	0.5731	0.5984	0.4856	0.3947	0.3433
AE+CAN	0.6598	0.7902	0.5824	0.2213	0.2044	0.0041
DCN	0.8000	0.6800	**0.6500**	0.6600	0.4700	0.3200
DEC	0.7105	0.7592	0.6317	0.8219	0.5095	0.5403
IDEC	0.7211	0.7560	0.6226	0.8245	0.4641	0.4852
DCCM	0.7370	0.3961	0.3760	0.3760	0.4960	-
Ours	**0.8907**	**0.7914**	0.6317	**0.8480**	**0.5760**	**0.5979**

Table 4. ARI of all methods on six public datasets.

Methods	MNIST	USPS	FMNIST	STL-10	CIFAR-10	REUTERS10K
AE+k-means	0.6958	0.5240	0.3390	0.4512	0.2716	0.1568
AE+SC	0.5876	0.4863	0.4468	0.3617	0.2820	0.3276
AE+CAN	0.6967	**0.8203**	**0.5778**	0.2397	0.2348	0.3930
DCN	0.7400	0.5800	0.4600	0.4100	0.3100	0.2500
DEC	0.6273	0.6690	0.4926	0.7841	0.3885	0.5867
IDEC	0.6548	0.6709	0.4818	0.8015	0.3707	0.4932
DMMC	0.6289	0.2841	0.1789	0.2620	0.4080	-
Ours	**0.9033**	0.7133	0.4899	**0.8358**	**0.4782**	**0.6057**

5.2 Effects of the Structured Graph Learning

In this subsection, we conduct experiments to verify the validity of the structured graph of the method. We design several variants of our method and compare their performance with our approach. Considering the differences between datasets and the time as well as space costs required for operation, we randomly select 10,000 samples from each dataset as the test set, and the effect of the structured graph of the model was tested on these datasets. The experimental results are shown in Fig. 2.

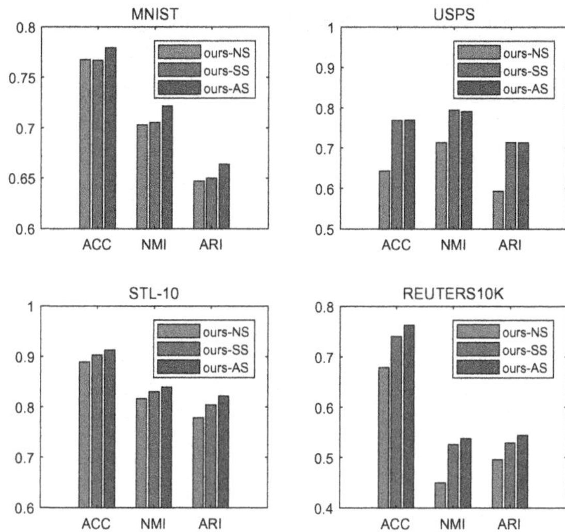

Fig. 2. Experimental results of our method and variants on public datasets, where ours-NS represents that similarity matrix is not used as a guide in the training process, ours-SS represents the use similarity matrix constructed by simple distances to guide the training process, and our-AS represents we obtain the similarity matrix adaptively by solving Eq. (15).

Model Without the Structured Graph Guidance. We first designed a variant method named ours-NS that performs clustering without the structured graph guidance. Under such circumstances, the variant method degenerates to a common embedding clustering model. According to the results in Fig. 2, we can clearly observe that the clustering effect of modes without structured graph guidance is significantly lower than that of other models with structure graph guidance.

Models with Different Structured Graph. We design a variant clustering model (ours-SS) based on the fixed graph constructed with the cosine similarity, we can observe that the model with the guidance of fixed structure graph can improve by about 3% points compared to the model without the structure graph. But on most datasets, it is still 1–3 percentage points behind the structured graph model with adaptive learning.

Through the above analysis, we can find that the guidance of the similarity matrix can significantly improve the accuracy of clustering. And the adaptive similarity matrix is better than the similarity matrix obtained by simple distance in guiding the clustering.

5.3 Parameter Experiment

To more accurately analyze the performance of the proposed method, the number of output neurons of different encoders is analyzed, and the variation curve of accuracy is shown in Fig. 3. When the dimension of output samples is too low, the information will be missing, when the dimension of output samples is too high, information redundancy will be caused and the clustering effect will be affected. From Fig. 3, we can find that for most datasets, when the number of neurons in the output layer o is the same as the number of clustering c, this method can achieve better results.

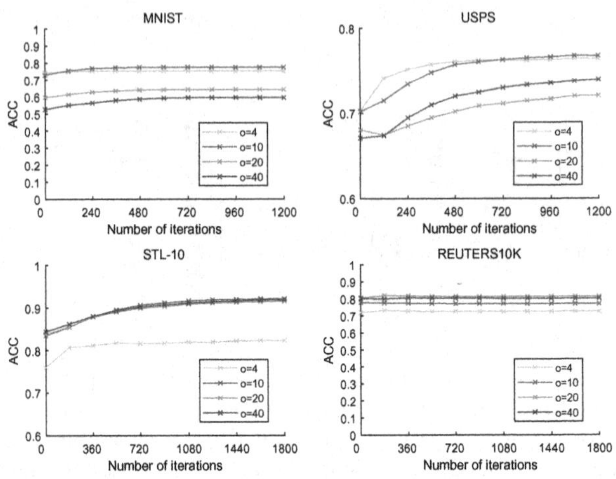

Fig. 3. Parameter analysis of the encoder construction on public datasets.

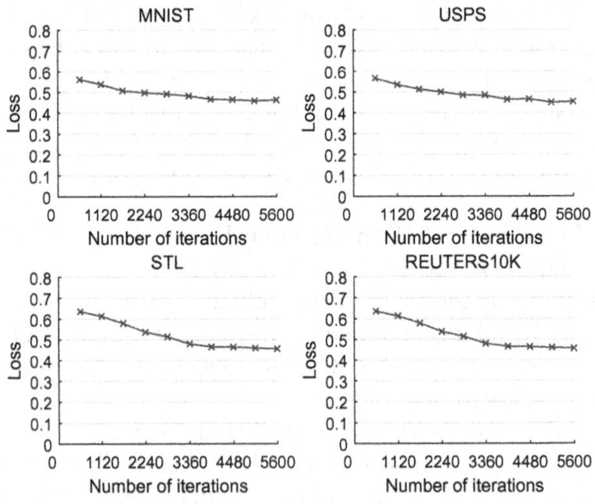

Fig. 4. The losses during training on public datasets

5.4 Convergence Experiment

Figure 4 shows the convergence curves that record the variations of the loss function value with the number of iterations. We can clearly find that as the number of iterations increases, the value of loss function decreases continuously. After a period of iteration, the value of loss function does not change significantly. The results validate that our proposed method could achieve convergence efficiently.

6 Conclusion

In this paper, we propose a clustering model that can adaptively learn a structured graph to guide the training of deep neural networks. To verify our claim, we conducted a series of experiments to verify the effect of the structure diagram on clustering results. By comparing the clustering performance of models with different structured graphs on each dataset, we verify the significant positive effect of structured graph guidance on clustering results.

Our future works are as follows. We will perform more methods to obtain the structured graph, try to achieve a better clustering effect, and solve the existing problem of excessive space and time occupancy.

References

1. Bellman, R.E.: Adaptive Control Processes: A Guided Tour. Princeton University Press (2015)
2. Ben-Hur, A., Horn, D., Siegelmann, H.T., Vapnik, V.: Support vector clustering. J. Mach. Learn Res **2**(Dec), 125–137 (2001)
3. Bottou, L., Bengio, Y.: Convergence properties of the k-means algorithms. In: NeurIPS, pp. 585–592 (1994)
4. Chen, G.: Deep Learning with Nonparametric Clustering. CoRR abs/1501.03084 (2015)
5. Coates, A., Ng, A.Y., Lee, H.: An analysis of single-layer networks in unsupervised feature learning. In: AISTATS, vol. 15, pp. 215–223 (2011)
6. D'Ambrosio, A., Amodio, S., Iorio, C., Pandolfo, G., Siciliano, R.: Adjusted concordance index: an extensionl of the adjusted rand index to fuzzy partitions. J. Classif. **38**, 1–17 (2020)
7. Deng, L.: The MNIST database of handwritten digit images for machine learning research [best of the web]. IEEE Signal Process. Mag. **29**(6), 141–142 (2012)
8. Fan, K.: On a theorem of weyl concerning eigenvalues of linear transformations i. Proc. Natl. Acad. Sci. USA **35**(11), 652 (1949)
9. Guo, X., Gao, L., Liu, X., Yin, J.: Improved deep embedded clustering with local structure preservation. In: IJCAI, pp. 1753–1759 (2017)
10. Guo, X., Liu, X., Zhu, E., Yin, J.: Deep clustering with convolutional autoencoders. In: ICONIP, vol. 10635, pp. 373–382 (2017)
11. Iandola, F.N., Moskewicz, M.W., Ashraf, K., Keutzer, K.: Firecaffe: near-linear acceleration of deep neural network training on compute clusters. In: CVPR, pp. 2592–2600 (2016)
12. Jain, A.K., Dubes, R.C.: Algorithms for Clustering Data. Prentice-Hall, Upper Saddle River (1988)
13. Ji, P., Zhang, T., Li, H., Salzmann, M., Reid, I.D.: Deep subspace clustering networks. In: NeurIPS, pp. 24–33 (2017)

14. Johnson, S.C.: Hierarchical clustering schemes. Psychometrika **32**(3), 241–254 (1967)
15. Lewis, D.D., Yang, Y., Rose, T.G., Li, F.: RCV1: a new benchmark collection for text categorization research. J. Mach. Learn. Res. **5**, 361–397 (2004)
16. Li, T., Ding, C.H.Q.: The relationships among various nonnegative matrix factorization methods for clustering. In: ICDM, pp. 362–371 (2006)
17. von Luxburg, U.: A tutorial on spectral clustering. Stat. Comput. **17**(4), 395–416 (2007)
18. Maaten, L.v.d., Hinton, G.: Visualizing data using t-SNE. J. Mach. Learn. Res. **9**(2605), 2605 2579–2605 (2008)
19. MacQueen, J., et al.: Some methods for classification and analysis of multivariate observations. In: BSMSP, pp. 281–297 (1967)
20. Mousavi, S.M., Zhu, W., Ellsworth, W., Beroza, G.: Unsupervised clustering of seismic signals using deep convolutional autoencoders. IEEE Geosci. Remote Sens. **16**(11), 1693–1697 (2019)
21. Nie, F., Wang, X., Huang, H.: Clustering and projected clustering with adaptive neighbors. In: ACM SIGKDD, pp. 977–986 (2014)
22. Nie, F., Zeng, Z., Tsang, I.W., Xu, D., Zhang, C.: Spectral embedded clustering: a framework for in-sample and out-of-sample spectral clustering. IEEE Trans. Neural Netw. **22**(11), 1796–1808 (2011)
23. Pearson, K.: On lines and planes of closest fit to systems of points in space. Lond. Edinburgh Dublin Philoso. Mag. J. Sci. **2**(11), 559–572 (1901)
24. Peng, X., Xiao, S., Feng, J., Yau, W., Yi, Z.: Deep subspace clustering with sparsity prior. In: IJCAI, pp. 1925–1931 (2016)
25. Pinto, D., Benedí, J., Rosso, P.: Clustering narrow-domain short texts by using the kullback-leibler distance. In: Proceedings of Computational Linguistics and Intelligent Text Processing. vol. 4394, pp. 611–622 (2007)
26. Rodriguez, M.Z., et al.: Clustering algorithms: a comparative approach. PLoS ONE **14**(1), 1–31 (2019)
27. Ruppert, D.: The elements of statistical learning: Data mining, inference, and prediction. Am. Soc. Anesth. **99**(466), 567–567 (2004)
28. Shi, D., Zhu, L., Li, Y., Li, J., Nie, X.: Robust structured graph clustering. IEEE Trans. Neural Netw. Learn. Syst. **31**(11), 4424–4436 (2020)
29. Tian, F., Gao, B., Cui, Q., Chen, E., Liu, T.: Learning deep representations for graph clustering. In: AAAI, pp. 1293–1299 (2014)
30. Vincent, P., Larochelle, H., Lajoie, I., Bengio, Y., Manzagol, P.A.: Stacked denoising autoencoders: Learning useful representations in a deep network with a local denoising criterion. J. Mach. Learn. Res. **11**(Dec), 3371–3408 (2010)
31. Wang, W., Yan, Y., Nie, F., Yan, S., Sebe, N.: Flexible manifold learning with optimal graph for image and video representation. IEEE Trans. Image Process. **27**(6), 2664–2675 (2018)
32. Wu, J., et al.: Deep comprehensive correlation mining for image clustering. In: ICCV, pp. 8149–8158 (2019)
33. Xie, J., Girshick, R.B., Farhadi, A.: Unsupervised deep embedding for clustering analysis. **48**, 478–487 (2016)
34. Yang, B., Fu, X., Sidiropoulos, N.D., Hong, M.: Towards k-means-friendly spaces: Simultaneous deep learning and clustering. In: ICML, vol. 70, pp. 3861–3870 (2017)

35. Yang, Q., Wang, H., Li, T., Yang, Y.: Deep belief networks oriented clustering. In: ISKE, pp. 58–65 (2015)
36. Yin, Q., Wu, S., Wang, L.: Multiview clustering via unified and view-specific embeddings learning. IEEE Trans. Neural Netw. Learn. Syst. **29**(11), 5541–5553 (2018)
37. Zhou, Y., Gu, K., Huang, T.S.: Unsupervised representation adversarial learning network: from reconstruction to generation. In: IJCNN, pp. 1–8 (2019)

Improved Clustering Strategies for Learning Style Identification in Massive Open Online Courses

Wei Song(✉) and Ziqiao Wang

School of Information Science and Technology, North China University of Technology, Beijing 100144, China
songwei@ncut.edu.cn

Abstract. Learning style identification is important for improving the learning and teaching experience in the massive open online courses (MOOCs). To identify learning styles automatically, a very large quantity of labeled data is necessary. However, labeling data manually is tedious and impractical. A known solution to this problem is to cluster MOOCs learning data and label them with the general characteristics of the cluster to which they belong. In this paper, we propose two distance measures suitable for forming canopies in MOOCs, and incorporate the canopy approach into the K-means clustering algorithm. This improves the stability of the clustering results and the quality of the data labeling. Experimental results with four popular classifiers show that the proposed method can improve both the overall identification of learning styles and the identification of each individual learning style.

Keywords: Massive open online courses · Learning styles · Clustering · K-means · Elbow method · Canopy approach

1 Introduction

Massive open online courses (MOOCs) are online teaching platforms that can offer unlimited enrollments in courses on rich learning topics for anyone via the internet. MOOCs play an increasingly important role in education because of the development of internet technology and people's increasingly diverse learning needs [16].

As the popularity of MOOCs has increased, their problems have also become more prominent. One of the earliest and most widely studied problems of MOOCs is their high dropout rate, which significantly reduces the number of learners successfully completing the courses in which they have enrolled. Various methods have been proposed to solve this problem from different perspectives [2, 10]. Another serious problem with MOOCs is their impersonal nature. In many cases, thousands of learners enroll in a single course with a single instructor and the same learning material. To improve personalization, data mining methods, such as pattern mining [14] and clustering [15], have been used to analyze students' learning behavior in depth. These methods discover learners' behavior from data collected via an e-learning or MOOC platform, thus avoiding the problems of

Y. Tan and Y. Shi (Eds.): DMBD 2022, CCIS 1744, pp. 240–254, 2022.
https://doi.org/10.1007/978-981-19-9297-1_18

traditional questionnaires, such as their complex design and the treatment of arbitrary answers.

Recently, Hmedna et al. demonstrated that exploiting domain knowledge can further improve the understanding of MOOC learners' behavior. In their work [8], the Felder–Silverman learning style model (FSLSM) [6] was used to guide the identification of learning styles. Specifically, K-means clustering was used to label learners according to their preferences for each learning style, and then four supervised models were used to identify their learning styles.

In this paper, we improve the performance of learning style identification by stabilizing the initial clusters with the elbow method [11] and canopy approach [9]. The elbow method is used to determine the number of clusters correctly, and the canopy approach can ensure that the initial cluster centers are suitable for stable clustering. The clustering results are used together with the FSLSM to label the MOOC learning data for automatic identification of learning styles. In experiments, the data were labeled separately using the proposed method and the method of [8], and learning styles were identified from two datasets using four popular classifiers. The experimental results show that the proposed method was superior to the method of [8] with respect to both the overall identification performance and the identification performance for each individual style.

2 Learning Style Identification

Learning styles can be defined in many ways, from the perspective of either psychology or pedagogy. Generally, a learning style is an overall pattern that provides direction to learning and teaching. A learning style can also be described as a set of factors and behaviors that facilitates learning for an individual in a given situation [4].

Among the various learning style models, FSLSM [6] is the most widely used. Originally designed for engineering education, FSLSM consists of four dimensions: perception, input, processing, and understanding. Recently, various studies have shown that identifying learners' learning styles automatically could improve the quality of online learning. El Aissaoui et al. extracted learning sequences from learners' log files using web usage mining techniques, and then used fuzzy c-means (FCM) to categorize learning styles with FSLSM [3]. Similarly, Azzi et al. also predicted learning styles in e-learning systems using FSLSM and FCM [1]. The difference between these two studies is that Azzi et al. considered several courses. Furthermore, neural networks (NNs) [5] and decision trees (DTs) [12] have also been used for identifying learning styles.

According to Hmedna et al. [8], FSLSM is also helpful for learning style identification in MOOCs. In their work, both unsupervised and supervised learning techniques were used to identify learning styles accurately.

3 Dataset and Preprocessing

The clickstream data of the "Statistical Learning" course was used throughout this study. The dataset was collected from edX and provided by the author of [8]. It should be noted that the data of only one dimension (the processing dimension) of FSLSM was provided to us; therefore, all of the work performed in this study was conducted on the processing dimension. According to FSLSM, the processing dimension has two poles: active and reflective.

The dataset contains the records of 18,475,724 events of 32,209 learners from January 19, 2015 to April 6, 2015. The main attributes include course content, learners' interactions in a forum, learning activities, video interactions, and events triggered by individual learners. Each event is described by a set of features, such as the learner identifier, event type, and date and time of the event.

We used the same preprocessing methods as those reported in [8]. First, each learner was represented as a *feature vector* that consists of the number of events, number of weeks, and status of certification. Second, eight anomalous learners were detected and deleted. Third, six features of the active pole and five features of the reflective pole were selected. Finally, their values were normalized to [0, 1] by min–max normalization.

4 Improved K-Means Clustering for Data Labeling

4.1 Basic Algorithm

Using the feature vectors constructed in the preprocessing phase, learners were divided into groups by clustering techniques in [8]. The purpose of clustering is to partition a set of objects such that objects in the same group (called a cluster) are more similar to each other than to those in other groups.

The clustering algorithm used in [8] was K-means. Given a predefined number of clusters K, the K-means algorithm starts with K randomly selected centers, which are used as the initial feature vectors for every cluster. At each step, every vector is assigned to its nearest cluster center, and each cluster center is updated to the average of the vectors assigned to it. This process repeats until either the cluster centers have stabilized or a predefined number of iterations has been performed.

K-means clustering has two main limitations. First, the user has to specify the number of clusters K in advance, which is a difficult task for those who are not familiar with the data. The second limitation is that the algorithm is sensitive to the initial cluster centers: choosing different initial centers often leads to very different results.

To overcome these two limitations and increase the accuracy of learning style identification, we improved the K-means clustering algorithm in two respects. First, the elbow method [11] was used to determine the number of clusters. Second, the canopy approach [9] was used to set the initial centers within each cluster. With these two improvements, the proposed K-means-CE (K-means with canopy and elbow) clustering method for data labeling is presented in Algorithm

Algorithm 1	**K-means-CE**
Input	Unlabeled feature vectors
Output	Labeled feature vectors
1	Determine K by the elbow method;
2	Calculate K initial centers using the canopy approach;
3	Perform K-means clustering with the K canopy centers as the initial cluster centers;
4	Label each vector with the clustering results.

4.2 Elbow Method

The first part of Algorithm 1 is the determination of K. We use the elbow method, which is based on the sum of squared errors (SSE). The SSE metric is defined as

$$\mathrm{SSE} = \sum_{i=1}^{K} \sum_{\mathbf{f} \in C_i} dis(\mathbf{f}, \boldsymbol{\mu}_\mathbf{i}), \tag{1}$$

where C_i is the i-th cluster, $\mathbf{f}$ and $\boldsymbol{\mu}_\mathbf{i}$ are an arbitrary feature vector and the center of C_i, respectively, and $dis(\mathbf{f}, \boldsymbol{\mu}_\mathbf{i})$ is the distance between $\mathbf{f}$ and $\boldsymbol{\mu}_\mathbf{i}$, which is defined as

$$dis(\mathbf{f}, \boldsymbol{\mu}_\mathbf{i}) = \sqrt{\sum_{j=1}^{m} (f_j - \mu_{ij})^2}, \tag{2}$$

where m is the number of elements of a feature vector, f_j is the j-th element of $\mathbf{f}$, and μ_{ij} is the j-th element of $\boldsymbol{\mu}_\mathbf{i}$.

We can observe from Eq. 1 that a smaller value of SSE corresponds to more compact clusters. Therefore, clusters that minimize SSE should be favored. However, SSE tends to decrease toward 0 as K increases. This is because, when K is maximized, each data point is its own cluster and there is no error between it and the center of its cluster. The value of K at which the improvement in SSE declines the most is called the *elbow*; this is the point at which we should stop dividing the data into more clusters. This process is usually realized by plotting a line chart of SSE for each value of K. If the line chart looks like an arm, then the "elbow" of the arm is the optimal value of K. In this study, K was set to 4.

4.3 Canopy Approach

After the number of clusters has been determined, the canopy approach is used to determine the initial center of each cluster.

A *canopy* is simply a set of the feature vectors that are within some distance threshold from a center. A feature vector may appear in more than one canopy, and every feature vector must appear in at least one canopy. Therefore, canopies usually overlap. The main idea underlying the canopy approach is that two feature vectors that do not appear in any common canopy are sufficiently far apart that they could not possibly be in the same cluster. Consequently, when performing a strict clustering algorithm, the distance between two feature vectors that are not in the same canopy can be ignored. The canopy approach is usually performed to obtain a rough partition of the dataset for a more accurate clustering result.

Canopies are usually generated as follows, given two distance thresholds T_1 and T_2, where $T_1 > T_2$. Select a feature vector $\mathbf{f}$ and approximately measure its distance to each canopy center. Add $\mathbf{f}$ to a canopy if the distance between $\mathbf{f}$ and its center is no greater than threshold T_1. Remove $\mathbf{f}$ from the dataset if its distance from the canopy center is no greater than threshold T_2. If $\mathbf{f}$ does not belong to any existing canopy, it is set as a new canopy center and deleted from the dataset. Repeat the above process until the dataset is empty.

The purpose of our proposed method is to generate stable clusters. Therefore, T_2 is defined as the average distance between each pair of feature vectors:

$$T_2 = \sum_{i=1}^{N} \sum_{j \neq i} dis(\mathbf{f_i}, \mathbf{f_j})/(N \times (N - 1)), \quad (3)$$

where $\mathbf{f_i}$ $(1 \leq i \leq N)$ and $\mathbf{f_j}$ $(1 \leq j \leq N)$ are two arbitrary feature vectors, and $dis(\mathbf{f_i}, \mathbf{f_j})$ is the Euclidean distance between points $\mathbf{f_i}$ and $\mathbf{f_j}$, defined in Eq. 2.

After outlining the approximate range, we attempt to determine the optimal value of T_1 by progressive refinement. Most importantly, to ensure that the number of canopies is equal to K, T_1 is defined as.

$$T_1 = 2 \times T_2. \quad (4)$$

4.4 K-Means Clustering

Using the K canopy centers as the initial centers of the K clusters, the next stage of K-means-CE is the K-means clustering.

In general, this stage processes a set of N feature vectors $F = \{\mathbf{f_1}, \mathbf{f_2}, \ldots, \mathbf{f_N}\}$ and K initial cluster centers $C = \{\boldsymbol{\mu}_\mathbf{1}, \boldsymbol{\mu}_\mathbf{2}, \ldots, \boldsymbol{\mu}_\mathbf{K}\}$, which are actually the centers of K canopies, and works as follows.

First, the distance from each feature vector $\mathbf{f_i}$ $(1 \leq i \leq N)$ to each center $\boldsymbol{\mu}_\mathbf{j}$ $(1 \leq j \leq K)$ is computed, using Euclidean distance (Eq. 2). The closest center is then assigned to each feature vector. For each center, the average of the feature vectors labeled with it is calculated, and these averaged feature vectors become the new centers of the clusters. The distance from each feature vector to each center is recalculated, the assignment is modified, and the procedure is repeated until the assignments are stabilized. Finally, the clusters are generated. It should be noted that step 3 of Algorithm 1 does not calculate the distance between two feature vectors that never appear in the same canopy.

Similar to the method of [8], we also use the Calinski–Harabasz index (CHI) and the Silhouette index (SI) to validate the clustering results.

CHI is the ratio of the sum of inter-cluster dispersion to the sum of intra-cluster dispersion for all clusters. It is defined as

$$CHI(K) = \frac{\text{SSB}}{K - 1} \times \frac{N - K}{\text{SSE}}, \quad (5)$$

where N is the number of feature vectors, K is the number of clusters, SSE (Eq. 1) denotes the intra-cluster sum of squares, and SSB denotes the sum of squares between clusters. SSB is defined as

$$\text{SSB} = \sum_{i=1}^{K} (N_i \times dis(\boldsymbol{\mu}_\mathbf{i}, \boldsymbol{\mu})), \quad (6)$$

where N_i is the number of feature vectors in the i-th cluster, $\boldsymbol{\mu}_\mathbf{i}$ is the center of the i-th cluster, $\boldsymbol{\mu}$ is the center of the whole dataset, and $dis(\boldsymbol{\mu}_\mathbf{i}, \boldsymbol{\mu})$ (Eq. 2) is the Euclidean distance between $\boldsymbol{\mu}_\mathbf{i}$ and $\boldsymbol{\mu}$.

It can be observed from Eq. 5 that a higher CHI corresponds to a better clustering because observations in each cluster are closer together, whereas clusters themselves are further away from each other.

Another metric used to validate clustering results is the SI, which measures the closeness of each point in one cluster to points in the neighboring clusters. SI is defined as

$$SI(\mathbf{f}) = \frac{b(\mathbf{f}) - a(\mathbf{f})}{max\{a(\mathbf{f}),\ b(\mathbf{f})\}}, \tag{7}$$

where $\mathbf{f}$ is a feature vector, $a(\mathbf{f})$ is the average distance between $\mathbf{f}$ and all other feature vectors in the same cluster, and $b(\mathbf{f})$ is the average distance between $\mathbf{f}$ and all objects in the closest cluster.

The value of SI lies in the range $[-1, 1]$. If $SI(\mathbf{f})$ is close to 1, $\mathbf{f}$ is well-clustered and already assigned to a highly appropriate cluster. If $SI(\mathbf{f})$ is close to 0, $\mathbf{f}$ could be assigned to another cluster close to it because $\mathbf{f}$ lies equally far away from both the clusters. If $SI(\mathbf{f})$ is close to -1, $\mathbf{f}$ is misclassified and is merely placed somewhere between the clusters.

The Silhouette validation technique calculates the SI for each feature vector, the average SI for each cluster, and the overall average SI for the entire dataset. Using the proposed approach, each cluster can be represented by its SI, which measures the compactness of the cluster and its separation from other clusters.

In the experiments reported in this paper, we generated four clusters for the active pole and four clusters for the reflective pole.

4.5 Data Labeling

In the final step of the algorithm, the clustering results are used for labeling each learner. For the active and reflective poles, four preference levels (very weak, weak, moderate, and strong) are used to describe the degree to which each learner belongs to each pole. These four labels correspond to the four clusters, and are determined by ranking the mean values of the corresponding attributes of each cluster. The main difference between the poles is that six features of the active pole and five features of the reflective pole are selected. The 11 features used in this paper are exactly the same as the 11 features used in [8].

The label of the cluster determines the degree of preference of each learner for both the active and reflective poles. For example, a learner with a strongly active learning style simultaneously shows a weak preference for a reflective learning style. We use the same weighting for the preference level as that used in [8]; the weights are shown in Table 1.

Table 1. Weights of learning style

	Very weak	Weak	Moderate	Strong
Active	0	1	2	3
Reflective	0	−1	−2	−3

By summing the active and reflective weights of each learner, a grid of the balance of learning styles is generated, in which each entry represents the *dominant learning style* (DLS) of a learner (Table 2).

Table 2. Balance of learning styles grid

		Active			
		Very weak (0)	Weak (1)	Moderate (2)	Strong (3)
Reflective	Very weak (0)	Balanced	Moderate active	Strong active	Strong active
	Weak (−1)	Moderate reflective	Balanced	Moderate active	Strong active
	Moderate (−2)	Strong reflective	Moderate reflective	Balanced	Moderate active
	Strong (−3)	Strong reflective	Strong reflective	Moderate reflective	Balanced

Table 2 shows that scores of ±2 and ±3 indicate a strong preference, ±1 indicates a moderate preference, and 0 indicates a balanced preference.

Each learner can be represented by a *global feature vector* (GFV), which includes the DLS, in the form.

$$GFV = \{x_{11}, x_{12}, \ldots, x_{16}, x_{21}, x_{22}, \ldots, x_{25}, \text{DLS}\}, \tag{7}$$

where x_{1i} $(1 \leq i \leq 6)$ is the value of the *i*-th feature of the active pole, x_{2j} $(1 \leq j \leq 5)$ is the value of the *j*-th feature of the reflective pole, and DLS ∈ {Balanced, Moderate active, Strong active, Moderate reflective, Strong reflective}.

5 Learning Style Identification by Supervised Learning

5.1 Classifiers for Learning Style Identification

The original dataset can be transformed to a labeled dataset that is ready for identifying learning styles by using popular classifiers. The DLSs of GFVs act as the labels. As in [8], DT, random forest (RF), K-nearest neighbors (KNN), and NN were used for learning style identification.

A DT is a tree of decision nodes. Beginning at the root node, each node tests the value of some feature of a GFV, and each leaf node assigns a class label to the GFV. A DT is easy to explain and efficient for classification. However, it is also sensitive to data change and prone to overfitting.

An RF combines the output of multiple DTs to obtain a single result. The RF method can be viewed as an extension of the bagging method because it uses both bagging and feature randomness to create an uncorrelated forest of DTs. Instead of relying on one DT, an RF takes a prediction from each tree and predicts the final output by a majority vote of the predictions. The main advantage of the RF method is that it reduces the overfitting problem of DTs; additionally, it reduces the variance and therefore improves the accuracy. However, an RF is harder to interpret than a single DT.

KNN is a data classification method for estimating the probability that a GFV will become a member of a specific group according to the groups to which the GFVs nearest to it belong. KNN is a lazy and non-parametric algorithm. Its main advantage is that it is simple and requires no training phase, but it has two main disadvantages. First, it does not perform well on a dataset containing a large number of records or a large number of dimensions. Second, it is sensitive to outliers.

An NN is a system whose structure is inspired by the action of the human brain. Generally speaking, the nodes of the network are distributed in several layers, which are interconnected with one another. Each node of an NN is a perceptron. NNs enable nonlinear process modeling, and this is one of the primary reasons for the immense popularity of NN technology.

5.2 Evaluation Metrics

We use the same measures to evaluate the performance of classifiers as those used in [8].

Accuracy is the fraction of true matches out of all possible samples, and is defined as

$$\text{Accuracy} = \frac{\sum_{i=1}^{M} (TP_i + TN_i)}{\sum_{i=1}^{M} (TP_i + TN_i + FP_i + FN_i)}, \tag{9}$$

where M is the number of classes, and TP_i, TN_i, FP_i, and FN_i are the numbers of true positives, true negatives, false positives, and false negatives of the i-th class, respectively.

Precision, also called positive predictive value (PPV), is the fraction of true positive matches out of all positive predicted samples. The precision of the i-th class is defined as

$$Precision_i = \frac{TP_i}{TP_i + FP_i}. \tag{10}$$

Recall, also called true positive rate (TPR), is the fraction of true positive matches out of all positive samples. The recall of the *i*-th class is defined as

$$Recall_i = \frac{TP_i}{TP_i + FN_i}. \tag{11}$$

The *F1-score* measures both precision and recall by harmonic meaning the two metrics, and is defined as

$$\mathrm{F1} = \frac{2 \times \mathrm{PPV} \times \mathrm{TPR}}{\mathrm{PPV} + \mathrm{TPR}}. \tag{12}$$

We also used two metrics that measure the general precision among multiple classes. *Macro-precision* is the average precision of all the classes, and is defined as

$$\text{Macro-Pre} = \frac{1}{M} \times \sum_{i=1}^{M} Precision_i. \tag{13}$$

Micro-precision is the sum of the numbers of true positives for all the classes divided by the total number of positive predictions, and is defined as

$$\text{Micro-Pre} = \frac{\sum_{i=1}^{M} TP_i}{\sum_{i=1}^{M} (TP_i + FP_i)}. \tag{14}$$

For all the above six measures, a larger value corresponds to a better classification performance.

6 Experimental Results

We compared our method for learning style identification (named K-CE-LS) experimentally with the method proposed in [8] (named K-LS). The source code of K-LS was provided by the author.

6.1 Clustering Results

We visualized the clustering results of K-LS and K-CE-LS to visually compare the performance of the two methods. Both methods returned four clusters.

To visualize the clustering results in the form of a scatter diagram, we used principal component analysis to transform the original features to two features for the active pole and two features for the reflective pole. The results of the comparison are shown in Figs. 1 and 2. In these two figures, each point is a learner, and points belong to different clusters are represented by different colors. Specifically, the green part represents the cluster 'Strong', the blue part represents the cluster 'Moderate', the yellow part represents the cluster 'Weak', and the purple part represents the cluster 'Very weak'.

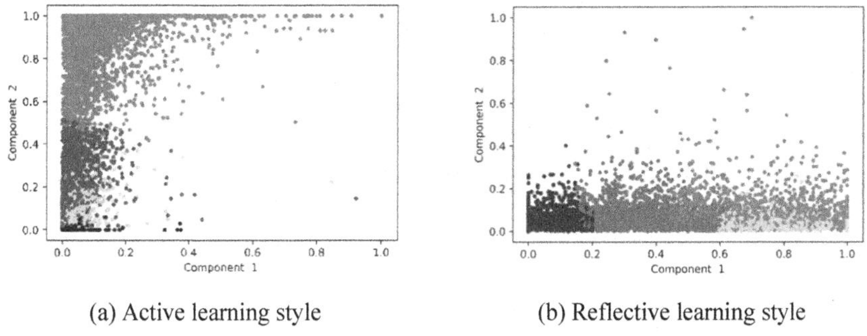

(a) Active learning style (b) Reflective learning style

Fig. 1. Clustering results of K-LS

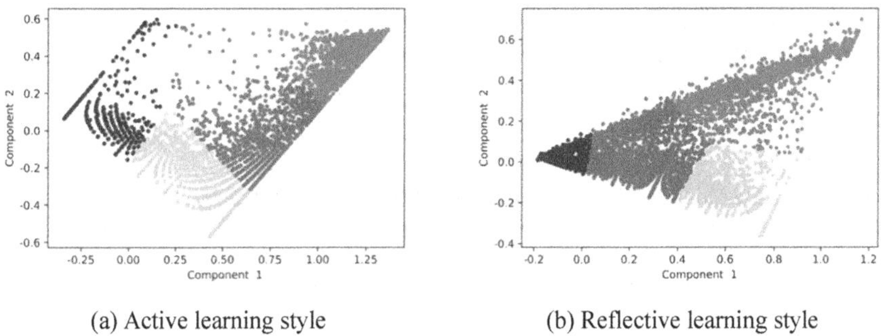

(a) Active learning style (b) Reflective learning style

Fig. 2. Clustering results of K-CE-LS

It is clear from Fig. 1 that the boundaries between clusters are not sufficiently clear and the clusters overlap. There are many points that are far away from any cluster, and the points within each cluster are scattered. In contrast to this, the boundaries between clusters in Fig. 2 are relatively clear. There are few points that are far away from any cluster, and the points within each cluster are compact.

We then further compared the clustering results quantitatively using CHI and SI; the numerical results are presented in Table 3.

Table 3. Comparison of clustering results of K-LS and K-CE-LS

	CHI		SI	
	K-LS	K-CE-LS	K-LS	K-CE-LS
Active	192985.01	198647.21	0.80	0.81
Reflective	99628.87	99660.80	0.78	0.79

The results in Table 3 show that incorporating the canopy approach into the clustering algorithm can improve the clustering results on clickstream data in the MOOC environment. This is mainly because the use of the canopy approach can solve the problem that the clustering results are not sufficiently stable because of the random selection of the initial centers.

Next, we labeled the original dataset with the clustering results of K-LS and K-CE-LS, separately, using the method described in Sect. 4.5. After labeling, the distributions of each learning style on the two datasets are shown in Figs. 3 and 4.

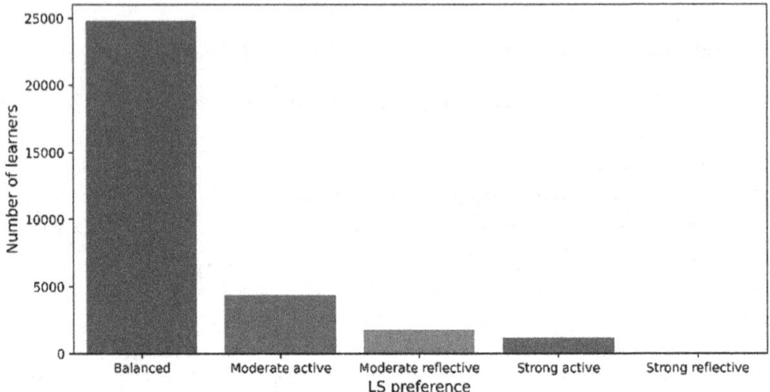

Fig. 3. Distribution of learning styles labeled by K-LS

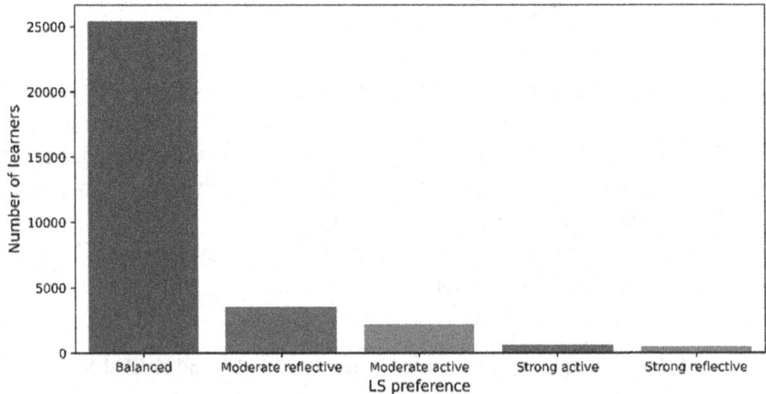

Fig. 4. Distribution of learning styles labeled by K-CE-LS

We can obtain two insights from Figs. 3 and 4. First, the labeled datasets transformed by both K-LS and K-CE-LS are highly imbalanced: the number of learners with the balanced style is far greater than the number of learners with other learning styles. Second, the number of learners with strong active and strong reflective styles is roughly equal in Fig. 4, whereas in Fig. 3, there are significantly more learners with the strong active style than with the strong reflective style. Using K-LS, only 64 learners were labeled as strong reflective, so they are barely visible in Fig. 3.

6.2 Classifiers for Learning Style Identification

We used DT, RF, KNN, and NN to identify learning styles on the datasets transformed by K-LS and K-CE-LS, separately. When comparing the classification performance, we used the same hyperparameters as those used in [8]. Training was performed using K-fold cross-validation with $K = 10$. Each dataset was divided into two parts, with 80% used as the training set and 20% used as the test set. Furthermore, we applied a learning curve to determine whether our learning algorithms suffer from overfitting or underfitting.

The overall classification performance on the two datasets are shown in Tables 4 and 5. Because these two tables present the performance results over all the classes, only the multiclass metrics are included.

Table 4. Overall classification performance on K-LS-labeled dataset

	Accuracy	F1	Macro-Pre	Micro-Pre
DT	0.990	0.990	0.980	0.990
RF	0.987	0.990	0.980	0.990
KNN	0.810	0.780	0.550	0.810
NN	0.979	0.980	0.920	0.980

Table 5. Overall classification performance on K-CE-LS-labeled dataset

	Accuracy	F1	Macro-Pre	Micro-Pre
DT	0.995	1.000	0.980	0.990
RF	0.990	0.990	0.980	0.990
KNN	0.849	0.840	0.620	0.850
NN	0.991	0.990	0.970	0.990

Similar to the clustering results presented in Table 3, these tables show that the general performance of the four classifiers on the K-CE-LS-labeled dataset is better than that on the K-LS-labeled dataset, particularly for KNN and NN.

To analyze the performance more concretely, we present the results of the four classifiers for identifying the five learning styles in Table 6. Because this experiment was designed to assess the classification performance for each specific class, we only include the single-class metrics.

Table 6 shows that, of the 60 results (obtained by identifying five styles using four classifiers and three metrics), 50 results (underlined) obtained on the K-CE-LS-labeled dataset are at least as good as those obtained on the K-LS-labeled dataset.

Interestingly, using KNN on the dataset labeled by K-LS failed to identify any learner with a strong reflective learning style. This can be explained by the results shown in Fig. 3.

The number of learners with a strong reflective learning style on the K-LS-labeled dataset is negligible, which makes it difficult for a lazy learner such as KNN to find neighbors whose learning style is strong reflective. Consequently, the values of the three metrics (precision, recall, and F1) obtained by KNN on this dataset are all zero. This extreme example also shows that labeling the dataset by the K-CE-LS method improves the performance of learning style identification.

Table 6. Identification performance of four classifiers for five learning styles

Learning styles	Classifier	K-LS-labeled dataset			K-CE-LS-labeled dataset		
		Precision	Recall	F1	Precision	Recall	F1
Balanced	DT	1.00	0.99	0.99	1.00	1.00	1.00
	RF	0.99	0.99	0.99	1.00	0.99	1.00
	KNN	0.85	0.96	0.90	0.90	0.95	0.93
	NN	0.99	0.99	0.99	1.00	0.99	1.00
Moderate active	DT	0.96	0.99	0.97	0.96	0.99	0.97
	RF	0.97	0.98	0.98	0.94	0.98	0.96
	KNN	0.55	0.42	0.47	0.54	0.36	0.43
	NN	0.95	0.94	0.95	0.98	0.97	0.97
Moderate reflective	DT	0.99	0.97	0.98	1.00	0.99	0.99
	RF	0.92	0.98	0.95	0.97	0.99	0.98
	KNN	0.50	0.16	0.24	0.58	0.56	0.57
	NN	0.95	0.94	0.94	0.96	0.99	0.97
Strong active	DT	0.98	0.99	0.99	0.99	0.99	0.99
	RF	0.99	0.92	0.95	1.00	0.96	0.98
	KNN	0.84	0.19	0.32	0.72	0.37	0.49
	NN	0.99	0.98	0.99	0.99	0.96	0.98
Strong reflective	DT	1.00	0.89	0.94	0.99	1.00	0.99
	RF	1.00	0.44	0.62	1.00	0.71	0.83
	KNN	0.00	0.00	0.00	0.33	0.07	0.12
	NN	0.70	0.78	0.74	0.94	0.97	0.96

7 Conclusions and Future Work

To identify learning style automatically, we clustered the MOOC learning data and labeled each learner according to the cluster to which it belongs, with the help of FSLSM. The main contribution of this work is that we set two appropriate distance thresholds for generating canopies, and incorporated the canopy approach into the clustering algorithm to determine the initial centers for K-means clustering. This enables stable clustering results to be generated. We demonstrated the superiority of the proposed method by comparing it with the method proposed in [8]. Comparison results on four popular classifiers showed that the proposed method can improve the performance of learning style identification both globally and locally.

The main purpose of learning style identification is to improve the teaching and learning quality of MOOCs. Thus, it is worth exploring whether descriptive methods such as pattern mining [7] can be used to improve the learning performance of students with different learning styles. Furthermore, providing different learning materials to learners with different learning styles is also a possible path. Therefore, using the identified learning styles to improve the performance of recommendation systems [13] in the MOOC environment is another objective of our future work.

Acknowledgments. We thank Dr. Brahim Hmedna for providing the source code of the K-LS method and dataset for experimentation. This work was partially supported by the National Natural Science Foundation of China (61977001) and the Great Wall Scholar Program (CIT&TCD20190305).

References

1. Azzi, I., Jeghal, A., Radouane, A., Yahyaouy, A., Tairi, H.: A robust classification to predict learning styles in adaptive E-learning systems. Educ. Inf. Technol. **25**(1), 437–448 (2019). https://doi.org/10.1007/s10639-019-09956-6
2. Blundo, C., Fenza, G., Fuccio, G., Loia, V., Orciuoli, F.: A time-driven FCA-based approach for identifying students' dropout in MOOCs. Int. J. Intell. Syst. **37**(4), 2683–2705 (2022)
3. El Aissaoui, O., El Alami El Madani, Y., Oughdir, L., El Allioui, Y.: A fuzzy classification approach for learning style prediction based on web mining technique in e-learning environments. Educ. Inf. Technol. **24**(3), 1943–1959 (2018). https://doi.org/10.1007/s10639-018-9820-5
4. Fatahi, S., Moradi, H., Kashani-Vahid, L.: A survey of personality and learning styles models applied in virtual environments with emphasis on e-learning environments. Artif. Intell. Rev. **46**(3), 413–429 (2016). https://doi.org/10.1007/s10462-016-9469-7
5. El Fazazi, H., Samadi, A., Qbadou, M., Mansouri, K., Elgarej, M.: A learning style identification approach in adaptive e-learning system. In: Rocha, Á., Serrhini, M. (eds.) Information Systems and Technologies to Support Learning. Smart Innovation, Systems and Technologies, vol. 111, pp. 82–89. Springer, Cham (2019). https://doi.org/10.1007/978-3-030-03577-8_10
6. Felder, R.M., Silverman, L.K.: Learning and teaching styles in engineering education. Engr. Education **78**(7), 674–681 (1988)
7. Fournier-Viger, P. et al.: Pattern mining: current challenges and opportunities. In: Rage, U.K., Goyal, V., Reddy, P.K. (eds) DASFAA 2022 Workshops. LNCS, vol.13248, pp. 34–49 (2022). https://doi.org/10.1007/978-3-031-11217-1_3
8. Hmedna, B., El Mezouary, A., Baz, O.: A predictive model for the identification of learning styles in MOOC environments. Clust. Comput. **23**(2), 1303–1328 (2019). https://doi.org/10.1007/s10586-019-02992-4
9. McCallum, A., Nigam, K., Ungar, L.H.: Efficient clustering of high-dimensional data sets with application to reference matching. In: Proceedings of the Sixth ACM SIGKDD International Conference on Knowledge Discovery and Data Mining, pp. 169–178 (2000)

10. Youssef, M., Mohammed, S., Hamada, E.K., Wafaa, B.F.: A predictive approach based on efficient feature selection and learning algorithms' competition: case of learners' dropout in MOOCs. Educ. Inf. Technol. **24**(6), 3591–3618 (2019). https://doi.org/10.1007/s10639-019-09934-y
11. Ramadhan, E.R., Sutoyo, E., Musnansyah, A., Belgaman, H.A.: Analysis of hotspot data for drought clustering using K-means algorithm. In: Proceedings of the International Confer-ence on Engineering and Information Technology for Sustainable Industry, pp. 1–6 (2020)
12. Sheeba, T., Krishnan, R.: Prediction of student learning style using modified decision tree algorithm in e-learning system. In: Proceedings of the 2018 International Conference on Data Science and Information Technology, pp. 85–90 (2018)
13. Song, W., Yang, K.: Personalized Recommendation Based on Weighted Sequence Similarity. In: Wen, Z., Li, T. (eds.) Practical Applications of Intelligent Systems. Advances in Intelligent Systems and Computing, vol. 279, pp. 657–666. Springer, Heidelberg (2014). https://doi.org/10.1007/978-3-642-54927-4_62
14. Song, W., Ye, W., Fournier-Viger, P.: Mining sequential patterns with flexible constraints from MOOC data. Appl. Intell. (2022). https://doi.org/10.1007/s10489-021-03122-7
15. Su, Z., Song, W., Lin, M., Li, J.: Web text clustering for personalized E-learning based on maximal frequent itemsets. In: Proceedings of the 2008 International Conference on Computer Science and Software Engineering, pp. 452–455 (2008)
16. Yousef, A.M.F., Sumner, T.: Reflections on the last decade of MOOC research. Comput. Appl. Eng. Educ. **29**(4), 648–665 (2021)

CSHEM - A Compressed Sensing Based Secure Data Processing Method for Electrical Data

Wei Wu, Haipeng Peng(✉), and Lixiang Li

State Key Laboratory of Networking and Switching Technology, Beijing University of Posts and Telecommunications, Beijing, China
{wuwei,penghaipeng,lixiang}@bupt.edu.cn

Abstract. Analyzing statistical features of electrical data is an important issue in the field of electrical data research, which often concerns collecting huge amounts of original data from various sources. Evidently, data compression and security issues are two key aspects of such process. However, a proportion of electrical data owners may agree to support electrical data analysis only when their private data are not disclosed to the public or even to the researchers. To address this problem, this paper proposes a secure data processing method named Compressed Sensing Homomorphic Encryption Method (CSHEM), which simultaneously achieves data compression and encryption. CSHEM also could allow researchers to reconstruct statistical analysis results of the original electrical data without requirements to possess these original data. We conduct experiments and simulations using real electrical data from over 100 households. The results show that the proposed method could realize data compression and encryption, and the reconstruction results could express the true statistical information of the original data.

Keywords: Compressed sensing · Homomorphic encryption · Electrical data

1 Introduction

During recent decades, information and communication technologies are developing rapidly, which supports the developments of smart grids. Simultaneously, many security issues are emerging during this progress [1–3]. As a result of the developments of smart grids, huge amounts of electrical data have been generated and may need to be collected or analyzed. Electrical data may contain records concerning various kinds of information, such as individual information of users, electrical capacities, electrical charges, etc., which may help to describe

This work is supported in part by the National Key Research and Development Program of China (Grant no. 2020YFB1805402), the National Natural Science Foundation of China (Grant nos. 61972051, 62032002) and BUPT Excellent Ph.D. Students Foundation (CX2022139).

Y. Tan and Y. Shi (Eds.): DMBD 2022, CCIS 1744, pp. 255–270, 2022.
https://doi.org/10.1007/978-981-19-9297-1_19

the status of individuals, households, enterprises or organizations [4]. Moreover, with the popularization of big data technology, more and more data may need to be shared with or to be processed by several different organizations or institutions. Big data businesses have facilitated people's life to a certain extent, but the risks brought by data opening may also follow [5–7]. How to obtain and to process data generated and collected from smart grids, and to achieve confidentiality and privacy during data sharing and processing, may become an issue to be studied.

Gentry constructed the concept of full homomorphic encryption in 2009 [15], which made homomorphic encryption technology obtain breakthrough progress, and opened the door to research on data sharing scheme based on homomorphic encryption technologies. Subsequently, researchers not only made contributions to the improvement of homomorphic encryption algorithms, but also began to try to apply homomorphic encryption algorithms in various fields. Zouari et al. proposed a privacy protection scheme that combined homomorphic encryption and secret sharing technologies. This scheme acted as a security intermediary and ensured data integrity and confidentiality by transmitting the collected data from the perception layer to the application layer [8]. Li et al. proposed a privacy protection computing scheme for the Internet of Things based on homomorphic encryption, which encrypted the encounter probability between nodes, so that the data information collected by nodes could be sent to the target node in the best path while protecting the privacy of related nodes [9]. Bringer et al. used the additive homomorphic encryption algorithm to complete the authentication of fingerprints, faces and irises [10]. You proposed a biometric authentication scheme based on homomorphic encryption and message encoding technology. The identity authentication process was carried out in the cryptographic domain, and the scheme proved to be well applicable in complex network environments [11]. Cramer et al. designed the first electronic voting system based on homomorphic encryption [12]. Alharbi et al. applied the data sharing technology based on homomorphic encryption to the smart grids, and proposed a smart grid data sharing framework, which enabled grid companies to analyze consumer data while maintaining consumer privacy [13]. Li et al. adopted an encryption system based on homomorphic encryption technology, mainly aiming at the two phases of the smart meters data processing, namely, the real-time data transmission phase and the accounting phase, which protected the user's privacy [14]. Applying homomorphic encryption methods to electrical data sharing and processing could effectively enhance data security and protect data privacy. However, as far as we know, data compression methods are rarely involved in such schemes, which is a worthy research direction in the era of big data when massive data may need to be collected and processed.

Compressed sensing (CS) is an efficient signal sampling method, which can sample signals beyond the Nyquist sampling rate [15,16]. CS makes use of the redundancy of original signals, reduces the sampling rate, and can use the sampled signals to reconstruct the nearly accurate original signal [17]. In recent years, compressed sensing technology has been widely used in various fields. Liu et al.

analyzed the inverse problem of sparse optimization of seismic random noise suppression under the compressed sensing framework and proposed an iterative soft threshold algorithm [18]. Cao et al. proposed an adaptive autocorrelation matrix reduction parameter pilot optimization algorithm achieving the minimization of channel reconstruction error rate based on the compressed sensing theory [19]. Zhao et al. applied the compressed sensing theory to the spectral experiments, reconstructed the spectral reflectance and improved the reconstruction accuracy [20]. Chen et al. proposed an image encryption algorithm based on depth learning, compressed sensing and compound chaotic systems, using bilinear interpolation and convolution neural network to compress images [21]. Compressed sensing methods can simultaneously realize data sampling, compression and encryption in solely one step. It has been applied in the field of smart grid in recent years. In order to meet the data collection requirements of smart grids, Yang et al. proposed a data collection method based on compressed sensing from the perspective of combining the same domain sampling and compression sampling [22]. Applying CS methods to the collection and transmission of electrical data could help to save data storage space and to improve data transmission efficiency. However, as far as we know, improvements still could be made in the aspect of data privacy protection, especially in scenarios concerning big data in smart grids. This issue could be studies in the future.

In summary, the research concerning electrical data sharing and processing technologies based on homomorphic encryption and compressed sensing is still in its early phase. Although there is existing research either on homomorphic encryption or compressed sensing, researchers are always considering the two theories separately. As far as we know, very little existing research covers the point of combining homomorphic encryption and compressed sensing technology. Wang et al. proposed a homomorphic aggregation method to process medical images [23]. There are two main differences between the method in reference [23] and the proposed one:

① The functions are different. The previous one only concerns data aggregation, while the proposed method in this paper extends the homomorphic method to provide privacy protection functions for statistical data analyzing.

② The application scenarios are different. The previous one is to process medical images, while the proposed method in this paper aims to process electrical data.

It is valuable to combine the homomorphic encryption and compressed sensing theories, especially in the big data era when information is exposing. To begin with, nowadays, huge amounts of data may be collected. How to efficiently and securely transmit and process these data becomes a burning issue. Compressed sensing methods are quite suitable to handle such scenarios because of their data dimensional reduction abilities. Namely, CS methods could compress data to make data sampling and transmission more efficient. In addition, since the CS measurement matrices could act as secret keys of symmetric cryptosystems, CS methods could also enhance the security level of data sampling and transmission [24]. Moreover, the original data to be processed may concern private or confidential information. Most traditional CS methods could not achieve the privacy protection goal for data owners during data processing by data analysts, while homomorphic encryption supports operations in the encrypted domain. So, it is significant to combine homomorphic encryption and compressed sensing theories, which could ensure efficiency, security and privacy protection during data sampling, transiting and processing. Electrical data may have characteristics such as multiple sources, multi-scale spatial and temporal distribution, etc., which makes research on electrical data processing methods based on the above two theories stimulating. The main contributions of this paper are as follows:

① This paper proposes an electrical data processing method called CSHEM, which could achieve data compression and encryption for data owners in only one step.

② CSHEM could realize sharing the operation results, that is, the reconstructed results of electrical data without disclosing original data of each data owner.

③ The data processed by CSHEM can compress the original data to 50 %. The experimental results show that the reconstructed results effectively reflect the statistical characteristics of the original data.

2 Preliminaries

This section briefly reviews the preliminaries concerning compressed sensing and homomorphic encryption. Specifically, in Sect. 2.1, research related CS is introduced, and in Sect. 2.2, research related homomorphic encryption is introduced.

2.1 Compressed Sensing

Compressed sensing is a signal processing method, which could represent original signals with dimensionally-reduced signals, i.e., observation values [25]. CS makes use of the redundancy of original signals. If there are at most k non-zero elements in vector x, we call the vector x is a k-sparse vector. Assume the original signal is $s \in \mathbb{R}^N$, and signal s is k-sparse or signal s is k-sparse under the sparse basis Ψ, namely, $x = \Psi s$, where $x \in \mathbb{R}^N$ is a k-sparse vector, the process of compressed sensing is taken as (1),

$$y = As = A\Psi^{-1}x = \Phi x \tag{1}$$

where $A \in \mathbb{R}^{M \times N}$ $(M < N)$ is the measurement matrix, $\Phi = A\Psi^{-1}$ is the sensing matrix and $y \in \mathbb{R}^M$ is the observation signal.

To reconstruct the original signals from the observation signals accurately, the Restricted Isometry Property (RIP) should be satisfied [17,26], that is to say, if there exists $\delta_k \in (0, 1)$ which satisfies (2),

$$(1 - \delta_k)\|x\|_2^2 \leq \|\Phi x\|_2^2 \leq (1 + \delta_k)\|x\|_2^2 \tag{2}$$

where x is a k-sparse vector.

2.2 Homomorphic Encryption

Homomorphic encryption is a data encryption method, which often has the data protection function [27]. It allows participants to directly perform specific operations in the ciphertext domain without decrypting the encrypted data. The data obtained after decrypting the operation results are consistent with the results obtained by directly performing the same operations with the plaintext.

Definition 1 (Homomorphic Encryption). *For plaintext domain P and ciphertext domain E, the cryptographic function $\psi : P \rightarrow E$ is called an additive homomorphic encryption when it satisfies the following properties:*

For $x, y \in P$, $Enc(x+y) = Enc(x) \oplus Enc(y)$ or $x+y = Dec(Enc(x) \oplus Enc(y))$ is a true statement, where $+$ and $\oplus$ are two kinds of operations, Enc and Dec are the encryption algorithm and the decryption algorithm of ψ.

3 CSHEM

In this section, the proposed method is introduced first. Then we discuss the feasibility of the proposed method.

3.1 The Proposed Method

CSHEM is a data processing method based on compressed sensing and homomorphic encryption, which could be used to share statistical features of original electrical data between participants.

As shown in Fig. 1, there are four kinds of participants of CSHEM: data owner, service provider, researcher and key distribution center.

1. Data Owner: Data owners possess the original data, that is, unencrypted data, and are willing to support researchers to study statistical features of the original data on the premise that data privacy is ensured. Data owners could be institutions or end users with original data, such as power companies, households with smart meters or other data collection terminals. The main work of data owners includes: ① Obtain and store the original data. ② Encrypt the original data with the key provided by the key distribution center. ③ Transmit the encrypted data to the service provider.

2. Service Provider: Service providers receive the encrypted data from data owners, and on the premise of ensuring data privacy, that is, do not decrypt the encrypted data, provide data processing services, and send the processing results to researchers. Service providers could be organizations or other entities with certain capacity of data processing and computing. The main work of service providers includes: ① Obtain and store the encrypted data. ② Process the encrypted data, i.e., conduct operations in the ciphertext domain without decrypting the encrypted data. ③ Transmit the results of data processing to researchers.

3. Researcher: Researchers receive the encrypted processing results from service providers, decrypt the results, and conduct further research on the decrypted

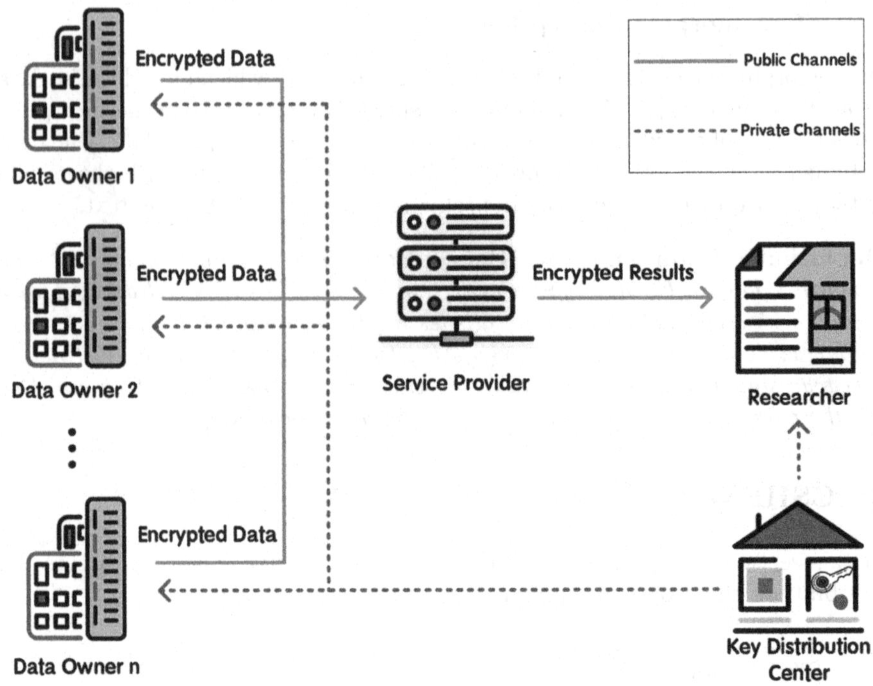

Fig. 1. The framework of CSHEM for data aggregation in Smart Grid

results. Researchers could be institutions or individuals who want to study features of the original data owned by multiple data owners, such as government regulatory authorities, colleges and universities. The main work of researchers includes: ① Obtain and store the encrypted data processing results. ② Decrypt the encrypted data processing results with the key provided by the key distribution center. ③ Conduct research using the decrypted results.

4. Key Distribution Center: Key distribution centers take charge of key generation, distribution and maintenance, and provide keys to data owners and researchers to accomplish data encryption and decryption. Key distribution centers could be independent and trusted third-party organizations or other entities. The main work of key distribution centers includes: ① Lead the processes of key generation. ② Securely distribute keys to data owners and researchers. ③ Lead the processes of key regeneration and destruction. Noticeably, the security level of secret keys may decide the security level of cryptographic schemes. Therefore, specific mechanisms should be deployed to protect the processing of key generation, distribution and destruction [28–30]. Such mechanisms could be sophisticated, which are not discussed in this paper.

We suppose that there are $n (n \in \mathbb{Z}^+)$ data owners, and the original data owned by the ith $(1 \leq i \leq n)$ data owner is $s_i \in \mathbb{R}^N$. In this paper, data s_i contain electrical records collected by smart meters from different households.

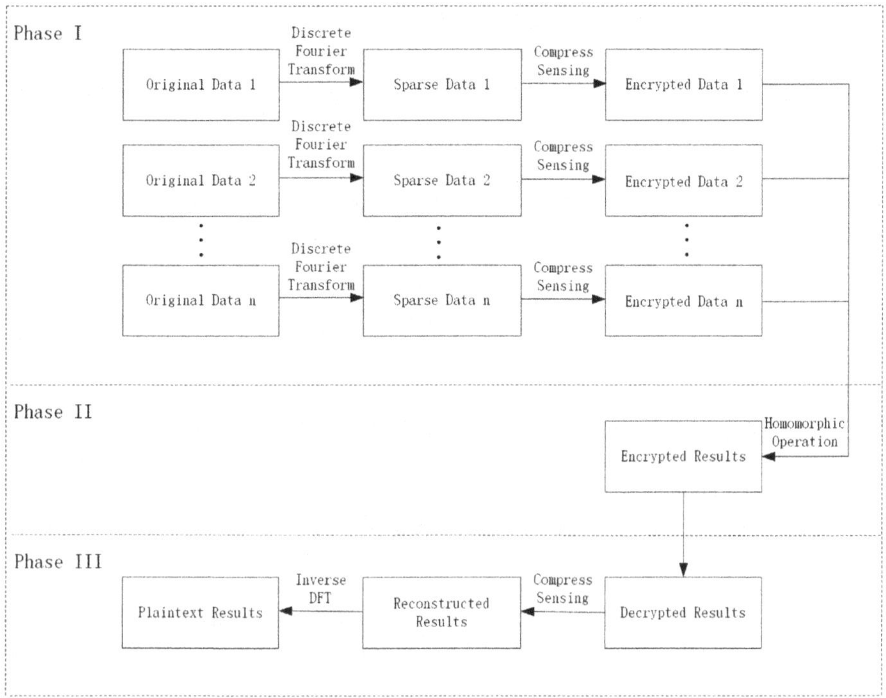

Fig. 2. The workflow of CSHEM for electrical data processing

Researchers want to study statistical features of the original data owned by data owners, such as the mean values of the samples, and do not care about the specific contents of these original data. Data owners are willing to support the work of researchers without exposing their own original data. The proposed method provides a solution for this demand. The main data processing flow of CSHEM is shown in Fig. 2, which includes three phrases.

Phase I: In order to protect the privacy of their original data, data owners firstly encrypt the original data using a CS method. Notably, this has the fringe benefit of compressing the original data while encrypting them, which may save both storage space and transmission bandwidth.

In Phase I, first, data owners need to increase the sparsity of the original data s_i, since in the real world, electrical data may not be sparse. The process is shown as (3),

$$x_i = \Psi s_i \tag{3}$$

where $x_i \in \mathbb{R}^N$ is the sparse signal of the ith data owner, and $\Psi \in \mathbb{R}^{N \times N}$ is the sparse basis. In this paper, we use orthogonal discrete Fourier matrices as sparse bases.

After that, data owners use a CS method to compress and encrypt signal x_i. The data compression and encryption process is shown as (4),

$$y_i = \Phi x_i \tag{4}$$

where $y_i \in \mathbb{R}^M$ is observation signal obtained by the ith data owner, and $\Phi \in \mathbb{R}^{M \times N}$ is the sensing matrix. In this paper, we use matrices padded by Tent chaotic sequences as sensing matrices, and these sensing matrices act as secret keys. The generation of a Tent chaotic sequence $z_l, l = 1, 2, 3 \cdots$ is as (5),

$$z_{l+1} = \begin{cases} z_l/b, & 0 < z_l < b \\ (1 - z_l)/(1 - b), & b < z_l < 1 \end{cases} \tag{5}$$

where b, $0 < b < 1$ is the Tent chaotic parameter, and z_0 is the initial value. Notably, when $b = 0.5$, the generated sequences perform short periods. Because of this, usually, the value of b is not set to be 0.5. Another thing to be noteworthy is that the initial value z_0 should not be equal to b. Chaotic sequences can be used to construct sensing matrices due to their good pseudo-randomness. Similar to Gaussian matrices and Bernoulli matrices, the sensing matrices padded by chaotic sequences also satisfy RIP with overwhelming probabilities [17,31,32].

Then the ith data owner transmits the compressed and encrypted data y_i to the service provider through open channels. At this point, the work of Phase I is completed.

Phase II: Service providers of CSHEM only provide their storage and computing capabilities. Since service providers do not own secret keys, they can only operate on the ciphertext in the encryption domain. Namely, the original data of data owners will not be exposed to the service providers.

In Phase II, after receiving the encrypted data sent by data owners, the service provider performs homomorphic operations without decrypting these data. In this paper, we suppose that researchers want to get the mean value of the original data owned by n data owners. The homomorphic operation process is shown as (6),

$$y_e = \frac{1}{n} \sum_{i=1}^{n} y_i \tag{6}$$

where y_e is the encrypted operation result calculated in the encryption domain.

Then the service provider transmits the encrypted operation result y_e to researchers through open channels. At this point, the work of Phase II is completed.

Phase III: Researchers want to study statistical features of the original data owned by data owners. In this paper, the research objectives are the mean values of the samples. Researchers do not care about the specific contents of the original data owned by data owners. In fact, even if researchers are interested in the contents of original data, they could not reconstruct the original data, since each y_i could not be calculated using y_e. That is to say, the original data owned by data owners will not be exposed to researchers.

In Phase III, first, researchers decrypt and decompress the encrypted mean value y_e which is calculated in the encryption domain using the secret key, i.e. the sensing matrix Φ. The decryption and decompression process of compressed sensing is actually the process of reconstructing the original signal using the observation signal. There has been much research on the CS signal reconstruction methods [33–35]. In this paper, we use orthogonal matching pursuit algorithm (OMP) for signal reconstruction [36,37], as shown in (7),

$$\hat{x}_e = \underset{x_e}{arg\,min} \|x_e\|_1 \quad subject\,to \quad y_e = \Phi x_e \tag{7}$$

where x_e is the sparse form of the mean value, and $\hat{x}_e$ is the estimate of x_e.

So far, Phase III is completed. Researchers obtain the statistical feature, that is the reconstructed mean value of the original data.

3.2 The Feasibility of CSHEM

The feasibility of the proposed method is based on the additive homomorphic character of compressed sensing process [23]. In this section, we briefly discuss the theoretical feasibility of the proposed method. From (1), (3) and (4), we could obtain,

$$Dec(Enc(\frac{s_1}{n}+\frac{s_2}{n}+\cdots+\frac{s_n}{n})) = s_e = \frac{1}{n}\sum_{i=1}^{n} s_i = \frac{1}{n}\sum_{i=1}^{n} \Psi^{-1}x_i = \frac{\Psi^{-1}}{n}\sum_{i=1}^{n} x_i \tag{8}$$

and

$$Enc(\frac{s_1}{n})+Enc(\frac{s_2}{n})+\cdots+Enc(\frac{s_n}{n}) = \frac{1}{n}\sum_{i=1}^{n} As_i = \frac{A}{n}\sum_{i=1}^{n} \Psi^{-1}x_i = \frac{A\Psi^{-1}}{n}\sum_{i=1}^{n} x_i \tag{9}$$

that is

$$Enc(\frac{s_1}{n}+\frac{s_2}{n}+\cdots+\frac{s_n}{n}) = Enc(\frac{s_1}{n})+Enc(\frac{s_2}{n})+\cdots+Enc(\frac{s_n}{n}) \tag{10}$$

where Enc and Dec are the encryption and decryption processes of CSHEM.

When implementing CSHEM, first, the ith data owner calculates $Enc(s_i)$ and transmits the encryption results to the service provider. After n results are received, the service provider calculates $Enc(s_1) + Enc(s_2) + \cdots + Enc(s_n)$ and transmits the encryption result to researchers. According to (10), researchers could decrypt the encryption result of $Enc(\frac{s_1}{n} + \frac{s_2}{n} + \cdots + \frac{s_n}{n})$, i.e., they could obtain the mean values of the original data owned by data owners.

It is worth noting that the premise of the above feasibility demonstration is that the original signal could be accurately reconstructed using the observation signal by CS method, i.e., $\hat{s}_e = s_e$. While in the real world, the reconstructed signal may not be exactly the same as the original signal, due to the influence of compression ratios, the constructions of sensing matrices and other factors. The application scenario of this paper is to help researchers analyze the statistical characteristics of electrical data. When the reconstructed signal is very close to the original signal, i.e., $\|\hat{s}_e - s_e\| < \varepsilon$, the reconstructed signal can express the statistical features of the original signal. Specifically, in this paper, the mean value of the original signal is the research object.

4 Experiment and Analysis

In this section, first, the feasibility of the proposed method is verified by experiments. Then the security of the proposed method is discussed from two aspects: the key space and the sensitivity of the initial values concerning the secret key.

4.1 Experiment to Verify Feasibility

In this paper, we use electrical data collected from 125 different households as experimental data set. The electrical data used in the experiments of this paper are obtained from the Smart project of the UMass Trace Repository, which could be accessed by visiting the website (traces.cs.umass.edu). To begin with, we randomly divide these 125 households into 5 groups, that is, each data group contains electrical data collected from 25 households. Then, we calculate the mean value of each data group and show the results by blue lines in Fig. 3. At the same time, we process the electrical data of each group with CSHEM: ① We compress and encrypt the original data under different compression ratios. Here the compression ratio refers to the ratio of the dimension of the compressed signal to the dimension of the original data. In Fig. 3, columns a to e show experimental results used electrical data from data group 1 to 5. The reconstruction results shown in a1-a5, b1-b5, c1-c5, d1-d5 and e1-e5 are obtain by experiments under compression ratios $\frac{1}{12}$, $\frac{1}{6}$, $\frac{1}{4}$, $\frac{1}{2}$ and $\frac{2}{3}$, respectively. ② We perform homomorphic operations on the encrypted data of each group, and obtain the encrypted forms of the mean values of the original data. ③ We reconstruct the mean values of data from each group and show the results by red lines in Fig. 3.

It can be implied from the experimental results shown in Fig. 3 that when the compression ratio is low, such as when the compression ratio is $\frac{1}{12}$ or $\frac{1}{6}$, the reconstructed mean values cannot truly express the real mean values. When the compression ratio rises to $\frac{1}{4}$, although the reconstructed mean values do not completely coincide with the real mean values, the reconstructed mean values can roughly express the real mean values. When the compression ratio is high, such as when the compression ratio is $\frac{1}{2}$ or $\frac{2}{3}$, the reconstructed mean values can express the real mean values more accurately. In summary, we consider that the proposed method is practically feasible according to the experimental results.

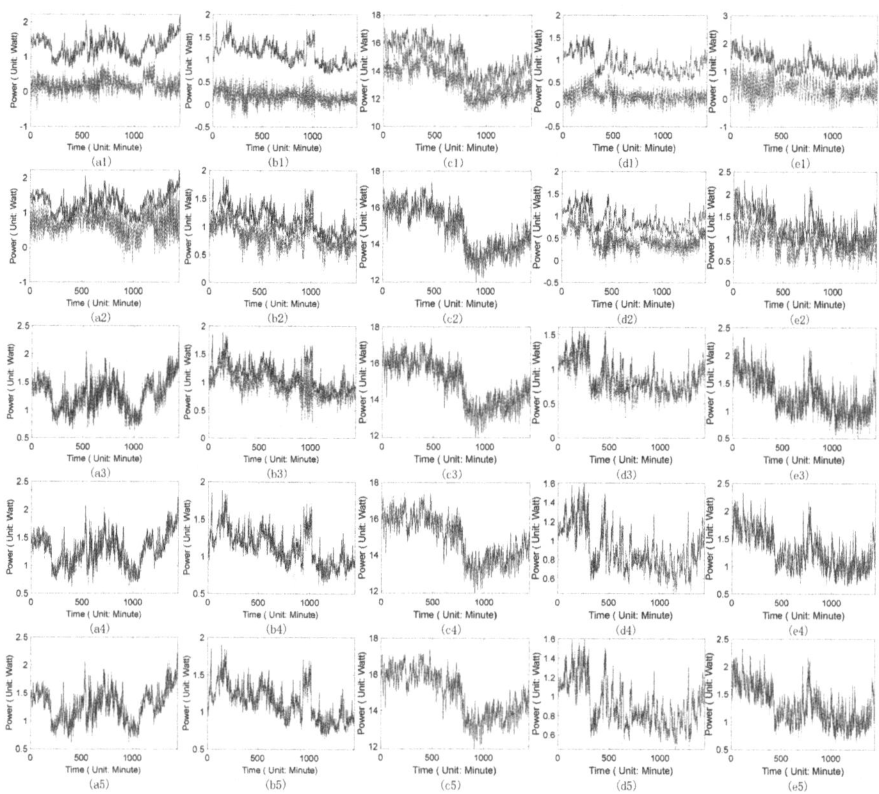

Fig. 3. The mean values of original electrical data and the reconstructed mean values

4.2 Security Analysis

A cryptosystem is considered to be secure if it satisfies $\mathrm{P}(c) = \mathrm{P}(c|p)$, where p is the plaintext and c is the ciphertext [38]. When designing modern cryptosystems, we often try to achieve computational security, i.e., the cryptosystem cannot be cracked by existing tools within polynomial time. More specifically, a cryptosystem could be considered to be secure, when it has the characteristics of large key space and initial value sensitivity [39]. The two characteristics of CSHEM are discussed as follows.

The CSHEM proposed in this paper uses sensing matrix Φ padded with Tent chaotic sequences as the secret key. The parameters involved in constructing sensing matrices are: ① the Tent chaotic parameter b, ② the initial value to generate Tent chaotic sequence z_0, ③ the initial sampling position r_0, ④ the sampling distance d. That is to say, the key space of the proposed method K_{CSHEM} could be calculated by (11),

$$K_{CSHEM} = K_1 \times K_2 \times K3 \times K_4 \tag{11}$$

where K_1, K_2, K_3 and K_4 are decided by parameters b, z_0, r_0 and d, respectively.

Table 1. Key space of CSHEM

Parameter name	Prameter type	Value range	Key space
b	Double precision floating point	$(0, 1)$	$K_1 \approx 1 \times 10^{16}$
z_0	Double precision floating point	$(0, 1)$	$K_2 \approx 1 \times 10^{16}$
r_0	Positive integer	$[1, 1000]$	$K_3 = 1000$
d	Positive integer	$[1, 100]$	$K_4 = 100$

The experiments in this paper use a 64-bit central processor, which processes double precision floating point numbers to 16 digits after the decimal point. The initial sampling position is selected from 1 to 1000. The sampling distance is selected from 1 to 100. So, the key space of the proposed method is 10^{37}. See Table 1 for details. Obviously, increasing the precision of parameters or expanding their value ranges could increase the key space of CSHEM, which may help to increase the security level of the proposed method. However, such practices may cause the proposed methods to require more storage space or more computational resources. Therefore, when using CSHEM, the key space should be reasonably designed according to the actual situations.

Sensitivity of initial values is one of the characteristics of chaotic sequences. Even if the initial value of a chaotic sequence changes slightly, the subsequent values of the sequence will change entirely. The proposed method uses Tent chaotic sequences to generate secret keys. Figure 4 shows the sensitivity of initial values of Tent chaotic sequences. The blue curves and the red curves show Tent chaotic sequences generated with different initial values. In Fig. 4(a), the difference between the initial values used by the blue curve and the red curve is 10^{-15}. The green curve shows the difference between the two sequences above. In Fig. 4(b), the difference between the initial values used by the blue curve and the red curve is 10^{-16}.

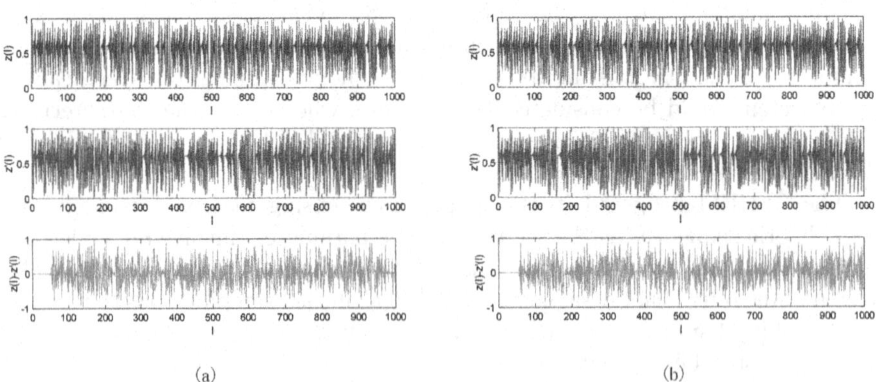

Fig. 4. Sensitivity to initial conditions of tent sequences

Figure 5 shows the impacts on reconstruction results of CSHEM when the initial values of the Tent chaotic sequences to construct the secret keys change slightly. Again, we use the electrical data of 125 households and divide them into 5 groups. Each group contains data from 25 households. In Fig. 5, columns a to e show the reconstruction results of groups 1 to 5. The blue lines show the meal values calculated using the original data. The red lines show the reconstructed mean values generated with different secret keys. The compression ratio is $\frac{1}{2}$. In lines 1 to 5, compared with the initial values of the Tent chaotic sequences to construct the right secret key, the initial values of the Tent chaotic sequences to construct secret keys have changed 0, $+10^{16}$, -10^{16}, $+10^{15}$ and -10^{15}, respectively.

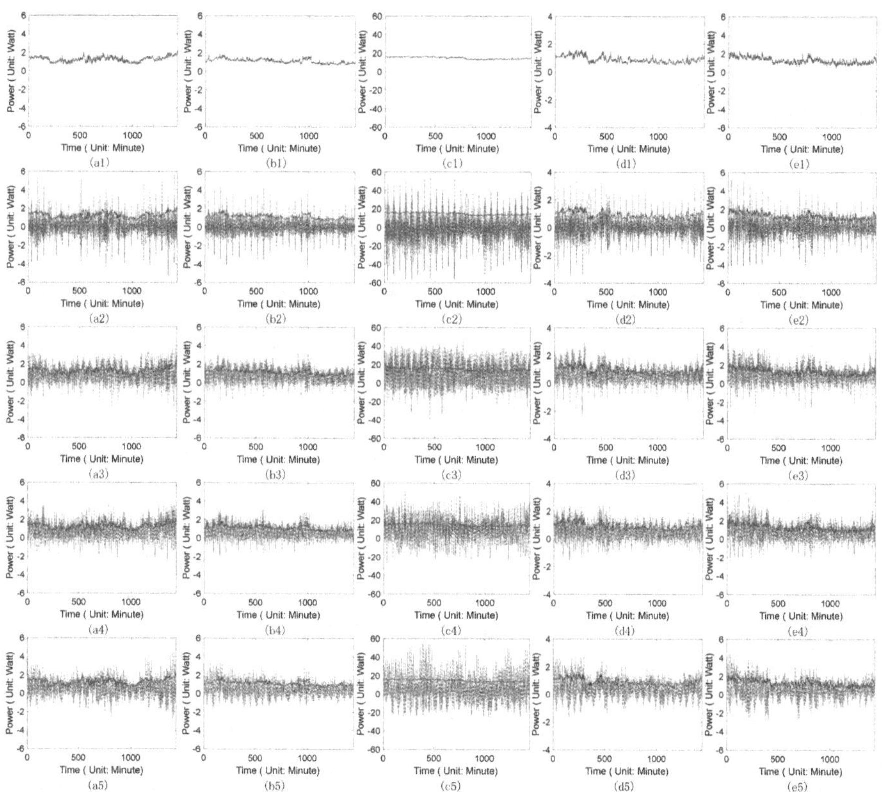

Fig. 5. The impact of changes of Tent initial values on CSHEM reconstruction results

From Fig. 5, we could imply that when using CSHEM to reconstruct the mean values of electrical data, even if the initial values of the Tent chaotic sequences to generate the secret keys have an extremely small change, such as $+10^{16}$, -10^{16}, $+10^{15}$ and -10^{15}, the reconstructed mean values have changed significantly.

5 Conclusion

This paper proposes a secure data processing method for electrical data, called CSHEM. The proposed method is motivated by the combination of compressed sensing and homomorphic encryption. CSHEM uses CS to compress and encrypt the original data to achieve both resource saving and security enhancement. At the same time, homomorphic encryption is used to ensure the privacy of electrical data, i.e., the original data does not need to be exposed in plaintext to researchers or other third-party organizations. In fact, encrypted data are operated in the encryption domain, and finally researchers only reconstruct the operation results. In the future, based on the work of this paper, expanding the types of homomorphic operations on the encryption domain could be a research direction, which may help researchers or other third-party institutions to research on the original data in greater detail.

References

1. Ni, J., Zhang, K., Lin, X., Shen, X.S.: Balancing security and efficiency for smart metering against misbehaving collectors. IEEE Trans. Smart Grid **10**(2), 1225–1236 (2019)
2. Smith, M.D., Paté-Cornell, M.E.: Cyber risk analysis for a smart grid: how smart is smart enough? a multiarmed bandit approach to cyber security investment. IEEE Trans. Eng. Manag. **65**(03), 434–447
3. Chen, B., Yu, X.: Research on the application and security of cloud computing in smart power grids. In: 2019 4th International Conference on Mechanical, Control and Computer Engineering (ICMCCE), pp. 784–7842 (2019)
4. Ma, G., Yang, X., Zhuo, J., Gao, Q.. Zhou, Q.: Research on early warning model of enterprise operational risk based on electric power data. Distrib. Utilization **38**(04), 16–21 (2011)
5. Rawat, D.B., Doku, R., Garuba, M.: Cybersecurity in big data era: from securing big data to data-driven security. IEEE Trans. Serv. Comput. **14**(6):2055–2072 (2021)
6. Samaraweera, G.D., Chang, J.M.: Security and privacy implications on database systems in big data era: a survey. IEEE Trans. Knowl. Data Eng. **33**(1), 239–258 (2021)
7. Dang, T.D., Hoang, D.: Nguyen, D.N.: Trust-based scheduling framework for big data processing with mapreduce. IEEE Transa. Serv. Comput. **15**(1), 279–293 (2022)
8. Zouari, .J, Hamdi, M., Kim, T.H.: A Privacy-preserving Homomorphic encryption scheme for the Internet of Things. In: 2017 13th International Wireless Communications and Mobile Computing Conference (IWCMC) 2007, pp. 1939–1944 (2007)
9. Li, C., Liu, Q., Xie, Y., Wang, G.: Privacy protection method in internet of things based on homomorphic encryption. Comput. Eng. Appl. **51**(06), 22–26 (2015)
10. Bringer, J., Chabanne, H.: Patey, A.: Privacy-preserving biometric identification using secure multiparty computation: an overview and recent trends. IEEE Signal Process. Mag. **30**(2), 42–52 (2013)
11. You, I., Liang, J.: Research on secure identity authentication based on homomorphic encryption and biometric. Netinfo Secur. **2018**(04), 1–8 (2018)

12. Cramer, R., Shoup, V.: A practical public key cryptosystem provably secure against adaptive chosen Ciphertext attack. In: Advances in Cryptology-Proceedings of CRYPTO 1998, pp. 13–35 (1998)
13. Alharbi, K., Lin, X., Shao, J.: A framework for privacy-preserving data sharing in the Smart Grid. In: 2014 IEEE/CIC International Conference on Communications in China (ICCC) , pp. 214–21 (2004)
14. Li, Z., Zou, Y., Zhang, J., Ma, A.: A Privacy preservation scheme for data exchange of smart grid based on homomorphic encryption. Netinfo Secur. **2016**(03), 1–7 (2016)
15. Candès, E.J., Tao, T.: Near-optimal signal recovery from random projections: universal encoding strategies? IEEE Trans. Inf. Theory **52**(12), 5406–5425 (2006)
16. Donoho, D.L.: Compressed sensing. IEEE Trans. Inf. Theory **52**(4), 1289–1306 (2006)
17. Candès, E.J.: The restricted isometry property and its implications for compressed sensing. Comp. Rendus Math. **346**, 589–592 (2008)
18. Liu, L., Liu, Y., Liu, C., Zheng Z.: Iterative seismic random noise suppression method based on compressive sensing. Chin. J. Geophys. **64**(12), 4629–4643 (2022)
19. Cao, H., Ye, Z.: Theoretical analysis and algorithm design of optimized pilot for downlink channel estimation in massive MIMO systems based on compressed sensing. Acta Physica Sinica **71**(05), 7–16 (2022)
20. Zhao, S., Li, X.: Research on reflection spectrum reconstruction algorithm based on compressed sensing. Spectro. Spect. Anal. **41**(04), 1092–1096 (2021)
21. Wei, C., Yuan, G., Shi-Wei, J.: General image encryption algorithm based on deep learning compressed sensing and compound chaotic system. Acta Phys. Sin. **69**(24), 99–111 (2020)
22. Yang, S., Tan, B.,. Guo, J.: A new data collection method based on compressed sensing for new generation energy internet. Renew. Energy Resour. **40**(07), 952–958 (2021)
23. Wang, L., Li, L., Li, J., Li, J., Gupta, B.B., Liu, X.: Compressive sensing of medical images with confidentially homomorphic aggregations. IEEE Internet Things J. **6**(2), 1402–1409 (2019)
24. Cho, W., Yu, N.Y.: Secure and efficient compressed sensing-based encryption with sparse matrices. IEEE Trans. Inf. Forensics Secur. **15**, 1999–2011 (2020)
25. Candes, E., Romberg, J., Tao, T.: Robust uncertainty principles: exact signal reconstruction from highly incomplete frequency information. IEEE Trans. Inform. Theory **52**, 489–509 (2006)
26. Candes, E.J., Tao, T.: Decoding by linear programming. IEEE Trans. Inform. Theory **51**, 4203–4215 (2005)
27. Armknecht, F., Boyd, C., Carr, C., et al.: A guide to fully homomorphic encryption. IACR Cryptol ePrint Arch **2015**, 1192 (2015)
28. Muramatsu, J., Yoshimura, K., Davis, P., Uchida, A., Harayama, T.: Secret-key distribution based on bounded observability. Proc. IEEE **103**(10), 1762–1780 (2015)
29. Kiktenko, E.O., et al.: Lightweight authentication for quantum key distribution. IEEE Trans. Inf. Theory **66**(10), 6354–6368 (2020)
30. Wei-jing, Z., He-chun, Z., Shi-ying, Y., Tong, L.: Decentralized lightweight group key management for dynamic access control in iot environments. IEEE Trans. Netw. Serv. Manage. **17**(3), 1742–1757 (2020)
31. Yu, L., Barbot, J.P., Zheng, G., Sun, H.: Compressive sensing with chaotic sequence. IEEE Signal Process. Lett. **17**(8), 731–734 (2010)

32. Hongping, G., Zhi, L., Jian, L., Xi, W., Cheng, Z:. Compressive sensing using chaotic sequence based on Chebyshev map. Nonlinear Dyn. **278**(4), 2429–2438 (2014)
33. Zhang, Q., Chen, Y., Chen, Y., Chi, Y., Wu. A.: A cognitive signals reconstruction algorithm based on compressed sensing. In: 2015 IEEE 5th Asia-Pacific Conference on Synthetic Aperture Radar (APSAR), pp. 724–727 (2017)
34. Sun, H., Ni, L.: Compressed sensing data reconstruction using adaptive generalized orthogonal matching pursuit algorithm. In: Proceedings of 2013 3rd International Conference on Computer Science and Network Technology, pp. 1102–1106 (2003)
35. Takeyama, P.: Ono, S.: Joint Mixed-noise removal and compressed sensing reconstruction of hyperspectral images via convex optimization. In: IGARSS 2020–2020 IEEE International Geoscience and Remote Sensing Symposium, pp. 1492–1495 (2020)
36. Mallat, S.G., Zhang, Z.: Matching pursuits with time-frequency dictionaries. IEEE Trans. Signal Process. **41**, 3397–3415 (1993)
37. Li, S., Cao, G. Wei. S.: Improved measurement matrix and reconstruction algorithm for compressed sensing. In: 2018 8th International Conference on Electronics Information and Emergency Communication (ICEIEC) 136–139 (2008)
38. Shannon, C.E.: Communication theory of secrecy systems. Bell Syst. Tech. J. **28**(4), 656–715 (1949)
39. Bansal R, Gupta S, Sharma G.: An innovative image encryption scheme based on chaotic map and Vigenère scheme. Multim. Tools Appl. **76**(15), 16529–16562 (2018)

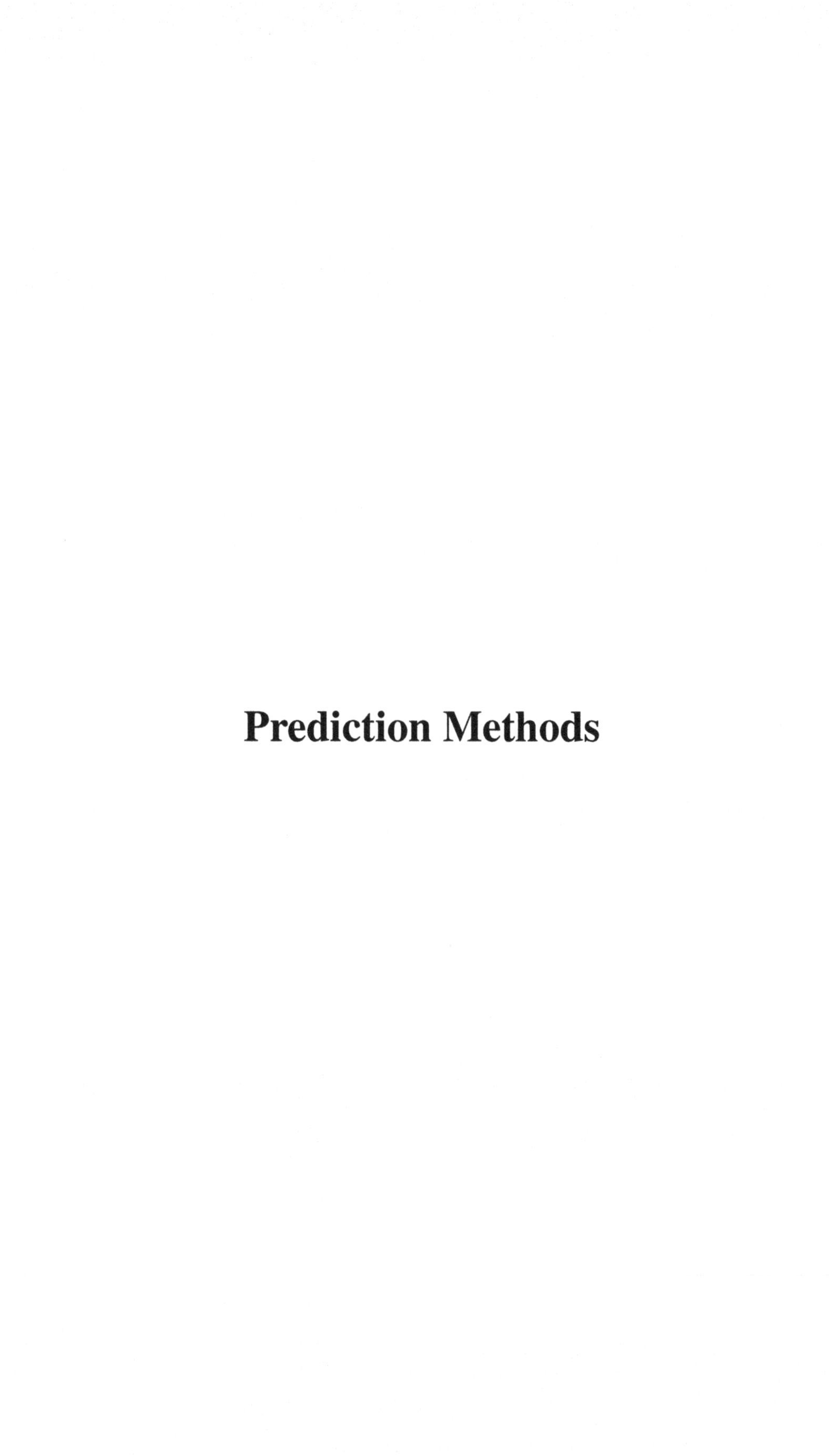

Prediction Methods

An Improved Multi-source Spatiotemporal Data Fusion Model Based on the Nearest Neighbor Grids for PM2.5 Concentration Interpolation and Prediction

Xiaxia Zhang(✉), Junjia Hu, Pengcheng Zhou, and Guoyin Wang(✉)

Chongqing Key Laboratory of Computational Intelligence,
Chongqing University of Posts and Telecommunications, No. 2 of Chongwen Road,
Nanan District, Chongqing 400065, China
{zhangxx,wanggy}@cqupt.edu.cn

Abstract. The acquisition of PM2.5 concentration mainly relies on small and provincial control air quality monitoring stations, respectively. The distribution of provincial control stations (PCSs) is sparse as its high cost, conversely the distribution of small stations is relatively dense and spread over the whole space as the relatively low cost, thus the observations of small stations can be employed to predict that of PCSs. Based on this considerations, in this paper, we propose a novel multi-source spatiotemporal data fusion method via the nearest neighbor grids, named MSF-NNG, to interpolate and predict PM2.5 concentration of PCSs by utilizing those data of small stations. Firstly, we divide the city into 1 km × 1 km grids, and then Cressman interpolation method is employed to fill the missing ones with the observations of small stations, wherein the observations include PM2.5 concentrations, humidity, temperature and wind speed. Secondly, it needs to find the neighbors of a PCS based on its grid partitions. Thirdly, MSF-NNG is proposed to interpolate and predict the PM2.5 concentrations of PCS by fusing the information of PM2.5 concentrations, humidity, temperature and wind speed of the corresponding neighbor grids. Finally, comparison experiments are conducted on several data sets, the results show MSF-NNG method with obvious advantages in interpolation and prediction for PM2.5 concentrations over fourteen and twelve algorithms, respectively.

Keywords: PM2.5 concentration prediction · Temporal convolutional network · Interpolation · Provincial control station data · Neural network · Small stations data

1 Introduction

Air pollution is a serious threat to people's health. According to the World Health Organization report, about 4.2 million people worldwide have died from

Y. Tan and Y. Shi (Eds.): DMBD 2022, CCIS 1744, pp. 273–287, 2022.
https://doi.org/10.1007/978-981-19-9297-1_20

diseases caused by air pollution [1]. Of all the air pollutants, particulate pollution (PM) has the most negative impact on people's lives, because PM accumulates toxic and harmful substances in the air, these harmful substances on the human body has induced respiratory disease, and increase the risk of cardiovascular and cerebrovascular diseases [2]. In China, with the process of urbanization and industrial agglomeration, the degree of environmental pollution is often aggravated [3]. Based on the above considerations, people pay more and more attention to the monitoring and prevention of air pollution because of the consideration of human health and sustainable development, many cities have set up their own air quality monitoring stations to measure the concentration of air pollutants [4]. But the significance of setting up monitoring stations is not only to monitor the concentration of air pollutants, the data collected from the concentration of air pollutants can not only be used for the government to formulate air pollutant prevention and control policies [5], the fine-grained data are also useful for public people make outdoor activities plans [6].

A city usualy own not enough pullution monitoring stations due to the expensive cost of buliding and maintaining [7], data collected from air quality monitoring networks also have the problem of missing data [8], and so on. In many scenarios which require real-time air pollutant concentrations in the monitored area, we have to predict pollutant concentrations at spatial and temporal scales. Similar to the data collected by the coastal environment monitor and the transmission error of the monitor, sensor failures and equipment maintenance problems often lead to data loss [9]. [10] experiments that use aerosol and other data to predict PM2.5 concentration for high-precision PM2.5 concentration is the same as missing values prediction. Sometimes, not only is the target data missing, but the data needed for the prediction is also missing, just like [11], the authors used interpolation algorithms to complete aerosol data with missing data and then used the completed data to make PM2.5 concentration predictions. We simulate the application of missing data and high-precision data prediction by predicting the PM2.5 concentrations of PCSs in our experiment. In short, we made the following three contributions:

1. The data of pollutant concentration monitoring points and meteorological monitoring points are interpolated into surface data by interpolation algorithm. Spatial information is integrated into surface data through point data to surface data, this is equivalent to incorporating new spatial information into the point data and then increasing the dimension of the point data.
2. A deep learning algorithm for multi-source data fusion is proposed, which extracts features from multi-source data and fuses different types of data and their spatial information, a mapping from multi-source data to PM2.5 concentration from PCS was constructed.
3. Two experiments are designed, the one is to investigate the spatial interpolation of PM2.5 concentrations by employing small air quality monitoring stations data and meteorological stations data at the current moment, it is named PM2.5 concentration interpolation, the other one is to predict the PM2.5 concentrations at the next moment of the PCS by fusing the small

air quality monitoring stations data and meteorological stations data in current moment, it is called PM2.5 concentration prediction. The experimental results show MSF-NNG with excellent ability in interpolation and prediction for PM2.5 concentration when compared to other methods.

The main contents are organized as follows: Sect. 2 introduces the related works, Sect. 3 introduces data preprocessing and MSF-NNG, Sect. 4 shows the experimental results and Sect. 5 gives the conclusion.

2 Overview

In this section, we discuss the algorithms about spatial resolution enhancement, which can be used to enhance the spatial resolution of PM2.5 monitoring stations.

In Ref. [12], Malings et al. proposed a spatial resolution enhancement algorithm which aims to improve the spatial resolution of air quality data by employing a dense sensor networks with low-cost. However, high spatial resolution of air pollution concentrations requires numerous air pollution monitoring stations to cover the target area, which is not feasible because of the high cost of installation and maintenance [13,14]. Li et al. [15] compares a number of spatial interpolation methods applied to the environment and divides them into non-geostatistical methods, geostatistical methods and combined methods, inverse distance weighting (IDW) and Kriging belongs to geostatistical methods, and support vector regression (SVR) and random forest (RF) are divided into new hybrid methods. Sekulic et al. [16] proposed a random forest spatial interpolation (RFSI) method for land surface temperature and humidity spatial interpolation.

In addition to the widespread use of machine learning algorithms for predicting PM2.5 concentrations, researchers have also developed a number of deep learning algorithms for predicting PM2.5 concentrations as deep learning becomes more and more popular. Li et al. [19] use a generalized regression neural network (GRNN) model to predict a national-scale PM2.5 concentrations in China. Huang et al. [20] proposed a gated recurrent unit (GRU) neural network based on the decomposition of an empirical model for predicting next hour PM2.5 concentrations which is greatly exceed single GRU model. Wu et al. [21] used a long short-term memory neural network (LSTM) [22] for PM2.5/PM10 ratio prediction. The experimental results show LSTM is superior than other algorithms in accuracy and stability for PM2.5/PM10 ratio prediction. Ahmed et al. [23] uses a convolutional neural network (CNN) input of seven different pollutant satellite images to estimate daily average PM2.5 concentrations. This work, however, requires plenty of satellite images.

In this paper, MSF-NNG is proposed for PM2.5 concentrations prediction by employing multi-source spatiotemporal data.

3 Method

This section aims to interpolate and predict the PM2.5 concentrations of PC stations by introducing a multi-source data fusion model based on nearest neighbor grids, wherein the multi-source data consist of PM2.5 concentrations, humidity, temperature and wind speed of small stations and meteorological stations. To achieve this accomplishment, we need to divide the entire city according to its location, and then get the corresponding interpolations or predictions for the PM2.5 concentrations, humidity, temperature and wind speed based on the observations.

3.1 Cressman Interpolation Method

Let $\mathbf{X}$ denote the region of entire city, we can get a division with $m \times n$ grids by dividing the region of entire city into 1 km × 1 km grids. Let $\mathbf{X}_l^t = \{x_{lij}^t, i = 1, \cdots, m, j = 1, \cdots, n\} \in \mathbb{R}^{m \times n} (l = 1, 2, 3, 4)$ be divisions of entire city $\mathbf{X}$ at time t corresponding to PM2.5 concentrations ($l = 1$), humidity ($l = 2$), temperature ($l = 3$) and wind speed ($l = 4$), where $\mathbf{X}_1^t$ denotes the division of PM2.5 concentrations, and $\mathbf{X}_l^t (l = 2, 3, 4)$ denotes that of the humidity, temperature and wind speed, respectively.

Crissman interpolation [24] is a fast spatial interpolation algorithm for spatial prediction, which is stable when the spatial resolution of the data used is higher than the grid resolution [25]. Suppose there are some grids with observations corresponding to each $\mathbf{X}_l^t$ and that of the rest ones are unknown and need to be filled, we fill the unknown values by Cressman interpolation method and obtain the corresponding dense matrix $\widehat{\mathbf{X}}_l^t = \{\hat{x}_{lij}^t\} (l = 1, 2, 3, 4)$.

As mentioned above, $\mathbf{X}_l^t (l = 1, 2, 3, 4)$ is incomplete with some grids are not monitored, which can be solved by introducing projection operator $\mathcal{P}_\Omega(\mathbf{X}_l^t)$ onto known entries of $\mathbf{X}_l^t$. The set of indices of the observed entries of $\mathbf{X}_l^t$ is denoted as $\Omega_l^t = \{(i_1, j_1), (i_2, j_2), \cdots, (i_m, j_m)\}$. The observation set is therefore $\{x_{l,i,j}^t : (i, j) \in \Omega_l^t\}$, and $(\mathcal{P}_\Omega(\mathbf{X}_l^t))_{ij} = \begin{cases} x_{lij}^t, (i, j) \in \Omega_l^t \\ 0, \text{otherwise} \end{cases}$. Especially, we treat the unobserved entries as 0 in $\mathbf{X}_l^t$.

Cressman interpolation method aims to compute the unobserved entry x_{lij}^t according to Eq. (1):

$$\hat{x}_{lij}^t = \sum_{(i,j) \in \Omega_l^t} \lambda_{lij}^t x_{lij}^t, \tag{1}$$

where λ_{lij}^t is the weight of the x_{lij}^t, and

$$\lambda_{lij}^t = \frac{\bar{w}_{lij}^t}{\sum\limits_{(i,j) \in \Omega_l^t} \bar{w}_{lij}^t}, \tag{2}$$

$$\bar{w}_{lij}^t = \frac{R_l^2 - (r_{lij}^t)^2}{R_l^2 + (r_{lij}^t)^2}, \tag{3}$$

where R_l^t represents the search radius of target grid $x_{li'j'}^t$, and r_{lij}^t is the distance between x_{lij}^t and $x_{li'j'}^t$. The interpolation process is shown in Fig. 1.

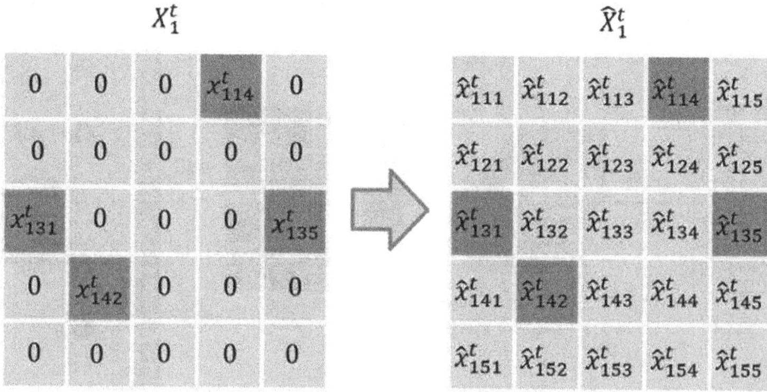

Fig. 1. Cressman interpolation method

3.2 Multi-source Data Fusion Model

As discussed in Sect. 3.1, we can get four dense matrices by Cressman interpolation method based on those observations of small air quality monitoring stations corresponding to PM2.5 concentrations, humidity, temperature and wind speed, respectively. The nearby observations are always more similar than the remote one in both time and space [10], so our goal is to predict the PCS's values based on the values of nine grid points of dense matrices around PCS.

Typically, suppose $\mathbf{X}_P^t = \{x_{pij}^t\}(l = 1, 2, 3, 4)$ denote the division of entire city correspond to PCS at time t, and $\mathbf{X}_P^{t+1} = \{x_{pij}^{t+1}\}(l = 1, 2, 3, 4)$ denote the division at time $t + 1$, the value of x_{pij}^t and x_{pij}^{t+1} are computed by the nearby grid points as follows, respectively:

$$x_{pij}^t = \mathcal{F}(G_1(x_{ij}^t), G_2(x_{ij}^t), G_3(x_{ij}^t), G_4(x_{ij}^t)), \tag{4}$$

$$x_{pij}^{t+1} = \mathcal{T}(G_1(x_{ij}^t), G_2(x_{ij}^t), G_3(x_{ij}^t), G_4(x_{ij}^t)), \tag{5}$$

wherein $G_l(x_{ij}^t)(l = 1, 2, 3, 4)$ are the collections of nearest neighbor grids around the PCS's location (i, j) from dense matrices $\widehat{\mathbf{X}}_l^t(l = 1, 2, 3, 4)$. $\mathcal{F}$ in Eq. (4) is an arbitrary mapping function which is used to interpolate the values of PCS at time t, and $\mathcal{T}$ in Eq. (5) is employed to predict the values of PCS at next time $t + 1$ by using the data sets collected at time t. Herein, $\mathcal{F}$ and $\mathcal{T}$ establish the fusion model frameworks for interpolation and prediction, where interpolation denotes the data fusion in a spatial sense, and prediction means the data fusion in a temporal sense, respectively. And both of $\mathcal{F}$ and $\mathcal{T}$ are composed of CNN and TCN, we collectively refers to this kind of fusion method as multi-source spatiotemporal data fusion model based on nearest neighbor grids, short for MSF-NNG. The detailed process can be shown in Fig. 2.

As shown in Fig. 2, MSF-NNG is composed of two parts where CNN is used for initial feature extraction, TCN is employed to multi-source data fusion, which are given as follows:

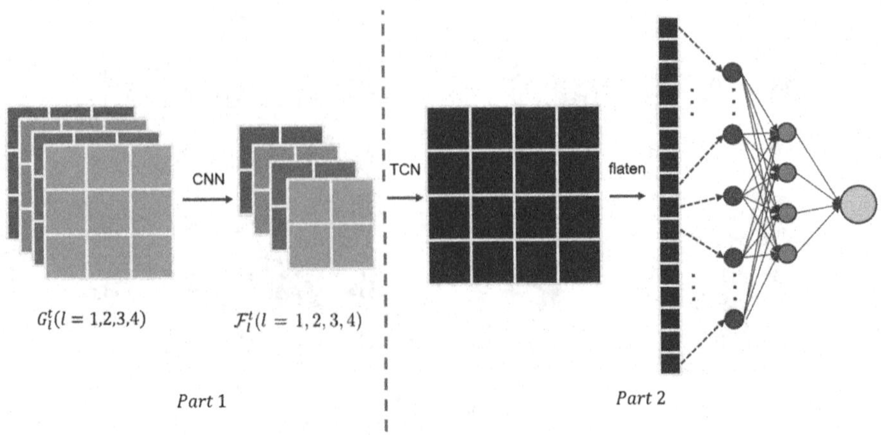

Fig. 2. The framework of MSF-NNG

- First part refers to feature extraction. We use CNN to extract the features of each $G_l^t(l = 1, 2, 3, 4)$, wherein those latent features can be represented as $\mathcal{F}_l^t(l = 1, 2, 3, 4)$, $G_l^t(l = 1, 2, 3, 4)$ consists of nine grid points around the PCS's location corresponding to PM2.5 concentrations, humidity, temperature and wind speed, respectively.
- Second part refers to feature fusion. Those latent features $\mathcal{F}_l^t(l = 1, 2, 3, 4)$ are extracted from multi-source $G_1^t, G_2^t, G_3^t, G_4^t$ can be employed as the inputs of TCN to get the integrated and unified latent features, which are explored to predict the values of PCS. Specifically, TCN integrates the features $\mathcal{F}_l^t(l = 1, 2, 3, 4)$ and outputs a 4 by 4 feature matrix $\mathcal{F}^t$, spatial characteristics of $\mathcal{F}_l^t(l = 1, 2, 3, 4)$ are integrated into a latent space, and they are structured as 4 by 4 feature matrix $\mathcal{F}^t$. To fit the spatial information, FCN flattens $\mathcal{F}^t$ into a 16 by 1 column vector and feeds it into a network of hidden layers.

We establish a multi-source data fusion framework which is composed of CNN and TCN based on above descriptions, by which we can predict the PM2.5 concentrations, PM10 concentrations and other air pollution concentrations.

4 Experiments

4.1 Data Set

As discussed in Sect. 3.1, we can get four dense matrices by Cressman interpolation method based on those observations of small air quality monitoring stations corresponding to PM2.5 concentrations, humidity, temperature and wind speed, respectively. The nearby observations are always more similar than the remote one in both time and space [10], so our goal is to predict the PCS's values based on the values of nine grid points of dense matrices around PCS.

The experiment is displayed on 8763 hourly data of PM2.5 concentrations, humidity, temperature and wind speed of one city in China from October 12, 2018 to October 12, 2019, which consist of 186 small air quality monitoring stations and 5 PCSs. To test the performance of the described algorithms, we first need to divide those data sets into training set, validation set and test set, wherein the training set with 7009 h of data from October 12, 2018 to July 31, 2019, the validation set consist of 889 h of data from August 1, 2019 to September 6, 2019, and the testing set contains 865 h of data from September 7, 2019 to October 12, 2019. We eliminate a small amount of missing hourly data which with few values and it doesn't affect the experimental results.

4.2 Algorithm Compared

To indicate the performance of our technique, we compare our MSF-NNG algorithm to Linear Regression (LR), KNN, Decision Tree (DT), IDW, OK, SVR, MLP, RF, Gradient Boosting (GB), ET, CNN and LSTM, the detailed description are giving as follows:

- K-Nearest Neighbor (KNN): KNN is a non-parametric method for outputting the average of K nearest input data [26].
- IDW and Ordinary Kriging (OK): IDW [27] and OK [28] are two traditional statistical interpolation methods, wherein IDW interpolation method gets its name from its definition of the relationship between weight and distance, which is inversely proportional to the distance; OK interpolation method employs observations to estimate the parameters of a random field and then predicts the values of an empty grid from the random field [16].
- Extremely Randomized Trees (ERT): ERT [30] is a tree-based ensemble learning algorithm, which can be used to solve complex regression problems. ERT divides the nodes of the tree by randomly selecting the cut points, and uses all the training samples to construct the tree during the training process [18].

4.3 Evaluation Metrics

To test the effectiveness of all algorithms, RMSE (Root Mean Squard Error) and R^2 are employed:

$$\mathrm{RMSE} = \sqrt{\frac{1}{n}\sum_{i=1}^{n}\left(\hat{y}_i - y_i\right)^2}, \quad R^2 = 1 - \frac{\sum_{i=1}^{n}\left(\hat{y}_i - y_i\right)^2}{\sum_{i=1}^{n}\left(\bar{y}_i - y_i\right)^2},$$

where $\hat{y}_i$ is the predicted value, y_i denotes real value, $\bar{y}_i$ is the mean value of real value, and n is the number of samples, the values of RMSE is smaller are better, whereas the larger the value of R^2 the better.

4.4 Performance Comparison

The spatial and temporal distribution of PM2.5 concentrations are different at the different stations, which can be shown in Fig. 3. It was noted in [17] that PM2.5 concentrations are strong correlated to the geographical environments which include meteorological factors, land changes and human activities and so on.

Table 1. RMSE comparison of PM2.5 concentration interpolation

Methods(RMSE)	Station 1	Station 2	Station 3	Station 4	Station 5	Average
LR	6.873	12.975	8.176	7.958	12.276	9.652
KNN	15.736	15.871	8.988	15.059	13.206	13.722
DT	11.294	15.585	8.257	10.533	12.273	11.588
SVR(Linear)	6.129	12.180	6.836	6.844	11.476	8.693
SVR(Poly)	8.896	14.283	8.884	8.058	12.560	10.536
SVR(RBF)	7.863	12.534	7.651	7.483	11.530	9.412
MLP	7.537	11.942	7.020	6.872	10.233	8.721
RF	10.728	12.593	7.274	7.404	10.125	9.625
GB	8.947	13.036	7.555	7.059	10.739	9.467
ERT	18.028	15.625	8.894	11.822	13.320	13.538
CNN	6.978	12.063	7.026	6.770	10.151	8.598
LSTM	7.398	11.947	7.093	7.371	9.278	8.617
OK	10.937	14.464	14.406	11.145	13.255	12.842
IDW	5.927	11.701	7.476	6.971	8.682	8.151
MSF-NNG	2.966	5.225	3.179	4.103	4.916	4.078

As can be seen from Tables 1, 2 and Figs. 4, 5, the RMSE of PM2.5 concentrations in spatial interpolation is smaller than that of prediction, some models like LR, RF, GB, and ERT, whose RMSE in spatial interpolation is higher than that of prediction.

Tables 3 and 4 verify the advantage of MSF-NNG by employing R^2, wherein the average R^2 are greater than 0.9 in both spatial interpolation and prediction, while the best IDW among other algorithms is only 0.7, and the rest are less than 0.5.

The results of Table 3 show MSF-NNG is superior to other methods in spatial interpolation of PM2.5 concentrations, except which SVR (Linear) perform best, and KNN and ERT perform worst, this is because PCS's observations with relatively large fluctuation at the different stations, and the relationships between the PCSs and their nearest neighbor grids are irregular. Specifically, when we use regression model to forecast the PM2.5 concentrations, it first needs to interpolate the missing values by using the Cressman interpolation methods,

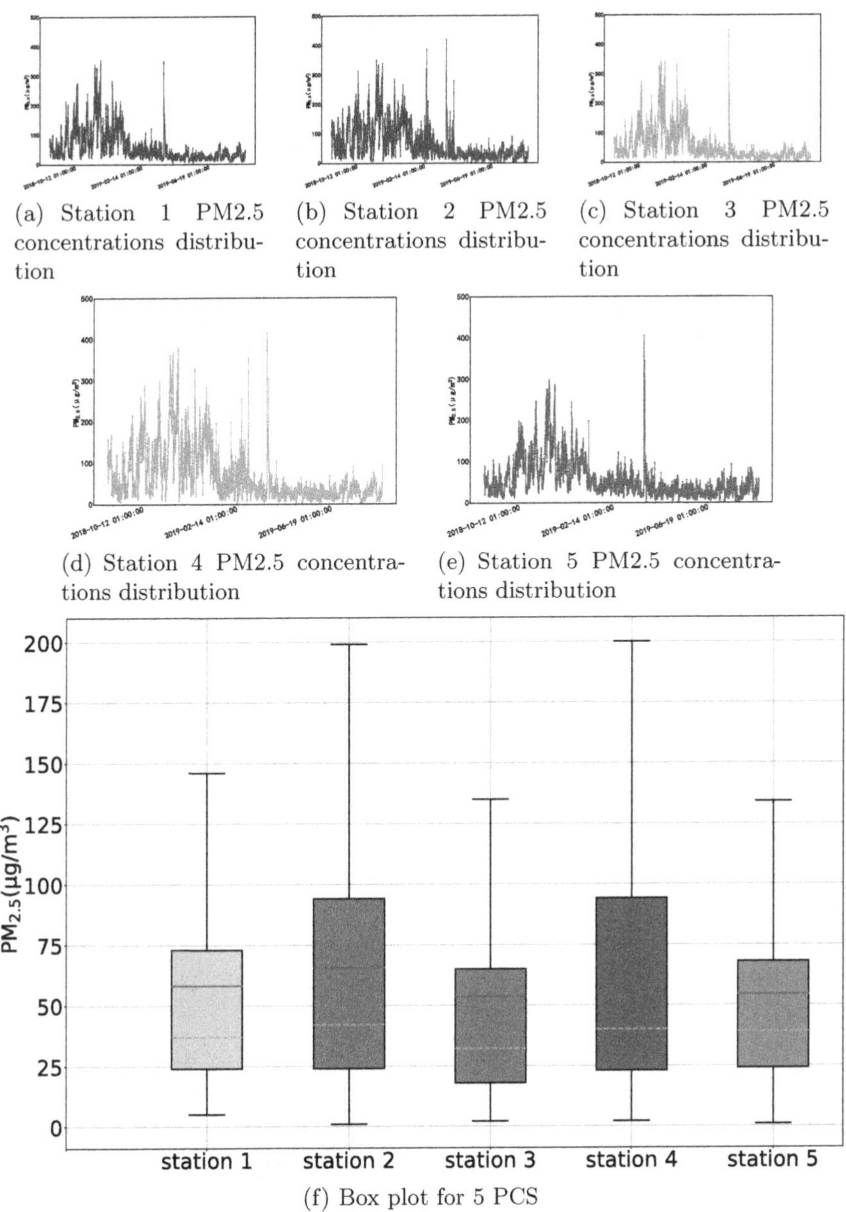

(a) Station 1 PM2.5 concentrations distribution

(b) Station 2 PM2.5 concentrations distribution

(c) Station 3 PM2.5 concentrations distribution

(d) Station 4 PM2.5 concentrations distribution

(e) Station 5 PM2.5 concentrations distribution

(f) Box plot for 5 PCS

Fig. 3. PM2.5 concentrations of 5 PCS in time series

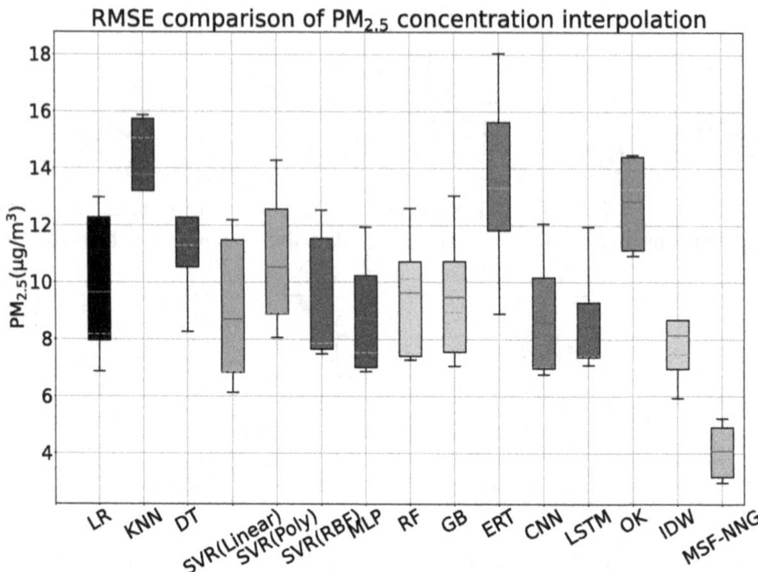

Fig. 4. The box plot for RMSE comparison of PM2.5 concentration interpolation

Table 2. RMSE comparison of PM2.5 concentration prediction

Methods(RMSE)	Station 1	Station 2	Station 3	Station 4	Station 5	Average
LR	6.656	13.377	8.052	8.756	12.389	9.846
KNN	10.603	15.772	9.105	14.123	14.210	12.763
DT	9.796	16.233	8.544	10.773	12.553	11.580
SVR(Linear)	5.869	12.351	6.668	7.009	11.519	8.683
SVR(Poly)	8.694	14.262	8.803	8.184	12.692	10.527
SVR(RBF)	7.651	12.641	7.673	7.589	11.695	9.450
MLP	7.961	12.367	7.905	6.564	9.510	8.861
RF	8.271	12.909	7.363	7.508	10.307	9.272
GB	8.041	13.773	7.575	7.458	11.458	9.661
ERT	11.51	15.985	9.718	12.275	13.569	12.612
CNN	6.818	12.404	7.032	6.893	10.367	8.703
LSTM	6.035	12.135	6.849	8.543	10.455	8.804
MSF-NNG	3.095	5.225	3.277	4.259	5.054	4.182

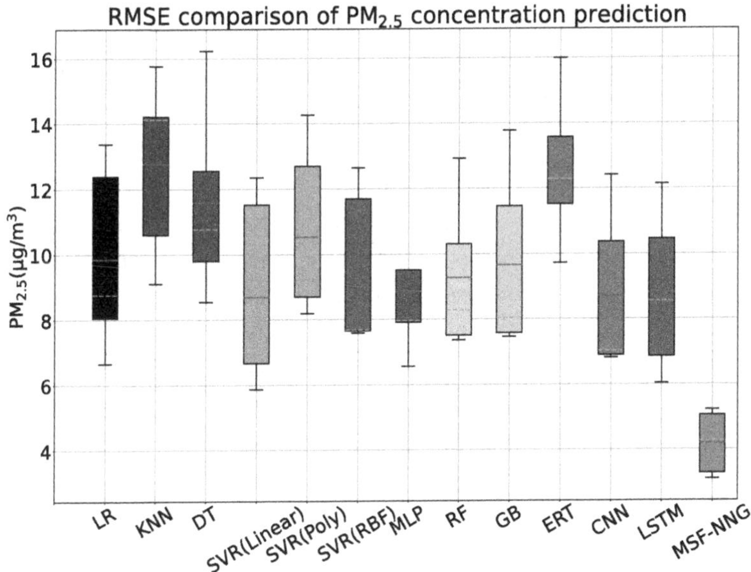

Fig. 5. The box plot for RMSE comparison of PM2.5 concentration prediction

Table 3. R^2 comparison of PM2.5 concentration interpolation

Methods(R^2)	Station 1	Station 2	Station 3	Station 4	Station 5	Average
LR	0.669	0.063	0.631	0.730	–0.180	0.382
KNN	–0.362	0.119	0.292	0.335	0.253	0.127
DT	0.151	–0.053	0.332	0.471	0.237	0.227
SVR(Linear)	0.746	0.266	0.723	0.805	–0.066	0.494
SVR(Poly)	–0.586	–1.001	–0.427	0.441	–1.323	–0.579
SVR(RBF)	0.075	–0.193	0.169	0.588	–0.409	0.045
MLP	0.321	0.145	0.447	0.695	0.254	0.373
RF	–0.329	0.031	0.399	0.680	0.357	0.228
GB	–0.292	–0.084	0.240	0.665	–0.013	0.103
ERT	–0.469	–0.138	0.295	0.489	0.159	0.067
CNN	0.417	0.099	0.467	0.715	0.051	0.350
LSTM	0.342	–0.160	0.480	0.553	0.583	0.359
OK	0.588	0.069	0.484	0.602	0.238	0.396
IDW	0.836	0.443	0.736	0.811	0.697	0.705
MSF-NNG	0.951	0.894	0.939	0.922	0.917	0.924

Table 4. R^2 comparison of PM2.5 concentration prediction

Methods(R^2)	Station 1	Station 2	Station 3	Station 4	Station 5	Average
LR	0.666	–0.051	0.620	0.661	–0.269	0.325
KNN	0.082	–0.041	0.276	0.370	0.238	0.185
DT	0.299	–0.091	0.343	0.460	0.252	0.252
SVR(Linear)	0.759	0.223	0.728	0.790	–0.081	0.484
SVR(Poly)	–0.457	–0.900	–0.312	0.425	–1.390	–0.527
SVR(RBF)	0.133	–0.236	0.184	0.564	–0.570	0.014
MLP	0.279	–0.105	0.278	0.752	0.362	0.313
RF	0.263	–0.111	0.362	0.645	0.290	0.290
GB	0.037	–0.307	0.273	0.624	–0.064	0.112
ERT	0.159	0.026	0.141	0.387	0.184	0.179
CNN	0.450	0.222	0.463	0.693	0.067	0.379
LSTM	0.698	–0.099	0.583	0.490	0.113	0.357
MSF-NNG	0.948	0.904	0.938	0.918	0.913	0.924

wherein those errors from interpolation stage will enlarge the regression model's deviations in prediction stage. However, MSF-NNG can reduce the influence of interpolation errors on the prediction, and it is easier to capture the relationship between the PCSs and their nearest neighbor grids.

The results of Table 4 show MSF-NNG is robust for PM2.5 concentrations prediction and it improves the accuracy by 50% on average. Among the remaining methods, MLP performs better than others, because it can captures the nonlinear relationship between PCSs and their nearest grids PM2.5 concentrations, whose most essential features are spatial and temporal heterogeneity [17], which are the import reasons that LR performs worse.

Based on above descriptions, we can see the performance of CNN and LSTM is better than that of LR, KNN, DT, MLP, RF, GB, and ERT, but they are still poor in comparison to MSF-NNG. The training dataset is multidimensional and each of them is depicted by its nearest neighbor grids, which reflects the spatial organization structure, and these data with the strong time correlation. CNN is robust to extract the spatial features, but it can not effectively fuse the spatial features. LSTM is good at extracting the temporal features of time series data, but it is not competent for refining spatial features well. However, MSF-NNG can integrate multi-source data information without altering the spatial structure of nearest neighbor grids, which contains abundant spatial information. If the spatial information can not fully be utilized and discovered, the data with spatial organization structure is redundant for the nonlinear model, that is why the performance of LR and SVR(Linear) is more robust than other traditional algorithms in interpolation and prediction.

5 Conclusion

In this paper, a multi-source spatiotemporal data fusion model named MSF-NNG is proposed to interpolate and predict the PM2.5 concentrations of PCSs, where multi-source are collected from the nearest neighbor grids around PCSs. Actually, two experiments are conducted in this paper to valid the effectiveness of MSF-NNG, one is related to interpolation, and the other one is referred to prediction. The experimental results demonstrate MSF-NNG with a higher accuracy than other methods both in interpolation and prediction, which further valid the necessity of introduction for the nearest neighbor grids. In the experimental stage, we select five regional data and each of them includes four kinds of data that related to PM2.5 concentrations, humidity, temperature and wind speed, which are highly correlated to the PM2.5 concentrations of PCSs. However, this paper only focuses on the interpolation or prediction by extrapolation from observations and incapability of those empty ones. Based on this considerations, we are dedicated to investigating the interpolation or prediction of entire city in the future, especially on those unobserved ones.

Acknowledgments. The authors would like to thank the support of the National Key R&D Program of China (2019YFB2103000), the State Key Program of National Nature Science Foundation of China (61936001), the Natural Science Foundation of Chongqing (cstc2019jcyj-cxttX0002, cstc2020jcyj- msxmX0737, cstc2021ycjh-bgzxm0013), the Key Cooperation Project of Chongqing Municipal Education Commission (HZ2021008), and the Science and Technology Research Program of Chongqing Education Commission of China (KJQN201900638).

References

1. Stafoggia, M., et al.: Estimation of daily PM 10 and PM 2.5 concentrations in Italy, 2013–2015, using a spatiotemporal land-use random-forest model. Environ. Int. **124**(1), 170–179(2019)
2. Chin, M.: Basic mechanisms for adverse cardiovascular events associated with air pollution. Heart **101**(4), 253–256 (2015)
3. Yao, C., Cao, Z., Han, Y.: Industrial agglomeration, population urbanization, land urbanization and environment pollution. Areal Res. Dev. **39**(5), 145–149 (2020)
4. Zheng, Y., et al.: Forecasting fine-grained air quality based on big da ta. In: 21th ACM SIGKDD International Conference on Knowledge Discovery Data Mining., pp. 2267–2276 (2010)
5. Jutzeler, A., Li, J., Faltings, B.: A Region-based model for estimating urban air pollution. In: 28th AAAI Conference on Artificial Intelligence, pp. 425–430 (2014)
6. Chen, L., Cai, Y., Ding, Y., Lv, M., Yuan, C., Chen, G.: Spatially fine-grained urban air quality estimation using ensemble semi-supervised learning and pruning. In: 2016 ACM International Joint Conference on Pervasive and Ubiquitous Computing, pp. 1076–1087 (2016)
7. Zheng, Y., Liu, F., Hsieh, H.: U-air: when urban air quality inference meets big data. In: 19th ACM SIGKDD The International Conference on Knowledge Discovery and Data Minin, pp. 1436–1444(2013)

8. Liu, X., Wang, X., Zou, L., Xia, J., Pang, W.: Spatial imputation for air pollutants data sets via low rank matrix completion algorithm. Environ. Int. **139**, Art. no. 105713 (2020)
9. Qin, M., Du, Z., Zhang, F., Liu, R.: A matrix completion-based multiview learning method for imputing missing values in buoy monitoring data. Inf. Sci. **487**(2), 18–30 (2019)
10. Qi, Z., Wang, T., Song, G., Hu, W., Zhang, Z.: Deep air learning interpolation, prediction, and feature analysis of fine-grained air quality. IEEE Trans. Knowl. Data Eng. **30**(23), 2285–2297 (2018)
11. Chen, Z., et al.: Extreme gradient boosting model to estimate PM2.5 concentrations with missing-filled satellite data in China. Atmos. Environ. **202**(1), 180–189 (2019)
12. Malings, C., et al.: Development of a general calibration model and long-term performance evaluation of low-cost sensors for air pollutant gas monitoring. Atmos. Meas. Tech. **12**(2), 903–920 (2019)
13. Liu, N., Ma, R., Wang, Y., Zhang, L.: Inferring fine-grained air pollution map via a spatiotemporal super-resolution scheme. In: 2019 ACM International Joint Conference on Pervasive and Ubiquitous Computing and the 2019 ACM International Symposium ACM, pp. 498–504 (2019)
14. Ma, R., et al.: Fine-grained air pollution inference with mobile sensing systems: a weather-related deep autoencoder model. In: 2020 ACM on Interactive Mobile Wearable and Ubiquitous Technologies, Art. no. 52 (2020)
15. Li, J., Heap, A.: Spatial interpolation methods applied in the environmental sciences-a review. Environ. Modell. Softw. **53**(12), 174–189 (2014)
16. Sekulic, A., Kilibarda, M., Heuvelink, G., Nikolic, M., Bajat, B.: Random Forest Spatial Interpolation. Remote Sens. 12, Art. no. 1687(2020)
17. Wei, J., et al.: Estimating 1-KM-resolution PM2.5 concentrations across China using the space-time random forest approach. Remote Sens. Environ. **231**, Art. no. 111221 (2019)
18. Wei, J., et al.: Improved 1 km resolution PM2.5 estimates across China using enhanced space-time extremely randomized trees. Atmos. Chem. Phys. **20**(6), 3273–3289 (2020)
19. Li, T., Shen, H., Zeng, C., Yuan, Q., Zhang, L.: Point-surface fusion of station measurements and satellite observations for mapping PM2.5 distribution in China: Methods and assessment. Atmos. Environ. **152**(1), 477–489 (2017)
20. Huang, G., Li, X., Zhang, B., Ren, J.: PM2.5 concentration forecasting at surface monitoring sites using GRU neural network based on empirical mode decomposition. Sci. Total Environ. **768**(3), Art. no. 144516 (2021)
21. Wu, X., Wang, Y., He, S., Wu, Z.: PM2.5_PM10 ratio prediction based on a long short-term memory neural network in Wuhan, China. Geosci. Model Dev. **13**(3), 1499–1511 (2020)
22. Hochreiter, S., Schmidhuber, J.: Long short-term memory. Neural Comput. **9**(8), 1735–1780 (1997)
23. Ahmed, M., Xiao, Z., Shen, Y.: Estimation of ground PM2.5 concentrations in pakistan using convolutional neural network and multi-pollutant satellite images. Remote Sens. **14**, Art. no. 1735 (2022)
24. Cressman, G.: An operational objective analysis system. Mon. Weather Rev. **87**(10), 367–374 (1959)
25. Liu, Z., Huang, R., Hu, Y., Fan, S., Feng, P.: Generating high spatiotemporal resolution LAI based on MODIS/GF-1 data and combined Kriging-Cressman interpolation. Int. J. Agric. Biol. Eng. **9**(5), 120–131 (2016)

26. Li, L., Zhang, J., Wang, Y., Ran, B.: Missing value imputation for traffic-related time series data based on a multi-view learning method. IEEE Trans. Intell. Transp. Syst. **20**(8), 2933–2943 (2019)
27. Willmott, C., Rowe, C., Philpot, W.: Small-scale climate maps: a sensitivity analysis of some common assumptions associated with grid-point interpolation and contouring. Am. Cartograph. **12**(1), 5–16 (1985)
28. Cormack, R., Cressie, N.: Statistics for spatial data. Int. Biometric Soc. **48**(4), 1300–1302 (1992)
29. Breiman, L.: Random forests. Mach. Learn. **45**(1), 5–32 (2001)
30. Geurts, P., Ernst, D., Wehenkel, L.: Extremely randomized trees. Mach. Learn. **63**(1), 3–42 (2006)

Study on the Prediction of Rice Noodle Raw Material Index Content by Deep Feature Fusion

Zhiyu Tian[1], Kang Zhou[1(✉)], Wangyang Shen[2], Weiping Jin[2], Qing Zhao[3], and Guangbin Li[4]

[1] College of Mathematics and Computer Science, Wuhan Polytechnic University, Wuhan 430023, China
zhoukang_wh@163.com

[2] College of Food Science and Engineering, Wuhan Polytechnic University, Wuhan 430023, China

[3] Xiangyang Tianyuan Lohas Rice Industry Co. Ltd., Xiangyang 441022, China

[4] Qianjiang Jujin Rice Industry Co. Ltd., Qianjiang 433115, China

Abstract. Rice noodle is a special snack in southern China. With the development of the grain industry and the improvement of living standards, choosing the right raw materials to produce high-quality rice noodles has become one of the problems to be solved at present. Therefore, on the premise of satisfying various characteristics of rice noodles, this paper proposed a deep feature fusion method, which combines with machine learning algorithm to achieve the backward prediction of raw material index content of rice noodles. Deep feature fusion can improve the prediction accuracy by multi-layer weighted feature fusion of rice noodles product index. It realizes feature selection and information extraction of multiple dimensions from the original data and makes the information of the original data play more fully. Experimental results show that the highest R^2 of the single index of the prediction result can reach 0.987, and the RMSE of single index only 0.0302. The errors between the predicted value and the actual value of the index of water content, starch content, protein content, swelling force and gelatinization temperature are small, which shows the method has a good prediction effect. It can provide a good reference for the selection of raw materials for the production of high-quality rice noodle.

Keywords: Raw material index · Value prediction · Deep feature fusion · Machine learning

1 Introduction

Rice noodles is a kind of special snacks in southern China. With the development of grain and food industry and the improvement of living standards, choosing the right raw materials to produce high-quality rice noodle is one of the problems to be solved at present. The basic condition for the production of high-quality products is to obtain high-quality raw materials. And choosing the proper raw materials to produce rice noodles has become the key to solve the problem.

Y. Tan and Y. Shi (Eds.): DMBD 2022, CCIS 1744, pp. 288–304, 2022.
https://doi.org/10.1007/978-981-19-9297-1_21

In terms of the influence of raw materials on the quality of rice noodles, Sun T.L [1] analyzed the correlation between the quality of 38 raw materials and the sensory score of rice flour, and established the regression equation of rice flour processing quality. Gao X X [2] made sensory evaluation of fresh rice noodles and determined the main evaluation indexes through correlation and cluster analysis. And the literature [3–5] also described the research of domestic and foreign researchers on rice noodle raw materials, which provides a theoretical basis for the selection of rice noodle raw materials, and confirms that the selection of different raw materials and processing way can improve the quality of rice noodles.

In different research fields of raw materials, Zhang Biao [6] used the artificial neural network algorithm to predict the quality of dried products with the indicators of apple raw materials, which provided a basis for the selection of apple dry specialized raw materials. Huang Yan [7] explored the influence of raw materials on the quality of sweet dumplings through correlation analysis and determined the key indicators affecting the quality of glutinous rice flour used for sweet dumplings. And the literatures [8–10] also discussed through various examples that the optimization of raw materials is absolutely necessary even in different fields.

This paper tries to predict the raw material index value of rice noodles through the index value of products and analyze the content of raw materials from the perspective of products. To obtain the relevant information of raw material index of rice noodles with high product evaluation, and provide suitable and scientific raw material optimization for the production of high-quality products. This will provide guidance for the production of rice noodles in related enterprises.

The core of rice noodles product index content prediction is to use appropriate prediction method to improve the prediction accuracy. For prediction methods, scholars from different fields at all over the world have made abundant research achievements in recent years. Obsie [11] used a variety of predictors to select features before the prediction and a variety of machine learning algorithms to predict the yield of wild blueberries. The results show that the prediction accuracy reaches the ideal effect. Zhang [12] extracted a large number of features from the remote maps of almond orchards as predictor variables, and used the stochastic gradient lifting model to predict almond yield with high accuracy. The literature [13–17] also described the methods used by domestic and foreign scholars on prediction problems, which can be summarized as machine learning model is a good method for prediction problems, and multi-source data also make a great contribution to the improvement of prediction accuracy.

2 Problem Analysis and Solution

2.1 The Research Question

In order to produce high-quality rice noodles with good taste, beautiful appearance and high nutritional value, it is necessary to analyze the index of rice noodle products, and make accurate reverse prediction of the product indexes after pretreatment. According to the relevant evaluation standards, the predicted raw material index content was analyzed and evaluated to provide a good reference for the selection of raw materials and quality control of high-quality rice noodle production. And the core of rice noodle product index content prediction is to use appropriate prediction method to improve the prediction accuracy.

2.2 Design Ideas

For the prediction problem of rice noodle raw material index, an excellent prediction process includes the following three stages. Firstly, the stage of data analysis and feature extraction. The next is the choice of prediction model. The last is the optimization of the prediction process. The prediction process is shown in Fig. 1.

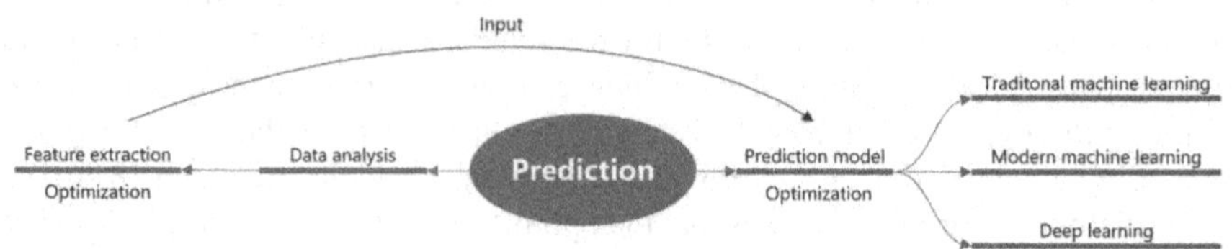

Fig. 1. Prediction process.

For the traditional prediction process, in the first stage of feature extraction, the traditional methods have certain limitations, such as using correlation analysis to remove features with high similarity, and using factor analysis to extract factors from data. These traditional methods may not give full play to the information expression of the original data. In addition, the optimization of the prediction process in the third stage is relatively less. For traditional machine learning models, such as regression, decision tree and neural network, their structure is relatively simple and the process of parameter optimization is not too complicated, which may make the accuracy of the prediction results fail to reach the expected expectation.

Aiming at the above two problems, this paper proposes the deep feature fusion technology applied in the whole prediction process to improve the prediction accuracy. The deep feature fusion prediction process is also divided into three parts. The first part is the feature extraction part. The deep feature fusion technology is used to extract multi-dimensional deep features from the original data to enhance the feature expression of the original data and improve the prediction accuracy. The second part is the selection of prediction model. The third part is the optimization of the deep feature fusion and prediction model together. Through the optimization, the extracted features can make greater contribution to the improvement of the prediction accuracy, so that the prediction performance of the prediction model can reach the best, and the prediction accuracy of the whole prediction process can be improved.

2.3 Methods

Based on the characteristics of rice noodles dataset (detailed below), deep feature fusion is used to predict the content of raw material index of rice noodles as follows.

Step One: Deep feature fusion is used to extract features from rice noodles data. The original data need to be preprocessed and feature extracted before being sent to the prediction model to reduce noise data and enhance data expressiveness. The deep feature fusion method is used to extract features and fuse the features from the original data. The multi-layer and multi-dimensional features are extracted, so as to play the information role of the data from the multi-dimension. In this paper, two-layer deep feature fusion will be adopted to process the data. Pearson correlation coefficient and factor analysis will be used for simple feature extraction in the first layer, and random forest and XGBoost will be used for deep feature score of the data in the second layer, so as to achieve the feature extraction of the original data from shallow to deep. Finally, the features will be weighted and fused, and the final fused features will be input into the prediction model.

Step Two: Selection of prediction model. According to the characteristics of the problem and the rice noodles data, it is necessary to choose the appropriate prediction model. The problem of this paper is to make numerical prediction, and the data is of the type of multi-feature and multi-label. Through investigation and simple experiment result analysis, we found several prediction models suitable for this kind of problems and data. For the experiment in this paper, Deep Neural Network (DNN) [18], Random Forest (RF) [19] and Extreme Gradient Boosting (XGBoost) [20] are selected.

The structure of DNN has greater capacity, which has the benefit of being able to represent complex functions with fewer parameters. In recent years, DNN has been frequently used in forecasting. Because of its relatively easy structure optimization, this model is selected as the prediction model.

Lately, RF and XGBoost have been using to predict yields by many agricultural and food researchers. Because of their excellent prediction performance, as well as their multi-feature and multi-label characteristics, were applicable to the data for this experiment, RF and XGBoost were selected as the prediction models used in this paper.

Step Three: Overall optimization of the prediction process. In this stage, the weights of deep feature fusion and the structure of different prediction models will be optimized. After reference and analysis, this paper decided to use PSO to optimize the fusion weight and model structure simultaneously with inner and outer nesting. The inner layer optimized the model structure and the outer layer optimized the fusion weight.

3 Implementation of Deep Feature Fusion

3.1 Introduction of Feature Fusion Process

Multi-dimensional feature fusion is an abstract module of deep feature fusion method, which is the single-layer basic operation part of deep feature fusion. In the process of feature fusion, the original data will be extracted by a variety of methods. The extracted features are weighted and then fused to generate the new data. The process of feature fusion is shown in Fig. 2.

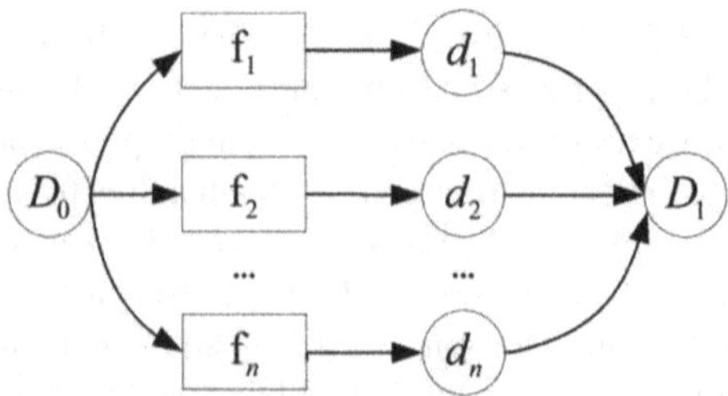

Fig. 2. Feature fusion process

In Fig. 2, $D_0 = \{X_1, X_2, X_3, ..., X_p\}$ is the input data of feature fusion at this layer, and $f = \{f_1, f_2, ..., f_n\}$ represents the various feature extraction methods at this layer. Each method f_i in f is used to extract features from D_0, and d_i is the different dimensions of the extracted features, which plays the role of information on different dimensions of data.

d_i will perform feature fusion calculation, and each d_i will be assigned the corresponding weight. The specific weighted fusion process is as follows: d_i is weighted internally by the assigned weight w_i, and the sum of the weights is 1, which can show the integrity of the data. The weighted d_i is spliced together to generate the fusion feature data $D_1 = \{X_1, X_2, X_3, ..., X_q\}$, and D_1 will be input into the next layer or prediction model. The process of feature fusion in a single layer is calculated as follows:

$$\begin{cases} d_i = f_i(D_0) \\ D_1 = \sum_{i=1}^{n} w_i d_i \\ w_i d_i = [w_i x_{i1}, w_i x_{i2}, ..., w_i x_{ik}] \\ \sum_{i=1}^{n} w_i = 1 or 0 \\ \tilde{y} = F(D_1) \end{cases} \quad (1)$$

Equation (1) shows the process of feature fusion, D_0 is the input, D_1 and $\tilde{y}$ is the output. $\tilde{y}$ is the predicted value, and F is the prediction model. $w_i d_i$ Shows the weighting process of feature d_i. The goal of Eq. (1) is to make the original data D_0 through feature fusion to generate the new data D_1. D_1 Will be input into the next layer or prediction model F for training and prediction, so as to minimize the loss value of the model.

A variety of feature extraction methods are used to extract features from data so that the extracted features can play the role of data information from different dimensions. This enhances the feature representation of the data and can also be viewed as an optimization of the feature extraction method. The weight allocation in feature fusion represents the contribution of various basic methods to the fusion feature. And the purpose of feature fusion is to improve the final prediction accuracy by processing the original data.

3.2 Introduction of Deep Feature Fusion Process

Deep feature fusion is a further improvement of multi-dimensional feature fusion. By setting multi-layer feature fusion, the feature fusion has its depth. This makes the feature extraction of the original data from simple to complex, and makes the information play more comprehensive. The deep feature fusion process of is shown in Fig. 3.

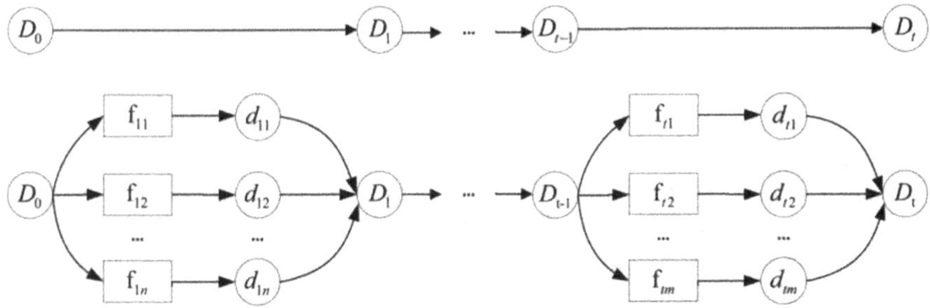

Fig. 3. Deep feature fusion process

D_0 is the original data, which generates D_t after multi-layer feature fusion. By setting the feature fusion of multiple layers, the feature extraction and fusion of each layer would be carried out. And saving the features extracted by each layer's methods, so that the features of each layer can be weighted when generating deep fusion features. Finally, deep fusion features are generated and input to the prediction model to maximize the performance of the original data as much as possible, so as to achieve the purpose of improving the final prediction accuracy.

Taking the data D_k obtained by feature fusion of the Kth layer as an example, to show how to save the features extracted by each layer's methods. The Kth layer feature fusion with multiple feature extraction methods set as $f_k = \{f_{k1}, f_{k2}, ..., f_{kp}\}$, and each method in f_k performs feature extraction on D_{k-1} to obtain d_{ki} respectively, and each d_{ki} generates $\{d_{k1}, d_{k2}, ..., d_{kp}\}$ by direct concatenation.

In the depth feature fusion process, in order to reflect the expressiveness of various feature extraction methods at each layer, $\{d_{k1}, d_{k2}, ..., d_{kp}\}$ would be processed in a weighted way, and then the fused feature D_k would be generated. The weighted process of each layer is independent, and the weighting order is from the first layer to the last layer. The process of deep feature fusion for prediction is as follows:

$$\begin{cases} d_{k1} = f_{k1}(D_{k-1}) \\ \cdots \\ d_{kp} = f_{kp}(D_{k-1}) \\ D_k = \sum_{i=1}^{p} w_{ki} d_{ki} \\ w_i d_i = [w_{ki}x_{k1}, w_{ki}x_{k2}, ..., w_{ki}x_{ki}] \\ \sum_{i=1}^{p} w_{ki} = 1or0 \\ \tilde{y} = F(D_k) \end{cases} \tag{2}$$

In Eq. (2), $\tilde{y}$ is the predicted value, and F is the prediction model. The goal of Eq. (3) is to make the original data D_0 operated by the deep feature fusion to generate the final data D_k, and the D_k is input into the prediction model to train and predict, so as to minimize the loss value of the model. Deep feature fusion enables feature fusion to obtain depth, further processing the data and enhancing the information expression of the original data.

3.3 Optimization of Weights and Models

Throughout the process of prediction with deep feature fusion, the assignment of fusion weights to each layer and the structure of the prediction model are to be optimized. However, the optimization of one may affect the optimization of the other. So this paper adopts an inner and outer nested optimization approach to optimize both. Then finding the combination that makes the final prediction result with the highest accuracy.

In the inner and outer nested optimization process, the inner layer optimizes the structure of the prediction model. This process can be regarded as local optimization. While the outer layer optimizes the assignment of the fusion weights of each layer, which needs to be optimized together with the model structure. This process can be regarded as the overall optimization of the prediction process.

Local Optimization: This is the optimization of the structure of three prediction models. In this paper, the structure of the models will be optimized by the PSO algorithm, which makes the prediction accuracy improved.

The PSO algorithm is suitable for the optimization of this paper because of its fast convergence, strong global search capability and fewer parameters. Therefore, the PSO algorithm is used to optimize the whole prediction process. The iterative process of the velocity and position of the particles is shown in Eq. (3):

$$\begin{cases} v_{id}^{k+1} = wv_{id}^{k} + c_1 r_1 (p_{id,pbest}^{k} - x_{id}^{k}) + c_2 r_2 (p_{d,gbest}^{k} - x_{id}^{k}) \\ x_{id}^{k+1} = x_{id}^{k} + v_{id}^{k+1} \end{cases} \tag{3}$$

In the optimization of each mode prediction model, it is necessary to encode its structural parameters into the position encoding of particles. The decimal encoding is used to encode the prediction model F into the form of particles:

$$\mathrm{F} = [X_1, X_2, ..., X_n] \tag{4}$$

where X_1 X_2... X_n are the parameters associated with the prediction model, which specifically decided by the prediction model. The structure of the three prediction models of DNN, RF, and XGBoost are coded respectively as F_{DNN}, F_{RF}, $F_{XGBoost}$:

$$\mathrm{F_{DNN}} = [[N_1, N_2, ..., N_i], Act, Opt] \tag{5}$$

where is the number of nodes in each hidden layer of DNN, Act is the selection of activation function, and Opt is the selection of optimizer.

$$\mathrm{F_{RF}} = [N,\ MaxD,\ MinSS,\ MinSL] \tag{6}$$

where N is the number of decision trees created by RF, MaxD is the maximum depth of the tree, MinSS is the minimum number of split samples of nodes, and MinSL is the min-number of samples of leaf nodes.

$$F_{XGBoost} = [N,\ LR,\ MaxD,\ \ MinCW] \tag{7}$$

where N is the number of decision trees of XGBoost, LR is the learning rate, MaxD is the maximum depth of the tree, and MinCW is the minimum sample weight sum of child nodes.

The encoded models F_{DNN}, F_{RF}, and $F_{XGBoost}$ are updated iteratively by the PSO algorithm and the loss values of the prediction model are used as the fitness function. When the iteration conditions are satisfied, the final output is the model structure with the minimum loss value, which is the optimal model-code in model optimization. The process of the PSO optimization prediction model is shown in Fig. 4.

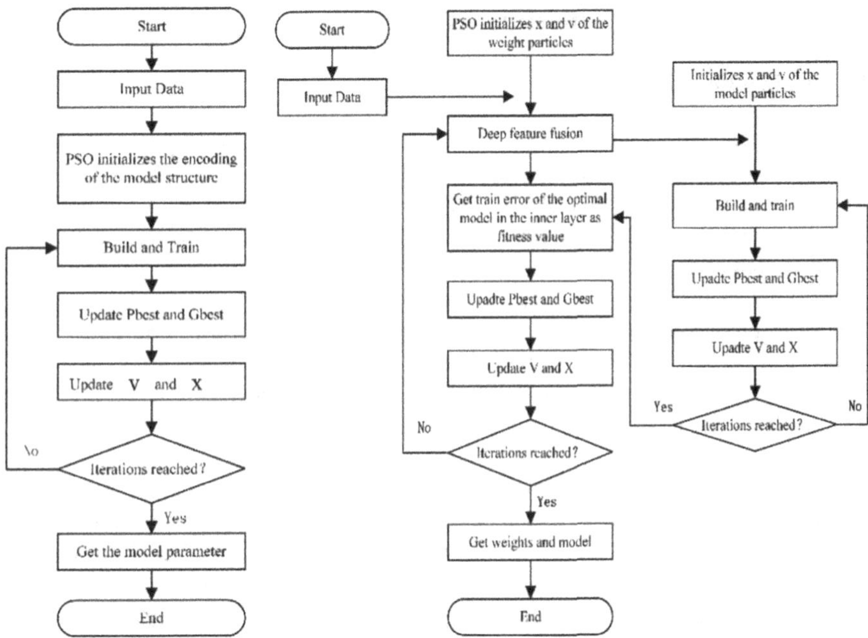

Fig. 4. Model optimization process

Fig. 5. Overall optimization process

Overall Optimization: The combined optimization of the fusion weights and the prediction model structure is defined as the overall optimization in the prediction process. Since the input is the fused feature data generated by deep feature fusion, when the fusion weights changed during the deep feature fusion process, the generated data also would change, which may cause the optimal structure of the prediction model to change as well. Therefore, in this paper, the structure of the prediction model and the fusion weights are optimized as a whole by using an inner and outer nesting approach. The process the overall optimization is shown in Fig. 5.

The inner fitness function is the loss value of the prediction model. In this paper, RRMSE is used as the loss value evaluation to the model, which is expressed as follows:

$$RMSE = \sqrt{\frac{1}{n}\sum\nolimits_{i=0}^{n}(Y_i - X_i)^2} \tag{8}$$

$$RRMSE = \frac{RMSE}{\tilde{Y}} * 100\% \tag{9}$$

where Y_i is the actual value, X_i is the model-predict value, $\tilde{Y}$ is the mean actual value. And the outer fitness function is the loss value of the inner optimal model. The number of iterations for both inner and outer is 20. When the number of iterations is satisfied, we can obtain the optimal combination of weights and prediction model.

4 Application and Experiments

4.1 Application

In this chapter, the method of deep feature fusion is used to predict the raw material index content from the product index content of rice noodle data. (D_0) [21]. And the prediction results were evaluated. In the experiment, deep feature fusion processing would be carried out on the original data to generate deep fusion features data, then it would be input into the prediction model.

In the experiment, we took two layers deep feature fusion (k = 2) with three prediction models to predict the materials index content of rice noodle. The framework of two layers deep feature fusion is as follows: the first layer uses Pearson coefficients and Factor Analysis (FA) to extract features from D_0. The second layer uses two algorithms, RF and XGBoost, to score the features input from the first layer and extract the features separately.

To increase the comparability, two sets of experiments with single-layer feature fusion (k = 1) were added: Pearson and FA were used to single layer feature fusion on D_0 for prediction, and RF and XGBoost were used to single layer feature fusion on D_0 for prediction. The results of multiple experiments were compared and analyzed, so as to provide relevant suggestions for the selection of raw materials to produce high quality rice noodles. The experimental process is shown in Fig. 6.

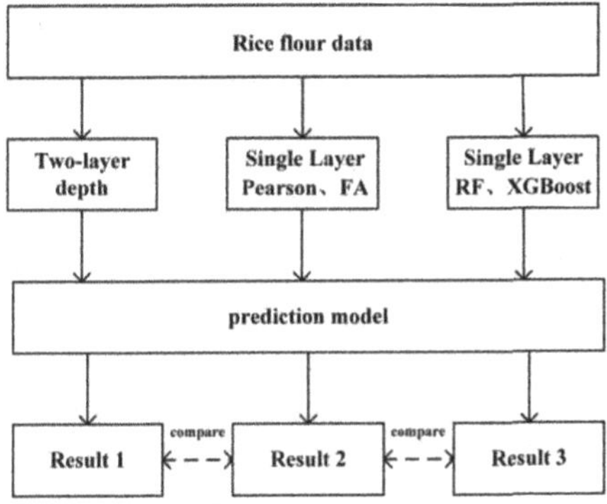

Fig. 6. Experimental process

4.2 Rice Noodle Data

Before the application experiments, a preliminary analysis of the rice noodles data is required. The total number of rice noodles data samples is 1074, and there are 22 data index, including 11 raw material index and 11 product index. Table 1 shows the statistical distribution of the raw materials. Table 2 shows the statistical distribution of the products.

Table 1. The statistical distribution of raw materials data.

Feature	Min	Max	Avg	Std
Water Content (WC)	11.302	14.346	12.602	0.554
Starch Content (SC)	69.451	74.789	72.759	1.341
Amylose Content (AC)	11.309	25.789	16.555	3.589
Gel Consistency (GC)	17.163	77.887	57.476	14.665
Protein Content (PC)	6.849	8.538	7.724	0.363
Fat Content (FC)	0.541	1.538	0.981	0.210
Fatty Acid Value (FAV)	16.271	196.878	74.559	46.078
Water Solubility (WS)	3.156	5.283	4.247	0.529
Swelling Force (SF)	6.916	8.523	7.793	0.424
Final Viscosity (FV)	2571.347	5020.148	3194.764	554.827
Gelatinzation Temperature (GT)	78.339	91.796	84.802	2.709

Table 2. The statistical distribution of products data

Feature	Min	Max	Avg	Std
Viscoelasticity (VIS)	2.500	7.199	4.171	1.389
Exquisite sexual (ES)	3.200	6.300	4.605	0.774
Softness (Softness)	3.511	7.297	5.038	0.893
Chewiness (Chewiness)	2.803	8.485	4.446	1.151
Colour and lustre (CAL)	14.007	18.000	16.544	0.880
Taste score (TS)	30.801	41.069	340804	2.672
Cooking loss (CL)	2.530	10.000	7.119	1.866
Rehydration time (RTime)	22.756	32.487	27.435	2.282
Taste	5.101	6.474	5.822	0.394
Product water content (PWC)	11.801	13.198	12.627	0.318
Breaking rate (BR)	1.159	28.494	10.370	5.938

4.3 Experimental Results of Two-Layer Depth Feature Fusion

The data D_{new} generated by two layers of deep feature fusion was input into three prediction models (DNN, RF and XGBoost). After using PSO to optimize the fusion weights and model structure, the index content of rice noodles was finally predicted. The optimized combinations of deep fusion features and prediction models are denoted as DNN-D_{new},RF-D_{new} and XGB-D_{new} respectively.

Table 3. Predicted results (k = 2)

	DNN-D_{new}			RF-D_{new}			XGB-D_{new}		
	R2	RMSE	Accuracy	R2	RMSE	Accuracy	R2	RMSE	Accuracy
WC	0.945	0.344	97.281%	0.975	0.090	99.287%	0.980	0.062	**99.505%**
SC	0.948	1.866	97.434%	0.974	0.215	99.109%	0.985	0.162	**99.777%**
AC	0.950	0.384	97.526%	0.951	0.350	97.932%	0.962	0.271	**98.345%**
GC	0.826	7.151	87.534%	0.945	1.920	96.640%	0.954	1.456	**97.506%**
PC	0.938	0.273	96.459%	0.978	0.053	**99.315%**	0.978	0.060	99.223%
FC	0.872	0.084	91.362%	0.947	0.035	96.530%	0.951	0.030	**96.894%**
FAV	0.870	7.954	90.102%	0.886	7.700	90.334%	0.912	4.986	**93.407%**
WS	0.932	0.120	96.243%	0.963	0.072	**98.310%**	0.960	0.077	98.196%
SF	0.933	0.287	96.309%	0.985	0.049	**99.357%**	0.979	0.050	99.356%
FV	0.924	103.175	95.241%	0.949	82.918	97.423%	0.958	67.092	**97.866%**
GT	0.933	3.056	96.397%	0.987	0.403	99.526%	0.982	0.379	**99.553%**

Table 3 shows the prediction results of DNN-D_{new}, RF-D_{new} and XGB-D_{new} on each index of rice noodles raw materials. R^2, RMSE and Accuracy were respectively shown to evaluate the prediction results.

It can be analyzed from Table 3 that RF-D_{new} and XGB-D_{new} have more stable prediction results, higher prediction accuracy and better overall prediction performance compared with DNN-D_{new}. Compared XGB-D_{new} with RF-D_{new}, the prediction accuracy of the former is a little higher. In conclusion, all the three can be effectively predicted in the prediction application of rice noodle raw material index, and XGB-D_{new} has the best prediction effect among the three.

From Table 3, it can be concluded that the RMSE of WC, SC, PC, SF and GT are relatively small and the prediction accuracy of XGB-D_{new} for each raw material index is more than 99%, which means that the prediction of XGB-D_{new} for these index is excellent. The prediction accuracy of SC, GC, FC, WS and FV are above 95%, and the prediction accuracy of FAV is above 90%. This indicates that the prediction of rice noodle index by XGB is very effective, and the predicted values of the index are very close to the real values, which can be well applied to the problem of predicting the rice noodle index content.

Table 4 shows the weights of the deep fusion features of DNN-D_{new}, RF-D_{new} and XGB-D_{new}. The weight distribution of the three has its own characteristics, and there is no case that a certain weight is too high to be close to one or too low to be close to zero. In other words, the basic methods of each layer in deep feature fusion have certain contributions to the final fused features. Among the weights of the three, w_{12} is greater than w_{11} and w_{22} is greater than w_{21}. It can be considered that in the first layer of deep feature fusion, the contribution of features extracted by factor analysis is greater than correlation analysis. In the second layer of deep feature fusion, the contribution of XGBoost is greater than RF.

Table 4. Feature fusion weight

	w_{11} (Pearson)	w_{12} (FA)	w_{21} (RF)	w_{22} (XGBoost)
DNN-D_{new}	0.301	0.699	0.298	0.702
RF-D_{new}	0.356	0.644	0.294	0.706
XGB-D_{new}	0.147	0.853	0.434	0.566

Table 5 shows the optimal structural coding of the three prediction models. We can obtain the model structure according to Eq. (5), Eq. (6), Eq. (7). This will provide an effective reference for the actual prediction of rice noodle.

Table 5. Model structure

Model	Structured coding
DNN	[[18, 22, 20], Selu, Adma]
RF	[480, 4, 7, 3]
XGB	[500, 0.05, 6, 3]

Table 6, Table 7 and Table 8 respectively show the predicted values of DNN-D_{new}, RF-D_{new} and XGB-D_{new} as well as the corresponding actual values and errors. And each sample is randomly selected from the rice noodle data as an example. By comparing the actual value with the predicted value, it is found that the error between each prediction index and the actual value is very small, among which XGB-D_{new} has the best prediction effect overall.

For example, the error between the actual and predicted values of WS in Table 8 is only 0.005, indicating that the prediction accuracy of this model combination is excellent. Although the error of FV is 55.9098, the accuracy of this index is 97%, which is within the error. In general, it can provide a reference for the prediction of rice noodle raw materials and help to select appropriate raw materials.

Table 6. Predicted and true values of DNN

	DNN				
	WC	SC	AC	GC	PC
Actual	13.2143	72.9255	17.0764	64.9421	7.9097
Predicted	12.9465	74.7397	16.7079	57.3485	7.8243
Error	0.2678	1.8148	0.3685	7.5926	0.0854

	DNN					
	FC	FAV	WS	SF	FV	GT
Actual	0.9561	46.9580	3.2602	8.2931	3378.0805	83.0449
Predicted	0.9995	49.2914	3.4210	7.9821	3246.7514	85.4788
Error	0.0434	2.3340	0.1608	0.3110	131.3291	2.4339

Table 7. Predicted and true values of RF

RF					
	WC	SC	AC	GC	PC
Actual	12.3244	74.0102	13.6870	71.4495	7.0179
Predicted	12.3390	73.9492	13.8281	69.7243	7.0851
Error	0.0146	0.061	0.1411	1.7252	0.0672

RF						
	FC	FAV	WS	SF	FV	GT
Actual	0.7951	28.7645	4.4436	7.4502	2685.7372	85.2922
Predicted	0.8004	33.6247	4.4269	7.4972	2606.1304	85.7216
Error	0.0053	4.8602	0.0167	0.0470	73.6068	0.4296

Table 8. Predicted and true values of XGBoost

XGBoost					
	WC	SC	AC	GC	PC
Actual	12.7803	70.9802	16.2490	54.4519	7.4479
Predicted	12.7725	70.8967	16.2130	53.5797	7.5271
Error	0.0078	0.0835	0.0360	0.8722	0.0792

XGBoost						
	FC	FAV	WS	SF	FV	GT
Actual	1.2784	66.4410	4.8202	7.4884	2576.8136	88.6146
Predicted	1.2856	62.2151	4.8152	7.5343	2632.7234	88.9814
Error	0.0072	4.2259	0.0050	0.0459	55.9098	0.3668

4.4 Experimental Results of Single-Layer Depth Feature Fusion

Two groups of comparative experiments were set. The first and second layers of deep feature fusion of two layers were respectively set as single-layer feature fusion.

The data after extracting features by Pearson and FA methods and performing weighted fusion is defined as D_{p_fa}. The data after extracting features by RF and XGBoost methods and performing weighted fusion is defined as D_{rf_xgb}. The prediction accuracy of D_{p_fa}, D_{rf_xgb} with three prediction models after optimization for each index is shown in Table 9.

Table 9. Predicted results (k = 1)

	D_{p_fa}			D_{rf_xgb}		
	DNN	RF	XGBoost	DNN	RF	XGBoost
WC	95.704%	98.766%	**99.393%**	96.300%	99.223%	99.317%
SC	97.040%	99.611%	**99.791%**	97.603%	99.740%	99.776%
AC	94.059%	95.835%	**97.902%**	91.430%	94.818%	97.720%
GC	84.580%	96.257%	97.114%	89.520%	96.820%	**97.275%**
PC	90.917%	98.714%	98.683%	96.065%	99.007%	**99.176%**
FC	92.950%	93.596%	95.613%	93.042%	94.316%	**97.017%**
FAV	87.891%	88.706%	**92.590%**	88.969%	87.317%	90.851%
WS	90.001%	96.546%	**98.264%**	90.411%	96.679%	97.627%
SF	95.452%	99.038%	**99.359%**	96.994%	98.651%	99.251%
FV	93.752%	97.445%	**97.605%**	93.951%	99.058%	96.973%
GT	95.155%	99.280%	99.343%	95.951%	99.388%	**99.671%**

Comparing Table 9 with Table 3, it can be found that the accuracy of the prediction results of rice noodle raw material index by using a single layer of feature fusion is overall lower.

This indicates that in the rice noodle raw material index prediction problem, the prediction performance of each model is improved after using two layers of deep feature fusion and optimization. So that the rice noodle raw material index content can be effectively predicted, which would provide an effective reference for the actual prediction application of rice noodle. And it will provide a good reference for the selection of raw materials in the process of producing high-quality rice noodle.

5 Conclusion

In order to solve the problem of rice noodle raw material index content prediction and improve the accuracy of prediction results, this paper proposes a deep feature fusion method to predict the raw material index content, and verifies the reliability of the results through experiments.

The experiment shows that the prediction accuracy of rice noodle raw material index values by taking two layers of deep feature fusion is improved compared with the single layer result. In the experimental results, the deep feature fusion combined with XGBoost has the best prediction effect. The accuracy of Water Content, Starch Content, Protein Content, Swelling Force and Gelatinzation Temperature are above 99%, the accuracy of Amylose Content, Gel Consistency, Water Solubility and Final Viscosity are above 97%, and the accuracy of the rest of the index are also above 90%, which is a very good result. The method improved the prediction accuracy of each raw material index by rice noodle products, which would provide a good reference to the selection of raw materials for producing high-quality rice noodle and provide guidance for the production of related enterprises.

Future Work: Further improvements to the overall optimization. More experiments: Compared with the experimental results of current mainstream feature fusion algorithms. Improved computational framework and theoretical description.

Acknowledgment. The work of this paper is supported by the subproject of National Key Research and Development Program of China (Grant No. 2017YFD0401102-02)

References

1. Sun, T.L., et al.: Prediction of sensory quality of fresh and wet rice noodle based on principal component analysis. Food Sci. Technol. **1**, 269–274 (2016)
2. Gao, X.X., et al.: Selection of special raw materials for fresh rice noodle processing. Chinese J. Cereals Oils **30**(2), 1–5 (2015)
3. Tong, L.T., et al.: Effects of semidry noodle milling on the quality attributes of rice noodle and rice noodles in China. J. Cereal Sci. **62**, 45–49 (2015)
4. Low, Y.K., Effarizah, M.E., Cheng, L.H.: Factors influencing rice noodles qualities. Food Rev. Intl. **36**(8), 781–794 (2020)
5. Yi, C., et al.: The texture of fresh rice noodles as affected by the physicochemical properties and starch fine structure of aged paddy. LWT **130**, 109610 (2020)
6. Biao, Z., Xuan, L., Jinfeng, B., et al.: Evaluation of suitability of apple drying based on BP artificial neural network algorithm. Chin. Agric. Sci. **52**(1), 129–142 (2019)
7. Yan, H.: Study on the Correlation Between Glutinous Rice Noodle Characteristics And Dumpling Quality. Jiangnan University, Wuxi (2014)
8. Chen, M., Zheng, W.: A study on optimum mixture ratio of reactive powder concrete. Adv. Mater. Sci. Eng. **2018** (2018)
9. Xu, C., et al.: Short-and medium-chain chlorinated paraffins in commercial rubber track products and raw materials. J. Hazard. Mater. **380**, 120854 (2019)
10. Barradas Filho, A.O., et al.: Application of artificial neural networks to predict viscosity, iodine value and induction period of biodiesel focused on the study of oxidative stability. Fuel **145**, 127–135 (2015)
11. Obsie, E.Y., Qu, H., Drummond, F.: Wild blueberry yield prediction using a combination of computer simulation and machine learning algorithms. Comput. Electron. Agric. **178**, 105778 (2020)
12. Zhang, Z., et al.: California almond yield prediction at the orchard level with a machine learning approach. Front. Plant Sci. **10**, 809 (2019)
13. Khaki, S., Wang, L.: Crop yield prediction using deep neural networks. Front. Plant Sci. **10**, 621 (2019)
14. Davies, T., et al.: A machine learning approach to predict the added-sugar content of packaged foods. J. Nutr. **152**(1), 343–349 (2022)
15. Wang, Y., et al.: Combining multi-source data and machine learning approaches to predict winter wheat yield in the conterminous United States. Remote Sens. **12**(8), 1232 (2020)
16. Zhang, L., et al.: Combining optical, fluorescence, thermal satellite, and environmental data to predict county-level maize yield in China using machine learning approaches. Remote Sens. **12**(1), 21 (2019)

17. Mokhtar, A., et al.: Using machine learning models to predict hydroponically grown lettuce yield. Front. Plant Sci. **13** (2022)
18. Liu, W., et al.: A survey of deep neural network architectures and their applications. Neurocomputing **234**, 11–26 (2017)
19. Breiman, L.: Random forests. Mach. Learn. **45**(1), 5–32 (2001)
20. Chen, J., et al.: Improved XGBoost model based on genetic algorithm. Int. J. Comput. Appl. Technol. **62**(3), 240–245 (2020)
21. Dataset: http://47.105.147.180:8080/rqcdp/a/log,2021.6.30

GAP: Goal-Aware Prediction with Hierarchical Interactive Representation for Vehicle Trajectory

Ding Li[1,2], Qichao Zhang[1,2(✉)], Shuai Lu[3], Yifeng Pan[3], and Dongbin Zhao[1,2]

[1] School of Artificial Intelligence, University of Chinese Academy of Sciences, Beijing, China
zhangqichao2014@ia.ac.cn

[2] State Key Laboratory of Management and Control for Complex Systems, Institute of Automation, Chinese Academy of Sciences, Beijing 100190, China

[3] Baidu Inc., Beijing 100085, China

Abstract. Predicting the future trajectories of surrounding vehicles plays a vital role in ensuring the safety of autonomous driving. It is extremely challenging for the pure imitation method due to the high degree of multimodality and uncertainty in the future. In fact, when driving in most traffic scenarios, vehicles should obey some traffic rules such as "vehicles follow the lane and do not collide with each other". Inspired by this, this paper proposes a goal-aware prediction (GAP) framework to predict the multimodal trajectories, where goals are chosen in the lanes with hierarchical interactive representation and a multi-task loss. Based on the graph-based vectorized input, a novel hierarchical interactive representation module is first designed to obtain the fine-grained goal features, which progressively models interactions between goal-to-goal, goal-to-lane, and lane-to-agent, corresponding to the individual, local and global levels, respectively. Then, an auxiliary collision loss is developed to take into account learning from demonstration and injecting common sense of collision avoidance, and is served as a part of the multi-task loss to guide the generation of multimodal plausible trajectories. In the end, the proposed method is verified on the Baidu In-house Cut-in dataset, which includes more than 370K interactive scenarios collected in the real road testing. The comparative results demonstrate the superior performance of our proposed GAP model than the mainstream prediction methods.

Keywords: Multimodal trajectory prediction · Hierarchical interactive representation · Graph neural network · Multi-task loss

1 Introduction

Predicting the future trajectories of surrounding vehicles (called target agents) is crucial for the Autonomous Vehicle (AV) system to conduct the subsequent

This work was supported by the National Natural Science Foundation of China (NSFC) under Grants No. 62173325, and also was supported by the Beijing Municipal Natural Science Foundation under Grants L191002.

Y. Tan and Y. Shi (Eds.): DMBD 2022, CCIS 1744, pp. 305–319, 2022.
https://doi.org/10.1007/978-981-19-9297-1_22

decision-making [1] and path planning [2] modules. Being different from Model Predictive Controller (MPC), this task not only makes a choice of the optimal path (i.e., spatial dimension) but also enriches the speed attribute (i.e., temporal dimension). However, trajectory prediction faces great challenges due to the high-degree uncertainties of target agents' future intents (e.g., a target agent could turn unprotected left or turn right at an intersection). Effective trajectory prediction model must be able to represent such a rich output space with the possible behavioral outcomes matching the underlying multimodal distribution.

Generally speaking, multimodal trajectories can be obtained via a direct regression model with pure imitation [3,4]. However, since such methods are trained with only one ground truth per data sample, all the predicted trajectories converge to the same solution which leads to mode collapse. To overcome these limitations, some researchers address the multimodality problem with the anchor-based method, which first predicts the probabilistic distribution over intent anchors, and then regresses multimodal trajectories conditioned on the predicted anchors. The intent anchors can be represented by different forms. On one hand, a family of methods describe the future intents by a candidate set of trajectory anchors which can be predefined [5,6] or generated by the planner [7]. On the other hand, when the high-definition (HD) map is available, a series of goal anchors can be retrieved by sampling the equally spaced waypoints along per future lane in a sequential order, which can be considered as the fine-grained representations of future intents. This is inspired by the fact that the future intents of vehicles are highly correlated with the topology of lanes. TNT [8], served as a typical representative for goal anchor-based methods, has achieved outstanding performance with the scene context encoder VectorNet [4]. This approach is flexible and can capture a diverse set of future intents. Unfortunately, the future interaction over vehicles is ignored for TNT, which means it can not reason about the danger of collision especially for the interactive scenarios such as cut-in scenarios. To address this problem, TrafficSim [9] augments the pure imitation method with an auxiliary common sense objective to avoid collision.

In this paper, we introduce a goal-aware prediction (GAP) framework, which builds upon TNT [8] and TrafficSim [10], taking concepts of goal anchors and the auxiliary collision loss, but reconsidering how to represent the fine-grained features of goal anchors and establish trajectory modeling via a multi-task loss. Our contributions are summarized as follows:

- A novel hierarchical interactive representation module is proposed to obtain the fine-grained features of goal anchors, which explicitly captures the sophisticated interactive relationships between goal-to-goal, goal-to-lane, and lane-to-agent, corresponding to the individual, local and global levels, respectively.
- A multi-task loss is established augmenting an auxiliary collision loss into the pure imitation loss of the goal anchor-based method, which takes into account learning from demonstration and injecting common sense of collision avoidance.

The experimental results indicate the proposed GAP framework can achieve superior performances on Baidu In-house dataset consisting of cut-in interactive scenarios than the existing mainstream prediction methods.

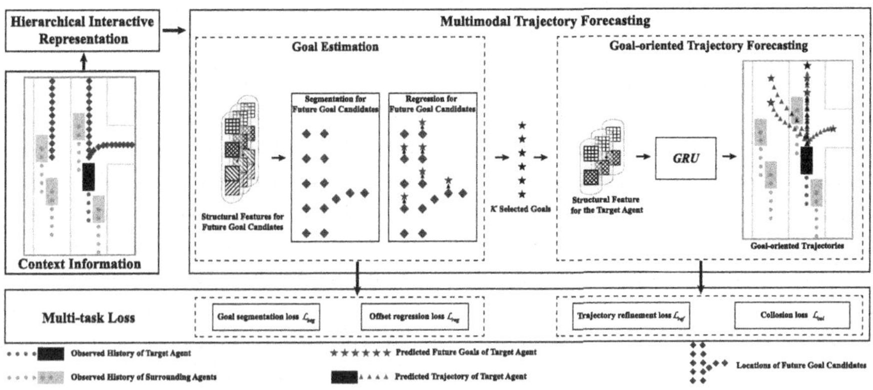

Fig. 1. An overall structure of our proposed GAP framework. The hierarchical interactive representation module is first applied to extract the fine-grained features over a candidate set of future goals. Followed by this, two main stages of goal anchor-based model are conducted in turn. Goal estimation stage is responsible to select the top $\mathcal{K}$ potential goals predicted by $\pi\left(\boldsymbol{g}_l^k \mid \boldsymbol{S}_p, \boldsymbol{G}, \boldsymbol{S}_p^{1:E}\right)$. Once the goal candidates are determined, the goal-oriented trajectory forecasting stage correspondingly produces $\mathcal{K}$ trajectories from the same initial state to the diverse final positions. Finally, a multi-task loss is proposed to optimize the end-to-end interpretable pipeline, predicting multimodal plausible trajectories with collision avoidance.

In recent years, deep learning-based methods have been widely used in the trajectory forcasting domain [11,12], which can be roughly divided into two categories: context-based and anchor-based methods.

Towards the context-based methods, the majority of them focus on how to design a scheme to encode the useful information from the environments. Numerous previous models [13,14] employ Convolutional Neural Network (CNN) to extract features by rendering as input a rasterized Birds-Eye-View (BEV) image, with different channels representing different types of semantic observations. However, the receptive fields of CNN may not be skilled at deducing the temporal and spatial sequential relationships between agent trajectories and future lanes. Hence, information aggregation methods, including Recurrent Neural Network (RNN), Graph Neural Network (GNN), Transformer layer, and max-pooling operator et al., have emerged to efficiently encode the vectorized representations instead, which characterizes the temporal and spatial sequences into entities with locations and attributes. More specifically, WIMP [15] applies an RNN-based encoder-decoder structure to capture temporal dependencies over time step movements. Further, VectorNet [4] treats both agent trajectories and future lanes as a unified graph-based vectorized representation, and encodes them via GNN. Besides, Scene Transformer [16] is proposed to predict multi-agent trajectories considering interactions over agents, time steps, and road elements three different axes by using the attention mechanism [17]. TrafficSim [10] utilizes the implicit latent variable model to capture useful information over future intents, and proposes an auxiliary collision loss to explicitly reason about multi-agent interactions.

As for another kind of methods, anchor-based approaches concentrate on modeling multimodality of future trajectories by abstracting diverse future intents as a pool of anchors. For instance, MultiPath [6] tackles trajectory prediction as a classification task over the candidate set of predefined trajectory anchors learned by k-means clustering algorithm. PRIME [7] relies on a model-based generator to produce multiple feasible trajectories under explicit constraints, and ranks them using a learning-based evaluator. Different from these methods above, TNT [8] samples fine-grained goal anchors along future lanes where the target agent potentially arrives, which makes the guidance of predicting various goal-oriented trajectories. Note that accurate descriptions of goal anchor features ease the difficulty of goal estimation.

Inheriting TNT and TrafficSim, the GAP framework further modifies the feature extraction and multi-task learning objectives to accurately forecast the future state with multimodality and collision avoidance.

2 Methodology

In the following, we first introduce our problem formulation in Sect. 2.1. We then define our hierarchical interactive representation module in Sect. 2.2. In Sect. 2.3, we explain how GAP predicts multimodal trajectories by means of goal-anchor based method. Finally, we show our multi-task loss in Sect. 2.4. An overall structure of our proposed GAP framework is shown in Fig. 1.

2.1 Problem Formulation

Given a sequence of the past states for the target agent $\boldsymbol{S}_p = \{\boldsymbol{s}_p^{-\tau+1}, \cdots, \boldsymbol{s}_p^{-t}, \cdots, \boldsymbol{s}_p^{0}\}$ throughout the observed τ time steps, our objective is to predict its future states $\boldsymbol{S}_f = \left\{\boldsymbol{s}_f^{1}, \cdots, \boldsymbol{s}_f^{\delta}, \cdots, \boldsymbol{s}_f^{T}\right\}$ over future T time steps. Let $\boldsymbol{s}_p^{-t}$ denote the coordinate of the target agent's centroid at the previous time step t relative to $\boldsymbol{s}_p^{0} = (0, 0)$. We represent $\boldsymbol{s}_f^{\delta}$ in a similar definition manner at the future time step δ. In addition, during the trajectory prediction process, the target agent interacts with the static HD map and its dynamic surrounding agents. On one hand, to effectively depict the topology of HD map, we sample K equally spaced waypoints on L future lanes in turn, *i.e.*, $\boldsymbol{G} = \{\boldsymbol{g}_l^k \mid l = 1 : L, k = 1 : K\}$, where $\boldsymbol{g}_l^k$ denotes the k-th waypoint coordinate extracted along the l-th future lane. On the other hand, we select E nearby agents in the neighbor region of the target agent to represent its dynamic surrounding agents. Likewise, let $\boldsymbol{S}_p^e = \{\boldsymbol{s}_p^{e,-\tau+1}, \cdots, \boldsymbol{s}_p^{e,-t}, \cdots, \boldsymbol{s}_p^{e,0}\}$ define the sequence of the past states for the e-th surrounding agent. In particular, $\boldsymbol{S}_p^1$ denotes the past trajectory of AV, which is also regarded as the surrounding agent for the target agent. Once all available observations are obtained, the trajectory prediction task can be formulated as a posterior distribution $p\left(\boldsymbol{S}_f \mid \boldsymbol{S}_p, \boldsymbol{G}, \boldsymbol{S}_p^{1:E}\right)$.

Inspired by the TNT model [8], we employ the goal anchor-based method to produce multimodal trajectories. In this paper, a candidate set of waypoints are served as goal anchors to guide the trajectory prediction. Thus, the probabilistic distribution $p\left(\boldsymbol{S}_f \mid \boldsymbol{S}_p, \boldsymbol{G}, \boldsymbol{S}_p^{1:E}\right)$ can be expressed as

$$\begin{aligned} p\left(\boldsymbol{S}_f \mid \boldsymbol{S}_p, \boldsymbol{G}, \boldsymbol{S}_p^{1:E}\right) &= \sum_{l=1}^{L}\sum_{k=1}^{K} p\left(\boldsymbol{S}_f, \boldsymbol{g}_l^k \mid \boldsymbol{S}_p, \boldsymbol{G}, \boldsymbol{S}_p^{1:E}\right) \\ &= \sum_{l=1}^{L}\sum_{k=1}^{K} p\left(\boldsymbol{S}_f \mid \boldsymbol{g}_l^k, \boldsymbol{S}_p, \boldsymbol{G}, \boldsymbol{S}_p^{1:E}\right) p\left(\boldsymbol{g}_l^k \mid \boldsymbol{S}_p, \boldsymbol{G}, \boldsymbol{S}_p^{1:E}\right). \end{aligned} \tag{1}$$

According to Eq. (1), the goal anchor-based method is implemented by two main stages including goal estimation and goal-oriented trajectory forecasting. In detail, the goal estimation is responsible to model the uncertainties over future intents of the target agent via the goal distribution $p\left(\boldsymbol{g}_l^k \mid \boldsymbol{S}_p, \boldsymbol{G}, \boldsymbol{S}_p^{1:E}\right)$, which can be further factorized by

$$p\left(\boldsymbol{g}_l^k \mid \boldsymbol{S}_p, \boldsymbol{G}, \boldsymbol{S}_p^{1:E}\right) = \pi\left(\boldsymbol{g}_l^k \mid \boldsymbol{S}_p, \boldsymbol{G}, \boldsymbol{S}_p^{1:E}\right) \mathcal{N}\left(\boldsymbol{\Delta g}_l^k \mid \boldsymbol{\mu}\left(\boldsymbol{\Delta g}_l^k\right), \boldsymbol{\Sigma}\left(\boldsymbol{\Delta g}_l^k\right)\right), \tag{2}$$

where $\pi\left(\boldsymbol{g}_l^k \mid \boldsymbol{S}_p, \boldsymbol{G}, \boldsymbol{S}_p^{1:E}\right)$ is a softmax distribution normalizing the predicted confidence over a discrete set of waypoints $\boldsymbol{G}$. Besides, a generalized Gaussian distribution $\mathcal{N}\left(\boldsymbol{\Delta g}_l^k \mid \boldsymbol{\mu}\left(\boldsymbol{\Delta g}_l^k\right), \boldsymbol{\Sigma}\left(\boldsymbol{\Delta g}_l^k\right)\right)$ is established to output the continuous offsets from the predicted goals to the real endpoint $\boldsymbol{s}_f^T$, with the mean $\boldsymbol{\mu}\left(\boldsymbol{\Delta g}_l^k\right)$ and the variance $\boldsymbol{\Sigma}\left(\boldsymbol{\Delta g}_l^k\right)$. Subsequently, once the potential goal is determined, the unimodal distribution $p\left(\boldsymbol{S}_f \mid \boldsymbol{g}_l^k, \boldsymbol{S}_p, \boldsymbol{G}, \boldsymbol{S}_p^{1:E}\right)$ is modeled to produce the plausible goal-oriented future states.

2.2 Hierarchical Interactive Representation

Figure 2 depicts the structure of our hierarchical interactive representation module. First, the prior knowledge, consisting of past trajectories and road topology, is encoded in a unified graph-based vectorized representation proposed by VectorNet [4]. Based on this, we build interactive representations at the individual, local and global levels by utilizing GNN, max-pooling operator and Transformer layer, respectively. Moreover, these three types of interactive representations exhibit a hierarchical progressive relationship, with the output at the lower level as the input to the higher level. Finally, the structural features of fine-grained goals are obtained by stacking these three interactive representations, which are used in the following multimodal trajectory forecasting module.

(1) Graph-based vectorized representation. Since all of the available observations are captured in the form of sequences, we formulate a unified graph-based vectorized representation $\mathcal{G}_a = (\boldsymbol{\mathcal{V}}_a, \boldsymbol{\mathcal{E}}_a)$ to be applied to any observed sequence. At the same time, we use the attribute index $a = \{0, e \in [1, E], l \in [1, L]\}$ to distinguish these observed sequences with different semantic information, *i.e.*, the temporal sequences over past states and the spatial sequences over future

lanes. Given a specific attribute index a, the set of nodes $\mathcal{V}_a$ and their edge relationships $\mathcal{E}_a$ are determined. More specifically, the node embeddings $\{\boldsymbol{v}_a^i\}$ with the temporal and spatial sequences are respectively given by

$$\boldsymbol{v}_0^i = [\boldsymbol{s}_p^i, \boldsymbol{s}_p^{i+1}, 0], \boldsymbol{v}_e^i = [\boldsymbol{s}_p^{e,i}, \boldsymbol{s}_p^{e,i+1}, e], \forall\ e \in [1, E]\ and\ i \in [-\tau+1, -1], \quad (3)$$

and

$$\boldsymbol{v}_l^i = [\boldsymbol{g}_l^i, \boldsymbol{g}_l^{i+1}, E+l], \forall\ l \in [1, L]\ and\ i \in [1, K-1]. \quad (4)$$

As shown in Eq. (3), the node embeddings of temporal sequences record the locations at the adjacent moments for the past trajectories of the target agent and its surrounding agents, which implicitly provides some extra useful information such as velocity and heading. Equation (4) gives a particular description over the node embeddings of the spatial sequences instead, which concludes the waypoint coordinates at the adjacent positions along per future lane the target agent desires to reach.

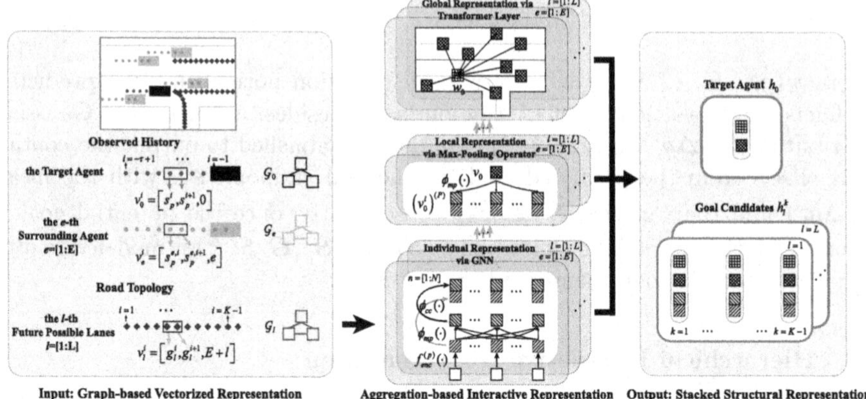

Fig. 2. An overview of the hierarchical interactive representation module. First, all observed sequences with different semantic information are transformed into a unified graph-based vectorized representation. Then, three information aggregation means, including GNN, max-pooling operator and Transformer layer, are adopted sequentially to model interactions at the individual, local and global levels, respectively. Finally, we obtain the structural representations of the target agent and its future goal candidates by stacking the interactive representations above in necessity.

(2) Aggregation-based interactive representation. Given the graph-based vectorized representations of all temporal and spatial sequences, we apply three typical aggregation means, *i.e.*, GNN, max-pooling operator and the Transformer layer, to model interactions at the individual, local and global levels, respectively. First, we use GNN to update each node feature $\left(\boldsymbol{v}_a^i\right)^{(n+1)}$ in a neighborhood aggregation manner, with $\left\{\left(\boldsymbol{v}_a^j\right)^{(n)}\right\}$ denoting the set of its neighbors in

the graph $\mathcal{G}_a$, as described by

$$\left(\boldsymbol{v}_a^i\right)^{(n+1)} = \phi_{cc}\left(f_{ec}\left(\left(\boldsymbol{v}_a^i\right)^{(n)}\right), \phi_{mp}\left(\left\{f_{ec}\left(\left(\boldsymbol{v}_a^j\right)^{(n)}\right)\right\}\right)\right), \tag{5}$$

where $\phi_{cc}(\cdot)$ denotes a concatenation operator, and $\phi_{mp}(\cdot)$ represents a max-pooling operator. Besides, a mapping function $f_{ec}(\cdot)$ is designed to iteratively encode the node features, which is realized by a single fully connected layer with Layer Normalization [18] and ReLU non-linearity. As the number of GNN layers increases, the number of hidden units grows twice as fast with its initial value set to 16. After $N = 3$ layers of iterations, we obtain the individual representations $\left\{\left(\boldsymbol{v}_a^i\right)^{(N)}\right\}$ over all node embeddings in each sequence. Then, a max-pooling operator is employed to capture the local representations $\{\boldsymbol{v}_a\}$ of the temporal and spatial sequences by aggregating the individual node representations belong to their own, which can be written as

$$\boldsymbol{v}_a = \phi_{mp}\left(\left\{\left(\boldsymbol{v}_a^i\right)^{(N)}\right\}\right). \tag{6}$$

Finally, built upon the local-level representations $\{\boldsymbol{v}_a\}$ above, the high-order information aggregation is established to modal global interactions between agent-to-agent and agent-to-lane by relying on the Transformer layer:

$$\boldsymbol{W} = \text{softmax}\left(\frac{\boldsymbol{Q}\left(\boldsymbol{K}\right)^{\mathrm{T}}}{\sqrt{d_k}}\right)\boldsymbol{V}, \tag{7}$$

where $\boldsymbol{W}$ denotes a matrix including the global-level representations $\{\boldsymbol{w}_a\}$ of all observed sequences. Besides, $\boldsymbol{Q}$, $\boldsymbol{K}$ and $\boldsymbol{V}$ represent the query, key and value matrix, respectively. Each of them is computed as a learned linear transformation over the local-level representations. Note that $d_k = 128$ denotes the dimension of the key matrix.

(3) Stacked structural representation. The fine-grained feature of a goal candidate needs to derive from three aspects: the individual node representations of a waypoint, the local and global sequence representations of the future lane along which the waypoint is sampled. Therefore, the structural representations are built to describe the fine-grained features over a candidate set of future goals by stacking the underlying representations from these three aspects above:

$$\boldsymbol{h}_l^k = \phi_{cc}\left(\left\{\left(\boldsymbol{v}_l^k\right)^{(N)}, \boldsymbol{v}_l, \boldsymbol{w}_l\right\}\right), \boldsymbol{h}_l^K = \boldsymbol{h}_l^{K-1}, \forall\, l \in [1, L] \text{ and } k \in [1, K-1]. \tag{8}$$

In addition, we also obtain the structural representations of the target agent by concatenating the corresponding local and global sequence representations of the past states:

$$\boldsymbol{h}_0 = \phi_{cc}\left(\{\boldsymbol{v}_0, \boldsymbol{w}_0\}\right). \tag{9}$$

2.3 Multimodal Trajectory Forecasting

This section exhibits the detailed implementation process of the goal anchor-based method.

(1) Goal estimation. As described in Sect. 2.1, this stage consists of two steps: goal selection and offset prediction. The goal selection can be treated a segmentation task, which is performed by a softmax distribution:

$$\pi\left(\boldsymbol{g}_l^k \mid \boldsymbol{S}_p, \boldsymbol{G}, \boldsymbol{S}_p^{1:E}\right) = \operatorname{softmax}\left(f_{seg}\left(\boldsymbol{g}_l^k, \boldsymbol{h}_l^k\right)\right). \tag{10}$$

Further, we select the top $\mathcal{K}$ goal candidates estimated by $\pi\left(\boldsymbol{g}_l^k \mid \boldsymbol{S}_p, \boldsymbol{G}, \boldsymbol{S}_p^{1:E}\right)$. For brevity, in the offset prediction step, we assume the variance $\boldsymbol{\Sigma}\left(\boldsymbol{\Delta g}_l^k\right)$ to be an identity matrix, and the mean $\boldsymbol{\mu}\left(\boldsymbol{\Delta g}_l^k\right)$ is learned by a regression task as denoted by

$$\boldsymbol{\mu}\left(\boldsymbol{\Delta g}_l^k\right) = f_{reg}\left(\boldsymbol{g}_l^k, \boldsymbol{h}_l^k\right). \tag{11}$$

In Eqs.(10) and (11), the mapping functions $f_{seg}(\cdot)$ and $f_{reg}(\cdot)$ are achieved by a three-layer multilayer perceptron (MLP), with the goal candidates $\boldsymbol{g}_l^k$ and their structural representations $\boldsymbol{h}_l^k$ as the input.

(2) Goal-oriented trajectory forecasting. In this paper, an encoder-decoder architecture is used to capture the sequential nature of past and future trajectories for the target agent. Here, both encoder and decoder are performed by a 2-layer bi-directional GRU network with a 128-dimension hidden state. More specifically, the encoder updates its hidden states by taking into input the past trajectory $\boldsymbol{S}_p$ of the target agent, and then the decoder inherits the hidden states of the encoding procedure to predict the future trajectory in a step-wise rollout manner. In addition to taking into account the structural representation $\boldsymbol{h}_0$, the decoding procedure also considers the selected $\mathcal{K}$ goal candidates $\boldsymbol{g}_l^k$, which are served as diverse anchors to guide the generation of $\mathcal{K}$ multimodal trajectories.

2.4 Multi-task Loss

To learn from demonstration and injecting common sense of collision avoidance, we train our model end-to-end with the multi-task loss function $\mathcal{L}$ augmenting pure imitation loss $\mathcal{L}_{imi}$ with an auxiliary collision loss $\mathcal{L}_{col}$, as described by

$$\mathcal{L} = \mathcal{L}_{imi} + \lambda \mathcal{L}_{col}, \ \mathcal{L}_{imi} = \mathcal{L}_{seg} + \mathcal{L}_{reg} + \mathcal{L}_{ref}. \tag{12}$$

where $\lambda = 1e-3$ is a scalar that balances the two loss terms. Determined by the pipeline of goal anchor-based method, the pure imitation loss $\mathcal{L}_{imi}$ consists of three parts: goal segmentation, offset regression, and trajectory refinement. More concretely, in the goal estimation stage, we adopt the binary cross entropy loss for $\mathcal{L}_{seg}$ and the mean square error loss for $\mathcal{L}_{reg}$, where both two loss functions are merely evaluated on the positive instances, *i.e.*, the top $\mathcal{K}$ closest goal candidates to the ground-truth endpoints. Further, $\mathcal{K}$ selected goals are represented as $\mathcal{K}$ different prediction modes to correspondingly produce $\mathcal{K}$ goal-oriented trajectories. In the goal-oriented trajectory forecasting stage, the trajectory refinement loss $\mathcal{L}_{ref}$ is measured by the mean square error loss between the predicted state and its ground-truth over each future time step for per prediction mode. Since the trajectory forecasting stage largely depends on the goal estimation stage, we employ the teacher forcing technique [19] by feeding the real end point as the goal to accelerate the training process. Different from that, in the inference process, the real endpoint is substituted by the predicted goals from the estimation $\pi\left(\boldsymbol{g}_l^k \mid \boldsymbol{S}_p, \boldsymbol{G}, \boldsymbol{S}_p^{1:E}\right)$ instead.

Since pure imitation loss can not reason about the danger of collision, an auxiliary collision loss $\mathcal{L}_{col}$ is designed to consider the future interaction with AV, as depicted by

$$\mathcal{L}_{col} = \frac{1}{\mathcal{K} \cdot T} \sum_{\kappa=1}^{\mathcal{K}} \sum_{\delta=1}^{T} \mathcal{L}_{or}^{\kappa,\delta}, \tag{13}$$

where $\mathcal{L}_{or}^{\kappa,\delta}$ denotes a single overlap loss between the target agent and AV at the future time step δ for the κ-th prediction mode. Approximately, we abstract each agent with 5 circles whose radiuses are determined by half of the agent widths. More concretely, we define the single overlap loss $\mathcal{L}_{or}^{\kappa,\delta}$ as follows:

$$\mathcal{L}_{or}^{\kappa,\delta} = \begin{cases} 1, \&\text{if } d\left(\hat{\boldsymbol{s}}_f^{\kappa,\delta}, \boldsymbol{s}_f^{1,\delta}\right) \leq R + R_1, \\ \qquad\qquad\qquad 0, \&\text{otherwise}, \end{cases} \tag{14}$$

where $\hat{\boldsymbol{s}}_f^{\kappa,\delta}$ represents the predicted state of the target agent at the time step δ for the prediction mode κ, and $\boldsymbol{s}_f^{1,\delta}$ is the ground truth future state of AV at the time step δ, and $d(\cdot)$ is responsible to compute L2 distance between centroids of the closest circles for two agents. In addition, R and R_1 are circle radiuses of the target agent and AV, respectively. From Eq. (14) we can intuitively conclude that the single overlap loss is set to 0 if no overlap between any circles while is set to 1 if two circles overlap with each other.

3 Experiment

In this section, we use the Baidu In-house Cut-in dataset to verify the effectiveness of our proposed GAP framework. Our model is trained on 4 A100 GPUs for 200 epochs with the batch size of 64. We use the Adam [20] optimizer with an initial learning rate of 5×10^{-3}, which is decayed by a factor of 0.5 per 30 epochs.

3.1 Dataset

Baidu In-house Cut-in dataset is a large-scale private dataset, which is collected from amounts of cut-in scenarios in Beijing, China. Given 2 s past observations, our task is to forecast 3 s future locations of the target agent to cut in front of the AV. According to different types of data collection scenarios, the Baidu In-house Cut-in dataset consists of two branches: Junction and Non-junction dataset. More specifically, the Junction dataset is further split into training and validation sets with 162381 and 17820 frames, respectively. Towards the Non-junction dataset, the number of the training and validation frames is 162556 and 30845, respectively. Also note that each frame is sampled 10 Hz. In addition to

5 s full trajectory of the target agent, each frame also includes 2 s past states of $E = 14$ surrounding agents, and some extra information, such as the agent's initial heading and the agent's length-width information. Moreover, we could query the map topology represented by $L = 6$ future lanes the target agent is likely to reach, each of which has the sequence of $K = 200$ equally spaced waypoints.

3.2 Evaluation Metrics

On one hand, we adopt three extensively used distance-error metrics [3], *i.e.*, minimum Average Displacement Error (minADE), minimum Final Displacement Error (minFDE) and Miss Rate (MR), for the performance evaluation over $\mathcal{K} = 6$ predicted future trajectories, respectively. minFDE is measured by L2 distance of the endpoint between the ground-truth and the best predicted trajectory. minADE is defined as the average L2 distance of all future time steps between the ground-truth and the predicted trajectory with minFDE. Besides, MR is also considered to compute the percentage of the predicted trajectory with minFDE, whose endpoint is more than 2.0 m away from ground-truth.

On the other hand, the Overlap Rate (OR) and Cut-in Rate (CR), served as the interactive metrics, are considered as well. OR is computed as the total number of collision frames divided by the total number of all the validation frames. In particular, a collision frame is determined by a overlap indicator $IsOR(\cdot)$ as described by

$$IsOR(\cdot) = \mathbb{1}\left(\sum_{\delta=1}^{T} IOU\left(b\left(\hat{\boldsymbol{s}}_f^{\bar{\kappa},\delta}\right), b\left(\boldsymbol{s}_f^{1,\delta}\right)\right) > 0\right), \tag{15}$$

where $b(\cdot)$ is a function to obtain the bounding box information (length, width and heading) from the specific predicted state $\hat{\boldsymbol{s}}_f^{\bar{\kappa},\delta}$ for the target agent, as well as the ground truth state $\boldsymbol{s}_f^{1,\delta}$ for AV. As the overlap indicator is measured by the full trajectories between the target agent and AV, the index $\bar{\kappa}$ is the number of the specific prediction mode belonging to the predicted trajectory with minADE. Once the bounding box information is obtained, $IOU(\cdot)$ computes the intersection-over-union between two bounding boxes of the two agents. From another aspect, due to the unique characteristics of the large-scale Baidu Inhouse Cut-in dataset, CR is assigned to count the number of the cut-in scenarios under the condition that no collision occurs. Moreover, a cut-in indicator is developed to identify the cut-in modality, which can be shown by

$$IsCutin(\cdot) = \mathbb{1}\left(lane\left(\hat{\boldsymbol{s}}_f^{\bar{\kappa},T}\right) = lane\left(\boldsymbol{s}_f^{1,T}\right)\right) \wedge \mathbb{1}\left(y\left(\hat{\boldsymbol{s}}_f^{\bar{\kappa},T}\right) > y\left(\boldsymbol{s}_f^{1,T}\right)\right), \tag{16}$$

where $lane(\cdot)$ is responsible to compute the index of the future lane where each of two agents locates at the last future time step, and $y(\cdot)$ is a function to retrieve the longitudinal coordinates of the endpoints for the target agent and AV, respectively.

Table 1. Performance comparison on Baidu In-house Cut-in dataset

Scenario	Method	minADE ↓ (m)	minFDE ↓ (m)	MR ↓ (%)	OR ↓ (%)	CR ↑ (%)
Junction	LSTM [3]	0.79	1.51	25.4	5.92e−1	83
	VectorNet [4]	0.54	1.06	13.4	4.97e−1	87
	GAP	**0.46**	**0.61**	**4.9**	**4.58e−1**	**90**
Non-junction	LSTM [3]	0.75	1.68	30.2	2.26e-2	82
	VectorNet [4]	0.55	1.19	17.4	1.93e-2	90
	GAP	**0.37**	**0.76**	**6.4**	**6.46e-3**	**92**

3.3 Quantitative Comparisons

We evaluate the performance of the proposed GAP framework on the junction and non-junction datasets. As shown in Table 1, towards each dataset, we compare the proposed GAP method with the existing mainstream methods including LSTM [3] and VectorNet [4], which are both served as the typical regression representatives trained by pure imitation loss.

Towards the distance-error metrics, compared with the competitive VectorNet in the junction dataset, we observe that our proposed GAP framework further promotes the performance of FDE and MR by 42.45% and 63.43%, respectively, which implies that our method is capable of learning accurate probabilistic distribution over goal anchors with a novel hierarchical interactive representation module.

Towards the interactive metrics, the proposed GAP framework adopts a multi-task loss to take into consideration learning from demonstration and injecting common sense of collision avoidance, resulting in largely better OR as compared to the mainstream trajectory prediction methods which are purely optimized by imitation loss. Besides, relying on the advantage of the goal anchor-based pipeline, the proposed GAP framework accurately captures the cut-in modality from the vast number of cut-in scenarios, which benefits the CR performance in contrast with the direct regression models.

3.4 Ablation Studies

As shown in Table 2, to highlight the contribution of each component in the proposed GAP framework, we conduct several ablation studies on the Baidu In-house Cut-in dataset. We consider the individual-level representation in GAP as the baseline model, and hierarchically add other level-based representation modules to aggregate interactive contextual information, and employ an auxiliary collision loss to encourage supervision from injecting common sense of collision avoidance.

Firstly, we observe that the model with a novel hierarchical interactive representation module boosts the minFDE and MR by a large margin. This validates

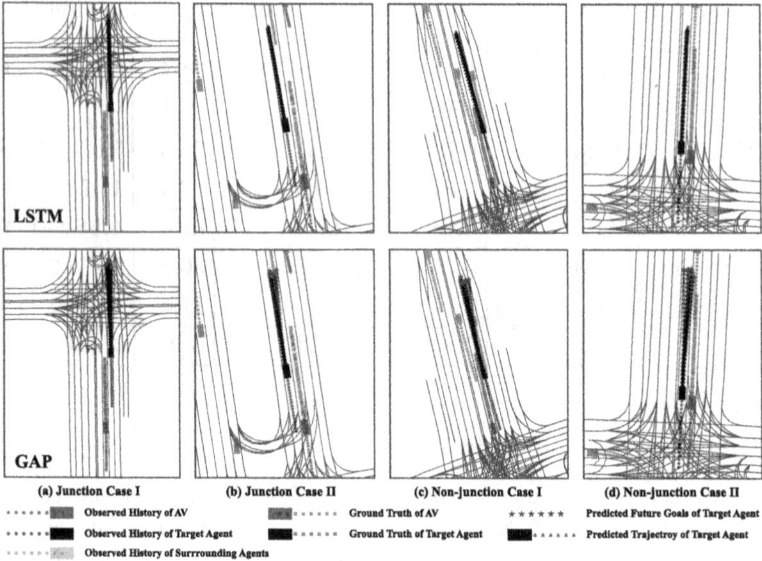

Fig. 3. Examples of $\mathcal{K} = 6$ predicted trajectories obtained with GAP (the lower row) and LSTM (the upper row) on the Baidu In-house Cut-in dataset: (a-b) junction dataset and (c-d) non-junction dataset.

that stacking the comprehensive understandings progressively contributes to the accurate distribution modeling over a candidate set of future goals, which takes into account the logical interactive relationships between goal-to-goal, goal-to-lane and lane-to-agent, correspondingly to the individual, local and global levels, respectively.

Besides, incorporating the additional constraints of collision avoidance, the proposed GAP framework with collision loss improves the interaction reasoning and prevents undesired collision behaviors in the future, reducing OR by a significant margin compared with our method without collision loss. More concretely, the proposed GAP framework with collision loss performs with 10.72% and 49.92% relative decrease in OR for the junction and non-junction dataset, respectively.

3.5 Qualitative Results

We showcase the qualitative comparisons between the proposed GAP framework and LSTM for junction and non-junction datasets. In Fig. 3, we observe that our method demonstrates good multimodalities which cover diverse future intents, such as cut-in and lane-keeping. On the contrary, the predictions provided by LSTM merely generate unimodal trajectories matching with the ground truth. From this result, we confirm that the future goal candidates provide the target agent different choices of admissible destinations and the proposed GAP frame-

Table 2. Ablation study of GAP on Baidu In-house Cut-in dataset

Scenario	Representation	minADE ↓ (m)	minFDE ↓ (m)	MR ↓ (%)	OR ↓ (%)	CR ↑ (%)
Junction	Individual	0.77	1.13	13.6	4.97e−1	86
	+Local	0.71	0.93	10.1	4.80e−1	87
	+Global	**0.46**	0.67	6.0	5.13e−1	**90**
	+Collision loss	**0.46**	**0.61**	**4.9**	**4.58e−1**	**90**
Non-junction	Individual	0.65	1.42	19.2	3.56e-2	87
	+Local	0.53	1.14	13.8	1.94e-2	89
	+Global	0.46	**0.62**	**5.3**	1.29e-2	**92**
	+Collision loss	**0.37**	0.76	6.4	**6.46e-3**	**92**

work exploits them to correspondingly generate the feasible goal-oriented trajectories in a given scenario. This also verifies the effectiveness of the hierarchical interactive representation module, which extracts the fine-grained features of future goal candidates for improving the accuracy of distribution modeling over future intents. Further, relying on the vast amounts of real cut-in scenarios, the proposed GAP framework has the ability to capture the cut-in modalities which are highly associated with the goal selection, even when they differ from the ground truth, especially as shown in Figs. 3 (b) and 3 (d). In the meanwhile, with the auxiliary collision loss considered in the multi-task loss, our model produces adequate trajectories with collision free behaviors and reasonable interactions.

4 Conclusion

In this paper, we propose a novel goal-aware prediction framework, GAP, by carefully considering fine-grained representation and multi-task loss design. Relying on information aggregation methods, a hierarchical interactive representation module is introduced to obtain the fine-grained features of goal candidates, which lays solid foundation to build accurate distribution over future intents. Moreover, an auxiliary collision loss is augmented in the multi-task optimization process to learn from injecting common sense of collision avoidance. These two components contribute to improve prediction quality in the aspect of multimodality and interactivity.

The experiments conducted on the Baidu In-house Cut-in dataset demonstrate that the proposed GAP framework achieves significant enhancements in nearly all metrics considered. Towards the junction dataset, the proposed GAP framework performs the competitive VectorNet with 63.43% reduction in MR. Besides, the auxiliary collision loss plays a vital role in producing collision avoidance behaviors in the future interaction process with AV, with about 49.92% improvements in OR as compared to our method without the collision loss for the non-junction dataset.

References

1. Wang, J., Zhang, Q., Zhao, D., Chen, Y.: Lane change decision-making through deep reinforcement learning with rule-based constraints. In: 2019 International Joint Conference on Neural Networks (IJCNN), pp. 1–6 (2019)
2. Li, H., Zhang, Q., Zhao, D.: Deep reinforcement learning-based automatic exploration for navigation in unknown environment. IEEE Trans. Neural Netw. Learn. Syst. **31**(6), 2064–2076 (2020)
3. Chang, M.-F., Lambert, J., Sangkloy, P., et al.: Argoverse: 3d tracking and forecasting with rich maps. In: 2019 IEEE/CVF Conference on Computer Vision and Pattern Recognition (CVPR), pp. 8740–8749 (2019)
4. Gao, J., Sun, C., Zhao, H., et al.: VectorNet: encoding HD maps and agent dynamics from vectorized representation. In: 2020 IEEE/CVF Conference on Computer Vision and Pattern Recognition (CVPR), pp. 11525–11533 (2020)
5. Phan-Minh, T., Grigore, E.C., Boulton, F.A., et al.: CoverNet: multimodal behavior prediction using trajectory sets. In: 2020 IEEE Conference on Computer Vision and Pattern Recognition (CVPR), pp. 14074–14083 (2020)
6. Chai, Y., Sapp, B., Bansal, M., Anguelov, D.: MultiPath: multiple probabilistic anchor trajectory hypotheses for behavior prediction. In: Conference on Robot Learning (CoRL) (2019)
7. Song, H., Luan, D., Ding, W., et al.: Learning to predict vehicle trajectories with model-based planning. In: Conference on Robot Learning (CoRL) (2021)
8. Zhao, H., Gao, J., Lan, T., et al.: TNT: Target-driveN trajectory prediction. In: Conference on Robot Learning (CoRL) (2020)
9. Suo, S., Regalado, S., Casas, S., Urtasun, R.: Trafficsim: learning to simulate realistic multi-agent behaviors. In: Proceedings of the IEEE/CVF Conference on Computer Vision and Pattern Recognition (CVPR), pp. 10400–10409 (2021)
10. Suo, S., Regalado, S., Casas, S., Urtasun, R.: TrafficSim: learning to simulate realistic multi-agent behaviors. In: 2021 IEEE/CVF Conference on Computer Vision and Pattern Recognition (CVPR), pp. 10400–10409 (2021)
11. Liu, Y., Zhang, J., Fang, L., et al.: multimodal motion prediction with stacked transformers. In: 2021 IEEE/CVF Conference on Computer Vision and Pattern Recognition (CVPR), pp. 7577–7586 (2021)
12. Chaochen, Z., Zhang, Q., Li, D., et al.: Vehicle trajectory prediction based on graph attention network. In: 2021 International Conference on Cognitive Systems and Information Processing (ICCSIP) (2021)
13. Bansal, M., Krizhevsky, A., Ogale, A.: ChauffeurNet: Learning to Drive by Imitating the Best and Synthesizing the Worst. arXiv preprint arXiv:1812.03079 (2018)
14. Cui, H., Radosavljevic, V., Chou, F.-C., et al.: Multimodal trajectory predictions for autonomous driving using deep convolutional networks. In: 2019 International Conference on Robotics and Automation (ICRA), pp. 2090–2096 (2019)
15. Khandelwal, S., Qi, W., Singh, J., Hartnett, A., Ramanan, D.: What-if motion prediction for autonomous driving. arXiv preprint arXiv:2008.10587 (2020)
16. Ngiam, J., Caine, B., Vasudevan, V., et al.: Scene Transformer: A unified architecture for predicting multiple agent trajectories. arXiv preprint arXiv:2106.08417 (2021)
17. Wang, J., Zhang, Q., Zhao, D.: Highway lane change decision-making via attention-based deep reinforcement learning. IEEE/CAA J. Autom. Sinica. **9**, 1–7 (2022)

18. Lei Ba, J., Kiros, J.R., Hinton, G.E.: Layer Normalization. arXiv e-prints. arXiv:1607.06450, July 2016
19. Williams, R.J., Zipser, D.: A learning algorithm for continually running fully recurrent neural networks. Neural Comput. **1**(2), 270–280 (1989)
20. Kingma, D.P., Ba, J.: Adam: a method for Stochastic Optimization. In: 3rd International Conference for Learning Representations (ICLR) (2015)

Multi-Cause Learning for Diagnosis Prediction

Liping Wang[1,2], Qiang Liu[1,2], Huanhuan Ma[1,2], Shu Wu[1,2(✉)], and Liang Wang[1,2]

[1] Center for Research on Intelligent Perception and Computing, Institute of Automation, Chinese Academy of Sciences, Beijing, China
wangliping2019@ia.ac.cn, {qiang.liu,shu.wu,wangliang}@nlpr.ia.ac.cn, huanhuan.ma@cripac.ia.ac.cn

[2] School of Artificial Intelligence, University of Chinese Academy of Sciences, Beijing, China

Abstract. Recently, Electronic Health Records (EHR) have become valuable for enhancing diagnosis prediction. Despite the effectiveness of existing deep learning based methods, one unified embedding fails to capture multiple disease causes of a patient. Even though naive adoption of multi-head attention could produce multiple cause vectors, a strong correlation between these cause representations might mislead the model to learning statistical spurious dependencies between cause vectors and diagnosis predictions. Hence, in this work, we propose a novel **Multi**-Cause Learning framework for **Diag**nosis Prediction, named **MulDiag**. Our Multi-Cause Network extracts multiple cause representations for a patient. We introduce HSIC (Hilbert-Schmidt Independence Criterion) to measure the dependencies among each pair of cause representations. Further, sample re-weighting techniques are utilized to conduct cause decorrelation. Experimental results on a publicly available dataset demonstrate the effectiveness of our method.

Keywords: Diagnosis prediction · Multi-cause · Decorrelation · Statistical dependency

1 Introduction

Recently, Electronic Health Records (EHR) have become valuable for enhancing medical decision making. EHR data are represented as a temporal sequence of visits, where each visit includes multiple medical codes, representing clinical diagnoses. One critical task is to predict future diagnoses based on historical EHR data of a patient, so as to intervene in advance, i.e., diagnosis prediction.

Meanwhile, deep learning models have achieved great success in various domains [7,8,20]. A lot of deep learning based methods have also been proposed to model sequential EHR data. Similar to word embedding [17], each diagnosis is parameterized by a real-valued vector. Recurrent neural networks [8] are adopted to model temporal correlation among EHR sequence data. With a patient's

Y. Tan and Y. Shi (Eds.): DMBD 2022, CCIS 1744, pp. 320–332, 2022.
https://doi.org/10.1007/978-981-19-9297-1_23

historical EHR data, these deep learning based methods usually generate an overall embedding as patient health status representation.

Despite the effectiveness of these deep learning based approaches, there remain some challenges demanding further exploration. A primary challenge is that it is hard for a unified embedding to reflect different aspects of disease progression. Take an old man as an instance, he may suffer from multiple diseases: diabetes and heart disease. Diagnoses of these two kinds of diseases appear during the historical EHR data. Information of different diseases is fused in the unified patient representation which produces difficulties for accurate predictions. Hence, we propose a multi-cause network to capture multiple disease causes of a patient.

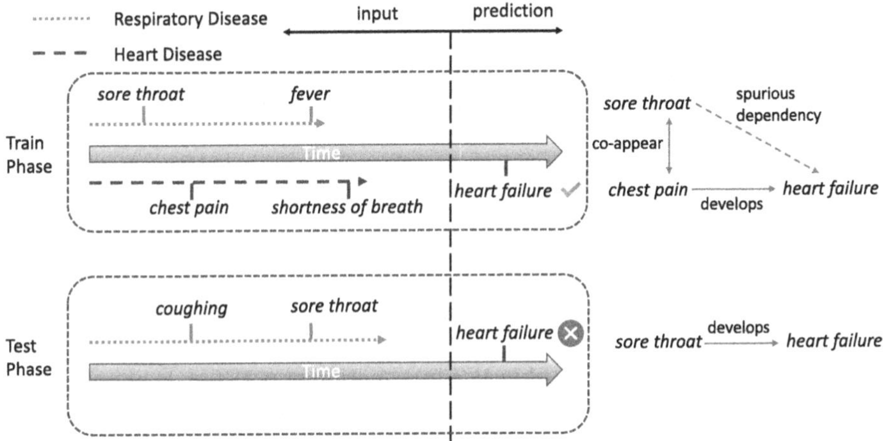

Fig. 1. Since the training dataset is collected in flu season, typical diagnoses of respiratory (*fever, sore throat*) and heart disease (*chest pain*) tend to appear at the same time. Hence, it is possible for the model to learn a spurious dependency between *sore throat* and *heart failure*. Then, in the test phase, the model may make predictions of heart failure according to *sore throat* symptoms.

Some existing methods [2] attempt to adopt multi-head attention mechanisms to capture different aspects of disease progression. However, the performance improvement is limited for two reasons. First of all, without proper regularization, it is hard to obtain a model which can produce diverse cause vectors. Instead, the obtained cause representations will be highly correlated which limits the capability of those methods. Further, the strong statistical correlation may mislead models to learn a statistical spurious dependency between diagnosis prediction and disease cause representation. As a result, when data distribution shifts, the learned statistical spurious dependency may generate false predictions. For instance, as illustrated in Fig. 1, during flu season, typical symptoms of respiratory (for example, cold) and heart disease tend to co-appear in some old patients. If a model which attempts to capture multiple disease causes is trained on these data, diagnoses of respiratory (*sore throat*) and heart disease (*heart failure*) would be statistically correlated. This kind of spurious dependency would result in false predictions of *heart failure* if symptom *sore throat* appears in historical visits.

To tackle the above two challenges, we propose a novel **Mul**ti-Cause Learning framework for **Diag**nosis Prediction, named **MulDiag**. With regard to the first challenge, we propose to represent one patient with multiple vectors through a multi-cause network. As for the second challenge, we introduce the Hilbert-Schmidt Independence Criterion (HSIC) to measure the degree of independence among captured disease causes. Inspired by sample re-weighting techniques [10, 25], the cause correlation regularizer aims to estimate a sample weight for each sample such that captured causes are decorrelated on the reweighted training data. These two modules are jointly optimized in our method.

The main contributions of this work are summarized as follows:

- We propose a multi-cause network to capture different causes of a patient.
- We introduce the Hilbert-Schmidt Independence Criterion (HSIC) to measure dependencies among captured causes.
- We adopt re-weighting techniques to conduct cause decorrelation for diagnosis prediction.

2 Related Work

2.1 Diagnosis Prediction

EHR data contain rich historical health information of patients. Building powerful health risk prediction models based on EHR data paves the way for personalized health care applications. Recently, deep learning techniques, including Convolutional Neural Networks (CNNs) and Recurrent Neural Networks (RNNs), have achieved great success in various applications among multiple domains, including health risk prediction and diagnosis prediction based on EHR data. In viewing that EHR data exist in temporal sequential form, it is natural to adopt RNNs or LSTMs to model disease progression in the time dimension. In comparison, CNNs are adopted to capture local dependence in EHR data.

In Dipole [14], bidirectional recurrent neural networks are employed to remember all the information of both the past visits and the future visits, and three attention mechanisms are introduced to measure the influence of different visits for the prediction. RETAIN [2] develops a reverse time attention model for EHR data which achieves high accuracy while remaining clinically interpretable. Its two-level neural attention detects influential past visits and significant clinical variables within those visits (e.g. key diagnoses). Some works try to model disease progression by taking time intervals into consideration. For example, StageNet [5] integrates inter-visit time information into LSTM cell states to capture the stage variation of patients' health conditions.

Another line of work proposes to incorporate existing medical knowledge into diagnosis prediction. For example, GRAM [3] infuses information from a medical ontology DAG (Directed acyclic graph) [19] into deep learning models via neural attention. GRAM can learn accurate and interpretable representations for medical concepts and show significant improvement in the prediction performance, especially on low-frequency diseases and small datasets. HAP [23] adopts the same medical ontology DAG with GRAM [3], but hierarchically propagates attention across the entire ontology structure with two rounds of knowledge propagation. Nevertheless, in both GRAM and HAP, medical ontology information is only used when learning code representations. Hence, Ma et al. [15] propose KAME which directly exploits medical knowledge in the whole prediction process, i.e. learning code representations, generating visit embeddings and making predictions. KnowRisk [24] and DG-RNN [22] incorporate a more powerful and larger scale knowledge graph KnowLife [4][1] to enrich the information extracted from insufficient inputs and guide the prediction. And they propose sophisticated knowledge graph attention to obtain the latent information from embeddings of the input events in the knowledge graph.

2.2 Stable Learning

In order to tackle the problem of statistical spurious dependency, researchers propose a stable learning framework. The framework usually consists of two steps: learning weights of training samples and training based on weighted data. To be more specific, sample weights are learned to reduce the correlation between features that could be measured by HSIC [6] or similar metrics. Under this framework, a lot of decorrelation methods [10,18] have been proposed to train linear stable models using re-weighted samples. Then, various deep stable models are also proposed. For instance, StableNet [25] proposes to remove dependencies between features by adopting sample weighting based on RFF (Random Fourier Features). OOD-GNN [12] designs a novel nonlinear graph representation decorrelation method.

For the diagnosis prediction task, Luo et al. [13] propose to use a causal representation learning method called Causal Healthcare Embedding (CHE) which aims at eliminating the spurious statistical relationship by removing the dependencies between diagnoses and procedures. In comparison, we propose MulDiag to eliminate spurious dependencies between different disease causes.

3 Preliminary

In this section, we mainly provide some background knowledge about EHR data and formulate the diagnosis prediction task.

3.1 Electronic Health Records

Electronic Health Records (EHR) is a special kind of data that consists of the medical history of a patient. For each visit to the hospital of a specific patient,

[1] http://knowlife.mpi-inf.mpg.de/.

the diagnoses are recorded as medical codes in a pre-defined system such as ICD[2] (International Classification of Diseases) or CUI[3] (Concept Unique Identifiers).

3.2 Basic Notations

In this paper, all the unique medical codes from EHR data are denoted as $\mathbf{c}_1, \mathbf{c}_2, \ldots, \mathbf{c}_{|C|} \in C$. For a specific patient, the EHR data are denoted as $V = \{v_1, v_2, \ldots, v_t\}$. Visit v_t is a subset of C, representing medical codes appearing in the t-th visit. For the convenience of calculation, v_t can also be represented as a $|C|$-length multi-hot vector $\mathbf{x}_t \in \{0,1\}^{|C|}$, where each element is zero or one, representing each medical code appears or not respectively. By stacking those multi-hot vectors, we reach a 0–1 valued matrix $\mathbf{X} \in \{0,1\}^{t \times |C|}$ to represent the EHR data.

3.3 Diagnosis Prediction Task

Diagnosis prediction is one of the most important tasks in the health care area which aims to predict potential diagnoses according to historical EHR data. Here, we give the formulation based on the notations provided above. For a specific patient, denote his or her EHR data for t consecutive visits as $\mathbf{X} \in \{0,1\}^{t \times |C|}$, the goal is to tell which diagnosis is likely to appear in the next visit, i.e. the value of $\mathbf{x}_{t+1}$.

4 Methodology

In Fig. 2, we provide an overview of the proposed MulDiag. In the following, we will describe each sub-module and optimization in detail.

4.1 Multi-Cause Network

In MulDiag, we employ a parameter embedding matrix $\mathbf{E} \in \mathbb{R}^{|C| \times d}$, where each row encodes a medical code. Given t-th visit code $\mathbf{x}_t$, we can obtain the vector representation for t-th visit as follows:

$$\mathbf{v}_t = \mathbf{E}\mathbf{x}_t. \tag{1}$$

Inspired by deep multi-interest recommendation models [1,11], we devise a Multi-Cause Network to generate multiple representations to reflect the disease causes of patients. In previous studies, the attention mechanism has shown strong capability in exploiting temporal EHR visit data. Hence, in this work, we adopt a similar temporal attention mechanism. First, visit embeddings $\mathbf{v}_1, \mathbf{v}_2, \ldots, \mathbf{v}_t$ are fed into an RNN to encode historical visits information into state vectors:

$$\mathbf{g}_1, \mathbf{g}_2, \ldots, \mathbf{g}_t = \mathrm{RNN}(\mathbf{v}_1, \mathbf{v}_2, \ldots, \mathbf{v}_t). \tag{2}$$

[2] https://www.cdc.gov/nchs/icd/icd9.htm.

[3] https://www.nlm.nih.gov/research/umls/new_users/online_learning/Meta_005.

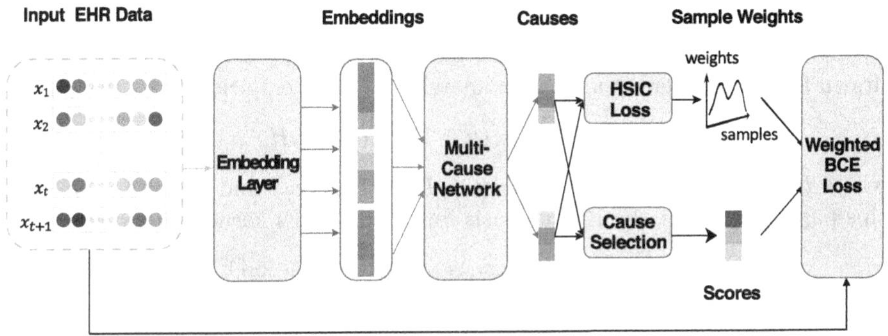

Fig. 2. The overview of the proposed MulDiag. The Embedding Layer first converts visits consisting of medical codes into dense embeddings. Then, Multi-Cause Network extracts multiple cause vectors given visit embeddings. Empirical HSIC statistics is calculated between each pair of cause representations and are optimized through sample weighting. Weighted BCE loss is adopted to optimize model parameters.

Then, based on these state vectors, attention coefficients are given by

$$\alpha_1, \alpha_2, \ldots \alpha_t = \mathrm{softmax}(a_1, a_2, \ldots, a_t), \tag{3}$$

in which $\alpha_i = \mathbf{w}_a^T \mathbf{g}_i + b$. Finally, we can obtain cause vector representations as follows:

$$\mathbf{c} = \sum_{i=1}^{t} \alpha_i \mathbf{v}_i. \tag{4}$$

We adopt the multi-head attention mechanism (for the sake of brevity, we omit the subscript in the previous text), so there are multiple cause vectors, i.e. $\mathbf{c}_1, \mathbf{c}_2, \ldots, \mathbf{c}_m$.

4.2 Cause Decorrelation

To decorrelate cause representations, we first need to measure the degree of dependence between each pair of cause representation vectors. Cause representations $\mathbf{c}_1, \mathbf{c}_2, \ldots, \mathbf{c}_m$ are samples of a high-dimensional distribution. In this paper, we introduce HSIC to reflect dependence among each pair of cause representations. HSIC is the Hilbert-Schmidt norm of the cross-covariance operator between distributions in Reproducing Kernel Hilbert Space (RKHS). Let $\mathbf{x}, \mathbf{y}$ be random vector variables, and they follow distribution $p_{\mathbf{xy}}$, HSIC is given by

$$\begin{aligned}\mathrm{HSIC}\left(p_{\mathbf{XY}}, \mathbf{x}, \mathbf{y}\right) = & \mathrm{E}_{\mathbf{x}_1, \mathbf{x}_2, \mathbf{y}_1, \mathbf{y}_2}\left[k\left(\mathbf{x}_1, \mathbf{x}_2\right) l\left(\mathbf{y}_1, \mathbf{y}_2\right)\right] + \mathrm{E}_{\mathbf{x}_1, \mathbf{x}_2}\left[k\left(\mathbf{x}_1, \mathbf{x}_2\right)\right] \\ & \cdot \mathrm{E}_{\mathbf{y}_1, \mathbf{y}_2}\left[l\left(\mathbf{y}_1, \mathbf{y}_2\right)\right] - 2\mathrm{E}_{\mathbf{x}_1, \mathbf{y}_1}\left[\mathrm{E}_{\mathbf{x}_2}\left[k\left(\mathbf{x}_1, \mathbf{x}_2\right)\right] \mathrm{E}_{\mathbf{y}_2}\left[l\left(\mathbf{y}_1, \mathbf{y}_2\right)\right]\right],\end{aligned} \tag{5}$$

in which $k(\cdot, \cdot)$ and $l(\cdot, \cdot)$ are kernel functions.

However, the definition of HSIC in Eq. 5 is only theoretically valuable. Luckily, given a series of n independent samples $Z := \{(\mathbf{x}_1, \mathbf{y}_1), \ldots, (\mathbf{x}_n, \mathbf{y}_n)\} \subset \mathcal{X} \times \mathcal{Y}$ drawn from $p_{\mathbf{xy}}$, there is an approximately unbiased empirical statistics [6]:

$$\mathrm{HSIC}(Z) = (n-1)^{-2} \operatorname{tr} KHLH, \tag{6}$$

where $H, K, L \in \mathbb{R}^{n \times n}$, $K_{ij} = k(\mathbf{x}_i, \mathbf{x}_j)$, $L_{ij} = l(\mathbf{y}_i, \mathbf{y}_j)$ and $H_{ij} = \delta_{ij} - n^{-1}$. In this paper, we adopt the Radial Basis Function (RBF) kernel functions, i.e.

$$k(\mathbf{x}_1, \mathbf{x}_2) = l(\mathbf{x}_1, \mathbf{x}_2) = \exp\left(-\frac{\|\mathbf{x}_1 - \mathbf{x}_2\|_2^2}{\sigma^2}.\right) \tag{7}$$

Algorithm 1: Training of MulDiag

Input: Training dataset
Parameters: $\boldsymbol{\Theta}, \mathbf{w}$
Initialize sample weights $\mathbf{w} \leftarrow \mathbf{1}$
Randomly initialize model parameters $\boldsymbol{\Theta}$
for $q \leftarrow 1$ **to** *max_epoch* **do**
  Keep $\mathbf{w}^{(q-1)}$ fixed and update parameters $\boldsymbol{\Theta}^{(q)}$ according to Eq. 10
  Keep $\boldsymbol{\Theta}^{(q)}$ fixed and update sample weights $\mathbf{w}^{(q)}$ according to Eq. 12
  if *early stopping condition reaches* **then**
    return $f_{\boldsymbol{\Theta}^{(q)}}$
  end
end

Inspired by sample re-weighting techniques, we propose a cause decorrelation framework that aims to estimate a weight for each sample. In this manner, cause representations for re-weighted data are decorrelated. We denote $\mathbf{w} \in \mathbb{R}^n$ as the sample weights, where n is the number of samples. Before training, $\mathbf{w}$ is initialized as $[1, 1, \ldots, 1]$. During training, sample weights $\mathbf{w}$ and model parameters are alternatively optimized as shown in Algorithm 1.

Model Optimization. During the optimization of model parameters, sample weights $\mathbf{w}$ is fixed. Given the k-th training sample $\mathbf{X}_k = (\mathbf{x}_1, \mathbf{x}_2, \ldots, \mathbf{x}_t, \mathbf{x}_{t+1})$, for target medical code i, cause selection is conducted by choosing a cause representation that is closest to the embedding vector $\mathbf{E}_i$:

$$\hat{s}_i = \max \mathbf{c}_j^T \mathbf{E}_i. \tag{8}$$

The normalized prediction score for i-th medical code will be $s_i = \frac{\exp(\hat{s}_i)}{\sum_j \exp(\hat{s}_j)}$. Hence, the BCE (Binary Cross Entropy) loss function for the k-th training sample would be

$$\mathcal{L}(\mathbf{X}_k) = -\sum_{i=1}^{|C|} s_i \log(\mathbf{x}_{t+1}[i]) + (1 - s_i) \log(1 - \mathbf{x}_{t+1}[i]). \tag{9}$$

Model parameters $\mathbf{\Theta}$ is updated through the weighted BCE loss:

$$\mathbf{\Theta} \leftarrow \operatorname{argmin} \sum_{k} \mathbf{w}_k \mathcal{L}(\mathbf{X}_k) \tag{10}$$

Weight Optimization. To obtain decorrelated cause representations, MulDiag finds optimal sample weights by minimizing the empirical HSIC statistics between each pair of weighted cause vectors. Formally, given a batch of B samples, let $\mathbf{c}_i^{(b)}$ be the i-th cause vector of the b-th sample and $\mathbf{w}(b)$ be the sample weight for the b-th sample, Then, the HSIC loss would be

$$\text{HSIC loss} = \sum_{i} \sum_{j} \text{HSIC}(\{(\mathbf{w}(1)\mathbf{c}_i^{(1)}, \mathbf{w}(1)\mathbf{c}_j^{(1)}), \ldots, (\mathbf{w}(B)\mathbf{c}_i^{(B)}, \mathbf{w}(B)\mathbf{c}_j^{(B)})\}), \tag{11}$$

where HSIC is defined in Eq. 6. With model parameters $\mathbf{\Theta}$ fixed, sample weights $\mathbf{w}$ is updated as:

$$\mathbf{w} \leftarrow \operatorname*{argmin}_{\mathbf{w}} \text{HSIC loss}. \tag{12}$$

4.3 Complexity Analysis and Model Comparison

In this subsection, we analyze the complexity of MulDiag and compare it with mainstream diagnosis prediction models.

For MulDiag, it takes $O(nmdLK)$ to obtain m cause vectors for n samples, in which d is embedding size, L is the average length of visit data and K is the average number of diagnoses appearing in one visit. Cause decorrelation process takes $O(Bnd)$ to compute the HSIC statistics in which B is the batchsize.

For mainstream diagnosis prediction models such as RETAIN and StageNet, computation complexity is usually $O(ndLK)$. Therefore, MulDiag is as asymptotically efficient as mainstream diagnosis prediction methods.

5 Experiments

In this section, we first provide details of experimental settings. Then, we discuss the experimental results of MulDiag and compare them with baseline methods. In addition, we also provide visualization and sensitivity analysis.

5.1 Experimental Setup

Dataset. In this paper, we conduct extensive experiments on a real-world EHR dataset MIMIC-III which includes 7,537 patients' health records from ICU. In the training phase, part of historical diagnoses are employed as an input of our model while future diagnoses serve as supervision signals. Similarly, in the test phase, diagnoses appearing later than those in the training set are adopted to compute the accuracy and precision of our model.

Baselines. To validate the effectiveness of the proposed MulDiag, we choose four competitive baseline models: LSTM, RETAIN [2], RAIM [21], StageNet [5].

LSTM: We adopt the same embedding method as Dipole [14]. Then, the embeddings of each visit are fed into an LSTM [8] layer. After that, all hidden states are added together to obtain a final feature vector. In the end, a linear classifier is employed to reach final predictions.

RETAIN: RETAIN is a competitive prediction model that adopts a two-level neural attention model that detects influential past visits and significant clinical variables with those visits.

RAIM: RAIM introduces an efficient attention mechanism for continuous monitoring data, which is guided by discrete clinical events. With guided multi-channel attention, high-density multi-channel signals are integrated with discrete events and prove very useful in risk prediction.

StageNet: StageNet is constituted of a stage-aware long-short-term memory (LSTM) module extracting health stage variations with no supervision and a stage-adaptive convolutional module that incorporates stage-related progression patterns.

Evaluation Metric. Following previous works [3,15], we adopt two metrics to measure the performance of all methods for the diagnosis prediction task, i.e. visit-level precision@k and code-level accuracy@k. In addition, we sort the medical codes by their frequencies in the training dataset in non-decreasing order, and then divide them into five different groups. We report code-level accuracy in each group to reflect the prediction performance for codes with varying frequencies.

Implementation Details. In this paper, all the baselines and our models are implemented with PyTorch[4] [16]. The dataset is randomly divided into training, validation and testing sets in a 0.7:0.1:0.2 ratio. Embedding size d is set to 64 for all approaches. The same dropout strategy with a 0.5 drop rate is applied to all the methods. All methods are trained with Adam optimizer [9] with a mini-batch of 128 samples. The learning rate is fixed at 0.001 for all methods.

5.2 Performance Comparison

Comparison results at both visit and code levels are reported in Table 1, in which, precision and accuracy for different values of k are included. From the table, we can observe that MulDiag outperforms all the baseline methods. In Table 2, in addition to the overall performance in code-level accuracy, we also report the results for each group which are obtained by dividing the medical codes according to the percentile of their frequencies in the training dataset. For example, 0–20 are the rarest diagnoses while 80–100 represent the most common ones. From the table, we can tell that in addition to the overall performance improvement,

[4] https://pytorch.org/.

Table 1. Visit level Precision@k and code level Accuray@k comparison on MIMIC-III. Average results for multiple values of k are also included.

Model	Visit level Precision@k						Code level Accuracy@k					
	10	15	20	25	30	Avg.	10	15	20	25	30	Avg.
LSTM	34.49	34.10	36.23	38.84	41.57	37.05	22.40	27.98	32.29	35.77	38.80	31.45
RETAIN	**39.22**	38.36	40.06	42.72	45.51	41.17	25.48	31.44	35.86	39.53	42.55	34.97
RAIM	23.49	23.50	25.31	28.17	30.75	26.24	15.93	20.27	24.15	27.61	30.55	23.70
StageNet	36.69	36.57	38.95	41.89	44.85	39.79	23.82	29.85	34.69	38.48	41.77	33.72
MulDiag	39.16	**38.77**	**40.93**	**43.71**	**46.47**	**41.81**	**25.49**	**31.73**	**36.55**	**40.27**	**43.40**	**35.49**

Table 2. Code-level accuracy@20. Diagnosis codes are divided into five groups according to their frequencies in the training set. For example, 0–20 are the rarest diagnoses.

Model	Code-level accuracy					
	0–20	20–40	40–60	60–80	80–100	Overall
LSTM	2.49	12.10	19.08	47.07	81.31	32.29
RETAIN	3.02	17.17	25.64	**51.31**	82.38	35.86
RAIM	0.00	0.00	0.00	26.56	**96.87**	24.15
StageNet	3.51	16.39	23.85	47.75	82.43	34.69
MulDiag	**5.80**	**20.53**	**28.26**	49.16	79.18	**36.55**

MulDiag achieves significant improvement in the prediction of rare diagnoses. In comparison, baseline models perform poorly for those infrequent diagnoses (Fig. 3).

5.3 Visualization Analysis

For an easier understanding of weight optimization, we visualize the change of HSIC on the test set while MulDiag and MulDiag-NWO are training on the MIMIC-III dataset. Compared with MulDiag, MulDiag-NWO is almost the same except that there is no sample weight optimization (i.e. each sample weight is 1). Since the parameters of models are initialized randomly, HSIC is near 0 at earlier epochs for both MulDiag and MulDiag-NWO. Then, the HSIC begins to decrease. After some epochs, the HSIC of MulDiag-NWO on the test set remains unchanged while the HSIC of MulDiag keeps decreasing. This makes it possible for our MulDiag to update more steps and achieve better performance.

5.4 Sensitivity Analysis

We also provide the experimental results for the sensitivity analysis of the number of causes. As Fig. 4 illustrates, the number of causes does not impact the performance very much. Cause decorrelation of MulDiag is capable of boosting the performance for various values of the number of causes.

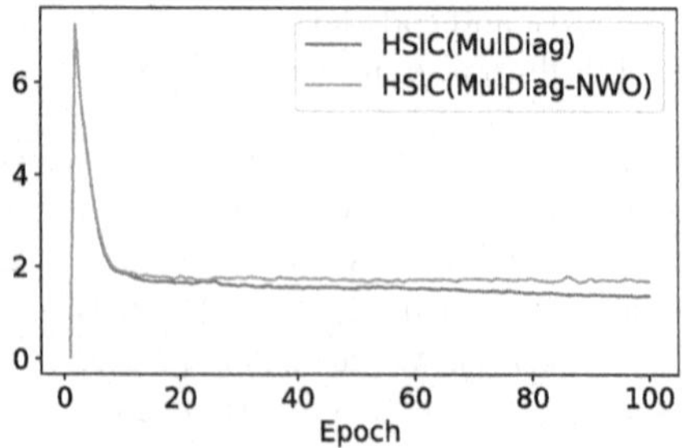

Fig. 3. The change of HSIC on the test set when MulDiag and MulDiag-NWO are trained on MIMIC-III.

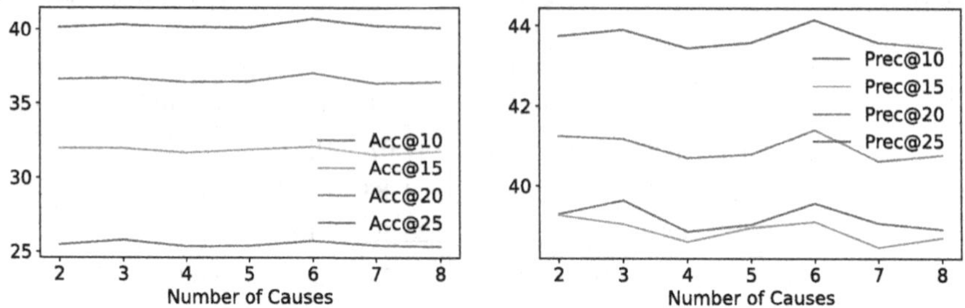

Fig. 4. Accuracy and precision of MulDiag with the number of causes varying from 2 to 8.

6 Conclusion

In this paper, we propose MulDiag which aims to capture multiple causes of diseases. To avoid learning statistical spurious dependency between cause representations and diagnosis predictions, we first introduce HSIC to measure the degree of independence among cause vectors. Then, re-weighting techniques are adopted to implement dependency decorrelation. Extensive experiments on the publicly available benchmark dataset demonstrate the effectiveness of our model.

References

1. Cen, Y., Zhang, J., Zou, X., Zhou, C., Yang, H., Tang, J.: Controllable multi-interest framework for recommendation. In: Proceedings of the 26th ACM SIGKDD International Conference on Knowledge Discovery & Data Mining (2020)
2. Choi, E., Bahadori, M.T., Kulas, J.A., Schuetz, A., Stewart, W.F., Sun, J.: Retain: an interpretable predictive model for healthcare using reverse time attention mechanism. In: Proceedings of the 30th International Conference on Neural Information Processing Systems (2016)
3. Choi, E., Bahadori, M.T., Song, L., Stewart, W.F., Sun, J.: Gram: graph-based attention model for healthcare representation learning. In: Proceedings of the 23rd ACM SIGKDD International Conference on Knowledge Discovery and Data Mining (2017)

4. Ernst, P., Meng, C., Siu, A., Weikum, G.: KnowLife: a knowledge graph for health and life sciences. In: 2014 IEEE 30th International Conference on Data Engineering (2014)
5. Gao, J., Xiao, C., Wang, Y., Tang, W., Glass, L.M., Sun, J.: Stagenet: stage-aware neural networks for health risk prediction. In: Proceedings of The Web Conference 2020 (2020)
6. Gretton, A., Bousquet, O., Smola, A., Schölkopf, B.: Measuring statistical dependence with Hilbert-Schmidt norms. In: Algorithmic Learning Theory (2005)
7. He, K., Zhang, X., Ren, S., Sun, J.: Deep residual learning for image recognition. In: 2016 IEEE Conference on Computer Vision and Pattern Recognition (2016)
8. Hochreiter, S., Schmidhuber, J.: Long short-term memory. Neural Comput. **9**, 1735–1780 (1997)
9. Kingma, D.P., Ba, J.: Adam: a method for stochastic optimization. In: International Conference on Learning Representations (2015)
10. Kuang, K., Xiong, R., Cui, P., Athey, S., Li, B.: Stable prediction with model misspecification and agnostic distribution shift. In: Proceedings of the AAAI Conference on Artificial Intelligence (2020)
11. Li, C., et al.: Multi-interest network with dynamic routing for recommendation at TMALL. In: Proceedings of the 28th ACM International Conference on Information and Knowledge Management (2019)
12. Li, H., Wang, X., Zhang, Z., Zhu, W.: OOD-GNN: Out-of-distribution generalized graph neural network. arXiv preprint arXiv:2112.03806 (2021)
13. Luo, Y., Liu, Z., Liu, Q.: Deep stable representation learning on electronic health records. arXiv preprint arXiv:2209.01321 (2022)
14. Ma, F., Chitta, R., Zhou, J., You, Q., Sun, T., Gao, J.: Dipole: diagnosis prediction in healthcare via attention-based bidirectional recurrent neural networks. In: Proceedings of the 23rd ACM SIGKDD International Conference on Knowledge Discovery and Data Mining (2017)
15. Ma, F., You, Q., Xiao, H., Chitta, R., Zhou, J., Gao, J.: Kame: knowledge-based attention model for diagnosis prediction in healthcare. In: Proceedings of the 27th ACM International Conference on Information and Knowledge Management, pp. 743–752 (2018)
16. Paszke, A., et al.: Pytorch: an imperative style, high-performance deep learning library. In: Advances in Neural Information Processing Systems (2019)
17. Pennington, J., Socher, R., Manning, C.D.: Glove: global vectors for word representation. In: Empirical Methods in Natural Language Processing (EMNLP) (2014)
18. Shen, Z., Cui, P., Kuang, K., Li, B., Chen, P.: Causally regularized learning with agnostic data selection bias. In: Proceedings of the 26th ACM International Conference on Multimedia (2018)
19. Thulasiraman, K., Swamy, M.N.: Graphs: Theory and Algorithms. John Wiley & Sons, New York (2011)
20. Vaswani, A.,et al.: Attention is all you need. In: Proceedings of the 31st International Conference on Neural Information Processing Systems (2017)
21. Xu, Y., Biswal, S., Deshpande, S.R., Maher, K.O., Sun, J.: RAIM: recurrent attentive and intensive model of multimodal patient monitoring data. In: Proceedings of the 24th ACM SIGKDD international conference on Knowledge Discovery and Data Mining (2018)
22. Yin, C., Zhao, R., Qian, B., Lv, X., Zhang, P.: Domain knowledge guided deep learning with electronic health records. In: 2019 IEEE International Conference on Data Mining (2019)

23. Zhang, M., King, C.R., Avidan, M., Chen, Y.: Hierarchical attention propagation for healthcare representation learning. In: Proceedings of the 26th ACM SIGKDD International Conference on Knowledge Discovery & Data Mining (2020)
24. Zhang, X., Qian, B., Li, Y., Yin, C., Wang, X., Zheng, Q.: KnowRisk: an interpretable knowledge-guided model for disease risk prediction. In: 2019 IEEE International Conference on Data Mining (ICDM) (2019)
25. Zhang, X., Cui, P., Xu, R., Zhou, L., He, Y., Shen, Z.: Deep stable learning for out-of-distribution generalization. In: Proceedings of the IEEE/CVF Conference on Computer Vision and Pattern Recognition (2021)

Prediction of Postoperative Survival Level of Esophageal Cancer Patients Based on Kaplan-Meier (K-M) Survival Analysis and Gray Wolf Optimization (GsWO)-BP Model

Enhao Liang[1,2], Yanfeng Wang[2], Lidong Wang[3], Xueke Zhao[3], and Changkai Sun[1](✉)

[1] Liaoning Key Lab of IC & BME System, The School of Biomedical Engineering, Dalian University of Technology, No. 2 Linggong Street, Ganjingzi District, Dalian 116024, Liaoning, China
cksun110@vip.sina.com

[2] Henan Key Lab of Information-Based Electrical Appliances, School of Electrical and Information Engineering, Zhengzhou University of Light Industry, Zhengzhou 450002, China

[3] State Key Laboratory of Esophageal Cancer Prevention & Treatment and Henan Key Laboratory for Esophageal Cancer Research of the First Affiliated Hospital, Zhengzhou University, Zhengzhou 450052, China

Abstract. Esophageal squamous cell carcinoma (ESCC) is a global safety problem, especially the low 5-year survival rate of patients after surgery, and their healthy life after surgery is directly threatened. Kaplan-Meier (K-M) survival analysis is used to screen the blood indexes of patients with ESCC. The gray wolf algorithm (GWO) is introduced to optimize the weight threshold of back-propagation (BP) neural network, and a prediction model based on K-M-GWO-BP is established. According to the influencing factors of postoperative survival, the postoperative survival level of patients is predicted. K-M survival analysis is used to analyze the relevant risk factors, the redundant variables are eliminated, and the whole structure of the neural network is simplified. The initial weight of BP neural network is optimized by GWO. Conclusions: BP neural network model, PSO-BP, GA-BP, SSA-BP, GWO-BP, K-M-BP, K-M-PSO-BP, K-MGA-BP, K-M-SSA-BP and K-M-GWO-BP are compared, the prediction accuracy of K-M-GWO-BP neural network model is the best.

Keywords: Esophageal Squamous Cell Carcinoma (ESCC) · Kaplan-Meier (K-M) survival analysis · BP network · K-M-GWO-BP model

1 Introduction

Esophageal cancer was one of the most common malignant tumors of digestive system in the world. Global Cancer Epidemiology Statistics (GLOBOCAN2018) shown that there are 572000 new cases of esophageal cancer worldwide, and 509000 cases were expected to die of esophageal cancer in 2018 [1]. The number of new cases of esophageal cancer

Y. Tan and Y. Shi (Eds.): DMBD 2022, CCIS 1744, pp. 333–349, 2022.
https://doi.org/10.1007/978-981-19-9297-1_24

in China ranked first in the world, accounting for about 50% of the global incidence of esophageal cancer [2, 3]. It was one of the countries with the highest incidence of esophageal cancer in the world [4, 5]. In China, squamous cell carcinoma was the main pathological type of esophageal cancer (EC), accounting for more than 90%. Surgery was the first choice for patients with resectable EC. With the progress of medical and health technology, the development of minimally invasive concept and the development of (ERAS) concept of accelerated rehabilitation surgery, the long-term prognosis of patients has been significantly improved [6, 7]. There are more problems like this, just to name a few. Due to the complexity of EC surgery, more postoperative complications, and a high recurrence rate after surgical resection, the 5-year survival rate was about 40% [8, 9].

In fact, the survival rate of all patients with ESCC more than 5 years after operation is less than 20% [12]. According to the low accuracy of predicting the survival rate of cancer patients, recent studies have shown that a computer-aided classification method for lung cancer prediction based on evolutionary system has been proposed [13]. The work demonstrated that the proposed probabilistic genetic algorithm optimized neural network models, integrating with the t-SNE dimensionality reduction algorithm, achieved accurate prediction of patient survival [14]. The proposed GPU-based training of BP neural network was tested on a breast cancer data, which shown a significant enhancement in training speed [16]. BP neural network model [17, 18], genetic algorithm model [19, 20], support vector machine model [21], decision tree method [22]and time series method [23] were commonly used prediction methods at present. However, BP neural network had some defects such as local optimization, irrelevant to physical meaning, strong dependence on training data and slow convergence speed, which hindered its application in practical engineering [17, 19]. Strong macro search and global optimization capabilities were the characteristics of genetic algorithm (GA) [20]. The problem of local minimization of network could be solved to improve network performance. Therefore, GA was widely used to optimize BP neural network [19]. Due to the characteristics of multi-media and multi factors in the blood of esophageal cancer, it was difficult to determine the influencing factors which had the optimal correlation with the prediction indexes of the model. In the process of neural network modeling, it was time-consuming and difficult to optimize the neural network.

The GWO had the characteristics of simple implementation and fast convergence speed, which shows excellent results in standard test functions. At the same time, the research shows that the GWO algorithm was better than other intelligent optimization algorithms in some application fields, such as particle swarm optimization algorithm (PSO) and GA [19]. The objectives of this work are summarized as follows.

1) A K-M-BP neural network model is proposed. The purpose of the model is to reduce the dimension of data and improve the accuracy of BP neural network prediction model. K-M analysis is used to screen the blood factors with high correlation with the survival level of patients to simplify the network structure. BP neural network is applied to predict the survival level of patients with esophageal cancer. Case study and experimental results demonstrate that K-M-BP neural network model is more effective than BP neural network model in predicting the survival level of patients.

2) Based on the proposed framework, a K-M-GWO-BP is proposed by adopting GWO as the optimizer for evolving the BP. GWO is used to optimize the BP neural network trained model to improve the prediction accuracy. The proposed GWO-BP is tested on a set of benchmark functions to verify its effectiveness. The prediction accuracy and applicability of BP, GWO-BP and K-M-GWO-BP prediction models are constructed to explore a new way of survival level prediction. The experimental results show that the proposed K-M-GWO-BP neural network model is superior to some of the latest BP neural network models in terms of calculation speed and prediction accuracy.

In the rest of this article, the sources of the data are described in Sect. 2. Then, the proposed K-M and GWO and GWO-BP are given in Sect. 3. Afterwards, the experimental results are detailed in Sects. 4 and 5. Finally, conclusions are drawn and future work is outlined in Sect. 6.

2 Objects and Analysis

2.1 Collect Patient Samples

A total of 331 patients with ESCC were treated in the affiliated Hospital of Zhengzhou University from January 2007 to December 2018, including 210 males (63.44%) and 121 females (36.56%). Patients were concentrated at age of 38 to 80 years old with average age of 60.61 years old.

2.2 Experimental Data

The patient data included 17 blood indexes, such as WBC count (109/L), lymphocyte count (109/L), monocyte count (109/L), neutrophil count (109/L), eosinophil count (109/L), basophil count (109/L), red blood cell count (109/L), hemoglobin concentration (g/L), platelet count (109/L), total protein (g/L), white blood protein (g/L), globulin (g/L), PT (s), INR, APTT (s), TT (s), FIB (mg/dL).

Blood indicators were regarded as important factors in the clinical manifestations of cancer patients. The relationship between neutrophil to lymphocyte ratio (NLR), platelet to lymphocyte ratio (PLR) and lymphocyte to monocyte ratio (MLR) and the prognostic and clinicopathological significance in patients with ESCC have been reported by many studies. NLR, PLR and LMR might be served as prognostic markers in patients with ESCC [24, 25]. Peripheral blood cell count ratio was suggested to evaluate clinical response and prognosis of patients with non-surgical ESCC. Serum TT may be an important factor in prognosis of ESCC patients confirmed. Preoperative serum FIB was validated to verify survival of ESCC, especially for the early pathological TNM stage (I–II) and N0 patients. The nomogram combined with C-reactive protein (CRP)/ALB ratio could be used as a predictive model for the efficacy and survival outcome of thoracic ESCC treated with received chemo radiotherapy (CRT) or single radiotherapy (RT), which was found by zhang research.

3 Composite Model for Predicting Survival Level of Patients with EC

3.1 K-M Survival Analyze

K-M survival analysis is a method to analyze the result and process of an event. K-M considers not only the occurrence of the event, but also the duration of the event. Therefore, survival analysis is also called time to event analysis. Survival analysis is very common for the study of survival time of cancer and other diseases in the medical field [34, 35]. In order to analyze the influencing factors of survival time of EC patients, the blood indicators of patients are used as input and the survival time is used as output. The statistical software SPSS20.0 is used for K-M survival analysis. The accuracy of variable selection is determined by the size of correlation.

3.2 GWO Algorithm

GWO is a new intelligent optimization algorithm proposed in 2014. The population system and predation behavior of grey wolves are imitated by GWO. In the Fig. 1, the goal of optimization is achieved by simulating the hunting process of wolves. The wolf pack is composed of 5–12 wolves, which can be divided into 4 grades according to the fitness value. The wolf in the first layer of the pyramid is the leader wolf, which is expressed as α, and has the decision-making power on all major issues of the whole wolf pack. The wolf in the second layer is represented as β, which helps the leader wolf to make decisions. The wolf in the third layer is represented as δ, which is responsible for sentinel, reconnaissance and other tasks. The wolf at the bottom is denoted as ω, which is under the command of the first three levels of gray wolf. In the process of predation, α, β, δ wolves constantly change their positions to pursue prey, and the remaining gray wolf ω follows the first three, and the optimal solution is the specific location of prey. Due to the uncertainty of the location of gray wolf, the distance between each wolf and its prey is expressed as follows:

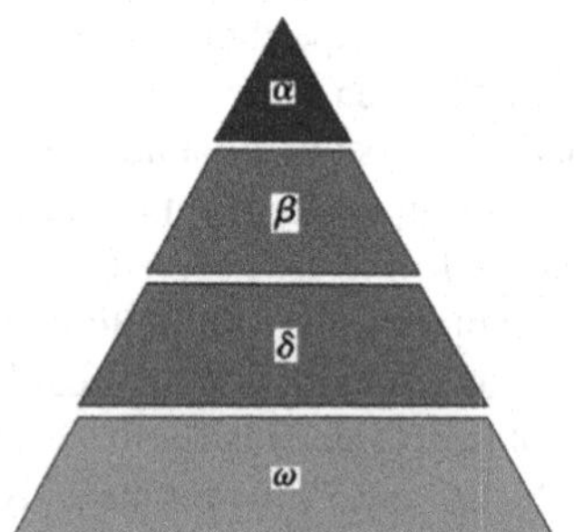

Fig. 1. Hierarchy of grey wolf

$$D(t) = |Cp(t) - X(t)| \tag{1}$$

The increasing number of iterations is represented by t. The prey of the t generation and the position of the wolf are expressed by $p(t)$ and $X(t)$, respectively. $C = 2r_1$, r_1 is a random number in [0,1]. The positions $X\alpha(0)$, $X\beta(0)$, $X\delta(0)$ and $Xw(0)$ of each gray wolf are randomly initialized. The location of the wolf is updated in formula.

$$\begin{cases} X(t+1) = p(t) - A(t)D(t) \\ A(t) = 2\alpha(t)r_2 - \alpha(t) \\ \alpha(t) = 2 - 2\frac{t}{\max} \end{cases} \tag{2}$$

r_2 is a random number at [0,1]. $a(t)$ is defined as the convergence factor. The custom maximum number of iterations is expressed as max. For the three wolves, there are the following mathematical descriptions:

$$\begin{cases} D_\alpha = |C_1 X_\alpha(t) - X(t)| \\ D_\beta = |C_2 X_\beta(t) - X(t)| \\ D_\delta = |C_3 X_\delta(t) - X(t)| \\ X_1 = X_\alpha - A_1 D_\alpha \\ X_2 = X_\beta - A_2 D_\beta \\ X_3 = X_\delta - A_3 D_\delta \end{cases} \tag{3}$$

The position of the next generation ω wolf is defined by Eq. (4).

$$X_\omega(t+1) = \frac{X_1 + X_2 + X_3}{3} \tag{4}$$

3.3 BP Neural Network Algorithm

(1) Determine the input layer, hidden layer and output layer

The number of nodes in the input layer, hidden layer and output layer of the network is expressed by l, m and n, respectively. α is a random number in the range of 1–10, in Fig. 2. The initial weight between input layer and hidden layer is determined by ω_{ij}, and that between hidden layer and output layer is determined by v_{jk}. The threshold of hidden layer is represented by a, $a = [a_1, a_2, \ldots, a_m]$. The threshold of the output layer is expressed by b, $b = [b_1, b_2, \ldots, b_n]$.

$$m = \sqrt{l+n} + \alpha \quad \alpha \in [1, 10] \tag{5}$$

(2) Calculate hidden layer output

$$h_j = f\left(\sum_{i=1}^{l} \omega_{ij} x_i - a_j\right) \tag{6}$$

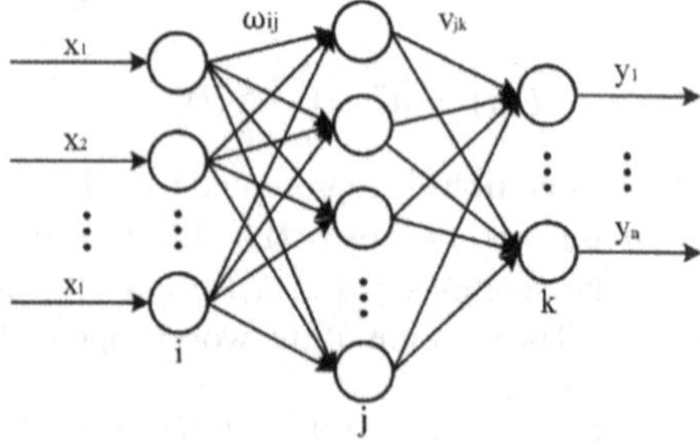

Fig. 2. Structure diagram of neural network

In formula (6), the output of the jth neuron in the hidden layer is h_j. x_i is the input of the i th neuron in the input layer. a_j is the jth threshold of the hidden layer.

(3) Calculate output of output layer

$$O_k = \sum_{j=1}^{m} h_j v_{jk} - b_k) \text{ k} = 1,2,\ldots.\text{n} \tag{7}$$

The kth threshold of the output layer is represented by b_k. The output of the output layer is O_k.

(4) Update connection layer weights.

The following objective functions are defined:

$$J = \frac{1}{2}\sum_{S=1}^{A}\sum_{k=1}^{n}(y_k^s - o_k^s)^2 \tag{8}$$

In Eq. (8), A is the number of training samples and n is the number of output nodes. y_k^s is the expected output of sample s; o_k^s is the output of the kth output node under the action of sample s.

The weight update function can be expressed as:

$$\omega_{ij}(t+1) = \omega_{ij}(t) + \mu[(1-\gamma)D(t) + \gamma D(t-1)] \tag{9}$$

$$v_{jk}(t+1) = v_{jk}(t) + \mu[(1-\gamma)E(t) + \gamma E(t-1)] \tag{10}$$

In Eq. (9) and Eq. (10), i = 1, 2, …, l, j = 1, 2, …, m, k = 1, 2, …, n. The learning efficiency is μ, and $\mu > 0$. The inertia coefficient is γ, and $0 \leq \gamma < 1$.

$$D(t) = -\frac{\partial J}{\partial \omega_{ij}(t)},\ E(t) = -\frac{\partial J}{\partial v_{jk}(t)}\circ$$

(5) Update threshold

$$\begin{cases} a_j(t+1) = a_j(t) + \mu h_j(1-h_j)\sum_{k=1}^{n} v_{jk}(y_k - o_k) \\ b_k(t+1) = b_k(t) + (y_k - o_k) \end{cases} \tag{11}$$

(6) Judge

Whether the algorithm reaches the maximum number of iterations is judged. If the maximum number of iterations is not reached, return to step (2). If the maximum number of iterations is reached, the network training ends.

3.4 GWO-BP Neural Network Algorithm

The convergence speed of BP neural network is slow and easy to fall into local minimum. Therefore, GWO algorithm is used to enhance the global search ability. As shown in Fig. 3, the gray wolf position is taken as the weight and threshold of BP neural network, and the gray wolf algorithm is iterated for many times. The location of prey is continuously judged and updated by gray wolf. The threshold and weight of BP neural network are constantly updated to calculate the global optimal result. The steps are as follows:

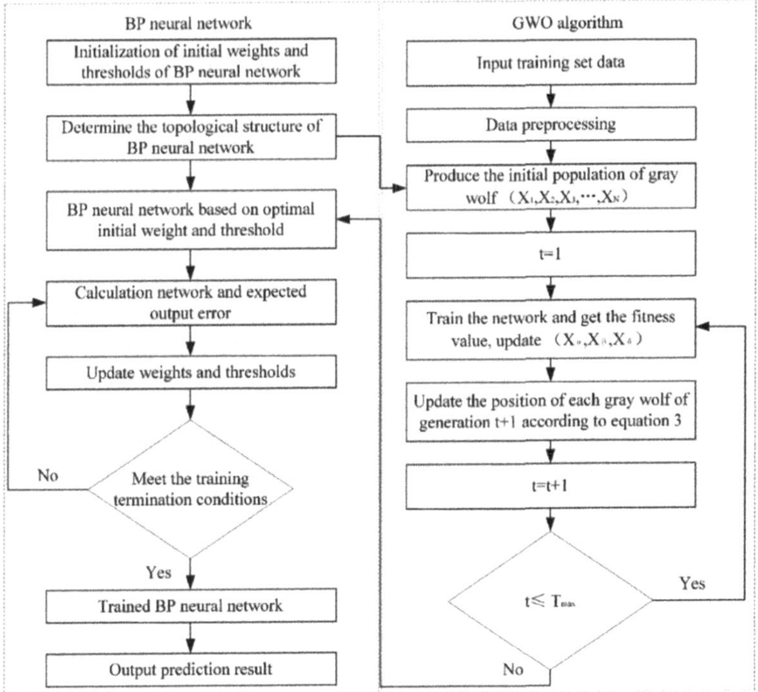

Fig. 3. Flow chart of GWO-BP neural network

Step 1: selecting appropriate training samples. The variables selected by K-M survival analysis are used as training input samples.

Step 2: the establishment of BP neural network model. The number of input layers is l. The number of output layers is n. The number of hidden layer neuron nodes m, as shown in formula (5). a is an arbitrary constant from 1 to 10. Therefore, after many experiments, it can be concluded that when a is 5, the convergence speed and fitting accuracy of the neural network model are the most suitable in the table.

Step 3: initialization of GWO optimization algorithm. The optimal positions X_α, X_β and X_δ are initialized.

Step 4: calculating individual fitness value. The weights and thresholds of BP neural network are set as the object of GWO algorithm. The error sum of each neural node of BP neural network is used as the fitness function of GWO optimization algorithm to measure the individual position, and the position of the current optimal fitness value is obtained.

$$F = \frac{1}{A}\sum_{S=1}^{A}\sqrt{\sum_{k=1}^{n}(y_k^s - o_k^s)^2} \tag{12}$$

Step 5: updating the parameters r_1, r_2, q in GWO. According to formula (1) and Eq. (2), the position of each wolf was updated, and a new BP neural network is constructed and trained. According to Eq. (12), the fitness function value of each wolf is calculated, and the new α, β, δ are determined again.

Step 6: determining the number of iterations. When the number of iterations reaches the upper limit, GWO optimization algorithm is finished, and the optimal initial weights and thresholds of BP neural network are obtained. If the number of iterations does not reach the upper limit, return to step (5).

Step 7: output of prediction results. BP neural network is trained and evaluated according to the weights and thresholds optimized by GWO optimization algorithm, and finally the prediction results are obtained.

In the process of building the network, Matlab simulation software is used to update the individual position in GWO optimization algorithm until the number of iterations reaches the set value. As shown in the Fig. 4, the optimal fitness value of GWO optimization algorithm before the number of iterations reaches 500. The optimal initial weights and thresholds of BP neural network are obtained by GWO optimization algorithm. When the number of iterations is 300, the optimal fitness value of GWO optimization algorithm before the number of iterations reaches 300. 300 iterations and 500 iterations are compared to calculate the speed and optimal value, and the optimal number of iterations 500 is obtained.

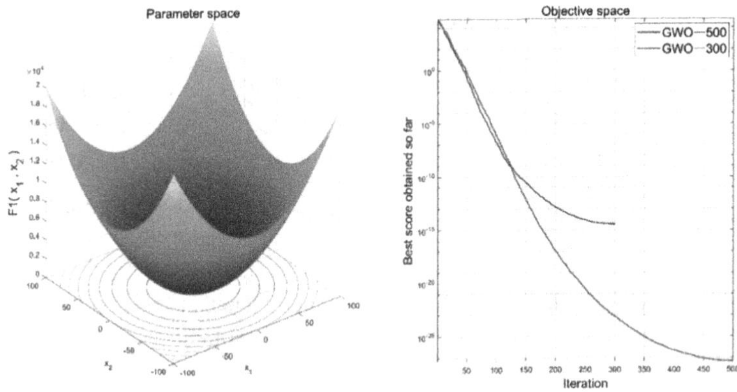

Fig. 4. Optimal fitness graphs for 300 and 500 iterations

4 Case Analysis

4.1 Selection of Input and Output Parameters

Table 1. Log rank test of K-M survival analysis

Variables	Chi square	Degrees of freedom	Sig
WBCC	315.765	86	**<0.001**
TLC	203.852	33	**<0.001**
MONO	32.085	15	0.006
NEUT	411.260	81	**<0.001**
EOS	174.795	9	**<0.001**
BOS	42.030	6	**<0.001**
RBC	412.880	151	**<0.001**
HGB	163.149	71	**<0.001**
PLT	756.434	191	**<0.001**
TP	59.369	37	0.011
ALB	41.551	29	0.062
GLB	37.363	27	0.088
PT	114.245	65	**<0.001**
INR	110.603	65	**<0.001**
APTT	578.811	188	**<0.001**
TT	135.878	77	**<0.001**
FIB	262.722	115	**<0.001**
LMR	416.955	107	**<0.001**

(continued)

Table 1. (*continued*)

Variables	Chi square	Degrees of freedom	Sig
NLR	1090.615	254	**<0.001**
PLR	1701.675	312	**<0.001**
PNI	254.672	61	**<0.001**

In the first step of prediction modeling, relevant data need to be obtained in Table 1. The input and output data in modeling are preprocessed to obtain accurate and applicable sample set. In view of the nonlinear complexity of the patient's blood system, K-M survival analysis is used to screen the input variables. The purpose of screening variables is related to survival level, and irrelevant variables are deleted. The significance of chi-square value is less than 0.05, and the two variables are significantly correlated. The degree of freedom refers to the number of variables whose values are not limited when calculating a unified measurement. Significance refers to the risk level of rejecting zero hypothesis when zero hypothesis is true, also known as probability level, or significance level.

4.2 Performance Test of GWO Algorithm

In order to verify the validity and generality of GWO, 23 benchmark tests are selected to test GWO algorithm. Among them, F1 and F2 are unimodal test functions, and F9, F11 and F13 are multi peak test functions, as shown in Table 2. Salp swarm algorithm (SSA), differential evolution (DE), particle swarm optimization (PSO), ant lion optimization (ALO), dragonfly algorithm (DA) and GWO are selected for comparative study. In order to make the algorithm fairer, the parameters of the five algorithms are set as follows. The population size is set to 30 and the cutoff iterations are set to 500. In SSA, c1 is between 0 and 2, c2 and c3 are random numbers between 0 and 1. In DE algorithm, the scale factor is set to 0.5 and the crossover constant is set to 0.2. In PSO algorithm, the maximum value of inertia weight is set to 0.9, and the minimum value is set to 0.4. The learning factor of PSO algorithm is set to ca = 2.5, cb = 0.5, and the maximum limit speed is set to 1. In ALO algorithm and DA the same dimension as GWO. The convergence accuracy and convergence rate of the algorithms are evaluated.

Table 2. Results of benchmark test function

Function		GWO	SSA	PSO	DE	ALO	DA
F_1	Ave	**1.69e−15**	4.51e−05	0.002195	0.010272	0.007754	8.208377
	Std	**1.54e−16**	3.43e−05	0.001589	0.022289	0.005202	5.867565
F_2	Ave	**1.30e−18**	0.041021	1.66e−04	0.019779	0.344763	0.485178
	Std	**2.38e−19**	0.114595	3.09e−04	0.040523	1.069088	0.626178
F_3	Ave	**5.37e−05**	9.344069	2.865525	0.012248	11.204666	17.469637

(*continued*)

Table 2. (*continued*)

Function		GWO	SSA	PSO	DE	ALO	DA
	Std	**2.36e−05**	6.754941	1.832225	0.027985	7.815729	16.309052
F_4	Ave	**8.94e−07**	5.601099	0.490286	0.306086	13.306136	16.960946
	Std	**1.96e−07**	2.719842	0.322861	0.169225	6.039672	8.004191
F_5	Ave	**0.076699**	**0.013783**	0.289451	0.525274	0.115306	2.742857
	Std	**0.208071**	**0.019954**	0.361101	0.357824	0.228265	1.101517
F_6	Ave	**0.434285**	0.499991	0.500024	0	0.500075	5.316411
	Std	**0.168623**	5.65e−05	**8.15e−04**	0	0.003769	3.671765
F_7	Ave	**0.016815**	0.133704	0.083586	0.230743	0.117537	0.127742
	Std	**0.020713**	0.071891	0.046507	0.176026	0.076103	0.1120653
F_8	Ave	**2.1242e+02**	3.1122e+02	**1.9815e+02**	**0.971742**	4.9405e+02	2.2939e+02
	Std	**1.4854e+02**	1.7010e+ 02	**1.3821e + 02**	**0.060516**	32.556011	1.6225e+02
F_9	Ave	**3.72e−09**	1.392938	1.162095	0.399364	1.757771	1.551829
	Std	**2.51e−09**	0.809567	0.786181	0.515579	1.582437	0.613495
F_{10}	Ave	**2.08e−14**	0.479007	0.121888	0.559262	2.786641	1.101415
	Std	**6.21e−15**	0.603006	0.309137	0.258891	2.566353	0.941039
F_{11}	Ave	**2.14e−08**	0.074052	0.001161	0.024587	0.146765	51.978504
	Std	**1.29e−08**	0.095434	0.001108	0.052775	0.163191	27.669841
F_{12}	Ave	**0.799699**	4.689853	1.000013	0.859562	5.624831	5.823162
	Std	**0.395535**	3.125309	0.005251	0.457892	3.101541	3.302272
F_{13}	Ave	**0.754019**	1.554161	1.000018	0.886953	3.777629	5.910301
	Std	**0.387561**	1.239284	3.94e−04	0.146431	1.138838	2.970171
F_{14}	Ave	**23.932545**	23.978367	31.978334	**0.029963**	31.978336	31.978334
	Std	**11.283171**	11.302351	1.003e−06	**0.003063**	**6.21e−06**	**7.23e−07**
F_{15}	Ave	**0.233314**	2.599323	7.270406	0.394241	1.063258	3.052731
	Std	**0.080406**	2.096767	5.048224	0.197431	0.867394	2.361489
F_{16}	Ave	**0.4012807**	0.401249	0.401249	0.353553	0.401249	0.401249
	Std	**0.440366**	0.440396	0.440396	0.500000	0.440396	0.440396
F_{17}	Ave	**2.708872**	0.537405	2.708296	1	2.708296	2.708296
	Std	**0.611744**	0.231406	0.612773	0	0.612773	0.612773
F_{18}	Ave	**0.500248**	0.500001	0.500001	0	0.500001	0.500001
	Std	**0.706892**	0.707106	0.707106	0	0.707106	0.707106
F_{19}	Ave	**0.508537**	0.507603	0.507603	0.496227	0.507603	0.508225
	Std	**0.369743**	0.371305	0.371305	0.364716	0.371304	0.370286
F_{20}	Ave	**0.345023**	0.479691	0.480745	0.364069	0.460785	0.433646
	Std	**0.189996**	0.322890	0.352831	0.185006	0.323137	0.287861
F_{21}	Ave	**8.000627**	4.000085	4.000085	0.982601	4.000085	7.999633
	Std	**0.006721**	5.55e-05	5.54e−05	0.021352	5.57e−05	1.25e−04
F_{22}	Ave	**4.001473**	4.000089	4.000089	0.994969	4.000089	4.001454

(*continued*)

Table 2. (*continued*)

Function		GWO	SSA	PSO	DE	ALO	DA
	Std	**0.001394**	6.28e-04	6.28e−04	0.005808	6.29e-04	0.005133
F_{23}	Ave	**4.007203**	5.293117	4.000128	0.975137	4.007192	7.999457
	Std	**2.305720**	1.960713	6.31e−04	0.049725	2.306840	1.84e−05

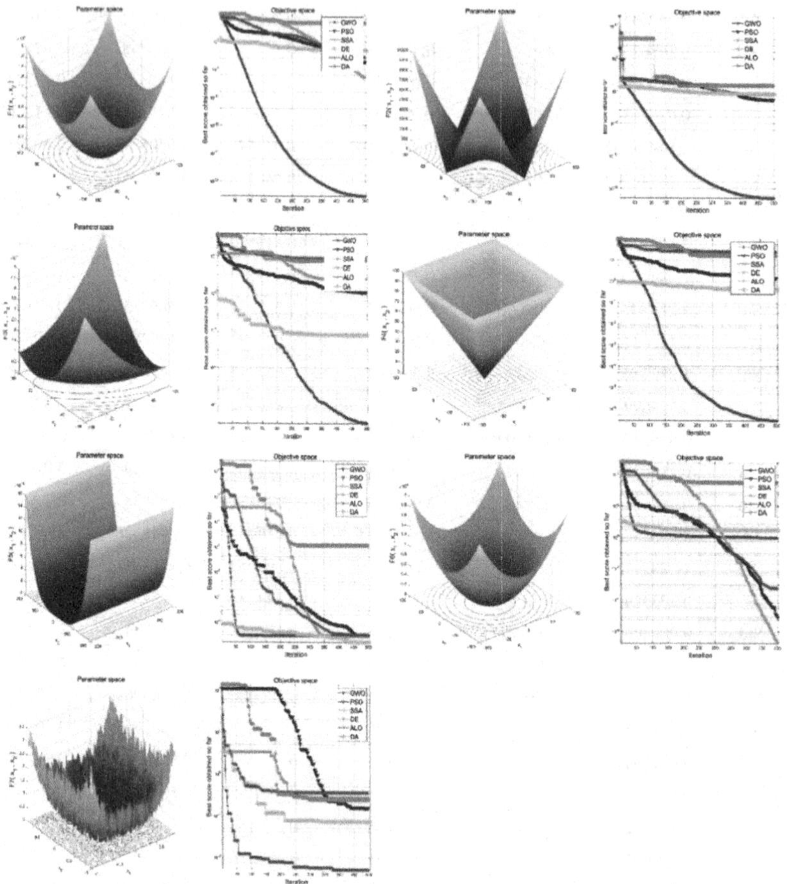

Fig. 5. Unimodal benchmark functions

Under the condition of the same population size and maximum iteration times, 30 tests are conducted on 23 functions by SSA, DE, PSO, ALO, DA and GWO. The average value and standard deviation are used as statistical data to observe the experimental results in Table 3. No matter in unimodal function or multimodal function, GWO is superior to other algorithms in convergence accuracy and stability. Therefore, GWO has good global convergence performance. Optimal fitness value diagram of benchmark functions are given in Fig. 5, Fig. 6. By comparing the advantages of the six algorithms, GWO has the advantages of fast computing speed and low fitness.

4.3 Prediction of Survival Level of Patients with EC by K-M-GWO-BP

In the construction of BP network model, the input layer is determined by the number of influence variables. The number of output layers is determined by the number of prediction. The number of input layer and output layer is 5 and 1 respectively. There is no unified way to determine the number of hidden layers, but it plays an important role in the accuracy of the prediction model. The number of hidden layers is selected by comparing the training errors under different numbers of hidden layers. Select the number of hidden layers from 3 to 13 for BP network training, and get the results as shown in Table 4 through 10 experiments. When the number of hidden layers is 11, the training error is 0.0173, and the training result is the best.

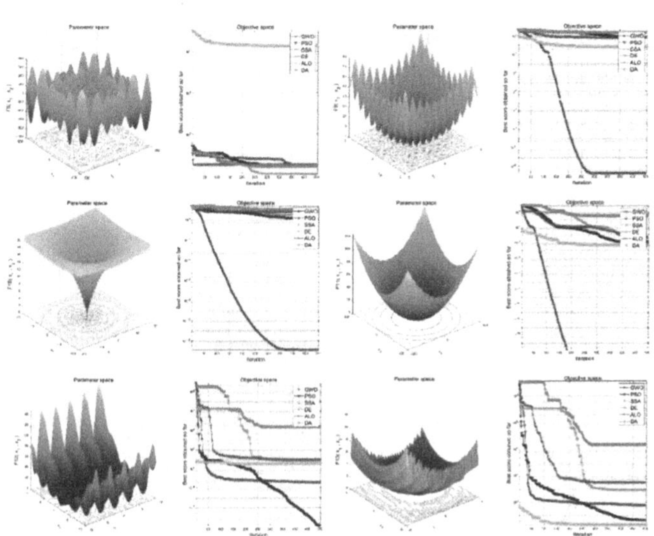

Fig. 6. Multimodal benchmark functions

Table 3. Network training error of node numbers in different implicit layer

Number of nodes	3	4	5	6	7	8	9	10	11	12	13
BP training error	6.6599	6.7328	6.7316	6.9328	6.6517	6.7726	6.8356	7.0237	6.9346	6.6637	6.8205
GWO-BP training error	4.8392	4.2302	5.2688	5.7011	4.6974	4.6812	4.8253	4.5574	4.8330	3.5871	5.0219

In order to comprehensively reflect the performance of the K-M-GWO-BP prediction model, the prediction results are evaluated by three indexes: the average value of the absolute error, the variance of the absolute error and the average value of the relative error. The agreement between the predicted value and the real value of test data in the prediction model is reflected by the average value of absolute error and relative error. The smaller the corresponding value is, the higher the prediction accuracy of the model is. The variance of the absolute error reflects the fluctuation of the difference, and the smaller the value is, the more stable the prediction result is. The predicted results for the normalized data are given in Table 5, with an average absolute error of 3.4156 for K-M-GWO-BP. The average relative error of 0.3277 is smaller than that of BP, PSO-BP, GA-BP, SSA-BP, GWO-BP, K-M-BP, K-M-PSO-BP, K-M-SSA-BP, K-M-GA-BP indicating that the prediction accuracy and fitting degree are higher. The average absolute error of PSO-BP is 7.3707 and the average relative error is 0.8831 higher than that of BP prediction model. The absolute error variance of BP is smaller than that of K-M-GWO-BP prediction model. The absolute error of the models without K-M analysis is given in Fig. 7. The absolute error of K-M-GWO-BP model is minimum. The comprehensive results show that the K-M-GWO-BP prediction model has better training accuracy and prediction effect.

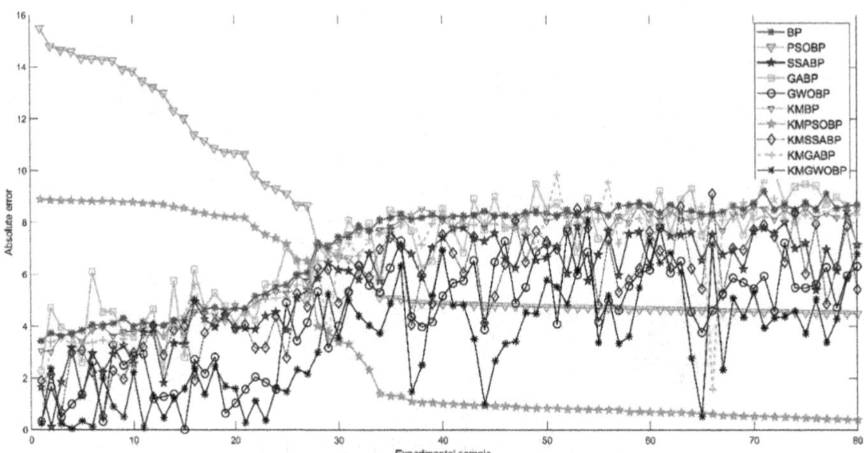

Fig. 7. Absolute error of the models

Table 4. Comparison of forecast results evaluation

Algorithm type	Average absolute error	Absolute error variance	Average relative error /%
BP	7.0483	3.6125	0.7098
PSO-BP	7.3707	13.7809	0.8831
ASSA-BP	5.7459	3.8047	0.5716
GA-BP	6.9386	3.9834	0.7007
GWO-BP	4.3486	4.2637	0.4232
K-M-BP	6.8245	3.7137	0.6852
K-M-PSO-BP	3.4979	12.5807	0.8744
K-M-ASSA-BP	5.4399	4.1366	0.5409
K-M-GA-BP	6.5191	4.6490	0.6522
K-M-GWO-BP	3.4156	4.4168	0.3277

5 Discussion

In this paper, a comprehensive model for predicting the survival level of patients with esophageal squamous cell carcinoma based on K-M survival analysis and gray wolf optimized backward propagation neural network is proposed. In view of the strong coupling and nonlinear characteristics of patient blood sample data, the sample data are analyzed by K-M survival analysis to reduce the impact of data correlation on modeling accuracy. On the basis of obtaining all kinds of sample data, the corresponding BP neural network model is distributed and constructed. The grey wolf algorithm with global optimization ability is used to optimize the parameters of error back propagation neural network, which avoids the blindness of artificial parameter selection and improves the prediction accuracy of the model.

Considering the influence factors of patients' blood, 250 groups of data are selected to train the network, and 80 groups of data are used to test the trained network. Compared with BP neural network model, PSO-BP, GA-BP, ASSA-BP, GWO-BP, K-M-BP, K-M-PSO-BP, K-M-ASSA-BP and K-M-GWO-BP, the prediction accuracy of K-M-GWO-BP is the best. The rapid and accurate prediction of patients' survival level is based on the solution method of K-M-GWO-BP neural network, which provides a new way for the healthy life of postoperative patients.

In this paper, 17 factors are found. Because there are many influence factors, the correlation is large. Reducing screened blood factors for ESCC is our next goal to improve the accuracy of predicting survival.

References

1. Bray, F., et al.: Global cancer statistics 2018: GLOBOCAN estimates of incidence and mortality worldwide for 36 cancers in 185 countries. CA Cancer J Clin **68**(6), 394–424 (2018)

2. Chen, W., et al.: Cancer statistics in China, 2015.CA cancer J. Clin. **66**(2), 115–132 (2016)
3. Siegel, R.L., Miller, K.D., Jemal, A.: Cancer statistics, 2015.CA cancer. J. Clin. **65** (1), 5–29 (2015)
4. Chen, W., et al.: Cancer statistics in China, 2015.CA cancer. J. Clin. **66**(2), 115–32 (2016)
5. Yang, M., Zhang, H., Ma, Z., et al.: Log odds of positive lymph nodes is a novel prognostic indicator superior to the number based and the ratio-based N category for gastric cancer patients with R0resection. Cancer **116**(11), 2571–2580 (2010)
6. Cao, J., Yuan, P., Ma, H., et al.: Log odds of positive lymph nodes predicts survival in patients after resection for esophageal cancer. Ann. Thorac. Surg. **102**(2), 424–432 (2016)
7. Hou, H.F., et al.: Survival of esophageal cancer in China. A pooled analysis on hospital-based studies from 2000 to 2018. Front. Oncol. **9,** 548 (2019)
8. Siegel, R.L., Miller, K.D.A.: Jemal, "cancer statistics," a cancer. J. Clin. **66**(1), 7–30 (2017)
9. Senthil, S., Ayshwarya, B.: Lung cancer prediction using feed forward back propagation neural networks with optimal features. Int. J. Appl. Eng. Res. **13**(1), 318–325 (2018)
10. Pan, X.Y., et al.: Survival prediction for oral tongue cancer patients via probabilistic genetic algorithm optimized neural network models. Br. J. Radiol. **93**(1112), 20190825 (2020)
11. Wang, Y., et al.: Prediction of survival time of patients with esophageal squamous cell carcinoma based on univariate analysis and ASSA-BP neural network. IEEE Access **8**, 181127–181136 (2020)
12. Song, W., et al.: A GPU-based training of BP Neural Network for Healthcare Data Analysis. Advanced Multimedia and Ubiquitous Engineering. Springer, Singapore, 518, 193–198 (2018)
13. Wu, X.Z., et al.: A study on the GA-BP neural network model for surface roughness of basswood-veneered medium-density fiberboard. Holzforschung **74**(10), 979–988 (2020)
14. Li, Z.M., Li, Y.N.: A comparative study on the prediction of the BP artificial neural network model and the ARIMA model in the incidence of AIDS. BMC Med. Inform. Decis. Making **20**(1), 1425–1431 (2020)
15. Mohamed, E.A.B.S., et al.: Novel hybridized adaptive neuro-fuzzy inference system models based particle swarm optimization and genetic algorithms for accurate prediction of stress intensity factor. Fatig. Fract. Eng. Mater. Struct. **43**(11), 2653–2667 (2020)
16. Guo, W.J., et al.: Using a genetic algorithm to improve oil spill prediction. Marine Pollut. Bull. **135**, 386–396 (2018)
17. Yoko, S., et al.: Diagnostic performance of the support vector machine model for breast cancer on ring-shaped dedicated breast positron emission tomography images. J. Comput. Assist. Tomogr. **44**(44), 413–418 (2020)
18. Imano, N., et al.: Evaluating individual radiosensitivity for the prediction of acute toxicities of chemoradiotherapy in esophageal cancer patients. Radiat. Res. **195**(3), 244–252 (2021)
19. Beukinga, R.J., et al.: Addition of HER2 and CD44 to 18F-FDG PET-based clinico-radiomic models enhances prediction of neoadjuvant chemoradiotherapy response in esophageal cancer. Eur. Radiol. **2021**(5) (2021)
20. Sk, A., et al.: Gastrointestinal cancer classification and prognostication from histology using deep learning systematic review. Eur. J. Cancer **155**, 200–215 (2021)
21. Carlson, D., et al.: Prediction of esophageal retention, a study comparing high-resolution manometry and functional luminal imaging probe panometry. Am. J. Gastroenterol. **116**(10), 2032–2041 (2021)
22. Southey, M.C., Dugue, P.A.: Improving breast cancer risk prediction with epigenetic risk factors. Nat. Rev. Clin. Oncol. **2022**(19–6) (2022)
23. Chu, F., et al.: Development and validation of MRI-based radiomics signatures models for prediction of disease-free survival and overall survival in patients with esophageal squamous cell carcinoma. Eur. Radiol. **32**(9), 5930–5942 (2022)

24. Zhang, H., et al.: Nomogram-Integrated C-Reactive protein/albumin ratio predicts efficacy and prognosis in patients with thoracic esophageal squamous cell carcinoma receiving chemoradiotherapy. Cancer Manag. Res. **11**, 9459–9468 (2019)
25. Xia, S.J., et al.: Overexpression of PSMA7 predicts poor prognosis in patients with gastric cancer. Oncol. Lett. **18**(5), 5341–5349 (2019)

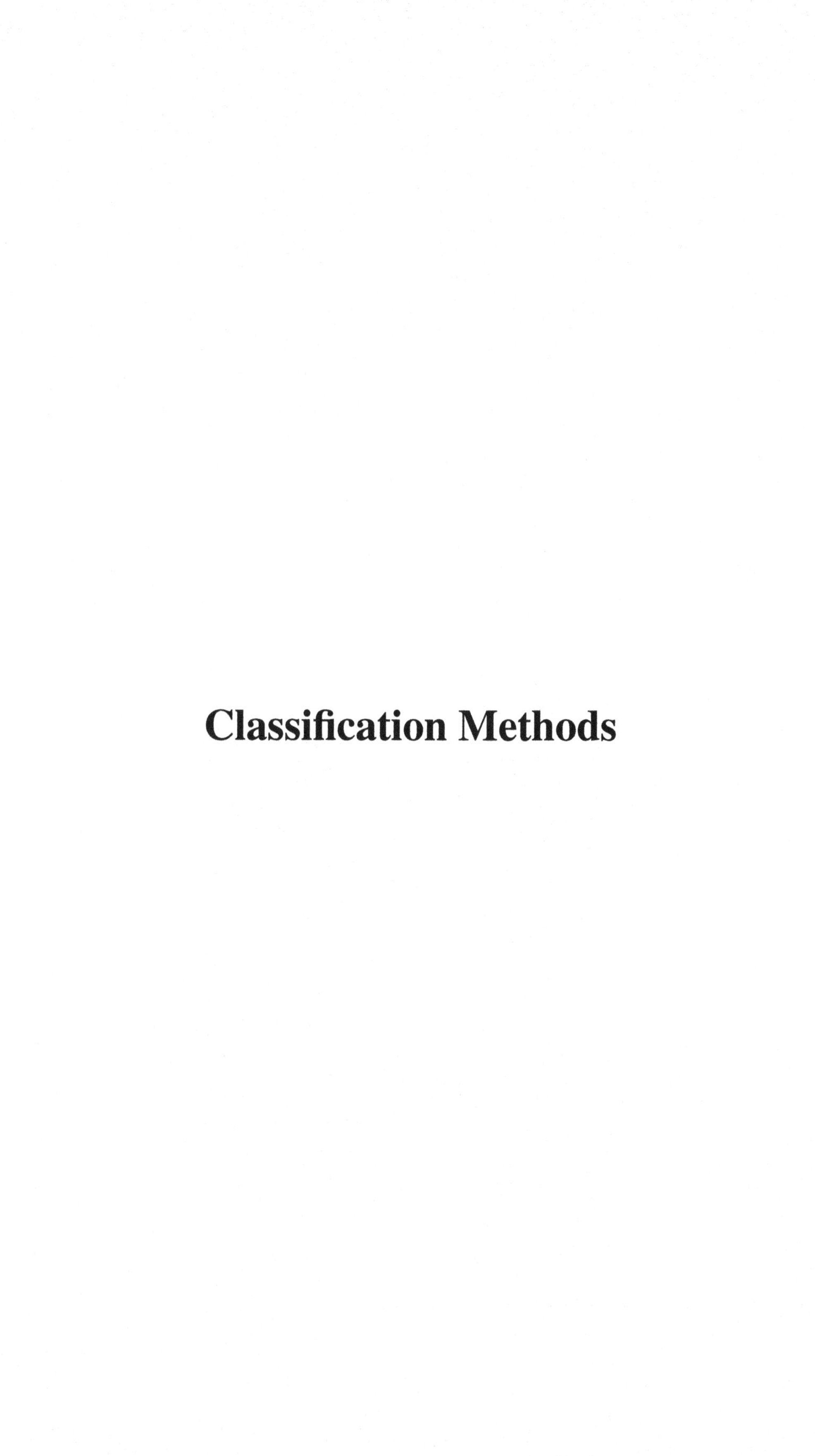

Classification Methods

Possibilistic Reject-Classification Based on Contrastive Learning in Vector Quantization Networks

Seyedfakhredin Musavishavazi(✉) and Maryam Alipour

Die Bundesanstalt für Arbeitsschutz und Arbeitsmedizin (BAuA), Fabricestraße 8, 01099 Dresden, Germany
musavishavazi.seyedfakhredin@baua.bund.de
https://www.baua.de/SharedDocs/Standorte/DE/Dresden.html

Abstract. In this paper, while considering **rejection** as an option, we attempt to tackle the problem of multiclass classification and the uncertainty that arises from the class possibility assignment of data. To address the challenge of classification based on possible class assignments, we use the likelihood ratio, which helps us develop a holistic approach that considers all the positive and negative effects of assigning a particular class as opposed to others to a data point. To this end, we propose a possibilistic variant of the **contrastive-learning** function, inspired by RSLVQ [20], and a **class-wise decision rule** based on it. The latter is used to define the total cost function. In addition, with the help of likelihood ratio, an error-rejection trade-off inspired by Chow [3], is proposed. Finally, modification of the cost function and integration of rejection into it result in an interpretable model whose capabilities in both aspects (classification/rejection) are demonstrated by application to different data sets.

Keywords: Reject-option · Possibilistic classifier · Contrastive learning · Multiclass classification · NN-Models

1 Introduction

In today's world, classification as a supervised machine learning method has gained a lot of credit, witnessed not only by many contributions with the promise of almost perfect classification in different kinds of applications [4,14,22], but also by a variety of practices for model evaluation [2,7,16,21]. Although, it should be pointed out that in the face of real-world data, classifying data safely and reliably, especially when a data point is too close to class boundaries, is an ongoing problem. To set an example for diagnosing a person with an illness sometimes it is impossible to call a person sick for **sure**. Hence, in this case, the idea of **crisp** labeling as a solution is off the table. After further investigation, it can be realized that sometimes people with the same symptoms may be diagnosed with

Supported by Die Bundesanstalt für Arbeitsschutz und Arbeitsmedizin (BAuA).

Y. Tan and Y. Shi (Eds.): DMBD 2022, CCIS 1744, pp. 353–366, 2022.
https://doi.org/10.1007/978-981-19-9297-1_25

different illnesses. So, here comes the problem of multi-labeling. But considering such a situation as **probability-based labeling** [11,18,23] is impossible since, in reality, we do not deal with random events which can be measured by probability functions. As a consequence, we have to consider any possible outcome and measure it with a possibility function. Even after narrowing the problem of diagnosis down to a possibilistic classification problem [12] the situation of **ambiguity** in symptoms and consecutive **uncertainty** leads us to consider a **rejection** as an option because here an incorrect classification is not just wrongdoing and it can cost a life. Despite many efforts and proposals from different models [5,24,25] almost all suffer from treating the problem of classification with or without rejection from a possibilistic point of view. In [12] we tried to close the gap between all previous solutions and the already existing problem, but the reject option is missing. In this paper, we try to tackle the latter with some fundamental modifications to the previous model.

The structure of the contribution is as follows; we start with LVQ [8] because it is simple, intuitive, and has a variety of applications that makes it a powerful method that can be compatible with almost any novel situation [6,13,19]. To this end, we hire the probabilistic version of LVQ, called robust soft LVQ or RSLVQ [20], to construct the first step to establish a model, called possibilistic soft LVQ or PSLVQ, that aims to fulfill the duty described previously.

The RSLVQ benefits from a function called **likelihood ratio** which helps us to introduce a prediction scheme followed by an error-reject trade-off, motivated by Chow [3], as a function of a threshold, t.

To evaluate the model's predicted class possibility assignment with the true class possibility label the Kullback-Leibler divergence [10] is hired. The application of the Kullback-Leibler divergence paves the way to introduce a local cost function. The goal is to minimize the recent function. But the resulted cost function does not have a lower bound i.e., without any extra constraint it cannot be minimized. To fix the problem we normalize the local cost function and obtain a **distance-based classifier** like the one in GLVQ [19]. Numerical experiments then follow the discussion. Finally, some remarks and discussions conclude the paper.

2 Model Description

2.1 Classifying in Absence of Rejection

We aim to classify a data point $\boldsymbol{x} \in \mathrm{X} \subseteq \mathbb{R}^n$ together with a label, called **class possibility assignment**, $\boldsymbol{y}(\boldsymbol{x}) = \left(y_1(\boldsymbol{x}), \ldots, y_{N_c}(\boldsymbol{x})\right) \in [0,1]^{N_c}$. Here $y_i(\boldsymbol{x})$ denotes the possibility of assigning a class $i \in C = \{1, ..., N_c\}$ to $\boldsymbol{x}$. To this end, we introduce a prototype-based scheme with a set of prototypes $\mathrm{W} = \{(\boldsymbol{w}_i, \mathrm{c}(\boldsymbol{w}_i)) \in \mathbb{R}^n \times C \mid i = 1, ..., N\}$ whereas $\mathrm{c}(\boldsymbol{w}_i)$ denotes the class label of $\boldsymbol{w}_i$.

In the beginning, the discussion is restricted to probability. After framing the primal model we relax the probability as a restriction and generalize the model to a possibilistic one. In all stages, stochastic gradient descent (SGD) [17] as a standard and efficient approach materializes the model optimization.

The RSLVQ as a Basis. We start this section with a quick review of the robust soft learning vector quantization (RSLVQ), introduced by S.Seo and K.Obermayer [20]. In a prototype-based classifier consisting of a set of prototypes $\mathrm{W} = \{(\boldsymbol{w}_i, \mathrm{c}(\boldsymbol{w}_i)) \in \mathbb{R}^n \times C \mid i = 1, ..., N\}$, let i be a mixture component that is parameterized by $\boldsymbol{w}_i$ and $\mathrm{c}(\boldsymbol{w}_i) = c_i$ as its label. We emphasize that each component is responsible for generating sample data for one and only one class. The model **density** of a data point $\boldsymbol{x}$ regarding a given class y is given by;

$$p_{\mathrm{W}}(\boldsymbol{x}, y) = \sum_{\{i, \mathrm{c}_i = y\}} p_i \cdot p_{\mathrm{W}}(\boldsymbol{x} \mid i) \tag{1}$$

here, p_i, typically chosen as a constant, is the **prior** probability and the conditional probability $p_{\mathrm{W}}(\boldsymbol{x} \mid i)$, called **likelihood-function**, is the probability that the component i generates a data point $\boldsymbol{x}$. As it can be seen all prototypes with the same label are involved in (1). So, this model is not a nearest prototype classifier.

Let $p_{\mathrm{W}}(\boldsymbol{x}, k)$ be the density of $\boldsymbol{x}$ and its **correct** class label. In contrast, the density of $\boldsymbol{x}$ and **incorrect** class labels is denoted by $p_{\mathrm{W}}(\boldsymbol{x}, \overline{k}) = \sum_{\{i, \mathrm{c}_i \neq k\}} p_i \cdot p_{\mathrm{W}}(\boldsymbol{x} \mid i)$. In the best-case scenario, the model benefits from a maximal $p_{\mathrm{W}}(\boldsymbol{x}, k)$ and a minimal $p_{\mathrm{W}}(\boldsymbol{x}, \overline{k})$ at the same time. Therefore, the RSLVQ sets the maximization of the following **Likelihood Ratio** as a goal;

$$\mathrm{L}_{\mathrm{W}}(\boldsymbol{x}, k) = \frac{p_{\mathrm{W}}(\boldsymbol{x}, k)}{p_{\mathrm{W}}(\boldsymbol{x}, \overline{k})} \tag{2}$$

and considers the respective following function as a cost-function.

$$\log(\mathrm{L}_{\mathrm{W}}(\mathrm{X})) = \sum_{\boldsymbol{x} \in \mathrm{X}} \log\left(\frac{p_{\mathrm{W}}(\boldsymbol{x}, k)}{p_{\mathrm{W}}(\boldsymbol{x}, \overline{k})}\right) \tag{3}$$

Inspired by RSLVQ, we propose a **modified** likelihood-ratio;

$$\hat{\mathrm{L}}_{\mathrm{W}}(\boldsymbol{x}, i) = \frac{p_{\mathrm{W}}(i \mid \boldsymbol{x})}{p_{\mathrm{W}}(\overline{i} \mid \boldsymbol{x})} \tag{4}$$

where $p_{\mathrm{W}}(i \mid \boldsymbol{x})$, called **posterior**, is inferred as the probability of assigning a label i to $\boldsymbol{x}$ as well as $p_{\mathrm{W}}(\overline{i} \mid \boldsymbol{x}) = \sum_{j \neq i} p_{\mathrm{W}}(j \mid \boldsymbol{x})$ denoting the probability of assigning any label to $\boldsymbol{x}$ except i. Unlike RSLVQ, i here does not necessarily refer to the correct label. The likelihood ratio (4) is utilized to predict a label for an unknown data point in a way that the higher is the value of $\hat{\mathrm{L}}_{\mathrm{W}}(\boldsymbol{x}, i)$ the more likely the class i assigned to $\boldsymbol{x}$. So,

$$\mathrm{argmax}_i \quad \hat{\mathrm{L}}_{\mathrm{W}}(\boldsymbol{x}, i) = i^* \implies \mathrm{c}^*_{\boldsymbol{w}}(\boldsymbol{x}) = i^*.$$

It must be noted the likelihood ratio (4) is a monotonically increasing function and obtains its maximum at $p_{\mathrm{W}}(i^* \mid \boldsymbol{x}) = \max_i\{p_{\mathrm{W}}(i \mid \boldsymbol{x})\}$. Due to the Bayes' theorem;

$$p_{\mathrm{W}}(i \mid \boldsymbol{x}) = p_{\mathrm{W}}(\boldsymbol{x} \mid i) \cdot \frac{p_i}{p_{\mathrm{W}}(\boldsymbol{x})} \tag{5}$$

so, the modified likelihood ratio (4) is rephrased as;

$$\hat{\mathrm{L}}_{\mathrm{w}}(\boldsymbol{x}, i) = \frac{p_{\mathrm{w}}(\boldsymbol{x} \mid i) \cdot p_i}{\sum_{j \neq i} p_{\mathrm{w}}(\boldsymbol{x} \mid j) \cdot p_j} \tag{6}$$

and in a special case with the assumption of $p_i = \frac{1}{N_c}$ the **likelihood-function**, $p_{\mathrm{w}}(\boldsymbol{x} \mid i)$, is a replacement for the **posterior** and has the same role. Here N_c stands for the number of classes. Using (6) in the next step helps us to introduce a contrastive learning function.

Introduction of a Contrastive-Learning Function. The RSLVQ proves that the expectation of the cost function (3) is given by;

$$\mathrm{E}(\log(\mathrm{L}_{\mathrm{w}}(\mathrm{X}))) = \sum_{\boldsymbol{x} \in \mathrm{X}} \mathrm{D}_{\mathrm{KL}}\big(\boldsymbol{P}(\boldsymbol{x}) \mid\mid \overline{\boldsymbol{P}_{\mathrm{w}}(\boldsymbol{x})}\big) - \mathrm{D}_{\mathrm{KL}}\big(\boldsymbol{P}(\boldsymbol{x}) \mid\mid \boldsymbol{P}_{\mathrm{w}}(\boldsymbol{x})\big) \tag{7}$$

where $\mathrm{D}_{\mathrm{KL}}(\bullet \mid\mid \bullet)$, called Kullback-Leibler divergence [10], distinguishes the similarity between the **true** distribution $\boldsymbol{P}(\boldsymbol{x}) = \big(p(\boldsymbol{x},1), ..., p(\boldsymbol{x}, N_c)\big)$ and **correct predicted** class probability assignment $\boldsymbol{P}_{\mathrm{w}}(\boldsymbol{x}) = \big(p_{\mathrm{w}}(\boldsymbol{x},1), ..., p_{\mathrm{w}}(\boldsymbol{x}, N_c)\big)$ as well as **incorrect predicted** class probability assignment $\overline{\boldsymbol{P}_{\mathrm{w}}(\boldsymbol{x})} = \big(p_{\mathrm{w}}(\boldsymbol{x},\overline{1}), ..., p_{\mathrm{w}}(\boldsymbol{x}, \overline{N_c})\big)$. In (7);

- $\mathrm{D}_{\mathrm{KL}}(\boldsymbol{P}(\boldsymbol{x}) \mid\mid \boldsymbol{P}_{\mathrm{w}}(\boldsymbol{x})) = \sum_{i=1}^{N_c} -p(\boldsymbol{x}, y_i) \cdot \log\left(\frac{p_{\mathrm{w}}(\boldsymbol{x}, y_i)}{p(\boldsymbol{x}, y_i)}\right)$,
- $\mathrm{D}_{\mathrm{KL}}(\boldsymbol{P}(\boldsymbol{x}) \mid\mid \overline{\boldsymbol{P}_{\mathrm{w}}(\boldsymbol{x})}) = \sum_{i=1}^{N_c} -p(\boldsymbol{x}, y_i) \cdot \log\left(\frac{p_{\mathrm{w}}(\boldsymbol{x}, \overline{y_i})}{p(\boldsymbol{x}, y_i)}\right)$

can be inferred as the positive- and negative-**reasoning**. So the expectation of the cost function (3) holds the property of a **contrastive learning** function. In analogy to (7), we introduce;

$$\hat{\mathrm{cl}}(\boldsymbol{x}) = \sum_{i=1}^{N_c} -y_i(\boldsymbol{x}) \cdot \log(\hat{\mathrm{L}}_{\mathrm{w}}(\boldsymbol{x}, i)) \tag{8}$$

which is actually $\hat{\mathrm{cl}}(\boldsymbol{x}) = \mathrm{D}_{\mathrm{KL}}(\boldsymbol{y}(\boldsymbol{x}) \mid\mid \boldsymbol{P}_{\mathrm{w}}(\boldsymbol{x})) - \mathrm{D}_{\mathrm{KL}}(\boldsymbol{y}(\boldsymbol{x}) \mid\mid \overline{\boldsymbol{P}_{\mathrm{w}}(\boldsymbol{x})})$. We aim to minimize (8) as a contrastive learning function. Here, $\boldsymbol{P}_{\mathrm{w}}(\boldsymbol{x}) = \big(p_{\mathrm{w}}(1 \mid \boldsymbol{x}), ..., p_{\mathrm{w}}(N_c \mid \boldsymbol{x})\big)$ and $\overline{\boldsymbol{P}_{\mathrm{w}}(\boldsymbol{x})} = \big(p_{\mathrm{w}}(\overline{1} \mid \boldsymbol{x}), ..., p_{\mathrm{w}}(\overline{N_c} \mid \boldsymbol{x})\big)$ with $p_{\mathrm{w}}(\overline{i} \mid \boldsymbol{x}) = \sum_{j \neq i} p_{\mathrm{w}}(j \mid \boldsymbol{x})$; $\forall i = 1, ..., N_c$.

Considering that $\mathrm{D}_{\mathrm{KL}}(\bullet \mid\mid \bullet) \geq 0$, the contrastive learning function (8), as a difference between two distinct Kullback-Leibler divergences, is not confined to a lower bound, i.e. it does not hold a necessary condition for minimization. Hence, (8) is not a good choice for being a cost function. The very next step is dedicated to tackling the problem through the deployment of the generalized learning vector quantization GLVQ [19].

An Objective Function Related to the GLVQ. To deal with the problem of minimizing the contrastive learning function (8) we need to review the GLVQ, introduced by A. Sato and K. Yamada [19], in the first place. Consider a set of prototypes $\mathrm{W} = \{(\boldsymbol{w}_i, \mathrm{c}(\boldsymbol{w}_i)) \in \mathbb{R}^n \times C \mid i = 1, ..., N\}$ with i as the class label of $\boldsymbol{w}_i$, denoted by $\mathrm{c}(\boldsymbol{w}_i) = i$. For a given data point $\boldsymbol{x} \in \mathrm{X}$ with the label $\mathrm{c}(\boldsymbol{x})$, let $\boldsymbol{w}^+$ be the closest prototype to $\boldsymbol{x}$ with the same label as $\boldsymbol{x}$ and $\boldsymbol{w}^-$ the closest prototype to $\boldsymbol{x}$ but with a different label. The GLVQ aims to minimize the cost function;

$$\mathrm{S_W} = \sum_{\boldsymbol{x} \in \mathrm{X}} \mathrm{f}(\mu(\boldsymbol{x})) \tag{9}$$

with $\mathrm{f}(\bullet)$ as a monotonically increasing function and $\mu(\boldsymbol{x})$ as a **distance-based classifier** function given by;

$$\mu(\boldsymbol{x}) = \frac{\mathrm{d}^+ - \mathrm{d}^-}{\mathrm{d}^+ + \mathrm{d}^-} \tag{10}$$

where d^+ and d^- denote the distances (dissimilarities) of $\boldsymbol{x}$ from $\boldsymbol{w}^+$ and $\boldsymbol{w}^-$, respectively. An investigation of the classifier function (10) shows $\mu(\boldsymbol{x}) \in [-1, 1]$ with $\mu(\boldsymbol{x}) < 0$ corresponding to a correct classification as well as $\mu(\boldsymbol{x}) > 0$ prompting an incorrect classification. It is worth to mention that different choices of $\mathrm{f}(\bullet)$ and $\mu(\bullet)$ provide LVQ and LVQ2.1 [9]. The corresponding learning step is given by;

$$\Delta\boldsymbol{\omega}^+ = \alpha \cdot \frac{\partial \mathrm{f}}{\partial \boldsymbol{\omega}^+} \tag{11}$$

and;

$$\Delta\boldsymbol{\omega}^- = (-1) \cdot \alpha \cdot \frac{\partial \mathrm{f}}{\partial \boldsymbol{\omega}^-} \tag{12}$$

with $0 < \alpha << 1$ as a learning **rate**. As a matter of different choices of $\mathrm{f}(\bullet)$ and $\mu(\bullet)$ in (9), we opt for the **sigmoid** function;

$$\mathrm{sgd}_\lambda(\tau) = \frac{\exp(\lambda \cdot \tau)}{\exp(1 + \lambda \cdot \tau)}; \ \ \lambda > 0 \tag{13}$$

and a **modified** distance(dissimilarity)-based classifier, like (10), as following;

$$\hat{\mu}(\boldsymbol{x}) = \frac{\mathrm{D_{KL}}(\boldsymbol{y}(\boldsymbol{x}) \ \ || \ \boldsymbol{P}_\mathrm{W}(\boldsymbol{x})) - \mathrm{D_{KL}}(\boldsymbol{y}(\boldsymbol{x}) \ \ || \ \overline{\boldsymbol{P}_\mathrm{W}(\boldsymbol{x})})}{\mathrm{D_{KL}}(\boldsymbol{y}(\boldsymbol{x}) \ \ || \ \boldsymbol{P}_\mathrm{W}(\boldsymbol{x})) + \mathrm{D_{KL}}(\boldsymbol{y}(\boldsymbol{x}) \ \ || \ \overline{\boldsymbol{P}_\mathrm{W}(\boldsymbol{x})})} \tag{14}$$

with $\mathrm{D_{KL}}(\bullet \ || \ \bullet)$, the Kullback-Leibler divergence [10], measuring the dissimilarities. Correspondingly, the **local** cost function is given by;

$$\mathrm{S_W}(\boldsymbol{x}) = \mathrm{sgd}_\lambda(\hat{\mu}(\boldsymbol{x})) \tag{15}$$

which as a bounded function does not suffer like (8) and paves the way for the following **total** cost function.

$$\mathrm{S_W} = \sum_{\boldsymbol{x} \in \mathrm{X}} \mathrm{sgd}_\lambda(\hat{\mu}(\boldsymbol{x})) \tag{16}$$

To justify the choice of the cost function (16), we simplify it as follows.

$$\mathrm{S_W} = \sum_{\boldsymbol{x} \in \mathrm{X}} \mathrm{H}(\hat{\mu}(\boldsymbol{x})) \tag{17}$$

where H(•), called the **Heaviside** function, returns 0 for negative- and 1 for non-negative- **inputs**. Accordingly, (17) counts the number of misclassifications regarding the sign of $\hat{\mu}(\boldsymbol{x})$. And, we aim to minimize (17). The application of H(•) makes (17) incompatible with gradient descent-based learning. In order to facilitate the optimization of the cost function, the **Heaviside** function is replaced by sgd(•), which on the one hand is differentiable and on the other hand, with a suitable choice of λ, acts as a soft variant of **Heaviside.**

2.2 Classifying in Presence of Rejection

Introduction of the Reject-Classifying Trade-Off. At this step we aim to introduce a **rejection** criterion and embed it in the cost function (16). But first we need to discuss the **error-reject** trade-off proposed by Chow [3]. Based on this model, the condition for rejecting a data point $\boldsymbol{x}$ is given by;

$$p_{i^*} \cdot p_{\mathrm{W}}(\boldsymbol{x} \mid i^*) < (1-t) \cdot \sum_{i=1}^{N_c} \Big(p_i \cdot p_{\mathrm{W}}(\boldsymbol{x} \mid i)\Big) \tag{18}$$

where $p_{i^*} \cdot p_{\mathrm{W}}(\boldsymbol{x} \mid i^*) = \max_i\{p_i \cdot p_{\mathrm{W}}(\boldsymbol{x} \mid i)\}$ and $t \in (0,1)$ is called **threshold.** A mathematical deduction from (18) leads us to the following reject condition;

$$\hat{\mathrm{L}}_{\mathrm{W}}(\boldsymbol{x}, i^*) \leq \frac{1-t}{t} \tag{19}$$

with the assumption that $\frac{1}{N_c-1} > \frac{1-t}{t} > 0$. The recent assumption guarantees $t \in (0,1)$ and (19) holds all specified properties. In [11] it was proved that not only such a threshold t exists but can also be optimized regardless of the choice of posterior as a probability or possibility function. Moreover, $\hat{\mathrm{L}}_{\mathrm{W}}(\boldsymbol{x}, i^*) = \frac{p_{\mathrm{W}}(i^* \mid \boldsymbol{x})}{\sum_{i \neq i^*} p_{\mathrm{W}}(i \mid \boldsymbol{x})}$ and i^* maximizes the $p_{\mathrm{W}}(i^* \mid \boldsymbol{x})$, and as a consequence $\hat{\mathrm{L}}_{\mathrm{W}}(\boldsymbol{x}, i^*)$.

To integrate the reject condition (19) in the cost function (16), first, we partition the data set X into two sets $\mathrm{A_C}$ and $\mathrm{A_R}$ called **classification-** and **reject-**area, respectively.

- $\mathrm{A_C} = \{\boldsymbol{x} \in \mathrm{X} \mid \hat{\mathrm{L}}_{\mathrm{W}}(\boldsymbol{x}, i^*) > \frac{1-t}{t}\}$
- $\mathrm{A_R} = \{\boldsymbol{x} \in \mathrm{X} \mid \hat{\mathrm{L}}_{\mathrm{W}}(\boldsymbol{x}, i^*) \leq \frac{1-t}{t}\}$

Accordingly, the cost function (16) is **modified** to the following statement.

$$\mathrm{S_W}(t) = \sum_{\boldsymbol{x} \in \mathrm{A_C}} \mathrm{sgd}_\lambda(\hat{\mu}(\boldsymbol{x})) + \sum_{\boldsymbol{x} \in \mathrm{A_R}} \mathrm{sgd}_\lambda(\hat{\mu}(\boldsymbol{x})) \tag{20}$$

Given the consideration of the modified distance-based classifier (14), A_C can be partitioned into **correct-** and **mis-**classification areas, denoted by A_{CC} and A_{MC}, respectively.

- $\mathrm{A_{CC}} = \{\boldsymbol{x} \in A_C \mid \hat{\mu}(\boldsymbol{x}) < 0\}$
- $\mathrm{A_{MC}} = \{\boldsymbol{x} \in A_C \mid \hat{\mu}(\boldsymbol{x}) \geq 0\}$

So we reformulate the cost function (20) as follows.

$$\mathrm{S_w}(t) = \sum_{\boldsymbol{x} \in \mathrm{A_{CC}}} \mathrm{sgd}_\lambda(\hat{\mu}(\boldsymbol{x})) + \sum_{\boldsymbol{x} \in \mathrm{A_{MC}}} \mathrm{sgd}_\lambda(\hat{\mu}(\boldsymbol{x})) + \sum_{\boldsymbol{x} \in \mathrm{A_R}} \mathrm{sgd}_\lambda(\hat{\mu}(\boldsymbol{x})) \tag{21}$$

In the absence of the reject condition (19), neither (20) nor (21) is a function of t. Hence, they are the same as (16).

Optimizing the Reject-Classifying Trade-Off. To find an optimum threshold, t^*, Chow's model introduces c_c and c_e as the rate for correct- and incorrect-classification, respectively, whereas c_r is the rate for the rejection assuming that $c_c < c_r < c_e$. The overall cost function is given by;

$$\hat{\mathrm{S}}_\mathrm{w}(t) = c_c \cdot \sum_{\boldsymbol{x} \in \mathrm{X}} C_{_\mathrm{w}}(t, \boldsymbol{x}) + c_e \cdot \sum_{\boldsymbol{x} \in \mathrm{X}} E_{_\mathrm{w}}(t, \boldsymbol{x}) + c_r \cdot \sum_{\boldsymbol{x} \in \mathrm{X}} R_{_\mathrm{w}}(t, \boldsymbol{x}) \tag{22}$$

where $C_{_\mathrm{w}}(t, \boldsymbol{x})$, $E_{_\mathrm{w}}(t, \boldsymbol{x})$ and $R_{_\mathrm{w}}(t, \boldsymbol{x})$ denote the cost of the correct classification, incorrect classification along with the rejection, in the same order. With the assumption that;

$$C_\mathbf{W}(t, \boldsymbol{x}) + E_\mathbf{W}(t, \boldsymbol{x}) + R_\mathbf{W}(t, \boldsymbol{x}) = p_\mathrm{w}(\boldsymbol{x}) \tag{23}$$

the optimum threshold $t^* = \frac{c_c - c_r}{c_c - c_e}$ is obtained from (22) where $p_\mathrm{w}(\boldsymbol{x}) = \sum_{i=1}^{N_c} p_\mathrm{w}(\boldsymbol{x}, i)$. In continuation to this idea and considering that;

- $0 \leq \mathrm{sgd}_\lambda(\tau) \leq 1$
- $\int_{\tau=-1}^{1} \mathrm{sgd}_\lambda(\tau)\, d\tau = 1$

$p_\mathrm{w}(\boldsymbol{x})$ in (23) can be replaced by $\mathrm{sgd}_\lambda\big(\hat{\mu}(\boldsymbol{x})\big)$ (15). To this end, we define;

- $C_\mathrm{W}(t, \boldsymbol{x}) = \mathrm{H}\big(\hat{\mathrm{L}}_\mathrm{w}(\boldsymbol{x}, i^*) - \frac{1-t}{t}\big) \cdot \mathrm{H}\big(-\hat{\mu}(\boldsymbol{x})\big) \cdot \delta_{\mathrm{c}_w^*(\boldsymbol{x})}^{\mathrm{c}_t(\boldsymbol{x})} \cdot \mathrm{sgd}_\lambda\big(\hat{\mu}(\boldsymbol{x})\big)$
- $E_\mathrm{W}(t, \boldsymbol{x}) = \mathrm{H}\big(\hat{\mathrm{L}}_\mathrm{w}(\boldsymbol{x}, i^*) - \frac{1-t}{t}\big) \cdot \mathrm{H}\big(\hat{\mu}(\boldsymbol{x})\big) \cdot \big(1 - \delta_{\mathrm{c}_w^*(\boldsymbol{x})}^{\mathrm{c}_t(\boldsymbol{x})}\big) \cdot \mathrm{sgd}_\lambda\big(\hat{\mu}(\boldsymbol{x})\big)$
- $R_\mathrm{W}(t, \boldsymbol{x}) = \mathrm{H}\big(\frac{1-t}{t} - \hat{\mathrm{L}}_\mathrm{w}(\boldsymbol{x}, i^*)\big) \cdot \mathrm{sgd}_\lambda\big(\hat{\mu}(\boldsymbol{x})\big)$

where $\mathrm{H}(\bullet)$ denotes the **Heaviside** function, while the Kronecker delta, as follows;

$$\delta_{\mathrm{c}_w^*(\boldsymbol{x})}^{\mathrm{c}_t(\boldsymbol{x})} = \begin{cases} 1\,; \mathrm{c}_w^*(\boldsymbol{x}) = \mathrm{c}_t(\boldsymbol{x}) \\ 0\,; \mathrm{c}_w^*(\boldsymbol{x}) \neq \mathrm{c}_t(\boldsymbol{x}) \end{cases} \tag{24}$$

examines if the **predicted** label $\mathrm{c}_w^*(\boldsymbol{x})$ and the **true** label $\mathrm{c}_t(\boldsymbol{x})$ are the same. As a matter of fact;

- $\mathrm{H}\big(\hat{\mathrm{L}}_\mathrm{w}(\boldsymbol{x}, i^*) - \frac{1-t}{t}\big) \cdot \mathrm{H}\big(-\hat{\mu}(\boldsymbol{x})\big) = 1 \implies \boldsymbol{x} \in A_{CC}$,

- $\mathrm{H}\big(\hat{\mathrm{L}}_{\mathrm{w}}(\boldsymbol{x}, i^*) - \frac{1-t}{t}\big) \cdot \mathrm{H}(\hat{\mu}(\boldsymbol{x})) = 1 \implies \boldsymbol{x} \in A_{MC}$,
- $\mathrm{H}\big(\hat{\mathrm{L}}_{\mathrm{w}}(\boldsymbol{x}, i^*) - \frac{1-t}{t}\big) = 0 \implies \boldsymbol{x} \in A_{R}$.

In summary, the cost function (22), using a **non-probabilistic** function $\hat{\mu}(\bullet)$, still holds all necessary properties like the **probabilistic** rejection classifier (21). Therefore (22) provides an optimal threshold, t^*.

3 Generalization

In the beginning, we restricted the discussion to probability functions. Now we relax the restriction and pivot towards **possibility** functions to generalize our model. But before moving further, we need the following assumptions.

- $y_i(\boldsymbol{x}) \in [0, 1]$ and $\sum_{i=1}^{N_c} y_i(\boldsymbol{x}) = y_{\boldsymbol{x}}$
- $p_{\mathrm{w}}(i \mid \boldsymbol{x}) \in [0, 1]$ and $\sum_{i=1}^{N_c} p_{\mathrm{w}}(i \mid \boldsymbol{x}) = p_{\boldsymbol{x}}$

It should be mentioned that $y_{\boldsymbol{x}}, p_{\boldsymbol{x}} \neq 1$, necessarily, and their indexing alludes that their values may change depending on $\boldsymbol{x}$. To measure the similarity between $y_i(\boldsymbol{x})$ and $p_{\mathrm{w}}(i \mid \boldsymbol{x})$ as well as $y_i(\boldsymbol{x})$ and $p_{\mathrm{w}}(\bar{i} \mid \boldsymbol{x})$, we have to use the **generalized** Kullback-Leibler divergence.

- $\mathrm{D_{GKL}}(\boldsymbol{y}(\boldsymbol{x}) \mid\mid \boldsymbol{P}_{\mathrm{w}}(\boldsymbol{x})) = \sum_{i=1}^{N_c} \Big[- y_i(\boldsymbol{x}) \cdot \log\Big(\frac{p_{\mathrm{w}}(i|\boldsymbol{x})}{y_i(\boldsymbol{x})}\Big) - \Big(y_i(\boldsymbol{x}) - p_{\mathrm{w}}(i \mid \boldsymbol{x})\Big)\Big]$
- $\mathrm{D_{GKL}}(\boldsymbol{y}(\boldsymbol{x}) \mid\mid \overline{\boldsymbol{P}_{\mathrm{w}}(\boldsymbol{x})}) = \sum_{i=1}^{N_c} \Big[- y_i(\boldsymbol{x}) \cdot \log\Big(\frac{\sum_{j \neq i} p_{\mathrm{w}}(j|\boldsymbol{x})}{y_i(\boldsymbol{x})}\Big) - \Big(y_i(\boldsymbol{x}) - \sum_{j \neq i} p_{\mathrm{w}}(j \mid \boldsymbol{x})\Big)\Big]$

As a consequence, the **generalized** contrastive learning function (8) is obtained as follows;

$$\mathrm{gcl}(\boldsymbol{x}) = \mathrm{D_{GKL}}(\boldsymbol{y}(\boldsymbol{x}) \mid\mid \boldsymbol{P}_{\mathrm{w}}(\boldsymbol{x})) - \mathrm{D_{GKL}}(\boldsymbol{y}(\boldsymbol{x}) \mid\mid \overline{\boldsymbol{P}_{\mathrm{w}}(\boldsymbol{x})}) + (N_c - 2) \cdot p_{\boldsymbol{x}} \quad (25)$$

In (25), $\mathrm{D_{GKL}}(\boldsymbol{y}(\boldsymbol{x}) \mid\mid \boldsymbol{P}_{\mathrm{w}}(\boldsymbol{x}))$ and $\mathrm{D_{GKL}}(\boldsymbol{y}(\boldsymbol{x}) \mid\mid \overline{\boldsymbol{P}_{\mathrm{w}}(\boldsymbol{x})})$ can be inferred as negative- and positive-reasoning, respectively. So, the $\mathrm{gcl}(\boldsymbol{x})$ is a contrastive-learning function. According to the current modifications, the **generalized** distance-based classifier (14) is obtained by;

$$\hat{\mu_g}(\boldsymbol{x}) = \frac{D^+ - D^- + (N_c - 2) \cdot p_{\mathrm{w}}(\boldsymbol{x})}{D^+ + D^- - (-1)^{\mathbf{H}(D^+ - D^-)} \cdot (N_c - 2) \cdot p_{\boldsymbol{x}}} \quad (26)$$

where D^+ stands for $\mathrm{D_{GKL}}(\boldsymbol{y}(\boldsymbol{x}) \mid\mid \boldsymbol{P}_{\mathrm{w}}(\boldsymbol{x}))$ and D^- for $\mathrm{D_{GKL}}(\boldsymbol{y}(\boldsymbol{x}) \mid\mid \overline{\boldsymbol{P}_{\mathrm{w}}(\boldsymbol{x})})$. For clarification, $(-1)^{\mathbf{H}(D^+ - D^-)}$ facilitates the normalization of (26) with the help of the Heaviside function, which leads to $\hat{\mu_g}(\boldsymbol{x}) \in [-1, 1]$. Similar to (10), $\hat{\mu_g}(\boldsymbol{x}) = -1$ determines the **best** predicted possibility function as $\hat{\mu_g}(\boldsymbol{x}) = 1$ does the same for the **worst** one. As a result, the cost function (22), regardless of the choice of a prediction function as a probability- or possibility-one, remains unchanged and works perfectly.

Table 1. Specification of datasets

Dataset	n-instances	n-attributes	n-targets
DBCW	569	32	2
CHD	1190	11	2

4 Experiments

Even though this paper aims to propose a concrete mathematical model, we believe that nothing better justifies the reasons for all the different choices when setting up a framework than pursuing its goal through experimental results. Also, we cannot confidently call a model **interpretable** unless we have a chance to compare the model's decisions with our expectations. This is the point at which the crucial role of comprehensive implementation is recognized.

As we already know a good choice of the likelihood function, $p_{\mathrm{w}}(\boldsymbol{x} \mid i)$, with the assistance of the Bayes' theorem (5) provides us with the posterior, $p_{\mathrm{w}}(i \mid \boldsymbol{x})$. To this end, we take the liberty to propose $p_{\mathrm{w}}(\boldsymbol{x} \mid i) = \exp\big(-\gamma \cdot \mathrm{d}^2(\boldsymbol{x}, \boldsymbol{w}_i)\big)$ as a likelihood function with $\gamma > 0$. Here $\mathrm{d}(\bullet, \bullet)$ is a distance function which in our case the standard Euclidean distance fulfills the job. To clarify;

$$\exp\left(-\gamma \cdot \tau\right) = \begin{cases} 1 & \tau = 0 \\ 0 & \tau \rightarrow \infty \end{cases} \tag{27}$$

in other words, (27) resembles a possibility function depending on τ as the relative distance between data points and prototypes. In addition, with the help of the likelihood-ratio (4) and a good choice of γ, (27) acts the same as the **Gaussian** distribution.

To start we implement the classification model **without** rejection. This includes implementing the core of the model and determining the necessary steps to design a training pipeline. In the next step, we add rejection as an option to the primal model and tune the parameters to ensure the stability of the model and prevent bad generalization in the long run. For this purpose, we use the k-fold cross-validation technique to find a trade-off between bias and variance. The **hyperparameter** k indicates the number of partitions into which the dataset should be divided. The whole process results in a robust estimation performance [7] that helps the better generalization of the model.

Here we use the Diagnostic Breast Cancer Wisconsin (DBCW) and Comprehensive Heart Disease (CHD) datasets. The description can be found in Table 1. In this table, the number of attributes(n-attributes) indicates the dimension of a single data point whereas the number of targets(n-targets) denotes the number of classes.

Table 2 shows the results of the model for investigating the accuracy of classification in **absence** and also **presence** of the rejection step.

As can be seen in Table 2, for the DBCW dataset, the test accuracy is slightly higher than the training accuracy. Although we are convinced that this phenomenon has nothing to do with the complexity of the model and the problem of bias-variance trade-off [15], we carry out the following experimental investigation. In this experiment, we try to investigate whether the trend (better test accuracy compared to training accuracy) can change due to the different values of parameters. In other words, is the trend sensitive to the model's parameters? We also check the cost function and find that it steadily decreases, which is another indication of the flawless performance of the model. So the only reason to justify this anomaly is that even though different data classes have the same proportion of train/test split, it doesn't mean that the underlying distribution of data in test split and train split equals fit. As a result, the test samples sometimes become the easier choice for the model to classify, which is the case in this dataset. Table 3 shows the selected part of the experiment.

Table 2. PSLVQ's Accuracy (train/test)

Dataset	Learning-rate	n-epochs	n-folds	Classification	Reject-classification
DBCW	0.2	25	60	81.785/88.88	83.67/88.88
CHD	0.1	20	60	80.78/74.57	81.36/78.94

Previously we discussed based on Chow [3] that the optimum $t^* = \frac{c_c - c_e}{c_c - c_r}$ is obtained from (22) as long as $c_e > c_r > c_c$. Without loss of generality, we assume $c_c = 0$ and try to investigate the model's behavior for different values of c_r and c_e. For this task, we focus on the CHD dataset.

Table 3. Model's parameters and their impact on the trend

Learning-rate	n-epochs	n-folds	Trend change	Cost function
0.05	30	53	No	Decreasing
0.10	10	53	No	Decreasing
0.10	20	53	No	Decreasing
0.10	20	27	No	Decreasing
0.15	10	53	No	Decreasing
0.15	20	53	No	Decreasing
0.15	20	27	No	Decreasing
0.15	25	27	No	Decreasing
0.15	30	27	No	Decreasing
0.20	20	53	No	Decreasing

As shown in Table 4, larger $\frac{1-t}{t}$ results in poorer performance and more rejected data. Since a larger $\frac{1-t}{t}$ means a smaller t, we can conclude that the more severe the impact of misclassification compared to rejection, the worse the outcome. In summary, to ensure an accurate classification, this model attempts to find a **balance** between severity of the impact of misclassification and rejection.

Table 4. Threshold-accuracy trade-off

$\frac{c_r}{c_e}$	$\frac{1-t}{t}$	Learning-rate	n-epochs	n-folds	Train/test	Rejection rate	n-acceptance
0.50	1.00	0.1	25	60	76.66/70.88	20.42	900
0.66	0.50	0.1	25	60	80.28/74.57	1.32	1131
0.75	0.33	0.1	25	60	81.36/78.94	0.59	1164

Finally, we compare our model, PSLVQ, with the RSLVQ. We open the discussion with Table 5. For this purpose, we consider the same rejection criterion which is used in the PSLVQ. As a drawback, it can be seen that the impressive accuracy (train/test) from the RSLVQ is compensated by rejecting almost half of the dataset. In our opinion, if not all but most of these rejections could be avoided. Besides, it seems in this special case the learning rate does not have any significant role. Considering that the original RSLVQ does not benefit from the reject option we decide to drop the rejection and compare the outcome of the PSLVQ with those from the RSLVQ. It is the point that the PSLVQ compared to the RSLVQ exhibits a big difference witnessed by Table 6.

In the end, it is worth mentioning that even though it is a tedious job to get the desired results from a model in practice but the outcomes are reasonably good enough to encourage us for taking further steps in the future and conduct a survey to compare other models with the PSLVQ.

Table 5. Applying RSLVQ with the reject-option on CHD

$(1-t)/t$	Learning-rate	n-epochs	n-folds	Train/test	Rejection percent.	n-acceptance
0.50	0.001	25	40	100/100	47.26	612
0.50	0.01	25	40	100/100	47.26	612
0.50	0.1	25	40	100/100	47.26	612

Table 6. Comparison between PSLVQ and RSLVQ

Model	Learning-rate	n-epochs	n-folds	Train/test
PSLVQ	0.15	25	60	82.24/79.00
RSLVQ	0.15	25	60	47.41/31.61
PSLVQ	0.1	25	60	80.87/78.94
RSLVQ	0.1	25	60	47.39/31.57
PSLVQ	0.1	25	40	78.16/74.57
RSLVQ	0.1	25	40	47.29/41.38

5 Conclusion

In this paper, we offer a trade-off between providing a reliable classification and omitting noisy data points in the case of ambiguity and uncertainty, bearing in mind that the lower the disparity between classes, the less reliable the model [1]. To this end, we try to maximize the disparity by proposing a contrastive learning method. The result is an *interpretable* mathematical model equipped with rejection as an option. Moreover, what sets this framework apart from other classifiers is the ability to process an unknown data point paired with a class-possibility assignment that does not sum up to one, i.e. this model can handle any positive measure like the membership function in fuzzy logic [26]. All challenges addressed in this work are supported by numerical experiments and are superior to RSLVQ, especially in classification. Finally, future work will consider studying unsupervised outlier detection as well as metric adaptation.

References

1. Bousquet, O., Elisseeff, A.: Stability and generalization. J. Mach. Learn. Res. **2**, 499–526 (2002)
2. Bradley, A.P.: The use of the area under the roc curve in the evaluation of machine learning algorithms. Pattern Recogn. **30**(7), 1145–1159 (1997)
3. Chow, C.: On optimum recognition error and reject tradeoff. IEEE Trans. Inf. Theory **16**(1), 41–46 (1970)
4. Devarakota, P.R., Mirbach, B., Ottersten, B.: Confidence estimation in classification decision: a method for detecting unseen patterns. In: Advances in Pattern Recognition, pp. 290–294. World Scientific (2007)
5. Fischer, L., Nebel, D., Villmann, T., Hammer, B., Wersing, H.: Rejection strategies for learning vector quantization – a comparison of probabilistic and deterministic approaches. In: Villmann, T., Schleif, F.-M., Kaden, M., Lange, M. (eds.) Advances in Self-Organizing Maps and Learning Vector Quantization. AISC, vol. 295, pp. 109–118. Springer, Cham (2014). https://doi.org/10.1007/978-3-319-07695-9_10
6. Hammer, B., Villmann, T.: Generalized relevance learning vector quantization. Neural Netw. **15**(8–9), 1059–1068 (2002)
7. Kohavi, R., et al.: A study of cross-validation and bootstrap for accuracy estimation and model selection. In: IJCAI, Montreal, Canada, vol. 14, pp. 1137–1145 (1995)

8. Kohonen, T.: Learning vector quantization. In: Kohonen, T. (ed.) Self-Organizing Maps, pp. 175–189. Springer, Heidelberg (1995). https://doi.org/10.1007/978-3-642-97610-0_6
9. Kohonen, T., Hynninen, J., Kangas, J., Laaksonen, J., Torkkola, K.: LVQ PAK: the learning vector quantization program package. Technical report (1996)
10. Kullback, S., Leibler, R.A.: On information and sufficiency. Ann. Math. Stat. **22**(1), 79–86 (1951)
11. Musavishavazi, S., Mohannazadeh Bakhtiari, M., Villmann, T.: A mathematical model for optimum error-reject trade-off for learning of secure classification models in the presence of label noise during training. In: Rutkowski, L., Scherer, R., Korytkowski, M., Pedrycz, W., Tadeusiewicz, R., Zurada, J.M. (eds.) ICAISC 2020. LNCS (LNAI), vol. 12415, pp. 547–554. Springer, Cham (2020). https://doi.org/10.1007/978-3-030-61401-0_51
12. Musavishavazi, S., Kaden, M., Villmann, T.: Possibilistic classification learning based on contrastive loss in learning vector quantizer networks. In: Rutkowski, L., Scherer, R., Korytkowski, M., Pedrycz, W., Tadeusiewicz, R., Zurada, J.M. (eds.) ICAISC 2021. LNCS (LNAI), vol. 12854, pp. 156–167. Springer, Cham (2021). https://doi.org/10.1007/978-3-030-87986-0_14
13. Nebel, D., Hammer, B., Villmann, T.: A median variant of generalized learning vector quantization. In: Lee, M., Hirose, A., Hou, Z.-G., Kil, R.M. (eds.) ICONIP 2013. LNCS, vol. 8227, pp. 19–26. Springer, Heidelberg (2013). https://doi.org/10.1007/978-3-642-42042-9_3
14. Provost, F., Fawcett, T.: Robust classification for imprecise environments. Mach. Learn. **42**(3), 203–231 (2001)
15. Raschka, S.: Model evaluation, model selection, and algorithm selection in machine learning. arXiv preprint arXiv:1811.12808 (2018)
16. Ravichandran, J., Kaden, M., Saralajew, S., Villmann, T.: Variants of dropconnect in learning vector quantization networks for evaluation of classification stability. Neurocomputing **403**, 121–132 (2020)
17. Robbins, H., Monro, S.: A stochastic approximation method. Ann. Math. Stat. 400–407 (1951)
18. Saralajew, S., Holdijk, L., Rees, M., Asan, E., Villmann, T.: Classification-by-components: probabilistic modeling of reasoning over a set of components. In: Advances in Neural Information Processing Systems, vol. 32 (2019)
19. Sato, A., Yamada, K.: Generalized learning vector quantization. In: NIPS, vol. 95, pp. 423–429 (1995)
20. Seo, S., Obermayer, K.: Soft learning vector quantization. Neural Comput. **15**(7), 1589–1604 (2003)
21. Varma, S., Simon, R.: Bias in error estimation when using cross-validation for model selection. BMC Bioinform. **7**(1), 1–8 (2006)
22. Villmann, A., Kaden, M., Saralajew, S., Hermann, W., Villmann, T.: Reliable patient classification in case of uncertain class labels using a cross-entropy approach. In: ESANN (2018)
23. Villmann, A., Kaden, M., Saralajew, S., Villmann, T.: Probabilistic learning vector quantization with cross-entropy for probabilistic class assignments in classification learning. In: Rutkowski, L., Scherer, R., Korytkowski, M., Pedrycz, W., Tadeusiewicz, R., Zurada, J.M. (eds.) ICAISC 2018. LNCS (LNAI), vol. 10841, pp. 724–735. Springer, Cham (2018). https://doi.org/10.1007/978-3-319-91253-0_67

24. Villmann, T., et al.: Self-adjusting reject options in prototype based classification. In: Merényi, E., Mendenhall, M.J., O'Driscoll, P. (eds.) Advances in Self-Organizing Maps and Learning Vector Quantization. AISC, vol. 428, pp. 269–279. Springer, Cham (2016). https://doi.org/10.1007/978-3-319-28518-4_24
25. Villmann, T., Kaden, M., Nebel, D., Biehl, M.: Learning vector quantization with adaptive cost-based outlier-rejection. In: Azzopardi, G., Petkov, N. (eds.) CAIP 2015. LNCS, vol. 9257, pp. 772–782. Springer, Cham (2015). https://doi.org/10.1007/978-3-319-23117-4_66
26. Zadeh, L.A.: Probability measures of fuzzy events. J. Math. Anal. Appl. **23**(2), 421–427 (1968)

A Classification Method for Imbalanced Data Based on Ant Lion Optimizer

Mengmeng Li, Yi Liu(✉), Qibin Zheng, Xiang Li, and Wei Qin

Academy of Military Sciences, Beijing, China
albertliu20th@163.com

Abstract. Imbalanced data will bring difficulties in data processing, which is very common in data engineering. These data usually have sophisticated distributions. Different resampling methods are required for dealing with data with different distributions, while fixed ones are adopted traditionally. Therefore, to select appropriate resampling methods for data with such characteristics, we propose a novel classification method for Imbalanced Data based on Ant Lion Optimizer, called ALOID. It combines adaptive resampling strategies, feature selection, and ensemble classifiers. The adaptive resampling strategy refers to utilizing roulette wheel selection to choose the most suitable resampling method with a greater probability for each dataset according to the variable probabilities of resampling methods. Then a two-stage approach is further used in feature selection: preprocessing and enhancing. In addition, we adopt an ensemble classifier with dynamic weights. The variable probabilities of resampling methods, features, and the weights of base classifiers are coded in individual solutions. A large number of comprehensive experiments have been carried out in this paper. ALOID is compared with 8 state-of-the-art algorithms on 33 publicly available imbalanced datasets. Using K-nearest neighbor as the base classifier, we have found ALOID outperforms other methods in most cases, especially on high-dimensional imbalanced datasets. Experiment results demonstrate the performance advantage of ALOID over other comparable algorithms.

Keywords: Ensemble · Feature selection · Imbalanced classification · Resampling

1 Introduction

In recent years, as more and more imbalanced data appear in computer science, natural science and management science, imbalanced classification problem has gradually become the focus in the field of pattern recognition, machine learning and data mining [1]. According to the number of classes, classification problems can be divided into binary classification and multi-class classification [2]. In this paper, we focus on the binary imbalanced classification problem. It refers to the number of instances between classes that are different. Specifically, one

Y. Tan and Y. Shi (Eds.): DMBD 2022, CCIS 1744, pp. 367–382, 2022.
https://doi.org/10.1007/978-981-19-9297-1_26

class (the majority/negative class) has more instances, while the other class (the minority/positive class) has fewer instances [3].

In standard binary classification research, it is usually assumed that the size of instances in majority class and minority class is approximately equal and the goal is to promote the overall accuracy of the classification model. But, when used in an imbalanced classification problem, such as cancer diagnosis [4], depression detection [5], fraud detection [6], network intrusion detection [7], gamma-ray spectral classification [8], standard classification algorithms become flawed or even ineffective [9]. That is because people tend to pay more attention to the minority classes which means the purpose is to improve the performance for the minority class without harming too much of it for the majority class [10]. If a standard algorithm is used in an imbalanced problem, it may be biased towards the majority class which goes against people's expectations.

In order to enhance the classification performance on imbalanced datasets, hundreds of methods have been proposed in the past few decades [1]. Existing algorithms improve the recognition of minority class and the performance of imbalance classification from different perspectives. However, they ignore that different datasets have different distributions, so different resampling methods should be used. If one method uses fixed resampling techniques, then it is probably not suitable for other datasets with different distributions. In addition, although feature selection has become the focus in an imbalanced classification problem, two-stage feature selection methods are relatively rarely used so far. Furthermore, how to set the weights of base classifiers in ensemble classifier is also a key issue. In order to solve these problems, we propose a classification method for imbalanced data based on Ant Lion Optimizer (ALOID) with adaptive resampling, two-stage feature selection, and ensemble classifiers with dynamic weights.

Our contributions and the advantages of ALOID are summarized as follows:

- Unlike existing methods, ALOID applies roulette wheel selection to choose resampling methods adaptively at iteration. This mechanism gives higher chance to the most resampling method for each dataset.
- We utilize a two-stage method in feature selection. First, we adopt filters to weigh and select features. It is considered feature preprocessing (rough selection). Then, a wrapper is employed subsequently. It is called enhanced feature selection (fine selection). Combining these two types of methods, ALOID can select more precise features based on the results of the previous step.
- An ensemble classifier is used in ALOID to ameliorate the classification performance. In ALOID, the weights of base classifiers are updated dynamically. This can make the performance better than those methods with artificial or fixed weights.

The rest of this paper is organized as follows. Section 2 reviews popular algorithms in four levels. Section 3 describes ALOID in detail. In Sect. 4, we show the results of experiments and then analyze them in three aspects. Finally, the conclusion is presented. And the possible future work is discussed in Sect. 5.

2 Related Work

In this part, we will introduce classification methods of imbalanced data. It is mainly divided into four categories: data level methods, algorithm level methods, cost-sensitive level methods, and ensemble level methods.

2.1 Data Level Methods

According to the resampling techniques, data level methods can be divided into two categories: oversampling and undersampling. Oversampling is usually to increase the number of minority instances by sampling from minority samples repeatedly or generating new minority instances. Undersampling usually decreases the number of majority samples by selecting part majority instances and combine them with all minority samples [11]. The simplest methods are random oversampling and random undersampling. However, random oversampling will cause an over-fitting problem because it copies minority samples simply and randomly [12]. In contrast, random undersampling may eliminate some valuable majority instances, which may lead to information missing and then affect classification performance.

In order to solve the over-fitting problem caused by random oversampling, Chawla et al. [13] propose the synthetic minority oversampling technique (SMOTE) which is a widely used and effective oversampling method. The idea of SMOTE is to synthesize new minority samples by random linear interpolation between each minority sample and its K neighbor samples in the same class. It generates new samples without repetition, which alleviates the over-fitting problem greatly.

Paria et al. [14] propose an improved method of SMOTE called the range-controlled SMOTE (RCSMOTE). It categorizes the minority instances into the border, safe and noisy samples, and give priority to border samples compared to the safe ones while ignoring the noisy samples in oversampling. In addition, it proposes a mechanism to control the location of synthetic samples by considering the characteristics of input datasets.

Outlier-SMOTE is a novel oversampling method proposed by Venkata et al. [15], which is an improvement to SMOTE and tests on the COVID-19 dataset. Original SMOTE resamples each instance equally, but the authors in this paper believe that more importance should be given to samples that are far away from the cluster, as they are the samples with a challenge to classify.

It is obvious that undersampling is a combinatorial optimization problem, so undersampling based on evolutionary algorithms is widely used. Javad et al. [16] employ the chaotic krill herd evolutionary algorithm to explore minority and majority class spaces for selecting some representative instances. In this algorithm, individuals are evaluated by a combined fitness function, which includes accuracy, Geometry mean (Gmean), and the penalties of minority and majority class reduction rates.

In response to how to identify the best mix of two classes in resampling, Li et al. [17] introduces a notion of swarm fusion and implements particle swarm optimization (PSO) as the optimizer to select sample subsets.

2.2 Algorithm Level Methods

Algorithm level methods don't generate new minority samples or remove majority samples during preprocessing, so they don't alter the original distribution of datasets. It is beneficial to learn unbiased models. But, when facing with imbalanced datasets, it is still very challenging. Algorithm level methods mainly include one class learning [18], feature selection, and feature extraction [19,20].

One class learning [21] which learns a model only using one class samples has attracted increasing attention in some costly fields [22]. Lee et al. [23] apply it to the industrial field for fault-detection. The proposed module consists of three submodules, time-series prediction, residual calculation, and one-class classification and each deep network used for time-series prediction is trained with the production success cases' data. Gao et al. [24] use one class learning to detect outliers in the medical field. The method uses imaging complexity to enable deep learning models and learn inherent imaging features of one class.

2.3 Cost-Sensitive Level Methods

In classification problems, standard methods assign the same weights to all samples and focus on improving overall accuracy. But the performance declines significantly in the case of learning from imbalanced data. If the classifier predicts all samples as negative classes, high accuracy can be got, but the classifier is useless obviously. To alleviate this problem, cost-sensitive level methods are proposed.

Li et al. [25] present a cost-sensitive approach that penalizes misclassification cost through a hybrid attribute measure. The measure is defined by the combination of the Gini index and information gain. Wang et al. [26] introduce a new algorithm called cost-sensitive fuzzy multiple kernel learning. It combines fuzzy memberships and multiple kernel learning. Fuzzy memberships are determined by both the entropies of samples and the cost of each class. Multiple kernel learning can easily extend existing algorithms to non-linear space by integrating different kernels.

Although cost-sensitive level methods are closer to the nature of people's expectations, there are two challenges: (1) Misclassification cost matrix is usually set by experts in that field, but most researchers are not. (2) Even for experts, it is very difficult to obtain an appropriate misclassification cost matrix. Therefore, cost-sensitive level methods have not received so much attention [27].

2.4 Ensemble Level Methods

Ensemble level methods have acquired popularity in the field of data mining and machine learning due to their superior performance than single base classifier [28]. Chen et al. [27] develop a hybrid data level ensemble method, which combines ensemble technology and the union of undersampling methods and oversampling methods. The proposed undersampling method deletes some unrepresentative majority samples based on margin theory [29], while oversampling method generates diverse minority samples according to a new distance measure comprising Euclidean distance and diversity of instances.

Seng et al. [30] propose a stacked ensemble method named neighborhood undersampling stacked ensemble, which replaces the standard cross-validation-like with the proposed Subset and Out-of-Subset prediction in the step of meta-data generation. Moreover, this paper further proposes a novel undersampling technique. It utilizes local neighborhood information to select majority samples by using K-Nearest Neighbors [31].

Due to the superior performance, ensemble learning has received increasing attention in imbalanced classification problems. However, existing ensemble methods exhibit some limitations. For example, how to maximize the performance of ensemble classifiers. Specifically, ensemble classifiers are combined by many base classifiers, and how to find the optimal weights of base classifiers is important and difficult.

3 Methods

In this section, we describe the proposed algorithm ALOID from four aspects: feature preprocessing, enhanced feature selection, adaptive resampling and ensemble classifier.

3.1 Feature Preprocessing

In order to attain a better input dataset, data preprocessing is often performed before building a learning model. ALOID uses three filter methods in feature preprocessing to delete irrelevant and redundant features. These three methods are symmetrical uncertainty (SU), chi-square test, and reliefF. Then *SU_list*, *Chi_list*, *ReliefF_list* are got by sorted the features in descending order, respectively. SU and chi-square test are good at measuring the correlation between features and classes. ReliefF is an expert in calculating the importance of features by using inter-sample information.

Then, we aggregate these three lists by median way. It chooses the median number as the ranking for each feature. Then, we select the first D features that are powerful in retrieving minority classes as the final result of feature preprocessing [32]. This stage can both reduce the solution space and provide guidance information for enhanced feature selection stage.

3.2 Enhanced Feature Selection

In this part, we will give the key component of ALOID based on Ant Lion Optimizer (ALO) [33]. ALO is an outstanding meta-heuristic algorithm by mimicking the hunting behavior of antlions. It's widely used in feature selection. In enhanced feature selection, we take ALO as the benchmark algorithm and each antlion is coded with $D+V+M$ values within the ranges of 0 to 1. Fig. 1 shows the composition of individuals.

3.3 Adaptive Resampling

Because the information from majority classes and minority classes is imbalanced, the learning classifier will perform better on the former than the latter. However, in the real world, people tend to pay more attention to minority classes. In order to increase the learning sensitivity to minority classes, lots of different resampling methods are proposed that is because no resampling method is valid for all datasets. But existing imbalanced classification methods often focus on fixed resampling methods. This may reduce classification performance significantly on datasets with different data distributions. Therefore, in order to select a more suitable resampling method for each dataset, we introduce an adaptive resampling strategy which selects a resampling method adaptively according to roulette wheel selection.

Roulette selection means that the probability of each resampling method being selected is proportional to the value of its variable probability. We set the variable probabilities of resampling methods in the middle part of individual solutions. In experiments, V is 3, and these three resampling methods are random oversampling (ROS), random undersampling (RUS), and SMOTE. The pseudo code of adaptive resampling strategy is described in Algorithm 1.

The process of normalizing the variable probability of each individual solution is shown in (1).

$$P_i = \frac{p_i}{\sum_{i=o,u,s} p_i} \tag{1}$$

where p_i and P_i are variable probability and normalized variable probability of each resampling method, respectively.

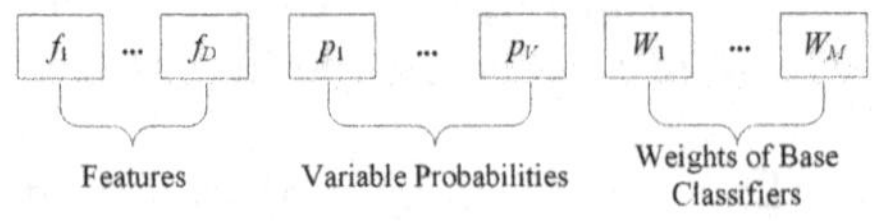

Fig. 1. The composition of individuals.

Algorithm 1. Pseudo code of Adaptive Resampling

Input: Number of balanced datasets M, variable probabilities of ROS p_o, variable probabilities of RUS p_u, variable probabilities of SMOTE p_s, dataset D_t
Output: M balanced datasets
1. According to the individual solution optimization process, the variable probability (p_o, p_u, and p_s) of each resampling method is obtained
2. FOR i from 1 to M
3. Use Equation (1) to normalize variable probability P_i
4. Use Equation (2) to calculate the cumulative probability q_j
5. IF rand() $<q_o$
6. Choose ROS as the resampling method
7. ELSEIF $q_o <$rand() $<q_u$
8. Choose RUS as the resampling method
9. ELSE
10. Choose SMOTE as the resampling method
11. END
12. Balance the dataset BD_i
13. END FOR
14. Output M balanced datasets

The process of calculating the cumulative probability of each resampling method is shown in (2).

$$q_j = \sum_{i=o}^{j} P_i, \quad j = o, u, s \tag{2}$$

where q_j is the cumulative probability of each resampling method.

3.4 Ensemble Classifier

To improve the classification performance of weak classifiers, ensemble algorithms are used in many imbalanced learning tasks. The classification performance of the ensemble classifier is usually greater than that of each single base classifier [1]. In addition, the diversity of base classifiers can improve classification performance significantly, especially in minority classes [34]. So, we make the weights of base classifiers update dynamically. Simple linear weight aggregation is employed in (3).

$$f(i) = W_1 * f_1(i) + W_2 * f_2(i) + \ldots + W_M * f_M(i) \tag{3}$$

where i is the ith samples. $f_j(\cdot)$ and $f(\cdot)$ are the results of jth base classifier and ensemble classifier, respectively. $W_j$is the jth element in the last M values of individuals.

3.5 ALOID

The pseudo code of ALOID is described in Algorithm 2.

The process of ALOID can be divided into four steps. Firstly, according to the feature dimension, it is judged whether the feature preprocessing process is needed. If the number of dimensions is more than the threshold (set to 30 in experiments), we make a rough feature selection. Secondly, we refine features in enhanced feature selection. Each antlion of ALOID, antlion, is coded as a candidate solution with three parts: features, variable probabilities, and weights. Thirdly, ALOID utilizes roulette wheel selection to choose a resampling method. Finally, we yield M balanced datasets to train M base classifiers and then combine them into an ensemble classifier.

4 Experimental Settings and Results

4.1 Datasets

In experiments, we select 33 binary imbalanced datasets from KEEL[1], UCI[2], and scikit[3] to test ALOID, including 23 low-dimensional datasets and 10 high-dimensional datasets with 30 features as the demarcation point. The characteristics of these datasets are shown in Table 1. The not bold part is low-dimensional datasets with less than 30 features, and the bold part is high-dimensional datasets with more than 30 features.

Samples denote the number of records (ranging from 62 to 2600). Features represent the number of features in each dataset (ranging from 4 to 22283). IR stands for the imbalanced ratio defined as the number of majority instances divided by that of minority instances [35] (ranging from 1.01 to 23.15). Chosen features indicate the number of features selected by ALOID (ranging from 38.88% to 75.00% in low-dimensional datasets and from 0.05% to 20.59% in high-dimensional datasets). The number of classifiers denotes how many base classifiers are integrated into ensemble classifiers.

The experiments are performed using Windows 10 operating system, Matlab R2018a, Intel i7-9700 3.00 GHz, 16.0 GB ram as the test platform. We adopt fivefold cross-validation for each dataset. In addition, in order to be objective and effective, every algorithm is executed ten times independently and the average value of ten outcomes is used as the final result.

4.2 Comparable Algorithms and Settings

To show the effectiveness of ALOID, eight algorithms are performed and compared with it. Binary Multi-Neighborhood Artificial Bee Colony (BMNABC) [36], Binary Differential Evolution (BDE) [37], Binary Grey Wolf Optimization-approach 1/2 (bGWO1/2) [38], and SYMON [32] are five popular wrapper methods for imbalanced data feature selection. Genetic Undersampling and Multiobjective Ant Colony Optimization based Feature selection (GU-MOACOFS) [11]

[1] https://sci2s.ugr.es/keel/imbalanced.php.

[2] https://archive.ics.uci.edu/ml/datasets.php.

[3] https://jundongl.github.io/scikit-feature/datasets.html.

Algorithm 2. Pseudo code of ALOID

Input: Train dataset D_t, test dataset D_s, population size N, max iterations T, the threshold of features D, number of chosen features F, number of classifiers M, number of resampling methods V
Output: Ensemble classifier
1.IF features of dataset $>D$
2. Generate *SU_list*, *Chi_list*, *ReliefF_list* on train dataset D_t
3. Integrate these three lists by median way into a *Ranking_list*
4. Choose the first D features from *Ranking_list*
5.END IF
6.Initialize N antlions and calculate their fitness
7.Find the best antlion as elite
8.WHILE (current iteration <T)
9. FOR every ant
10. Select an antlion based on roulette wheel selection
11. Create a random walk around the selected antlion and elite
12. Update the position of the ant
13. Select F features from the ant's first D dimension, and choose a resampling method based on variable probabilities from the middle V dimensions of ants
14. Generate M balanced datasets based on the F chosen features and the chosen resampling method
15. Learn M base classifiers and combine them into an ensemble classifier with weights from ant's last M dimensions
16. Evaluate ALOID on test dataset D_s
17. END FOR
18. Update elite
19. END WHILE

is the preliminary work of our team. SVM-RFE [39] and SVM-RFE+CBR [40] are two filter methods for imbalanced data feature selection.

The parameters of algorithms are set as follows, the number of iterations T is 200, population size N is 40. Hyperparameters are the same as original papers. About ALOID, the threshold of features D is 0.2 times of dataset's dimension, and the number of chosen features F is shown in Table 1. We take KNN as the base classifier, and K is set to 5. The number of base classifiers M is set according to the results of preliminary experiments.

4.3 Evaluation Metrics and Functions

In order to reflect the performance of ALOID, we take Gmean [41], and Kappa [42] as evaluation metrics. Among them, Gmean is popular in classification problems, which can reflect the classification result objectively. Kappa is adopted to verify and contrast these algorithms because it can imply the credibility of classification models. Moreover, in order to analyze ALOID comprehensively, we conduct a time cost analysis.

4.4 Experiment Results and Analysis

Table 1. Characteristics of experiment datasets.

No.	Datasets	Samples	Features	IR	Chosen features	Number of classifiers	Websites
1	ecoli0vs1	220	7	1.86	4	15	keel
2	wisconsin	683	9	1.86	5	15	keel
3	pima	768	8	1.87	4	30	keel
4	iris0	150	4	2	3	3	keel
5	glass0	214	9	2.06	5	15	keel
6	vehicle0	846	18	3.25	7	15	keel
7	ecoli1	336	7	3.36	4	15	keel
8	glass	214	9	8.44	5	3	keel
9	ecoli3	336	7	8.6	4	15	keel
10	ecoli067vs35	222	7	9.09	4	5	keel
11	ecoli01vs235	244	7	9.17	4	9	keel
12	ecoli0347vs56	257	7	9.28	4	24	keel
13	glass016vs2	192	9	10.29	5	22	keel
14	ecoli01vs5	240	6	11	3	6	keel
15	cleveland0vs4	177	13	12.62	7	13	keel
16	ecoli0146vs5	280	6	13	3	4	keel
17	zoo-3	101	16	19.2	8	3	keel
18	shuttlec2vsc4	129	9	20.5	5	3	keel
19	yeast	1484	8	23.15	4	15	keel
20	poker9vs7	244	10	29.5	5	4	keel
21	ecoli0137vs26	281	7	39.14	4	4	keel
22	Statlog (heart)	270	12	1.25	6	20	UCI
23	Planning Relax	182	12	2.5	6	24	UCI
24	**sonar**	208	60	1.14	7	3	UCI
25	**ionosphere**	351	34	1.79	7	27	UCI
26	**madelon**	2600	500	1.01	5	18	scikit
27	**Prostate_GE**	102	5966	1.04	6	3	scikit
28	**SMK_CAN_187**	187	19993	1.08	11	3	scikit
29	**arcene**	200	10000	1.27	9	19	scikit
30	**colon**	62	2000	1.82	7	4	scikit
31	**leukemia**	72	7070	1.88	8	20	scikit
32	**ALLAML**	72	7129	1.88	8	18	scikit
33	**GLI_85**	85	22283	2.27	13	4	scikit

Comparative Experiments and Analysis. In this section, we analyze the results of comparative experiments with all algorithms on all datasets. Table 2 and Table 3 shows the values of Gmean and Kappa, respectively. The upper part is the results of low-dimensional datasets and the lower part is that of high-dimensional datasets. Then, the bolded values represent the best. In addition, the number of first best, second best, third best, and others are recorded at the bottom of tables by F/S/T/O, respectively.

Table 2 displays the value of Gmean. From it, we can find that ALOID's performance is the best in most cases. ALOID is top three on all 33 datasets, with 23 times reaching the best, 8 times reaching the second best, and 2 times being the third best. According to the values in low-dimensional datasets, ALOID can get 1 on 5 datasets iris0, glass, zoo-3, shuttlec2vsc4, and poker9vs7. Then, ALOID can get the first best on 15 datasets out of 23 cases, that is 65.22%. In addition, ALOID's Gmean is improved significantly by 0.9667 with BMNABC in dataset poker9vs7. Furthermore, when compared with bGWO2 which is the second-best among the remaining algorithms, ALOID's result also can improve up to 0.2244 on dataset poker9vs7. Based on the values in high-dimensional datasets, ALOID can get 1 on 3 datasets Prostate_GE, leukemia, and ALLAML. Then, ALOID can get the first best on 8 datasets out of 10 cases, that is 80.00%. In addition, ALOID's Gmean is improved significantly by 0.4767 with SVM-RFE+CBR in dataset GLI_85. When compared with bGWO2, the value of ALOID can improve up to 0.1393 on dataset SMK_CAN_187.

Table 2. Gmean value of all algorithms on all datasets.

Gmean	BMNABC	BDE	bGWO1	bGWO2	SYMON	GU-MOACOFS	SVM-RFE	SVM-RFE+CBR	ALOID
ecoli0vs1	0.9852	0.9873	0.9873	0.9873	0.9873	**0.9895**	0.9790	0.9682	0.9873
wisconsin	0.9698	**0.9868**	0.9841	0.9866	0.9832	0.9468	0.9562	0.9681	0.9857
pima	0.6643	0.7132	0.7119	0.7117	0.7025	0.4422	0.6605	0.5934	**0.7433**
iris0	0.9972	**1.0000**	**1.0000**	**1.0000**	**1.0000**	**1.0000**	**1.0000**	**1.0000**	**1.0000**
glass0	0.8053	0.8630	0.8643	0.8629	0.7954	0.6673	0.7746	0.7776	**0.8715**
vehicle0	0.9374	0.9670	0.9714	0.9784	0.9529	0.9619	0.9324	0.9168	**0.9799**
ecoli1	0.8589	0.8870	0.8895	0.8905	0.8907	0.7080	0.8370	0.8426	**0.9171**
glass	0.8912	0.9838	0.9929	0.9995	0.9715	0.9991	0.8551	0.8479	**1.0000**
ecoli3	0.6094	0.8024	0.8216	0.7710	0.7566	0.4832	0.7517	0.7198	**0.8887**
ecoli067vs35	0.8253	0.8778	0.8721	0.8746	0.8733	**0.9473**	0.7785	0.8419	0.9419
ecoli01vs235	0.7948	0.9102	0.9077	0.9135	0.9097	**0.9516**	0.7769	0.7088	0.9463
ecoli0347vs56	0.8440	0.9217	0.9217	0.9235	0.9116	0.9509	0.8572	0.8016	**0.9564**
glass016vs2	0.0856	0.5228	0.5228	0.5699	0.0974	0.4203	0.0632	0.0787	**0.7665**
ecoli01vs5	0.8645	0.9730	0.9707	0.9755	0.9638	**0.9860**	0.7840	0.7612	0.9841
cleveland0vs4	0.4527	0.7429	0.7712	**0.9104**	0.7240	0.7593	0.6518	0.6991	0.8581
ecoli0146vs5	0.8654	0.9562	0.9458	0.9599	0.9520	**0.9680**	0.8244	0.6944	0.9649
zoo-3	0.0667	0.6667	0.6667	0.8000	0.7333	0.4000	0.4000	0.2667	**1.0000**
shuttlec2vsc4	0.5805	**1.0000**	0.9805	**1.0000**	**1.0000**	0.0667	0.7886	0.2552	**1.0000**
yeast	0.8367	0.8566	0.8566	0.8584	0.8482	0.9316	0.8251	0.8266	**0.9437**
poker9vs7	0.0333	0.6190	0.6385	0.7856	0.5661	0.5632	0.7523	0.7718	**1.0000**
ecoli0137vs26	0.6334	0.8612	0.8612	0.8612	0.8612	0.4734	0.7786	0.7775	**0.9476**
Statlog (heart)	0.7947	0.8640	0.8600	**0.8763**	0.8157	0.7454	0.7860	0.7962	0.8607
Planning Relax	0.3948	0.5762	0.5715	0.5964	0.5546	0.5478	0.3385	0.3833	**0.6924**
sonar	0.8463	0.9300	0.9411	**0.9732**	0.9120	0.8352	0.7751	0.7330	0.9578
ionosphere	0.8731	0.8929	0.9054	0.9474	0.8916	0.8852	0.8513	0.8461	**0.9547**
madelon	0.8230	0.8274	0.8248	**0.9200**	0.7416	0.8083	0.4960	0.4998	0.8873
Prostate_GE	0.9256	0.9027	0.9123	0.9193	0.9152	0.9711	0.9215	0.9352	**1.0000**
SMK_CAN_187	0.6946	0.7142	0.7357	0.7483	0.7160	0.6821	0.6466	0.6798	**0.8876**
arcene	0.8752	0.8775	0.8971	0.9027	0.8824	0.8831	0.7668	0.7138	**0.9632**
colon	0.8322	0.8463	0.8610	0.8851	0.8447	0.9426	0.7007	0.7240	**0.9912**
leukemia	0.9072	0.9020	0.9224	0.9222	0.9163	0.9811	0.9482	0.7458	**1.0000**
ALLAML	0.8383	0.7906	0.8167	0.8397	0.8245	0.8054	0.8452	0.7524	**1.0000**
GLI_85	0.8516	0.9064	0.9397	0.9414	0.9201	0.9879	0.7757	0.5180	**0.9947**
F/S/T/O	0/1/1/31	3/4/6/20	1/5/7/20	6/12/8/7	2/3/1/27	6/6/1/20	1/1/4/27	1/0/1/31	23/8/2/0

From Table 3, ALOID's Kappa values stay top three in 27 out of 33 cases, including 18 best, 5 s best, 4 third best. In low-dimensional datasets, ALOID can get 1 on 5 datasets iris0, glass, zoo-3, shuttlec2vsc4, and poker9vs7. Then, ALOID can get the first best on 10 datasets out of 23 cases, that is 43.48%. In addition, ALOID's Kappa values stay above 0.8 in 14 out of 23 cases, that is 60.87%. In high-dimensional datasets, ALOID can get 1 on 3 datasets Prostate_GE, leukemia, and ALLAML. Then, ALOID can get the first best on 8 datasets out of 10 cases, that is 80.00%. In addition, ALOID's Kappa values stay above 0.8 in 8 out of 10 cases, that is 80.00%.

Based on the analysis of Table 2 and Table 3, we can draw the following three conclusions. Firstly, ALOID can get the best results in most cases, that prove the effectiveness of ALOID. Secondly, the results obtained by ALOID on high-dimensional datasets are better than those on low-dimensional datasets. Therefore, it can be considered that ALOID is more suitable for the classification of high-dimensional imbalanced datasets. Thirdly, in most cases, the Kappa value of the model trained using our proposed algorithm ALOID is higher than that of the model trained using other comparison algorithms, which proves that the model trained using ALOID is more reliable. Specifically, ALOID's Kappa values stay above 0.8 in 22 out of 33 cases, which stands for the almost perfect credibility of ALOID [43], and stay above 0.4 in 32 out of 33 cases, which represents that ALOID can train a stable and credible model in most cases.

Table 3. Kappa value of all algorithms on all datasets.

Kappa	BMNABC	BDE	bGWO1	bGWO2	SYMON	GU-MOACOFS	SVM-RFE	SVM-RFE+CBR	ALOID
ecoli0vs1	0.9767	0.9800	0.9800	0.9800	0.9800	**0.9833**	0.9667	0.9497	0.9800
wisconsin	0.9331	**0.9667**	0.9632	0.9677	0.9600	0.9123	0.9100	0.9328	0.9632
pima	0.3793	0.4648	0.4627	0.4681	0.4532	0.2229	0.3633	0.2436	**0.4709**
iris0	0.9953	**1.0000**	**1.0000**	**1.0000**	**1.0000**	**1.0000**	**1.0000**	**1.0000**	**1.0000**
glass0	0.5998	0.7117	0.7122	**0.7137**	0.5354	0.5077	0.5372	0.5417	0.6893
vehicle0	0.8738	0.9284	0.9341	**0.9511**	0.8993	0.8547	0.8519	0.8065	0.9232
ecoli1	0.7322	0.8003	0.8016	**0.8041**	0.7890	0.6017	0.7017	0.7107	0.7498
glass	0.6212	0.9798	0.9912	0.9974	0.9640	0.9912	0.6841	0.5472	**1.0000**
ecoli3	0.5045	0.6901	**0.7108**	0.6761	0.6622	0.3731	0.5673	0.5263	0.6272
ecoli067vs35	0.7570	0.8497	0.8446	0.8476	0.8459	0.8525	0.6897	0.7845	**0.8947**
ecoli01vs235	0.7131	0.8915	0.8899	0.8956	0.8908	0.8706	0.6354	0.5191	**0.9132**
ecoli0347vs56	0.7555	0.9025	0.9025	**0.9045**	0.8856	0.8502	0.7726	0.6738	0.8949
glass016vs2	0.0757	0.4411	0.4411	**0.4848**	0.0392	0.0000	(0.0056)	0.0279	0.4352
ecoli01vs5	0.8127	0.9685	0.9636	0.9691	0.9551	0.9362	0.6372	0.5703	**0.9762**
cleveland0vs4	0.4075	0.6850	0.7148	**0.8947**	0.6802	0.0000	0.5402	0.5855	0.7644
ecoli0146vs5	0.8096	0.9497	0.9352	**0.9505**	0.9430	0.8859	0.7244	0.5038	0.9050
zoo-3	0.0667	0.6667	0.6667	0.8000	0.7333	0.0000	0.4000	0.2667	**1.0000**
shuttlec2vsc4	0.5766	**1.0000**	0.9765	**1.0000**	**1.0000**	0.0667	0.7729	0.2396	**1.0000**
yeast	0.7270	0.7700	0.7690	**0.7711**	0.7550	0.7302	0.7086	0.7111	0.7704
poker9vs7	0.0253	0.6094	0.6323	0.7681	0.5452	0.0000	0.7428	0.1627	**1.0000**
ecoli0137vs26	0.5970	0.8485	0.8485	0.8485	0.8485	0.4624	0.7615	0.7358	**0.9131**
Statlog (heart)	0.5961	0.7319	0.7273	**0.7627**	0.6414	0.5716	0.5796	0.5995	0.7302
Planning Relax	0.0451	0.3761	0.3679	**0.4037**	0.3359	0.3349	(0.0525)	0.0002	0.3379
sonar	0.6916	0.8661	0.8828	**0.9470**	0.8259	0.6748	0.5484	0.4724	0.9163
ionosphere	0.7912	0.8224	0.8427	0.9108	0.8284	0.8110	0.7257	0.7144	**0.9238**
madelon	0.6463	0.6550	0.6496	**0.8398**	0.4835	0.6329	(0.0049)	0.0008	0.7747
Prostate_GE	0.8461	0.7984	0.8200	0.8355	0.8274	0.9378	0.8386	0.8691	**1.0000**
SMK_CAN_187	0.4016	0.4365	0.4773	0.5027	0.4399	0.1592	0.2998	0.3634	**0.7731**
arcene	0.7473	0.7515	0.7893	0.8013	0.7600	0.7535	0.5297	0.4243	**0.9289**
colon	0.7020	0.6917	0.7292	0.7691	0.6872	0.8354	0.4189	0.4459	**0.9824**
leukemia	0.8417	0.8298	0.8707	0.8723	0.8526	0.9270	0.8802	0.5500	**1.0000**
ALLAML	0.7329	0.6807	0.7246	0.7547	0.7331	0.7084	0.7525	0.6089	**1.0000**
GLI_85	0.7341	0.7901	0.8628	0.8731	0.8246	0.9563	0.5670	0.1863	**0.9896**
F/S/T/O	0/1/1/31	2/9/8/14	2/8/8/15	15/12/4/2	2/2/2/27	2/5/1/25	1/0/4/28	1/0/1/31	18/5/4/6

Time Cost Experiment. In Fig. 2, we show the average time cost of all algorithms. From it, we can find that ALOID takes less time only than GU-MOACOFS on low-dimensional datasets, GU-MOACOFS and SYMON on high-dimensional datasets, and GU-MOACOFS on all datasets. It is because that ALOID uses a two-stage feature selection method which employs filters first and a wrapper next. This method improves ALOID's performance but consumes more time accordingly. On the other hand, ALOID even needs to synthesize some minority samples on some datasets. And multiple base classifiers also need to be trained in ALOID. Both of these skills are designed to improve performance but are time-consuming.

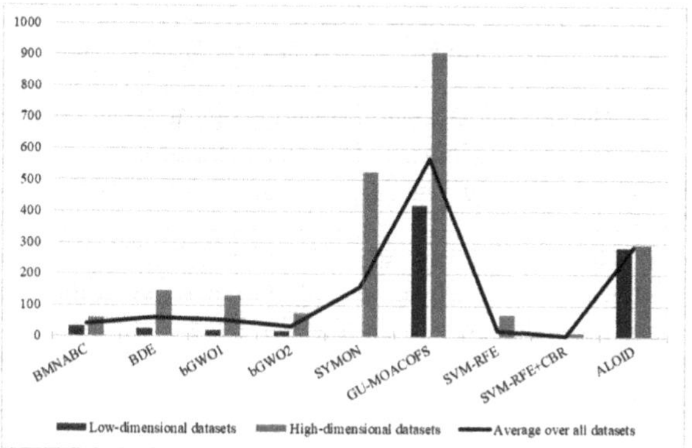

Fig. 2. Combination chart of the average results of time cost on low-dimensional datasets, high-dimensional datasets, and all datasets. (s)

5 Conclusion

In this paper, we propose a classification method for imbalanced data based on Ant Lion Optimizer, called. In ALOID, we adopt a two-stage feature selection method. In feature preprocessing stage, three filter methods are used and in enhanced feature selection stage, a wrapper method based on ALO is employed. Then, in order to select an appropriate resampling method adaptively for each dataset, ALOID uses the roulette wheel selection strategy. Moreover, an ensemble classifier with dynamic weights is also utilized to improve classification performance. A large number of comprehensive experiments have been performed with 8 comparable algorithms on 33 imbalanced datasets. The results show the effectiveness and superiority of ALOID, especially on high-dimensional datasets.

Although the classification performance of ALOID is superior to comparable algorithms, it also has some shortcomings. For example, ALOID is time-consuming when compared with other algorithms. In the future, we will reduce the time overhead of ALOID.

References

1. Guo, H., Li, Y., Jennifer, S., Gu, M., Huang, Y., Gong, B.: Learning from class-imbalanced data: review of methods and applications. Expert Syst. Appl. **73**, 220–239 (2017)
2. Branco, P., Torgo, L., Ribeiro, R.P.: A survey of predictive modeling on imbalanced domains. ACM Comput. Surv. **49**(2), 1–50 (2016)
3. Wang, C., Deng, C., Yu, Z., Hui, D., Gong, X., Luo, R.: Adaptive ensemble of classifiers with regularization for imbalanced data classification. Inf. Fusion **69**, 81–102 (2021)
4. Alkuhlani, A., Nassef, M., Farag, I.: Multistage feature selection approach for high-dimensional cancer data. Soft Comput. **21**, 6895–6906 (2017)
5. Mousavian, M., Chen, J., Greening, S.: Feature selection and imbalanced data handling for depression detection. In: Wang, S., et al. (eds.) BI 2018. LNCS (LNAI), vol. 11309, pp. 349–358. Springer, Cham (2018). https://doi.org/10.1007/978-3-030-05587-5_33
6. Sun, J., et al.: FDHelper: assist unsupervised fraud detection experts with interactive feature selection and evaluation. In: Proceedings of the 2020 CHI Conference on Human Factors in Computing Systems, pp. 1–12. Association for Computing Machinery (2020)
7. Al-Mandhari, I., Guan, L., Edirisinghe, E.A.: Impact of the structure of data pre-processing pipelines on the performance of classifiers when applied to imbalanced network intrusion detection system dataset. In: Bi, Y., Bhatia, R., Kapoor, S. (eds.) IntelliSys 2019. AISC, vol. 1037, pp. 577–589. Springer, Cham (2020). https://doi.org/10.1007/978-3-030-29516-5_45
8. Sharma, S., Somayaji, A., Japkowicz, N.: Learning over subconcepts: strategies for 1-class classification. Comput. Intell. **34**, 440–467 (2018)
9. Zhang, X., Hu, B.: A new strategy of cost-free learning in the class imbalance problem. IEEE Trans. Knowl. Data Eng. **26**(12), 2872–2885 (2014)
10. Rodríguez, J.J., Díez-Pastor, J.F., Arnaiz-González, l., Kuncheva, L.I.: Random balance ensembles for multiclass imbalance learning. Knowl.-Based Syst. **193**, 105434 (2020)
11. Liu, Y., Wang, Y., Ren, X., Zhou, H., Diao, X.: A classification method based on feature selection for imbalanced data. IEEE Access **7**, 81794–81807 (2019)
12. He, H., Garcia, E.A.: Learning from imbalanced data. IEEE Trans. Knowl. Data Eng. **21**(9), 1263–1284 (2009)
13. Chawla, N.V., Bowyer, K.W., Hall, L.O., Kegelmeyer, W.P.: Smote: synthetic minority over-sampling technique. J. Artif. Intell. Res. **16**(1), 321–357 (2002)
14. Soltanzadeh, P., Hashemzadeh, M.: RCSMOTE: range-controlled synthetic minority over-sampling technique for handling the class imbalance problem. Inf. Sci. **542**, 92–111 (2021)
15. Turlapati, V.P.K., Prusty, M.R.: Outlier-smote: a refined oversampling technique for improved detection of COVID-19. Intell.-Based Med. **3–4**, 100023 (2020)
16. Hamidzadeh, J., Kashefi, N., Moradi, M.: Combined weighted multi-objective optimizer for instance reduction in two-class imbalanced data problem. Eng. Appl. Artif. Intell. **90**, 103500 (2020)
17. Li, J., Fong, S., Wong, R.K., Chu, V.W.: Adaptive multi-objective swarm fusion for imbalanced data classification. Inf. Fusion **39**, 1–24 (2018)
18. Trittenbach, H., Englhardt, A., Böhm, K.: An overview and a benchmark of active learning for outlier detection with one-class classifiers. Expert Syst. Appl. **168**, 114372 (2021)

19. Almaghrabi, F., Xu, D., Yang, J.: An evidential reasoning rule based feature selection for improving trauma outcome prediction. Appl. Soft Comput. **103**, 107112 (2021)
20. Effrosynidis, D., Arampatzis, A.: An evaluation of feature selection methods for environmental data. Eco. Inform. **61**, 101224 (2021)
21. Mena, L.J., Gonzalez, J.A.: Symbolic one-class learning from imbalanced datasets: application in medical diagnosis. Int. J. Artif. Intell. Tools **18**(2), 273–309 (2009)
22. Tsai, C.F., Lin, W.C.: Feature selection and ensemble learning techniques in one-class classifiers: an empirical study of two-class imbalanced datasets. IEEE Access **9**, 13717–13726 (2021)
23. Lee, J., Lee, Y.C., Kim, J.T.: Fault detection based on one-class deep learning for manufacturing applications limited to an imbalanced database. J. Manuf. Syst. **57**, 357–366 (2020)
24. Gao, L., Zhang, L., Liu, C., Wu, S.: Handling imbalanced medical image data: a deep-learning-based one-class classification approach. Artif. Intell. Med. **108**, 101935 (2020)
25. Li, F., Zhang, X., Zhang, X., Du, C., Xu, Y., Tian, Y.: Cost-sensitive and hybrid-attribute measure multi-decision tree over imbalanced data sets. Inf. Sci. **422**, 242–256 (2018)
26. Wang, Z., Wang, B., Cheng, Y., Li, D., Zhang, J.: Cost-sensitive fuzzy multiple kernel learning for imbalanced problem. Neurocomputing **366**, 178–193 (2019)
27. Chen, Z., Duan, J., Kang, L., Qiu, G.: A hybrid data-level ensemble to enable learning from highly imbalanced dataset. Inf. Sci. **554**, 157–176 (2020)
28. López, V., Fernández, A., García, S., Palade, V., Herrera, F.: An insight into classification with imbalanced data: empirical results and current trends on using data intrinsic characteristics. Inf. Sci. **250**(250), 113–141 (2013)
29. Guo, L., Boukir, S.: Margin-based ordered aggregation for ensemble pruning. Pattern Recogn. Lett. **34**(6), 603–609 (2013)
30. Seng, Z., Kareem, S.A., Varathan, K.D.: A neighborhood undersampling stacked ensemble (NUS-SE) in imbalanced classification. Expert Syst. Appl. **168**, 114246 (2021)
31. Napierala, K., Stefanowski, J.: Identification of different types of minority class examples in imbalanced data. In: Corchado, E., Snášel, V., Abraham, A., Woźniak, M., Graña, M., Cho, S.-B. (eds.) HAIS 2012. LNCS (LNAI), vol. 7209, pp. 139–150. Springer, Heidelberg (2012). https://doi.org/10.1007/978-3-642-28931-6_14
32. Moayedikia, A., Ong, K.L., Boo, Y.L., Yeoh, W.G., Jensen, R.: Feature selection for high dimensional imbalanced class data using harmony search. Eng. Appl. Artif. Intell. **57**, 38–49 (2017)
33. Mirjalili, S.: The ant lion optimizer. Adv. Eng. Softw. **83**, 80–98 (2015)
34. Wang, S., Yao, X.: Diversity analysis on imbalanced data sets by using ensemble models. In: 2009 IEEE Symposium on Computational Intelligence and Data Mining, pp. 324–331 (2009)
35. Fernández, A., García, S., Galar, M., Prati, R.C., Krawczyk, B., Herrera, F.: Learning from Imbalanced Data Sets (2018)
36. Beheshti, Z.: BMNABC: binary multi-neighborhood artificial bee colony for high-dimensional discrete optimization problems. Cybern. Syst. **49**, 452–474 (2018)
37. He, X., Zhang, Q., Sun, N., Dong, Y.: Feature selection with discrete binary differential evolution. In: 2009 International Conference on Artificial Intelligence and Computational Intelligence, vol. 4, pp. 327–330 (2009)
38. Emary, E., Zawbaa, H.M., Hassanien, A.E.: Binary grey wolf optimization approaches for feature selection. Neurocomputing **172**(8), 371–381 (2016)

39. Guyon, I., Weston, J., Barnhill, S., Vapnik, V.: Gene selection for cancer classification using support vector machines. Mach. Learn. **46**(1), 389–422 (2002)
40. Yan, K., Zhang, D.: Feature selection and analysis on correlated gas sensor data with recursive feature elimination. Sens. Actuators B Chem. **212**, 353–363 (2015)
41. Kubat, M., Holte, R.C., Matwin, S.: Machine learning for the detection of oil spills in satellite radar images. Mach. Learn. **30**(2), 195–215 (1998)
42. Viera, A.J., Garrett, J.M.: Understanding interobserver agreement: the kappa statistic. Fam. Med. **37**(5), 360–363 (2005)
43. Chen, Y., Lin, C.: Combining SVMs with various feature selection strategies. In: Guyon, I., Nikravesh, M., Gunn, S., Zadeh, L.A. (eds.) Feature Extraction, pp. 315–324. Springer, Heidelberg (2006). https://doi.org/10.1007/978-3-540-35488-8_13

Learnable Relation with Triplet Formulation for Semi-supervised Medical Image Classification

Yiming Sun, Zhiqiang Xie, Kun Fang, Enmei Tu, and Jie Yang(✉)

Institute of Image Processing and Pattern Recognition, Shanghai Jiao Tong University, Shanghai, China
{ymsun_sjtu,qiang839,fanghenshao,jieyang}@sjtu.edu.cn

Abstract. For medical image classification, annotations for images are laborious and expensive, which is suitable for the application of semi-supervised learning. Mainstream semi-supervised learning methods develop a consistency regularization to leverage the unlabeled data but they neglect the relations among data. This paper proposes a novel learnable relation semi-supervised method with triplet formulation to not only jointly achieve feature extraction and distance metric learning but restrict the relations among features properly. With the learnable distance metric, the proposed method could learn the features and the metric via one single network to much better characterize the relations among features. Besides, triplet formulation is employed to constraint the relations among features. Experiments on skin lesion diagnosis data set indicate that the proposed method outperforms other state-of-the-art semi-supervised learning methods.

Keywords: Semi-supervised · Medical image classification · Learnable relation · Triplet formulation

1 Introduction

Medical image classification [10,11,25] plays an important role in clinical treatment and computer-aided diagnosis, e.g., skin lesion classification [14,16] which aims to identify melanoma apart from nevus. Recently, deep learning has boosted the development of medical image classification [10,25]. However, the demand for a large amount of labeled training data is especially hard to satisfy for medical images since expertise medical knowledge is involved while labeling. By contrast, unlabeled data is much easier to collect through clinical equipment. Thus, semi-supervised learning (SSL, [4,9,15,22]), which could effectively leverage the numerous unlabeled data and the scarce labeled data to achieve great performance, has its natural advantages in medical image classification [2,12,26].

Among the diverse researches in semi-supervised learning, Mean Teacher (MT, [23]) is a popular framework that exploits the student and teacher models

Y. Tan and Y. Shi (Eds.): DMBD 2022, CCIS 1744, pp. 383–393, 2022.
https://doi.org/10.1007/978-981-19-9297-1_27

to regularize the consistency hidden in the labeled and unlabeled data. Based on MT, SRC-MT [13] and MT-SNTG [15], have shown remarkable performance in the task of skin lesion classification. SRC-MT [13] additionally enforces the sample relation consistency to extract the semantic information from images. MT-SNTG [15] encourages the features of data in the same class to be similar. These methods regularize the relations in the feature space by employing standard distance functions, e.g., Euclidean distance, cosine distance, and l_1-norm distance. However, in the encoded feature space, these standard distance functions might not be the optimal choices to characterize the relations [15], which indicates that the performance could even be further improved.

To address this issue, in this paper, we consider a novel learnable relation semi-supervised method that incorporates the feature encoding and the distance metric learning into a unifying framework. In this framework, the distance functions are not fixed forms and instead are learned simultaneously with the encoded features via one single network, which brings better compatibility between the features and the distance metric. Besides, to further better characterize the relations, we construct a triplet formulation [5,8] to constrain the distribution of feature space with respect to both intra-class and inter-class relations, which is more effective than other existing constraints. Experiments show that our method achieves state-of-the-art results on the ISIC 2018 [3,24] skin lesion analysis dataset.

Our main contributions are summarized as follows:

- We propose a novel learnable relation semi-supervised method by jointly performing the feature extraction and the distance metric learning via one single network.
- The proposed triplet formulation achieves stronger compactness of the intra-class features and stronger separability of the inter-class features to enhance the relation learning for semi-supervised learning.
- Extensive empirical results on the task of the skin lesion classification reveal the superior effectiveness of the proposed method over the other state-of-the-art methods. The ablation studies further indicate the necessity of distance metric learning.

2 Related Works

In this section, we discuss the existing methods related to our approach, including consistency-based semi-supervised learning and skin lesion classification.

2.1 Consistency-based Semi-supervised Learning

The consistency-based semi-supervised learning leverages the unlabeled data by encouraging consistency of predictions for the same input with different perturbations. Earlier Π model [9] predicts the labels for unlabeled data twice every epoch and encourages the two predictions to be the same. Since random perturbations are added to unlabeled data, it achieves the consistency regularization.

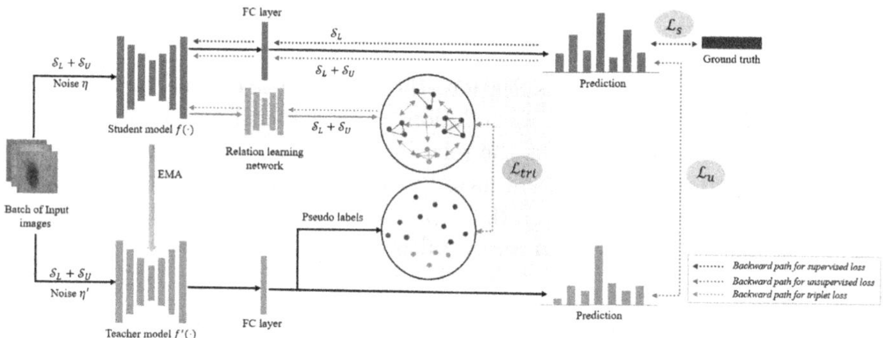

Fig. 1. The overview of learnable relation semi-supervised framework with triplet formulation. There is an MT semi-supervised backbone, whose student model is updated via supervised loss $\mathcal{L}_s$ and unsupervised loss $\mathcal{L}_u$, while teacher model weights are updated as the EMA of student weights. The proposed method utilizes a relation learning network to achieve better compatibility between feature extraction and distance metric, and a triplet formulation $\mathcal{L}_{tri}$ to enhance the relation learning.

Temporal Ensembling (TE, [9]) improves Π model by altering one prediction with an ensembling of previous predictions for the same input through *exponential moving average* (EMA). TE needs lots of storage to preserve the predictions for each epoch. MT [23] avoids this issue by adding a teacher network whose parameters are updated as the EMA of parameters of student model. There are also some improvements for MT, e.g., MT-SNTG [15] constructs a graph based on the predictions of the teacher model, and the graph guides the features in the same class to be similar on the low-dimensional manifold. SRC-MT [13] enforces a sample relation consistency to extract the semantic information from images. Besides, there are a series of consistency-based semi-supervised methods which do not employ the teacher network. MixUp [27] trains the model using the convex combination of data and label which simply learn the linear behavior in-between training samples. MixMatch [1] follows MixUp and develop a unified loss to reduce entropy and keep traditional regularization. MutexMatch [6] utilizes a novel mutex-based consistency regularization for low-confidence samples, which finally achieves better use of unlabeled data.

2.2 Skin Lesion Classification

Early detection for melanoma is important for decreasing the mortality rate of skin cancer. Thus, skin lesion classification, especially melanoma recognition which assists diagnosis, is essential and crucial. Lopez et al. [18] propose a deep-learning approach based on VGGnet [20] to classify dermoscopic images containing a skin lesion as malignant or benign. Gyawali et al. [7] present a novel semi-supervised approach that trains network on linear mixing of labeled and unlabeled data at both the input and latent space and achieves improved performance.

3 Method

To achieve medical image classification, the proposed learnable relation semi-supervised method with triplet formulation, see Fig. 1, utilizes MT as the backbone and additionally constrains the relations among features to achieve better classification performance. We will introduce our pipeline from four aspects: the backbone MT network (Sect. 3.1), the triplet formulation (Sect. 3.2), the relation learning network (Sect. 3.3), and the overall semi-supervised objective (Sect. 3.4).

3.1 The Backbone Semi-supervised Learning Network

In this subsection, we first introduce MT [4], which is the basis of our method. We denote the labeled set as $\mathcal{S}_L = \{(x_i, y_i)\}_{i=1}^{N}$ and the unlabeled set as $\mathcal{S}_U = \{x_i\}_{i=N+1}^{N+M}$, where $x_i \in \mathbf{R}^{H\times W\times 3}$ is the input image from the data space $\mathcal{X}$ and y_i is the ground truth from label space $\mathcal{Y}$. MT contains two networks named teacher model $f'(\cdot)$ and student model $f(\cdot)$. The student model is trained with the *stochastic gradient descent* (SGD) algorithm [19], while the teacher network updates its parameters θ' as the *exponential moving average* (EMA) parameters of student model:

$$\theta'_{\tau} = \alpha \cdot \theta'_{\tau-1} + (1-\alpha)\cdot \theta_{\tau}, \tag{1}$$

where α denotes the EMA coefficient and τ represents the global training iteration.

As a semi-supervised method, MT encourages a supervised loss $\mathcal{L}_s$ between student model prediction and ground truth, and a consistency loss $\mathcal{L}_u$ between student model prediction and teacher model prediction. The total semi-supervised loss can be denoted as:

$$\mathcal{L}_{mt} = \frac{1}{N}\sum_{i=1}^{N}\mathcal{L}_s(f(x_i;\theta), y_i) + \lambda_u \sum_{i=1}^{N+M}\mathcal{L}_u(f(x_i;\theta,\eta), f'(x_i;\theta',\eta')), \tag{2}$$

where η and η' represent different perturbations (e.g. random affine). $\mathcal{L}_s$ is cross entropy loss and $\mathcal{L}_u$ is mean square error loss. More details can be referred to [4].

3.2 Triplet Formulation

Recent improvements on MT have shown that learning relations between data can benefit classification [13,15]. As previous work only encourages features in the same class to be similar, we propose a more effective constraint to restrict the intra-class as well as inter-class relations of features named triplet formulation, which encourages the features in the same class to be closer and the features in different classes to be far away, and thus contributes to classification. For unlabeled data $x_i \in \mathcal{S}_U$, the predictions of teacher model are employed as the pseudo labels which can determine their class.

To regularize the relations between data, firstly, we need to map each image to a latent feature h_i in feature space $\mathcal{H}$. To achieve this, the student model $f(\cdot)$

can be decomposed to feature encoder $\widetilde{f}(\cdot)$ and classifier $\hat{f}(\cdot)$, where $\widetilde{f}(\cdot)$ maps the input image x_i to a latent feature h_i, and the $\hat{f}(\cdot)$ maps h_i to y_i. Then in latent space, each feature is regarded as an anchor h_a, the features in the same class with the anchor are regarded as the positive samples h_p, and the features in different classes with the anchor are regarded as the negative samples h_n. Then distances between the anchor and the positive as well as negative samples are measured using a distance function $D(\cdot,\cdot)$. Finally, the formulation requires: a). minimize the distance between the anchor and the positive samples, b). at the same time maximizing the distance between the anchor and the negative samples until it is larger than the distance between the anchor and positive samples by a margin $\mathcal{M}$. The specific constraint can be denoted as:

$$\mathcal{L}_{tri} = \max(0, D(h_a, h_p) - D(h_a, h_n) + \mathcal{M}) \tag{3}$$

3.3 Relation Learning Network

To further improve the effect of triplet formulation with a more suitable distance function $D(\cdot,\cdot)$, a learnable relation semi-supervised network which combines student model in MT with a relation learning network is proposed. The proposed network implements feature encoding and distance metric simultaneously by coupling the feature encoder of student model $\widetilde{f}(\cdot)$ with a relation learning network $g(\cdot)$ and achieving end-to-end training. Relation learning network is composed of four blocks and in each block there is a convolution layer, a BatchNorm and a ReLU function. Features for different data are concated and then relation learning network computes distance for the concated two features and output a distance matrix. The relations learned from the proposed network can represent the encoded feature distribution better. Learnable relations for feature distribution can be presented as:

$$\begin{aligned} D(h_i, h_j) &= g(h_i, h_j; \theta_r) \\ &= g(\widetilde{f}(x_i; \theta), \widetilde{f}(x_j; \theta); \theta_r) \end{aligned} \tag{4}$$

where $x_i, x_j \in \mathcal{S}_L \cup \mathcal{S}_U$, h_i, h_j are features from latent space $\mathcal{H}$. θ_r and θ respectively represents the parameters of relation learning network and student network.

3.4 Overall Loss Function

The total objective function of the proposed method can be concluded as:

$$\mathcal{L} = \mathcal{L}_s + \lambda_u \mathcal{L}_u + \lambda_t \mathcal{L}_{tri} \tag{5}$$

where λ_u and λ_t are the loss weights for consistency loss and triplet loss respectively.

4 Experiments

4.1 Data Sets and Experimental Setup

To validate the proposed method in the skin lesion classification task, experiments are conducted on the data set of ISIC 2018: Skin Lesion Analysis Towards Melanoma Detection [3,24]. ISIC 2018 is a multi-class skin lesion data set which contains 10,015 images of 7 classes. We mainly follow the settings in SRC-MT [13]. Specifically, 70%, 10% and 20% of the data are partitioned into the training, validation and test sets respectively for a fair comparison. Besides, 4 different metrics, i.e., AUC, sensitivity, specificity and accuracy [21], adopted in [13] are also included in the comparison on the ISIC 2018 data set. The proposed method is implemented in Python with PyTorch library [17]. The network is trained using an SGD optimizer with a learning rate $1e^{-4}$. The batch size is set as 48, where 12 labeled images and 36 unlabeled ones are included. The number of epochs in each experiment is set as 70. For those hyper-parameters of the model, λ_u and λ_t are initialized as 100 and 0.001 respectively with exponential ramp-up [9]. Both the 2 margins m_1 and m_2 are set as 100.

Table 1. Comparison results of different models on the ISIC 2018 data set with multiple percentages of labeled data.

Methods	Percentages		Metrics			
	Labeled	Unlabeled	AUC	Sensitivity	Specificity	Accuracy
Upper bound	100%	0%	95.43	75.20	94.94	95.10
Baseline	5%	0%	84.24	59.69	87.28	84.73
MT	5%	95%	89.58	53.20	89.88	90.66
MT-SNTG			90.11	53.84	89.73	**90.74**
SRC-MT			87.61	62.04	89.36	88.77
Ours			**90.75**	**64.02**	**90.49**	90.44
Baseline	10%	0%	87.04	64.22	89.88	87.45
MT	10%	90%	92.49	66.36	90.97	92.18
MT-SNTG			92.67	68.56	90.48	91.88
SRC-MT			90.31	66.29	90.47	89.30
Ours			**92.89**	**72.56**	**91.42**	**92.22**
Baseline	20%	0%	90.15	65.50	91.83	92.17
MT	20%	80%	92.96	69.75	92.20	92.48
MT-SNTG			93.68	71.67	91.03	**93.04**
SRC-MT			93.58	71.47	**92.72**	92.54
Ours			**94.03**	**74.34**	92.47	92.66
Baseline	30%	0%	91.80	71.63	92.78	92.96
MT	30%	70%	94.55	72.03	92.65	92.75
MT-SNTG			94.73	76.39	92.51	**93.48**
SRC-MT			94.27	74.59	92.85	93.11
Ours			**95.05**	**76.96**	**92.87**	93.11

Table 2. Ablation studies on the proposed relation learning network.

Distances	Metrics			
	AUC	Sensitivity	Specificity	Accuracy
Euclidean distance	92.12	71.62	91.13	91.17
Cosine distance	91.89	67.69	90.58	91.30
Manhattan distance	92.37	70.65	91.18	91.82
Ours (*relation learning network*)	**92.89**	**72.56**	**91.42**	**92.22**

In the following subsections, comprehensive empirical results are presented to verify (1) the superiority of the proposed method in the skin lesion classification task over other MT-based methods (see Sect. 4.2), (2) the individual impacts of the relation learning network and the triplet formulation in the proposed method (see Sect. 4.3), and (3) the robustness of the proposed method towards the variations of the hyper-parameter $\mathcal{M}$ in the triplet loss $\mathcal{L}_{tri}$ in Equation (3) (see Sect. 4.4).

4.2 Main Results

In this subsection, the proposed method is compared with several MT-based semi-supervised methods, i.e., MT [23], MT-SNTG [15] and SRC-MT [13]. Specifically, for a comprehensive comparison, a wide range of different percentages of the labeled data is adopted in experiments, including 5%, 10%, 20% and 30% labeled data. Aside from the compared MT-based methods, we further list the results of "Upper Bound" and "Baseline". To be specific, the former indicates a supervised model trained with all the data fully-labeled, which can be viewed as an upper bound that semi-supervised methods could achieve. While the latter implies also a supervised model but trained only with limited labeled data of the specified percentage, which appears as a baseline or lower bound of semi-supervised methods. The results can be found in Table 1.

In Table 1, the proposed method outperforms the baseline and other MT-based methods a lot in the terms of AUC, sensitivity and specificity under all the multiple percentages of labeled data. Specifically, with 30% labeled data, the proposed method achieves 76.96% sensitivity, which even exceeds that of the fully-supervised model (75.20%) by nearly 2% points. Regarding to the accuracy, the proposed method also achieves competitive performance on the skin lesion classification. Nevertheless, considering the fact that the positive samples are only of a really small number of the total data (less than 1/7), the accuracy metric is less convincing and comprehensive in demonstrating the model performance, and the other 3 metrics play a more importance role, which are exactly the advantages of the proposed method. In short, compared with other MT-based methods, the proposed relation learning and triplet formulation together boost the performance. Their individual impacts are further empirically shown in detail in the next subsection via the ablation studies.

Table 3. Ablation studies on the proposed triplet formulation.

Methods	Metrics			
	AUC	Sensitivity	Specificity	Accuracy
Model 1	92.49	66.36	90.97	92.18
Model 2	92.67	68.56	90.48	91.88
Model 3	92.23	66.86	90.96	**92.35**
Ours (*Model 4*)	**92.89**	**72.56**	**91.42**	92.22

4.3 Ablation Studies

Effectiveness of Relation Learning Network. In this subsection, we evaluate the effectiveness of the relation learning network. Via this learnable network, the proposed method could learn to capture better relations in the feature space than other fixed distance functions. In experiments, keep MT framework with triplet formulation in proposed method and substitute the relation learning network with the following 3 widely-used distance functions respectively. The corresponding models w.r.t. 4 different distances trained with 10% labeled data and 90% unlabeled data are involved into a comparison.

$$\begin{aligned} \textit{Euclidean distance}(h_i, h_j) &= (\sum_{k=1}^{K}(h_{ik} - h_{jk})^2)^{1/2}, \\ \textit{Cosine distance}(h_i, h_j) &= \frac{h_i \cdot h_j}{\|h_i\|\|h_j\|} = \frac{\sum_{k=1}^{K} h_{ik}h_{jk}}{(\sum_{k=1}^{K} h_{ik}^2)^{1/2}(\sum_{k=1}^{K} h_{jk}^2)^{1/2}}, \\ \textit{Manhattan distance}(h_i, h_j) &= \sum_{i=1}^{K} |h_{ik} - h_{jk}|, \end{aligned} \tag{6}$$

where $h_i = (h_{i1}, ..., h_{iK})$ and $h_j == (h_{j1}, ..., h_{jK})$ are learned features with K dimensions in latent space.

The results are listed in Table 2. The relation learning network shows the best performance on the 4 metrics over other three fixed distance functions which confirms the effectiveness of relation learning network. It may because the deep neural network have greater modeling capabilities than fixed functions.

Effectiveness of Triplet Formulation. In this subsection, we evaluate the effectiveness of the proposed triplet formulation, which considers both the intra-class and the inter-class relationship in the feature space for better classification performance. Specifically, based on an MT framework, the experiments are executed by training the following multiple models where the triplet loss $\mathcal{L}_{tri}$ (Eq. (3)) is replaced:

- Model without the triplet formulation (*Model 1*).

Table 4. Robustness analysis on the hyper-parameter $\mathcal{M}$.

Different $\mathcal{M}$-s	Metrics			
	AUC	Sensitivity	Specificity	Accuracy
$\mathcal{M}$=0.1	92.21	71.93	**91.47**	91.53
$\mathcal{M}$=1	92.65	72.19	90.81	91.03
$\mathcal{M}$=10	92.80	68.65	90.21	91.38
Ours ($\mathcal{M}$=100)	**92.89**	**72.56**	91.42	**92.22**
$\mathcal{M}$=*1000*	92.68	70.89	91.51	91.73

- Model trained with the intra-class formulation only (*Model 2*). Equation (7) shows the intra-class formulation where features h_i and h_j are of the same class. $\mathcal{M}_1$ is a hyper-parameter.

$$\mathcal{L}_1 = \max(0, D(h_i, h_j) - \mathcal{M}_1) \tag{7}$$

- Model trained with the inter-class formulation only (*Model 3*). Equation (8) shows the inter-class formulation where features h_i and h_j are of different classes. $\mathcal{M}_2$ is also a hyper-parameter.

$$\mathcal{L}_2 = \max(0, \mathcal{M}_2 - D(h_i, h_j)) \tag{8}$$

- Our model trained with the complete triplet formulation (*Model 4*).

Again, all the models are trained on a data partition of 10% labeled and 90% unlabeled data. The results are listed in Table 3. Clearly, the complete triplet formulation brings the highest model performance, which indicates that simultaneously considering both the intra-class and inter-class benefits classification performance the most.

4.4 Analysis of Hyper-parameter $\mathcal{M}$

In this subsection, we analyse the robustness of the proposed method towards the hyper-parameter $\mathcal{M}$ in Equation (3). $\mathcal{M}$ is a significant hyper-parameter, indicates the exceeding distance margin and controls the separability of inter-class samples and the clusterity of intra-class ones. To evaluate the impact of $\mathcal{M}$, multiple models are trained w.r.t. different values of $\mathcal{M}$, i.e., $\mathcal{M} \in \{0.1, 1, 10, 100, 1000\}$, on 10% labeled data and 90% unlabeled data. The results are listed in Table 4.

In Table 4, as $\mathcal{M}$ increases from 0.1 to 100, values of the 4 metrics becomes better. It is observed that specificity and accuracy are not very sensitive to the value of $\mathcal{M}$. Meanwhile, there is a limitation of $\mathcal{M}$ that it can not be too high (e.g., 1000). Finally we set $\mathcal{M}$ as 100 in our experiments.

5 Conclusion

We propose a novel learnable relation semi-supervised method with triplet formulation for medical image classification in this paper. Based on the widely-used MT framework, a triplet formulation is devised to better characterize the intra-class and inter-class feature relations. Besides, a relation learning network is proposed to learn the feature relations instead of adopting any fixed distance functions. By considering the feature encoding and the distance metric learning together, the proposed semi-supervised method shows stronger classification performance. Extensive empirical results demonstrate the superiority of our method over other state-of-the-art semi-supervised learning methods and reveal the robustness of our method with little labeled data.

References

1. Berthelot, D., Carlini, N., Goodfellow, I., Papernot, N., Oliver, A., Raffel, C.A.: Mixmatch: a holistic approach to semi-supervised learning. In: Advances in Neural Information Processing Systems, vol. 32 (2019)
2. Cheplygina, V., de Bruijne, M., Pluim, J.P.: Not-so-supervised: a survey of semi-supervised, multi-instance, and transfer learning in medical image analysis. Med. Image Anal. **54**, 280–296 (2019)
3. Codella, N., et al.: Skin lesion analysis toward melanoma detection 2018: a challenge hosted by the international skin imaging collaboration (ISIC). arXiv preprint arXiv:1902.03368 (2019)
4. Cui, W., et al.: Semi-supervised brain lesion segmentation with an adapted mean teacher model. In: Chung, A.C.S., Gee, J.C., Yushkevich, P.A., Bao, S. (eds.) IPMI 2019. LNCS, vol. 11492, pp. 554–565. Springer, Cham (2019). https://doi.org/10.1007/978-3-030-20351-1_43
5. Dong, X., Shen, J.: Triplet loss in Siamese network for object tracking. In: Ferrari, V., Hebert, M., Sminchisescu, C., Weiss, Y. (eds.) ECCV 2018. LNCS, vol. 11217, pp. 472–488. Springer, Cham (2018). https://doi.org/10.1007/978-3-030-01261-8_28
6. Duan, Y., et al.: Mutexmatch: semi-supervised learning with mutex-based consistency regularization. arXiv preprint arXiv:2203.14316 (2022)
7. Gyawali, P.K., Ghimire, S., Bajracharya, P., Li, Z., Wang, L.: Semi-supervised medical image classification with global latent mixing. In: Martel, A.L., et al. (eds.) MICCAI 2020. LNCS, vol. 12261, pp. 604–613. Springer, Cham (2020). https://doi.org/10.1007/978-3-030-59710-8_59
8. Hermans, A., Beyer, L., Leibe, B.: In defense of the triplet loss for person re-identification. arXiv preprint arXiv:1703.07737 (2017)
9. Laine, S., Aila, T.: Temporal ensembling for semi-supervised learning. arXiv preprint arXiv:1610.02242 (2016)
10. Li, Q., Cai, W., Wang, X., Zhou, Y., Feng, D.D., Chen, M.: Medical image classification with convolutional neural network. In: 2014 13th International Conference on Control Automation Robotics & Vision (ICARCV), pp. 844–848. IEEE (2014)
11. Litjens, G., et al.: A survey on deep learning in medical image analysis. Med. Image Anal. **42**, 60–88 (2017)

12. Liu, P., Zheng, G.: Semi-supervised learning regularized by adversarial perturbation and diversity maximization. In: Lian, C., Cao, X., Rekik, I., Xu, X., Yan, P. (eds.) MLMI 2021. LNCS, vol. 12966, pp. 199–208. Springer, Cham (2021). https://doi.org/10.1007/978-3-030-87589-3_21
13. Liu, Q., Yu, L., Luo, L., Dou, Q., Heng, P.A.: Semi-supervised medical image classification with relation-driven self-ensembling model. IEEE Trans. Med. Imaging **39**(11), 3429–3440 (2020)
14. Lopez, A.R., Giro-i Nieto, X., Burdick, J., Marques, O.: Skin lesion classification from dermoscopic images using deep learning techniques. In: 2017 13th IASTED international conference on biomedical engineering (BioMed), pp. 49–54. IEEE (2017)
15. Luo, Y., Zhu, J., Li, M., Ren, Y., Zhang, B.: Smooth neighbors on teacher graphs for semi-supervised learning. In: Proceedings of the IEEE Conference On Computer Vision And Pattern Recognition, pp. 8896–8905 (2018)
16. Mahbod, A., Schaefer, G., Wang, C., Ecker, R., Ellinge, I.: Skin lesion classification using hybrid deep neural networks. In: ICASSP 2019–2019 IEEE International Conference on Acoustics, Speech and Signal Processing (ICASSP), pp. 1229–1233. IEEE (2019)
17. Paszke, et al.: Pytorch: An imperative style, high-performance deep learning library. In: Advances in Neural Information Processing Systems, vol. 32 (2019)
18. Romero Lopez, A., Giro-i Nieto, X., Burdick, J., Marques, O.: Skin lesion classification from dermoscopic images using deep learning techniques. In: 2017 13th IASTED International Conference on Biomedical Engineering (BioMed), pp. 49–54 (2017). https://doi.org/10.2316/P.2017.852-053
19. Saad, D.: Online algorithms and stochastic approximations. Online Learn. **5**, 3–6 (1998)
20. Simonyan, K., Zisserman, A.: Very deep convolutional networks for large-scale image recognition. arXiv preprint arXiv:1409.1556 (2014)
21. Šimundić, A.M.: Measures of diagnostic accuracy: basic definitions. EJIFCC **19**(4), 203 (2009)
22. Sohn, K., et al.: Fixmatch: simplifying semi-supervised learning with consistency and confidence. Adv. Neural. Inf. Process. Syst. **33**, 596–608 (2020)
23. Tarvainen, A., Valpola, H.: Mean teachers are better role models: Weight-averaged consistency targets improve semi-supervised deep learning results. In: Guyon, I., Luxburg, U.V., Bengio, S., Wallach, H., Fergus, R., Vishwanathan, S., Garnett, R. (eds.) Advances in Neural Information Processing Systems. vol. 30. Curran Associates, Inc. (2017). https://proceedings.neurips.cc/paper/2017/file/68053af2923e00204c3ca7c6a3150cf7-Paper.pdf
24. Tschandl, P., Rosendahl, C., Kittler, H.: The ham10000 dataset, a large collection of multi-source dermatoscopic images of common pigmented skin lesions. Sci. Data **5**(1), 1–9 (2018)
25. Wang, W., et al.: Medical image classification using deep learning. In: Chen, Y.-W., Jain, L.C. (eds.) Deep Learning in Healthcare. ISRL, vol. 171, pp. 33–51. Springer, Cham (2020). https://doi.org/10.1007/978-3-030-32606-7_3
26. Wang, X., Chen, H., Xiang, H., Lin, H., Lin, X., Heng, P.A.: Deep virtual adversarial self-training with consistency regularization for semi-supervised medical image classification. Med. Image Anal. **70**, 102010 (2021)
27. Zhang, H., Cisse, M., Dauphin, Y.N., Lopez-Paz, D.: mixup: Beyond empirical risk minimization. arXiv preprint arXiv:1710.09412 (2017)

Multi-view Classification via Twin Projection Vector Machine with Application to EEG-Based Driving Fatigue Detection

Xiaobo Chen(✉) and Yuxiang Gao

Shandong Technology and Business University, Yantai 264005, Shandong, China
xbchen82@live.cn

Abstract. Multi-view learning based on a variety of multiple hyperplane classification (MHC) models has shown promising performance for multi-view data classification in recent years. However, seeking for a single fitting hyperplane for each class might be insufficiently expressive for the datasets with complex feature distribution. Moreover, in the presence of outlier data, most approaches tend to produce degraded results due to the adverse impact of outliers. In this paper, we put forward a new multi-view MHC model termed as multi-view twin projection vector machine (MvTPVM) which aims to seek for multiple projection vectors. Following the consensus principle, multi-view co-regularization is introduced to constrain the projected features of two views. To further achieve robust multi-view classification, we propose a robust variant called RMvTPVM where the distance involved in this model is measured by $L_{1,2}$-norm. To solve the resulting model, an elegant iteration algorithm is further proposed. The experimental results on both standard UCI datasets and driving fatigue detection based on EEG signals verify the effectiveness of our models in multi-view classification.

Keywords: Multi-view classification · Multi-hyperplane model · Support vector machine · Driving fatigue detection

1 Introduction

In many real-world applications, data in specific domain can be frequently described by multiple representations or views. For example, for driving fatigue detection [1], we can expect spectrum features as well as functional connectivity network extracted from the collected EEG data characterizes the activities and relations occurred in the brain from different viewpoints. Multi-view learning [2, 3] has been proposed to exploit complementary information from multiple sources. One popular multi-view learning strategy called consensus principle attempts to maximize the agreement among multiple distinctive prediction results of the data. Multi-view co-regularization [4] which conforms to the consensus principle has been widely applied and shows excellent performance.

To data, the multi-view classification algorithms based on support vector machines (SVM) [5] have received increasing popularity. As early as 2005, an SVM-based two-view learning method called SVM-2K [6] was developed to implement a regularization

Y. Tan and Y. Shi (Eds.): DMBD 2022, CCIS 1744, pp. 394–407, 2022.
https://doi.org/10.1007/978-981-19-9297-1_28

framework for multiple view learning. Despite the ability of traditional SVM-based models to combine multiple views, these algorithms suffer the problem of high cost since the model training has to solve a convex quadratic programming (QP) problem with time complexity $O(N^3)$ where N is the total size of training samples. Recently, multiple hyperplane classification (MHC) models such as generalized eigenvalue proximal SVM (GEPSVM), twin SVM (TSVM), have attracted much attention. Instead of seeking for a single separating hyperplane between different classes as SVM does, MHC try to find multiple nonparallel hyperplanes, each of which is associated with a class, such that each plane is closest to its own class while furthest from the other class. Due to the excellent performance of MHC models and reduced training cost, the combination of MHC model and multi-view information has emerged as a promising direction for classification task. Many effective models such as MvGSVM [7], multi-view TSVM (MvTSVM) [8], Regularized multi-view LSTSVM (RMvLSTSVM) [9], Robust double-sided TSVM (MvRDTSVM) [10] have been developed in the literature.

Although the existing multi-view MHC methods have achieved remarkable success, there are still some problems. One major challenge is that all of these models are dedicated to generate a fitting plane for each class. Using a single plane to characterize the data with complex distribution has been proved to be insufficient for many real-world applications. To address this challenge, in this paper, we first present a novel algorithm termed as multi-view twin projection vector machine (MvTPVM). MvTPVM attempts to find multiple projection vectors for each class such that in its own projected subspace, the samples belonging to the same class are closest to its class mean and the samples of the other class are separated as far as possible. Then, in order to alleviate the adverse impact of outliers, we further present a robust MvTPVM model (RMvTPVM) based on $L_{2,1}$-norm. Experiments are used to verify the effectiveness of our models.

In summary, our models have the following merits:

(1) Different from the existing multi-view MHC models, our proposed MvTPVM is capable of producing multiple projection vectors such that the samples of one class can be well separated from those of the other class in its own projected space. Intuitively, multiple projection vectors which span a linear subspace with higher dimension will contribute to extract more informative features and therefore probably cause better performance for complex problems.
(2) Considering MvTPVM may be prone to the presence of outliers since the involved distance measure is based on squared L_2-norm which will magnify the effect of outliers, the enhanced RMvTPVM formulation purely based on $L_{2,1}$-norm is further proposed with the expectation of suppressing the influence of outliers and thus promoting the classification performance.

The rest of this paper is organized as follows. Section 2 presents our proposed MvTPVM for classification. In Sect. 3, the robust variant RMvTPVM is further introduced. Section 4 reports extensive experiment on standard UCI machine learning datasets. Subsequently, our proposed models are applied to EEG based driving fatigue detection. Finally, some conclusions and future works are discussed in Sect. 5.

2 Multi-view Twin Projection Vector Machine

2.1 Problem Formulation

Suppose that there are two views with different dimensions, and each view contains samples from positive and negative class denoted as $\left\{\mathbf{x}_i^{1,+}, \mathbf{x}_i^{2,+}\right\}_{i=1}^{n_1}$ and $\left\{\mathbf{x}_j^{1,-}, \mathbf{x}_j^{2,-}\right\}_{j=1}^{n_2}$, $\mathbf{x}_i^{1,+}, \mathbf{x}_j^{1,-} \in \mathrm{R}^{d_1}$, $\mathbf{x}_i^{2,+}, \mathbf{x}_j^{2,-} \in \mathrm{R}^{d_2}$ where the superscript 1 and 2 denotes two view, superscript $+$ and $-$ represents two class, subscript i and j denote the i th and j th sample in each class, d_i is the dimension of view i, n_1 and n_2 are the number of samples in positive and negative class, $n = n_1 + n_2$.

Different from the most MHC models [7–10] which find two nonparallel fitting hyperplanes for each view, the goal of MvTPVM is to find view-specific projection matrices $\mathbf{W}_1 \in \mathbf{R}^{d_1 \times m_1}$, $\mathbf{W}_2 \in \mathbf{R}^{d_2 \times m_1}$ for the positive class, and $\mathbf{V}_1 \in \mathbf{R}^{d_1 \times m_2}$, $\mathbf{V}_2 \in \mathbf{R}^{d_2 \times m_2}$ for the negative class, where m_1 and m_2 denote the number of projection vectors for the two views, respectively. By projecting the samples along these projection matrixes, we expect that the samples in the same class are closest to the center of the corresponding class while the samples in other class scatter away as far as possible from that center. In addition, the multi-view information is further incorporated by following the consensus principle. Therefore, we present the following formulations of MvTPVM for positive class as follows

$$
\begin{aligned}
\text{(MvTPVM1)} \min_{\mathbf{W}_1, \mathbf{W}_2} & \frac{\sum_{i=1}^{n_1} \|\mathbf{x}_i^{1,+}\mathbf{W}_1 - \boldsymbol{\mu}^{1,+}\mathbf{W}_1\|^2 + \sum_{i=1}^{n_1} \|\mathbf{x}_i^{2,+}\mathbf{W}_2 - \boldsymbol{\mu}^{2,+}\mathbf{W}_2\|^2}{\sum_{j=1}^{n_2} \|\mathbf{x}_j^{1,-}\mathbf{W}_1 - \boldsymbol{\mu}^{1,+}\mathbf{W}_1\|^2 + \sum_{j=1}^{n_2} \|\mathbf{x}_j^{2,-}\mathbf{W}_1 - \boldsymbol{\mu}^{2,+}\mathbf{W}_1\|^2} \\
+ & \frac{\delta_1 \sum_{i=1}^{n_1} \left\|\left(\mathbf{x}_i^{1,+} - \boldsymbol{\mu}^{1,+}\right)\mathbf{W}_1 - \left(\mathbf{x}_i^{2,+} - \boldsymbol{\mu}^{2,+}\right)\mathbf{W}_2\right\|^2 + \tau_1\left(\|\mathbf{W}_1\|_F^2 + \|\mathbf{W}_2\|_F^2\right)}{\sum_{j=1}^{n_2} \|\mathbf{x}_j^{1,-}\mathbf{W}_1 - \boldsymbol{\mu}^{1,+}\mathbf{W}_1\|^2 + \sum_{j=1}^{n_2} \|\mathbf{x}_j^{2,-}\mathbf{W}_1 - \boldsymbol{\mu}^{2,+}\mathbf{W}_1\|^2}
\end{aligned}
\tag{1}
$$

whereδ_1, $\tau_1$are non-negative weight parameters, $\boldsymbol{\mu}^{1,+} = \sum_{i=1}^{n_1} \mathbf{x}_i^{1,+}/n_1$, $\boldsymbol{\mu}^{2,+} = \sum_{i=1}^{n_1} \mathbf{x}_i^{2,+}/n_1$, $\boldsymbol{\mu}^{1,-} = \sum_{j=1}^{n_2} \mathbf{x}_j^{1,-}/n_2$, $\boldsymbol{\mu}^{2,-} = \sum_{j=1}^{n_2} \mathbf{x}_j^{2,-}/n_2$, denotes the class mean of positive and negative class for two views. $\|\cdot\|$is the L_2-norm of a vector, and $\|\cdot\|_F$is the Frobenius norm of a matrix. The explanation of (1) is shown below. The first two terms in the numerator are used to reduce the within-class scatter in the projected subspace for the two views, respectively. The third term is the classic multi-view co-regularization which constrains the prediction of the same sample across two views to be consistent. The final term often called Tikhonov regularization is used to penalize the norm of projection matrices so as to avoid overfitting. The two terms in the denominator are used to push the samples in negative class far away from the mean of positive class in the two views.

In the spirit of similar idea, the MvTPVM model for the negative class can be expressed as

$$
\begin{aligned}
&(\text{MvTPVM2}) \min_{\mathbf{V}_1,\mathbf{V}_2} \frac{\sum_{j=1}^{n_2} \|\mathbf{x}_j^{1,-}\mathbf{V}_1 - \mu^{1,-}\mathbf{V}_1\|^2 + \sum_{j=1}^{n_2} \|\mathbf{x}_j^{2,-}\mathbf{V}_2 - \mu^{2,-}\mathbf{V}_2\|^2}{\sum_{i=1}^{n_1} \|\mathbf{x}_i^{1,+}\mathbf{V}_1 - \mu^{1,-}\mathbf{V}_1\|^2 + \sum_{i=1}^{n_1} \|\mathbf{x}_i^{2,+}\mathbf{V}_2 - \mu^{2,-}\mathbf{V}_2\|^2} \\
&+ \frac{\delta_2 \sum_{j=1}^{n_2} \|\left(\mathbf{x}_j^{1,-} - \mu^{1,-}\right)\mathbf{V}_1 - \left(\mathbf{x}_j^{2,-} - \mu^{2,-}\right)\mathbf{V}_2\|^2 + \tau_2(\|\mathbf{V}_1\|_F^2 + \|\mathbf{V}_2\|_F^2)}{\sum_{i=1}^{n_1} \|\mathbf{x}_i^{1,+}\mathbf{V}_1 - \mu^{1,-}\mathbf{V}_1\|^2 + \sum_{i=1}^{n_1} \|\mathbf{x}_i^{2,+}\mathbf{V}_2 - \mu^{2,-}\mathbf{V}_2\|^2}. \quad (2)
\end{aligned}
$$

2.2 Solution Algorithm to MvTPVM

Let matrix $\mathbf{A}_1 \in \mathbf{R}^{n_1 \times d_1}$ and $\mathbf{A}_2 \in \mathbf{R}^{n_1 \times d_2}$ represent the positive class in the first and second view of the positive class. Similarly, we can get the matrix representation of netive samples in the two views, $\mathbf{B}_1 \in \mathbf{R}^{n_2 \times d_1}$ and $\mathbf{B}_2 \in \mathbf{R}^{n_2 \times d_2}$. Some definitions are given as follows

$$
\begin{aligned}
&\mathbf{S}_1 = \mathbf{A}_1 - \mathbf{e}_1\mu^{1,+},\ \mathbf{S}_2 = \mathbf{A}_2 - \mathbf{e}_1\mu^{2,+},\ \mathbf{S}_1^* = \mathbf{B}_1 - \mathbf{e}_2\mu^{1,+},\ \mathbf{S}_2^* = \mathbf{B}_2 - \mathbf{e}_2\mu^{2,+}. \\
&\mathbf{L}_1 = \mathbf{B}_1 - \mathbf{e}_2\mu^{1,-},\ \mathbf{L}_2 = \mathbf{B}_2 - \mathbf{e}_2\mu^{2,-},\ \mathbf{L}_1^* = \mathbf{A}_1 - \mathbf{e}_1\mu^{1,-},\ \mathbf{L}_2^* = \mathbf{A}_2 - \mathbf{e}_1\mu^{2,-}.
\end{aligned} \quad (3)
$$

Then, the optimization problems (1) and (2) for MvTPVM can be rewritten as

$$
\min_{\mathbf{W}_1,\mathbf{W}_2} \frac{\|\mathbf{S}_1\mathbf{W}_1\|_F^2 + \|\mathbf{S}_2\mathbf{W}_2\|_F^2 + \delta_1\|\mathbf{S}_1\mathbf{W}_1 - \mathbf{S}_2\mathbf{W}_2\|_F^2 + \tau_1\left(\|\mathbf{W}_1\|_F^2 + \|\mathbf{W}_2\|_F^2\right)}{\|\mathbf{S}_1^*\mathbf{W}_1\|_F^2 + \|\mathbf{S}_2^*\mathbf{W}_2\|_F^2}. \quad (4)
$$

$$
\min_{\mathbf{V}_1,\mathbf{V}_2} \frac{\|\mathbf{L}_1\mathbf{V}_1\|_F^2 + \|\mathbf{L}_2\mathbf{V}_2\|_F^2 + \delta_2\|\mathbf{L}_1\mathbf{V}_1 - \mathbf{L}_2\mathbf{V}_2\|_F^2 + \tau_2\left(\|\mathbf{V}_1\|_F^2 + \|\mathbf{V}_2\|_F^2\right)}{\|\mathbf{L}_1^*\mathbf{V}_1\|_F^2 + \|\mathbf{L}_2^*\mathbf{V}_1\|_F^2}. \quad (5)
$$

First, we will solve the optimization problem (4) for MvTPVM1. According to the properties of matrix trace, the problem (4) is equivalent to

$$
\min_{\mathbf{W}} \frac{\mathrm{tr}\left(\mathbf{W}^{\mathrm{T}}\begin{bmatrix} (1+\delta_1)\mathbf{S}_1^{\mathrm{T}}\mathbf{S}_1 & -\delta_1\mathbf{S}_1^{\mathrm{T}}\mathbf{S}_2 \\ -\delta_1\mathbf{S}_2^{\mathrm{T}}\mathbf{S}_1 & (1+\delta_1)\mathbf{S}_2^{\mathrm{T}}\mathbf{S}_2 \end{bmatrix}\mathbf{W}\right) + \tau_1\mathrm{tr}(\mathbf{W}^{\mathrm{T}}\mathbf{W})}{\mathrm{tr}\left(\mathbf{W}^{\mathrm{T}}\begin{bmatrix} \mathbf{S}_1^{*\,\mathrm{T}}\mathbf{S}_1^* & 0 \\ 0 & \mathbf{S}_2^{*\,\mathrm{T}}\mathbf{S}_2^* \end{bmatrix}\mathbf{W}\right)}. \quad (6)
$$

where $\mathbf{W} = \begin{bmatrix} \mathbf{W}_1 \\ \mathbf{W}_2 \end{bmatrix}$, $\mathrm{tr}(\cdot)$ is the trace operation of a matrix. We define

$$
\mathbf{Q}_1 = \begin{bmatrix} (1+\delta_1)\mathbf{S}_1^{\mathrm{T}}\mathbf{S}_1 & -\delta_1\mathbf{S}_1^{\mathrm{T}}\mathbf{S}_2 \\ -\delta_1\mathbf{S}_2^{\mathrm{T}}\mathbf{S}_1 & (1+\delta_1)\mathbf{S}_2^{\mathrm{T}}\mathbf{S}_2 \end{bmatrix} + \tau_1\mathbf{I},\ \mathbf{U}_1 = \begin{bmatrix} \mathbf{S}_1^{*\,\mathrm{T}}\mathbf{S}_1^* & 0 \\ 0 & \mathbf{S}_2^{*\,\mathrm{T}}\mathbf{S}_2^* \end{bmatrix}. \quad (7)
$$

Then the optimization problem (6) can be simplified to the following form

$$
\min_{\mathbf{W}} \frac{\mathrm{tr}(\mathbf{W}^{\mathrm{T}}\mathbf{Q}_1\mathbf{W})}{\mathrm{tr}(\mathbf{W}^{\mathrm{T}}\mathbf{U}_1\mathbf{W})}. \quad (8)
$$

Following the previous studies [11, 12], the unconstrained minimization problem (8) is equivalent to

$$\min_{\mathbf{W}} \operatorname{tr}\left(\mathbf{W}^{\mathrm{T}}\mathbf{Q}_1\mathbf{W}\right) \text{ s.t.} \mathbf{W}^{\mathrm{T}}\mathbf{U}_1\mathbf{W} = \mathbf{C}_1. \tag{9}$$

where $\mathbf{C}_1$ is a constant matrix with all elements being constants. The above objective function is a constrained optimization problem, so we can solve it by Lagrangian multiplier method. Finally, it can be concluded that MvTPVM1 boils down to the following eigenvalue decomposition problem

$$\mathbf{Q}_1\mathbf{W} = \mathbf{U}_1\mathbf{W}\Delta_1. \tag{10}$$

As a result, the optimal projection matrix $\mathbf{W}$ is composed of eigenvectors corresponding to the first m_1 smallest eigenvalues except zeros of the Eigen-equation $\mathbf{Q}_1\mathbf{w}_k = \lambda_k\mathbf{U}_1\mathbf{w}_k (k = 1, \ldots, m_1)$.

In the same way as the first optimization problem, the second problem (5) can be reformulated as

$$\min_{\mathbf{V}} \operatorname{tr}\left(\mathbf{V}^{\mathrm{T}}\mathbf{Q}_2\mathbf{V}\right) \text{ s.t.} \mathbf{V}^{\mathrm{T}}\mathbf{U}_2\mathbf{V} = \mathbf{C}_2. \tag{11}$$

where $\mathbf{V} = \begin{bmatrix} \mathbf{V}_1 \\ \mathbf{V}_2 \end{bmatrix}$, $\mathbf{C}_2$ is a constant matrix, and

$$\mathbf{Q}_2 = \begin{bmatrix} (1+\delta_2)\mathbf{L}_1^{\mathrm{T}}\mathbf{L}_1 & -\delta_2\mathbf{L}_1^{\mathrm{T}}\mathbf{L}_2 \\ -\delta_2\mathbf{L}_2^{\mathrm{T}}\mathbf{L}_1 & (1+\delta_2)\mathbf{L}_2^{\mathrm{T}}\mathbf{L}_2 \end{bmatrix} + \tau_2\mathbf{I}, \mathbf{U}_2 = \begin{bmatrix} \mathbf{L}_1^{*\mathrm{T}}\mathbf{L}_1^{*} & 0 \\ 0 & \mathbf{L}_2^{*\mathrm{T}}\mathbf{L}_2^{*} \end{bmatrix}. \tag{12}$$

Then, the optimal solution of (11) is given by

$$\mathbf{Q}_2\mathbf{V} = \mathbf{U}_2\mathbf{V}\Delta_2. \tag{13}$$

The optimal projection matrix $\mathbf{V}$ is thus composed of eigenvectors corresponding to the first m_2 smallest eigenvalues except zeros of the Eigen-equation $\mathbf{Q}_2\mathbf{v}_k = \lambda_k\mathbf{U}_2\mathbf{v}_k (k = 1, \ldots, m_2)$.

3 Robust MvTPVM

3.1 Problem Formulation

MvTPVM uses the squared L_2-norm as distance metric as the other methods mentioned above. However, it is generally recognized that [13, 14] the squared L_2-norm are not robust enough to outliers in that the samples with large distance will dominate the total loss and thus make the resulting solution deviate from the optimal one. Therefore, we further develop a robust MvTPVM model termed as RMvTPVM based on $L_{2,1}$-norm. The $L_{2,1}$-norm is able to reduce the influence of outliers by using the L_2-norm instead of the squared version as distance metric on the data points, thereby improving the robustness of the model.

First, we give the definition of $L_{2,1}$-norm of an arbitrary matrix $\mathbf{A}$

$$\|\mathbf{A}_{L_{2,1}}\| = \sum_{i=1}^{n_1} \sqrt{\sum_{j='1}^{d_i} (\mathbf{A}(i,j))^2} = \sum_{i=1}^{n_i} \|\mathbf{A}(i,:)\|. \tag{14}$$

We replace the squared L_2-norm in the MvTPVM objective function (4) and (5) with the $L_{2,1}$-norm, and the objective function after replacement is shown as follows:

$$\text{(RMvTPVM1)} \min_{\mathbf{W}_1,\mathbf{W}_2} \frac{\|\mathbf{S}_1\mathbf{W}_1\|_{L_{2,1}} + \|\mathbf{S}_2\mathbf{W}_2\|_{L_{2,1}} + \delta_1\|\mathbf{S}_1\mathbf{W}_1 - \mathbf{S}_2\mathbf{W}_2\|_{L_{2,1}}}{\|\mathbf{S}_1^*\mathbf{W}_1\|_{L_{2,1}} + \|\mathbf{S}_2^*\mathbf{W}_2\|_{L_{2,1}}} + \frac{\tau_1\left(\|\mathbf{W}_1\|_{L_{2,1}} + \|\mathbf{W}_2\|_{L_{2,1}}\right)}{\|\mathbf{S}_1^*\mathbf{W}_1\|_{L_{2,1}} + \|\mathbf{S}_2^*\mathbf{W}_2\|_{L_{2,1}}} \tag{15}$$

$$\text{(RMvTPVM2)} \min_{\mathbf{V}_1,\mathbf{V}_2} \frac{\|\mathbf{L}_1\mathbf{V}_1\|_{L_{2,1}} + \|\mathbf{L}_2\mathbf{V}_2\|_{L_{2,1}} + \delta_2\|\mathbf{L}_1\mathbf{V}_1 - \mathbf{L}_2\mathbf{V}_2\|_{L_{2,1}}}{\|\mathbf{L}_1^*\mathbf{V}_1\|_{L_{2,1}} + \|\mathbf{L}_2^*\mathbf{V}_2\|_{L_{2,1}}} + \frac{\tau_2\left(\|\mathbf{V}_1\|_{L_{2,1}} + \|\mathbf{V}_2\|_{L_{2,1}}\right)}{\|\mathbf{L}_1^*\mathbf{V}_1\|_{L_{2,1}} + \|\mathbf{L}_2^*\mathbf{V}_1\|_{L_{2,1}}} \tag{16}$$

3.2 Solution Method to RMvTPVM

Let $\mathbf{W} = \begin{bmatrix} \mathbf{W}_1 \\ \mathbf{W}_2 \end{bmatrix}$ and according to the definition of $L_{2,1}$-norm, the objective function (15) is equivalent to

$$\min_{\mathbf{W}} \frac{\left\|\begin{bmatrix} \mathbf{S}_1 & 0 \\ 0 & \mathbf{S}_2 \end{bmatrix}\mathbf{W}\right\|_{L_{2,1}} + \delta_1\left\|\begin{bmatrix} \mathbf{S}_1 & 0 \\ 0 & -\mathbf{S}_2 \end{bmatrix}\mathbf{W}\right\|_{L_{2,1}} + \tau_1\|\mathbf{W}\|_{L_{2,1}}}{\left\|\begin{bmatrix} \mathbf{S}_1^* & 0 \\ 0 & \mathbf{S}_2^* \end{bmatrix}\mathbf{W}\right\|_{L_{2,1}}}. \tag{17}$$

Given the following notations:

$$\mathbf{S}_{p_1} = \begin{bmatrix} \mathbf{S}_1 & 0 \\ 0 & \mathbf{S}_2 \end{bmatrix}, \mathbf{S}_{p_2} = \delta_1\begin{bmatrix} \mathbf{S}_1 & 0 \\ 0 & -\mathbf{S}_2 \end{bmatrix}$$
$$\mathbf{S} = \left[\mathbf{S}_{p_1}^{\mathrm{T}}\mathbf{S}_{p_2}^{\mathrm{T}}\tau_1\mathbf{I}\right]^{\mathrm{T}}, \mathbf{S}^* = \begin{bmatrix} \mathbf{S}_1^* & 0 \\ 0 & \mathbf{S}_2^* \end{bmatrix}. \tag{18}$$

where $\mathbf{I}$ is an unit matrix of appropriate dimensions, the objective function (17) can be transformed into

$$\min_{\mathbf{W}} \frac{\|\mathbf{SW}\|_{L_{2,1}}}{\|\mathbf{S}^*\mathbf{W}\|_{L_{2,1}}}. \tag{19}$$

According to the definition of $L_{2,1}$-norm and through simple algebra, the numerator of the above problems can be written as

$$\|\mathbf{SW}\|_{L_{2,1}} = \mathrm{tr}\left(\mathbf{W}^{\mathrm{T}}\mathbf{S}^{\mathrm{T}}\mathbf{D}_1\mathbf{SW}\right). \tag{20}$$

where $\mathbf{D}_1 = \mathrm{diag}\left(\frac{1}{\|\mathbf{SW}(1,:)\|_2}, \ldots, \frac{1}{\|\mathbf{SW}(N_1,:)\|_2}\right)$, $N_1 = 4n_1 + d_1 + d_2$, diag(·) denotes a diagonal matrix.

Similar to the numerator, the denominator of the problem (19) can be written as

$$\left\|\mathbf{S}^*\mathbf{W}\right\|_{L_{2,1}} = \mathrm{tr}\left(\mathbf{W}^{\mathrm{T}}\mathbf{S}^{*\mathrm{T}}\mathbf{E}_1\mathbf{S}^*\mathbf{W}\right). \tag{21}$$

where $\mathbf{E}_1 = diag\left(\frac{1}{\|\mathbf{S}^*\mathbf{W}(1,:)\|_2}, \ldots, \frac{1}{\|\mathbf{S}^*\mathbf{W}(N_2,:)\|_2}\right)$ $N_2 = 2n_2$.

Replacing the numerator and denominator in the objective function (19) with Eq. (20) and Eq. (21) we can get

$$\min_{\mathbf{W}} \frac{\mathrm{tr}\left(\mathbf{W}^{\mathrm{T}}\mathbf{S}^{\mathrm{T}}\mathbf{D}_1\mathbf{SW}\right)}{\mathrm{tr}\left(\mathbf{W}^{\mathrm{T}}\mathbf{S}^{*\mathrm{T}}\mathbf{E}_1\mathbf{S}^*\mathbf{W}\right)}. \tag{22}$$

Similar to (9), objective function (22) can be reformulated as

$$\min_{\mathbf{W}} \mathrm{tr}\left(\mathbf{W}^{\mathrm{T}}\mathbf{S}^{\mathrm{T}}\mathbf{D}_1\mathbf{SW}\right) \text{ s.t. } \mathbf{W}^{\mathrm{T}}\mathbf{S}^{*\mathrm{T}}\mathbf{E}_1\mathbf{S}^*\mathbf{W} = \mathbf{T}_1. \tag{23}$$

where $\mathbf{T}_1$ is a constant matrix, and we define

$$\mathbf{Q}_1 = \mathbf{S}^{\mathrm{T}}\mathbf{D}_1\mathbf{S}, \mathbf{U}_1 = \mathbf{S}^{*\mathrm{T}}\mathbf{E}_1\mathbf{S}^*. \tag{24}$$

In the same way as MvTPVM, the optimal solution of (23) is given by $\mathbf{Q}_1\mathbf{W} = \mathbf{U}_1\mathbf{W}\Lambda_1$. Therefore, the optimal projection matrix $\mathbf{W}$ is composed of eigenvectors corresponding to the first m_1 smallest eigenvalues except zeros of the Eigen-equation $\mathbf{Q}_1\mathbf{w}_k = \lambda_k\mathbf{U}_1\mathbf{w}_k (k = 1, \ldots, m_1)$.

However, it should be emphasized that $\mathbf{Q}_1$ and $\mathbf{U}_1$ in (25) are actually depending on the unknown $\mathbf{W}$ due to the definition of $\mathbf{D}_1$ and $\mathbf{E}_1$. As a result, the optimal solution of needs to solved in an iterative way, that is, solving $\mathbf{W}$ while fixing $\mathbf{D}_1$ and $\mathbf{E}_1$ and updating $\mathbf{D}_1$ and $\mathbf{E}_1$ while fixing $\mathbf{W}$. The convergence of this iterative algorithm will be proved in the following section.

In a similar way, for the second problem (16), we can reformulate the model as

$$\begin{aligned} &\min_{\mathbf{V}} \mathrm{tr}\left(\mathbf{V}^{\mathrm{T}}\mathbf{L}^{\mathrm{T}}\mathbf{D}_2\mathbf{LV}\right) \\ &\text{s.t.} \mathbf{V}^{\mathrm{T}}\mathbf{L}^{\mathrm{T}}\mathbf{E}_2\mathbf{L}^*\mathbf{V} = \mathbf{T}_2. \end{aligned} \tag{25}$$

where $\mathbf{T}_2$ is a constant matrix, and we have

$$\mathbf{L}_{p1} = \begin{bmatrix} \mathbf{L}_1 & 0 \\ 0 & \mathbf{L}_2 \end{bmatrix}, \mathbf{L}_{p2} = \delta_2\begin{bmatrix} \mathbf{L}_1 & 0 \\ 0 & -\mathbf{L}_2 \end{bmatrix}, N_3 = 4n_2 + d_1 + d_2 .$$

$$\mathbf{L}=\left[\mathbf{L}_{p1}^{\mathrm{T}}\ \mathbf{L}_{p2}^{\mathrm{T}}\ \tau_2\mathbf{I}\right]^{\mathrm{T}},\ \ \mathbf{L}^{*}=\begin{bmatrix}\mathbf{L}_1^{*} & 0\\ 0 & \mathbf{L}_2^{*}\end{bmatrix},\ N_4=2n_1\ .$$
$$\mathbf{D}_2=\mathrm{diag}\left(\frac{1}{\|\mathbf{LV}(1,:)\|_2},\ldots,\frac{1}{\|\mathbf{LV}(N_3,:)\|_2}\right).$$
$$\mathbf{E}_2=\mathrm{diag}\left(\frac{1}{\|\mathbf{L}^{*}\mathbf{V}(1,:)\|_2},\ldots,\frac{1}{\|\mathbf{L}^{*}\mathbf{V}(N_4,:)\|_2}\right). \tag{26}$$

Let us define

$$\mathbf{Q}_2=\mathbf{L}^{\mathrm{T}}\mathbf{D}_2\mathbf{L},\quad \mathbf{U}_2=\mathbf{L}^{*\mathrm{T}}\mathbf{E}_2\mathbf{L}^{*}. \tag{27}$$

Then, the optimal solution for (26) is given by

$$\mathbf{Q}_2\mathbf{V}=\mathbf{U}_2\mathbf{V}\Lambda_2. \tag{28}$$

The optimal projection matrix $\mathbf{V}$ is composed of eigenvectors corresponding to the first m_2 smallest eigenvalues except zeros of the Eigen-equation $\mathbf{Q}_2\mathbf{v}_k = \lambda_k\mathbf{U}_2\mathbf{v}_k(k=1,\ldots,m_2)$. It is worthy of note that, $\mathbf{Q}_2$ and $\mathbf{U}_2$ actually depend on the current estimation of $\mathbf{V}$, therefore, the optimal solution should be calculated iteratively.

Now we have obtained a total of four optimal projection matrices $\mathbf{W}_1, \mathbf{W}_2, \mathbf{V}_1, \mathbf{V}_2$ corresponds to the positive and negative class under the two views respectively. Given a new sample with two views $\mathbf{x}^1$ and $\mathbf{x}^2$, we can assign the corresponding category based on the distance between the projections of this sample and the class mean in each view. Concretely, if

$$\sum_{i=1}^{2}\|\mathbf{x}^i\mathbf{W}_i-\boldsymbol{\mu}^{i,+}\mathbf{W}_i\|_2<\sum_{i=1}^{2}\|\mathbf{x}^i\mathbf{V}_i-\boldsymbol{\mu}^{i,-}\mathbf{V}_i\|_2. \tag{29}$$

the sample is classified to positive class, otherwise negative class.

3.3 Convergence Analysis

In order to ensure the convergence of RMvTPVM, we hope to prove the monotonically decreasing behavior. Specifically, we have the following conclusion.

Theorem 1. Algorithm will monotonically decrease the objective (23) in each iteration until convergence. Mathematically, in the t-th iteration of algorithm, we will have

$$\mathrm{tr}\left(\left(\mathbf{W}^{(t+1)}\right)^{\mathrm{T}}\mathbf{S}^{\mathrm{T}}\mathbf{D}_1^{(t+1)}\mathbf{S}\mathbf{W}^{(t+1)}\right)\le\mathrm{tr}\left(\left(\mathbf{W}^{(t)}\right)^{\mathrm{T}}\mathbf{S}^{\mathrm{T}}\mathbf{D}_1^{(t)}\mathbf{S}\mathbf{W}^{(t)}\right). \tag{30}$$

4 Experiments and Analysis

4.1 Experimental Specification

In order to evaluate the classification performance and computational efficiency of our proposed MvTPVM and RMvTPVM, we compare with some state-of-the-art multi- view MHC models, including MvGSVM [7], MvTSVM [8], and RMvLSTSVM [9]. As for the parameter selection of each method, we employ 10-fold cross-validation technique and grid search strategy. We carry out experiments on both standard UCI datasets and EEG signal dataset for driving fatigue detection.

4.2 Classification Results on UCI Datasets

For the UCI dataset shown in Table 1, we take the original data as the first view. For the second view, we follow the previous methods [8, 9] where PCA is used to reduce the dimension of original data. Then the resultant representation is regarded as the second view. The classification accuracy averaged over 10-fold cross-validation of five algorithms on 8 UCI datasets are reported in Table 2. In order to investigate whether the proposed RMvTPVM has advantages in noise resistance, for each UCI datasets, we perform experiment in label noise settings. Specifically, we randomly choose a portion of training samples and reverse labels of the selected samples. The classification and training time of all algorithms when the proportions of label noise are set equal 10% and 20% are shown in Table 3 to Table 4. The training time when no label noise is added is shown in Table 5. The convergence behavior of RMvTPVM on three datasets is shown in Fig. 1.

Table 1. Information about UCI datasets.

Data	Datasets	Numbers	Positive	Negative	Dimension
D1	Diabetes	768	500	268	8
D2	Monks1	432	216	216	6
D3	Monks3	554	288	266	6
D4	Hepatitis	155	32	123	19
D5	Sonar	208	97	111	60
D6	Spect	267	212	55	44
D7	TicTacT	958	626	332	9
D8	E Votes	435	168	267	16

From these results, we can find that the proposed MvTPVM and RMvTPVM outperform the other algorithm on most datasets which indicates our proposed multi-view methods are effective. Given label noise, we can find that the proposed RMvTPVM works better than other algorithms for most datasets, although the performance of all algorithms tends to drop as the label noise increases. In addition, RMvTPVM is more stable with the increase of noise ratio on most datasets. We observe that MvGSVM cannot work well on these datasets and RMvTPVM is superior than MvTPVM in most cases. In terms of training time, our proposed MvTPVM is very fast and RMvTPVM is slower because a series of eigenvalue problem needs to be solved.

Table 2. The classification accuracy on UCI datasets.

Data	MvGSVM	MvTSVM	RMvLSTSVM	MvTPVM	RMvTPVM
D1	75.14	77.08	**77.09**	76.69	75.40
D2	82.88	75.05	76.43	91.44	**93.29**
D3	83.05	88.47	87.03	**96**	9
D4	69.67	80.71	85.38	**87.1**	86.58
D5	77.36	80.76	81.67	85.62	**87.45**
D6	69.99	82.01	**82.76**	79.42	77.48
D7	66.29	67.44	68.80	**76.40**	75.46
D8	95.41	**96.77**	96.31	96.09	**96.77**

Table 3. Classification accuracy on UCI datasets for 10% noise.

Data	MvGSVM	MvTSVM	RMvLSTSVM	MvTPVM	RMvTPVM
D1	74.48	**76.18**	76.05	71.22	70.58
D2	77.55	68.79	73.20	85.66	**86.58**
D3	81.96	81.60	83.06	92.80	**93.69**
D4	61.50	72.42	80.17	**84.63**	83.46
D5	70.21	75.40	73.55	75.95	**78.43**
D6	61.38	76.01	73.09	**76.38**	74.54
D7	62.94	65.77	67.44	72.44	**72.54**
D8	91.97	94.27	89.62	**95.17**	94.50

Table 4. Classification accuracy on UCI datasets for 20% noise.

Data	MvGSVM	MvTSVM	RMvLSTSVM	MvTPVM	RMvTPVM
D1	73.70	74.62	**75.13**	69.54	69.41
D2	69.48	57.90	69.49	81.24	**82.17**
D3	75.48	75.63	77.64	89.90	**90.44**
D4	54.96	61.87	77.54	80.04	**80.92**
D5	64.48	64.90	68.74	70.71	**74.60**
D6	57.71	73.03	72.29	72.64	**73.38**
D7	60.63	64.83	64.72	**70.55**	70.25
D8	87.36	**92.15**	87.3	90.80	91.26

Table 5. Training time of different algorithms on UCI datasets.

Data	MvGSVM	MvTSVM	RMvLSTSVM	MvTPVM	RMvTPVM
D1	0.0039	2.5362	0.0012	0.0017	0.0702
D2	0.0009	0.6246	0.0007	0.0017	0.0245
D3	0.0009	1.0151	0.0008	0.0018	0.0307
D4	0.0011	0.0763	0.0014	0.0026	0.0113
D5	0.008	0.227	0.0024	0.0069	0.0319
D6	0.0068	0.2561	0.0023	0.0067	0.0425
D7	0.0011	3.8297	0.001	0.0030	0.1066
D8	0.0019	0.8739	0.0011	0.0031	0.0237

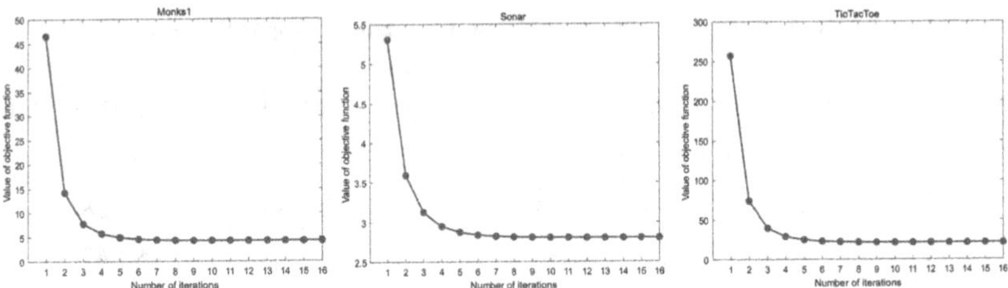

Fig. 1. Convergence curves on Monks1, Sonar, and TicTacToc datasets.

4.3 Application to EEG Based Driving Fatigue Detection

Driver fatigue is one of the most influential factors causing traffic accidents. Electroencephalography (EEG), as a direct manifestation of brain inherent neurophysiological activities in response to particular stimulus, has been widely to detect the driving fatigue due to its high temporal resolution as well as non-invasive acquisition method. Traditionally, the amplitude information related fatigue evaluation indicators including EEG power spectrum density (PSD), approximate entropy, fuzzy entropy, are used to extract feature from raw EEG signal channel. Taking the whole brain as a complex network where node represents specific brain region or electrode and edge describes the relation between nodes, functional connectivity [15] can be utilized to measure the statistical correlation between different nodes. Based on this analysis, we attempt to leverage the proposed multi-view MHC models for driving fatigue detection based on the fusion of local activation and functional connectivity.

The experimental data [16, 17] was originally collected by a highway driving simulator. A total of 12 young, healthy men participated in the experiment. The EEG recordings from 32 channels (including 30 effective channels and 2 reference channels) at 1000 Hz. For the detailed procedure, please refer to the studies [16, 17]. After necessary data preprocessing, for each subject, 5 min EEG data during the normal and fatigue driving was recorded from 30 electrodes. The data was further segmented into 1s epochs to generate about 300 samples. The whole flowchart for driving fatigue detection is shown in Fig. 2.

Considering that EEG signal suffers from serious mental and physical drifts across different subjects [18], we carry out experiment for two class within-subject fatigue detection. The accuracy and the training time obtained by different models on twelve subjects from S1 to S12 is shown in Table 6. As we can see, our methods achieve better results for most subjects. Moreover, we also notice that the detection performance is varied to a large extent for different subjects. For example, for some subject (e.g., S1) the accuracy can reach about 90% while for other subject (e.g., S11) the accuracy is about 70%.

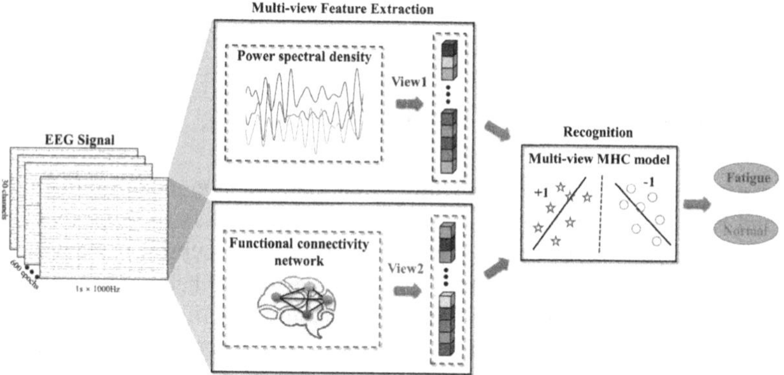

Fig. 2. Flowchart of multi-view classification for driving fatigue detection.

Table 6. Classification accuracy on EEG datasets.

	MvGSVMs	MvTSVMs	RMvLSTSVMs	MvTPVM	RMvTPVM
S1	85.67	87.33	87.67	94.01	**94.83**
S2	86.01	87.67	**88.17**	86.33	87.17
S3	75.92	68.94	76.23	**79.08**	78.91
S4	93.51	96.17	**96.34**	96.01	95.84
S5	82.17	86.17	**90.67**	90.50	90.17
S6	73.73	68.73	78.55	**81.19**	80.37
S7	**73.51**	72.33	73.33	67.00	68.00
S8	80.67	83.33	83.33	**84.17**	83.83
S9	73.54	73.71	**75.04**	72.21	73.04
S10	73.01	77.01	76.83	84.83	**85.50**
S11	65.51	66.83	68.33	70.33	**71.50**
S12	68.38	67.21	71.21	71.72	**73.05**

5 Conclusions and Future Works

In this paper, we proposed two novel multi-view classification models termed as MvTPVM and RMvTPVM by learning multiple projection vectors for each class so as to achieve better separation of different class in the projected subspace. RMvTPVM can be regarded as a robust variant of MvTPVM thus leading to better performance in the presence of outliers. The solution of MvTPVM is given by eigenvalue problem while that of RMvTPVM can be obtained by an efficient iterative algorithm in which a series of eigenvalue problem needs to be solved in each iteration. The experiments on eight UCI benchmark datasets verify the effectiveness and efficiency of these algorithms. We also apply the proposed algorithms to detect driving fatigue based on EEG data where the results also indicate the advantages of our proposed methods over other related techniques in most cases.

In the future works, a straightforward extension of this study is to investigate the fusion of data with more than two views. This will be beneficial to integrate more information from different sources thus boosting the performance. We also try to apply the proposed models for other applications, such as brain disorder related disease diagnosis.

References

1. Wang, F., Wu, S., Ping, J., Xu, Z., Chu, H.: EEG driving fatigue detection with PDC based brain functional network. IEEE Sens. J. **21**, 10811–10823 (2021)
2. Zhao, J., Xie, X., Xu, X., Sun, S.: Multi-view learning overview: recent progress and new challenges. Inf. Fus. **38**, 43–54 (2017)
3. Yan, X., Hu, S., Mao, Y., Ye, Y., Yu, H.: Deep multi-view learning methods: a review. Neurocomputing **448**, 106–129 (2021)

4. Sun, S.: A survey of multi-view machine learning. Neural Comput. Appl. **23**(7–8), 2031–2038 (2013). https://doi.org/10.1007/s00521-013-1362-6
5. Cortes, C., Vapnik, V.: Support-vector networks. Mach. Learn. **20**, 273–297 (1995)
6. Farquhar, J., Hardoon, D., Meng, H., Shawe-Taylor, J.S., Szedmak, S.: Two view learning: SVM-2K, theory and practice. In: Advances in Neural Information Processing Systems, pp. 355–362 (2006)
7. Sun, S., Xie, X., Dong, C.: Multiview learning with generalized eigenvalue proximal support vector machines. IEEE Trans. Cybernet. **49**, 688–697 (2018)
8. Xie, X., Sun, S.: Multi-view twin support vector machines. Intell. Data Anal. **19**, 701–712 (2015)
9. Xie, X.: Regularized multi-view least squares twin support vector machines. Appl. Intell. **48**(9), 3108–3115 (2018). https://doi.org/10.1007/s10489-017-1129-3
10. Ye, Q., Huang, P., Zhang, Z., Zheng, Y., Fu, L., Yang, W.: Multiview learning with robust double-sided twin SVM. IEEE Trans. Cybernet. **52**, 1–14 (2021)
11. Liao, S., Gao, Q., Yang, Z., Chen, F., Nie, F., Han, J.: Discriminant analysis via joint euler transform and ℓ2,1-norm. IEEE Trans. Image Process. **27**, 5668–5682 (2018)
12. Fukunaga, K.: Introduction to Statistical Pattern Recognition. Elsevier (2013)
13. Wang, C., Ye, Q., Luo, P., Ye, N., Fu, L.: Robust capped L1-norm twin support vector machine. Neural Netw. **114**, 47–59 (2019)
14. Nie, F., Wang, H., Wang, Z., Huang, H.: Robust linear discriminant analysis using ratio minimization of L1, 2-Norms. arXiv preprint arXiv:1907.00211 (2019)
15. Wang, P., Min, J., Hu, J.: Ensemble classifier for driver's fatigue detection based on a single EEG channel. IET Intel. Transp. Syst. **12**, 1322–1328 (2018)
16. Simon, M., et al.: EEG alpha spindle measures as indicators of driver fatigue under real traffic conditions. Clin. Neurophysiol. **122**, 1168–1178 (2011)
17. Stam, C.J., Van Dijk, B.W.: Synchronization likelihood: an unbiased measure of generalized synchronization in multivariate data sets. Phys. D **163**, 236–251 (2002)
18. Min, J., Wang, P., Hu, J.: Driver fatigue detection through multiple entropy fusion analysis in an EEG-based system. Public Libr. Sci. **12**, 1–19 (2017)

An Interpretable Conditional Augmentation Classification Approach for Imbalanced EHRs Mortality Prediction

Tianhao Li, Najia Yin, Penghao Gao, Dengfeng Li(✉), and Wei Lu

School of Management and Ecomonics, University of Electronic Science and Technology of China, Sichuan, China
lidengfeng@uestc.edu.cn

Abstract. One of the most crucial tasks in the ICU is mortality prediction. The number of deceased patients is significantly lower than the number of survivors, and it is simple to over-identify the survivors. Additionally, the clinical use of present machine learning and deep learning models is challenging due to their lack of interpretability. To address the aforementioned issues, we innovatively propose the Interpretable Conditional Augmentation Classification (ICAC) method. By using CWGAN to create balanced samples, ICAC learns the distribution of minor samples. In order to make better clinical suggestions, the Shapley value is utilized to examine the marginal contribution of patient characteristics to the prediction model. We test the model on the latest released MIMIC-IV, and the experimental results show that the AUC index of our model is superior than that of the basic model. Our proposed method can successfully address the class imbalance issue in EHRs, clarify how features affect model outcomes, and offer useful recommendations for clinical practice.

Keywords: Mortality prediction · Conditional Wasserstein Generative Adversarial Nets · Interpretable classification

1 Introduction

Electronic Health Records (EHRs) are digital collections of clinical information. They are generated from one or more encounters in any healthcare delivery setting. EHRs include information about patient demographics, laboratory indicators, medication use, vital signs, laboratory results, and reports of diagnostic procedures [4]. In recent years, EHRs have become a major source for treatment assessment, quality of care improvement, side effect reduction, disease prediction, and patient care optimization [18]. Dissimilar with other sources of data, EHRs

Supported by National Key R&D Program of China (2018AAA0101003) and National Natural Science Foundation of China (Grant No. 71901050).

Y. Tan and Y. Shi (Eds.): DMBD 2022, CCIS 1744, pp. 408–422, 2022.
https://doi.org/10.1007/978-981-19-9297-1_29

have a lot of noise, irregular sampling, missing values, and heterogeneous data. These characteristics of EHRs pose many challenges for data modeling [24].

Patient mortality risk prediction using EHRs has been a popular topic among scholars in recent years, especially for ICU mortality prediction [12,28]. One of the major challenges in performing mortality risk prediction is to build a valid prediction model. This is a promissing technique to improve the patient's prognosis by providing physicians the pertinent information. The other challenge is to achieve high accuracy or performance of the model. Thus, there are two main challenges when dealing with this kind of work.

Class Imbalance: Class imbalance is a ubiquitous problem in medical data [8]. Class imbalance leads the model to focus on the major proportion of the category, thus ignoring the minor samples. Minor samples, however, should raise greater concerns. For instance, the proportion of ICU deceased patients is substantially lower than that of those who survived [13]. Further, as deep learning algorithms continuously evolve, deep learning methods will be impractical in prediction even with high accuracy when the sample classes are severely imbalanced [27]. Typically, class imbalance is solved by adding minor samples to achieve balance, or by emphasising minor sample learning in the loss function, etc.

Interpretability: There is general agreement that deep learning and advanced machine learning exhibit excellent performance but lack interpretability in healthcare [14]. There seems to be a trade-off between predictive accuracy and interpretability, deeper and larger neural networks consistently outperform shallow structures in some tasks at the expense of simpler representations. However, the consensus is often not true [22]. When considering the problem that contains structured data with meaningful features, there is often no significant difference betweeen more complex classifiers and simpler classifiers [1]. However, interpretability of models is important and necessary in medical fields [6] and accuracy is equally important. Studies that may fail to be explained to healthcare professionals and physicians are meaningless with a high accuracy.

To address these challenges, we propose an Interpretable Condition Augmentation Classification (ICAC) Approach, which aims at mortality prediction of ICU patients with class imbalance EHRs data. The model addresses the imbalance category of ICU patients in EHRs and selects Conditional Wasserstein Generative Adversarial Nets (CWGAN) to generate a batch of new minor class samples (deceased patients), thus expanding the original data to make the sample balance. Then Shapley value is used to interpret the CWGAN augmentation model. Our results show that CWGAN can significantly enhance the performance and interpretability of the model and achieve superior outcomes to the baseline model.

2 Related Work

Class Imbalence in Healthcare: Imbalanced data classification is an important research topic in the field of data mining, especially in the medical field, such as diagnosis of malignant tumors [9], mortality prediction [26] and so on.

Without sample processing, research findings may lack practical significance in the diagnosis of tumors [8], even with a high accuracy. Usually, we need to generate a balanced training set from the original training sample set, which is used to train medical classification models and improve the recognition rate of minor class samples. In addition, the class imbalance problem can be ameliorated by changing the class weights of the loss function, as well as using undersampling for major class samples, which lose the diversity of the samples.

Data Augmentation for Class Imbalance: Data augmentation is a data generation strategy commonly used for supervising problems in machine learning [20]. Data augmentation improves model performance by algorithmically adding relevant data points. Common data augmentation algorithms are mainly classified into oversampling and undersampling, with oversampling as Synthetic Minority Oversampling Technique (SMOTE), Borderline-SMOTE and so on. With the superior performance of Generative Adversarial Nets (GAN) [10] for various tasks, such as generating realistic images, transforming image styles, predicting temporal data, etc. GAN is also utilized for data augmentation, which provides more distributed information about the sample [7]. Variant of GAN, CGAN [16] can generate images of specified categories by adding conditional variables to the generator and discriminator. WGAN has also been applied to EHRs data with good performance [3]. Inspired by those, we extract the minor class samples in dataset and use CWGAN to expand the samples so that the categories can be balanced.

Interpretability with Shapley Value: Interpretability of deep learning models is significant and inevitable for medical applications, as clinicians increasingly rely on data-driven solutions for patient monitoring and decision making [6]. Model interpretability is a major limitation in existing healthcare research. Though various techniques are proposed in recent years like LIME [21], LRP [2] and DeepLift [23], they can not portion the feature importance while maintaining local accuracy and consistency. However, Shapley value provides a theoretically sound method for allocating coalition benefits among coalition members of a cooperative game. In foresight, the set of variables is the input characteristics of the model, which can be viewed as a set of coalitions. The output values are the predicted values of the model given these special input features.

3 Methods

3.1 Architecture

We provide a structural diagram of the model, as shown in Fig. 1. We divide the class imbalanced EHRs data into training set and test set evenly by category proportion. The training set is added to CWGAN for training to obtain a trained generator. Then we get the new samples by trained generator, which is generated according to the labels of the deceased patients. Finally, the generated data is pasted with the original data to obtain a class balanced dataset.

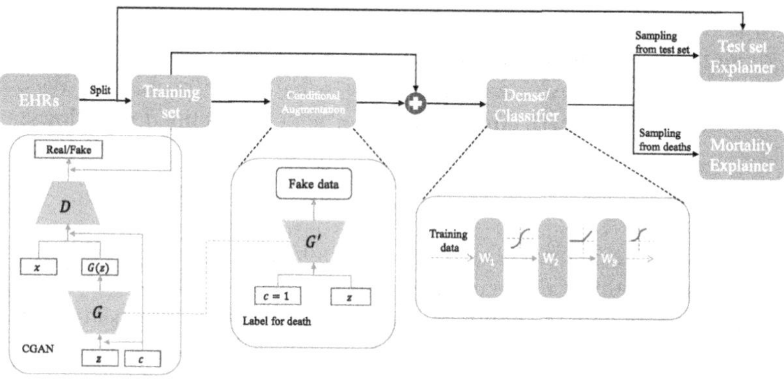

Fig. 1. Structure of our propose work

For the binary classification task, we use this class balanced data and a multilayer perceptron consisting of two hidden layers with activation functions tanh, relu, and sigmoid with weight W_i in Fig. 1. Subsequently, we perform interpretable analysis of the trained model with sampling from the test set, and obtain interpretable mortality risk analysis at the dataset level. Meanwhile, we take a sample of the test data from deceased patients to analyze the causes of explainable death for these individuals.

3.2 Conditional Wasserstein Generative Adversarial Nets

GAN is a deep learning model, which originates from the two-player zero-sum game in game theory, i.e. One party's loss is the other party's gain. GAN consists of a generator (G) and a discriminator (D). Generator is fed by input noise variables $p_z(z)$ and generates fake data. Discriminator is a binary classifier and outputs a single scalar, which represents the probability that x is from the data rather than generator distribution p_g. The two models compete with each other until the generator has enough fake data to make the discriminator indistinguishable and equilibrium is reached. The value function $V(G, D)$ originated from two-player minimax game is defined by:

$$\min_G \max_D V(D,G) = E_{x \sim p_{data(x)}} \log(D(x)) - E_{z \sim p_z(z)} \log(1 - D(G(z))) \quad (1)$$

where the first part is the sum of expectation of correctly recognizing real data $D(x)$, and the other is the expectation of 1 minus truly recognizing the generated data. Compared with unconstrained generative models such as GAN and Deep Convolution GAN [19], CGAN can generate specific data based on label information, which adds category information to GAN so that the generators can generate according to categories with the following value function:

$$\min_G \max_D V(D,G) = E_{x \sim p_{data(x)}} \log(D(x|y)) - E_{z \sim p_z(z)} \log(1 - D(G(z|y))) \quad (2)$$

where y is the one-hot labels that condition discriminator and generator inputs. The original GAN faces training instability, mode collapse and other problems, WGAN (Wasserstein GAN) can effectively solve these problems. Wasserstein distance is also called Earth-Mover distance, which is defined as follows:

$$W\left(p_{data}, p_g\right) = \inf_{\gamma \sim \Pi\left(p_{\mathrm{data}}, p_g\right)} E_{(x,y)\sim y}\left[\|x - y\|\right] \tag{3}$$

where $\Pi\left(p_{\mathrm{data}}, p_g\right)$ represents the joint distribution of $\left(p_{\mathrm{data}}, p_g\right)$. For every possible γ, which contains a real sample x and a generated sample y, the expected value of the distance of the samples can be calculated. The expected value can be lower bounded in the joint distribution of all possible values, which is defined as Wasserstein distance.

3.3 Interpretable Learning with Shapley Value

In statistical models, it is simple to comprehend how characteristics affect the results, but it is more challenging for deep learning models. To address this, we use feature importance to characterize the impact of each feature on the model, where the impact is represented by Shapley value, which is the only way to add the feature importance to the model and keep two important properties at the same time. Below, we provide a brief description of the properties.

Local Accuracy. The local accuracy assumes the attribution of each specific input can directly capture the difference between the expected model output and the predict output, this property is defined by following equation:

$$f(x) = \phi_0(f, x) + \sum_{i=1}^{M} \phi_i(f, x) \tag{4}$$

where $\phi_0 = E[f(x)]$ is the expected value of trained model, and M is the number of the input with different groups of input features.

Consistency. There are two models f and $f^{'}$, if

$$f_x^{'}(S \cup \{i\}) - f_x^{'}(S) \geq f_x(S \cup \{i\}) - f_x(S) \tag{5}$$

for all $S \in Z \backslash \{i\}$, where Z presents the set of all M input features, then $\phi_i(f^{'}, x) \geq \phi_i(f, x)$. This property describes that if a feature is more important in one model than in the other, then the attribution of this feature should be higher to the model regardless of the other features.

There seems to be only allocation of attibution can satisfy those property, which is given by Shapley value [15]. Given a particular prediction $f(x)$, we use a weighted sum that allows us to calculate Shapley value. The impact of each feature is calculated by averaging the marginal impact produced, and accumulated by the model with the feature added to all possible feature orders:

$$\phi_i(f,x) = \sum_{S \subseteq S_{all \setminus i}} \frac{|S|!(M-|S|-1)!}{M!} \left[f_x(S \cup \{i\}) - f_x(S) \right] \tag{6}$$

In practice, the Shapley value is very complex to calculate, with too many terms to estimate, but they can be calculated by a sampling procedure [25]

4 EHRs Benchmarks and Data Processing

4.1 Data Sources

Our work is conducted on MIMIC-IV (Version 1.0) [11]. MIMIC (Medical Information Mart for Intensive Care) is a large, freely-available EHRs database, and contains information about patients such as biochemical test results, demographics, clinical notes, survival etc. MIMIC-IV v1.0 was officially released in March 2021, and consists of EHRs data from 2008 to 2019.

Table 1. Laboratory measurements

Laboratory Measurements
Hematocrit, Platelets, white blood cell (WBC), Aniongap,
Bicarbonate, Blood urea nitrogen (BUN), Calcium, Chloride,
Creatinine, Glucose, Sodium, Potassium, Basophils,
Eosinophils, Monocytes, International normalized ratio (Inr),
Prothrombin time (Pt), Partial thromboplastin time (Ptt),
Alanine aminotransferase (Alt), Alkaline phosphatase (Alp),
Aspartate aminotransferase (Ast), Bilirubin, Neutrophils,
Cv (coefficient variation of glucose), Count_hypoglycemia

4.2 Patient Cohort Feature Extracting

We extract the basic information of the patients who are first admitted to the ICU, including gender, age, height, and weight. Laboratory measurements within 24 h after the patient's admission to the ICU, which is shown in Table 1. In order for the measurements to be correctly identified in the subsequently performed interpretable analysis, we provide a few abbreviations for the measurements.

Indicators chosen before 24 h of a patient's admission to the ICU are more prognostic than those chosen after 72 h or a longer period of time [17]. The longer span of time, the lower the timeliness of prediction, and the less practical significance of predicting death, especially in the ICU. One of the most serious challenges in using temporal data is the lack of data, especially for MIMIC data sets. Nearly one-third of the variables have missing values of more than 90%, and only the characteristics of clinical monitoring such as heart rate and blood pressure have missing values of less than 10% [5]. We try to extract six sets of features every 8 h as a time point over 48-h, most of the variables are missing more than 60%. So we select data within 24 h of admission to the ICU to be more predictive. In addition, we consider the following five physiological scores as indicators: (1) Acute Physiology Score III (APSIII). (2) Simplified Acute Physiology Score II (SAPSII). (3) Systemic inflammatory response syndrome (SIRS). (4) Logistic Organ Dysfunction Score (LODS). (5) Oxford Acute Severity of Illness Score (OASIS).

We filter the cohort for patients with one or more missing basic information and age less than 18 years old. Meanwhile the patients with missing values of laboratory indicators more than 1/3 are deleted. Finally, we leave a total of 25450 patients in the cohort, and 31 variables are included for each patient. The summary of patients' basic information is in Table 1.

The summary of part variables is shown in Table 2, and p value indicates the value of the Independent-Samples T-test to test whether there is a significant difference in the two patient groups of death and survival. As shown in Table 2, the ratio of deceased to survival patients is close to 1:10, which implies the dataset is imbalanced. We use the label '1' indicates the patient died in hospital and '0' indicates the survival. Then we preprocess the extracted data. For structural data, We fill the empty value with the mean value of the measurements to obtain the complete data, and we code the gender with one-hot encoding. Finally, the variables except gender, are normalized using maximum-minimum.

Table 2. Summary of our patient cohort

	ALL N = 25450	Survivor N = 22973	Non-survivor N = 2477	p value
Demographic data				
Age (years)	65.3(16.1)	64.8(16.1)	69.79(15.6)	<0.01
Sex (male)	15397(60.5%)	14016(61%)	1381(55.8%)	<0.01
Body Mass Index	28.7(7.5)	28.7(7.4)	28.5(8.7)	0.25
Laboratory data				
Platelets (K/uL)	166.4(114.1)	167(113.4)	161(119.9)	<0.05
Potassium (mEq/L)	4.3(0.6)	4.3(0.6)	4.4(0.7)	<0.01
Aniongap (mEq/L)	13.4(5.4)	12.8(5.1)	15.9(6.8)	<0.01
Bicarbonate (mEq/L)	21.4(6.9)	21.7(6.8)	19(7.7)	<0.01
BUN (mg/dL)	21.8(19)	21.7(17.9)	31.7(25)	<0.01
Criteria				
APSIII	48.8(25.6)	45.5(22.7)	78.9(30.3)	<0.01
SAPSII	36.9(14.5)	35.4(13.6)	50.1(16)	<0.01
SIRS	2.6(0.9)	2.6(0.9)	3(0.8)	<0.01
LODS	5.1(3.4)	4.7(3)	8.8(3.8)	<0.01
OASIS	32.9(9.5)	31.9(9)	42.1(9.3)	<0.01

4.3 Length of Stay

There is a basis for setting appropriate prediction time span according to the length of stay of our patient cohort. On the one hand, if the average length of stay is short, then the variable time-span used for prediction should be shorter. Only then the prediction is time-sensitive. The summary of length of stay is shown in Table 3. We can see that the average length of stay is 55 h, only 11.58% of patients are hospitalized less than 24 h. If we choose longer span of features, such as 48 h, there are near 42.15% of patients with length of stay less than 48 h, which make the value of mortality prediction models greatly discounted. Therefore, we select the data of the first 24 h after patients are admitted to the ICU. Most of the existing studies have missed this specification, and there are even mortality prediction studies using the first 72 h of patient characteristics in the MIMIC dataset [26], which is low in practical value. On the other hand, the missing values of MIMIC's time series are very serious. The missing values of some variables are more than 60% when using time series data, some variables are more than 90% [5], in order to better explain the attribution, we have no choice but to use cross-sectional data.

Table 3. Length of stay quartiles for our patient cohort

Quantile	Min	11.58%	25%	42.15%	50%	58.21%	75%	Max
Stay hours	0.67	24	30.71	48	55.73	72	120	2391.3

4.4 Conditional Augmentation

Expanding the dataset is one of the means to solve the class imbalance problem. The conditional generative model is necessary for the expansion of minor class samples. CWGAN provides a generative model with labels. Compared with traditional models such as Borderline-SMOTE and ADAptive SYNthetic sampling (ADASYN), which are prone to overfitting and other problems. CWGAN is able to capture the characteristics of the data distribution. In EHRs, we utilize the CWGAN model for expanding death cases. The structure of CWGAN is shown in Fig. 2.

The generator (G) consists of noise and label information as input layers, and the number of neurons in the output layer is equal to the number of variables. The input layer of the discriminator (D) consists of neurons with the number of variables combined with labels, and the output is a sigmoid value of probability. The details of the parameters are presented in the hyperparameter section.

We use the trained generator with given the labels to generate the spurious data of death, thus expanding the original dataset and making the classes balanced.

In order to verify the validity of the generated data, we adopt Quantile-Quantile (QQ) plot as the visual inspection. QQ plot is often used to compare

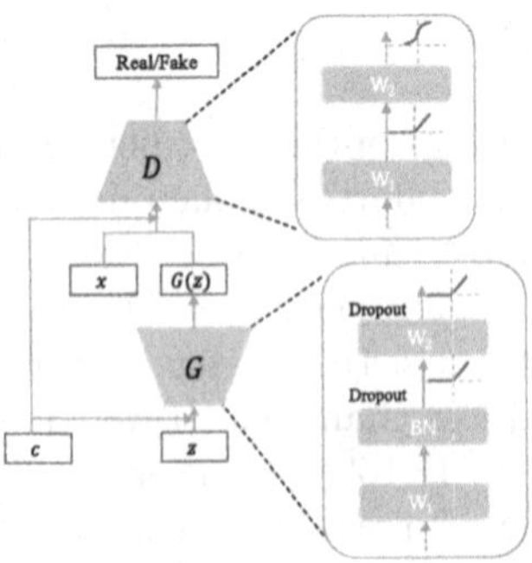

Fig. 2. Structure of CWGAN

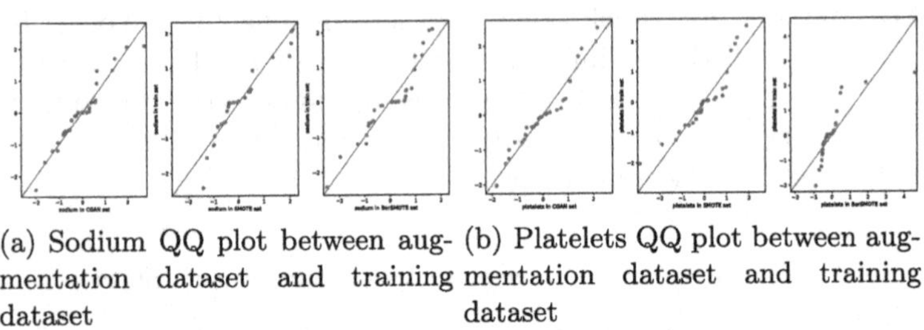

(a) Sodium QQ plot between augmentation dataset and training dataset

(b) Platelets QQ plot between augmentation dataset and training dataset

Fig. 3. QQ plot of augmentation data and training data in sodium and platelets

the quantile of sample data with the known data, and to test whether the data distribution is consistent. We conduct 5-fold cross-validation of experiments, and this is shown in Fig. 3 with a sample of the first fold. The Fig. 3 shows the QQ plot of augmentation data and original training data and only shows two variables due to space limitation. The X-axis represents with augmentation data of platelets and sodium. In the figure, the X-axis represents the data sets from different augmentation methods, while the Y-axis represents the original training set. We can see that in the features, most data are evenly distributed on both sides of the red line ($Y = x$) indicating that the generated data is relatively consistent with the distribution of the original data.

4.5 Details of the Model and Hyperparameters

To evaluate the performance of the model and optimize the neural network structure, we partition the dataset by training and test set at the ratio of 8:2. Since our cohort is a class imbalanced dataset, we divide the sets in such a way that the ratio of the deaths/survivals is consistent in each set.

Our model consists of two parts, CWGAN and MLP classifier. In CWGAN, we set the binary cross-entropy loss function for both the generator and the discriminator. ADAM and SGD are selected as the optimizer respectively, with a learning rate of 0.001. In order to ensure the characteristics of the generated data, we selecte a model with the accuracy of the discriminator converging at 0.5, and the latent noise distribution is uniform distribution on [0, 1].

In MLP, we use hidden layers with 64 and 32 neurons respectively, and an output layer with 1 neuron. The activation functions are tanh, relu and sigmoid, respectively. The dropout layers are with a ratio of 0.4. The experimental environment is Python 3.7 with Tensorflow 1.15 and all the experiments run on our experimental computer with CPU: Intel I7-10700F, RAM: 16G and GPU: GEFORCE RTX 2060 SUPER.

5 Performance Evaluation

5.1 Comparable Methods

As the features extracted from the dataset are one-dimensional, the data structure requirements of algorithms such as CNN or RNN are not applicable. To evaluate the effectiveness of our model, we test the performance of the following models on the same original and expanded datasets: eXtreme Gradient Boosting (XGB), Support Vector Machines (SVM), and Logistic Regression (LR). The parameters of the models are optimized by the grid search method.

To demonstrate our algorithm on data augmentation performance, we use the ADASYN and Borderline-SMOTE for comparison. Traditional SMOTE algorithm generates new data from the following:

$$x_{new} = x + \text{Rand}(0, 1) \times (x - x_n) \tag{7}$$

where x denotes a sample in the minor class and x_n denotes a randomly selected nearest neighbor after k nearest neighbors. Rand is the random sampling function.

Borderline-SMOTE is a modified algorithm of SMOTE, which selects only the minority samples on the boundary to synthesize new samples, thus improving the class distribution of the samples. Borderline-SMOTE sampling process is to divide the minor class samples into 3 categories: Safe, Danger and Noise. Only the minor class samples with the Danger are sampled by SMOTE. ADASYN (adaptive synthetic sampling), is similar to Borderline-SMOTE. Which gives different weights to different minority samples for generating data.

5.2 Evaluate Indicator

We apply Area Under the Receiver Operating Characteristic Curve (AUROC) score and Area Under the Precision-Recall Curve (AUPRC) score to evaluate the performance of the model. AUROC and AUPRC are highly diagnostic of the classification ability of the model under class imbalance. The higher the AUROC and AUPRC, the more capable the model is.

To ensure the reliability of the experiment, we conduct 5-fold cross-validation of experiments with fixed random seeds and take the mean and standard deviation for reporting.

Table 4. Experimental results in different classifiers

	AUROC	AUPRC
MLP	0.825(0.008)	0.372(0.021)
C_MLP	**0.854(0.06)***	**0.413(0.016)***
BS_MLP	0.84(0.007)*	0.314(0.014)*
AD_MLP	0.805(0.007)*	0.304(0.007)*
XGB	0.733(0.017)	0.488(0.048)
C_XGB	**0.746(0.029)***	**0.549(0.057)***
BS_XGB	0.728(0.009)*	0.535(0.01)*
AD_XGB	0.705(0.021)*	0.541(0.027)*
SVM	0.532(0.003)	0.381(0.023)
C_SVM	0.534 (0.004)	0.377(0.02)
BS_SVM	0.771(0.01)*	0.525(0.012)*
AD_SVM	0.772(0.006)*	0.529(0.007)*
LR	0.578(0.004)	0.401(0.013)
C_LR	0.582(0.004)	0.407(0.019)
BS_LR	0.74(0.079)*	0.505(0.055)*
AD_LR	0.741(0.078)*	0.508(0.056)*

Note: * significance level of 10%

5.3 Performance Analysis

The results of the experiment using data within 24 h of admission to the ICU to predict patient death are shown in Table 4. Where the prefixes C, BS, and AD represent dataset augmentation by using CWGAN, Borderline-SMOTE and ADASYN, respectively. In order to ensure the robustness of the results, Independent-Samples T-test is performed on the augmentation models and benchmark models results respectively.

As shown in the table, our model achieves the best performance in all indicators in the MLP and XGB. The MLP model achieve a significant AUC score at 0.854 under the balanced data after adding CWGAN. Meanwhile, comparing the results of the ADASYN and Borderline-SMOTE algorithm, they are significantly improved in SVM and LR models compared with the benchmark model. But CWGAN augmentation has little impact on the performance of the indicators of the model. These results indicate that these augmentation algorithms are able to enrich the diversity of samples and thus improve the model performance.

5.4 Interpretable Analysis

For the interpretable analysis of the model, we use Shapley value to calculate the marginal contribution of the variables to the model. Deepshap provides a visualization toolkit to get an intuitive view of the impact of features on the model. Here, we build two explainers for interpretable analysis, one is the whole test set and the other is death cases in the test set. Each explainer repeats ten times for the stability of the results.

We use the first interpreter to calculate the effect of each variable on the MLP model, which gets the best AUC score, and the result is shown in Fig. 4(a). The Base value indicates the expected output of test features by the trained model, and the final output $f(x)$ represents the result impacted by features on the model, as Eq. (5) indicated.

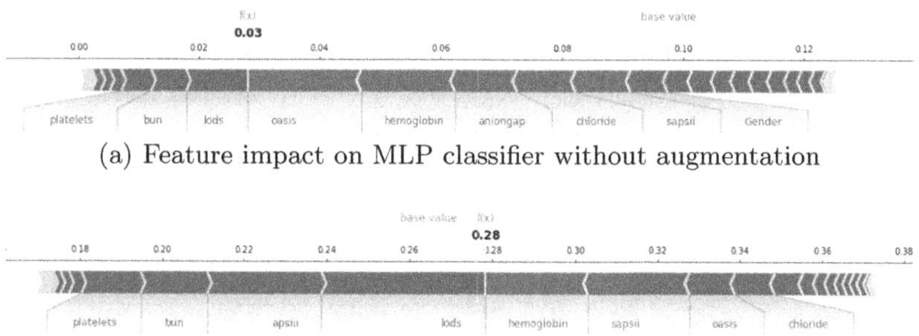

(a) Feature impact on MLP classifier without augmentation

(b) Feature impact on MLP classifier after the CWGAN data expansion

Fig. 4. Feature impact on MLP output with Shapely value

The final output of the model goes through the marginal contribution of the features from 0.096 to 0.03 of base value in Fig. 4(a). The degree of marginal contribution of each variable is indicated by the length of the bar, and red features imply to push the mortality higher, while vice versa in blue. We can see that characteristics such as lods and bun increase the risk of death, while oasis and hemoglobin can decrease the risk in this test set explainer.

Figure 4(b) shows the performance of each feature on the classifier after the CWGAN data augmentation. The results differ from those without data augmentation. Firstly in base value and model output, the categories of data are balanced after data augmentation, so that the expected output value (base value) and output of the model are increased to 0.264 and 0.28, respectively. Thus we can get an observation of the effects of the variables on the model. After the data expansion, one more variable that increases the risk of death is apsiii. While the main variables that decrease the risk only change their order compared to the previous results. The results indicate that data augmentation increases the diversity of the samples, but as the model changes, the order of main variables also changes. The results can likewise provide more informative clinical information, such as the effect of apsiii score on the risk of patient mortality is not negligible.

After performing an analysis of explainable factors at the dataset level, we further extract the cases that died in the test set for explainable analysis. To fully observe each feature, we find the impact of each feature in the sample on the model, as shown in Fig. 5.

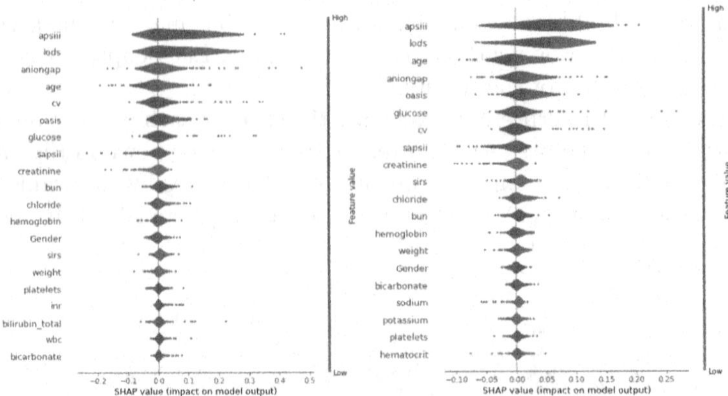

(a) Feature impact on MLP classifier output

(b) Feature impact on MLP classifier output with augmentation

Fig. 5. Feature impact on MLP classifier output Between train and augmentation data

The Fig. 5 shows the effect of each feature on the model output, with red representing high feature value and blue representing low feature value. Taking the apsiii score as an example, a higher feature value has a positive effect on the model output (increasing the risk of death). Similarly, we can conclude that higher age may increase the risk of death, while part of the samples with a lower age show that age decreases the risk of death.

When considering the results of the experiments with data augmentation, as shown in Fig. 5(b), it can be seen that the order of the top three variables influencing the model changes slightly. CWGAN gives more clear prominence to some variables, such as apsiii and lods scores. Lower apsiii and lods scores may reduce the risk of death. However, we cannot get such a distinct analysis of these two variables in Fig. 5(a). This extra information leads our model to outperform the benchmark classifier. For the remaining features, the distribution of the original features is well maintained, such as creatinine, which has no effect on the model output at lower feature value, while higher feature value has a negative effect on the model, which is unified with that in Fig. 5(a).

Overall, CWGAN is able to capture the importance of features to the model, both at the test set level and the death case level. The feature importance of the model is further riched so that the classification model has more information and thus obtains better performance.

6 Conclusion

In this paper, we design the Interpretable Conditional Augmentation Classification (ICAC) method to creatively solve the class imbalance problem and interpretability in EHRs. The classification task results of the balanced dataset achieve better performance than the benchmark model on AUROC and AUPRC.

In addition, we use Shapley value for interpretable analysis of mortality risk factors for different level sets and explain the classification impact of CWGAN generated data on the model. Our method can give practical clinical advice and thus improve patient prognosis.

References

1. Agrawal., D., et al.: Challenges and opportunities with big data. Cyber Center Technical Reports (White Paper 1) (2012)
2. Bach, S., Binder, A., Montavon, G., Klauschen, F., Müller, K.R., Samek, W.: On pixel-wise explanations for non-linear classifier decisions by layer-wise relevance propagation. PLoS ONE **10**(7), e0130140 (2015). https://doi.org/10.1371/journal.pone.0130140
3. Baowaly, M.K., Lin, C., Liu, C., Chen, K.: Synthesizing electronic health records using improved generative adversarial networks. J. Am. Med. Inform. Assoc. **26**(3), 228–241 (2019)
4. Baumann, L.C., Ylinen, A.: Electronic Health Record, pp. 744–745. Springer International Publishing, Cham (2020)
5. Caicedo-Torres, W., Gutierrez, J.: ISeeU: visually interpretable deep learning for mortality prediction inside the ICU. J. Biomed. Inform. **98**, 103269 (2019). https://doi.org/10.1016/j.jbi.2019.103269
6. Che, Z., Purushotham, S., Khemani, R., Yan, L.: Interpretable deep models for ICU outcome prediction. In: AMIA Annual Symposium Proceedings/AMIA Symposium. AMIA Symposium 2016, pp. 371–380 (2016)
7. Che, Z., Cheng, Y., Zhai, S., Sun, Z., Liu, Y.: Boosting deep learning risk prediction with generative adversarial networks for electronic health records. In: Raghavan, V., Aluru, S., Karypis, G., Miele, L., Wu, X. (eds.) 2017 IEEE International Conference on Data Mining, ICDM 2017, New Orleans, LA, USA, 18–21 November 2017, pp. 787–792. IEEE Computer Society (2017)
8. Devarriya, D., Gulati, C., Mansharamani, V., Sakalle, A., Bhardwaj, A.: Unbalanced breast cancer data classification using novel fitness functions in genetic programming. Expert Syst. Appl. **140**, 112866 (2020)
9. Fotouhi, S., Asadi, S., Kattan, M.W.: A comprehensive data level analysis for cancer diagnosis on imbalanced data. J. Biomed. Inform. **90**, 103089 (2019)
10. Goodfellow, I.J., et al.: Generative adversarial nets. In: Advances in Neural Information Processing Systems 27: Annual Conference on Neural Information Processing Systems 2014, 8–13 December 2014, Montreal, Quebec, Canada, pp. 2672–2680 (2014)
11. Johnson, A., Bulgarelli, L., Pollard, T., Horng, S., Celi, L., Mark, R.: Mimic-iv (version 1.0) (2020)
12. Alghatani, K., Ammar, N., Rezgui, A., Shaban-Nejad, A.: Predicting intensive care unit length of stay and mortality using patient vital signs: machine learning model development and validation. JMIR Med. Inform. **9**(5), e21347 (2021)
13. Li, T.H., Wang, Z.S., Lu, W., Zhang, Q., Li, D.F.: Electronic health records based reinforcement learning for treatment optimizing. Inf. Syst. **104**(3), 101878 (2021)
14. Lipton, Z.C.: The mythos of model interpretability. Commun. ACM **61**(10), 36–43 (2018)
15. Lundberg, S.M., et al.: Explainable machine-learning predictions for the prevention of Hypoxaemia during surgery. Nature Biomed. Eng. **2**(10), 749–760 (2018)

16. Mirza, M., Osindero, S.: Conditional generative adversarial nets. CoRR abs/1411.1784 (2014). arxiv:1411.1784
17. Nowroozilarki, Z., Pakbin, A., Royalty, J., Lee, D.K., Mortazavi, B.J.: Real-time mortality prediction using mimic-iv ICU data via boosted nonparametric hazards. In: 2021 IEEE EMBS International Conference on Biomedical and Health Informatics (BHI), pp. 1–4 (2021)
18. Poucke, S.V., Gayle, A.A., Vukicevic, M.: Secondary analysis of electronic health records in critical care medicine. Ann. Transl. Med. **6**(3), 52 (2017)
19. Radford, A., Metz, L., Chintala, S.: Unsupervised representation learning with deep convolutional generative adversarial networks. In: Bengio, Y., LeCun, Y. (eds.) 4th International Conference on Learning Representations, ICLR 2016, San Juan, Puerto Rico, 2–4 May 2016, Conference Track Proceedings (2016). arxiv:1511.06434
20. Ramponi, G., Protopapas, P., Brambilla, M., Janssen, R.: T-CGAN: conditional generative adversarial network for data augmentation in noisy time series with irregular sampling. CoRR abs/1811.08295 (2018)
21. Ribeiro, M.T., Singh, S., Guestrin, C.: "Why should I trust you?": explaining the predictions of any classifier. In: Proceedings of the 22nd ACM SIGKDD International Conference on Knowledge Discovery and Data Mining, pp. 1135–1144. KDD 2016. Association for Computing Machinery, New York, NY, USA (2016)
22. Rudin, C.: Stop explaining black box machine learning models for high stakes decisions and use interpretable models instead. Nature Mach. Intell. **1**(5), 206–215 (2019)
23. Shrikumar, A., Greenside, P., Kundaje, A.: Learning important features through propagating activation differences. In: Precup, D., Teh, Y.W. (eds.) Proceedings of the 34th International Conference on Machine Learning, ICML 2017, Sydney, NSW, Australia, 6–11 August 2017. Proceedings of Machine Learning Research, vol. 70, pp. 3145–3153. PMLR (2017)
24. Si, Y., et al.: Deep representation learning of patient data from electronic health records (EHR): a systematic review. J. Biomed. Inform. **115**, 103671 (2021)
25. Strumbelj, E., Kononenko, I.: Explaining prediction models and individual predictions with feature contributions. Knowl. Inf. Syst. **41**(3), 647–665 (2014)
26. Xu, Y., Biswal, S., Deshpande, S.R., Maher, K.O., Sun, J.: RAIM: recurrent attentive and intensive model of multimodal patient monitoring data. In: Guo, Y., Farooq, F. (eds.) Proceedings of the 24th ACM SIGKDD International Conference on Knowledge Discovery & Data Mining, KDD 2018, London, UK, 19–23 August 2018, pp. 2565–2573. ACM (2018)
27. Xu, Z., Shen, D., Nie, T., Kou, Y.: A hybrid sampling algorithm combining m-smote and ENN based on random forest for medical imbalanced data. J. Biomed. Inform. **107**, 103465 (2020)
28. Ye, J., Yao, L., Shen, J., Janarthanam, R., Luo, Y.: Predicting mortality in critically ill patients with diabetes using machine learning and clinical notes. BMC Med. Inform. Dec. Making **20**(Suppl 11), 295 (2020)

Combining Statistical and Semantic Features for Trajectory Point Classification

Jian Xu(✉), Xin Xu, and Guoqing Ruan

Science and Technology on Information System Engineering Laboratory, Nanjing Research Institute of Electronic Engineering, Nanjing 210023, China
461629348@qq.com

Abstract. Trajectory point classification can be described as a supervised sequence labeling problem, in which a model is trained by labeling data to predict the category of unknown points and identify key events in the trajectory. Due to the difficulty of labeling trajectory point, a large amount of trajectory data is either unlabeled or labeled in an imbalanced way. To make matters worse, traditional trajectory point classification methods are generally constrained to utilize the statistical features of the labeled data and the semantic features as well as the large amount of unlabeled data have not been well studied yet. For this reason, the performance of traditional trajectory point classification methods is far from satisfactory. To solve this problem, we transfer existing language model knowledge to construct the semantic features and construct a trajectory point classification model by combining both the motion features and semantic features. The simulation results show that, compared with the traditional methods, our method has improved the accuracy of trajectory point classification by three and seven percentage points in the classification of circular and turning movements respectively.

Keywords: Trajectory point classification · Sequence labeling · Motion features and semantic features · Language model

1 Introduction

In recent years, with the development of intelligent data acquisition equipment, a large amount of spatiotemporal trajectory data can be obtained. Aircraft trajectory is a structured time series data, which describes the longitude and altitude of aircrafts sequentially. The movement category of each data point could be labeled accordingly. And then the trajectory point classification algorithm uses the labeled data to build a point classification model to predict the category of unknown trajectory points. Trajectory point classification is useful for detecting the change of target movement status, such as when the target enters a turning state or a hovering state.

Trajectory classification can be summarized into three steps [1], trajectory data preprocessing, feature extraction and point classifier building. Trajectory data preprocessing mainly includes trajectory resampling, denoising and segmentation. Feature extraction

Y. Tan and Y. Shi (Eds.): DMBD 2022, CCIS 1744, pp. 423–431, 2022.
https://doi.org/10.1007/978-981-19-9297-1_30

aims to extract features that play a key role in classification, including moving features, shape features, location and time features. Point classification is a process of building a classifier with features extracted from trajectory points.

Existing trajectory classification methods include decision tree, support vector machine, Bayes network, conditional random field, k-nearest neighbor, random forest, boosted decision tree and so on [2–4]. Paper [2] first extracts the target trajectory length, moving speed and acceleration features, and then use Machine learning methods for classification. Paper [5] adopts three new features: direction change rate, stop rate and speed change rate to improve the classification accuracy. Paper [6] extracts global and local motion features (velocity and acceleration) from trajectory for classification, integrating global and local features, support vector machine is used for trajectory classification. However, these methods only consider a limited number of motion features, such as velocity and acceleration, and the spatiotemporal characteristics of trajectories have not been interpreted well.

In natural language processing, a sentence is composed of a sequence of words. Word2vec [7] algorithm is an algorithm for word sequence vectorization. It makes use of the context of a word to infer the semantic representation of this word. The aircraft trajectory is a kind of time series. In that case, each point corresponds to a "word" in a sentence, and the whole trajectory corresponds to a "sentence". In reference [8], the word sequence vectorization algorithm word2vec is applied for trajectory sequence processing. However, word2vec is just a static word vector algorithm which cannot deal with the phenomenon of "polysemy".

The main challenges of trajectory point classification are as follows: The first challenge is the small labeled sample size due to the time-consuming labeling process. Meanwhile, a large amount unlabeled data is easy to obtain. So, the key problem is how to reasonably use a small amount of labeled data and a large amount of unlabeled data. The second challenge is the category imbalance. This is because some categories of movement occur rarely. Thirdly, the spatiotemporal trajectory data could not be handled directly by existing machine learning algorithms.

In this paper, we propose a novel trajectory point classification method by combining both motion and semantic features. Firstly, the background of trajectory point classification and the data annotation process are introduced. Secondly, the target motion characteristics are calculated based on the dynamic sliding window. Then, a mask language model is constructed to extract the semantic features of target trajectories. Finally, a focal loss function is introduced to solve the problem of category imbalance. The experimental results indicate that our classifier beats the traditional methods by 3 and 7 percentage of f1 score in circling and turning points classification respectively.

2 Problem Description

2.1 Trajectory Representation

Trajectory data is the real-time longitude, latitude, altitude and other information of the aircraft captured by radar, the trajectory data obtained by radar consists of a series of discrete trajectory points, and the degree of discretization depends on the scanning period of the radar. If all points of a given trajectory are connected into lines in chronological order, a line is formed. This process is called trajectory diagram, as shown in Fig. 1. Trajectory F can be represented as a set composed of multiple tracks $F = \{T_1, T_2 \ldots T_n\}$, where T_i indicates the i-th trajectory, T_i can be represented as $T_i = \{P_{i1}, P_{i2} \ldots P_{ij} \ldots P_{im}\}$, where P_{ij} indicates the j-th trajectory point in the i-th trajectory. Each trajectory point P_{ij} = (x,y,h,t) is defined as a 4-dimensional vector, indicates the latitude, longitude, altitude at a given time.

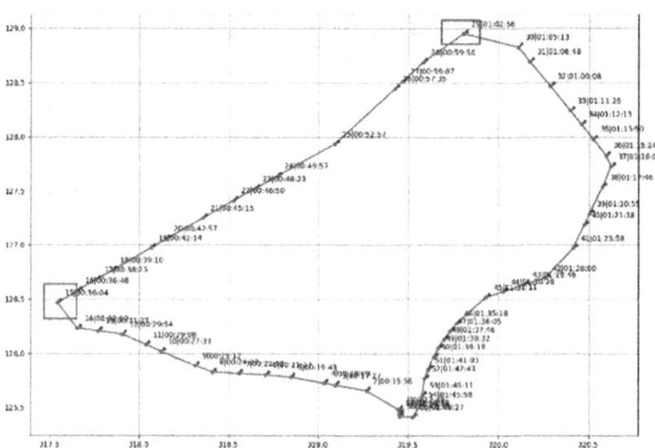

Fig. 1. Turning events trajectory drawing

2.2 Trajectory Annotation

Given a trajectory sequence, the trajectory point classification algorithm hopes to tag each point with the corresponding category label sequence $L_i = \{l^{(1)}, l^{(2)} \ldots l^{(j)} \ldots l^{(m)}\}$, where $l^{(j)} \in$ {turn, circle, O} represents the label of j point in the trajectory. The event types concerned in this paper include turning, circling and others.

3 Motion Feature Extraction

3.1 Feature Extraction of Trajectory Point Motion

The local motion features mainly include speed (v_i), acceleration (a_i), curvature (s_i), direction (θ_i) and rotation angle ($diff_i$), and the calculation is shown in formulas (1)-(7). The curvature represents the ratio of the moving distance between two points to the straight-line distance between the two points, which can describe the degree of curvature of the path. The definition of the direction and the angle of rotation is shown in Fig. 2. The direction represents the direction of movement between two consecutive points, and the angle of rotation represents the difference between two consecutive angles.

$$a_i = \frac{v_{i+1} - v_i}{t_{i+1} - t_i}. \tag{1}$$

$$v_i = \frac{distance(P_{i+1}, P_i)}{t_{i+1} - t_i}. \tag{2}$$

$$s_i = \frac{distance(P_i, P_{i-1}) + distance(P_{i+1}, P_i)}{\text{distance}(P_{i-1}, P_{i+1})}. \quad (3)$$

$$distance(P_i, P_j) = \sqrt{(P_i - P_j)^2}. \quad (4)$$

$$diff_i = \theta_{i+1} - \theta_i. \quad (5)$$

$$\theta_{i+1} = \arctan(y_{i+2} - y_{i+1}, x_{i+2} - x_{i+1}). \quad (6)$$

$$\theta_i = \arctan(y_{i+1} - y_i, x_{i+1} - x_i). \quad (7)$$

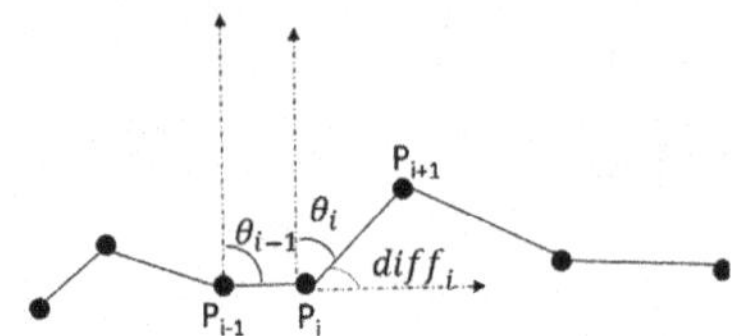

Fig. 2. Definition of direction and turn angle

3.2 Aggregate Feature Extraction Based on Sliding Window

In this paper, the sliding window is used as a unit to count the motion characteristics in a single window. A sliding window w of size n is constructed with the current point as the center, and local features are calculated in units of windows.

Let's mark trajectory points in the window are $[P_0, P_{n-1}]$, and calculate the curvature and turning angle of the window respectively. The curvature of the window is calculated as shown in formula (8), which is the ratio of the sum of the moving distance in the entire window to the straight-line distance between the start and end positions of the window, where n represents the window size, and the distance between the two points of the trajectory pull the distance. The direction of the window is defined as shown in formula (9), which is the direction angle of the line connecting the start point and the end point of the window. The corner of the window is defined as shown in formula (10), which is the difference between the direction angle of the window and the direction angle of the entire trajectory.

$$s_{window} = \frac{\sum_{i=1}^{n-1} \text{distance}(P_i, P_{i-1})}{\text{distance}(P_{n-1}, P_0)}. \quad (8)$$

$$\theta_{window} = \arctan(y_{n-1} - y_0, x_{n-1} - x_0). \quad (9)$$

$$\theta_{track} = \arctan(y_{T-1} - y_0, x_{T-1} - x_0). \quad (10)$$

4 Semantic Feature Extraction Based on Transfer Learning

In natural language processing, a sentence is composed of words, which can be regarded as a time series composed of words. The success of the pre training language model represented by Bert [9] has created a new paradigm for NLP research, which contain two steps: First, a large number of unsupervised corpora are used for language model pre training; Second, a small number of labeled corpus are used for fine-tuning for specific tasks. In the pre training stage, some words in the sentence will be masked according to the probability to form noisy input, and the training model will predict the masked words. In this way, the model can learn the context representation of words, so as to obtain the context semantic representation vector of words.

Literature [10] attempts to transfer the pre-training model learned by Bert in the source domain to the target domain. Because the trajectory data and natural language sentence are all time series data, this paper draws lessons from the ideas of the above literature, try to transfer the language model knowledge in natural language to trajectory point classification. The existing language model is directly used to encode the trajectory sequence, then in trajectory sequence train mask language model. It includes three steps: longitude and latitude discretization, word frequency alignment between trajectory data and pre training model, and the process of training mask language model on trajectory data.

4.1 Longitude and Latitude Discretization

Because the trajectory sequence exists in the form of longitude and latitude with time stamp, in order to train the word vector algorithm, it needs to be discretized first. In this paper, geohash algorithm [11] is used to discretize the trajectory points, geohash is an address coding method, which can encode two-dimensional longitude and latitude coordinates into one-dimensional string. The coding process is regarded as the process of spatial region division. Take longitude as an example, the longitude is divided into two sections [−180, 0] and [0,180]. If the longitude to be coded falls in the left section, it is coded as 0, otherwise it is 1.

4.2 Word Frequency Alignment

The trajectory sequence encoded by geohash is converted into a discrete string sequence, formed the vocab of trajectory sequences. In order to load the pre-trained language model, it is necessary to align the vocabulary of trajectory sequence with the vocabulary of existing language model. First, according to the longitude and latitude coordinates in the geohash coding trajectory, get the dictionary set of trajectory sequence. Then count the frequency of each code, and sorted in descending order of word frequency. Similarly, the word in Bert vocab are also arranged in descending order of word frequency. This ensures that words with the same ranking have the same initialization vector. For example, the longitude and latitude coordinates encoded as "9y6c" have the same word frequency ranking as "week" in Bert vocabulary, so they have the same initialization vector.

4.3 Feature Extraction Network

In this paper, transformer [12, 13] is used as the feature extractor. As shown in Fig. 3, the network is composed of multiple blocks with the same architecture, each block is independent, and learn their own information. Each block consists of a multi head self-attention layer and a feedforward network layer, normalization layer and residual connection are inserted between the two layers. The input of each block is the output vector of the previous block, and the operation of each block does not change the input dimension.

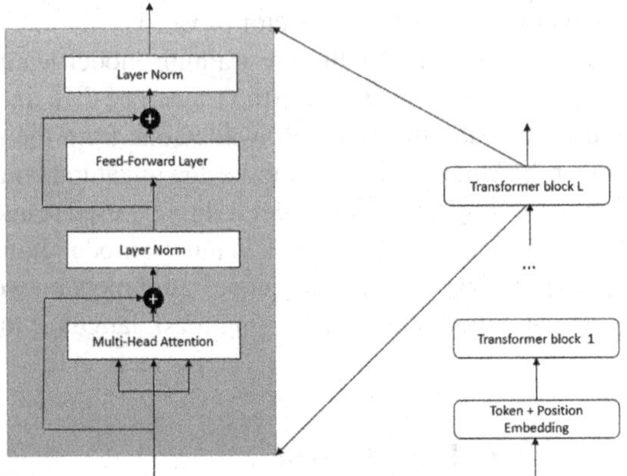

Fig. 3. Architecture of transformer

4.4 Mask Language Model Based on Trajectory Sequence

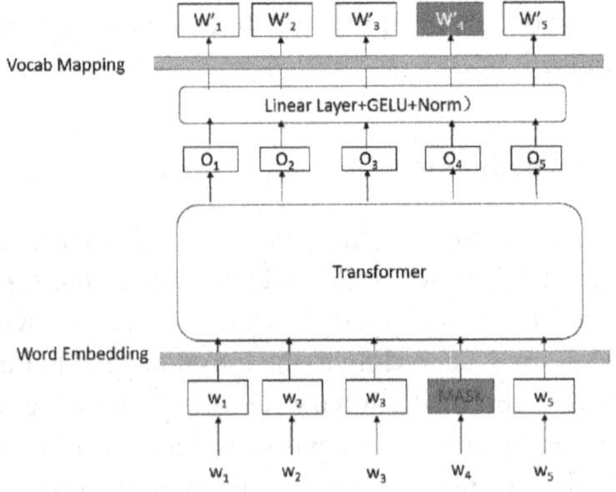

Fig. 4. Masked language model by using trajectory

Mask language model is an auto encoding language model, which can recover the original input from noisy data. Firstly, noise is introduced into the original data by masking, then train a model to predict the masked words. Through this process, we learn the contextual representation for the masked words. As is showed in Fig. 4, firstly adding noise to the original input, then get the hidden vector by transformer encoder, after a fully connected layer, the probability distribution over the vocabulary is obtained.

After aligning the trajectory sequence vocabulary in Sect. 3.2 with the existing language model vocabulary, the existing language model weight can be applied to initialize the trajectory sequence, then mask language model is used to pre-train the trajectory sequence.

5 Construction of Aircraft Trajectory Point Classification

Because the number of turn event type in the labeled data is less, it is a typical label imbalance problem. This paper introduces focal loss [14] to solve this problem, focal loss mainly solves the problem by setting different weights for different samples. For the samples that are easy to distinguish, we want to reduce their weight, and for the samples that are difficult to distinguish, we want to increase their weight. Extend focal loss to the case of multi classification, note that the model output is shown in Eq. (11), and the prediction probability is obtained by softmax normalization according to Eq. (12); if the real category is y, the sample is based on multi classification focal loss, as shown in Eq. (13).

$$Z : (Z_1, Z_2 \ldots Z_y \ldots Z_C). \tag{11}$$

$$\mathrm{p} = \frac{\exp(\mathrm{Z_y})}{\sum_{\mathrm{j}=1}^{\mathrm{C}} \exp(\mathrm{Z_j})}. \tag{12}$$

$$\mathrm{FL(Z, y)} = -(1-p)^{\gamma} \mathrm{logp}. \tag{13}$$

6 Results and Analysis

In this paper, the simulation platform LabVIEW [15, 16] is used to simulate the fighter, its maneuvering process includes straight-line flight, ascent, turning and circling, this paper limits the fluctuation range of longitude and latitude coordinates within 50 degrees. Under the above restrictions, 50000 pieces of trajectory data are generated. We manually mark 1400 trajectories, annotate the turning and circling points.

After analyzing the annotation data, we found each trajectory has an average of 63 points. For the distribution of event categories, turning events account for 2%, circling events account for 26% and other events account for 72%, is a typical category imbalance (Table 1).

In this experiment, we only measure the effect of combination features, and do not consider the difference of classifiers. Therefore, we choose the Xgboost [17] as base classifier, and we also fixes its parameters: setting the maximum depth of the tree to 18, the number of iterations to 20. The classifier needs to perform three label classifications for each trajectory point, that is circle, turning and other. We use F1 to measure the difference of models. For semantic features, we use Bert as the basic model to train the mask language model, the learning rate is setting to 4e−4, each word has a 15% probability of being replaced, of which 80% remains unchanged, 10% is replaced with [mask], and 10% is randomly replaced with a word in the dictionary. Table 2 shows the f1 score of classifier using only motion features, and Table 3 shows the effect of combination of motion and semantic features. It can be seen that compared with motion features, the combined features in this paper has an improvement of 3 and 7 percentage points of f1 score in the classification of turning and circling.

Table 1. Distribution of event type.

	Others	Circle	Turning
Count	62811	22712	1460
Ratio	0.72	0.26	0.02

Table 2. Result of classifier (motion features only).

	Precision	Recall	F1	Support
Circle	0.81	0.87	0.84	4449
Turning	0.26	0.71	0.38	293
Others	0.96	0.89	0.92	11103

Table 3. Result of classifier (motion and semantic features)

	Precision	Recall	F1	Support
Circle	0.85	0.90	0.87(+3)	4449
Turning	0.33	0.73	0.45(+7)	293
Others	0.98	0.94	0.96	11103

7 Conclusion

Aiming at the problem of aircraft trajectory point classification, a trajectory point classification method integrating motion features and semantic features is proposed in this paper. Based on the sliding window, we extract moving features, including velocity, acceleration, curvature, direction and rotation angle. We train mask language model on a large number of unlabeled data, and get context semantic features. We then combine moving features and semantic features to train a point classifier. For the problem of category imbalance, we introduce focal loss, reduce the weight of easily distinguishable samples. The experimental results show that compared with existing motion features only, the method proposed in this paper has an improvement of 3 and 7 percentage points of f1 score in the classification of turning and circling events, respectively.

References

1. Zhao, Z.J., Ji, G.L.: Research progress of spatial-temporal tra-jectory classification. J. Geo-Inf. Sci. **19**, 289–297 (2017)
2. Zheng, Y., Liu, L., Wang, L., Xie, X.: Learning transportation mode from raw gps data for geographic applications on the web. In: Proceedings of the 17th international conference on World Wide Web, pp. 247–256 (2008)
3. Jahangiri, A., Rakha, H.A.: Applying machine learning techniques to transportation mode recognition using mobile phone sensor data. J. IEEE Trans. Intell. Ttransp. Syst. **16**, 2406–2417 (2015)
4. Shafique, M.A., Hato, E.A.: Comparison among various classification algorithms for travel mode detection using sensors' data collected by smartphones. In: International Conference on Computers in Urban Planning and Urban Management, pp. 175–181 (2015)
5. Zheng, Y., Li, Q., Chen, Y., Xie, X., Ma, W.Y.: Understanding mobility based on GPS data. In: Proceedings of the 10th International Conference on Ubiquitous Computing, pp. 312–321 (2008)
6. Dodge, S., Weibel, R., Forootan, E.: Revealing the Physics of Movement: Comparing the Similarity of Movement Characteristics of Different Types of Moving Objects, pp. 419–434. Computers, Environment and Urban Systems (2009)
7. Mikolov, T., Sutskever, I., Chen, K., Corrado, G.S., Dean, J.: Distributed representations of words and phrases and their compositionality. J. Adv. Neural Inf. Process. Syst. **26**, 1–9 (2013)
8. Li, Y., Fei, T., Zhang, F.: A regionalization method for clustering and partitioning based on trajectories from NLP perspective. Int. J. Geogr. Inf. Sci. **33**, 2385–2405 (2019)
9. Yang, Z., Dai, Z., Yang, Y., Carbonell, J., Salakhutdinov, R.R., Le, Q.V.: XlNet: Generalized autoregressive pretraining for language understanding. J. Adv. Neural Inf. Process. Syst. **32**, 1–18 (2019)
10. Chiang, C.H., Lee, H.Y.: Pre-training a language model without human language. arXiv preprint arXiv:2012.11995 (2020)
11. Balkić, Z., Šoštarić, D., Horvat, G.: GeoHash and UUID identifier for multi-agent sys-tems. In: KES International Symposium on Agent and Multi-agent Systems: Technologies and Applications, pp. 290–298 (2012)
12. Han, K., Xiao, A., Wu, E., Guo, J., Xu, C., Wang, Y.: Transformer in transformer. In: Advances in Neural Information Processing Systems, pp. 15908–15919 (2021)
13. Parmar, N., et al.: Image transformer. In International Conference on Machine Learning, pp. 4055–4064 (2018)
14. Lin, T.Y., Goyal, P., Girshick, R., He, K., Dollár, P.: Focal loss for dense object detec-tion. In: Proceedings of the IEEE International Conference on Computer Vision, pp. 2980–2988 (2017)
15. Salim, J.O.: Fuzzy based PID controller for speed control of DC motor using LabVIEW. J. WSEAS Trans. Syst. Control. **10,** 154–159 (2015)
16. McGrew, J.S., How, J.P., Williams, B., Roy, N.: Air-combat strategy using approximate dynamic programming. J. Guidance Control Dyn. **33**, 1641–1654 (2010)
17. Chen, T., Guestrin, C.: Xgboost: A scalable tree boosting system: In: Proceedings of the 22nd ACM SIGKDD International Conference on Knowledge Discovery and Data Mining, pp. 785–794 (2016)

Author Index